1400 DAYS

THE US CIVIL WAR DAY BY DAY

1400 DAYS

THE US CIVIL WAR DAY BY DAY

Chris Bishop

Ian Drury

Illustrated by Tony Gibbons

PARKGATE
BOOKS

First published in 1990

This edition published in 1997 by
Parkgate Books Ltd
London House, Great Eastern Wharf
Parkgate Road, London SW11 4NQ, Great Britain
9 8 7 6 5 4 3 2 1

© Collins & Brown Ltd, 1990
© Text Chris Bishop and Ian Drury, 1990
© Illustrations Tony Gibbons of Bernard Thornton Artists,
London, 1990

All rights reserved

British Library Cataloguing in Publication Data

Designer Tony Gibbons
Editorial Trish Burgess, Diana Steedman
Editorial Director Pippa Rubinstein

ISBN 1 85585 325 6

Printed in Italy

Monitor Merrimack battle, March 1862

CONTENTS

Introduction

The April morning was dark. The defenders of the fortress in the harbor looked into the blackness with foreboding. For some, it was a sense of personal danger. Others, gifted with second sight, might have foreseen that a cataclysmic struggle was about to commence. A nation was about to tear itself apart. The bloody banner of rebellion had been raised, but the final irrevocable step had yet to be taken.

At 4.30 on the morning of April 12, a mortar was fired from a battery on Sullivan's Island, at Charleston, South Carolina. Shrieking into the sky, the shell curved over and plummeted to burst directly over Fort Sumter in the middle of the entrance to the harbor. No comet in ancient days ever foretold more death and suffering than did that mortar shell. For with that shot, the United States of America was at war. A nation forged in the fires of a struggle against tyranny was launching into a life and death struggle with the worst of all possible enemies. It was at war with itself.

From the moment General Robert E. Lee surrendered the Confederate Army of Virginia at Appomattox Court House, the Civil War has exerted a considerable fascination on succeeding generations. It was one of the formative experiences that made the United States what it is today, settling once and for all the question of the indivisibility of the Union, and bringing slavery to an end.

It was one of the last of the old-style wars, in which many of the participants, amateurs at the start, still cherished the notion of chivalry. It had its romantic swashbucklers, like the Southern cavalrymen led by such larger-than-life figures as Jeb Stuart and Wade Hampton. It was a war fought by volunteers, men who enlisted in their hundreds of thousands for the cause. As in all wars since the dawn of time, it was fought by young men. It was a war when

brother fought brother, at the same time as picket lines from opposing armies would fraternize between the battles. Officers fought against West Point classmates, men who had shared the hardships and triumphs of the war with Mexico a decade and a half before.

The War between the States was one of the last in which large numbers of soldiers marched everywhere on foot. They marched to a hundred songs, like "Dixie," "Marching through Georgia," "Lorena," and "Tenting Tonight on the Old Camp Ground." They sang to keep in step, or to while away the long weary hours slogging through mud, or rain, or snow, or dust. Around fires at the end of day they sang to remember family and loved ones. Later generations of soldiers, moved into battle by train, road transport, or helicopter, had no such need to give voice. This may be why no American war since 1865 has produced so many songs which still, a century later, have the power to tug at the heart.

It is not only in song that the Civil War made its mark. The body of literature which it has generated is without parallel. Walt Whitman's *Drum Taps*, Stephen Crane's *Red Badge of Courage*, even Buster Keaton's *The General* — all have the war as their inspiration. But the most telling contribution to the literature of the War comes from its participants, for this was the first literate war. Never before had the ability to read been so widespread. Newspapers were everywhere, reporting on everything from high policy through the doings in the industrial towns of the North and the plantations of the South to the conditions in the trenches on some remote field half a continent away. They were read avidly in the front lines, giving the ordinary soldier a more thorough picture of the conduct of the war than had been possible with any preceding army. Being educated, well-informed, and imbued with a spirit of equality, the soldiers were not afraid to hold their own views, and they debated the issues with spirit.

And after the war there was a veritable explosion of memories committed to print. Many, from the highest to the lowest, had kept diaries. This meant that in addition to the heavyweight tomes in which the generals re-fought their battles, there were as many which recorded everyday life in the trenches before Petersburg, or on the gunboats of the Mississippi, or on any of the many and varied battlefields which saw Billy Yank and Johnny Reb fight to the last desperate inch.

The Civil War created a thousand images which have become an integral part of American history, from General Thomas J. Jackson at Manassas, "standing like a stone wall," to General Ulysses S. Grant's uncompromising message to the Confederate defenders of Fort Donelson that "No terms except conditional and immediate surrender can be accepted. I propose to move immediately upon your works." The writings cover moments of triumph and tragedy, recording the changing character of the war. Less than four years separate William Howard Russell's account of the Battle of Bull Run for the London *Times* and the events at Appomattox recorded by General Joshua L. Chamberlain, yet they seem to come from different eras. The gaily dressed Washington socialites who went to watch the battle as if it were some kind of spectator sport could have had no conception of the years of blood and horror to come. No more at the end of the day could the victorious Southerners have foreseen the final shame of defeat so vividly depicted in Chamberlain's moving account of the surrender of Lee's army when "The whole column seemed crowned with red."

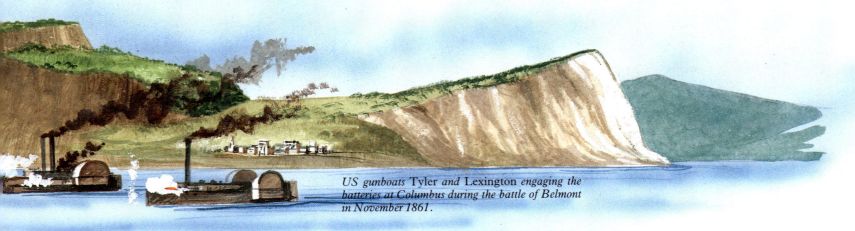

US gunboats Tyler *and* Lexington *engaging the batteries at Columbus during the battle of Belmont in November 1861.*

Although it can never lose a certain romantic aura, the Civil War had another, darker side. It was one of the first major conflicts of the industrial age. Battles like Shiloh, Antietam, and Gettysburg were bloody, awful struggles. Antietam, one of the bloodiest, saw the mass-production of maiming and death to an unprecedented degree. After the battle, the sunken road there became known as Bloody Lane, with Confederate dead lying three deep for a mile. Some 5000 men died at Antietam, and nearly 20,000 were wounded during the bloodiest 24 hours in American history.

It was the North who found the commanders to match the new kind of warfare. U.S. Grant knew that the North had an enormous advantage over the South when it came to resources and manpower. While careful of the welfare of his men, considered by many to have been a real "soldier's general," he was willing to accept losses in a long, grinding struggle of attrition, knowing that the South would run out of fighting men first.

William T. Sherman was the man who declared that "War is hell," and then set out to prove it. He held firmly to the belief that the quickest way of winning a war was to destroy the Southern people's willingness to support the fight. His march of destruction through Georgia was a strike at the Confederate spirit itself. He wanted to show the citizens of the South that a Union army could burst the heart of the Confederacy, and that the Southern army could not protect its own homes and families. It was the first step toward total war, and Grant and Sherman have some claim to having been the first modern generals.

New warfare required new weapons. The war started with the troops on both sides being armed with rifled muskets, with which you had to be a pretty good shot to hit anything more than 100 yards away. As the war progressed, however, a number of more advanced weapons appeared. The Sharps Carbine, much favored by the rebel cavalry, was a breech-loading weapon which utilized a metaliic cartridge, and had a much greater rate of fire than previous, muzzle-loading weapons. Magazine-fed rifles, such as the Spencer and the Henry (precursor to the famous Winchester used in the west after the war), increased the fire-power of the individual soldier tremendously.

Edged weapons had little place in this new kind of combat. The classic cavalry charge with sabres drawn would have been shot to pieces. Instead, the cavalry became mounted infantrymen, using their horses to get to places quickly but fighting on foot. As their "shock action" role diminished, however, their other tasks became even more important. Cavalry reconnaissance could win or lose battles, and cavalry raids against enemy lines of communication were a particular Southern speciality.

CORN FIELD

ROAD TO FORT DONELSON

RIFLE PITS

SWAMP

FORT HENRY

QUARTERS

Apart from making breech-loading magazine rifles a practical proposition, the development of the metallic cartridge also meant that, for the first time, rapid-fire weapons were feasible. The Gatling gun was the most successful of many designs, but made little contribution to the war. Although capable of firing nearly 300 rounds per minute, it was ignored by the Union authorities, primarily because its inventor was Southern born and a number of senior Northern officials thought that he was trying to get the Union to spend money on a worthless weapon!

Repeating small arms, modern artillery, and mortars made the infantry lines and columns of the Napoleonic Wars obsolete, and by the end of the struggle soldiers were fighting from entrenchments protected by barbed wire entanglements. Formal European tactics were found wanting: battles generally became gigantic skirmishes, although there were still plenty of occasions when massed columns of men charged the enemy and engaged hand to hand. Sometimes it worked. More often it ended like Pickett's charge at Gettysburg, with the Confederates storming up Missionary Ridge almost to the top before being cut down by Union musketry and artillery fire.

Innovations did not stop at small arms. The telegraph and the railroad were vital to the successful control of far-flung armies. At sea, iron-clad, steam-powered warships were dominant, and the submarine made its first tentative contribution to battle. Balloons were used for reconnaissance. Economic warfare in the shape of a naval blockade was instrumental in choking off the South's overseas trade. The entire resources of one divided nation were being used in ever more ingenious ways—to preserve the Union on one side, or to bring it to an end on the other.

What created this fatal divide? The United States had been in existence less than 90 years, but in that time had grown rapidly in size, wealth, and influence. Progress was built into the culture, education was widespread, the people were generally contented. Why would any nation go to war with itself? Historians to this day argue about the causes, but to discover the roots of the war we have to go back in time to the first European settlement on the eastern seaboard of North America.

Union gunboats attack Fort Henry in February 1862.

ROAD OF RETREAT

9

The Roots of War

Man has been in residence in North America for at least 15,000 years. Great civilizations arose in Central and South America from the second century A.D., but the greater part of North America was a wilderness, peopled by simple, hunter-gatherer cultures whose way of life remained unchanged for millenia. In the eleventh century Scandinavian adventurers left traces of occupation on the northeast coast of what is now Canada, but in general the Amerindians were undisturbed.

The European Renaissance saw the beginnings of a new sense of adventure. The world was there to be explored, and naval expeditions set off in all directions from the maritime states of Western Europe. Columbus made landfall in the Caribbean in 1492, and in further voyages explored the region, but he is unlikely to have had any conception of the vastness of the New World, and probably never realized the importance of his voyages.

It was not long before other, more far-sighted mariners followed. Amerigo Vespucci explored the coasts of the southern landmass which was to bear his name. Spain took the lead in the voyages of discovery, and over the next 50 years the Spanish empire in America was founded by men like Balboa, Cortez, Pizzarro, de Vaca, de Soto and Coronado. But Spain was not the only power interested in the New World.

John Cabot was a Florentine in the service of England, and in 1497 he made the first landfall on the continent of North America. Around 80 years later the English naval hero Francis Drake circumnavigated the Earth, putting into what was to become San Francisco Bay in the process. His reports of the New World and the riches the Spanish and Portuguese were ripping from what is now Latin America provided the impetus for the northern European nations to mount their own colonization efforts. In 1603 Samuel de Champlain became the first governor of Canada, taking possession of Nova Scotia, Newfoundland, and New France. In 1607 the first English colony was established at Jamestown, Virginia, by Sir Walter Raleigh. The Dutch established the New Netherlands in 1616, and in 1620 English Puritans, persecuted for religious reasons, crossed the Atlantic to found New England.

There was a difference between the various colonies from the beginning. The Spanish *conquistadores* were often feuding or dispossessed noblemen driven by missionary zeal, the desire for fame and renown, and above all, by the craving for gold. They brutally subjugated the native peoples, enslaving them and forcibly converting them to Christianity. In 1510 and 1511 the first slaves were imported from Africa, where the Portuguese had begun to establish the roots of the trade.

The French colony in the North was a smaller affair, consisting of about 10,000 settlers by the end of the seventeenth century, but where it made its mark was in the interior. French backwoodsmen made long journeys in search of furs, and they provided the first glimpse of the scale of the sparsely settled continent. The Dutch colony of New Netherlands was small, and was absorbed by the surrounding English speakers in the 1660s after the Anglo-Dutch wars.

It was the English who came to settle. Britain was a small country, with no land available for the adventurous, and the persecuted could not escape their persecutors. What the Americas had in plenty was room. The non-conformists of New England were only the first to flee religious strife. In 1632, with the English Civil War looming and the heavy hand of Puritanism hovering over them, English Catholics settled in Maryland.

Whatever the cause of emigration, by the middle of the seventeenth century the eastern seaboard of North America was English. New France had a small population; Virginia and Maryland had 20,000 settlers, and New England as many. About half of the 3000 settlers in the New Netherlands were English, and the Swedish colony at the mouth of the Delaware was so small as not to count.

Even though the English colonies were settled by people from the same culture speaking the same language, there were great differences between North and South. It is in this basic divide that one of the root causes of the Civil War can be found. The people in the North sought freedom to worship as they wished, a freedom they austerely denied to others. They clustered in small farming communities centered on the Church, where they sought to win a living from the soil. They sought a thrifty, independent, "godly" life. Above all, they sought to educate the people. Grammar schools were established for all the children of the colonies, and the foundations of a number of colleges date from this period.

The South was very different. The colonies were planted, not settled, by men of wealth and rank, who remained in Europe to reap the profits from their investments. The land was split up into large estates, cultivated first by felons and later by slaves. The first of these arrived in Jamestown as early as 1619. Religion in the South was paid lip-service, but it did not pervade society as it did in the North. Education was for the rich, and to obtain it they had to go North, or obtain Northern tutors for their children. The vast mass of people were ignorant. After all, how much knowledge did you need to work in the fields?

It can be seen that the basic conditions for the Civil War were in place from the foundations of the first colonies, 250 years before Fort Sumter was fired upon. It seems strange that such disparate societies could have formed the United States, but people will band together in the face of a common foe. A common foe there was, but not the French or Spanish one as might have expected. It was misrule from Great Britain, the mother country, that was the spur to the formation of the United States.

Battle of Bunker Hill and the destruction of Charlestown in June 1775. The British paid a high price in casualties to dislodge American militia men.

The Birth of Independence

It was the policy of the British Government from the 1750s onward that began to set the colonies on the road to independence. At first, all they wanted was for their rights as Englishmen to be respected. But for many years before that time the colonists were thought of as hardly more than beasts of burden, creators of wealth for the benefit of Britain, not free and equal citizens. When, in the 1690s, Virginia sent a petition for the establishment of a theological college on the grounds that there were souls to be saved, the attorney-general replied, "Souls? Damn your souls! Plant more tobacco!"

The increase in taxation bore heavily on people who had no say in their governance. The concept that the Americans were there solely for the benefit of British commerce and to provide a ready market for British-manufactured goods naturally grated on the colonists. This pressure told on all, Puritan New Englander and cavalier from Virginia alike.

There was also America's involvement in the many conflicts of the period. The Seven Years' War was a triumph for Britain. Under the leadership of William Pitt, Lord Chatham, Britain emerged as the pre-eminent world power. The colonists had made their contribution to that success in the French and Indian War. A young commander named George Washington distinguished himself, and many other names, later to become famous, got their first taste of battle. A certain Henry Lee commanded a detachment of the 16th Light Dragoons during

Action at Spuyten Devil where the British were slow to follow up victory at Brooklyn in September 1776. They were halted in this battle against the defenses on the bluffs but it was enough to cause the Americans to destroy two unfinished frigates.

12

the campaign in Portugal in 1762, under the command of Colonel Burgoyne. Later known as "Light Horse Harry" Lee, he was to become a hero of the Revolutionary War and was, incidentally, the father of Robert E. Lee.

Although some of the ruling classes profited from British wars, to the vast majority of Americans they simply meant higher taxes, unemployment, and poverty. Although scattered over a vast expanse of land, with very different local government and customs, there was considerable contact between the various colonies, and shared blood and culture began to seem more important to them than differing ideas on how to run their lives. They began to organize—not, at first, to make the break with Britain, but to achieve for themselves their rights as Englishmen.

In 1765 the first Colonial Congress was convened at New York. They drew up a declaration of rights and grievances, they petitioned King George III, they sent appeals to the British Parliament. Above all, they claimed their birthright as Englishmen, that they should not be taxed by a body within which they were not represented.

The British ignored them. Indeed, they began to tighten the screws against the protests of many of their own politicians, such as Chatham, now out of office, and Edmund Burke. With the French out of the war, they could look to the colonies for the revenues needed to pay for the war. The Stamp Act of 1765 was the measure which inflamed colonial opinion most, and unrest in the cities and in the countryside grew considerably. Over the next few years further measures inflamed opinion, including taxes such as the one on tea, and the law stating that colonists were not to settle in the Indian lands beyond the Appalachians.

It was against the background of such unrest that the Continental Congress gathered in Philadelphia in 1774. This body, set up as a deliberative chamber, quickly became the director of the common interests of the colonies. There was already a powerful sentiment toward breaking with Britain, but it was not until the clashes at Lexington and Concord in 1775 that the Congress decided upon making the final break with Britain. On July 4, 1776, the Declaration of Independence was proclaimed. The colonies had now become the United States of America.

But although now a nation, with people of one blood, speaking one language, joined in a common struggle for survival, the United States lacked formal unity. There was no sovereign authority. The colonies had possessed no sovereignty under the British, all laws having to have the assent of a governor appointed by the Crown. The Continental Congress had no powers to raise revenue, to sign treaties, or to maintain an army.

The colonies had declared their independence as "united colonies," not as individual states. Yet the states, having thrown off one overlord, were loath to place another of their own making over themselves. The Articles of Confederation, proposed by the Continental Congress of 1777, were not completely ratified until 1781. It was the Constitution of the United States that formally set the seal on the Nation, but not until Rhode Island, last of the former colonies to adopt it, consented to join the Union in 1790.

All the declarations in the world would not have sufficed, however, without the military victory in the War of Independence.

The Struggle for Independence

When the colonies rose in revolt against the British Government, most of that government believed that it would quickly be put down. Nobody thought that European tactics would be of much use in the often trackless forests of North America, or that tough, determined men fighting for a principle would form stern opposition. The logistical problems of fighting a war across 3000 miles of ocean were soon encountered, but knowing about them and being able to do something about them without incurring crippling costs are two different things.

Even so, the colonists would have been unlikely to survive, were it not for the the clandestine support, later to become open alliance, with France and Spain. And that intervention would not have been enough had King George III and his prime minister, Lord North, attempted to take measures to rally the loyalties of the colonists. But once a colonist, always a colonist, and even those loyal to Britain were scorned. Later on, as Hanoverian and Hessian troops ravaged the property of all Americans, and the British used Indians to fight their battles on the frontier, all but a hard core were alienated.

In June 1775, following the clashes between British troops and colonial minutemen at Lexington Green and Concord, the Second Continental Congress appointed Virginia plantation-owner George Washington as commander-in-chief of the army of the 13 colonies.

The colonial army attempted the invasion of Canada in 1775, but the largely militia force was unable to match military skill to martial will, and at the end of the year was roughly handled at the siege of Quebec. General Montgomery was killed and Benedict Arnold wounded. Even so the siege continued, but by July 1776 Arnold had been forced back to Ticonderoga. American ambitions were dealt a further blow in August when Lord Howe, who had evacuated Boston in March, landed a force on Long Island. Skillfully turning the American line, he forced his opponents back in confusion to the Brooklyn Heights. A few days later Washington abandoned New York.

During the winter Washington made amends by winning victories at Trenton and Princeton, which proved great boosts to rebel morale.

The British mounted two major offensives in 1777, but that toward Albany was to end in the American victory over Burgoyne at Saratoga. Lord Howe was more successful in his drive on Philadelphia, defeating Washington at the Battle of Brandywine, occupying Philadelphia, and again beating Washington at Germantown. The Continental Army spent a miserable winter at Valley Forge, but the tide was turning. In February 1778 the French formed an alliance with the United States.

The war had now changed from a colonial struggle into a general war, and the outcome of the naval campaign in the Atlantic was vital to the war on land. French assistance added professional skill to Washington's armies, as was to become clear during the British invasion of the Southern states in 1780 and 1781.

Russia declared an armed neutrality in February 1780, with Catherine the Great declaring that her navy would be used against anybody trying to interfere with Russian trade. Denmark and Sweden quickly followed suit, and within two years the Baltic nations had been joined by The Netherlands, Prussia, Portugal, Austria, and the Kingdom of the Two Sicilies. Britain was totally isolated, with no European allies, and her resources were fatally overstretched.

The year 1780 saw some British success in the Southern states. Charleston was taken after a three-month siege in the worst American defeat of the war. General Cornwallis's heavy-handed methods of pacification only inflamed the country, however, and the British found themselves with a guerrilla war on their hands. Nevertheless, the British smashed an American force at Camden in August. Over the winter the Americans, under General Nathaniel Greene, regained some of the initiative. In a number of mostly indecisive battles, he persuaded Cornwallis that he could not with certainty hold on to Georgia and the Carolinas.

Cornwallis moved on to Virginia, and for several months attempted to bring the Americans and French to battle. By September, however, he was besieged in Yorktown on the York River. The French landed reinforcements for Washington's army and managed to keep the British from doing the same for Cornwallis. The *coup de grâce* for Britain's attempt to regain control of the colonies came on October 19, 1781, when General Cornwallis and 8000 British troops marched out of Yorktown to surrender.

Although the War of Independence was to drag on for another two years, until the treaty of Versailles, after Yorktown Britain had lost her American colonies for good. Admiral Rodney's success at sea in the Battle of the Saintes restored British command of the oceans, but it was too late to affect the outcome of the war. The United States of America was a fact.

The deliberate burning of Washington in August 1814 by British forces under Rear Admiral Sir George Cockburn. Although the raw militia men put up a stiff resistance, they were no match for the British and their mercenaries.

15

The New Nation

After the Revolution, the United States had to settle the question of sovereignty. In the Constitutional Convention of 1787 at Philadelphia, Benjamin Franklin and James Madison mediated between two opposing points of view. Federalists, like Alexander Hamilton, John Adams, and George Washington, wanted a strong central government, while the Republicans, headed by Thomas Jefferson, felt that the rights of the individual states should be paramount. A compromise solution to the argument saw the establishment of a federal republic under an executive president.

On September 17, 1787, the Constitutional Convention presented the Constitution of the United States of America. This was the center of the first modern democracy. Its essential characteristic was the separation of powers, with a system of checks and balances between the executive and the legislature, between the federal government and the individual states, and between the states themselves. The president became the head of state and the chief administrator, but he was subject to the political control of Congress, and constitutionally subject to the Supreme Court.

The written constitution was ratified, in some cases somewhat reluctantly, by all 13 states by 1790. Vermont became the fourteenth state in 1791, followed by Kentucky in 1792, and Tennessee in 1796.

The foreign policy of the United States tended from the start toward isolationism. In spite of the 1778 alliance with France, the United States remained neutral when war blazed over Europe in 1793. In his farewell address in 1796, George Washington, the first president, warned against "lasting entanglements" in Europe.

Even had Congress wanted such entanglement, it did not have the means. The Continental Army was disbanded after the Revolution,

and the tiny regular army established in 1784 was formed in response to the wave of Indian unrest which had swept the frontier. At first the force was less than effective, since on two occasions, in 1790 and 1791, it was badly defeated by Maumee Indians in the Ohio Valley.

In 1794 a new, larger army, trained and led by Revolutionary War veteran General Anthony Wayne, defeated the Maumee near what is now Toledo, Ohio, and brought peace to the frontier for several years.

That same year also saw the birth of the US Navy. Warships were needed to protect American trade in the Mediterranean, where merchantmen of all nations were threatened by the Barbary pirates.

The first overseas adventure came in 1801. The Pasha of Tripoli declared war on the United States because the nation would not meet his demands for protection money on the Mediterranean. For two years a small American naval force blockaded Tripoli, but to no effect. In 1803 a more vigorous policy was established, and Barbary corsairs were hunted down. Unfortunately, the frigate USS *Philadelphia* ran aground and was captured. Lieutenant Stephen Decatur led a daring mission into Tripoli to board and burn the *Philadelphia* as she lay at anchor. Eventually, for a ransom of $60,000, the crew of the *Philadelphia* was released and the Pasha agreed to cease demands for payments from American vessels.

Although America vowed to stay clear of the European conflict, it became involved in a war with Britain in 1812. The British claimed a "right of search" of vessels on the high seas, taking contraband off and impressing British nationals in the crews of foreign ships. President James Madison saw this as a chance to seize Canada, and the high-handed British actions at sea gave him the excuse to declare war.

Four invasions were planned, but the United States lacked the men or the experience to bring them off. The first operations in 1812 were defeated by British Brigadier-General Isaac Brock. In 1813 Commodore Oliver Hazard Perry won control of Lake Erie, which enabled the Americans to gain a victory on the Canadian side at Moravian Town. However, the advance by General Wilkinson toward Quebec ended in ignominious failure when his army of 8000 men was defeated at Crysler's Farm by a British force one tenth the size.

At sea the British had a shock. Since Trafalgar, the Royal Navy had felt itself invincible, but now it was coming up against men with a similar maritime tradition and manning better ships. The US Navy inflicted a series of stinging reverses in single ship action on the British, but once the Royal Navy was able to bring its full strength to bear, it won almost complete control of the seas. That control was used to mount a series of punitive raids on the American coast, including the operation in which General Ross's army seized and burned Washington.

The final act of a war which should never have been fought took place in January 1815, when the British were defeated by Major-General Andrew Jackson in the Battle of New Orleans. It was a singularly pointless battle, fought before news could reach the armies that a peace treaty had been signed in Belgium on December 24, 1814.

During the war against Tripoli in 1803 USS Philadelphia *accidentally ran aground and was lost, in spite of frantic efforts by the crew to get her afloat.*

The Expansion of the United States

The growth of the United States was explosive. Thomas Jefferson, president from 1801 to 1809, led a reaction to the previous centralist policies of the Federal Government. The maxim of the time was "a minimum of government and governing." The energies and interests normally expended on foreign policy were channelled into westward expansion by settlement.

In 1790 the population of the nation was about 3,900,000. Most people lived within 50 miles of the Atlantic. Within 40 years that population had more than trebled to 13,000,000. By 1840 nearly 5,000,000 people had crossed the Appalachians into the huge expanse of land drained by the Mississippi. The only stumbling block was the Indian, and in the quarter century from 1820 his numbers in the region had declined from 120,000 to less than 30,000.

The westward expansion led to the creation of new states. Kentucky and Tennessee were the first, established in 1792 and 1796. In 1803 Jefferson almost doubled the size of the United States by purchasing Louisiana from the French, who had received it from Spain. Stretching from the Mississippi in the south to the Rockies in the north, "the greatest real estate deal in American history" opened up even more of the west for settlement. More states came into being: Ohio in 1803, Louisiana in 1812, Indiana in 1816, Mississippi in 1817, Illinois in 1818, Alabama and Florida (the latter purchased from Spain) in 1819.

The expansion of the country, however, was far from peaceful. Someone had to make room for the whites, and that someone was the Indian.

In 1818 the first Seminole War began when Seminole Indians raided and massacred into the United States from strongholds in Spanish Florida. Andrew Jackson, the hero of the Battle of New Orleans, set off from Nashville with some 7800 men, his task being to end the Seminole threat. Without authority he invaded Spanish territory, taking Pensacola in May 1818. He sent columns into the swamps, which destroyed numerous villages, and broke up Seminole power. Two English traders found in the villages were tried and executed, which almost brought war with the British, but that danger was averted when the captured territory was returned to the Spanish. Clearly, the United States could take Florida whenever it wanted to, and the Spanish decided that negotiation was better than fighting.

By the Adams-Onis Treaty of 1819 Spain ceded Florida to the United States, and they also dropped claims to the Pacific northwest. The boundary of Spanish Mexico was established from the Sabine River on the Gulf of Mexico northwest to the northern boundary of California.

In 1823 the Monroe Doctrine held that America was for the Americans, and that foreign interference would be strongly resisted.

The continued westward expansion had no place for the Indian. Prime land held by Indian tribes was eyed greedily by the white men, and solemn treaties were callously disregarded. Andrew Jackson forced the Choctaws and Cherokees to leave their homes. The fact that gold had been found on Cherokee tribal land in Georgia probably had a great deal to do with the decision. The dispossessed Indians were told to settle beyond the Mississippi, where they would find, according to Jackson, "Beyond the limits of any state, land of their own, which they shall possess as long as grass grows or water runs." The grass did not grow long—only until such time as the ever-growing white population needed the land.

In the North the Sac and Fox tribes of Illinois and Wisconsin tried to stem the tide. But with too few men to have any great effect on white settlers moving into their lands, they were moved on just like the Indians of the South. Under their chief, Black Hawk, they fought, but soon the tribes were starved, hunted, and driven across the Mississippi. Black Hawk tried to surrender under a white flag, but the pursuing soldiers opened fire, killing women and children as well as tired warriors. Black Hawk fled, but was eventually captured by Sioux Indians working for the white man. The Sioux themselves were to learn the worth of treaties with the Americans over the next half century.

Although the treatment of the native American is a dark stain on America's history, the movement west was a period of great achievement. The population of the country was growing by leaps and bounds, fuelled by massive immigration from the Old World. Although the direction of the nation remained in the hands of the Protestant Anglo-Americans, 40 percent of the 5,000,000 who crossed the Atlantic between 1830 and 1860 were Irish, and another 30 percent came from Germany.

While many of the new Americans settled in the east, it was the wagon trains of settlers pushing further and further westward that stitched together the vast fabric of the modern United States. Oregon was originally to be settled jointly by Britain and the United States, but a flood of American settlers eroded the agreement. America's "Oregon Claim" was accepted by the British in 1846 as a fact, and the boundary dispute was settled by agreeing to the 49th Parallel as the border between Canada and the USA.

The acquisition of southern Oregon territory brought the United States into close contact with Mexico, and it was not long before relations between the two countries became strained. In 1846 the ill-feeling generated over decades by the Texas War of Independence and by America's "Manifest Destiny" to rule the continent from sea to sea exploded into war.

Alamo during a night bombardment in March 1836.

War with Mexico

The westward tide of settlement saw many Americans moving into Mexican territory. In Texas those settlers began to feel that they could rule themselves better than the Mexican Government did.

In 1836 they rose in revolt against Mexico. The president of Mexico, General Santa Anna, set out with 3000 regular soldiers to put the rebellion down, besieging 188 rebels in the Alamo mission in San Antonio. After a heroic defense, they fell to a Mexican assault. All within the mission died, but in the process the Mexicans lost 1500 men.

Santa Anna moved on to the east, where an insurgent force was gathering after a declaration of independence. The Mexicans massacred 300 Texans at Goliad, but at the Battle of San Jacinto they were routed by the army of the infant Republic of Texas under Sam Houston. Santa Anna, captured in the battle, recognized the new state, although his action was repudiated by his own government. The United States immediately recognized the Republic of Texas, which aroused considerable Mexican resentment.

In 1845 Texas was annexed, at the request of its inhabitants, by the United States. Mexico had already threatened war if this occurred. A further incentive to war was the revolt of American colonists in northern California, which was used by General Frémont as an excuse for armed intervention. The real reason for the war was expansionist sentiment in the USA, where the nation's "Manifest Destiny" to control the lands north of the Rio Grande was taken as a matter of faith.

In 1846 General Zachary Taylor established a camp at Fort Brown, near Matamoros on the Rio Grande. On April 25, 1846, a small force of US Dragoons was attacked by Mexican troops. After a series of skirmishes, Taylor occupied Matamoros, then moved on Monterey with

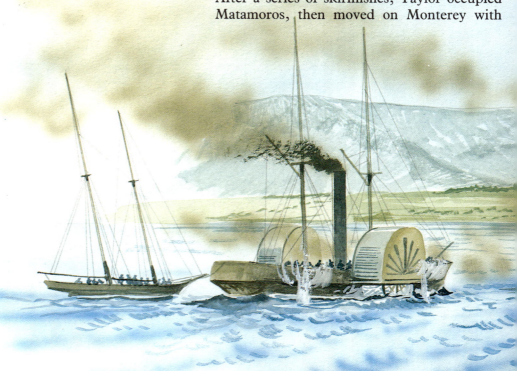

6000 men. In five days of combat he defeated General Pedro de Ampudia's 10,000-strong army. Moving on, he was reinforced at Saltillo by a column of 3000 men under Brigadier-General Wool.

Far to the north, a force of 1700 men under Colonel Kearney set out from Kansas for Santa Fe. Detaching half of his column for a raid into Chihuahua, he continued on toward California. Defeating a Mexican cavalry force at San Pasqual, he continued on to San Diego, where he was reinforced by troops landed by Commander Stockton of the US Navy. Moving north, the combined column won a battle at San Gabriel near Los Angeles, resulting in Mexico's loss of California.

Meanwhile, the force under Colonel Doniphan, which had been detached into Chihuahua, won a crushing victory at Sacramento, killing 600 Mexicans for the loss of just seven men. Doniphan carried on to join Taylor at Saltillo, having marched over 2000 miles.

Command of the war against Mexico had been taken from Taylor because of his refusal to march over miles of desert to San Luis Potosi, and thence to Mexico City. President Polk was forced to appoint General Winfield Scott, a man with whom he shared a mutual animosity, as overall commander. Scott's plans called for a landing at Vera Cruz from where he would attack toward Mexico City. Taylor had to give up 5000 veterans to Scott's command, and was ordered to remain on the defensive.

President Santa Anna, learning of the American plan, determined to deal with Taylor before the Vera Cruz landings. He moved north from San Luis Potosi with 20,000 men, losing as many as 4000 in the desert which Taylor had refused to cross. Arriving at Saltillo in February 1847, he met the American Army in the hard-fought battle of Buena Vista. Well-handled artillery broke up the main Mexican attack, and an attempt to turn the American flank was beaten off by Colonel Jefferson Davis. Santa Anna then retreated back toward San Luis Potosi, leaving northern Mexico firmly in American hands.

Scott arrived off Vera Cruz on March 9, and landed his force without opposition. After a short siege, the garrison of 5000 surrendered on March 27. Advancing inland, Scott encountered Santa Anna at Cerro Gordo, and in the ensuing battle killed or captured 4000 out of the 12,000 Mexicans on the field. Pausing at Puebla after 4000 of his troops returned home on the expiry of their enlistments, he continued when further reinforcements brought his strength up to 14,000. Effective strength was less than this, however, as at least 3000 of his command were sick.

Reaching Mexico City in August, he whipped Santa Anna in two battles on August 20, inflicting 10,000 casualties on the Mexican Army of 30,000. After further battles at Molina del Rey and at Chapultepec, the capital was occupied on September 14. Meanwhile, Puebla, where Scott had left his sick, had been surrounded, but a relief force from Santa Cruz raised the siege.

Negotiations to end the war were by now under way, and in February 1848 the war was brought to an end. Mexico ceded land which was later to become the states of New Mexico, Arizona, Nevada, Utah, and California, together with parts of Colorado and Wyoming. In two years the USA had again virtually doubled in size.

There was one further outcome of the war. Among the young officers who gained experience of battle were many whose names would rise to prominence in years to come, not the least of whom would be Jefferson Davis, Robert E. Lee, Ulysses S. Grant, Thomas J. Jackson, D. H. Hill, William T. Sherman, Joseph E. Johnston, George B. McClellan, A. P. Hill, and George H. Thomas.

Lieutenant David Dixon Porter of USS Spitfire *in action during the Mexican War of 1847.*

The Shadow of War

Slavery lay at the heart of the road to war. By the middle of the nineteenth century it had been abolished throughout most of the civilized world, and by 1846 it had been outlawed in all of the Northern states. But in the South, the "Peculiar Institution" persisted to a remarkable degree.

Most of the reason was economic. The Industrial Revolution was booming in the North, but the South was predominantly agrarian. Most Southern capital was tied up in plantation land, and in speculation on crops like tobacco, cotton, and sugar. Cheap labor was essential, and the cheapest of such labor was provided by slaves.

It was an inefficient industry, yet such was the demand for cotton, particularly by the booming British textile industry, that the crop seemed to offer limitless economic possibilities. It was the nation's premier export; not for nothing was it known as "King Cotton."

Yet the slave trade was not alone a cause for war. From the earliest days of the United States, political control had been in the hands of the South. Any time the delicate balance was threatened, compromises would be reached to keep things pretty much as they always had been.

But in the 1850s it was clear that the old order was changing. The rapidly industrializing North began to outstrip the South economically and demographically. Before long, that economic muscle would begin to be flexed in the political field, especially with the formation in 1854 of the Republican Party.

The threat to their oligarchy forced the Southern aristocrats to band together. Throughout the 1850s Southerners began to press their own interpretation of the Constitution, which was parochial in the extreme and placed States' rights above all other loyalties.

Things got worse in 1854 with the passing of the Kansas-Nebraska Act. Instead of laying down the law as to whether these new territories were to become free or slave states, Congress left it up to the citizens to vote on the issue. This meant that both sides attempted to sway the issue in their favor. It was not long before the arguments had turned to violence, as the pro-

slavery "Border Ruffians" crossed over from Missouri, only to be opposed by anti-slavery fanatics like John Brown. Kansas became a battleground, as the two sides fought it out with often horrific violence.

The violent emotions spread throughout the Union, even to the halls of Congress. Senator Charles Sumner of Massachusetts was beaten up by Preston Brooks from South Carolina after a notable anti-slavery speech in the Senate. Newspapers on both sides whipped up the fervor even more.

In 1859 John Brown attempted to raise a slave rebellion in Virginia. Together with a number of followers, he took the arsenal at Harper's Ferry, and called for the oppressed to join him. He was captured by Federal troops commanded by Colonel Robert E. Lee, who had a young lieutenant called J.E.B. Stuart in his force. Although Brown was tried and hanged, he was looked on as a martyr in the North, while in the South he had raised the specter of slave rebellion—a serious matter when there were as many slaves as free men in some of the Southern states.

Secessionist talk, which had been heard for years in the South, began to be more seriously regarded. It became a real possibility when two new states were admitted to the Union. Both Minnesota and Oregon were free states and weighed the balance in Congress in favor of the abolitionists. Worse was to come, however, in the presidential election of 1860. Northern industrial power was now being felt in the political field, and the Southern Democrat vote was split due to the "fire-eaters" inability to agree on a single candidate. The Democrats lost badly to the Republicans, whose candidate, Abraham Lincoln from Illinois, was duly elected to the highest office of the land. This meant that Southern control of the United States was a thing of the past. Their fears were confirmed when prominent Northern politicians announced that "The country has once and for all thrown off the domination of the slaveholders."

Lincoln's election also hit at the South's most vital economic area. Northern industries could now be protected against European competition by the imposition of trade tariffs. This was the last thing the South needed. Most of the South's trade was with Europe, and they needed the free trade of an open market to compete effectively.

Southern leaders now actively urged secession. In the four months of the "secession winter" between Lincoln's election and his inauguration, the final split, which had been implicit in the very make-up of the United States, took place. On December 20, 1860, the state legislature of South Carolina voted unanimously to secede from the Union. Over the next six weeks Mississippi, Florida, Alabama, Georgia, Louisiana, and Texas followed suit. They formed the Southern Confederacy, raised an army, and seized Federal forts, arsenals, and customs houses. Jefferson Davis was elected president of the Confederacy at a Provisional Congress in Montgomery, Alabama.

For two months, an informal truce existed between the two sides. But in the early morning darkness of April 12, 1861, the sound of gunfire echoed around Charleston, South Carolina. Fort Sumter had been fired on. The Civil War was under way.

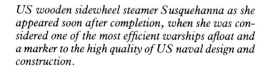

US wooden sidewheel steamer Susquehanna as she appeared soon after completion, when she was considered one of the most efficient warships afloat and a marker to the high quality of US naval design and construction.

April 1861

Friday, April 12, 1861

War starts at 4.30 a.m. when the Confederates open fire on Fort Sumter in Charleston Harbor, the order to commence being given by Captain George S. James at Fort Johnson. Firing continues throughout the day. Further south, on Santa Rosa Island in Florida, Union reinforcements land and secure the vital Gulf Coast stronghold at Fort Picken.

Saturday, April 13

Major Robert Anderson surrenders the Federal Garrison at Fort Sumter. Undermanned, and with no food, he has no other option. In spite of more than 40,000 shells having been fired, casualties on both sides are light, with no lives lost.

Sunday, April 14

The North Washington receives official notice of the fall of Fort Sumter. President Lincoln meets his Cabinet and decides the call for volunteers to "still the insurrection in South Carolina." At Fort Sumter itself, two Union soldiers are killed by an accidental explosion during the ceremony to lower the United States flag. They are the first fatalities of the war.

Monday, April 15

The North Lincoln issues the call for 75,000 volunteers willing to fight to save the Union. Northern states respond positively and instantly.

Tuesday, April 16

Governors of Virginia, North Carolina, Kentucky, Tennessee, Missouri, and Arkansas (all of which are slave states but not yet part of the Confederacy) make hostile responses to the president's appeal for volunteers. Indeed, Governor Harris of Tennessee goes so far as to reply, "Tennessee will not furnish a single man for coercion, but 50,000, if necessary, for the defense of our rights, or those of our Southern brethren."

Wednesday, April 17

The Confederacy At the urging of Governor Letcher, a hastily called meeting of the Virginia Convention passes the Ordinance of Secession. Further secessionist meetings are held at Baltimore, Maryland. Jefferson Davis announces that the Confederacy will be issuing letters of marque, so opening the way for privateering on the high seas.

Thursday, April 18

The North At the prompting of the aging General Winfield Scott, Lincoln offers command of the Federal Armies to Colonel Robert E. Lee, the highly regarded former superintendent of West Point. Lee it was who, at the head of a column of United States Marines, had put down John Brown's "insurrection" at Harper's Ferry in 1859. Lee considers his reply, but decides to serve his home state of Virginia.

Union troops abandon the huge military arsenal at Harper's Ferry on the Potomac.

Friday, April 19

The North The president declares the Union's intention to blockade all Confederate ports from Texas to South Carolina.

Confederate sympathizers riot in Baltimore, and attack the 6th Massachusetts Regiment passing through the city. Four soldiers and nine civilians die.

Saturday, April 20

The Confederacy Robert E. Lee resigns from the US Army. Commandant Charles S. Macauley orders the burning of the navy yards at Norfolk, Virginia, to prevent their falling into Confederate hands. The loss of this important facility hampers Federal military operations along the Virginia coast, and in spite of the burning, the Confederates manage to salvage much of value, including the hull and machinery of a

powerful steam frigate, the USS *Merrimac*, which will reappear in a very different form as the USS *Virginia*.

Sunday, April 21

The North Rioting continues in Baltimore, which has the effect of cutting off Washington's rail link to the north. Troops are moved by sea.

In western Virginia, anti-secessionists meet and resolve to support the Union. This highland region is very different topographically and socially from the lush fields and slave-worked plantations of the eastern part of the state, and the hill-farmers feel no kinship to the old-established Southern "aristocracy."

Monday, April 22

The Confederacy Jefferson Davis hopes that Virginia will be able to support Confederate sympathizers rioting in Baltimore.
Western Theater In the west, Illinois state troops garrison Cairo, which will become strategically important in later years.
Trans-Mississippi Across the Mississippi, the Federal arsenal at Fayetteville in Arkansas is taken for the Confederacy.

Tuesday, April 23

The North Rioting continues unabated in Baltimore, and a slave insurrection is feared. General B.F. Butler, moving toward Washington with the Massachusetts volunteers, offers the services of his troops to help to restore order.
The Confederacy Robert E. Lee takes command of the land and naval forces of Virginia in the rank of general.

Wednesday, April 24

The North As Washington awaits reinforcements, the threat to the national capital from the South continues to grow.

Thursday, April 25

The North The 7th New York Regiment arrives in Washington, much to the relief of its inhabitants and the Federal Government.

Friday, April 26

The North Washingtonians, back in communication with the north after a week, begin to take down barricades set up when an immediate Southern invasion seemed imminent.

Saturday, April 27

The North North Carolina and Virgina having officially seceded, the US Navy's blockade is extended to include the ports in those states.

President Lincoln suspends habeas corpus between Philadelphia and Washington to allow the military to handle the unrest in Baltimore.
The Confederacy Virginia offers Richmond as the capital of the Confederacy, which is currently seated at Montgomery in Alabama.

In the late 1850s Fort Sumter was in an unfinished state, and in November 1860 $80,000 was appropriated to complete the fort which was to have had a full garrison of 650 men. At the time of the attack upon the fort it housed three 10-inch guns which were intended to cover the salient angles.

There was also a plentiful supply of 8-inch columbiads, as well as 42-, 32- and 24-pounders, plus some 8-inch sea-coast howitzers. The top tier of guns stood some 50 feet above the parade ground and the heavy weapons were hoisted up by means of legs. Under the roof were large iron tanks containing the water supply for the fort.

Sumter was manned by a small Union garrison, and after a token resistance gave in to the powerful Southern forces that surrounded it. It went on to defy massive attacks by Union forces and eventually became little better than a huge mound of rubble.

SHELL BIN

HOSPITAL

TRAVERSE

BARRACKS

April–May 1861

Rallying proudly to the flag, Charleston Zouaves parade at Castle Pinckney. South Carolina contained many such fire-eating secessionists, eager to pull their state out of the Union. Of all those hostile to the Union and eager for war, none was more so than Edmund Ruffin, a 70-year-old Virginian to whom was given the honor of firing the first shot upon Fort Sumter, and the first shot of the war.

Sunday, April 28, 1861
The North Turmoil in Baltimore and uncertainty about secession in the rest of Maryland still threatens the Federal capital's communications with the industrial states of the north.

Monday, April 29
The North Maryland's state legislature votes against secession.
The Confederacy At Montgomery, Alabama, Jefferson Davis outlines the reasons for secession to the second Provisional Confederate Congress and vows "with a firm reliance on that Divine Power which covers with its protection the just cause, we will continue to struggle for our inherent right to freedom, independence, and self government."

Tuesday, April 30
Trans-Mississippi Federal troops abandon the Indian territory forts, leaving the tribes which make up the "Five Civilized Nations" under Confederate control.

Wednesday, May 1, 1861
Eastern Theater General Robert E. Lee sends Virginia troops under Colonel T.J. Jackson to seize Harper's Ferry. At sea the US Navy blockades the mouth of the James River.
Trans-Mississippi In the west, the Union issues a call for volunteers in Nebraska.

Thursday, May 2
Eastern Theater The hitherto unknown Colonel Jackson makes considerable changes in the troops under his command. He picks officers for their ability, instead of having the militia elect them, as has previously been the rule. He also establishes the principles of discipline, administration, and drill, which will turn volunteers into effective fighting men in the minimum time.

Friday, May 3
The North President Lincoln sets out to enlarge the regular armed forces and calls for over 42,000 three-year volunteers for the army and 18,000 for the navy. General Winfield Scott, commander of the Federal Army, reveals the "Anaconda Plan" which is to destroy the Confederacy by striking down the length of the Mississippi and cutting the Confederacy in two. Superior Federal industrial capability should then strangle the rebellion. Implicit in the plan are two main areas of conflict, with a Western Theater centered on the Mississippi, and an Eastern Theater whose battles will largely be contested in the "cockpit of the war" between Washington and Richmond. Also vital to the prosecution of the war are the naval operations, principally those of blockade, which will cut the South off from overseas assistance.

Western Theater Major-General George B. McClellan is given command of the newly formed Department of the Ohio.
Overseas Abroad the United States protests the "unofficial" meeting between the British foreign minister and the Southern commissioners attempting to gain international recognition for the Confederacy.

Saturday, May 4
Naval Operations In a letter to Mr G.W. Childs, veteran US Navy Commodore Stewart throws an interesting light on the reason for the war. Recalling conversations with John C. Calhoun during the war of 1812, he quotes the Southerner as saying, "That we are inherently aristocratic I cannot deny . . . it is through our affiliation with [the Democratic Party] that we hold power; but when we cease thus to control this nation through a disjointed democracy, or any material obstacle in that party which shall tend to throw us out of that rule and control, we shall then resort to the dissolution of the Union."

Sunday, May 5
Eastern Theater Virginia troops abandon the city of Alexandria, directly across the Potomac from the District of Columbia.

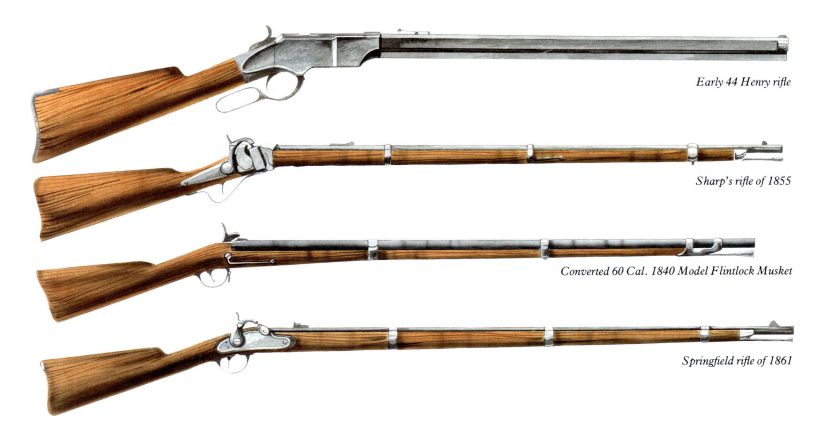

Early 44 Henry rifle

Sharp's rifle of 1855

Converted 60 Cal. 1840 Model Flintlock Musket

Springfield rifle of 1861

Monday, May 6

The Confederacy Jefferson Davis approves a bill from the Confederate Congress confirming a state of war between the Confederacy and the Union. Arkansas announces its secession from the Union after the state legislature votes 69–1 in favor.

Tuesday, May 7

Western Theater The Union steps up its drive to recruit volunteers from the borderline areas of western Virginia and from Kentucky.

Tennessee forms an alliance with the Confederacy which has the same effect as an official secession from the Union. This is pending the result of a state referendum on secession to take place before June 8. Not all Tennessee citizens are for the Confederacy, however. One person is killed during clashes between Southern and Federal supporters at Knoxville.

Wednesday, May 8

The North Major Robert Anderson, whose command at Fort Sumter has made his name known throughout the Union, has been given the task of raising volunteers for the Union from the borderline states.

Thursday, May 9

Naval Operations The Federal gunboat *Yankee*, on blockade duty off Virginia, exchanges shots with Confederate guns on Gloucester Point. The Naval Academy is moved north from Annapolis, due to the uncertain nature of Maryland's allegiance.

Friday, May 10

The Confederacy President Davis and Navy Secretary Mallory set in motion the purchase of a force of ironclads for the Confederate Navy. James D. Bullock has already been ordered to Britain for this purpose.

Trans-Mississippi Federal troops under Captain Nathaniel Lyon march to Camp Jackson at St Louis, and take 637 pro-Confederate state militiamen prisoner, as well as seizing 10,000 muskets. On the way back to the city curious onlookers are incited to riot, and four soldiers are killed along with 27 or more civilians.

Saturday, May 11

Trans-Mississippi Unrest continues at St Louis. Seven more people are killed in clashes between rioters and the 5th Missouri Reserve Regiment of the United States Army.

Far West Large pro-Union demonstrations take place in San Francisco, California.

Infantry formed the bulk of both armies and the Union alone was able to raise 1666 infantry regiments plus over 300 independent infantry companies. This vast number of troops had as its main weapon the rifle which appeared in many forms and varying numbers. The Union Government establishments could not handle all the work and many private firms were used. The 1861 model US percussion rifle musket totaled over 700,000 alone. Specialist rifles were also produced in large numbers as the war ground on with a consequent increase in type and variety.

May 1861

Sunday, May 12, 1861
The North General Benjamin Butler moves troops into Baltimore without authorization. He claims that he has received information that a major disturbance is being planned, and his action will nip a potentially serious riot in the bud.

Monday, May 13
Overseas Queen Victoria announces that Great Britain will remain neutral in the war. The British Government does not, for the moment, accord the Confederacy diplomatic recognition, but does regard it as a belligerent with all the rights that that entails. The British decision is helped by the president's mistake in calling the stopping of Southern sea trade a blockade. Blockade is something that is done to the ports of another nation, not your own. The president would have been better advised to have informed the world that the Federal Government was simply closing the ports held by insurgents.

Tuesday, May 14
The North President Lincoln decides that Union supporters in Kentucky are to receive every assistance, in spite of the increasingly neutral stance of the state government.

Wednesday, May 15
The North General Butler continues with his occupation of Baltimore. Although Maryland has repudiated secession, there is still a large body of pro-Confederate sentiment in the state, and Butler's actions can be seen to be safeguarding the Federal capital.

Thursday, May 16
The Confederacy The Confederate Provisional Congress authorizes the recruitment of 400,000 volunteers.
Western Theater Commodore John Rodgers is instructed to take command of Union riverine operations in the west. The legislature in Kentucky proposes to make its neutral stance official.

Friday, May 17
The Confederacy The Confederate Provisional Congress (so called because it has voted itself a life of only one year until it can be replaced by a permanent body) continues in session at Montgomery, Alabama.

Saturday, May 18
Eastern Theater The Union launches its first attack against the Confederacy, engaging rebel batteries at Sewall's Point, Virginia.

Naval Operations The Federal Navy seals off the mouth of the Rappahannock River, completing the blockade of Virginia.

Sunday, May 19
The North Although the threat to Washington caused by unrest in Baltimore has receded, the capital is still vulnerable to a thrust by Confederate forces. Fortunately for the Federal cause such a coup requires more troops than can currently be mustered by Virginia, which is the only rebel state with forces within striking distance of Washington. This allows the Union the time and space to set about improving the defenses of the national capital.

Monday, May 20
The Confederacy At a convention in Raleigh, the state of North Carolina officially secedes from the Union. Deeply divided Kentucky resolves to remain neutral in the war.

Tuesday, May 21
The Confederacy The Confederate Provisional Congress votes to accept Virginia's offer of facilities and elects to move the capital to Richmond.

Above: *Engineers of the 8th New York State Militia pose in their camp. The larger Northern states bore much of the burden of the war, both in financial terms and in terms of providing manpower. These first volunteers went to war without any conception of the horrors which awaited them, but it was not long before the true nature of the struggle became apparent.*

Right: *Private Thomas Bagley of the Richmond Home Guard was typical of the many young men, both Northern and Southern, who volunteered to serve their respective causes. As the war progressed, however, the smart European-influenced uniforms became drab, utilitarian items, at least for the rank and file soldier.*

Wednesday, May 22

Eastern Theater General Benjamin Butler arrives at Fortress Monroe, Virginia. This is a large Union-held fortification at the end of the peninsula between the James and the Charles rivers, and which overlooks Hampton Roads. Butler is to command a new military department intended to occupy the whole Atlantic coast. Possession of Fortress Monroe allows the Union to severely restrict Virginia's water-borne commerce.

Thursday, May 23

The Confederacy Virginia votes overwhelmingly to accept the state legislature's decision to join the Confederacy. The western portion of the state, however, remains strongly pro-Union, and a formal break with the rest of the state is a real possibility.

Friday, May 24

Eastern Theater 13,000 Federal troops under General Mansfield cross the Potomac and occupy the town of Alexandria and the Arlington Heights. This is the first stage in securing the defenses of Washington, so vulnerable to attack from Virginia. During the occupation, Elmer Ellsworth is shot dead while trying to remove a Confederate flag from a hotel. Ellsworth, commander of the Zouaves of the 11th New York Regiment, is killed by hotel owner James Jackson, who is himself immediately shot by a Private Brownell. The events are extensively and colorfully reported by newspapers North and South, and both men are regarded as martyrs by their respective causes.

Saturday, May 25

Eastern Theater While Mansfield's troops are occupying the Virginia side of the Potomac, on the peninsula Butler launches a reconnaissance in force toward the Confederate-occupied village of Hampton, north of Fortress Monroe. Occupying the village, Butler establishes an encampment, which he garrisons strongly. Occupation of Newport News, eight miles to the west, will give him control of the whole of the tip of the peninsula. His force can be resupplied by sea and stands poised like a dagger aimed at the heart of the Confederacy's strongest state. Richmond, the capital of Virginia, is less than 70 miles to the northwest.

Above: *The graceful wooden 3765-ton sidewheel steamer* Powhatan *saw much service during the Civil War. She had been completed in the early 1850s and went on to enjoy a long and active career, being withdrawn from service in 1886. Although steam-powered, much reliance was placed upon the large spread of canvas carried because of the high coal consumption of the early machinery.*

In spite of these negative points vessels such as Powhatan *marked the end of the reign of the graceful sailing men-of-war. In service* Powhatan *was a popular ship, being roomy and comfortable, and weathering many a severe storm in safety in spite of her increasing age.*

Above left: *Mary Tippee was a sutler, or supplier of goods, to the 114th Pennsylvania Regiment, otherwise known as Collis's Zouaves. In the first bright flush of the war, many volunteer regiments patterned themselves on the highly colorful French colonial regiments. But flashing uniforms do not a soldier make, and the armies were armies of amateurs.*

Left: *Black laborers work on a wharf on the James River of Virginia. Although differing ideas on the morality of slavery were major reasons for the war, it was actually fought in the first instance over state rights, and emancipation did not become a major issue of the war for at least a year.*

May–June 1861

Sunday, May 26, 1861
The Confederacy Surprisingly, postal communications with the Confederacy have continued past the outbreak of war, but today in Washington the postmaster-general announces that, with effect from May 31, they will cease.

Monday, May 27
Eastern Theater Units of General George B. McClellan's Army of the Ohio cross the Ohio River into Virginia to reinforce Colonel Kelly's 1st Virginia Regiment, which, like most of western Virginia, is loyal to the Union.

Tuesday, May 28
Eastern Theater Brigadier-General Irvin McDowell is appointed to command the Department of Northeastern Virginia and the Army of the Potomac. A graduate of West Point, he has combat experience from the Mexican War, although he is more highly regarded as an administrator.

Wednesday, May 29
The North Dorothea Dix offers to help set up hospitals for the Union Army, which is accepted by Secretary of War Simon Cameron.
Eastern Theater General Butler's troops occupy Newport News at the mouth of the James River and across the Hampton Roads from Norfolk, Virginia. This action makes the Union's grip on the strategically placed peninsula between the James and the York rivers even more secure, at the same time providing a base from which to threaten Richmond.

Butler's command at Fortress Monroe and the encampments at Hampton and Newport News now totals some 12,000 men.

Thursday, May 30
Eastern Theater Grafton, in western Virginia, is occupied by troops of McClellan's Army of the Ohio. Their main function is to protect Virginian citizens who have remained loyal to the Union, and to guard the important Baltimore and Ohio Railroad.

Friday, May 31
Eastern Theater General Pierre Gustave Toutant Beauregard is appointed to the command of the Confederate Army of the Potomac. From a Creole family, Beauregard is a professional soldier who had been superintendent of West Point at the beginning of the year. He was the first Confederate-appointed brigadier-general, and he commanded the troops which took Fort Sumter at the start of the war.
Trans-Mississippi Union troops from the Indian Nations reach Fort Leavenworth in Kansas. Guided by the half-Scottish, half-Indian Jesse Chisholm, the trail they take will become known as the Chisholm Trail, and will see some of the first great cattle drives after the war.

Saturday, June 1, 1861
Eastern Theater There is a skirmish at Fairfax Court House between Virginia troopers and Company B, 2nd US Cavalry. Both sides sustain some of their earliest battle casualties (as against deaths during rioting), with one killed and four wounded on the Union side and one killed and 14 wounded on the Confederate side.

Sunday, June 2
Eastern Theater The 3000 Union troops at Grafton are ordered by General McClellan to advance on the small Confederate cavalry force commanded by Colonel Porterfield at Philippi. Porterfield had been sent by General Lee to recruit troops for the Confederacy, but has had little success in staunchly pro-Union western Virginia. Under the command of Colonel Crittenden, the Union force marches south through the night.

Monday, June 3
The North In Chicago the distinguished Democratic politician Stephen A. Douglas dies of typhoid fever at the age of 48. Lincoln's great rival defeated the future president in the Illinois senatorial election of 1858, but was himself defeated in the presidential contest two years later. Known as the "Little Giant," he worked hard before the war for reconciliation between North and South, but stood firmly behind the president when war became inevitable.
Eastern Theater McClellan's troops attack Philippi, catching Porterfield's outnumbered cavalry troopers by surprise. The speed of the Confederate retreat leads to the engagement becoming known as the "Philippi Races."

Tuesday, June 4

Eastern Theater The almost bloodless victory at Philippi gives the Union troops in western Virginia great confidence, or, more accurately, over-confidence. Philippi shows, they argue, that Confederate troops have no stomach for a fight, and that the war will be quickly over. Although McClellan shares his soldiers' confidence, he prefers to move more carefully. The campaign in western Virginia is thus a series of marches and skirmishes with few casualties being inflicted on either side.

Wednesday, June 5

The North Arms and ammunition destined for the South are seized by Federal marshals from the Dupont works in Delaware and from factories in Baltimore.

Thursday, June 6

The North In Washington it is decided that once the individual states' fulfil their responsibilities to mobilize their volunteers, the Union Government will bear the cost of the war.

Friday, June 7

Eastern Theater McClellan's campaign in western Virginia highlights the conflict between the region and the rest of the state. Mountainous, rather than flat, and with ten free men for every slave, as compared with one to one which is the proportion in eastern Virginia, it is different in almost every way.

Saturday, June 8

The North The United States Sanitary Commission is established in Washington. It is one of the first official bodies to have been set up to look after the health of the troops, and is a major innovation in nineteenth-century warfare.

The Confederacy Tennessee's secession from the Union is confirmed by a state referendum.

The formidable outline of the powerful Union ironclad Benton *which saw extensive service along the Mississippi. She started life as a catamaran-hulled salvage vessel and was taken over by the army for conversion into an ironclad gunboat.*

In October 1862 she, together with other warships being used by the army, was transferred to the navy. Like many of the vessels that served along the rivers of the Confederacy, the heat of summer took its fearful toll of the crew, who soon fell ill. At one time Admiral Porter requested 600 replacemments for crew on the sick list.

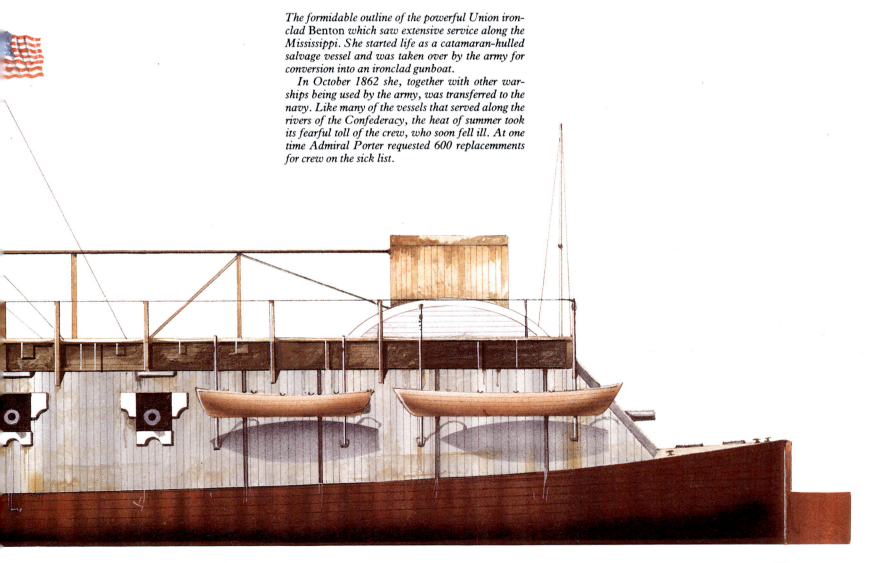

June 1861

Sunday, June 9, 1861

Eastern Theater On the peninsula Butler prepares to ferry troops across Hampton Creek. There they will operate in conjunction with a column from the encampment at Newport News, which is moving towards an isolated enemy outpost at Little Bethel Church. This is the most advanced position of a strong enemy force centered on Yorktown, about 25 miles from Fortress Monroe. Five miles from Little Bethel is the Church at Big Bethel, around which is entrenched a 2000-strong Confederate force under the command of Colonel John B. Magruder. A graduate of West Point, the hot-tempered Virginian is known as "Prince John" from his elaborate personal lifestyle.

Monday, June 10

Eastern Theater Setting out at midnight, the two Union columns on the peninsula intend to catch the Confederate outpost at Little Bethel by surprise. After a dawn attack, the confused rebels are to be driven into Magruder's position at Big Bethel and in the ensuing confusion that too should be taken. Unfortunately, the confusion in the dark is all on the Union side. Colonel Duryea's regiment is ferried into position and moves behind the enemy as planned. Colonel Phelps's regiment comes up from Newport News and advances toward Little Bethel, leaving a rear guard under Colonel Bendix at the junction of the Hampton and Newport News roads. The 3rd New York Regiment, under Colonel Townsend, is the last unit to arrive, and

Above: Washington in 1861 was not the sophisticated capital which it has become in the twentieth century. It was a city under construction; its streets were largely mud, and hot, humid summer weather made it unbearable. But as the nation's capital, it was a major target for the Southern states, and Virginia, the most important of them, lay across the Potomac River.

is expected to join with Bendix and continue with the attack. As the regiment approaches the crossroads, it is led by two officers on horseback. In the dim light Bendix assumes the two riders are part of a cavalry unit. As there is no Union cavalry on the peninsula, he assumes that they are hostile. Ten of Townsend's force are wounded when Bendix opens fire.

The Union forces at the crossroads now fall back and, alarmed by the firing, the regiment already in advance does likewise. Of course, the whole thing has alerted the Confederate outpost at Little Bethel, and the troopers there move to join Magruder's formidable and now fully alert position. With the coming of daylight, the Union forces try a direct assault upon the Confederate entrenchments, and although they take the outer line of defenses, the dug-in Confederates eventually throw them back in a sharp engagement. The Union sustains some 50 casualties, including 16 dead, while the better protected Confederates report only one killed and seven wounded.

Tuesday, June 11

The North In western Virginia anti-secessionist counties set up a pro-Union state government, which is recognized as such by Washington.

Eastern Theater In a skirmish at Romney, two Confederates are killed in a fight with the 11th Indiana Regiment, who have a single, non-fatal casualty.

Trans-Mississippi Nathaniel Lyon, now brigadier-general commanding the Department of the West, meets the pro-Southern Governor Claiborne Jackson of Missouri and militia Major-General Sterling Price. They try to persuade Lyon that the state is neutral and should not have United States troops quartered in or passing through the state. Lyon, however, knows that Jackson and Price have organized a State Guard in secret for their own secessionist purposes. But even had he wanted to, Lyon cannot accept their demands since, even by holding itself neutral, Missouri is taking a secessionist stance. Meanwhile, a Confederate force under the noted Texas ranger Ben McCulloch has crossed the southern boundary of the state and is heading toward Springfield.

Wednesday, June 12

Trans-Mississippi Governor Jackson makes a proclamation in Jefferson City, Missouri, claiming he had tried to compromise with the "invaders," and calling for 50,000 volunteers to fight the Union forces. General Sigel is sent toward Springfield to ward off McCulloch's force.

Above: *Confederate troops stand ready for battle before their tents. Although they were just as amateur as their Northern counterparts, the Southernners had greater motivation, in that they were fighting for the very survival of their fledgling nation.*

Above: *Mass is celebrated by members of the 69th New York State Militia in camp at Fort Corcoran, Washington, D.C. Many of the first East Coast volunteers were needed to protect the national capital, which was threatened by the first great Confederate advances from Virginia.*

Thursday, June 13
Trans-Mississippi Jackson and all available troops retreat south from Jefferson City, while Lyon advances from St Louis with 1500 men.

Friday, June 14
Eastern Theater In Virginia, McClellan's and Patterson's commands are advancing east and south respectively toward Harper's Ferry, which is abandoned by the Confederates in the face of this threat.

Saturday, June 15
Trans-Mississippi Further Confederate formations are in the field in Missouri: under Price, heading for Booneville and Lexington, and under Rains on the western border.

Sunday, June 16
Trans-Mississippi Lyon's strategy in Missouri is to prevent the Confederate forces from concentrating and to take the opportunity to defeat them in detail.

Monday, June 17
The North At Washington, Professor Thaddeus Lowe demonstrates his hot-air balloon to President Lincoln and to his military advisers. A number see the possibilities the device offers for battlefield reconnaissance.

Eastern Theater Gregg's Confederate cavalrymen raid to within sight of Washington. On their return they ambush a Union troop train at Vienna, Virginia.

Trans-Mississippi In Missouri, Nathaniel Lyon leaves part of his force in Jefferson City and embarks 2000 men in three river steamers for Booneville. Landing his troops before they can be taken under fire by rebel batteries, he advances on the Confederate force. Feigning a retreat, Lyon draws the enemy under the fire of his own guns, and within 20 minutes has them in full retreat, leaving 14 killed and 20 wounded.

Tuesday, June 18
Trans-Mississippi In a clash between Union and Confederate Home Guards at Camp Cole, Missouri, 70 Union casualties include as many as 25 killed, while four rebels are killed and some 20 are wounded.

Wednesday, June 19
The North Anti-secessionists in the western part of Virginia meet to elect Francis H. Pierpont governor of what will eventually become the state of West Virginia.

Thursday, June 20
Trans-Mississippi State forces in Missouri now make every effort to concentrate with McCulloch's force in the south of the state, away from the Union-controlled north.

Friday, June 21
Trans-Mississippi In Missouri, Rains' force hurries to join with Governor Jackson, pursued by a regular army column under Major Sturgis. Reaching the Osage River, the Confederates cross the bridge and destroy it behind them. Faced with a river in full spate, the Union troops are forced to set up camp until the waters subside.

Saturday, June 22
Trans-Mississippi Governor Jackson, who had been an onlooker at Booneville, flees southward with 500 men.

June–July 1861

Sunday, June 23, 1861

Eastern Theater It is obvious that the Confederates plan to make Virginia their major battlefield. General Beauregard, having won laurels at Fort Sumter, is in command of the Army of the Potomac, which is well positioned to be able to threaten Washington or to come to the defense of Richmond. The key to the Southern position is the vital railroad junction at Manassas, less than 30 miles west of Washington. A second force, the Army of the Shenandoah, is in position in the Shenandoah Valley under the command of General Joseph E. Johnston.

Monday, June 24

Naval Operations Virginia batteries at Mathias Point are attacked by Union gunboats.

Tuesday, June 25

Eastern Theater General Patterson marches toward Winchester in the Shenandoah Valley. His force had crossed the Potomac two days before. Unfortunately for the aging Union general, most of his troops are three-month volunteers, who are indicating that they will not stay one minute beyond their terms of enlistment. Joe Johnston's command slowly retires, with some inconsequential skirmishes taking place between the forces.

Wednesday, June 26

Eastern Theater In a clash at Patterson Creek, Virginia (also known as the engagement at Kelley's Island) seven Confederates are killed for one Union loss.

Thursday, June 27

The North In one of the more useful committees of the war, army, navy and coastal survey representatives meet in Washington to discuss problems likely to be encountered in on-shore and off-shore operations around the Southern coast.

Naval Operations A Federal amphibious attack on Mathias Point mounted from the gunboats *Pawnee* and *Freeborn* is repelled by Confederate defenders.

Friday, June 28

The North An article published two days previously in the *New York Tribune* becomes widely quoted in Washington. In just 30 words it strikes a chord with the public. "Forward to Richmond!" was the heading, and it continued, "The Rebel Congress must not be allowed to meet there on the 20th July! By that date the place must be held by the National Army!" Repeated time and time again, like Cato's denunciation of Carthage, it demands action. In purely military terms, a drive into the heart of Virginia from Washington promises to be a risky affair, but saner military counsels are overwhelmed by the public's demand for action.

Saturday, June 29

The North Civil and military leaders of the Union meet the president and his Cabinet to consider long-term strategies for the war. General Scott outlines his plans, and because age and infirmity preclude him from undertaking any strenuous activity, he delegates the field command to General Irvin McDowell. McDowell is a military academy graduate, with a good record from the Mexican War, but who spent the 12 years following the war in administrative posts in the Adjutant-General's Department. His first task in command must be to carry out the "Forward to Richmond" campaign.

Sunday, June 30

Naval Operations CSS *Sumter*, formerly the Spanish vessel *Marques de Habana*, breaks out from New Orleans. Taking advantage of the USS *Brooklyn* being off station chasing an English blockade runner, the *Sumter* eludes the Federal blockade. Under the command of 52-year-old Captain Raphael Semmes, the *Sumter* sets off on a six-month cruise, during which she will capture or destroy 18 Federal vessels.

Monday, July 1, 1861

The North In an attempt to bolster the Union's fighting power, the War Department intends recruiting for volunteers in Tennessee and Kentucky, even though Kentucky is trying to stay neutral and Tennessee has actually voted to join the Confederacy.

Tuesday, July 2

The North General John C. Frémont, the noted explorer, meets with President Lincoln. In Europe at the outbreak of war, he has returned to take command of Union forces in Missouri, currently with many small skirmishes and violent civil unrest the most active area of conflict.

Eastern Theater The Confederates under Beauregard are massing in strong positions at Manassas only a few miles west of Washington. Johnston has established himself at Winchester in the Shenandoah Valley. Patterson's 18,000 men once again move out toward the Confederates from their positions near Harper's Ferry to keep an eye on Johnston, and to prevent him from uniting with the main Confederate Army of the Potomac at Manassas.

Wednesday, July 3

Eastern Theater Patterson's approach to Martinsburg leads Johnston to pull back yet again toward his fortified positions at Winchester.

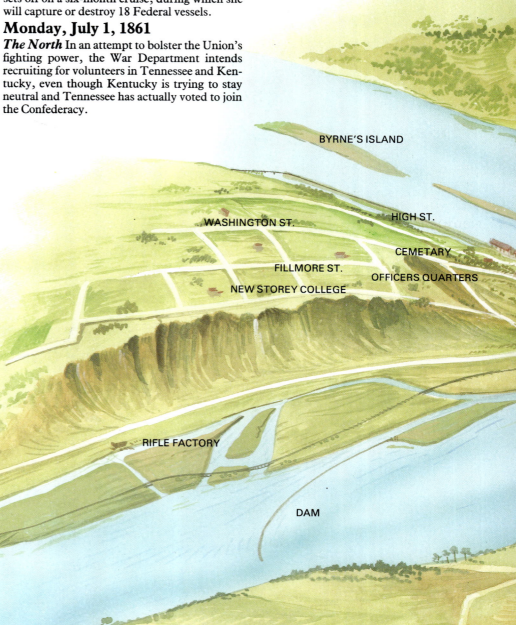

BYRNE'S ISLAND

WASHINGTON ST.

HIGH ST.

FILLMORE ST.

CEMETARY

OFFICERS QUARTERS

NEW STOREY COLLEGE

RIFLE FACTORY

DAM

Thursday, July 4

The North Today is the 84th anniversary of the Declaration of Independence, and in Washington Congress meets in extraordinary session. The president sets forth the causes of the present trouble, the measures that had been taken to try to avert the war, and the indivisibility of the Union. The House is addressed by Simon Cameron, the secretary for war, who recommends volunteers be enlisted for three years; Salmon P. Chase, the secretary of the treasury, who asks for $240 million for the running of the war and $80 million for current government expenses; and Gideon Wells, the secretary of the navy, who asks Congress to approve his actions and also to appoint a commission to examine the possibility of building ironclad steamers and floating batteries.

Friday, July 5

Trans-Mississippi Northern troops out of Springfield, Missouri, under General Franz Sigel attack Governor Claiborne Jackson's troops at Carthage, where they have joined with Rains' and Price's commands. Although outnumbered, Sigel attacks across the open countryside, beginning the battle with a cannonade which is returned by the Confederates. Although getting the better of the artillery duel, Sigel is outflanked by Confederate cavalry, so he falls back to his baggage wagons, beating off attacks on the way. Finding the town of Carthage occupied by the enemy, he decides to retire to Mount Vernon, between Carthage and Springfield, there to unite with a further Federal force. Although Union casualties are much lighter than Confederate losses (13 killed and 31 wounded against up to 50 rebel dead, 125 wounded, and 45 rebels captured), the battle at Carthage is a setback for the Union in Missouri, slowing the otherwise successful Federal drive for control of the state.

Saturday, July 6

Eastern Theater In a skirmish at Buckhannon, western Virginia, Union troopers kill seven Confederates.

Trans-Mississippi In Missouri Sigel marches his troops through the night, fighting off rebel attacks in the woods in the early stages of the maneuver. Sigel's advantage lies in his artillery, that of his opponents being of poor quality and very poorly managed. Not stopping to rest in the morning, he returns his command to Mount Vernon.

Harper's Ferry in 1861. It was here in 1859 that John Brown tried to free the slaves by force of arms. His small band of supporters was soon overwhelmed by troops under Robert E. Lee.

MARYLAND HEIGHTS

POTOMAC RIVER

MUSKET FACTORY

ENGINE HOUSE

ARSENAL

GAULT HOUSE

LOUDOUN HEIGHTS

July 1861

Sunday, July 7, 1861

Eastern Theater In a skirmish at Great Falls, Virginia, 12 Confederates are killed for the loss of two Union soldiers.

Monday, July 8

Far West The Confederacy moves to take control of New Mexico territory, appointing General H.H. Sibley to command. His task is to force the Federals completely out of the southwest.

Tuesday, July 9

Trans-Mississippi Missouri remains the scene of skirmishing. Reports are received of a July 8 attack on a Confederate camp at Florida, Missouri. The camp is dispersed.

Wednesday, July 10

The North President Lincoln, in an attempt to keep Kentucky out of the Confederacy, sends a letter to Simon Bolivar Buckner stating that Union troops will not enter the state. Buckner, personally against secession, is Kentucky's inspector general of militia.

Eastern Theater In western Virginia McClellan sends a force under the command of General William B. Rosecrans toward the Confederates at Rich Mountain. Among the units Rosecrans has at his disposal are the 8th, 10th, and 13th Indiana, and the 19th Ohio regiments.

Trans-Mississippi In a battle at Monroe Station, Missouri, troops from the 16th Illinois Regiment, the 3rd Indiana Regiment, and the Hannibal Home Guards defeat a Confederate force for the loss of three men. Confederate casualties total four killed, 20 wounded, and 75 prisoners.

Above: *The ruins of the Stone Bridge over the Bull Run mark the point where McDowell's flank attack at Manassas first came into contact with the Confederate line.*

Thursday, July 11

Eastern Theater Rosecrans defeats Pegram's Confederates at the Battle of Rich Mountain in western Virginia. In the most costly battle of the war to date the defeated Confederate casualties total 300, including 60 killed, 140 wounded, and 100 taken prisoner. The cost to the Union is much lighter, with 11 lives lost and 35 other casualties. Meanwhile, a second Union force is in action nearby under General Morris. Attacking Laurel Mountain, Morris forces General Robert S. Garnett's Confederates to retreat toward the Cheat River valley.

Friday, July 12

Eastern Theater At Beverley in western Virginia McClellan's 4th and 9th Ohio regiments occupy the town, taking 600 defeated Confederates prisoner. Meanwhile, a Union force under the command of Jacob Cox prepares to meet former Virginia governor Henry Wise's troops in the Great Kanawah Valley.

Saturday, July 13

Eastern Theater McClellan completes the Union domination of western Virginia by crushing Garnett's command at Carrick's Ford. Confederate casualties total 20 killed (including General Garnett), 10 wounded, and 50 prisoners taken by the 7th and 9th Indiana, and the 14th Ohio regiments. Union casualties total 53, including 13 dead.

Sunday, July 14

Eastern Theater Success in western Virginia leaves McClellan and the Union in command of several important railroads, and also provides a secure base from which to conduct operations into the rest of Virginia. It also encourages the North to press forward elsewhere, and General McDowell plans to cross into Virginia with 40,000 troops. His first advance will be toward Fairfax Court House.

Monday, July 15

Naval Operations The USS *Daylight* has been blockading Wilmington, North Carolina, for a day. The task is too much for a single ship, however, and the blockade is less than effective. More vessels are called for.

Tuesday, July 16

Eastern Theater McDowell's army begins to move out from the defenses of Washington toward the Confederates at Manassas Junction.

Trans-Mississippi In Missouri the skirmishing continues, with both sides losing seven men at Wentzville.

Wednesday, July 17

There is a small-scale action on all of the main battle fronts, with casualties reported at Fulton, Missouri, Martinsburg, Missouri, Scarrytown, western Virginia, and Bunker Hill, Virginia.
Eastern Theater The engagement at Bunker Hill involves a detachment from General Patterson's command, which is supposed to be holding Joe Johnston's Confederates in the Shenandoah Valley. However, Johnston has been instructed to move the bulk of his troops from the valley to reinforce Beauregard's command. By skilful use of deception, Johnston convinces Patterson he is still at Winchester and will remain there.

Thursday, July 18

Eastern Theater McDowell's army is camped at Centreville. Morale is high. "It is ardently hoped," writes a newspaper correspondent, "that the rascals will stand and fight at Manassas. But it is greatly feared that they will run again." Tyler's division is in the van, and pushes forward in force toward Blackburn's Ford on the Bull Run Creek.

In the woods at the ford a considerable force of Confederates under James Longstreet are dug in, and in an exchange lasting several hours, the Union sustains 19 killed, 38 wounded, and 26 missing, to the Confederate loss of 15 dead and 53 wounded. In the valley Johnson leaves a rear guard to hold Patterson's attention and, with all but the sick and wounded, marches through Ashby's Gap to the Manassas railroad. From there he moves toward Manassas Junction.

Friday, July 19

Eastern Theater McDowell expects to meet Beauregard at Fairfax Court House, but finds nothing there. He does not expect the army to be engaged near Centreville, so is not even with it at the time of the engagement with Longstreet. Coming to Centreville, he soon realizes that the Confederates have pulled back to the line of the Bull Run and, even if he forces his way across, he will be faced with the strong position at Manassas. But he must do something. It is not just public opinion; many of his troops have volunteered for just three months, and in a few days he will have lost 10,000 men whose enlistments will have expired. His first plan, a wide-sweeping march to the left to outflank the enemy, is found to be impractical. He decides to use an apparently unguarded ford across the Bull Run at Sudley Springs to outflank the Confederates on the right. What he does not know, however, is that Johnston is making his way toward Manassas with all possible speed.
Trans-Mississippi In Missouri there is a running fight between a Confederate force and Van Horne's Missouri Battalion with the Cass County Home Guards.

Saturday, July 20

The Confederacy The Confederate Congress meets at Richmond for the first time.
Eastern Theater Johnston reaches Beauregard's army at Manassas with 9000 fighting men from the Shenadoah Valley. Beauregard's strategy is the same as McDowell's—making a flank attack to the right and sweeping around the enemy's left. McDowell has some 30,000 men under his command, although two units of three-month volunteers reach the end of their enlistment today and cannot be persuaded to

Above: *The Confederate victory at Bull Run meant that a Southern move against Washington was a real possibility, so hasty steps were taken to beef up the defenses of the capital. Before long, the city was ringed by encampments, where volunteers like this Pennsylvania regiment drilled to stand off the rebels everybody believed were just over the horizon. However, Bull Run had another effect. Far from rolling the rebellion over, the people of the Union now realized that they were in a real war, and that a real army would be needed. Ironically, the Southern populace formed an opposing opinion, as the inept Federal performance at Manassas convinced many that the war would soon be over.*

stay, leaving McDowell with about 28,000 effectives. Beauregard has just under 22,000, with 6000 reinforcements from the Shenandoah Valley almost on the scene, and a further 2500 not far behind. With the armies in position, an "ominous stillness" settles over Manassas.

July–August 1861

Sunday, July 21

Eastern Theater McDowell's plan of striking the Confederate left flank at Manassas is good. He reasons that the partly trained Confederate volunteers will not easily be able to make the complex change of direction necessary to respond to the Federal attack. Unfortunately, the Federal Army is hardly better trained, and the attack takes longer to form up than had been expected. This gives the rebels time to prepare their defenses.

The first part of the Union plan involves Tyler's division, including a brigade commanded by Colonel William T. Sherman, making a diversionary attack against Stone Bridge while the bulk of the army is to continue to Sudley Springs, fording the river and enveloping the Confederate left.

At 6.30 a.m. Tyler's artillery, including a large 30-pound Parrot rifled gun, opens up on Stone Bridge, which is held by 1100 Confederates under Captain N.G. Evans. At first the attack holds their attention, but then the main Federal force is spotted, and Evans moves to cover the approach from Sudley Springs.

Evans' small force holds the main Union Army, which is spearheaded by Colonel Ambrose Burnside's Rhode Island Brigade, until about noon. The remnants of Evans' command then fall back toward Henry House, where the newly arrived Confederate brigades of Bartow and Bee are positioned. Bee's brigade joins Evans', but the combined Southern line is still threatened by the overwhelming force of the advancing Federal Army.

Further Confederate reinforcements are dispatched to the embattled left of the line, in the shape of Jackson's brigade and Wade Hampton's legion. Meanwhile, Generals Johnston and Beauregard are concentrating on the planned Confederate attack against the Union left flank and toward Centreville.

The rapidly worsening situation on the left makes Johnson realize that the battle can be lost there, however, with the rebel line being hammered unmercifully by the Union artillery. Both generals head for Henry Hill. The rebel line is on the point of disintegrating when Wade Hampton's legion of aristocratic Southern cavalrymen secures the right flank of a Confederate line now forming along the Henry Plateau. The meat of the line is Jackson's brigade, which, "Standing like a stone wall," holds fast. Eventually, the Federals pull back, but in the process are shattered by an attack from Jackson's left flank regiment, heavily reinforced by Confederate troops recently arrived on the battlefield, followed by a cavalry charge led by Colonel J.E.B. Stuart. Panic breaks out in parts of the Union force, which retreats in disorder through the by now hysterical civilians who had come out from Washington to watch the battle as if it were a sporting event. The situation is made worse by the upsetting of an artillery caisson on the bridge over the Bull Run, blocking the way to safety. The panic caused by those trying to force their way past the bottleneck is contagious, and soon, with a few courageous exceptions, the entire Union Army is in full flight.

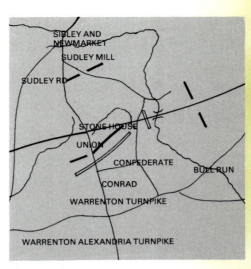

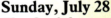

What had looked to be a Union victory at midday, the first stage of the march "Forward to Richmond," has in a few hours been turned into a Confederate triumph. But it is at some cost; Confederate losses are listed at 400 dead and missing, with 1582 wounded. Union casualties total 2896, including 460 dead, and 1312 missing. Far from being a triumphal march on Richmond, the battle at Bull Run makes the North realize that this is going to be a long and costly war.

Monday, July 22

Trans-Mississippi In Missouri, conflicting state governments arise, with a convention at Jefferson City declaring for the Union, while the secession-minded Governor Claiborne Jackson continues to claim authority.

Tuesday, July 23

Western Theater John C. Frémont is now in place as commander of Union forces in the west.

Wednesday, July 24

Eastern Theater Union troops attack Confederates under General Henry Wise at Tyler Mountain, western Virginia. Wise evacuates the area of Charleston.

Thursday, July 25

The North Congress passes the Crittenden Resolution, which declares that the war is being fought to preserve the Union and not to abolish slavery.

Trans-Mississippi The situation remains confused, with fighting at Harrisville and Dug Springs, Missouri.

Far West In New Mexico Federal troops at Fort Fillmore repel Confederate attempts to eject the Union from the southwestern states.

Friday, July 26

Far West At Fort Fillmore Major Isaac Linde retreats with the 500 troops under his command, in spite of the fact that Baylor's Confederates facing him are only 250 strong.

Saturday, July 27

The North President Lincoln removes the defeated McDowell from command of the Washington area and gives the responsibility to the confident General George B. McClellan, fresh from his successful campaign in western Virginia.

Sunday, July 28

The Confederacy Following the victory at Bull Run, Confederate president Jefferson Davis urges further action in Virginia.

Monday, July 29

Eastern Theater Success at Manassas is not matched for the South elsewhere in Virginia. After the battle of Carrick Ford, the position in the western part of the state is precarious. President Davis resolves to send his military adviser, General Robert E. Lee, to take command in the region.

Tuesday, July 30

Eastern Theater At Fortress Monroe General Butler has about 900 former slaves on his hands, and presses Washington as to what he should do about them.

Wednesday, July 31

The North Ulysees S. Grant, a West Point graduate with Mexican War experience and serving as a volunteer colonel in Illinois, is appointed general of volunteers by President Lincoln, and will become a brigadier-general within two months.

Thursday, August 1, 1861

Far West Captain Baylor at Fort Fillmore claims Arizona and New Mexico for the Confederacy.

Friday, August 2

Trans-Mississippi In Missouri General Nathaniel Lyon clashes with part of McCulloch's command near Dug Springs, losing four men but killing 40 of the enemy.

Far West Baylor continues to push the Union out of New Mexico, forcing the Federal garrison to evacuate Fort Stanton.

SHERMAN ADVANCES
VIA FORD

McDOWELL
WITH 2 DIVISIONS

STONE HOUSE

ROBINSON HOUSE

STONE BRIDGE

JACKSON'S
BRIGADE MAKING A STAND

HENRY HOUSE

KIRBY SMITH ATTACKING

WARRENTON TURNPIKE

MATHEW'S HOUSE

BALD HILL

JUBAL EARLY
DRIVES UP FROM SOUTH

Saturday, August 3

Trans-Mississippi Southwestern Missouri remains unsettled, and General Lyon predicts more trouble to come. He is reinforced by troops sent by General Frémont.

Far West In New Mexico Union troops from the 7th US Infantry Regiment and the US Mounted Rifles get slightly the better of a small Confederate force in a skirmish at Mesilla.

In the opening, heady days of 1861 the North predicted a speedy victory over the forces of the South, and one of the early actions was that of Bull Run, where Union forces under General McDowell clashed with 29,000 Confederates under Beauregard. On July 1 the Federals crossed Bull Run, forcing the Confederates back to Henry House Hill where General Jackson checked their advance. Late in the day the Confederates went on the attack, driving through the Union's exposed wing.

39

August 1861

Sunday, August 4, 1861

The North Following an appropriation of $1,500,000 at the close of the Congressional session, the Union places an advertisement requesting proposals for one or more ironclad warships to improve Federal naval capability. At the same time, a commission is established which will examine any plans suggested. This will eventually see 17 presentations, ranging from vessels costing $38,000 up to a plan for a 400-foot monster that would use up the entire appropriation.

Monday, August 5

Trans-Mississippi In Missouri a large Confederate force advances on General Lyon's position at Dug Springs in the southwest of the state.

Naval Operations The Confederate blockade runner *Alvarado* is captured and burned by the USS *Vincennes* off Florida.

Tuesday, August 6

The North Congress passes a Confiscation Act, declaring that property used in insurrection, including slaves where slave laws apply, shall be forfeit. The president is given extraordinary powers by Congress, specifically when dealing in military and naval matters.

Wednesday, August 7

Eastern Theater On the peninsula General John B. Magruder leads a force against the Federal-held town of Hampton and burns it to the ground. He claims that the action is in reprisal for General Butler's harboring of fugitive slaves.

Thursday, August 8

The North In response to General Butler's persistent inquiries, Secretary of War Cameron states that the Union must adhere to fugitive slave laws, but only in states which possess such laws, and then only if they are not in insurrection. Further, escaped slaves must not be returned to states in insurrection.

Friday, August 9

Trans-Mississippi Nathaniel Lyon, having fallen back on Springfield from his earlier position at Dug Spring, Missouri, knows that he does not have enough strength to protect the city. McCulloch's Confederate force, having joined with Price, Rains, and Jackson, is pushing north, and Frémont has troubles of his own in St Louis and is unable to send any help. Nevertheless, Lyon sets out with 5200 men on a night march to Wilson's Creek, where he proposes to use his heavily outnumbered force at least to delay the advancing Confederates, and even drive them back if he can mount a surprise attack.

Saturday, August 10

Trans-Mississippi Lyon divides his command into two columns. One, under Sigel, is to flank the Confederate right and attack from the rear, while Lyon himself will lead a frontal attack with 4000 men. The Confederate force numbers between 15,000 and 20,000 men. In the battle, the largest of the year after Bull Run, things do not go well for the Union. Sigel is more of a political general than a fighting commander, and his force is repelled and driven from the field. Although Lyon's force beats off two overwhelming attacks from a position known as Bloody Ridge, the general himself is killed while at the head of the 1st Iowa Regiment. Command devolves upon Major Sturgis, who holds the position until it becomes clear that his alternatives are retreat or oblivion. Union losses are 223 killed, 721 wounded, and 291 missing, while Confederate losses are variously reported as between 265 and 421 killed, and between 800 and 1300 wounded. Although Wilson's Creek is a significant Confederate victory, McCulloch's army has received a severe mauling and is unable to pursue the retreating Union troops. The Union's loss is only heightened by the death of Brigadier-General Lyon, a fine leader who could well have risen to the very highest of Union commands had he survived.

Below: *The Civil War was the first people's war. A generally literate population was interested in every detail of the campaigns, and that interest was catered to by the press. Reporters like these accompanied the armies into battle, filing their stories over the telegraph wires to appear the next day in newspapers 1000 miles away.*

Below: *General P.G.T. Beauregard had commanded the rebellious forces at Fort Sumter and was, with General Joseph E. Johnston, commander of the victorious Confederate troops at the Battle of Manassas.*

Sunday, August 11

Eastern Theater General George B. McClellan is well into the task of reorganizing a Union Army disrupted by defeat at Manassas. In a memo requested by the president immediately after Bull Run, and considered and written over the next few weeks, he outlines his ideas. The main tenor of his argument is that the war is not like normal wars, where the aim is usually to gain a strong enough hand to win an advantageous peace settlement. In this case, it is necessary to crush an intelligent and warlike population numerous enough to constitute a nation. He urges the formation of the massive military force necessary for the prompt and irresistable actions which would end the war quickly.

Monday, August 12

Far West A Confederate force in West Texas is attacked by hostile Apache Indians, who kill 15 of the white men.

Tuesday, August 13

Eastern Theater The chaos in the Union Army makes the still firmly held belief by the populace that the rebels can be defeated in the field within two or three months unreasonable. Indeed, those in the know say that it will take the army longer to learn how to build a single pontoon bridge than the people seem to think it will take to settle the Confederacy once and for all.

Major General Irvin McDowell (below), a fine administrative officer but no field commander, was reluctant to fight the Confederates with his untrained troops, but popular pressure forced him forward with disastrous results. After the battle, the defenses of Washington, like the Fort (right) took priority for troops over almost any other military activity.

Wednesday, August 14

Eastern Theater Unrest and indiscipline in the Union Army defending Washington is turned to mutiny in the 79th New York Regiment. The ringleaders are arrested.

Trans-Mississippi General John C. Frémont, troubled by continuing unrest amounting almost to ferment, puts a blanket of martial law over St Louis.

Thursday, August 15

Eastern Theater Missouri is not the only place that the Union is in trouble. All is not well in the army defending Washington. Following the mutiny in the 79th New York, there is further trouble in the 2nd Maine Volunteers. Ringleaders are sent to the Dry Tortugas off the Florida Keys as as punishment. It is clear that the new army commander will have to institute a major reorganization of what is currently an amateur collection of militia groups if it is to be turned into an army capable of meeting and defeating a Confederate Army currently riding a victorious wave.

Trans-Mississippi The position in Missouri grows more serious, and President Lincoln directs the War Department to send reinforcements to Frémont.

Friday, August 16

Trans-Mississippi Contact is reported between Union and Confederate troops at Fredricktown and at Kirkville, Missouri, although there are no casualties reported at either location.

Saturday, August 17

Trans-Mississippi There is a skirmish at Brunswick, Missouri, involving the (Union) 5th Missouri Reserves.

August 1861

Sunday, August 18, 1861
The North Even in places like New England there are those who sympathize with the secessionist cause, but it is a dangerous thing to make known. A number of New York newspapers have been brought to court to answer charges of publishing pro-Confederate material. In other states newspaper offices are attacked by outraged citizens, one Massachusetts editor being tarred and feathered.
Eastern Theater General Butler is relieved of his command in the Department of Virginia by General Wool. Having no other orders, he remains at Fortress Monroe in a subordinate position.

Monday, August 19
The Confederacy The Confederate Congress declares an alliance with Missouri, probably with a view to establishing a Confederate state government. This only makes the North/South division in the troubled state even more pronounced.
Trans-Mississippi In a fight at Charlestown, or Bird's Point, Missouri, the 22nd Illinois Regiment kill at least 40 Confederates at a cost to themselves of only one killed and six wounded.

Tuesday, August 20
The Confederacy The Confederate Government announces that it will appoint more commissioners, who will have the task of securing war material and supplies from the European powers, particularly from Britain and France.
Eastern Theater A skirmish is reported at Hawk's Nest, western Virginia.
Trans-Mississippi Fighting is reported at Jonesboro, Missouri, but no casualties are inflicted on either side.

Wednesday, August 21
Eastern Theater With Fortress Monroe at the end of the James/Charles peninsula secure, it is time to think of what to do with such a stronghold, pointed as it is like a dagger at the heart of the Confederacy. It is a potential base of operations from which land forces could drive up the peninsula toward the Confederate capital at Richmond, but as yet the Union Army is not strong enough for such an ambitious operation. It also promises to be a fine springboard for naval operations along the weakly defended southern coasts. Indeed, General Wool finds a raid along these lines being planned when he arrives in Fortress Monroe to take command of the Department of Virginia. General Butler volunteers to command the expedition, which in any case is largely of his own planning.

Thursday, August 22
The Confederacy Northern military and naval commanders are not the only people to notice the South's vulnerability to attack from the sea, The *Augusta Chronicle and Sentinel* runs an article which sounds a note of alarm in setting out the reasons for organizing a coastal defense—an alarm which is to be illustrated graphically less than a week later at Cape Hatteras.

"1. There are many places where the enemy might raid and do damage before we could drive them off . . . Beaufort district opposite Savannah has several fine ports and inlets, navigable for large vessels, wholly unprotected . . . several inlets on our coast which the enemy knows like a book from surveys . . . are equally unprotected.

"2. In two months more they will not fear our climate. By that time they might be ready to make a sudden descent and find us unprepared.

"3. A small force might eject them if ready to move at once; . . . if we have to wait, a much larger one will be necessary.

"4. By organizing and drilling infantry and guerrillas at home there will be no need to call on the president for troops, and a feint from the enemy would not injure our Virginia operations."

Friday, August 23
Eastern Theater General Wise, the Confederate commander in western Virginia, has too small a force to oppose General Rosecrans' Federal Army effectively, and manages to squeeze reinforcements out of the authorities in Richmond. Unfortunately, the reinforcement is under the command of General Floyd, a buffoon whose supercilious air immediately arouses hostility in the hard-pressed Wise. Floyd it is who appoints the editor of the *Lynchburg Republican* as his chief of staff, a sub-editor as his aide-de-camp—perhaps intended for his victories to be set in print as quickly as possible—and a farmer as his cavalry commander on the grounds that he should know something about horses. In his plans to drive Rosecrans out of Virginia in two weeks or so, he forgets his baggage trains, and it is some time before his force is supplied.

Saturday, August 24
The Confederacy James Mason, John Sliddel, and Pierre Rost are appointed Confederate commissioners to Britain, France, and Spain respectively.

ROANOKE ISLA

PAMLICO SOUND

EGG SHOALS

SWASH CHANNEL

FORT HATTERAS

FORT CLARK

HATTERAS POINT

Sunday, August 25

The North General McClellan continues rebuilding Washington's defenses. Characteristically, he overestimates the enemy's strength, expecting a frontal attack on Washington, as well as a flanking Confederate drive into Maryland. Being such a cautious commander, he refuses to contemplate taking the offensive actions being demanded by the populace. McClellan believes that battles should be planned in the greatest detail and won with a single decisive blow. But a month after Bull Run, the Federal Army is as yet in no fit state to give him what he wants, so he remains on the defensive.

Monday, August 26

Eastern Theater Union and Confederate troops meet in combat in a number of skirmishes in western Virginia. In a setback for Union arms, the 7th Ohio Regiment is badly mauled in a battle at Cross Lanes (also known as Summerville). Although only five Union soldiers are killed, 50 are wounded, and over 200 are taken prisoner. Other actions are fought at Wayne Court House and at Blue's House.

Naval Operations Eight vessels under Commodore Silas Stringham, carrying 900 troops drawn from the 9th, 20th, and 99th New York regiments, set sail from the Union-held positions around Hampton Roads, Virginia. Their destination is Cape Hatteras, North Carolina.

Tuesday, August 27

Eastern Theater At Ball's Cross Roads in Virginia two companies of the 23rd New York Regiment skirmish with Virginian troops.

Wednesday, August 28

Eastern Theater/Naval Operations Under the command of Benjamin F. Butler, Union forces mount an amphibious assault on Hatteras Inlet. Because of heavy seas, only a small number of Federal troops can be landed. In the war's first major use of gunboats, the Federal ships launch a heavy bombardment of the two forts commanding the inlet. By nightfall, Fort Clark has been evacuated and the flag over Fort Hatteras is hauled down. However, when the USS *Monticello* steams to within 600 yards of the position, it is almost overwhelmed by heavy artillery fire and is lucky to escape. The Union vessels, far from being able to protect the small Union landing force, are in danger of being driven ashore by worsening weather, and have to withdraw out to sea for their own safety.

Western Theater Ulysses S. Grant is appointed commander of Union troops in southern Illinois and southeastern Missouri.

Thursday, August 29

Eastern Theater/Naval Operations Although the small Union landing party on Cape Hatteras is vulnerable to superior Confederate forces, it is not attacked. Dawn sees the resumption of the bombardment of Fort Hatteras, and after several hours the Confederate commander, Commodore Barron, offers to surrender the position to Butler if the garrison might be allowed to retire with all the honors of war. General Butler, while returning all compliments to Barron, states that no terms are admissible but those of an unconditional surrender. Reluctantly, Barron agrees, and passes into captivity. Ironically, one of the vessels under whose guns he has to pass is the USS *Wabash*. Only six months previously he had been her commander. The attack at Hatteras Inlet is a Federal success, when for the cost of one killed and two wounded the Union force inflicts 56 casualties on the Confederates, and takes more than 700 prisoners.

Trans-Mississippi Missouri Home Guards fight a brief engagement at Lexington, Missouri.

Friday, August 30

Eastern Theater/Naval Operations General Butler has been instructed to destroy the port at Hatteras Inlet and withdraw, but once on the spot he sees that it will be of much greater value if it is kept in Union hands. Its location means that it can be used as a base to dominate the sea routes followed by Confederate blockade runners. It could also provide a springboard for further actions along the Carolina coast. Such is Hatteras Inlet's importance in General Butler's view that he returns to Washington to present his case to General Scott.

Trans-Mississippi Frémont's continuing troubles in Missouri lead him to proclaim martial law. At the same time, he orders the confiscation of all property and slaves belonging to any Missourian supporting the Confederacy, a measure considerably in excess of the Confiscation Act which has been passed through Congress, and likely to rouse feelings against the Union in that turbulent state.

Saturday, August 31

Eastern Theater Two companies of the 23rd New York Regiment lose two men in an action at Munson's Hill, Virginia.

GULL ISLAND

ATTACKING UNION SOLDIERS

HATTERAS BANK

With the Union setback at Bull Run, Federal confidence got a nasty jolt and more care would need to be taken in future assaults on the South. Some 850 troops under Major-General Ben Butler were landed at Cape Hatteras on August 28 under the protection of guns of the fleet.

The two small Confederate forts mounted 15 guns between them but they were no match for the large batteries of the fleet.

43

September 1861

Sunday, September 1, 1861

Eastern Theater The 1st Kentucky Regiment kills 30 Confederates at Boone's Court House, western Virginia, without loss to themselves. Small engagements also occur at Blue Creek and Burlington as General Rosecrans' command pushes into the state with a view to defeating Floyd's Confederates.

Trans-Mississippi At Cape Girardeau Ulysses S. Grant takes up his command in Missouri. In a skirmish with Confederates at Bennet's Mills, Missouri, the local home guards lose one man and six wounded.

Monday, September 2

The North President Lincoln feels that General Frémont's actions in Missouri are ill-advised, and could turn the population away from the Union. Furthermore, such actions as the declaration of martial law, the confiscation of property from Southern sympathizers, and the emancipation of slaves could also have an effect in nominally neutral Kentucky swinging further toward the South.

Trans-Mississippi Skirmishing continues in Missouri, with actions reported at Dallas, and at Dry Wood, also known as Fort Scott.

Tuesday, September 3

Western Theater General Leonidas Polk orders Confederate troops into Kentucky. He commands Confederate Department Number 2, which includes most of the west. Polk was a classmate of Jefferson Davis at West Point, and at the outbreak of war was a bishop in the Episcopal Church. With the start of the war, he resigned from the Church because of its support for the Union, and joined the Confederate Army.

Wednesday, September 4

Western Theater Polk's troops seize Columbus, bringing the war into Kentucky and thus ending that state's attempt to remain neutral in the conflict.

Thursday, September 5

The North The president discusses General Frémont's performance in Missouri with General Scott. It is clear that, whatever his fame as an explorer, Frémont is at the very least out of his depth in his current position.

Western Theater Union Troops under Brigadier-General U.S. Grant prepare to march on Paducah, Kentucky, to secure the mouth of the Cumberland River. This move is in response to the Confederate capture of Columbus.

Friday, September 6

Western Theater Grant's troops occupy Paducah without bloodshed. The town's location will be vital to the river campaigns which will dominate the Western Theater over the next year or so. Having established this foothold in Kentucky, Grant returns to his headquarters at Cairo, Illinois, leaving General Charles F. Smith in command in western Kentucky.

Saturday, September 7

Eastern Theater General Rosecrans' campaign in Virginia begins to take shape. Leaving a force under General John Reynolds at Cheat Mountain to occupy Robert E. Lee, Rosecrans, with the bulk of his force, moves south over Kreitz and Powell mountains.

Sunday, September 8

Eastern Theater Reaching Summershill, Rosecrans drives back the enemy's advanced posts. From there, he force-marches his command the 17$\frac{1}{2}$ miles to the Gauley River.

Monday, September 9

The North President Lincoln is advised by a number of military advisers to relieve Frémont in Missouri. The president does not do so for the moment, possibly still having a measure of belief in the man's international reputation, but it is becoming clear that the great explorer is an ineffectual commander. The president directs General David Hunter to go to Frémont's assistance.

Authors' impression of the giant Confederate ironclad Mississippi *had she been completed in time to see action against the Union fleet at New Orleans in April 1862.*

The massive 1400-ton vessel was laid down in the suburbs of New Orleans in October 1861 and work continued as rapidly as the supply of materials and the availability of workers would allow. Over 2 million feet of timber went into the construction, and the hull was 2 feet thick at the sides.

Mississippi *was launched only four days before New Orleans fell and she had to be destroyed to prevent her capture as no suitable vessel was available to tow the uncompleted ironclad to safety further up the river.*

In armored vessels the Confederacy were well ahead of the US Navy. In the early weeks of the war the Confederates had five such vessels under construction and it was left to the US Army to order the first ironclads to see service for the North.

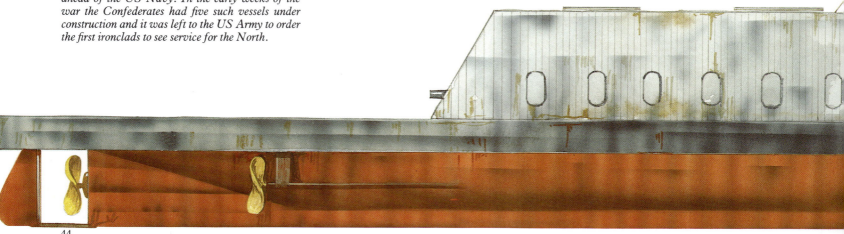

Tuesday, September 10

The Confederacy General Albert Sidney Johnston, a soldier of the highest reputation, is given command of the Confederate Armies of the West.

Eastern Theater While Rosecrans is moving his army south, his opponent General Floyd advances toward Carnifax Ferry in western Virginia. Expecting to meet a division under General Cox at the ferry, he finds it gone. Pushing his infantry across the river, Floyd finds that in their withdrawal, Cox's men have sunk all the ferry boats. He now has his infantry on one bank of the river and his artillery, unable to cross without boats, on the other. Floyd sends for engineers to start building him some boats, but now comes under attack from a small Union force commanded by Colonel Tyler. Hardly have the Confederates beaten back Tyler's attack when Rosecrans' force arrives from Summerville. The weary Union troops attempt to carry the Confederate positions, but it is almost nightfall and the engagement ceases with the Union having lost 15 killed and 102 wounded.

Wednesday, September 11

The North President Lincoln, worried about the effects of Frémont's slave and property confiscations in Missouri, orders the general to modify his proclamation in order to bring it into line with the Congressional Confiscation Act. To emphasize his desires, Lincoln sends Judge Joseph Holt to St Louis to urge Frémont toward moderation.

Eastern Theater Floyd's Confederate troops retreat from Carnifax Ferry in the night, destroying bridges behind them. This effectively blocks any Union pursuit. Floyd continues on to Meadow Bridge.

Meanwhile, at Cheat Mountain, Lee mounts a surprise attack on Reynolds, sending Jackson to attack the position on Cheat Mountain Summit, and personally leading the assault on the other main Union position at Elkwater. However, heavy rain makes the already difficult terrain almost impossible to cross, and the Federal troops hold off the Confederate attack.

Lee pulls back to join with Floyd at Meadow Bridge, leaving Jackson at Cheat Mountain to hold Reynolds.

Thursday, September 12

Eastern Theater Lee now has the bulk of the Confederate forces in western Virginia—about 30,000 men—under his command at Meadow Bridge. Rosecrans is approaching from Carnifax Ferry, and Lee anticipates that the two main armies will meet at Sewell's Mountain. But in a sudden change of direction, Rosecrans lunges for Cheat Mountain, where he meets and comprehensively beats Jackson, before pulling back to the Gauley River.

Trans-Mississippi Sterling Price attacks the town of Lexington, Missouri. The large Confederate force outnumbers the Union defenders at least five-to-one. Elsewhere in Missouri, three companies of the 1st Indiana Cavalry defeat a small Confederate force in an action at Black River, near Ironton. In a battle close to the Missouri, 500 Union troops of the 3rd Iowa Regiment are attacked by some 4000 rebels. After sustaining 120 casualties, the Federals retreat, and the Confederates ride away to cross the Missouri. As they approach the river, however, they run into a Union column commanded by Colonel Smith. His four cannon soon make short work of the rebels, and they are driven off in disorder.

Friday, September 13

Eastern Theater After the battles in western Virginia, Lee and Wise are recalled to Richmond, leaving the much less effective Floyd in command. Floyd immediately goes into winter quarters. Cheat Mountain costs the Union nine killed and 12 wounded, while Confederate casualties total between 80 and 100.

Trans-Mississippi Missouri Home Guards kill 12 Confederates and wound 30 at Booneville, sustaining only one dead and four wounded in the process.

Saturday, September 14

Naval Operations USS *Colorado*, the Federal flagship, sinks the Confederate blockade runner *Judah* off Pensacola, Florida.

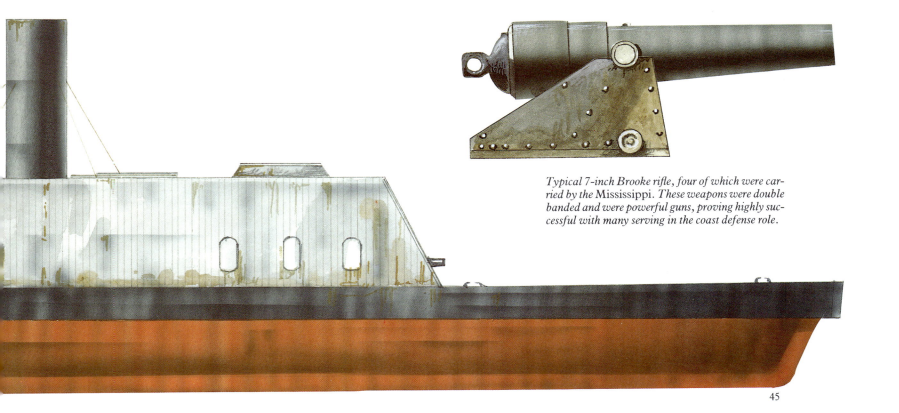

Typical 7-inch Brooke rifle, four of which were carried by the Mississippi. *These weapons were double banded and were powerful guns, proving highly successful with many serving in the coast defense role.*

September 1861

Above: *The Union never lost sight of other routes to the Confederate heartlands. A number of coastal fortifications from Florida to Virginia were to be used as bases from which to strike at the South.*

Above: *Sister Mary Joseph, who served in a North Carolina hospital, is typical of many who sought to provide humanitarian services on both sides of an increasingly brutal war.*

Sunday, September 15, 1861

Eastern Theater In an action at Pritchard's Mills near Darnestown, Virginia, the 28th Pennsylvania and 13th Massachusetts regiments meet a Confederate force upon which they inflict over 80 casualties.

Trans-Mississippi The Confederate attack on Lexington, Missouri, continues. Sterling Price leads a Confederate force 18,000 strong. Colonel Mulligan, the Union commander, has 3600 troops to defend the town. He waits for General Frémont to send reinforcements, not knowing that many of his messengers to St Louis have been captured by the Confederates.

Monday, September 16

Trans-Mississippi Price continues to besiege Lexington, Missouri, although the Confederates, waiting for a resupply of ammunition, have not made a major assault since the first day. Colonel Mulligan is still waiting for reinforcements from Frémont, but what little help sent is in penny packets, and most are captured or defeated by the Confederates. The great river system of the west is the scene of a number of actions. USS *Conestoga* takes two Confederate vessels on the Cumberland River, and far to the south the Confederates evacuate Ship Island in the Mississippi. When occupied by the Union, Ship Island will become an important Federal base in the war along the Gulf.

Tuesday, September 17

The Confederacy Changes in the Confederate Government see Judah P. Benjamin moving from his position as attorney-general to the post of secretary of war, replacing Leroy P. Walker. Thomas Bragg succeeds Benjamin as attorney-general.

Wednesday, September 18

The North The situation in Missouri is again the subject of discussion in Washington, with moves to replace Frémont gaining strength.

Trans-Mississippi Having been resupplied with ammunition, Price begins an all-out assault on Lexington. One part of his command, under General Rains, attacks from the east and northeast, while General Parsons attacks from the southwest. Confederate artillery is well to the fore, smashing at the Federal defenses.

The Union garrison is soon in a difficult position, after Confederate sharpshooters manage to cut it off from its main water supply.

Thursday, September 19

Western Theater The Confederates establish a strong defensive line in Kentucky, stretching from the Cumberland Gap to Bowling Green and Columbus.

Trans-Mississippi In Missouri the defenders of Lexington are in increasingly desperate straits. Confederate troops take the hills north of the town, and a sortie from Lexington is unable to dislodge them from this vital position. An attempt is made to send fresh provisions and ammunitions into the town by river, but the steamer carrying the supplies is captured by the rebels, who make good use of its cargo.

Friday, September 20

Trans-Mississippi Sterling Price finally captures Lexington. Colonel Mulligan surrenders the Union garrison at two o'clock, after 52 hours of fighting. Among the booty captured is a Federal payroll of nearly $1 million. Confederate losses are 25 killed and 75 wounded, while the Union losses include 42 dead, 108 wounded, and over 1600 taken prisoner or reported missing. Frémont's apparent inaction during the siege, and his failure to send Mulligan the reinforcements he needed, is another piece of ammunition for the general's critics.

Saturday, September 21

Trans-Mississippi The big battles are only one part of the all-pervading violence in the state of Missouri. "Neither life nor property were secure from violence; murders were committed by the wholesale; bridges were ruthlessly destroyed; and everywhere indiscriminate plunder and outrage attempted to shelter itself under the Confederate flag, and to claim privileges not even accepted to regularly organized combatants."

Sunday, September 22

Trans-Mississippi In a skirmish at Papinsville, Missouri, a Federal cavalry force, including three Kansas regiments, lose at least 17 troopers killed. Action is also reported at Elliot's Mills, or Camp Crittenden, Missouri.

Left: *Alexander H. Stephens (left) was chosen as vice-president of the rebellious Confederacy. An able lawyer and congressman, he had been opposed to secession, but remained loyal to his state when Georgia broke with the Union.*

Below left: *Jefferson Davis, the president of the Confederacy, was not a statesman. He was a calm, adroit political manager who had been a good soldier, and was possessed of coolness under pressure and tenacity of purpose. He had been President Pierce's secretary of war, and had introduced a number of army reforms, as well as overseeing the modernization of the defenses of the coast.*

Monday, September 23

Eastern Theater In an action at Hanging Rock, western Virginia, the 4th and 8th Ohio regiments kill 35 rebels for the loss of three men.

Tuesday, September 24

Trans-Mississippi General Frémont's actions in Missouri continue to cause disquiet to the leaders of the Union. Because the *St Louis Evening News* questioned his inactivity during the siege of Lexington, the general closed the paper and arrested the editor. Interfering with the freedom of the press comes perilously close to striking at the Constitution, and to do so because of a personal sensitivity to criticism makes the action worse.

Wednesday, September 25

Eastern Theater The Union and Confederate armies in and around the Kanawha Valley of western Virginia maintain their positions in close proximity to each other, with minor skirmishing taking place. In an action at Chapmansville, the 1st Kentucky and 34th Ohio regiments inflict 50 casualties on their rebel opponents.

Elsewhere in Virginia, a Federal reconnaissance-in-force under General Smith crosses the Potomac. Reaching Lewinsville, the Union troops come under attack by a large Confederate force. Beating the rebels back in a sharp action, the northern column then captures enemy supplies in the town.

Western Theater Union troops engage Confederates in a minor clash in Kentucky near the Cumberland River.

Far West No casualties are reported in an action at Cañada Alamosa, New Mexico.

Thursday, September 26

Western Theater In a skirmish at Lucas Bend, Kentucky, Stewart's Union cavalry kill four rebels.

Above: *Richmond became the capital of the Confederacy after a meeting of the Confederate Government at Montgomery, Alabama. This view looks toward the Capitol.*

Friday, September 27

The North Although the army is by no means ready, overwhelming public opinion demands that the Union take the offensive. General McClellan confers with the president and his Cabinet, where they discuss a possible offensive south from Washington into Virginia.

Eastern Theater As a result of the skirmish at Lewinsville on the 25th the Confederates abandon the fortifications atop Munson's Hill, which they have held since Bull Run.

Saturday, September 28

The North McClellan wildly overestimates the size of the Confederate force at Manassas, partly due to faulty intelligence, but also because he rejects any facts which do not fit his preconceived ideas. It is unlikely that the rebels have more than 50,000 men available, but he believes that they have at least 150,000. He tells the president that the Union requires 35,000 men to garrison Washington, and a further 23,000 to guard the Potomac and to garrison Annapolis and Baltimore. Taking these from the 134,000 armed and equipped troops present for duty, he has a force of 76,000 available for an advance. He will not consider an aggressive move toward Richmond until he has at least 150,000 men. Thus, there is no advance for the moment.

September–October 1861

Sunday, September 29, 1861

Eastern Theater Federal troops occupy Munson's Hill, Virginia. Although the Confederates have withdrawn from the area, there are Union casualties at Camp Advance when elements of the 69th Pennyslvania Regiment fire into the 71st Pennsylvania Regiment in error. Nine soldiers are killed and 25 are wounded.

Monday, September 30

The North Although there have been no battles on the scale of Manassas during September, a month of mostly brief skirmishes has left the president dissatisfied. Frémont continues to cause concern in Missouri, and the large Confederate force in Kentucky stands ready to contest any Union attempt at control of the state. Things are better in western Virginia, but nearer to Washington public opinion is pressing hard for an offensive toward Richmond.

Tuesday, October 1, 1861

The North President Lincoln confers with General Scott, General McClellan, and the Cabinet, ordering the preparation of a major operation on the east coast of the Confederacy. He also appoints General Benjamin Butler to the command of the Department of New England, where his major task will be the recruitment and training of soldiers for more active war zones.
The Confederacy President Davis meets with his senior commanders at Centreville, Virginia. Ironically, he suffers from many of the same difficulties as President Lincoln. The populace demands an offensive in Virginia, while Generals Johnston, Beauregard, and Smith advise that there are not enough suitably equipped and provisioned troops available. The consensus is to wait until spring, unless forced to respond to a Union advance.
Naval Operations Rebels seize a Federal supply steamer in Pamlico Sound, capturing a large quantity of military material along with 31 soldiers.

Wednesday, October 2

Eastern Theater In the continuing series of skirmishes in western Virginia, a Confederate force is beaten at Chapmanville on the Guyandot River.
Trans-Mississippi Several days of clashes between Union and Confederate sympathizers at Charleston, Missouri, are interrupted when Union troops manage to find and scatter a rebel camp.

Thursday, October 3

The Confederacy The governor of Alabama bans cotton exports in an attempt to put pressure on the European industrial nations. Governor Thomas O. Moore reasons that with their textile industries feeling the pinch, public opinion in Britain and France will force their respective governments to recognize the Confederacy.
Eastern Theater A large Union reconnaissance-in-force, including troops from three Ohio regiments and six Indiana regiments, together with artillery, probe toward Greenbriar, western Virginia. Routing the Confederates there, the Union force takes large quantities of horses and cattle as booty. Northern casualties include eight killed and 32 wounded, in exchange for over 100 rebels dead and close to the same number wounded.

Friday, October 4

The North In a day which looks into the future of battle, the president observes a second balloon flight by Professor Lowe.
At a Cabinet meeting the seemingly perennial subject of Missouri and Frémont's conduct in command of the Department of the West are discussed. The Cabinet also examines and approves of a contract for a new warship proposed by John Ericson of New York.
The Confederacy Treaties are signed with a number of eastern Indian tribes, including the Cherokee. As a result, many Indians will fight for the South.
Western Theater 20 Union soldiers and 50 rebels die in a sharp skirmish at Buffalo Hill, Kentucky.
Far West Regular and volunteer cavalry fight an action at Alamosa, near Fort Craig, New Mexico.
Naval Operations Two Confederate blockade runners trying to break out of New Orleans are taken by the USS *South Carolina* off the Louisiana coast.
The vitally important Federal bases on Cape Hatteras are attacked by rebels, but without success.

Saturday, October 5

The North The contracts for Ericsson's revolutionary new ironclad fighting ship are signed. To be armed with a pair of heavy guns in a revolving turret, the first vessel will be the USS *Monitor*, and will lend its name to a whole new type of warship.
Far West Union troops from Los Angeles mount an expedition to flush reported Confederate sympathizers out of Temecula Ranch in the Santa Ana Mountains of southern California.

Sunday, October 6

Eastern Theater Confederate actions in Virginia have two main aims: to close the lower Potomac to navigation, and to find fords to cross over the upper Potomac into Maryland, thus outflanking the Federal armies around Washington and threatening the vital Baltimore and Ohio Railroad.

Monday, October 7

The North Rapidly losing patience with General Frémont's performance in the Department of the West, the president sends Secretary of War Cameron to Missouri to investigate.
Trans-Mississippi Unaware of Cameron's mission, Frémont has at last gathered together his troops in an attempt to intercept Sterling Price after his victory at the siege of Lexington. Finally taking action 17 days after the fall of the town does little to help Frémont's reputation, and even less to endear him to President Lincoln.

Tuesday, October 8

Western Theater General Robert Anderson, the defender of Fort Sumter, is suffering from nervous strain and cannot effectively carry out his duties as commander of the Union's Army of the Cumberland. He is relieved, and retires from active duty, being replaced by General William T. Sherman. He too soon suffers a nervous

Right: *Robert Anderson became a popular hero in the North after his defense of Fort Sumter; following the surrender of the fort, he was sent on a recruiting tour of the Union. Later he was to command the Department of Kentucky, but the post proved too much for him and he had to be replaced after a few weeks due to ill health.*

breakdown, but has the confidence of his immediate superior, General U.S. Grant. "Grant stood by me when I was crazy," Sherman is later to recall, "and I stood by him when he was drunk." It is out of such unlikely material that a war-winning partnership will be forged.

In a skirmish at Hillsborough, Kentucky, Confederate and Union home guards clash, with three Union soldiers killed compared with 11 Confederates.

Wednesday, October 9

Eastern Theater The Union-held fortifications and batteries along the Atlantic and Gulf coasts of the Confederacy are a direct threat to rebel seaborne trade, but prove difficult to handle as they can be supplied and reinforced by the US Navy. Fort Pickens, on Santa Rosa Island, is just such a fortification which dominates Pensacola harbor, the finest anchorage on the Gulf. It is garrisoned by regular infantry and artillery. They are supported by a Zouave regiment, the 6th New York, which is encamped a mile further down the island. Although there is a large Confederate Army under General Braxton Bragg on the mainland, the Zouaves neglect to mount more than a token guard down the island. In the early hours, the Confederates land a force of up to 2000 men not four miles down the island. Although Colonel Billy Wilson has little more

than 200 effectives under his command, they put up a stern resistance when the rebels attack. Soon, laden with plunder, the Confederates retire. But as they are boarding their boats they are in turn attacked by a column from the fort, coming to the aid of the Zouaves. Confederate losses are great at this point, and they retreat back across the bay.

Thursday, October 10

The Confederacy President Jefferson Davis, addressing a possible shortage of manpower in the South, is not convinced that slaves should be used by the Confederate Army, although demographics mean that the prosperous and populous North states will always have the advantage of numbers over the South.

Friday, October 11

Eastern Theater While the two main armies face each other in Virginia, there is considerable activity on the upper Potomac. General Banks, who succeeded the aged General Patterson after Bull Run, has pushed his outposts up the Potomac Valley from Harper's Ferry. This is partly to guard against a Confederate drive into Maryland, but also in response to the Southern army's wide-ranging foragers. Having consumed everything around Manassas and Centreville, the Confederate Army must look for supplies as far north as Leesburg, some 40 miles from Harper's Ferry.

Saturday, October 12

The Confederacy Confederate commissioners John Slidell and James Mason begin their journeys to Europe from Charleston aboard the blockade runner *Theodora*. Their first stop will be in Cuba, from where they will take the British steamer, the *Trent*, to Europe.

Western Theater Skirmishes are fought at Bayles Cross Roads, Louisiana, and at Upton Hill, Kentucky.

Trans-Mississippi Missouri continues as dangerous as ever. Frémont's harsh rule has many Southern sympathizers taking active measures, and fighting is reported at Clintonville, Pomme de Terre, Cameron, and Ironton.

Naval Operations The Confederates attempt to break the blockade of New Orleans. The Union fleet is attacked by the Confederate ironclad ram *Manassas*, and by fireships. In the darkness and confusion, both the steamer USS *Richmond* and the sloop of war USS *Vincennes* run aground, but work free. The long-planned raid does not have the shattering effect expected, however, and the next day the blockade is as tight as ever.

Confederate ironclad privateer Manassas *started life as the icebreaker* Enoch Train *built in 1855.*

At the start of the war the vessel was converted into an armed privateer and underwent a major rebuild, finally emerging in 1861 coated with 1.5 inches of armor over 12 inches of wood. The bow was filled in solid with timber to form a massive 20-foot-long ram.

She was taken into the Confederate Navy but sank in action against Union forces off New Orleans in April 1862.

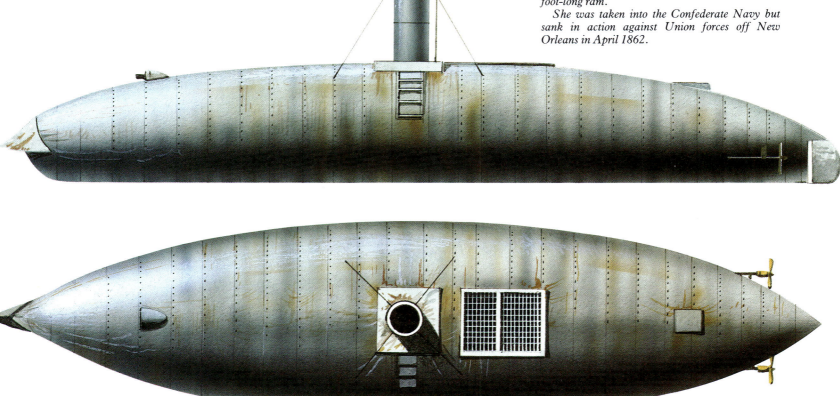

October 1861

Sunday, October 13, 1861

Eastern Theater Confederate raiders under the command of noted cavalryman Turner Ashby make a daring assault on Harper's Ferry from their base at Charlestown in the Shenandoah Valley. Although of little value, the raid is a foretaste of the actions of Confederate cavalrymen later in the war.

Monday, October 14

The North President Lincoln reluctantly suspends the writ of habeas corpus, this curtailment of civil rights being thought necessary as a war measure.

Trans-Mississippi Jeff Thompson, the Virginia-born secessionist former mayor of St Louis, announces his intentions of ridding the southeastern corner of Missouri of Northern "invaders."

Tuesday, October 15

The North Federal gunboats are dispatched to search for the Southern blockade runner believed to be carrying the Confederate commissioners to Europe, unaware that they are aboard the *Theodora* and heading for Cuba.

Trans-Mississippi Under the command of Jeff Thompson, a rebel force captures 33 Union soldiers and burns the Big River Bridge near Potosi, Missouri.

Elsewhere in the state a fierce fight at Lime Creek leaves 63 Confederates dead and 40 wounded.

Above: Any Union advance into Virginia had to go through certain routes. Alexandria across the Potomac was one gateway, and it was defended by guns like this 15-inch Rodman.

Wednesday, October 16

Eastern Theater The Confederate General Evans, with a brigade of four regiments, has been dispatched to Leesburg. He is severely outnumbered by Union troops along the upper Potomac, with General Banks at Harper's Ferry, General Geary at Sugarloaf Mountain to the north, General Stone at Edward's Ferry, and General McCall at Drainsville to the east. McCall is within striking distance of Evans' main supply route to Manassas, but the Union generals are deceived into thinking the Southern force is much larger than it is, so they are cautious. Nevertheless, there is a skirmish at Bolivar Heights, when three Union soldiers are killed.

Trans-Mississippi Lexington, the Missouri town which had fallen to Sterling Price's Confederates at such cost, is retaken by the Union without a fight, as the rebels withdraw.

Three Confederates are killed in a skirmish at Warsaw, Missouri.

Thursday, October 17

Trans-Mississippi Jeff Thompson's Missouri partisans start a series of engagements with strong Union forces in the area around Fredricktown and Ironton.

Above: Lieutenant-General Winfield Scott was the most senior man in the Union Army, but at 76 this veteran of the War of 1812 was too old for the challenge facing the North.

Friday, October 18

The North General Winfield Scott's future at the head of the Union Army is discussed in Cabinet. The old general is a veteran of both the war of 1812 and the Mexican War, and because of his age a number of the president's advisers recommand that he should be asked to retire. The ambitious George McClellan is prominent among those who hold this view. McClellan is also reluctant to provide General T.W. Sherman with troops for a major landing operation currently being planned.

Western Theater Federal gunboats start a move down the Mississippi.

Trans-Mississippi Federal troops from Cape Girardeau and Jeff Thompson's Confederates continue to skirmish around Ironton.

Saturday, October 19

Trans-Mississippi Federal units involved in the battles around Ironton include the 17th, 20th, 21st, 33rd, and 38th Illinois regiments, the 8th Wisconsin Regiment, the 1st Indiana Cavalry, and a company of the 1st Missouri Light Infantry.

Also in Missouri, 14 rebels are killed for the loss of two Union soldiers at Big Hurricane Creek.

Sunday, October 20

Eastern Theater A Confederate force under Nathan Evans holds Leesburg. To General McClellan he threatens an advance into Mary-

The Federal Army is slowly taking a more effective shape, a far cry from the gaudy volunteer outfits of the summer. Armaments are being produced, and manpower built up for the push toward Richmond that the Northern populace still demands. By the end of the war, the hard lessons of combat will have been learned, and the citizen armies will have become highly professional formations commanded by men who understand the realities of total war.

land, in spite of the fact that Union forces along the upper Potomac greatly outnumber the rebels. As has been seen, however, McClellan vastly overestimates the strength of his enemy. By contrast, General Charles Stone, in command at Edward's Ferry about five miles from Leesburg, has received erroneous reports that the town is held by only two or three Southern companies. He resolves to cross the river and force an engagement. After cannonading a rebel fortification, he throws a small force across the river but they return before nightfall. Stone then orders Colonel Charles Devens to make a night crossing from his position on Harrison's Island to Ball's Bluff, and then make a reconnaissance toward Leesburg, scattering any rebels he may find in the thickly wooded terrain. With few boats, it takes Devens time, and it is morning before he is across the river.

Monday, October 21

Eastern Theater Devens proceeds to Leesburg, but finds that Evans' brigade of four regiments is there. Stumbling across a Mississippi regiment on picket duty, the Union troops are forced to make a fighting retreat to the clearing near Ball's Bluff that was their landing place. There they come under punishing fire from Confederates positioned at the edge of the wood. Meanwhile, Colonel Edward Baker's Californian regiment has been ordered across the river from Harrison's Island, but the transportation problems remain. Baker, a highly regarded former senator from Oregon and a personal friend to the president, is to take command as acting-brigadier when on the Virginia side of the river. Initially, the only way of getting across is by an old scow, which holds about 40 troops at a time. It takes almost nine hours for the regiment to cross, with some loss to Confederate sharpshooters. Baker now takes command of all the

Federal troops on the Virginia side of the river, a total of over 1700 men. This would be enough to defeat the weak Confederate force Stone believes to be in Leesburg, but is not enough to cope with Evans' brigade, which is taking up positions in the woods higher up the bluff in ever-increasing strength. Climbing up the steeply wooded banks of Ball's Bluff, the Union troops are stunned to come under increasingly heavy fire from a large, well-placed Confederate force. For two hours the Union troopers press on into murderous fire. There is nothing else to do, as without an adequate supply of boats there is no quick way back across the river. Baker falls at the head of an attack, and his subordinates decide to try to cut through the Confederates to Edward's Crossing. By this time, however, the Union troopers have had enough, and are streaming back to the river. In the panic which sets in, the old scow is swamped, troops roll down the banks into the river, and many who try to swim to safety drown. And all under a continuous hail of Confederate fire.

Losses are severe. US Army records show 223 killed, 226 wounded, and 445 captured or missing, many of whom are drowned. Confederate losses are estimated at 36 killed and up to 260 wounded. A public outcry in the North after the disaster lays the blame on General Stone, and Colonel Baker is regarded as a martyr. By contrast, Nathan Evans is seen as a hero in the South.

Trans-Mississippi Five days of fighting around Ironton, Missouri, come to a halt, Union troops sustaining 66 casualties to 200 on the Confederate side.

Tuesday, October 22

The North The Cabinet meets to discuss Ball's Bluff, but another topic is raised. As usual, it concerns General Frémont's performance in the west.

Wednesday, October 23

Western Theater Troops from the extended Union and the Confederate lines in Kentucky are in action. At West Liberty, Ohio, infantry, artillery, and cavalry kill 10 Confederates without loss. There is a smaller skirmish at Hodgeville.

Thursday, October 24

Trans-Mississippi President Lincoln decides to change the western command. He sends General Curtis to order General Frémont to hand over his command to General David Hunter with immediate effect, unless he is in contact with the enemy "in expectation of a battle."

Friday, October 25

Trans-Mississippi General Frémont, knowing he has little time to make his mark, has his force chasing Confederate General Price around Springfield, Missouri. Unfortunately, Price is nowhere near Springfield, but that does not stop Frémont's bodyguards and White's prairie scouts from fighting a battle with the Confederates that are in the town.

Naval Operations An important event occurs on Long Island, when the keel is laid of a small ironclad warship called the USS *Monitor*.

Saturday, October 26

Eastern Theater Skirmishing takes place at Romney, in the northern part of western Virginia. The 4th Ohio, 8th Ohio, 7th West Virginia, Maryland Volunteers, Potomac Home Guards, and Ringgold (Pennyslvania) Cavalry regiments clear the Confederates out of Mill Creek Mills. The Union side loses two killed and 15 wounded, while Confederate casualties include 20 dead, 15 wounded, and 50 captured.

Western Theater There is a small skirmish reported at Saratoga, Kentucky.

October–November 1861

Sunday, October 27, 1861
Trans-Mississippi Frémont arrives in Springfield, although Price has in fact joined with McCulloch at Neosho, some 60 miles to the southwest. However, the two Confederate commanders are not on the best of terms.

Monday, October 28
Trans-Mississippi The Federal advance into southwestern Missouri is made in five divisions, under Hunter, Pope, Sigel, Asboth, and McKinstry. There are no major encounters with Confederate troops, although brief skirmishes taken place at Plattsburg and at Spring Hill. Meanwhile, at Neosho, Price is making a lengthy and emotional appeal for more volunteers to aid the Southern cause. "Where are our Southern rights friends? . . . I must have 50,000 men . . . Come with your guns of any description that can be made to bring down a foe. If you have no arms, come without them . . . Give me those men and, by the help of God, I will drive the hireling thieves and marauders from the state."

Tuesday, October 29
Eastern Theater/Naval Operations A Federal fleet of 77 vessels leaves Hampton Roads under the command of Commodore Samuel Du Pont, one of the most influential commanders of the pre-war US Navy. Aboard are 12,000 men commanded by General Thomas W. Sherman. To the rebels watching from the Virginia shore, it is clear that a major landing is to take place somewhere on the coast of the Confederacy, although carefully leaked information leads them to suppose it will be an attack on a major port, such as Charleston, or Savannah, or even New Orleans. The majority of the Union force are no better informed, having sailed under sealed orders. In fact, their eventual destination is Port Royal, South Carolina.

Wednesday, October 30
Eastern Theater/Naval Operations The Union force heads south into worsening weather off the Carolinas' coast.

Thursday, October 31
The North Winfield Scott requests of the president that he be relieved of his post at the head of the army. Born just after the revolution, a hero of the War of 1812, general-in-chief of the army since 1841, once again a hero in the Mexican War, the 75-year-old Scott lacks the vigor both to prosecute the war and to cope with the opposition of younger, more ambitious commanders. It is the 34-year-old George B. McClellan, the most ambitious of these younger generals who will succeed him.
Western Theater Skirmishing continues in Missouri, with the 17th Kentucky Regiment and the 3rd Kentucky Cavalry seeing some action around Morgantown.

Friday, November 1, 1861
The North George B. McClellan officially replaces Lieutenant-General Winfield Scott as general-in-chief of the United States Army.
Eastern Theater Three days of ineffectual skirmishing begin in western Virginia between the Confederates of General John B. Floyd and the Union force commanded by General Rosecrans.
Trans-Mississippi Frémont and Price agree on a prisoner exchange in Missouri, although the Union commander does not have the authority to take such action without the approval of the president.

Naval-Operations The Port Royal expedition encounters a southeasterly gale after rounding Cape Hatteras, and is scattered. Some warships have to jettison in order to ride out the storm, and the USS *Sabine* is lost.

Saturday, November 2
Trans-Mississippi Frémont is finally relieved as commander of the Department of the West. His replacement, General David Hunter, is a West Point graduate who had commanded the 2nd Union Division at Bull Run. However, his massive command, from the Mississippi to the Pacific, is soon to be reorganized by the army's new general-in-chief.

Sunday, November 3
The Confederacy As in the North, there is disagreement between the president and his commanders as to the best course of action. President Davis begins to look for supporters, and sounds out Generals Lee and Cooper to see if they will take his side against General Beauregard.
Eastern Theater Clashes continue in western Virginia between Rosecrans and Floyd, but casualties, if any, are light.

Monday, November 4
Eastern Theater/Naval Operations The Union fleet arrives at Port Royal Bar, some 10 miles out from the coast. Port Royal Sound offers an anchorage midway between Savannah and Charleston from which Union forces will be able to dominate Confederate shipping along the whole coast of South Carolina. Commodore Du Pont sends vessels to scout out the approaches. The channel is dominated by powerful batteries at Fort George on Hilton Head, and at Fort Beauregard on St Philip's Island. The original

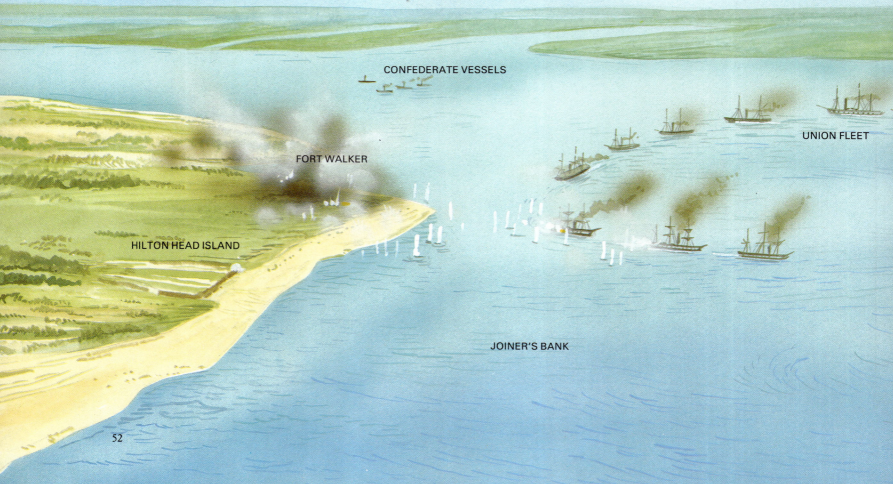

CONFEDERATE VESSELS

UNION FLEET

FORT WALKER

HILTON HEAD ISLAND

JOINER'S BANK

plan, to attack the forts both from the sea and by means of troops landed on the islands, has to be changed after the storm has damaged many of the smaller vessels which would have been used to cross the shallow waters from the bar to the islands.

Tuesday, November 5

Eastern Theater/Naval Operations The weather is still against the Port Royal expedition, and it is decided to postpone the attack on the rebel fortifications until November 7.

Wednesday, November 6

The Confederacy In the first Southern general election, Jefferson Davis is elected president for a six-year term. Until now, he has been acting as provisional president. Alexander Stephens is his vice-president.

Western Theater General U.S. Grant leads a force of 3500 men downriver from Cairo, Illinois. Troops from the 22nd, 27th, 30th, and 31st Illinois, and the 7th Indiana regiments, together with a battery of artillery and a company of cavalry, embark upon six river vessels and set off as night falls.

Thursday, November 7

Eastern Theater/Naval Operations Commodore Du Pont's naval squadron mounts its attack on Port Royal. Thirteen fighting ships sweep up the channel in the early morning light, exchanging fire with the batteries on Hilton Head and St Philip's Island. Fort Beauregard has been silenced by 11 o'clock, while Fort Walker continues until a little after noon. Soon both islands are in Union hands. For the loss of eight seamen killed and 43 wounded, the North

has captured 43 guns, and now has a base from which to sustain the blockade of the coast of South Carolina.

Elsewhere, the US frigate *Santee* takes and burns the blockade runner *Royal Yacht* trying to make the run from Galveston, Texas.

Western Theater Confederate General Polk is led to suppose that Columbus is the object of the Union attack down the Mississippi, but with only 3500 men Grant is not strong enough to take the heavily fortified position. When Grant lands at Belmont, on the Missouri side of the river, Polk is slow to send aid, still thinking that Columbus must be the main target for attack. Union forces come close to driving the weaker Confederates into the river. But at last Polk sends reinforcements to Belmont, and Grant is driven back to his boats, fighting all the way. Collecting his reserve troops, Grant then mounts another fierce assault on the Confederates, but the heavy guns from Columbus firing across the river, and reinforcements bringing enemy strength up to 13,000, force him back again. Retreating in good order, he re-embarks his force and returns to Cairo. In seven and a half hours of fighting, Union losses are between 90 and 120 killed, and some 400 wounded and missing. Confederate casualties, initially reported to exceed 2000, are later estimated to be 261 dead, and over 700 wounded or missing.

Friday, November 8

Naval Operations/Overseas Confederate commissioners James Mason and John Slidell take passage aboard the British packet *Trent* out of Havana. Hearing of this, Captain Charles Wilkes of the USS *San Jacinto* forces the British vessel to heave to in the Old Bahama Channel. In spite of being in international waters, he forces the British captain to surrender his passengers before allowing the *Trent* to continue. The *San Jacinto* heads for Hampton Roads, while the *Trent* heads for Britain, still carrying the families of Mason and Slidell. This action comes close to changing the course of the war.

Saturday, November 9

Western Theater A pro-Union uprising by the independent mountain men of eastern Kentucky forces Confederate general Felix Zollicoffer to send for reinforcements. At Piketown five Union regiments rout a Confederate force, capturing 200 rebels in the process.

The expedition to Port Royal was delayed because of fears for the safety of Washington after the Union's defeat at Bull Run. Delays in equipping the troops caused more postponements, and the expedition launched its attack on November 17, quickly overcoming the two Confederate forts.

The Union fleet was commanded by Du Pont, and by this bold stroke he secured a base for future operations deep within the South.

ST. HELENA ISLAND

BEAUFORT RIVER

BAY POINT

FORT BEAUREGARD

ST PHILIP'S ISLAND

FISHING RIP

UNION TRANSPORTS

53

November 1861

Sunday, November 10, 1861
Eastern Theater In a skirmish on the Guyandot River in western Virginia, recruits of the 9th West Virginia Regiment are attacked by rebels, and in the ensuing fight lose seven dead and 20 wounded to a Confederate loss of three killed and 10 wounded. There is a second, smaller action in western Virginia at Gauley Bridge.

Monday, November 11
The North The national capital celebrates General George McClellan's appointment as general-in-chief of the Union Army with a torchlight parade through Washington.

Tuesday, November 12
The North General McClellan initiates a major reform of the Union command structure. The huge Department of the West is split into three parts: the Department of New Mexico is to be commanded by Colonel Canby; the Kansas Department, a vast area which covers much of the great plains, including Kansas, the Indian Territory, Nebraska, Colorado, and Dakota, is given to General Hunter, who had replaced Frémont earlier in the month; the Department of Missouri, comprising Missouri, Iowa, Minnesota, Wisconsin, Illinois, Arkansas, and Kentucky west of the Cumberland River, is to be commanded by General Henry W. Halleck from California. A former lecturer at West Point, and something of a military intellectual, Halleck has written well-regarded works on military science, and is an able administrator. Elsewhere, General Don Carlos Buell's Department of the Ohio includes the rest of Kentucky, Ohio, Michigan, Indiana, and Tennessee. The Department of Western Virginia, under Rosecrans, and the Department of the Potomac remain unchanged.

Wednesday, November 13
The North President Lincoln pays a call on his new army chief, but after keeping the president waiting, McClellan retires to bed without meeting his superior.

Thursday, November 14
The North McClellan, writing to General Halleck, expresses dissatisfaction at Frémont's handling of the Department of the West. "You will have extraordinary duties . . . Chaos must be reduced to order . . . staff personnel will have to be changed . . . a system of reckless expenditure and fraud, perhaps unheard of before in the history of the world, will have to be reduced to the limits of an economy consistent with the interests and necessities of the state." This last is a calumny, possibly motivated by McClellan's dislike of Frémont; there is no evidence that Frémont's command was in any way more corrupt than those nearer to Washington.

Friday, November 15
The North The Young Men's Christian Association plans to provide help for Union hospitals, as well as gathering supplies and the like.

The North/Overseas The USS *San Jacinto* reaches Fortress Monroe, Virginia, with prisoners Mason and Slidell. When news of the affair reaches Washington, first reaction from the Department of the Navy is entirely favorable. The secretary of the navy writes in congratulation to Captain Wilkes, only regretting that he had not gone further and taken the British vessel *Trent* as a prize. However, even as Wilkes is being regarded as the hero of the moment, other saner heads are questioning the advisability of antagonizing the world's greatest naval power, and even setting the European nations firmly on the side of the Confederacy.

Saturday, November 16
The North Prominent Northern politicians, including Postmaster-General Blair and Senator Sumner of Massachusetts, hold that the *Trent* affair is a violation of international law, and that Mason and Slidell should be released to continue on their journey.

Sunday, November 17
The Confederacy Confederate congressmen gather in Richmond.

Monday, November 18
The Confederacy The fifth session of the provisional Congress of the Confederacy meets at Richmond. Only 12 members are present, but they represent six out of the 11 states in secession, and so constitute a quorum. Meanwhile, in North Carolina pro-Union sentiment is expressed at a meeting at Hatteras. In Kentucky a meeting of soldiers passes a secessionist ordinance and sets up an administration. This means that Kentucky now has two governments, one on each side of the war.

Trans-Mississippi General Halleck reaches Missouri and takes command of the Department of the Missouri from General Hunter, who moves on to Kansas.

Naval Operations Commodore David Porter is given the task of obtaining the necessary vessels to allow the Union to mount an attack on New Orleans.

Tuesday, November 19
The Confederacy Jefferson Davis's presidential message is given to the provisional Congress. Amid the usual optimistic military statements, condemnations of the North, and financial reports, President Davis suggests one practical measure. This is for the completion of a railroad through the center of the Confederacy to match the ones from Richmond down the coast, and from western Virginia down to New Orleans. The third line would allow for the rapid movement of supplies and troops right through the heartland of the Confederacy.

Above: *Commodore David Dixon Porter was charged with obtaining and provisioning the Federal gunboats required for the proposed expedition against New Orleans. From a naval family, Porter was one of the most successful military commanders of the war, although overshadowed most of the time by Farragut, his senior officer. Nevertheless, he contributed greatly to the success of the campaigns on the Mississippi, as well as to actions on the coast of the Confederacy late in the war.*

Wednesday, November 20
Eastern Theater In Washington George B. McClellan reviews 60,000 troops from the Department of the Potomac.

Trans-Mississippi A brief skirmish is reported at Butler, Missouri.

Far West Union troops chase Southern supporters into the mountains of southern California. Some 18 rebel sympathizers will eventually be captured southeast of Los Angeles.

Thursday, November 21
The Confederacy Jefferson Davis reshuffles his Cabinet, replacing Judah Benjamin with Leroy Walker as secretary of war. Thomas Bragg is appointed attorney-general.

Western Theater General Lloyd Tilghman is appointed commander of Forts Henry and Donelson, rebel bastions on the Tennessee and Cumberland rivers against the possibility of a "backdoor" Union invasion of the South.

Left: *George B. McClellan was appointed to the command of all the Union armies at the young age of 35. He was a hero of the Mexican War, and in the early stages of the Civil War had been one of the few Union generals to have made a success of his command by clearing the Confederates out of western Virginia. He was a superb organizer and trainer of men, being able to turn hordes of raw recruits into an effective army in record time. McClellan was thoughtful, he paid considerable attention to detail, and he was extremely careful about his approach to battle. But the qualities which made him so effective administratively were not the ones required by a president and public demanding instant, decisive action against the Confederate capital.*

Below: *In spite of the rise in spirits caused by the appointment of a new general-in-chief, Washington and its surrounds remained armed against Confederate attack.*

Friday, November 22
Eastern Theater/Naval Operations Fort Pickens, on Santa Rosa Island in Pensacola Bay, is threatened by a build-up of Confederate troops around the bay. The biggest danger comes from the batteries at Fort McRea, at Fort Barrancas, and at the Pensacola Navy Yard. During the morning, the fort opens fire on the Confederate positions, assisted by Commodore McKean's force of USS *Niagara*, *Richmond* and *Montgomery*. Although Fort McRea is quickly silenced, the other Confederate batteries exchange vigorous fire with the Union guns all day.

Saturday, November 23
Eastern Theater/Naval Operations Fort Pickens, under the command of Colonel Harvey Brown, continues to bombard Pensacola. Tidal conditions and shallow water mean the naval vessels play no part on the second day of this 48-hour bombardment. There are few fatalities on either side, but the whole affair goes to show that shore batteries around Pensacola can not harm Fort Pickens, and that General Braxton Bragg is wasting his time trying to blast the Union into submission.

November–December 1861

Sunday, November 24, 1861
The North The ramifications of the *Trent* affair are beginning to be appreciated in Washington. Retaining the two Confederate commissioners in custody could lead to Britain recognizing and actively aiding the Confederacy. Worse, it could lead to war, and while there are as yet few British troops in Canada, the powerful Royal Navy could wreak havoc upon Federal trade.

Meanwhile, the USS *San Jacinto* arrives at Fort Warren, Massachusetts, with the Confederate commissioners and their secretaries aboard.

Eastern Theater/Naval Operations Northern troops land on Tybee Island in the mouth of the Savannah River, threatening Fort Pulaski which is Savannah's main defense against seaborne attack.

Monday, November 25
Naval Operations The Confederate raider CSS *Sumter* takes another Federal vessel while on its highly destructive Atlantic cruise. There is some compensation for the North, however, when a blockade runner is captured off South Carolina.

Tuesday, November 26
The North Union loyalists meet at Wheeling, in western Virginia, where they call for the establishment of the state of West Virginia, independent of the rest of Virginia.

In Boston Captain Wilkes of the *San Jacinto* is feted by citizens for his capture of Mason and Slidell.

Eastern Theater/Naval Operations Rebel gunners at Fort Pulaski engage Federal warships supporting the landings at the mouth of the Savannah River, but without hitting anything.

Naval Operations The highly active CSS *Sumter* takes yet another Federal vessel in the Atlantic.

Wednesday, November 27
The North Plans for the occupation of New Orleans are proceeding apace. The first stage of the operation will involve the seizure of Ship Island, a low sandbank at the mouth of the Mississippi but which possesses that vital commodity, fresh water.

Overseas News of the seizure of Mason and Slidell from the *Trent* reaches London and the outcry is immediate.

Thursday, November 28
The Confederacy Missouri is admitted to the Confederacy. It now has two governments, and is represented on both sides of the war.

Eastern Theater The Port Royal expedition is authorized to seize agricultural products and slaves, and put them to work building Federal defenses. This is possible because of the Confiscation Act passed by Congress earlier in the year. Slaves in slave states still represented in the Union are, for the moment, untouchable, but for states in rebellion property rights have been suspended.

Friday, November 29
The Confederacy/Naval Operations The Naval Department of the Confederacy orders the former US Navy frigate *Merrimac*, whose hull and machinery had been captured at Norfolk during the early days of the war, to be converted into an ironclad. The vessel is renamed the CSS *Virginia*.

Saturday, November 30
Overseas In response to the *Trent* affair, British Foreign Secretary Lord John Russell writes to Lord Lyons, the British envoy in Washington, expressing the British Government's extreme displeasure at what is seen as a violation of international law. Lyons is to demand the release of the Confederate diplomats, and also to ask for an apology from the Federal Government. In a private note, Lyons is instructed to allow the Union 10 days before closing the embassy and cutting off diplomatic relations. Further steps to be taken by the British include putting the Royal Navy on alert, and the dispatch of the élite Guards regiments to Canada.

Sunday, December 1, 1861
The North Once again, the president is seemingly worried about the lack of activity apparent in the forces of the Union, and in a letter to General McClellan he asks sarcastically about the time it would take to actually get the Army of the Potomac moving.

Naval Operations The USS *Penguin* seizes the blockade runner *Albion*, together with its military cargo worth $100,000.

Monday, December 2
The North The 37th Congress of the United States meets in Washington.

Western Theater/Trans-Mississippi General Halleck is given permission to suspend habeas corpus in the Department of Missouri.

Naval Operations Four Federal gunboats damage the Confederate vessel *Patrick Henry* off Newport News, Virginia.

Tuesday, December 3
The North The president makes his State of the Union address to Congress.

Eastern Theater A detachment of the 3rd Pennyslvania Cavalry is captured in its entirety by the Confederates at Vienna, Virginia.

Western Theater/Naval Operations USS *Constitution* carries the 26th Massachusetts Regiment and the 9th Connecticut Regiment to Ship Island, at the mouth of the Mississippi. This is the first part of the Union's expedition to New Orleans, which will be under the command of General Benjamin Butler.

Trans-Mississippi In a sharp action at Salem, Missouri, a detachment of the 10th Missouri Cavalry kills 16 Confederates and wounds 20 for the loss of six men killed and 10 wounded.

Wednesday, December 4
Eastern Theater Some 30 men of the 3rd New Jersey Regiment meet a similar sized Confederate force and kill seven for the loss of one man.

Trans-Mississippi General Henry Halleck announces that anyone arrested for aiding the enemy in St Louis will be executed.

At Dunksberg, Missouri, the citizens repel a Confederate raid.

Overseas Britain announces an embargo on all exports to the United States.

Thursday, December 5
The North The secretary of war announces that the strength of the army has reached 660,971. Of that total, 640,637 are volunteers for three years or the duration of the war. Of that total, more than half are from the four states of New York, Pennsylvania, Ohio, and Illinois.

Friday, December 6
The North The secretary of the treasury reports that if the war ends by the middle of 1862, then receipts from customs, taxes, and loans should be sufficient, but if the war should go on for another year then expenditure would approach half a billion dollars and receipts less than $100 million. Although increased duty on tea, sugar, and coffee, and taxes on incomes, liquor, tobacco, carriages, banknotes, and other evidences of debt would raise some of the balance, it would still require a doubling of the public debt to finance the war.

Saturday, December 7
Eastern Theater There is a small clash on the Potomac River Dam Number Five.

Trans-Mississippi Confederate troops capture the town of Glasgow, Missouri.

Naval Operations USS *Santiago de Cuba* stops the British vessel *Eugenia Smith* and takes off J.W. Zacharie of New Orleans, a Confederate purchasing agent. Coming on top of the *Trent* affair, this action is bound to heighten the tension between the USA and Britain, although there might be a case for considering a person who is setting out to purchase war materials as contraband, and hence a legitimate target for seizure.

Left: *The seizure of the Trent gave the United States its most tricky diplomatic problem, failure to resolve which could have caused war with Britain. Charles Sumner of Massachusetts was prominent among the senators who favored releasing the Confederate envoys.*

Top: *San Jacinto was an early type of wooden screw sloop found in many of the world's navies of the period. She was laid down in 1847 and at the start of the Civil War was one of the few warships available to the US Navy.*

In 1861, under the command of Captain Wilkes, she seized the English mail steamer Trent, then carrying the Confederate commissioners Slidell and Mason. This event caused severe tension between the US and the UK.

Later in the war San Jacinto suffered two serious outbreaks of yellow fever aboard which curtailed her active career.

Above: *Confederate raider Sumter was one of the first vessels that the South let loose on the Union merchant fleet. During a six-month cruise she was commanded by Captain Raphael Semmes and seized 18 merchant vessels. This eventually caused insurance rates to rise, so forcing Northern shipowners to sell vessels to foreign buyers.*

December 1861

Sunday, December 8, 1861

Naval Operations CSS *Sumter* destroys the northern whaler *Eben Dodge* in the Atlantic.

Monday, December 9

The North The United States Senate approves overwhelmingly the establishment of the Joint Committee on the Conduct of the War. This is to be set up following the hard-taught lesson that the rebellion of the Southern states is far stronger than had been recognized only six months previously, and that to win the struggle will demand the use of every means within the Union's power. A measure of the change in mood of the Congress can be seen in the vote to table the Crittenden Resolution passed almost unanimously during the summer. This was originally drafted to reassure the South that the war was being fought solely to uphold the supremacy of the Constitution, and that individual states' sovereignty and rights would not be interfered with. This time, however, Congress is saying that it might, and probably would have to, interfere with the civil and domestic institutions of the insurgent states.

Trans-Mississippi A skirmish at Chusto-Talasah, in the Indian Territories, is notable for the fact that most of the protagonists are Indians. Confederate Indians attempt to force pro-Union Creek Indians from the region, but Creek tenacity is enough to ensure that they hold their ground.

Tuesday, December 10

The Confederacy In spite of the fact that the majority of its citizens are firmly in the Northern camp, and that Union forces are poised to drive the rebels from the state, the Confederacy admits Kentucky to membership.

Wednesday, December 11

The Confederacy Charleston, the most important port of South Carolina, is ravaged by a fire which sweeps through the city.

Thursday, December 12

The Confederacy Charleston is not the only thing burning on Southern coasts. The success of Union amphibious operations has led owners of coastal plantations to burn their crops to prevent the seizure of cotton by the North.

Friday, December 13

Eastern Theater In a sharp but inconclusive action at Camp Allegheny on Buffalo Mountain in western Virginia, troops from the 9th and 13th Indiana regiments, the 25th and 32nd Ohio regiments, and the 2nd West Virginia Regiment attack a rebel encampment. The Union force suffers 20 killed and 107 wounded, while the Confederates sustain 116 casualties, including 20 dead. Both sides retreat from the action, the Northern troops back to Cheat Mountain, and the rebels to Staunton in the Shenandoah Valley.

Saturday, December 14

Great Britain Prince Albert, consort to Queen Victoria, dies at Windsor Castle. Until falling ill of typhoid fever, the prince had counselled moderation in dealing with the *Trent* affair, and his death adds to the uncertainty over possible military confrontation.

Sunday, December 15

The North During this session of Congress, it is apparent that the question of slavery is becoming more important. Slavery is recognized as one of the fundamental causes of the war, and in order to put down the rebellion it will become necessary to interfere directly with the institution in the insurrectionist states. Among the many bills that are proposed and will be enacted in the next few months are those which outlaw slavery in the District of Columbia, which ban military and naval officers from returning fugitive slaves, and which offer financial assistance to any slave state undertaking the gradual abolition of slavery.

Trans-Mississippi General Pope moves from Sedalia to cut off Sterling Price's Confederate Army as it tries to move into Kansas. Pope makes a feint toward Warsaw on the Osage River, then moves into Henry County. He places his 4000 men between Price's main force and scattered bodies of recruits camped along the north side of the Osage.

Above: *As 1861 drew to a close, both sides faced the prospect of continuing the struggle into the New Year. But few could have foreseen the amount of blood and death that this New York drummer boy and the like would face and succumb to in the years that followed.*

Right: *The* Trent *affair simmered through December, straining relations between Britain and the United States. It took some skilled diplomatic work, as well as some concessions by Secretary of State William H. Seward, ably assisted by the British minister in Washington and the American minister in London, to heal the rift.*

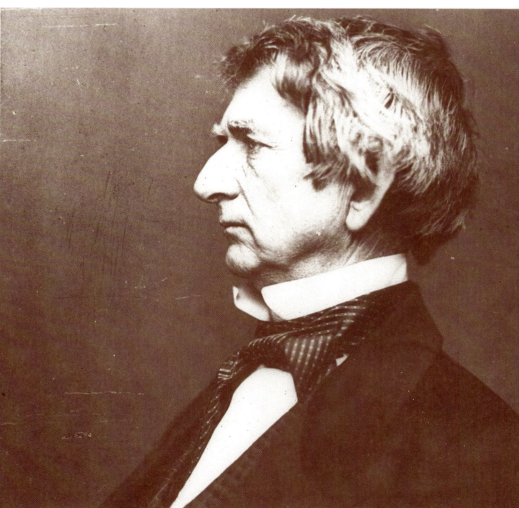

Monday, December 16

Trans-Mississippi Pope's cavalry disperses many of the Confederate recruits on the Osage River, including an encampment of 2200 some six miles north of Chilhouse.

Tuesday, December 17

Eastern Theater General Thomas J. "Stonewall" Jackson moves his command along the Potomac near Harper's Ferry. In South Carolina there are skirmishes and confrontations at Rockville, on Chisolm Island, and on Hilton Head.

Western Theater In a skirmish at Rowlett's Station (also called Mumfordsville, or Woodsonville), Kentucky, the 32nd Kentucky Regiment lose 10 dead and 22 wounded, but inflict 83 casualties (including 33 dead) on the Confederates.

Trans-Mississippi Union troops surround an encampment of rebel recruits at the mouth of Clear Creek, near Milford. In the one-sided fight which follows, the North loses two dead and eight wounded in capturing 1300 rebels.

Wednesday, December 18

The North Lord Lyons, the British minister in Washington, receives his instructions from London to demand the release of Confederate commissioners Mason and Slidell, together with the secret instruction to break off diplomatic relations if the Federal Government does not respond within 10 days.

Thursday, December 19

The North Lord Lyons presents Britain's demands to Secretary of State Seward. Previously, Seward has been known to make vote-grabbing motions against the British, but in this instance he is much more circumspect. He is assisted by the efforts of two highly effective diplomats, Lord Lyons in Washington and Charles Francis Adams, the American minister in London. The exchange of views clears the air and makes a graceful withdrawal by the US Government more feasible. Ironically, the meat of the affair, that Americans could stop and search British vessels on the high seas and remove passengers from the protection of the British flag, was almost identical to the British practice, of stopping American merchantmen and impressing those thought to be British citizens, that had brought about the War of 1812.

Friday, December 20

Naval Operations The US Navy continues in its only partially effective attempt to block the passage into Charleston, South Carolina, by sinking more blockships in the main channel.

Two British warships arrive in Canada, having been sent as a result of the *Trent* affair.

Saturday, December 21

The North Meetings between Lord Lyons and Secretary Seward continue. Both the president and the secretary of state recognize that the British demand must be complied with, or the Union would risk war with the United Kingdom, and possibly with France.

Former lawyer, Brigadier General Ben Butler was a classic political general. He commanded New Orleans in 1862 where his ruthless policies earned him the nickname "The Beast."

The Civil War was the first great war to leave a comprehensive photographic record. Personalities, battlefields, cities, or ordinary soldiers like this fife and drum corps were committed to posterity by the traveling photographers, the most famous of which was Matthew Brady (right).

December 1861

Sunday, December 22, 1861

Eastern Theater In a skirmish at Newmarket Bridge near Newport News, Virginia, 10 Confederate soldiers are killed without loss to the Union side.

Monday, December 23

The North Lord Lyons once again requests the release of Mason and Slidell. President Lincoln and the Cabinet are advised by Senator Sumner of Massachusetts to comply. The question exercising both sides comes down to the definition of "contraband." Secretary Seward argues that "persons as well as property may become contraband, since the word means 'contrary to proclamation, illegal, unlawful.'" The secretary then goes on to cite precedents in international law for the seizure of enemy ambassadors on passage. Similarly, "'Dispatches are not less clearly contraband, and the bearers or couriers who undertake to carry them fall under the same condemnation.'" Seward then goes on "that the *Trent* was proceeding from one neutral port to another does not modify the right of the belligerent captor." Seward considers that Captain Wilkes was within his rights to stop and search the *Trent*, but he was in error in removing Mason and Slidell from the vessel. The correct procedure should have been to have taken the vessel, which he believed had forfeited its neutrality, to a prize court for judicial examination. It was this error alone which made the seizure of the Confederate commissioners unlawful.

Tuesday, December 24

The North Congress passes the duties on coffee, tea, sugar, molasses, and similar luxury goods that had been requested by the secretary of the treasury earlier in the session.
Trans-Mississippi A minor skirmish is reported at Wadesburg, Missouri.

Wednesday, December 25

The North It is a working Christmas for the president and the Cabinet, as they discuss what to do with Mason and Slidell.
Eastern Theater The first Christmas of the war sees fighting at Cherry, in western Virginia, and at Fort Frederick, in Maryland.

Thursday, December 26

The North Lord Lyons is informed that the Confederate commissioners James H. Mason and John Slidell were seized illegally, and that instructions had been sent by Secretary of State Seward ordering their release from custody at Fort Warren, Massachusetts. Furthermore, it is repeated that "Captain Wilkes' actions were without the authority or knowledge of the government, which had neither meditated, nor practiced, nor approved any deliberate wrong." Accepting this, Lord Lyons immediately dispatches a steamer for Boston.
Trans-Mississippi General Halleck, who seems to be having as little enjoyment out of Missouri as his predecessor, declares martial law in St Louis and on all the railroads of the state.

Pro-Union Creek Indians are driven from the Indian Territories into Kansas after a battle with superior Confederate forces at Christenahlah.

Friday, December 27

Trans-Mississippi Missouri, never quiet, is the scene of more skirmishing, with action reported at Hallsville, and at Mount Zion.

Saturday, December 28

Western Theater Union cavalry troopers win a fight at Sacramento, Kentucky, killing 30 Confederates for the loss of one man.
Trans-Mississippi At Mount Zion a Union force comprising Birge's Sharpshooters and the 3rd Missouri Cavalry scatter a rebel force 900 strong. Union casualties are five killed and 63 wounded. Rebel casualties total 175, including 25 dead.

Sunday, December 29

Trans-Mississippi Skirmishes are reported at a number of places in Missouri, and the Confederates also attack and try to take a river steamer.

Monday, December 30

The North/Overseas James Mason and John Slidell are handed over to Lord Lyons, who immediately gets them aboard ship and safely on their way to England. While accepting the Union action, and pleased at the immediate lessening of tension between the two governments, Lord Lyons still cannot accept Secretary Seward's arguments. Indeed, he prepares his own paper on the *Trent* affair, which many Americans accept as being perhaps a more appropriate interpretation of the law than that of the secretary of state. Briefly, Lyons holds that "The neutral country has a right to preserve its relations with the enemy, and you are not at liberty to conclude that any communication between them can partake in any degree of the nature of hostility against you." He goes on to

One of the Cairo *class ironclad gunboats during an all too rare rest period. Life on board these craft during the hot season on the Mississippi was unpleasant and crew sickness was very common.*

cite other authorities, and quotes the Earl Russell's exposition of the British position: "'You may stop an enemy ambassador in any place where you yourself are the master, or in any other place where you have a right to exercise acts of hostility. Your own territory or ships of your country are places of which you are yourself the master. The enemy's territory or the enemy's vessels are places where you have the right to exercise acts of hostility. Neutral vessels guilty of no violations of the laws of neutrality are places where you have no right to exercise acts of hostility.'" Lord Lyons concludes, "An ambassador to a neutral power is inviolable on the high seas and in neutral waters while under the protection of the neutral flag."

Leaving such points of law aside, however, the resolution of the *Trent* affair allows relations between the United States and the United Kingdom to continue on a far more friendly footing.

Tuesday, December 31
The North President Lincoln ends the year in familiar fashion, pressing his generals into some sort of action. In this instance, it is to General Halleck he addresses his inquiries, General McClellan having fallen ill.

As the Civil War gathered momentum, so the navies of both sides were forced to expand to meet the new demands.

The cruiser in particular carried a major part of the war burden as they were forced to spend long spells at sea hunting down the elusive Confederate raiders. They also performed a myriad of duties as blockaders, as well as ascending the rivers of the South to back up the ironclads and gunboats. Here the cruisers would find themselves many miles from their natural habitat—the open sea.

Top: *Impressive outline of* Vanderbilt, *the flagship of Commodore Vanderbilt's steamship line. She was a large, 3360-ton wooden sidewheel steamer and typical of her type when laid down in the 1850s. On the cruise which lasted a year, she went on a worldwide foray in search of the Confederate raider* Alabama *but without success.*

By being forced to use such merchant vessels, the US Navy showed its weakness in purpose-built cruisers, a situation made worse by the fears of British intervention in the war after the Trent *affair.*

Center: *US sloop* Brooklyn *was part of a group of cruising vessels laid down in the 1850s. Upon entering service she proved to be a good sailer, although lightly built, serving until 1889 after showing the US flag worldwide.*

Below: *US single-screw sloop* Worcester *was one of a ten-strong class of warship that formed part of the rapidly expanded navy, which, by the war's end, totalled nearly 400 vessels of all types.*

January 1862

Wednesday, January 1, 1862

Eastern Theater Union artillery shells Confederate positions at Pensacola from the batteries at Fort Pickens. Further up the coast, Federal troops at Port Royal, South Carolina, exchange fire with Confederate forces as the Union continues in its efforts to establish a presence in this strategic location.

Western Theater General Halleck is urged by Washington to initiate some action. He is expected to begin an advance on Nashville, Kentucky, and on Columbus, Kentucky. He is to operate in conjunction with General Buell, currently commanding Union troops in Kentucky.

Thursday, January 2

Confederate commissioners James Mason and John Slidell are now well away from the Union coast aboard the British schooner *Rinaldo*. With their release the Federal Government brings to a close the *Trent* affair. At its height, the differences between the North and the United Kingdom came close to precipitating an armed conflict between them, but tension is now considerably eased.

Friday, January 3

The Confederacy Jefferson Davis communicates his worry over the Union force stationed on the low bank of shifting white sand that is Ship Island at the mouth of the Mississippi. In the center of the Mississippi Sound, Ship Island is only 65 miles from New Orleans and 50 from Mobile, and the presence of Union troops under General Phelps points to an amphibious operation in the near future.

Eastern Theater General Jackson leaves his winter quarters at Winchester in the Shenandoah Valley to begin a campaign intended to disrupt the North's movement of goods and troops. His targets are the vital Baltimore and Ohio railroad, and the Chesapeake and Ohio canal.

Saturday, January 4

Eastern Theater Jackson is already demonstrating some of the skills which will make him legendary. His force of 10,000 men seems to be twice the size. "The rapidity of his marches," says a contemporary writer, "is something portentious. He is heard of by the enemy at Bone Point, and before they can make up their minds to follow him, he is off at another. He keeps so constantly in motion that he never has a sick list, and no need of hospitals." His force is in action on both sides of the Potomac, at Bath and Great Cacapon Bridge in Virginia, and at Hancock in Maryland.

Sunday, January 5

Eastern Theater Confederate batteries on the Potomac shell Federal troops who have retreated to positions around Hancock, Maryland.

Monday, January 6

The North Because of his seeming inaction, it is suggested that General McClellan be replaced as commander of the Union Army. Although urged on by members of the Senate, President Lincoln keeps faith with the general. Inaction in Virginia is not the president's sole worry, however, and he writes to suggest that General Buell in Kentucky advance into east Tennessee.

Tuesday, January 7

Eastern Theater Federal troops at Hancock are directed to intercept the Confederate raiders at Romney, western Virginia. At Blue Gap, near Romney, a Northern force under the command of Colonel Dunning, and made up from the 4th, 5th, 7th, 8th Ohio, and 14th Indiana regiments, together with the 1st West Virginia Cavalry, scatter a small Confederate force, killing 15.

Western Theater The Union gunboats *Essex*, *Lexington*, and *Tyler*, under the command of Commodore Andrew Foote, make a reconnaissance down the Mississippi to within two or three miles of the important rebel strongpoint at Columbus. At the same time, General U.S. Grant begins preparations to move toward Columbus by land.

Wednesday, January 8

Eastern Theater A company of Union cavalry skirmishes with a similar sized Confederate force at Dry Forks, on the Cheat River of western Virginia.

Trans-Mississippi Confederates get the better of the 10th Indiana Regiment at Charleston, Missouri, killing eight and wounding 16. Elsewhere in the state, the situation is reversed. At Silver Creek, also called Sugar Creek and Roan's Tan Yard, Union troops inflict at least 60 casualties on the rebels for the loss of five dead and six wounded.

Thursday, January 9

Western Theater Although neither Halleck nor Buell appear to have responded to the president's request that the Union should advance in the west, there is some movement in Kentucky, with Colonel James A. Garfield's Union force, about 2200 strong, and Humphrey Marshall's Confederates approaching each other.

At the same time, Grant begins his operation against Columbus. Under the immediate command of General John A. McClernand, 1000 Illinois cavalry cross the Ohio and secure the approaches from Columbus.

Trans-Mississippi A skirmish is reported at Columbus, Missouri.

Friday, January 10

Eastern Theater As Jackson's troops approach Romney, Union troops in the town begin to evacuate the area. The Confederates will remain here for some time, as a period of cold weather makes campaigning difficult.

Western Theater Marshall and Garfield clash in a confused battle at Middle Creek, Kentucky. Both sides claim victory, but both are in retreat at the end. At least 40 Confederates are killed, however, compared with a Union casualty bill of two dead and 25 wounded. Garfield is promoted brigadier general after the battle. (Later in the war, he will enter politics, and after the war be elected to the presidency, only to die at an assassin's hand three months after taking office.) Some 4000 infantry and two batteries of artillery cross from Cairo to join McClernand's cavalry.

Saturday, January 11

The North Simon Cameron, under pressure because of irregularities in the running of his department, ranging from plain incompetence to swindling, resigns from the position of secretary of war. The president is likely to offer the post to former attorney-general Edwin Stanton.

Eastern Theater/Naval Operations A large US Navy fleet of some 100 vessels transports 15,000 Federal troops down the Atlantic coast. These troops, under the command of General Ambrose E. Burnside, are to reinforce Port Royal, where Union forces already pose a severe threat to the Confederates in North Carolina.

Western Theater McClernand mounts reconnaissances from his position on the Mississippi, particularly toward Columbus.

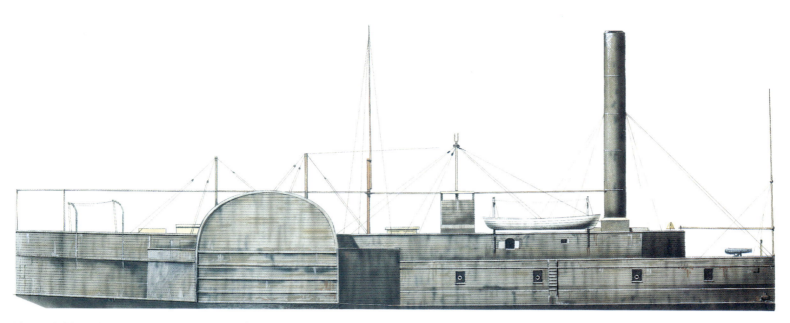

Above: *USS Lexington was yet another early US Army initiative for setting up a force able to control the all-important routes along the rivers. At first Lexington was under army control but later transferred to the navy.*

She was one of the warships that saved the day for the Union Army as it was about to suffer defeat at Shiloh.

Below: *Dumpy outline of the powerful, shallow-draft ironclad Essex completed early in the war for use against the defenses set up by the Confederates along the riverbanks. Essex started life as a typical river steamer but was taken over by the army who were convinced of the use of ironclads right from the start.*

January 1862

Sunday, January 12, 1862

The North The US Navy has grown tremendously in less than a year, with nearly 25,000 seamen in service, as compared with 7500 before the attack on Fort Sumter. But more will be required. The old navy had 76 vessels mounting 1783 guns. When all vessels purchased or building are armed and equipped, the navy will have 264 vessels mounting 2557 guns.

Monday, January 13

The North President Lincoln makes Edwin Stanton secretary of war in place of Simon Cameron. Stanton is close to General McClellan, and is a strong supporter of emancipation.

Western Theater George H. Thomas, detached from General Buell's command in Kentucky, rests his command at Columbia. His seven regiments have been on the march from Lebanon for two weeks, aimed at the Confederate stronghold of Mill Spring in eastern Kentucky. Thomas, a former instructor in artillery at West Point, remained loyal to the Union when his native state of Virginia declared for the Confederacy, and will make a considerable contribution to the Union's war effort in the next few years.

Tuesday, January 14

The North The president dispatches a letter to Generals Buell and Halleck designed to spur them into action in the west. He states his desire that the Confederacy should be menaced by coordinated attacks, but at widely spaced locations. While this is in principle similar to General McClellan's plans, the president wants action to occur as soon as possible, while the ever-cautious commander of the army wants to wait until what he considers the right moment. "I soon found," he wrote shortly after replacing General Scott, "that the labor of preparation and organization had to be performed [in the west]; transportation, arms, clothing, artillery, discipline, all were wanting."

Western Theater McClernand takes up a position near Blandville, commanding the Paducah to Columbus road.

Wednesday, January 15

The North The Senate formally approves of Edwin Stanton's appointment, and the Washington lawyer becomes President Lincoln's secretary of war.

Western Theater McClernand crosses Mayfield Creek, meeting with General Grant at Weston's. The expedition proceeds to Milburn, 10 miles east of Columbus. Communications are established with General Smith, who has marched several columns from Paducah to Mayfield. To Confederate General Polk, this could either be a demonstration against Columbus, or be aimed at the Confederate-held railroad from Columbus to Union City.

Thursday, January 16

Western Theater General Felix Zollicoffer has commanded a Confederate force guarding against a Union drive through the Cumberland Gap since the middle of 1861. Five regiments of infantry and 12 guns are at Mill Spring on the Cumberland, while on the north bank at Beech Grove he has a further two regiments and a strong cavalry force. At first glance the positions appear strong, on bluffs high above the river, but the terrain gives artillery no real field of fire, and lines of communication are terrible. The rebels have exhausted local sources of provisions, and few supplies are crossing the 130 miles from Knoxville. By the time General Thomas Crittenden arrives and assumes command, the Confederate troops are surviving on half or even one-third rations.

Friday, January 17

Western Theater General Charles Smith leads a Federal river-borne assault near Fort Henry.

General Thomas pushes his command to Fishing Creek, west of Somerset, and only 10 miles north of Mill Spring. Here he pauses to regroup his force which has been strung out by the bad roads. Half of his command is yet to arrive, still struggling along the road from Columbia. The plan is to coordinate with a Union force under General Alvin Schoepf, which has been fighting the Confederates around Somerset on and off for several months. The attack is planned for the 20th. However, as night falls, Union pickets exchange fire with Confederate reconnaissance patrols.

Saturday, January 18

Western Theater General Crittenden has managed to scrape together enough supplies and provisions for three days, and resolves to take the offensive rather than wait for the Union attack. He hopes to attack Thomas's column before it can unite with Schoepf, planning to make his assault at dawn in the hopes of surprising Thomas. He underestimates the size of Thomas's command, however, misled by inaccurate reconnaissance reports.

Sunday, January 19

Western Theater At midnight eight regiments and six pieces of artillery march from Beech Grove. At dawn skirmishers from the 15th Mississippi Regiment encounter two companies of the 10th Indiana Regiment. The rest of the regiment quickly comes to their support, and the

TO COLUMBIA

LOGAN'S FARM

KINNEY'S FERRY ROAD

MILL SPRINGS ROAD

Indiana troops stand for an hour in the face of three rebel regiments. Although reinforced by two other regiments, the Union troops have almost exhausted their ammunition and are forced to give way. They fall back to woods on the crest of a hill, with the Confederates pushing forward hard. At this point, General Zollicoffer is killed by Colonel S.S. Fry, of the 4th Kentucky Regiment. The battle comes to the closest of quarters; at one point Confederate and Union troopers are fighting each other from either side of a single fence. Eventually, however, superior Northern artillery begins to tell, and the Southerners begin to fall back. When their line is flanked by Carter's brigade, and a bayonet charge is ordered along the whole Union line, the Confederate retreat is turned into a rout. By nightfall they have been driven the 10 miles back to their entrenchments at Beech Grove. Schoepf joins Thomas, and their artillery begins a cannonade on the Confederate lines.

Monday, January 20

Western Theater Thomas and Schoepf plan to carry the rebel entrenchments at Beech Grove by assault, but find that the demoralized Confederates have retreated across the river to Mill Spring during the night. The battle of Mill Spring (also known as the battle of Somerset, although it actually took place at Fishing Creek between the two) costs the victorious Union Army under 40 dead and some 200 wounded. Confederate losses are estimated at between 125 and 190 dead, with around 200 wounded or taken prisoner.

Naval Operations The Federal Navy sinks block ships in the channel at Charleston, South Carolina. The stone-filled wrecks are designed to keep Confederate blockade runners in port, or at least to limit the number of ways out of a port so as to make the Union task of blockade less difficult.

Tuesday, January 21

Western Theater Grant withdraws McClernand's force from its position threatening Columbus and returns to Cairo. Only now do the Confederates realize that all the activity in this region, together with General Buell's apparent massing of troops for an attack on the Cumberland Gap, has been a feint. The real attack is likely to be at one of the weaker points of the Confederate defensive line in Kentucky, at Forts Donelson and Henry between the Tennessee and Cumberland rivers. However, it is unlikely that the Union commanders will give their opposite numbers time to react.

Wednesday, January 22

Eastern Theater General Henry Wise is appointed to command the rebel troops on Roanoke Island, South Carolina, and is given the task of deterring the rapidly growing Union force at Port Royal from seizing another position on the Confederate coast.

Thursday, January 23

Naval Operations More block ships are sunk in Charleston Harbor, South Carolina. At the mouth of the Mississippi a rebel vessel attempting to reach the open sea is taken by the Union blockade.

Friday, January 24

Trans-Mississippi General Halleck declares that under the provisions of the martial law in force in St Louis, he will have anyone arrested who tries to subvert previous measures, such as the confiscation of pro-Southern property for various offenses.

Naval Operations Two more Confederate vessels try to use the myriad channels of the mouth of the Mississippi to evade the blockade, but both are run aground and burnt.

Saturday, January 25

Western Theater The remnants of the Confederates beaten at Mill Spring begin to reassemble around Gainsboro, almost 100 miles to the southwest. The Confederate defensive line, which reaches from Columbus on the Mississippi right back to the Manassas in Virginia, now has a large gap punched through it.

CAMP SITE

OLD ROAD

Action at Logan's Cross Roads at the time of the Confederates' final attack upon the Federal force.

CONFEDERATES MAKING FINAL RALLY

BLACKSMITH SHOP

January–February 1862

Sunday, January 26, 1862
Eastern Theater/Naval Operations Union vessels carrying General Ambrose Burnside's troops have been anchored off Cape Hatteras for nearly two weeks trying to negotiate the treacherous shallows of Hatteras Inlet to get to the sheltered waters of Pamlico Sound. Once into the sound, the Union force will be able to strike at any one of a number of locations on the North Carolina coast.

Monday, January 27
The North After months of frustration, and a war that so far has not been successful for the Union, President Lincoln takes steps to galvanize his cautious commanders. Issuing General War Order Number One, he commands "That the 22nd day of February 1862 be the day for the general movement of the land and naval forces of the United States against the insurgent forces. That especially, the army at and about Fortress Monroe; the Army of the Potomac; the Army of Western Virginia; the army near Munfordsville, Kentucky; the army and flotilla at Cairo; and a naval force in the Gulf of Mexico be ready to move on that day."

Tuesday, January 28
Naval Operations The US force probing into the waters of North Carolina finally breaks through into Pamlico Sound.

Wednesday, January 29
Eastern Theater Union cavalry skirmishes with a Confederate force at Occoquan Bridge, Virginia, losing one killed and four wounded in exchange for 10 Southern fatalities.

Thursday, January 30
The North The *Monitor* is launched. This revolutionary new vessel, designed by John Ericsson and built at great speed, marks a new stage in the construction of ironclad warships.
Overseas Confederate commissioners James Mason and John Slidell arrive in England considerably later than they had expected when leaving Charleston in late October.

Friday, January 31
The North Supplementing his General War Order of January 27, President Lincoln issues his Special War Order Number One, commanding "That all the disposable force of the Army of the Potomac, after providing safely for the defense of Washington, be formed into an expedition for the immediate object of seizing upon the railroad southwestward of what is known as Manassas Junction, all details to be in the discretion of the commander-in-chief, and the expedition to move before or on the 22nd day of February next."
Overseas Britain once again makes plain its position of neutrality, dashing Confederate hopes of obtaining immediate support from Europe.

Saturday, February 1, 1862
Western Theater General A.S. Johnston realizes that his Confederate defenses in the west are vulnerable to Federal attack in a number of places. General Beauregard has arrived from Manassas, but he informs Johnston that there are ominous signs of activity along the length of the line from Virginia to the Mississippi. This means that Johnston can expect no reinforcements from the east to help repel what he is beginning to suspect may be an attack on Fort Henry or Fort Donelson.

Sunday, February 2
Western Theater Confederate General Johnston takes comfort from the fact that although the Union fleet is preparing for action, many of the Federal ironclads and mortar-boats essential to operations on the Cumberland or Tennessee rivers have not yet been completed. He is not aware of President Lincoln's determination that the Union armies will attack come what may, and that at Cairo, Illinois, General Grant is making final preparations for a major expedition.

Monday, February 3
The North The President writes to his general-in-chief, pressing for the Army of the Potomac to make an advance into Virginia aimed at the Confederate capital of Richmond. McClellan, disagreeing with his commander-in-chief in this as in almost everything else, proposes to transport the army by sea to the Virginia Peninsula and then push the 40 or so miles to Richmond, but only when he feels that the army is ready.
Western Theater Grant's expedition sets off from Cairo under the protection of Foote's gunboats. Ten regiments, together with cavalry and artillery, are convoyed up the Tennessee River to Paducah. Each man carries three days' field rations.
Naval Operations USS *Tuscarora* attempts to seize the Confederate vessel *Nashville* as it leaves Southampton, England, but is prevented by a Royal Navy warship with a name well known to the US Navy. HMS *Shannon* is a successor to the frigate which fought the epic battle with USS *Chesapeake* in 1813.

Tuesday, February 4
Western Theater The Union force advancing on Fort Henry moors on the east bank of the Tennessee, about 10 miles below the fort. The *Essex*, a gunboat converted from a St Louis ferryboat, makes a reconnaissance upstream, but is hit by a 32-pound shot from Fort Henry. Meanwhile, the Union troops have landed and are moving south toward a night camp at Bailey's Ferry, about four miles north of the fort.

Wednesday, February 5
Western Theater General Grant holds his troops at Bailey's Ferry while waiting for the rest of his force to arrive from Cairo. He orders Commodore Foote to commence bombardment of

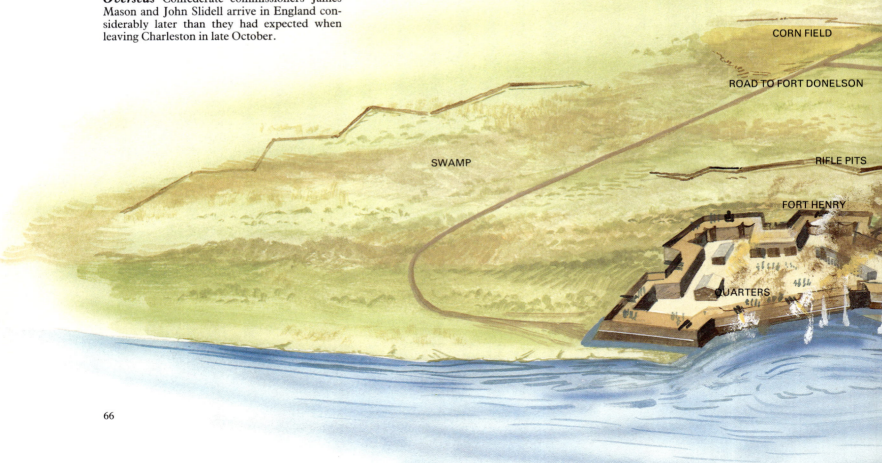

CORN FIELD

ROAD TO FORT DONELSON

SWAMP

RIFLE PITS

FORT HENRY

QUARTERS

Fort Henry in the morning, and prepares to mount the attack in the afternoon. General Lloyd Tilghman, the Confederate commander at Fort Henry, pulls all of his 3200 troops into the fort, and recalls the small force he had established at Fort Heiman on the opposite bank. He is reinforced during the day by two Tennessee regiments, but opposing him Grant has 15,000 troops divided into two columns; McClernand's division of 11 regiments and General C.F. Smith's division of a further 10 regiments. Being outnumbered is the least of Tilghman's worries, however. Fort Henry is not on high ground, and is surrounded on all sides by elevated positions. He does not have enough men to hold these vantage points, and a rise in the level of the river forces him to order the abandonment of his outlying rifle pits around the fort.

Naval Operations The Federal fleet in Pamlico Sound leaves its anchorage at Hatteras Inlet and moves on Roanoke Island, 38 miles to the north. During the night, a force is landed on the mainland to hire or impress by force a pilot familiar with the shoals of the sound.

Thursday, February 6

Western Theater Seven gunboats set off at 10.30 to begin the bombardment of Fort Henry. The *Essex, Carondelet, Cincinnati, St Louis, Conestoga, Tyler,* and *Lexington* approach the fort from behind an island in the river, being hidden from the Confederate guns until they are within a mile of the enemy. Even before they commence firing, however, Tilghman is aware of the movement of Grant's vastly superior force, and he evacuates all but the gunners from the fort, sending them on to Fort Donelson. Had McClernand's division been able to make their way more quickly through the woods, the whole Confederate force would have been cut off, but a rainstorm during the night has turned the ground to mud, and the rebel garrison escapes. The Federal vessels open fire just after noon, and in an engagement lasting little over an hour, during which the range falls to 1000 yards, disable 13 out of 17 Confederate guns. In the process, the *Essex* is damaged and drifts downstream. Once the walls begin to collapse, Tilghman hauls down the flag and surrenders the 62 men left in the fort. Informing Foote of his willingness to surrender to a brave man, Tilghman receives the following reply from the commodore: "You do perfectly right in surrendering; but you should have blown me out of the water before I would have surrendered to you." Soon after the end of the battle, Tilghman's second-in-command marches into Fort Donelson with more than 3000 men, and the garrison immediately begins to prepare for the inevitable Union assault.

The surrender of Fort Henry is a blow to the South, the Tennessee River being a navigable waterway passing through the heart of the western states of the Confederacy. Immediately after the surrender, Foote sends the gunboats *Conestoga, Tyler,* and *Lexington* on a reconnaissance up the Tennessee, which reaches as far as the mouth of the Muscle Shoals River in northern Alabama.

Friday, February 7

Western Theater General Grant immediately begins pushing his troops toward Fort Donelson, and the general personally goes to examine the ground in order to prepare for an assault on the position. Fort Donelson is a much tougher nut than Fort Henry. Built amid uneven, timbered terrain on a bluff 100 feet above the Cumberland River, it is a strong position, but suffers from being commanded by neighboring ridges.

Naval Operations Flag officer Goldsborough commences the bombardment of Confederate positions on Roanoke Island. Before opening the attack, he sends the signal, "This day our country expects every man to do his duty." But Roanoke is no Trafalgar, and before long Fort Bartow is mostly ablaze. General Burnside's troops begin landing at Ashby's Harbor in the afternoon.

Saturday, February 8

Eastern Theater General Henry Wise, the Confederate commander on Roanoke, lies ill at Nag's Head. Commanded in his absence by Colonel Shaw, the Confederate garrison consists of some 1600 men drawn from the 8th, 17th, and 31st North Carolina regiments, augmented by almost 1000 men of the Wise legion. General Wise continues to maintain overall control from his sickbed. Outnumbered by the 7500 troops under the command of Burnside, the rebels surrender after futile resistance. At the cost of 35 killed and 200 wounded, the Union force inflict only 55 casualties on the Confederates, including 16 dead, but take 2527 prisoners.

Western Theater Union forces take two Confederate vessels at Chickasaw, Mississippi.

ROAD OF RETREAT

In order to prevent Confederate reinforcements being sent from Columbus to oppose General Buell who was about to start his own campaign, it was planned to attack Fort Henry. After a fierce, two-hour battle on February 6, the fort surrendered, leaving the way clear for the Union gunboats to mop up fleeing Confederate vessels.

Union gunboats had successfully captured this strong, defensive position without the aid of the army. Lack of ground support meant that the garrison was able to make good its escape.

February 1862

Sunday, February 9, 1862

Eastern Theater/Naval Operations Following the Union success at Roanoke Island, Federal gunboats cross Albemarle Sound toward the mouth of the Pasquatonk River in search of remaining Confederate vessels in the area.

Monday, February 10

Eastern Theater/Naval Operations Thirteen Union gunboats encounter Confederate vessels near Elizabeth City in North Carolina's Pasquatonk River, and destroy them. Three sailors are killed in the action.

Western Theater General Grant issues preparatory orders to his army at Fort Henry, indicating that his troops will begin to move on Fort Donelson within a day. Federal gunboats *Conestoga*, *Tyler*, and *Lexington* seize three Southern supply vessels on the Tennessee River, while six more are burned by their crews to prevent their capture by the Union.

Tuesday, February 11

Western Theater McClernand's division begins to move the 12 miles from Fort Henry to Fort Donelson. General Grant and his superior, General Halleck, both know the virtues of speedy movement, but the six days' delay has been necessary both to replenish the army (which had set off from Cairo with only three days' rations) and to allow more gunboats to arrive to replace the ones damaged in exchanges with the guns of Fort Henry. Even as the first division moves, Federal gunboats are entering the Cumberland River and moving upstream to Fort Donelson.

Wednesday, February 12

Western Theater Grant gets General Smith's division under way toward Fort Donelson. The 20,000 Union troops outnumber the Confederate garrison, under the command of General Gideon Pillow, but the rebel position is strong. The true Confederate strength is difficult to assess, since in the last week the garrison has been reinforced a number of times: by Heiman's troops from Fort Henry, by the 2nd Kentucky Regiment under Bushrod Johnson, which came from Bowling Green by rail, by Brown's brigade, and by Simon Bolivar Buckner's division. Still to come are General Floyd's Virginians, and he makes it known even as Grant's men are within two miles of the fort that he feels that the main Confederate force should pull back. Total rebel strength is estimated at some 18,000 troops, including a cavalry battalion under an unknown commander named Nathan Bedford Forrest.

Thursday, February 13

Floyd finally arrives at Fort Donelson, even as Grant launches his attack. McClernand's division is on the left while Smith attacks from the right, although the absence of the gunboats mean this is not a full-strength assault. However, three Illinois regiments try to carry a Confederate redoubt by frontal assault and are driven back. Federal artillery bombards Fort Donelson through the day, and continues into the night, forcing the Confederates to stand to in the trenches. An added complication to both sides is the weather, which until now has been unseasonably mild for February. However, a sudden unforeseen change brings snow and sleet, which makes the night a trial for the unsheltered soldiers.

Southern troops at Bowling Green are in danger of being cut off by the action at Fort Donelson, and begin to withdraw from the town.

Friday, February 14

The North The secretary for war decrees that a general amnesty is in force for all those who will take an oath of allegiance to the United States.

Western Theater At midnight Union reinforcements arrive at Fort Donelson, convoyed by six Union gunboats. Fourteen transports land the 10,000 men of General Lew Wallace's division downstream of the battle, and the troops spend most of Friday marching around the Union lines to take up a position to the left of General McClernand's division. Meanwhile, the gunboats steam up the river to bombard the fort. The ironclads *St Louis*, *Carondelet*, *Louisville*, and *Pittsburgh* lead the unarmored *Tyler* and *Conestoga*, and between them add another 70 guns to the Federal artillery force. At 3.00 p.m. they begin to engage the Confederate batteries, but are temporarily forced to withdraw. *St Louis* and *Louisville* are damaged, Commodore Foote is injured, and the Union flotilla sustains 54 casualties. General Grant decides to complete the encirclement of Fort Donelson and wait for more gunboats. In spite of the lack of Union success, Confederate General Floyd considers that with more Union reinforcements Fort Donelson will fall. During an evening conference with General Pillow and all rebel division and brigade commanders, he resolves to attack the Federal right flank to the south, cutting through the Union lines and retiring into open country.

Saturday, February 15

Western Theater The Confederate attack out of Fort Donelson an hour before dawn catches McClernand's division by surprise. Fierce fighting through the morning forces the division back, although as General Pillow will record, "he did not retreat, but fell back, fighting us and contesting every inch of ground." However, Buckner's supporting attack on the right has, after initial gains, been pushed back by the rest of McClernand's division. Pillow's attack has created a gap, but instead of pouring through to safety, the Confederates now try to defeat the Union Army. Unfortunately for them, McCler-

nand's division is rapidly being reinforced, and by late afternoon the Confederates have been driven back to their old defenses. To add to their problems, Smith's division of fresh Federal troops is now thrown into action, and by nightfall the rebels are totally encircled.

Sunday, February 16

Western Theater At three in the morning Floyd meets with Pillow and Buckner to discuss what to do next. Surrender is the only real option, but neither Floyd nor Pillow want to take the responsibility. It falls upon Buckner to take command, while his seniors run for safety with their own men. As dawn breaks, a white flag over Fort Donelson pre-empts the Union forces lined up for the final assault. A note is delivered to Grant from Buckner (who had been a classmate at West Point) to ask for capitulation terms. Grant's reply will greatly enhance his reputation with the populace in the North.

"Yours of this date proposing an armistice and appointment of commissioners to settle terms of capitulation is just received. No terms other than an unconditional and immediate surrender can be accepted.

"I propose to move immediately upon your works. I am, sir, very respectfully, your immediate servant,

U.S. Grant"

To this ultimatum Buckner has no recourse but to surrender.

THIRD UNION DIVISION (WALLACE)

INDIAN CREEK

DOVER

The victory at Fort Donelson is of major importance, ensuring that Tennessee and Kentucky are lost to the Confederacy. But it does not come cheaply: 446 Union soldiers are killed, with over 1700 wounded, and 150 missing. Confederate losses include 231 dead, over 1000 wounded, and nearly 14,000 taken prisoner.

Monday, February 17
The Confederacy The Provisional Congress of the Confederacy is dismissed for the last time.
Trans-Mississippi In a skirmish at Sugar Creek, Missouri, Union cavalry lose five killed and nine wounded.

Tuesday, February 18
The North News of the victory at Fort Donelson reaches Washington, where there is considerable rejoicing. "Unconditional Surrender" Grant has now become a name to be noticed.
The Confederacy The First Congress of the Confederate States of America meets, a new two-tier permanent government which replaces the Provisional Congress.

Wednesday, February 19
Western Theater The loss of Forts Henry and Donelson has unhinged the whole Confederate defensive line in Kentucky and Tennessee, and commanders in previously safe positions have to think about evacuation.

Thursday, February 20
Western Theater Columbus, Kentucky, is evacuated by the Confederates. The Confederate Army at Nashville is ordered by General A.S. Johnston to move southeast to Murfreesboro, the better to resist any Union drive on the capital of Tennessee.

Friday, February 21
Far West In a battle at Fort Craig, New Mexico, General H.H. Sibley's 2600 Confederates drive Colonel Canby's 3800-strong Union force from the field. The Confederates seize six guns, and advance on Santa Fé. More than 60 Union soldiers are killed and 160 or more wounded. Confederate losses are estimated at 31 dead and 154 wounded.

Saturday, February 22
The Confederacy At Richmond, Jefferson Davis is inaugurated president of the Confederate States of America. Although elected unopposed at the end of 1861, he has been provisional president until the establishment of a permanent Confederate Congress.

In spite of large reinforcements, Fort Donelson surrendered to the combined attack of Grant's Union forces and the armored gunboats led by Foote on February 14, 1862. The gunboats were subjected to a deadly plunging fire but they were to contribute to the victory that compelled the Confederates to withdraw along a broad front.

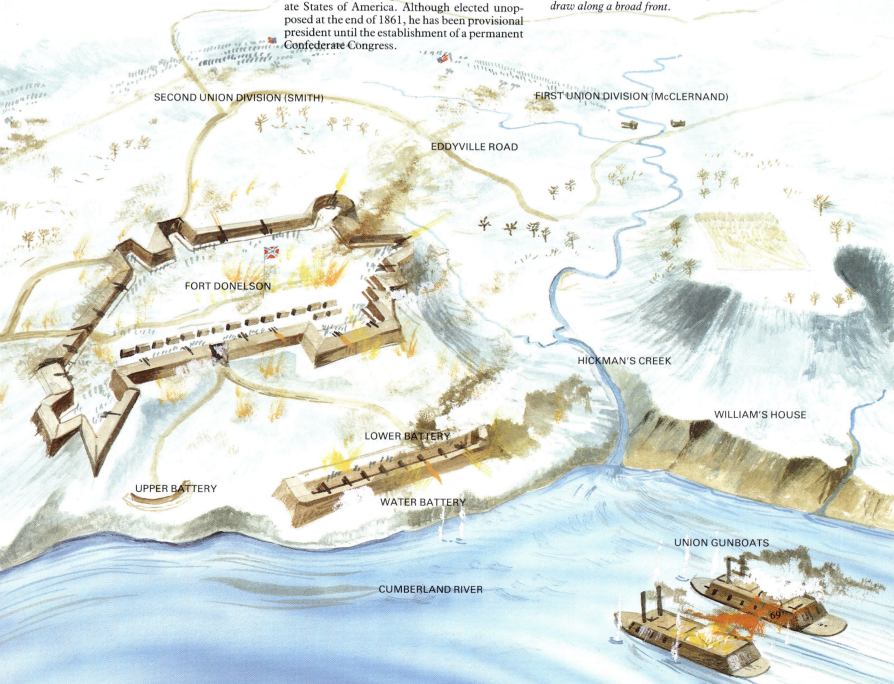

SECOND UNION DIVISION (SMITH)

FIRST UNION DIVISION (McCLERNAND)

EDDYVILLE ROAD

FORT DONELSON

HICKMAN'S CREEK

WILLIAM'S HOUSE

UPPER BATTERY

LOWER BATTERY

WATER BATTERY

UNION GUNBOATS

CUMBERLAND RIVER

February–March 1862

Sunday, February 23, 1862
Trans-Mississippi Confederate forces in southwest Missouri continue to retreat toward Arkansas. Sterling Price had abandoned his headquarters at Springfield in January under the pressure of a Union force commanded by General Samuel R. Curtis advancing along the railroad to Rolla and to Lebanon. Price feels he is not strong enough to stand up to the Northern army unless he unites with General McCulloch in Arkansas.

Monday, February 24
Eastern Theater Skirmishing occurs in Virginia, near Pohick Church, and at Mason's Neck, Occoquan. Casualties are light. Harper's Ferry changes hands yet again, when Union troops commanded by General Nathaniel Banks take over.
Western Theater Troops from Don Carlos Buell's command occupy Nashville, driving Nathan Forrest's Confederate cavalry aside to do so.

Tuesday, February 25
Trans-Mississippi General Halleck has been sending a series of telegraph messages over the past 10 days, saying first that the Union flag was flying over Springfield, then that it had moved into Arkansas, that Price had been driven over the border in disarray, and that his rear guard had been badly disrupted and that vast quantities of supplies were being captured. The Eastern public, already delighted at the fall of Fort Donelson, feel that victory in Missouri is assured. The truth is, however, that the Army of the Southwest has yet to accomplish anything decisive, and in fact could be marching into a trap. Far from any Northern bases, General Curtis has to guard his supply lines with troops from his army, and when he crosses into Arkansas with little more than 12,000 men, he is faced with an enemy who is concentrating a greater number of troops in his path as each day goes by.

Wednesday, February 26
Trans-Mississippi In a mounted skirmish at Keytesville, Missouri, the 6th Missouri Cavalry lose two men in exchange for one rebel.

Thursday, February 27
The Confederacy The Confederate Congress gives Jefferson Davis the authority to suspend the writ of habeas corpus, should it become necessary. At the same time, the president asks for martial law to be established at the important Virginia naval sites of Norfolk and Portsmouth.
Naval Operations The Federal ironclad *Monitor* steams out of New York and heads south.

Friday, February 28
The Confederacy There is a day of fasting through the South, held at the request of President Davis.
Eastern Theater Charleston, in western Virginia, is occupied by Federal troops. The town is destined to become the capital of the new state of West Virginia.

Saturday, March 1, 1862
The Confederacy Richmond is under martial law. In a crackdown on "traitors," a number of prominent citizens are arrested for saying that the war should end.
Western Theater General Halleck directs newly promoted Major-General of Volunteers U.S. Grant to advance toward Mississippi. There is a naval skirmish at Pittsburg Landing on the Tennessee River, where Federal gunboats destroy a Confederate battery. Union losses of five killed and five wounded are far outweighed by the Confederate casualty list of 20 dead and some 200 wounded.

Sunday, March 2
Western Theater General Leonidas Polk abandons the Confederate stronghold of Columbus, Kentucky. The "Gibraltar" of the Mississippi has been made vulnerable by Union advances after the fall of Fort Donelson.

Trans-Mississippi General Earl Van Dorn reaches the Confederate camp at Boston Mountain, where he takes overall command of rebel forces across the Mississippi, and incidentally defuses the ongoing feud between Sterling Price and Ben McCulloch.

Monday, March 3
Western Theater General Halleck claims credit for Grant's victory at Fort Donelson, in spite of the fact that he was opposed to Grant's plans for much of the time. He telegraphs a message to General McClellan in Washington accusing his subordinate of "neglect of duty, inefficiency, and drunkenness." McClellan replies, with the authority of President Lincoln, that Halleck is free to arrest General Grant if it should prove necessary.
Trans-Mississippi There is a skirmish at New Madrid, Missouri.

Tuesday, March 4
The North President Lincoln appoints Andrew Johnson as military governor of Tennessee.
The Confederacy General Robert E. Lee is recalled from his command of South Carolina and Georgia to become President Davis's military adviser. He is replaced in the South by General John Pemberton.
Western Theater Grant is removed from command of his army, replaced by his former subordinate, General C.F. Smith. To add insult to injury, Halleck is soon to be given command of all of the Union's western armies, largely as a result of "his" triumph at Fort Donelson.

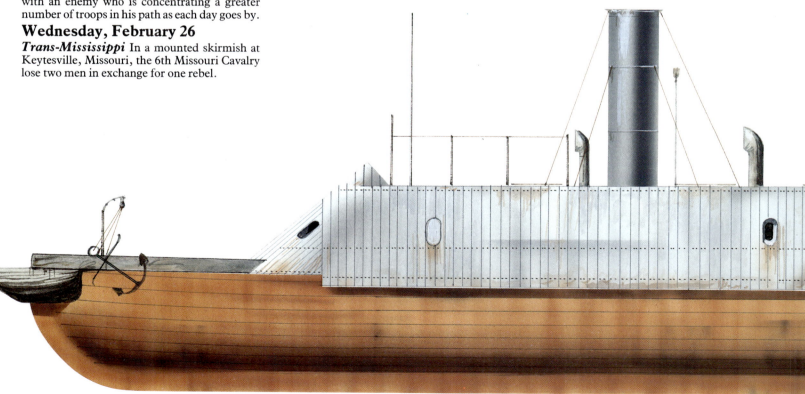

Trans-Mississippi General Earl Van Dorn begins an advance toward the Union Army operating in northern Arkansas. His strength of 20,000 men includes Pike's Indian division, largely composed of Cherokee and Creek Indians. His route of advance will take the army through Fayetteville and Bentonville.

Wednesday, March 5

Western Theater General P.T. Beauregard takes command of Confederate troops in the Mississippi Valley. In Tennessee, General Smith's Federal Army is at Savannah, where it is joined by three gunboats and a large troop transport flotilla.

Trans-Mississippi In Arkansas, Union General Sigel is operating at Bentonville, to the south of General Curtis's main Union force. His scouts report the advance of Van Dorn's Confederate Army, and he immediately pulls back toward the Union position at Sugar Creek. Using the terrain to his benefit, Sigel avoids being cut off, although at one point his supply train of 200 wagons is surrounded by Confederates.

Thursday, March 6

The North President Lincoln asks Congress to approve of Federal funding to help states contemplating emancipation legislation.

The Confederacy The Confederate Congress proclaims a scorched earth policy in the event of a Federal advance into Virginia, with the military being given orders to burn cotton and tobacco to prevent it falling into Northern hands.

Trans-Mississippi Van Dorn attacks the Union Army drawn up along Sugar Creek, Arkansas. The fighting is little more than skirmishing for position, as yet. Sigel manages to join up with the main Federal force in the afternoon, but an attack on the Federal right threatens to turn the whole Union position, and by the evening the Confederates have managed to get onto Pea Ridge and menace the Northern positions at Lee Town and at Elkhorn Tavern. Fed-

eral defenses have been built assuming an attack from the south, but Van Dorn's maneuver means that Curtis has to change his front to cover an attack from the west along Pea Ridge.

Friday, March 7

Eastern Theater General George McClellan moves the Army of the Potomac from Alexandria into Virginia, toward Joe Johnston's Confederate Army at Manassas. There is skirmishing at Winchester, Virginia, at the entrance to the Shenandoah Valley.

Trans-Mississippi General Van Dorn launches a heavy attack on the Federal positions at Pea Ridge. The brush-covered terrain favors the Confederates, many of whom are armed with shotguns which are ideal for the close-quarter fighting. The Federal troops are pushed back from Lee Town, and the Confederate left reaches as far as Elkhorn Tavern, dominating any Federal line of retreat to Missouri. The Confederate right, however, is not as successful, and in a local counter-attack they are forced back, leaving General McCulloch and his second-in-command, General McIntosh, dead on the battlefield. As night falls, neither side is dominant, but the Confederates have the slight edge.

Saturday, March 8

Eastern Theater General McClellan persuades the president to agree with his plan to invade Virginia from the coast, in a campaign up the peninsula toward Richmond. The president does insist on an adequate force being left behind to defend Washington.

Trans-Mississippi At Pea Ridge, Union troops advance on Van Dorn's Confederates accompanied by a fierce cannonade. Within two hours, the Southern army is in retreat. The North wins a significant victory at Pea Ridge. After the battle, the Confederate armies are withdrawn to reinforce Southern positions along the Mississippi, giving up any attempt to drive the Union out of Missouri. But it is not a cheap victory. Union losses include 203 killed, 972 wounded, and 174 missing. Confederate casual-

ties total between 600 and 800, with another 1000 captured.

Naval Operations Off Hampton Roads, Virginia, the steam frigates *Minnesota* and *Roanoke* (the latter with a broken shaft) lie in company with the sailing frigates *Cumberland* and *Congress*. At midday the Confederate ironclad *Virginia* approaches from the Elizabeth River. The *Virginia* is the former US frigate *Merrimac*, burned but salvaged during the first days of the war. It has been fitted with heavy armor, which stands up to six full broadsides without significant damage. Ramming the *Cumberland*, the Confederate ironclad then opens fire and within minutes sinks the wooden vessel. The *Virginia* then batters the *Congress*, which is hard aground, into submission. The shattered US Navy vessel is left ablaze to blow up when the fire reaches her magazines.

Minnesota is a helpless witness from where she has stuck on a mud bank, but before the seemingly invincible rebel vessel can repeat the act, darkness falls and the *Virginia* steams back to port. She has destroyed two Union vessels and inflicted over 250 fatal casualties, in exchange for a loss of two dead and eight wounded. Losses on other rebel vessels bring the total Confederate casualty bill to some 10 killed and a similar number of wounded. The next morning seems likely to see the end of the *Minnesota*. However, a new player enters the action that evening, when the USS *Monitor* enters Hampton Roads after a stormy passage from New York.

The Confederate ironclad Virginia, *better known as* Merrimack, *after her conversion into an ironclad. She had been abandoned by retreating Union forces at Norfolk and then quickly seized by the triumphant Confederate forces.*

In early March 1862 the lone ironclad very nearly raised the blockade at Hampton Roads but was checked by the timely arrival of the diminutive ironclad Monitor.

March 1862

Sunday, March 9, 1862

Eastern Theater Troops from the Army of the Potomac move out from Alexandria, but find the Confederates have moved toward the Rappahannock, away from their previous positions, and the Federal force returns without having made contact.

Naval Operations The *Virginia* moves out into Hampton Roads to complete the destruction of Union naval forces in the area, but this time encounters a new opponent, the USS *Monitor*. Looking like a tin can stuck onto a plank, the *Monitor* is a much worthier opponent than she seems. The *Virginia*, looking as one observer puts it, "as if a barn had somehow put to sea," comes out to finish the USS *Minnesota*, still stuck fast. The *Monitor*, only a fifth the size of the Confederate vessel, moves to cover the helpless frigate. In one of the most dramatic naval battles of the war, the two unusual opponents set about each other. *Virginia* opens fire first, but most of her heavy broadside passes right over the low-slung, Northern vessel, only one shot from a 100-pound Armstrong gun even partially penetrating the thick iron of the *Monitor*'s turret. In the maneuvering which now takes place, the *Virginia* runs aground, and *Monitor* moves in to batter her with 168-pound cast iron shot. All bounce harmlessly off the larger vessel's sloping armor. After refloating, *Virginia* breaks off to attack the *Minnesota*, and in spite of being hit at least 50 times by the wooden frigate's broadside, shows no damage. *Monitor* again intervenes, and in another exchange of shot, neither side much harms the other. After *Virginia* attempts to ram the smaller vessel, again with no effect, both sides break off the engagement.

Monday, March 10

Eastern Theater In a skirmish at Burke's Station, Virginia, a company of Federal cavalry gets slightly the better of a Confederate force.

Western Theater There is a skirmish reported at Jacksborough, in Big Creek Gap, Tennessee.

Tuesday, March 11

The North President Lincoln issues War Order Number Three, in which he declares the position of general-in-chief in temporary abeyance, General McClellan now having command only of the Army of the Potomac.

The Confederacy Generals Floyd and Pillow are removed from their commands following the disaster at Fort Donelson.

Eastern Theater General "Stonewall" Jackson takes 4600 Confederate troops southward from Winchester, Virginia.

Western Theater There is a skirmish at Paris, Tennessee, in which five Union cavalry troopers are killed.

Wednesday, March 12

Trans-Mississippi In spite of the Confederate defeat at Pea Ridge, Arkansas, there is still rebel activity in Missouri. At Lexington in that state, one Union soldier is killed in a skirmish in exchange for nine dead and three wounded rebels.

Naval Operations Jacksonville, Florida, is occupied by a Federal naval force.

Thursday, March 13

Eastern Theater General McClellan is told by the secretary of war that his plan of moving on Richmond by sea and then up the Virginia Peninsula must not leave the capital undefended.

General Burnside expands his operations on the North Carolina coast by landing near the town of New Berne.

Trans-Mississippi Union General Pope takes control of the area around Point Pleasant, Missouri, capturing over a million dollars worth of abandoned rebel supplies in the process. In the skirmishing there are some 50 Union and 100 Confederate casualties, few on either side being fatal.

Friday, March 14

Eastern Theater Burnside attacks and takes New Berne with 11,000 men, driving Confederate General Branch's larger army from the town. Union casualties are reported as 91 dead and 466 wounded. Confederate losses include 64 killed, 106 wounded, and 413 captured.

Insert map shows the relative position at Pea Ridge on March 7, 1862.

Main picture shows the last hours of the battle when Union forces seized Elkhorn Tavern.

Trans-Mississippi General Pope takes New Madrid, Missouri, thus opening the way for an attack on the Confederate-held Island Number 10 in the Mississippi. Possession of this strategic position is the key to the control of the whole of eastern Tennessee.

Saturday, March 15

Western Theater Grant's brief period in wholly unearned disgrace is over, as he once again takes command of Union forces in the field in Tennessee.

Sunday, March 16

Western Theater There is a minor skirmish at Black Jack Forest, Tennessee.

Monday, March 17

Eastern Theater Transport of McClellan's Army of the Potomac to Fortress Monroe begins. This is the first step in the Peninsular Campaign.

Tuesday, March 18

The Confederacy Judah Benjamin, until now Jefferson Davis's much criticized secretary of war, is appointed secretary of state. He replaces Robert M.T. Hunter, a sluggish Virginian noted for his constant repetition of ponderous political platitudes, which has in the past been mistaken for profundity.

Western Theater Confederate troops from the General Albert Sidney Johnston's main western army begin arriving at Corinth, Kentucky, from their previous positions near Murfreesboro.

Wednesday, March 19

Western Theater The Confederate strategy in Tennessee centers on the railroads. There are two main routes by which the Federals can advance into the heart of the South. One way is through Chattanooga into Georgia, and the main nexus at Atlanta. The other is via Corinth and Memphis, and then on into Mississippi and Alabama. General Buell's army is at Nashville, threatening Chattanooga, but is covered by A.S. Johnston at Murfreesboro. However, General Grant has moved up the Tennessee to Pittsburg Landing, and it seems that Buell will join him there for a major attack on Corinth. The Confederates can concentrate enough force to deal with Grant, but should Buell reach him from Nashville, the Union Army will be the larger. Johnston's plan is to join forces with Beauregard's Confederate Army, and to attack Grant at Pittsburg Landing.

Thursday, March 20

Eastern Theater General Jackson's Confederates advance toward Winchester, Virginia. It is the opening move in a campaign in the Shenandoah Valley. Jackson is chasing an apparently retreating Union force, but it is in fact a feint by General James Shields, with the aim of drawing Jackson away from the main Confederate Army under Joe Johnston.

Friday, March 21

Naval Operations There is a short action at Mosquito Inlet, Florida, when the Federal gunboats *Penguin* and *Harry Andrew* are fired upon.

Saturday, March 22

Eastern Theater In the valley, Jackson's troops drive through the Union pickets outside Winchester, believing the town to be all but unoccupied. The Confederates do not know that Shields' division, which they have been chasing, is dug in within two miles of the town near the hamlet of Kernstown. The Confederates are pushed back in a sharp action, during which General Shields is wounded. Although some Union officers feel that the Confederates will now withdraw, Shields orders his command to prepare to receive an attack in the morning.

CONFEDERATES ON BIG MOUNTAIN

ELKHORN TAVERN

March–April 1862

Sunday, March 23, 1862

Eastern Theater A sharp exchange of artillery at noon opens the battle of Winchester, known as the battle of Kernstown to the Confederates. At three o'clock Tyler's brigade assaults and takes the Confederate batteries on the left. This success is followed by a general assault on the Confederate center and right, forcing Jackson to retreat. The Confederate dead and wounded are left on the battlefield. Jackson's force loses some 270 men killed and missing, with estimates of the wounded ranging from 375 to as high as 1000. Union losses are reckoned at 103 killed, 440 wounded, and 24 missing.

In North Carolina, Burnside's Union troops move on Fort Macon, at Beaufort.

Western Theater General Grant has established his headquarters at Savannah on the Tennessee River, eight miles to the north of Pittsburg Landing. One division, under Brigadier-General William T. Sherman, has been in camp at Pittsburgh Landing since March 17, and more Federal troops are arriving. The site is called Camp Shiloh, after a small log-built meeting house called Shiloh Church, two miles from the landing. Although Grant's army is concentrating within a day's march of the growing Confederate force at Corinth, a belief that the Confederates are demoralized leads the Union commander to make light of the risks.

Monday, March 24

Eastern Theater Jackson's attack on Kernstown is thought to presage another attack on Harper's Ferry, so General Banks is instructed to stop his move toward McClellan and to rejoin Shields at Winchester. Furthermore, President Lincoln fears that it may be the start of a Confederate drive on Washington, so he withdraws General McDowell's command from the troops allotted to the peninsula; they are instead to defend Washington.

In North Carolina, a division of Burnside's force requests the surrender of Fort Macon, which is refused. As a result, the Union troops under the command of General John Parke now mount a siege.

Tuesday, March 25

Eastern Theater The 30-mile pursuit of Jackson's troops in the valley is called off at Woodstock, as the Union troops are exhausted.

Wednesday, March 26

Trans-Mississippi There are clashes at Hammondsville and at Warrensburg, Missouri, with Missouri state militia and Unionist sympathizers repelling the Confederates in both cases. At Warrensburg, 60 militia cavalrymen lose one dead and 22 wounded, while inflicting nine killed and 17 wounded on their opponents.

Far West Some 50 Confederate cavalrymen are captured in a clash near Denver, Colorado Territory.

In New Mexico, Federal troops from the 1st and 2nd Colorado cavalry, on their way from Fort Union to Sante Fé, encounter a Confederate force at Apache Canyon.

Thursday, March 27

Far West The Union troopers involved in the action at Apache Canyon fall back toward La Glorietta Pass, where Federal units await a Confederate force pushing into northern New Mexico.

Friday, March 28

Eastern Theater Federal troops occupy Shipping Point, Virginia. Skirmishing is reported along the Orange and Alexandria Railroad.

Western Theater Further skirmishing is reported at Warrensburg, Missouri, with three Union cavalrymen killed in exchange for 15 Confederates.

Far West In New Mexico, 1100 Confederates advance on 1300 Federals at La Glorietta. The Union force commanded by Colonel John Slough is pushed back by Colonel W.R. Scurry's Confederates. Nearby, however, Federals under Major John Chivington attack the Confederate supply train at Johnson's Ranch. The loss of the supplies forces the rebels to fall back on Santa Fé, effectively ending their offensive operations for the moment. Confederate casualties in the three days of fighting total 36 killed, 60 wounded, and 93 missing. Union losses are 32 killed, 75 wounded, and 35 missing.

Saturday, March 29

Eastern Theater General William Rosecrans hands command of the Mountain Department of western Virginia to General Frémont.

Western Theater The Confederate concentration of forces at Corinth, Mississippi, continues. Albert Sydney Johnston is in command, with General Beauregard his deputy.

Sunday, March 30

Eastern Theater Stonewall Jackson's troops have pulled back toward Harrisonburg, where they will remain licking their wounds for some three weeks. In the meantime, Union troops in the valley are pushing slowly toward the Confederate positions.

Monday, March 31

Western Theater More Northern troops are ferried up the Tennessee River toward Pittsburg Landing and Camp Shiloh.

Tuesday, April 1, 1862

Eastern Theater Twelve divisions of General McClellan's Army of the Potomac dwarf the Union Fortress Monroe garrison of 12,000 men under General John Wool.

Wednesday, April 2

The North The Senate considers President Lincoln's plan to provide Federal financial support to states emancipating slaves.

Western Theater A.S. Johnston orders his army to move out of Corinth, Mississippi, toward the Federal camp at Pittsburg Landing.

Trans-Mississippi Three Confederates are killed in a skirmish at Putnam's Ferry, near Doniphan, Missouri.

Thursday, April 3

The North The Senate passes a bill to outlaw slavery in the District of Columbia. This important act establishes the concept that slavery should be prohibited in all areas over which the Federal Government has jurisdiction. In terms of numbers freed, it is unimportant: the Territories have a total population of 220,000, only 63 being slaves. But it establishes a precedent.

Eastern Theater The president removes another corps from McClellan's command to bolster what is seen as a weakness in the defenses of Washington. Nevertheless, with a strength of 112,000 men, Union forces in the peninsula can hardly be said to be weak.

Friday, April 4

Eastern Theater McClellan's peninsular campaign gets under way. There is a skirmish at Great Bethel as the Union III Corps moves out, part of the general Union advance on Yorktown. General Joseph Johnston has a massive task; he has some 17,000 Confederates to defend an eight-mile front on the peninsula, but opposed to him is the huge Union Army of the Potomac, 100,000 strong.

Left: *An engraving of 1863 made from a sketch drawn at the time of the Battle of Hampton Roads records one of the most important fights in naval history.*

Saturday, April 5

The North Andrew Johnson, the Northern-appointed military governor of Tennessee, suspends the city government of Nashville after some aldermen refuse to take the oath of allegiance to the Union.

Eastern Theater McClellan continues to push his huge army toward Yorktown.

Western Theater Southern scouts can hardly believe what they see as they look over the Union positions at Camp Shiloh. None of the Union commanders seem to believe a Confederate attack is imminent. In spite of skirmishes between the picket lines of the two forces, the atmosphere in the Federal camp is almost festive. It is not fortified; the Northern commanders apparently believe that entrenching will convey an impression of weakness to the Confederates and ruin their own army's morale. It is an attitude which will soon prove very costly.

Left: *Confederate positions at Manassas. These were a threat to Washington and had to be dealt with before the Army of the Potomac could move down to Virginia for the peninsular campaign.*

Unusual shape of Monitor. *The Union's answer to the threat of the* Merrimack *came about because of lack of time available to build a more conventional warship.*

Monitor *was the brainchild of one of the world's most talented designers, John Ericsson, who saw entire fleets of these diminutive warships forcing the South to surrender. She displaced less than 1000 tons and was only a fraction of the size of her opponent* Merrimack.

April 1862

Sunday, April 6, 1862

Western Theater At 5.15 a.m. 40,000 Confederates bear down on the Union camp at Shiloh, smashing into Sherman's and Prentiss's divisions. The rebels are formed into four lines across three miles of front, Hardee's corps being followed by those of Bragg, Polk, and Breckinridge. The almost medieval formation is met by a hastily assembled Northern line of battle, with the divisions of W.H.L. Wallace and Hurlbut together with McClernand's veterans of Fort Donelson rushing to the assistance of Sherman's and Prentiss's inexperienced troops. The Confederate steamroller soon smashes through the outer edges of the Union camp, and by 9.30 a.m. is pushing against the main Union line about a mile behind Prentiss's camp. Known as the Hornet's Nest, this sees some of the fiercest and deadliest fighting of the war, with Confederate brigades making repeated attacks. On the right, General Johnston personally leads attacks against Hurlbut's division in a position known as the Peach Orchard, and sustains a fatal wound while so doing. He is the highest ranking officer on either side to be killed in battle during the war.

Grant, who has made his way from his headquarters at the first distant sound of firing, asks Prentiss to hold on for as long as possible until Lew Wallace's division and the first units of General Don Carlos Buell's Army of the Ohio can make their presence felt. Prentiss is finally overwhelmed, and surrenders with 2200 men at the Hornet's Nest, while W.H.L. Wallace is seriously wounded leading an attempted breakout through a ravine to the landing. Later known as Hell's Hollow, the ravine is lined with Confederates and the Union losses are fearful. As night falls, the Federals are stretched to breaking point, but the Confederates have themselves sustained crippling losses and have yet to win a decisive advantage.

During the evening, the Federals are reinforced by General Lew Wallace's division and by the divisions of Nelson and Crittenden from Buell's Army of the Ohio. This brings Union strength up to 54,000, against a Confederate effective strength of some 34,000.

Monday, April 7

Western Theater At Shiloh, a Union counterattack supported by gunboats on the Tennessee River gets under way at dawn. Confederate resistance is fierce, but weight of numbers forces them back. General Beauregard, in command since the death of Johnston, has been expecting reinforcements under Earl Van Dorn, but as it becomes clear that these will not be coming, he disengages and retreats back to Corinth. "Bloody Shiloh" is over. Technically a draw, it is strategically a Union victory because it leaves them in virtual possession of the Mississippi basin. Losses are an order of magnitude greater than in any other battle of the war so far, with 1754 killed, 8408 wounded, and 2885 captured on the Union side, while Confederate losses total 1728 killed (including the army commander), 8102 wounded, and 959 captured.

Elsewhere in the theater, Federal gunboats run past the fortifications of the strategic Island Number Ten on the Mississippi, with four regiments under the direction of General John Pope being landed below the Confederates.

Tuesday, April 8

Western Theater General Pope's command takes Confederate positions on Island Number Ten, capturing 3000 prisoners; 17 Confederates are killed.

Wednesday, April 9

Far West There is a skirmish at Owen's River, California.

Thursday, April 10

Eastern Theater General Quincy Adams Gillmore launches a Union attack on Fort Pulaski in the harbor of Savannah, Georgia. He mounts 11 batteries of heavy guns, the nearest being almost a mile from the fort. Before opening fire, he demands that the strongpoint surrender, but Olmstead, the Confederate commander, replies that he has been placed there to defend the fort, not to surrender it. Although the Confederates have at least 40 guns, the great range means that they have no answer to the Union bombardment, which commences at 8 a.m.

Western Theater General W.H.L. Wallace dies of wounds sustained in Hell's Hollow at Shiloh.

Friday, April 11

The North The House of Representatives pass the bill to abolish slavery in the District of Columbia, which has been passed by the Senate eight days before.

Eastern Theater After a bombardment of 18 hours, Fort Pulaski surrenders. The Federals take 360 prisoners and capture 47 guns.

Western Theater General Halleck, in command of the armies of Grant, Buell, and Pope, begins preparations for the Union to move upon Corinth, Mississippi. The town of Huntsville, Tennessee, is captured by Federals, who are now almost astride the Memphis and Charleston railroad.

Naval Operations At Newport News there is another confrontation between the *Monitor* and the *Virginia*, but no shots are exchanged.

Saturday, April 12

Eastern Theater James Andrews leads a raid behind the Confederate lines, seizing the locomotive *General* on the Western and Atlantic railroad. After a long chase, in which the Confederates use the locomotive *Texas*, Andrews and his 21 raiders are captured. Andrews and six others are eventually executed.

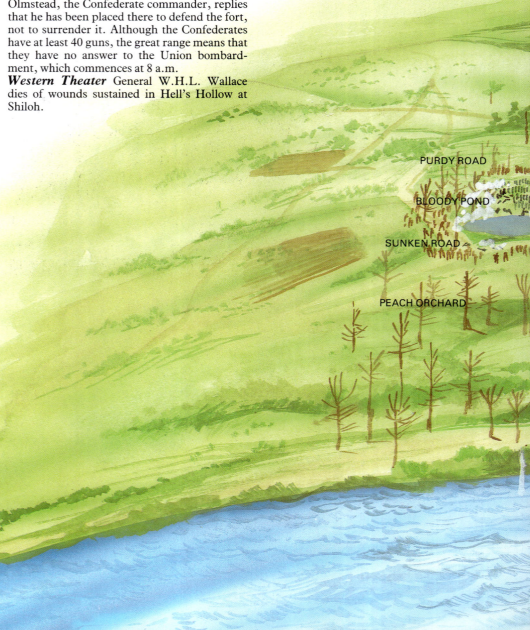

PURDY ROAD

BLOODY POND

SUNKEN ROAD

PEACH ORCHARD

Sunday, April 13

Far West The Union advance in New Mexico, arising from the battles near Santa Fe, continues. Confederate troops are almost driven from the territory, being forced back to El Paso on the Texas border.

Monday, April 14

Eastern Theater Seven Confederates are wounded in a skirmish at Pollocksville, North Carolina.

Trans-Mississippi In spite of Union successes elsewhere in the west, Missouri is still the scene of much activity. Small actions are reported at Montavallo, Diamond Grove, and Walkersville.

Tuesday, April 15

Far West Three Union troopers from the 1st California Cavalry are killed at Pechacho Pass, Arizona Territory.

Wednesday, April 16

The North President Lincoln signs the bill to outlaw slavery in the District of Columbia.

The Confederacy President Davis approves the proposal to make "all persons residing within the Confederate states between the ages of 18 and 35 years" liable for military draft. The vastly greater population of the Federal states makes this move necessary, unpopular though it will be.

Eastern Theater In a sharp clash at Lee's Mills, Virginia, 35 Union troops are killed and 128 wounded. Confederate losses are 20 dead, 75 wounded, and 50 captured.

A skirmish takes place at White Marsh, Georgia.

Western Theater Five rebels are killed and 65 wounded at Savannah, Tennessee.

Thursday, April 17

A minor action is reported at Holly River in western Virginia.

Friday, April 18

Eastern Theater A Confederate attack at Yorktown is repulsed. Cavalry from the 2nd New York Regiment, part of General McDowell's command, take Falmouth, Virginia. Five troopers are killed and 16 wounded, while 19 Confederates are captured.

Naval Operations The Federal build-up at Ship Island, off the mouth of the Mississippi delta, now has an objective. With Federal forces moving south down the Mississippi, a Federal fleet under Commodore David Farragut and a mortar fleet under Commander David Porter begin to move upon New Orleans. First targets are the Confederate strongpoints of Fort Jackson and Fort St Philip.

Saturday, April 19

Eastern Theater In a skirmish at South Mills, near Camden, North Carolina, 12 Union soldiers are killed and 98 are wounded. Confederate casualties total 25, including six dead.

Naval Operations Federal vessels moving on New Orleans continue their bombardment of the areas around Fort Jackson and Fort St Philip.

RIVER ROAD

HORNET'S NEST

UNION LINE REFORMED

PITTSBURG LANDING

LEXINGTON

TYLER

TENNESSEE RIVER

Critical time at the battle of Shiloh, when the rapidly advancing Confederate forces were about to drive Union forces from the field. Union gunboats Lexington *and* Tyler *arrived just in time to drive off the attacking enemy by firing over the heads of their own soldiers.*

Grant was able to patch together a defensive line and thus save the day. Prior to this, six hours of savage fighting had seen the camps of Sherman and Prentiss overrun with heavy losses. On the next day, April 7, Grant attacked with fresh troops and secured victory, thus opening up the Mississippi to eventual capture.

April–May 1862

Sunday, April 20, 1862
Naval Operations/Western Theater Forts Jackson and St Philip are 75 miles below New Orleans and, according to reports in Southern newspapers, are impregnable. Manned by 3000 men, the forts are reputed to mount 173 rifled 63-pounder cannon. Below the forts a dam blocks the river. This will take an attacking fleet several hours to force, during which time it would be under a constant fire of heated shot from both sides of the river. Above the forts a chain of redoubts all the way to New Orleans makes the passage of the river even more hazardous. However, the Federal Government is of the opinion that the Confederate position is nowhere as strong as has been claimed.

Monday, April 21
Naval Operations/Western Theater Farragut's fleet is convoying the 15,000 men of General Benjamin Butler's army, which is intended to capture New Orleans. Butler's orders from General McClellan, general-in-chief at the time the operation was set in motion, state, "The object of your expedition is one of vital importance—the capture of New Orleans. The route selected is up the Mississippi River, where the first obstacles to be encountered will be Forts St Philip and Jackson. It is expected that the navy can reduce the works. Should the navy fail to do so, you will land your forces and siege train, and endeavor to breach the works, silence their fire, and carry them by assault." To all appearances, Butler may have to do just that, since the forts seem unharmed by being the targets of more than 4000 mortar bombs in three days of bombardment.

Tuesday, April 22
Naval Operations/Western Theater Farragut learns from a deserter that the shelling has in fact done fearful damage inside the Confederate forts. Nevertheless, he feels that the mortar boats will never reduce them completely. He also feels that landing Butler's army will not bring the final goal of New Orleans any closer.

The gunboats *Pinola* and *Itasca* had cut the cables of the boom across the river two nights before, so Farragut resolves to run past the forts.

Wednesday, April 23
Eastern Theater A skirmish is reported at Grass Lick, western Virginia.
Naval Operations/Western Theater Farragut prepares to run the forts. The mortar fleet is to remain behind, providing support if necessary. If the fleet could not manage to force a passage, it will engage the forts in close action "and abide the result; conquer or be conquered; drop anchor, or keep under way, as in my opinion shall be the best." The plan calls for the fleet to advance through the gap in the barricade in two columns. Bailey, Farragut's second-in-command, will take the right column and deal with Fort St Philip. Bell, captain of the fleet, will take the left column through to deal with Fort Jackson.

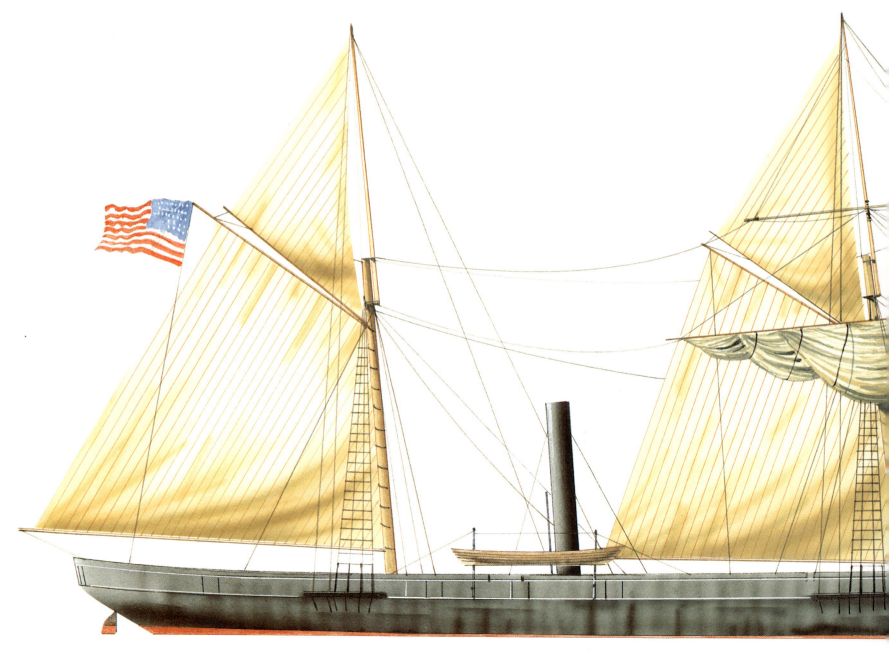

Thursday, April 24

Naval Operations/Western Theater By 3.30 in the morning, the Federal fleet is making its way up the Mississippi. Under Farragut's command are the steam ships *Hartford* (flag), *Brooklyn*, *Richmond*, *Pensacola*, and *Mississippi*, together with the gunboats *Cayuga*, *Oneida*, *Varuna*, *Katahdin*, *Kineo*, *Wissahickon*, *Sciota*, *Iroquois*, *Pinola*, *Kennebec*, *Itasca*, and *Winona*. The fleet mounts 294 guns, although this total is soon reduced when the three last named gunboats fail to find the gap in the barricade and have to turn back.

After passing through the gap, the Federal fleet and the Confederate forces exchange fire in a fierce fight, complicated by the Confederate river flotilla which now joins in. Among the Confederate vessels is the armored ram *Manassas*, armed with a single gun but very heavily protected. Most of the rebel vessels are disabled or driven ashore in the fight. As dawn breaks the Union fleet is safely past the fortifications, heading up for New Orleans. Only the *Manassas* gives chase, but she is driven onto a sandbank by the *Mississippi*. Riddled by shot and afire, the Confederate ram is abandoned and set adrift.

Farragut continues to steam up the Mississippi, leaving the forts isolated behind him. He drops anchor nine miles south of the city, although it is 18 miles by the river's winding course. The seven days of bombardment and the three-hour battle have cost the Union 37 killed and 171 wounded. One gunboat and one mortar boat are lost. Fourteen Confederates have been killed in the forts and 38 wounded, but the death toll must be much greater (some estimate it to be as high as 400) as between eight and 12 Confederate gunboats have been sunk or burned.

Friday, April 25

Eastern Theater In North Carolina the siege of Fort Macon is ended after nearly a month. Some 450 Confederates are taken prisoner by Union troops under the command of General John Parkes.

Naval Operations/Western Theater The garrison of New Orleans is 4000, not the 32,000 which has been reported in the Southern press. At the imminent arrival of the Union fleet, Mansfield Lovell, the Confederate commander, orders his troops to withdraw. In the chaos which follows, Commodore Farragut arrives to claim the city for the Union.

Saturday, April 26

Eastern Theater The Army of the Potomac continues to press upon Yorktown. The Confederates continue to resist, but all know that the town will soon fall.

Trans-Mississippi Skirmishes are reported at Turnback Creek and at Neosho, Missouri. In the latter action the 1st Missouri Cavalry take over 60 Confederate prisoners.

Sunday, April 27

Eastern Theater A skirmish is reported at Horton's Mills, North Carolina.

Western Theater Following the occupation of New Orleans, four Confederate forts to the north of the city surrender. At the bypassed Fort Jackson there is a mutiny of enlisted personnel, and many flee before the fort is surrendered to the Union.

Monday, April 28

Western Theater General Butler arrives in New Orleans ahead of his troop transports, which are still making their way up the river. He confers with Farragut, who has hoisted the Union flag above the New Orleans Customs House, City Hall, and the Mint, but is not sure how to go about taking control of the city. Back down the river, Union forces demand the surrender of the two Mississippi forts. Fort Jackson has been badly knocked about, but still functions as a strongpoint. Fort St Philip has hardly been touched by the actions of the last 10 days, but both are irretrievably cut off from any help so they surrender.

In Mississippi General Halleck prepares for the advance on Beauregard's Confederate Army at Corinth.

Tuesday, April 29

Western Theater In an action at Bridgeport in Northern Alabama, the 3rd Division of the Army of the Ohio fight an action during which they kill 72 Confederates and capture a further 350.

Union troops begin to move on Corinth. Halleck has over 100,000 men under his command.

Wednesday, April 30

Eastern Theater General Ewell's division, detached from the Confederate Army in the peninsula, arrives in the Shenandoah Valley where it reinforces Stonewall Jackson's command.

Western Theater Skirmishes are reported in Tennessee. In the last two days there have been actions at Cumberland Mountain and at Monterey.

Thursday, May 1, 1862

Eastern Theater In a skirmish at Clark's Hollow, western Virginia, a company of the 23rd Ohio Regiment loses one man killed and 21 wounded.

Western Theater General Butler occupies New Orleans, beginning an administration that will cause considerable controversy in the days and weeks to come.

Friday, May 2

Eastern Theater McClellan masses his troops and readies his batteries for the assault on Yorktown. Confederate General Joseph E. Johnston knows that his heavily outnumbered troops will not be able to stand up to such an attack, and he prepares to evacuate.

Saturday, May 3

Eastern Theater Joe Johnston's Confederate Army evacuates Yorktown, Virginia. McClellan's siege tactics have worked, with the Southern troops being defeated without fighting a major battle. Johnston pulls his men back toward Richmond.

Western Theater As Halleck advances toward Corinth, Mississippi, troops from his command skirmish with Confederates from Beauregard's army. In the fight at Farmington 30 Southerners are killed in exchange for two from the North.

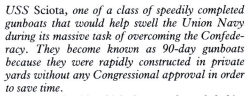

USS Sciota, *one of a class of speedily completed gunboats that would help swell the Union Navy during its massive task of overcoming the Confederacy. They become known as 90-day gunboats because they were rapidly constructed in private yards without any Congressional approval in order to save time.*

The speed with which these much needed ships entered service shows just how powerful Union industry was.

May 1862

Sunday, May 4, 1862

Eastern Theater Federal forces from the Army of the Potomac occupy Yorktown, Virginia, after its evacuation by Joseph E. Johnston's Confederates the day before. Johnston shows great ability in the retreat toward Richmond. He leaves a strong rear guard behind defensive works at Williamsburg, whose task it is to delay any Federal advance. Although McClellan is convinced that the Confederates are far stronger than in fact they are, he appears to have no inkling that they are standing at Williamsburg, and remains in Yorktown while Stoneman's division, reinforced by all available cavalry, marches further up the peninsula. They soon come under heavy fire from Fort Magruder, and stand at bay until reinforced by General "Fighting Joe" Hooker's division, which comes up in the night.

There is a skirmish reported at Cheese Cake Church, Virginia.

Trans-Mississippi One Union soldier is reported killed in a skirmish at Licking, Missouri.

Monday, May 5

Eastern Theater President Lincoln, Secretary of War Stanton, and Secretary of the Treasury Chase leave Washington by steamer for Fortress Monroe, from where they will confer with General McClellan and witness the Federal advance into the peninsula.

At Fort Magruder, Hooker resolves to attack, though he has only 9000 men. However, with two Union corps within three hours' march he is confident of his ability to hold the Confederates until they can come up. The assault on Fort Magruder goes in at 7.30 and for several hours the division fights the Confederate rear guard alone. Confederate General James Longstreet, who had taken his corps beyond Williamsburg, returns to the battle and makes repeated charges on the Union line. Hooker stands them off until about four in the afternoon, when Kearney comes up and relieves him and his weary troops. At the right of the line, where Hancock's brigade has come up and joined the battle, the Union is having some success against determined opposition. Feigning a withdrawal, Hancock turns and pours volleys into the Confederate line, followed by a bayonet charge by the whole brigade. This routs the enemy and brings the battle to a close. McClellan, who has just arrived on the scene, declines to order a further attack in the morning, and the Confederates make their way in good order toward Richmond. Union losses to III and IV Corps at Williamsburg are severe, with 456 dead, 1400 wounded, and 372 missing. Three fourths of the casualties are in Hooker's division, which had carried the fight alone for much of the day. Confederate losses are estimated at between 1000 and 1700.

Western Theater An action at Lebanon, Tennessee, results in three regiments of Kentucky cavalry taking 66 Confederate prisoners. However, at Dresden, Kentucky, the 5th Iowa Cavalry sustains four killed, 16 wounded, and 68 missing.

Tuesday, May 6

Eastern Theater Federal forces in the Shenandoah Valley are widely scattered, with General Irvin McDowell about to be ordered to move on Richmond; Banks, who has been stripped of Shields' division, which is now attached to McDowell, is 70 miles away at Strasburg, and Frémont is on the other side of the Shenandoah Mountains at Franklin. In the middle of these dispositions lies the reinforced army of Stonewall Jackson, who is closer to each individual Federal force than they are to each other.

Wednesday, May 7

Eastern Theater McClellan transports four divisions up the York River. They disembark at Eltham's Landing, Virginia, near West Point, where they come under attack from a Confederate force continuing the retreat from Yorktown. In a sharp exchange of musketry which lasts for several hours, Union losses total 49 killed, 104 wounded, and 41 missing before the rebels continue their retreat toward Richmond.

Thursday, May 8

Eastern Theater Robert H. Milroy commands a column from Frémont's Mountain Department, which advances along the slopes of the Shenandoah Mountains toward the Confederate positions in the valley. At the town of McDowell he is attacked by Jackson, and in spite of being reinforced by a small unit under Robert C. Schenck, is forced to retreat. The Federal's loss

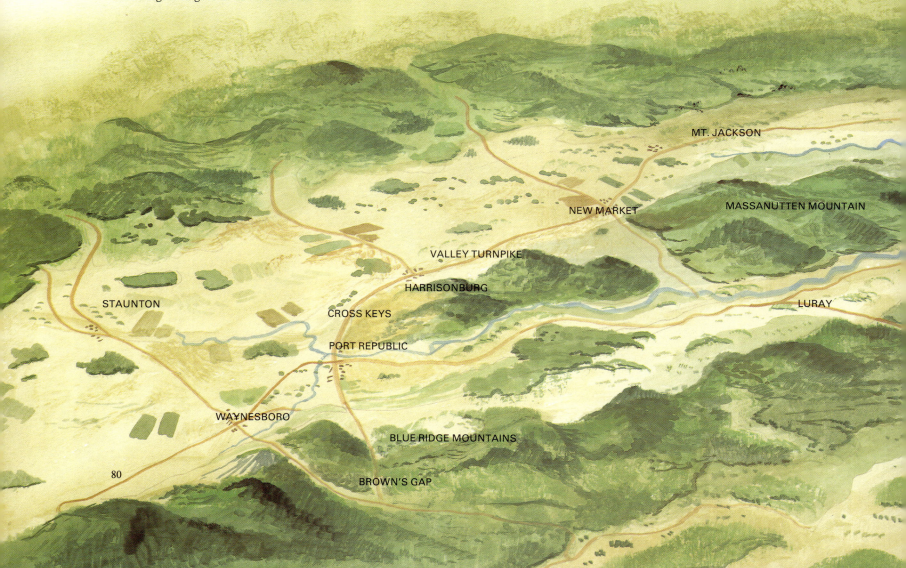

MT. JACKSON

MASSANUTTEN MOUNTAIN

NEW MARKET

VALLEY TURNPIKE

HARRISONBURG

STAUNTON

LURAY

CROSS KEYS

PORT REPUBLIC

WAYNESBORO

BLUE RIDGE MOUNTAINS

BROWN'S GAP

is not as high as that of the Confederates: 28 killed and 225 wounded, compared with over 100 rebels killed and twice as many wounded. At the end of the day the Federal force is fleeing toward Franklin, pursued by Jackson's command, but the Confederates will give up the chase after a couple of days and return to the valley.

Western Theater Skirmishing continues around Corinth, Mississippi. There is an action at Glendale, near the town.

Friday, May 9

Eastern Theater President Lincoln confers with McClellan. The advance of the Army of the Potomac forces the Confederates to abandon the important navy yards at Norfolk, leaving much of their stores and equipment intact to fall into Federal hands.

Western Theater A company of the 37th Indiana Regiment is worsted at Elkton Station, near Athens, Alabama. Five troopers are killed and 43 are captured, against a Confederate loss of 13 dead.

Saturday, May 10

Eastern Theater Pensacola, Florida, is occupied by the Federals.

Western Theater There is an exchange of fire between Confederate batteries and the Union gunboats *Cincinnati* and *Mound City* at Fort Pillow, Tennessee.

Sunday, May 11

Eastern Theater The CSS *Virginia*, the former USS *Merrimac*, draws a great deal of water due to the weight of armor she carries. Because of her draft she is unable to navigate the shoals of the James River to get to Richmond. She is destroyed by the Confederates to prevent her from falling into Federal hands.

Trans-Mississippi A minor skirmish is reported at Bloomfield, Missouri.

Monday, May 12

The North President Lincoln opens the Southern ports of Beaufort, North Carolina, Port Royal, South Carolina, and New Orleans, Louisiana. They had been subject to Federal blockade since the first days of secession, but now are in Federal hands.

Western Theater Federal troops occupy Baton Rouge, Louisiana.

Tuesday, May 13

The Confederacy The approach of the Union Army prompts large numbers of citizens to leave Richmond.

Western Theater There is a minor skirmish at Monterey, Tennessee.

Wednesday, May 14

Eastern Theater In the Shenandoah Valley General Jackson concentrates his whole force at Harrisonburg preparatory to striking at one of the widely dispersed Federal units in the area. The smallest and weakest of these is General Banks's weakened command at Strasburg, which Jackson resolves to cut off and eliminate.

Thursday, May 15

Eastern Theater Federal troops attack Fort Darling, near Drewry's Bluff, Virginia. The assault is supported by gunfire from the *Monitor* and the gunboats *Galena, Port Royal, Naugatuck*, and *Aroostock*. The attack is repulsed by the guns of the fort, manned in part by the crew of the now destroyed CSS *Virginia*.

Western Theater General Butler's administration of New Orleans becomes controversial. While the men of the city have been quieted by the Union's military presence, the woman of the city, safe behind the shield of their sex, make their feelings known in a number of unpleasant ways. Butler's method of dealing with the repeated insults is original and will lead to a storm of protest through the South and in Europe. His General Order Number 28 states: "As the officers and soldiers of the United States have been subject to repeated insults from the women (calling themselves ladies) of New Orleans, in return for the most scrupulous non-interference and courtesy on our part, it is ordered that hereafter, when any female shall, by word, gesture, or movement insult or show contempt for any officer or soldier of the United States, she shall be regarded and held liable to be treated as a woman of the town plying her avocation."

Friday, May 16

Eastern Theater In a three-day action at Princeton, western Virginia, Union troops lose 30 killed and 70 wounded to the Confederate two killed and 14 wounded.

Saturday, May 17

Eastern Theater McDowell, at Fredericksburg, is ordered to advance toward Richmond from the North.

Western Theater More action occurs before Corinth, Mississippi.

KERNSTOWN
WINCHESTER
STRASBURG
HARPER'S FERRY
SHENANDOAH RIVER
FRONT ROYAL
MANASSAS GAP
CULPEPER

The fertile Shenandoah Valley was rich in farmland and served as a vital source of food to the Confederacy. Over this fine country Jackson marched to numerous victories, pushing back one army after another in a series of brilliant moves. Later, in 1864, Sheridan at the head of the Union forces, with orders from the North's high command, would carry out a policy of total war, leaving this once beautiful valley a blackened wasteland.

May 1862

Sunday, May 18, 1862

Eastern Theater Federal troops take the town of Suffolk, Virginia.

Western Theater Farragut advances up the Mississippi with a Federal fleet. His objective is Vicksburg, which holds a commanding position on the lower Mississippi.

Monday, May 19

The Confederacy In a letter to his wife, President Jefferson Davis indicates the uncertainty exercising the minds of the defenders of Richmond.

Trans-Mississippi A Confederate force is defeated at Searcy Landing, Arkansas. Federal casualties total 18 dead and 27 wounded. Some 150 Confederates are reported killed, wounded, or missing.

Tuesday, May 20

The North Even at the height of the war. President Lincoln is looking to the future. He signs the Homestead Act, making quarter sections (160 acres) of government land available to homesteaders willing to improve the land over a period of five years. It is this act which will prove crucial to the post-war taming and settlement of the vast spaces of the American west.

Eastern Theater General Thomas J. Jackson moves into the Luray Valley, with the aim of stopping Federal troops in the Shenandoh Valley from joining in the attack on Richmond.

On the peninsula advanced units of the Army of the Potomac are within eight miles of the Confederate capital.

Wednesday, May 21

Eastern Theater McClellan, still feeling short of troops, asks the president to assign him McDowell's command which is advancing toward Richmond from Fredericksburg.

Western Theater There is a minor skirmish at Phillip's Creek, Mississippi.

Thursday, May 22

Eastern Theater Jackson's troops push toward Front Royal, in western Virginia. Their objective is the small Federal force under Colonel J.R. Kenley, which is positioned there as an anti-guerrilla force. A skirmish is reported outside New Berne, North Carolina.

Trans-Mississippi The vicious guerrilla war in Missouri continues, with a small action occurring at Florida in that state.

Friday, May 23

Eastern Theater The president confers with General McDowell at Fredericksburg.

In the valley Jackson falls on the small Union force at Front Royal. The Confederates strike at Colonel Kenley's command just before noon and, in spite of brave resistance, the Union troops are swept away. Three-fourths of the 1400 Union troops are killed or captured. At the same time, at Lewisburg, 50 miles to the southwest, Crook's brigade of Frémont's command wins a battle with a superior Confederate force. Union casualties total 14 killed and 60 wounded, compared with Confederate losses of 40 dead, 66 wounded, and 100 captured. Colonel George Crook will later become one of America's most famous Indian fighters.

Far West There is a minor skirmish at Fort Craig, New Mexico.

Saturday, May 24

Eastern Theater President Lincoln sends an order to General Frémont commanding him to take the field against Jackson, moving from Franklin to Harrisonburg to take the Confederates in the rear. Furthermore, far from giving McClelland McDowell's troops, Lincoln orders McDowell to send 20,000 men into the Shenandoah Valley to counter the threat presented by the 16,000 Confederates led by Jackson and Ewell.

On the peninsula, in an action at New Bridge, the 4th Michigan Regiment causes 60 Confederate casualties and captures 27 prisoners for the loss of one killed and 10 wounded.

Sunday, May 25

Eastern Theater Jackson races his command toward Winchester in the hope of cutting off Banks's force which is retreating from Strasburg. Before daybreak, Jackson attacks, and after five hours of contact forces the Union force to retreat hurriedly toward Williamsport on the Potomac. In his 53-mile retreat, Banks has lost over 1000 men, mostly captured. The Confederates lose 68 dead and 330 wounded.

On the peninsula McClellan is given an ultimatum by the president: either attack Richmond, or give up and come to the defense of Washington.

Western Theater Halleck at last has his whole army in place at Corinth, Mississippi, after taking 26 days to advance 20 miles.

Monday, May 26

Eastern Theater Banks crosses the Potomac to safety just before Jackson arrives. Confederate actions with 16,000 men in the valley cause as much consternation in Washington as Federal actions with 100,000 men on the peninsula cause in Richmond.

Tuesday, May 27

Eastern Theater A strong enemy force is positioned at Hanover Court House, Virginia. McClellan orders FitzJohn Porter's corps, on the right flank of the Army of the Potomac, to dislodge them. Emory's brigade drives off an enemy force, with the main Union body being ordered to follow. Three regiments under John H. Martindale are ordered westward to cut the railroad and telegraph lines, and find themselves under attack by a superior force. Asking Porter for help, Martindale is ordered to move to his right where the main Union column is chasing the rebels. Rightly believing that the enemy are in fact attacking him, he keeps 1000 men back, who are soon assailed by a Confederate force of 5000 or 6000 men. Standing their ground for two hours, Martindale's men are in trouble when FitzJohn Porter decides he has been "pursuing a myth" and brings his corps about to hit the Confederates on the flank. The Southern force is routed, leaving 200 casualties and 730 prisoners.

Trans-Mississippi A skirmish occurs at Big Indian Creek, near Searcy Landing, Arkansas.

Wednesday, May 28

Eastern Theater Potomac home guards are involved in a skirmish with rebels at Wardensville, Virginia.

Thursday, May 29

Eastern Theater Union forces are massing at Harper's Ferry to counter Jackson's depredations in the Shenandoah Valley. Starting with 16,000 men, the Confederate general has managed to divert 40,000 Union troops away from the peninsular campaign, troops that McClellan had been relying on to conclude that campaign.

Union troops capture the town of Ashland, a few miles north of Richmond.

Friday, May 30

Eastern Theater Jackson, retreating in the face of the much larger Union force at Harper's Ferry, skirmishes with General Shields who is reoccupying Front Royal.

Western Theater General Beauregard evacuates Corinth, Mississippi, which is occupied by Halleck's army. During the operation the 2nd Iowa Cavalry and the 2nd Michigan Cavalry capture 2000 Confederate prisoners at Booneville.

Saturday, May 31

Eastern Theater General Joseph E. Johnston launched a long-delayed Confederate offensive against the Army of the Potomac at Fair Oaks. McClellan's left wing, 30,000 men of Keyes' and Hentzelman's corps are entrenched across the Chickahominy River between Seven Pines on the Williamsburg Road, and Fair Oaks farm. Johnston intends to attack at daybreak with the divisions of Huger, Longstreet, D.H. Hill and G.W. Jones, but Longstreet in the van waits in vain for Huger's division. He attacks at noon and drives Casey's Union division back toward Fair Oaks farm. Here the 5000 Federal troopers hold for three hours, until being forced back to Seven Pines. By now, Union reinforcements from Hentzelman's division have been brought up, but the Confederate pressure continues to force the Union line back. Eventually, at about six in the evening, fragments of various divisions form a line which stops the Confederate advance.

Meanwhile, at Fair Oaks Station, G.W. Smith's Confederate division, which had taken no part in the battle at Seven Pines, attacks a hastily formed Union line at 5 p.m. The Union troops have been stiffened by Sedgwick's division of Sumner's corps, which McClellan had sent across the Chickahominy just in time. Sumner orders a charge at six o'clock, which throws the Confederates back. General Johnston, who has been observing this battle, is seriously wounded by flying fragments. As night falls, the various armies bivouac on the battlefield.

Western Theater A minor skirmish occurs near Neosho, Missouri.

Fair Oaks was an inconclusive battle fought out on May 31 and June 1, 1862, between the Federals under McClellan and the Confederates led by Johnston.

After reaching a point on the Chickahominy River only six miles from Richmond, McClellan halts while he dispatches two corps across the river, leaving them open to attack by Johnston.

McClellan waits for reinforcements from the Shenandoah Valley but these are involved in battles with Jackson, so cannot be moved to their intended position.

The Confederates take advantage of the situation and drive the Federals back, but the Confederate drive was slow and the Union line holds.

The main picture shows the line of Union earthworks thrown up near the twin houses.

June 1862

Sunday, June 1, 1862
The Confederacy Following the wounding of Joseph E. Johnston at Fair Oaks, Robert E. Lee takes command of the defense of Richmond.
Eastern Theater G.W. Smith takes command of the Confederate forces at Fair Oaks and Seven Pines in place of Johnston. He decides the Federal entrenchments of Seven Pines are too strong to attack, but renews the assault at Fair Oaks. Sumner's Union corps, supported by artillery, stands firm, until Hooker's division comes up on the left and after an hour's hard fighting drives the Confederates from the wood in which they are sheltering. As the Southern lines break, a bayonet charge by Richardson's division, holding the center of Sumner's corps, completes the rout. However, the Federal forces are too scattered to pursue. Union losses in this bloody battle are 890 killed, with 3627 wounded, and 1222 missing. Confederate losses are reported as 2800 killed, with 3897 wounded and 1300 missing.

Monday, June 2
Eastern Theater In the Shenandoah Valley there is skirmishing at Strasburg and Staunton Road between Jackson's retreating force and McDowell's Federals.

Tuesday, June 3
Eastern Theater Union troops advancing on Charleston, South Carolina, meet and skirmish with a Confederate force at Legare's Point on James Island.
Western Theater Union troops, having taken Corinth, Mississippi, advance on Memphis, Tennessee. The Confederate garrison at Fort Pillow prepares to evacuate, leaving the city wide open.

Wednesday, June 4
Eastern Theater The Army of the Potomac prepares to move on Richmond, following a couple of days' rest for the troops involved at Seven Pines and Fair Oaks. In the Shenandoah Valley Stonewall Jackson continues to withdraw from larger Union forces.
Western Theater Fort Pillow is evacuated, leaving Memphis unguarded.
Skirmishes are reported at Jasper, Tennessee, and at Blackland, Mississippi.

Thursday, June 5
Eastern Theater There is a brief fight at Tranter's Creek, North Carolina, during which seven Union soldiers are killed and 11 wounded.

Friday, June 6
Eastern Theater In a skirmish at Harrisonburg, Virginia, the Confederates lose one of their most gifted cavalry leaders. Turner Ashby, left behind to command Jackson's rear guard, is killed during an ambush which captures 60 Federal cavalrymen, including the commander of the Union reconnaissance, Colonel Wyndham.
Western Theater A Federal river fleet moving down the Mississippi engages the Confederate flotilla defending Memphis. Eight Confederate vessels, mounting a total of 28 guns, confront a Federal force of five gunboats and two river rams mounting a total of 68 guns. The contest, lasting little more than an hour, ends with three Federal sailors wounded, compared with seven out of eight rebel boats sunk, and a Confederate casualty bill of 80 killed and wounded, and over 100 sailors captured. As a result, Memphis surrenders to the North before noon. The Mississippi is now open to Federal navigation along most of its length.

Saturday, June 7
Eastern Theater Federal reconnaissance units come within sight of Richmond, where Robert E. Lee is preparing to try to force the Union Army of the Potomac back down the peninsula.
Western Theater General Butler causes more controversy in New Orleans when he sentences William Mumford, who had torn down the Union flag flying over the New Orleans Mint, to be hanged.

Sunday, June 8
Eastern Theater In the Shenandoah Valley Jackson is in danger of being caught between the two Federal forces of Frémont and Shields. He cannot allow them to combine against him, so he leaves Ewell with 8000 men to engage Frémont's army of 18,000 at Cross Keys, while he continues a further four miles to Port Republic. The fight at Cross Keys lasts from 11 in the morning till four in the afternoon, until Ewell disengages and rejoins Jackson during the night. In the meantime, Jackson has been skirmishing with Shields, whose main force is on the far side of the South Fork of the Shenandoah.

Monday, June 9
Eastern Theater Jackson throws his whole army across the Shenandoah against Shields, burning the bridge behind him. Several Confederate attacks are repulsed, until a brigade marches through dense forest to make a flank attack coordinated with another frontal assault, and throws the Federals back. Frémont arrives at the end of the action, but is on the wrong side of the river and can contribute nothing. Surprisingly, the Federal forces in the valley now give up the pursuit of Jackson, having received orders to take various posts in the Shenandoah Valley to "guard against the operations of the enemy." The battle of Cross Keys has cost Frémont 125 killed and 500 wounded, while Ewell's division loses 42 dead and 230 wounded. Port Republic has cost Shields 67 killed, 361 wounded, and 574 missing. Jackson's losses in the same battle total 88 killed, 535 wounded, and 34 missing.

Tuesday, June 10
Eastern Theater A skirmish on James Island, South Carolina, results in three Union killed and 13 wounded in exchange for 17 dead and 30 wounded Confederates.

Wednesday, June 11
Western Theater In an action at Monterey in Owen County, Kentucky, Captain Blood's Mounted Provost Guard, together with a battery of Indiana artillery, capture 100 rebels.

Thursday, June 12
Eastern Theater Stonewall Jackson crosses the South Fork of the Shenandoah, where he rests for three days before beginning the march back to Lee's Army of Northern Virginia at Richmond. With a force never exceeding 20,000 men, Jackson has neutralized at least 60,000 Federal troops under McDowell, Frémont, and Banks. His actions mean that the defenders of Richmond can concentrate on the task of beating off McClellan without having to worry about a second Union attack from the North.

A further blow to Federal morale is dealt by flamboyant Brigadier-General J.E.B. Stuart, who takes a force of cavalry and horse artillery on a reconnaissance mission that will in four days take him right around the Army of the Potomac.
Trans-Mississippi A detachment of Federal cavalry meets a Confederate force at Waddell's Farm, near Village Creek in Arkansas.

Friday, June 13
Eastern Theater Skirmishing continues on James Island, South Carolina. This day's action costs three Union and 19 Confederate lives.

Saturday, June 14
Eastern Theater J.E.B. Stuart's cavalry force of some 1500 men attacks a number of lightly guarded Federal supply depots and shoots up a train at Turnstall's Station. By midnight his force is crossing the Chickahominy by means of an improvised footbridge, the horses being swum across.

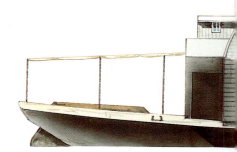

Above: *Confederate river gunboat* General Bragg *formed part of the River Defense Fleet that patrolled the upper waters of the Mississippi. She was a former passenger vessel built in 1851, and was converted into a gunboat in early 1862, having a thick covering of oak over the lower parts for protection. Unfortunately, the side wheels, always a source of weakness in a warship, were still exposed.*

Note the difference to another Confederate gunboat, the General Price *(below), which was also pressed into service at the same time. She later fell into Union hands and was one of the few vessels to serve both sides.*

During early 1862 the Confederate War Department was to set up a River Defense Force made up of 14 lightly-armed rams intended to help the Confederate Navy resist the Union forces now rapidly expanding along the Mississippi. Heavy timbers, plus a liberal helping of iron, were added to the bows to form a powerful ram. Protection was also added to the machinery by surrounding it with compressed cotton bales—a commodity that was in abundant supply in the South!

By running downriver with the current, a good speed could be developed, which enabled the ram to be used with effect. The group, stationed at Memphis, commanded by Captain Montgomery, and crewed by army personnel, put up a good fight against Union forces on several occasions but were eventually defeated in early June off Memphis.

The local population lined the heights, hoping for a successful outcome for the Confederate force, but like so many actions in the long war, the Confederate flag fell to superior forces.

June 1862

Sunday, June 15, 1862

Eastern Theater J.E.B. Stuart returns to Confederate lines after his ride around the Army of the Potomac. His force has captured 165 prisoners and over 300 horses for the loss of a single man. McClellan brushes off the raid as being of no consequence, but apart from improving Confederate morale, it proves to General Robert E. Lee that Federal communications are all but unprotected. He immediately instructs General Jackson to move down from the Shenandoah Valley with all possible speed to join the Army of Northern Virginia on the north side of the Chickahominy. At the same time, as a ruse, he sends 10,000 troops in Jackson's direction, ostensibly to reinforce the Confederates in the valley.

Monday, June 16

Eastern Theater The Federal drive against Charleston, South Carolina, continues, with an attack on Confederate entrenchments on James Island. The strongly fortified Confederate line, stretching from Secessionville to Fort Johnson, is attacked by 6000 men under General Henry Benham. However, in spite of their best efforts, the Union forces are repulsed. Union losses are high, with 85 killed, 472 wounded, and 138 missing. Confederate losses total 51 killed and 144 wounded. After this battle, Union actions against Charleston are suspended for a year.

Tuesday, June 17

The North President Lincoln, in his continuing search for generals who will win, initiates a further rearrangement of the high command. General John Pope is given command of the new Army of Virginia, and Frémont resigns after being placed under the new commander. He is replaced by Franz Sigel.
Eastern Theater Stonewall Jackson's army begins its march from the Shenandoah Valley to join Robert E. Lee in front of Richmond.
Trans-Mississippi A Federal naval expedition is moving up the White River, Arkansas, with the aim of making contact with General Curtis's army, which had been operating in the state after the battle of Pea Ridge. Approaching St Charles, the four gunboats and the single transport came under fire from concealed Confederate batteries. Troops from the transport are landed and eventually take the batteries, but not until the gunboat *Mound City* suffers a boiler explosion which kills or severely scalds many of her crew of 175. Total casualties on the Federal side are 105 dead and 30 wounded. Confederate losses in the batteries total 155 killed, wounded, and captured.

Elsewhere in the region, there are minor skirmishes reported at Smithville, Arkansas, and at Warrensburg, Missouri.

Centreville, Virginia, was one of those places about which many of the main battles of the Civil War was fought. Not far from the Bull Run battlefield, it changed hands several times during the war, and is seen here guarded by Union troops.

Wednesday, June 18

Eastern Theater Lincoln writes to McClellan indicating that the Union high command has been taken in by Lee's deception. The president urges McClellan to attack the Confederate lines at Richmond, stating that with 10,000 fewer men the Confederates are ripe for the plucking. Characteristically, McClellan sees in the move an illustration of the strength and confidence of the enemy he faces.

The only action reported this day is on the Williamsburg Road, close to the scene of the battles of Seven Pines and Fair Oaks, where a skirmish results in seven Union fatalities and 57 other casualties. Confederate losses are much lower.

Thursday, June 19

The North Emancipation becomes an even more important factor in the war when the president indicates that he intends to outlaw slavery in all states in rebellion against the Federal Government.

Friday, June 20

Western Theater General Thomas Williams leaves Baton Rouge with a large part of the Federal garrison of that city. He is moving against Vicksburg on the Mississippi, which is the last major Confederate strongpoint on the river. A Federal fleet under Farragut, now promoted rear-admiral, has been near the city for a month.

Saturday, June 21

Western Theater There is a skirmish at Battle Creek, Tennessee.

Sunday, June 22

The North President Lincoln sets out to confer with retired Lieutenant-General Winfield Scott, still the most revered figure in the Northern armies.
Western Theater A minor action is reported at Raceland, near Algiers, Louisiana.

Monday, June 23

Trans-Mississippi Missouri remains a cockpit of guerrilla warfare, with minor but bitterly fought actions occurring almost daily. On this day, a skirmish is reported at Raytown, Missouri.

Below: *General Thomas J. Jackson was one of the few commanders of true military genius. In this Shenandoah Valley campaign, he manages with a very inferior force to occupy a large Union Army and distract the Washington Government from the peninsular campaign.*

Tuesday, June 24

Eastern Theater As McClellan's troops press on toward Richmond, there is an exchange of fire with Confederates at Mechanicsville.

Western Theater Williams reaches Vicksburg after his march from Baton Rouge, setting up camp across the peninsula (caused by the meandering of the great river in its lower course) on which the city stands. With only four regiments, a total of 3000 men, he is outnumbered by the 10,000 defenders of the city, but he is supported by Farragut's fleet and Porter's mortar boats on the river.

Wednesday, June 25

Eastern Theater The Army of the Potomac before Richmond is divided in two by the Chickahominy River. McClellan, at last deciding that his bridges and entrenchments are ready, orders the picket lines on the left of the Army of the Potomac to advance and reconnoiter some woods a mile or so in front of Fair Oaks. Confederate reaction is swift and vigorous, and there is an inconsequential fight lasting for some hours. Federal casualties are in excess of 500, with 61 killed, while Confederate losses are about half that. Characteristically, McClellan has a number of worries. At 6.30 p.m. he cables Washington stating that Stonewall Jackson is at Hanover Court House; that Beauregard's army is in Richmond; that the Confederate force exceeds 200,000 men; that he expects to be attacked the next day; that if the army is destroyed by overwhelming numbers, he could at least die with it; that if the coming action is a disaster, it would not be his fault; that even if he wanted reinforcements, he would not get any. Of course, there are some errors in McClellan's assessment, although many of these arise from faulty intelligence by his secret service, which is headed by Allen Pinkerton. Far from being in overwhelming strength, the Confederates actually have slightly fewer men than the Union Army at Richmond. Beauregard is in semi-disgrace in Alabama, after the fall of Corinth. But Jackson is indeed close to Hanover Court House, with his whole force, and the general himself has been into Richmond to confer with Lee.

Thursday, June 26

Eastern Theater Lee launches his assault on the Federal Army. His plan is to demonstrate against the bulk of the Union Army, four corps on the south bank of the Chickahominy, while launching a heavy attack on the single Union corps, commanded by Fitz John Porter, isolated on the north side of the river. By driving it back, he hopes to fall on the Federal supply lines and capture the main supply base at White House, which is, in fact, a Lee family estate. The battle of Mechanicsville opens with "Prince John" Magruder operating against the main Union force. A.P. Hill's division is supposed to attack Fitz John Porter in the morning, in conjunction with Jackson. When Jackson's veterans of the Shenandoah are delayed, Hill decides to attack anyway. Crossing the Chickahominy at 3 o'clock, his division drives in the first Federal units it meets, but the Confederates soon come under withering fire from the massed Union artillery, and are driven into cover. Similarly, D.H. Hill's division comes under heavy fire while trying to turn the Union left. Jackson arrives on Porter's right wing at 5 o'clock, but decides his men are in no condition to fight, so he bivouacs for the night. At night falls, Lee pulls A.P. Hill's division back, and he prepares his forces for an attack the next day.

Even though Porter has stopped a larger force with cool professionalism, and is confident in his corps' ability to do the same again, he is overruled by McClellan. Fearing that his entire army will be cut off, he gives the order to withdraw. Once the supplies have been moved away from the White House base, the entire Army of the Potomac is to withdraw from the siege lines.

Western Theater Farragut commences the bombardment of Vicksburg.

Friday, June 27

Eastern Theater A.P. Hill again forms the spearhead for the Confederate attack, but this time it is on a retiring Federal Army. The scene of battle has by now moved on to Gaines Mill. Hill's division once again bears the brunt of the fighting, and by 4.00 p.m. is no longer an organized fighting force. However, by now D.H. Hill, Jackson, Ewell, and Longstreet are in the field, and begin forcing Porter back. As twilight falls, Porter's corps is forced back across the river, and Robert E. Lee has won his first major victory. As a result of the battle, the Confederates have gained the initiative, as well as a vast amount of supplies. McClellan's army is now in full, if disciplined, retreat. Its commander, already at odds with his president, no longer has any of Lincoln's confidence.

Western Theater Farragut runs his fleet up the Mississippi, past the shore batteries of Vicksburg.

General Braxton Bragg is appointed to command the Confederate Army of the Mississippi, replacing General Beauregard.

Trans-Mississippi Skirmishes occur on the Armite River in Louisiana, and at Village Creek and Waddell's Farm in Arkansas.

Saturday, June 28

Eastern Theater The Northern retreat from Richmond continues, with skirmishing at Garnett's and Golding's Farms. Much of the stockpile of supplies at White House Landing is destroyed by the retreating Federals to save it from being captured by the Confederates.

Below: *The luckless Union ironclad* Mound City *was severely damaged while taking part in the White River expedition, when she came under heavy enemy fire from a battery high up on the riverbank.*

A boiler exploded upon being struck and over 100 men were killed or reported missing. Only 26 escaped injury. This loss was among the worst suffered by any vessel during the war.

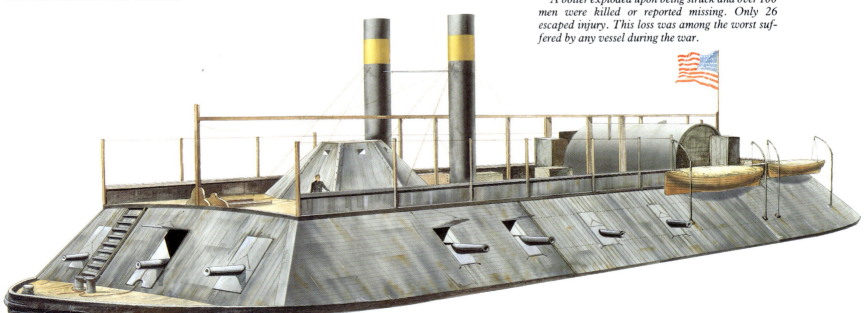

June–July 1862

Sunday, June 29, 1862

Eastern Theater Lee's pursuit of the retreating Army of the Potomac continues, as McClellan fights a series of rear guard actions. He is moving his army toward the James River, from where it can be supported more effectively than from the York River, along the banks of which he had placed his supply dumps.

Today's action takes place at Savage's Station, where, in a two-hour action before dark, Sumner's corps holds off two brigades of Magruder's division. Sumner's force withdraws toward White Oak Swamp having delayed the Confederates, but he leaves behind 2500 sick and wounded together with their attendants.

Monday, June 30

Eastern Theater Lee attempts to cut off McClellan's army with a co-ordinated attack by his whole force of 80,000 men. Jackson's command is to attack from the rear, while the rest of the army is to attack the Federal flank. Unfortunately for Lee, the plan fails because the Confederate Army cannot be made to attack in unison. Jackson is delayed on the White Oak Creek, the bridges across which have been destroyed, while at about 4.00 a.m. Longstreet and A.P. Hill fall on the Federals at Frazier's Farm. The battle rages furiously, with McCall's division bearing the brunt of the Confederate attack.

Night falls with the Union line holding. Once again the Federal troops withdraw, but thanks to the check to the Confederates, McClellan is now able to concentrate his army on the James River.

Tuesday, July 1, 1862

The North President Lincoln signs the bill to introduce Federal income tax at rates between 3 percent and 5 percent.

Eastern Theater McClellan's army is dug into a commanding position on Malvern Hill, overlooking the James River. A.P. Hill fears that a Confederate attack on such a strong position will be a bloody failure, but Lee, eager for a total defeat of the Union Army, orders an assault. However, the lack of co-ordination which has plagued the Confederates means that Longstreet and A.P. Hill are not engaged at all, and Jackson is hardly any more involved.

The divisions of D.H. Hill, Magruder and Huger are cut to pieces by the Federal artillery, and by the end of the day, the whole Confederate line is in confusion. If McClellan were not so worried by the overwhelming Confederate force, which has existence in his imagination alone, a general attack by the Army of the Potomac could finish the Confederate Army.

So ends six days of fighting, which for some reason goes into the history books as the Seven Days' Battle, or the Seven Days' Retreat. Casualties are high, with Union losses being tallied at 1582 dead, 7709 wounded, and 5958 missing. Southern losses are even higher: some 3000 dead, around 15,000 wounded and almost 1000 missing.

The Union Army is still a powerful fighting force, but even as Malvern Hill ends, McClellan is ordering the army to retreat further to Harrison's Landing. Lee has not beaten the Army of the Potomac, but the one incontrovertible fact is that Richmond is no longer besieged.

Wednesday, July 2

The North President Lincoln calls for a further 300,000 men to enlist for three-year terms.

Eastern Theater McClellan's Army of the Potomac begins arriving at Harrison's Landing on the James River.

Thursday, July 3

Eastern Theater McClellan begins fortifying his army's positions at Harrison's Landing.

In an action at Elvington Heights, western Virginia, Union troops kill and wound more than 100 Confederates.

Friday, July 4

The North Celebrations for the 86th Anniversary of the Declaration of Independence are enthusiastically held in spite of the bad news from the peninsula.

Western Theater Colonel John Hunt Morgan, a wealthy planter from Kentucky, begins a long raid deep into Union territory which will place him at the forefront of the roll of Confederate raiders. His regiment is joined by some Rangers from Georgia, a Texas squadron and two companies of Tennessee cavalry.

RAVINES

CONFEDERATE

CORNFIELD

Saturday, July 5

The North Even as the war proceeds, the Federal Government is laying the groundwork for the post-war settlement of the vast territories of the American west. In the first week in July, Congress authorizes the construction of the first transcontinental railroad, and the president signs the Morrill Land Grant Act. Originally introduced to give public land for individual states to build agricultural colleges, it will eventually allow settlers to take up land and tame the prairies.

Sunday, July 6

Trans-Mississippi In a skirmish at Grand Prairie, near Aberdeen in Arkansas, the 24th Indiana Regiment inflicts 81 casualties on a Confederate force for the loss of one man killed and 21 injured.

Monday, July 7

The North McClellan writes to President Lincoln claiming that many of the difficulties experienced by the Army of the Potomac were caused by the president's insistence upon keeping troops back for the defense of Washington. He continues to request more troops, because "the rebel army is in our front, with the purpose of overwhelming us by attacking our positions, or reducing us by blocking our river communication. I cannot but regard our position as critical." In fact, Lee is in the process of pulling his force back toward Richmond, but McClellan will not become aware of this for some days.

Trans-Mississippi A battle is fought near Cotton Plant, between the Bayou de View and the Bayou Cache tributaries of the White River in Arkansas. Union casualties in this action are seven dead and 57 wounded, while the Confederates lose 110 killed and over 200 wounded.

Tuesday, July 8

Eastern Theater Lee's army continues to move back toward Richmond. A cavalry screen prevents McClellan from learning of its departure.

Trans-Mississippi The struggle in Missouri continues, with a minor skirmish being reported at Black River in that state.

Wednesday, July 9

Eastern Theater/Naval Operations Confederate positions along the banks of the Roanoke River are seized, and a number of Confederate vessels are taken. Only one sailor is killed in the operation, which involves the Federal gunboats *Perry*, *Ceres* and *Shawseen*.

Western Theater Morgan's Confederate raiders seizes Tomkinsville, Kentucky.

Trans-Mississippi Skirmishing continues around Aberdeen in Arkansas.

Thursday, July 10

Eastern Theater General Pope, in command of the Federal Army of Virginia, announces that he will deal harshly with Confederate sympathizers in the Shenandoah Valley.

Friday, July 11

The North General Halleck, an efficient if unimaginative administrator, is appointed general-in-chief of the Federal Armies. It will be some days, however, before he can arrive from the Western Theater to take up his post.

Eastern Theater Three Confederates are killed in a skirmish at Williamsburg, Virginia.

Western Theater Morgan's raiders attack Lebanon, south of Frankfort. The town is defended by less than 100 soldiers, who are unable to prevent the destruction of a large Federal supply depot.

Trans-Mississippi The guerrilla war in Missouri continues, with 10 Federals and six rebels killed in an action at Pleasant Hill.

Saturday, July 12

Eastern Theater There is a skirmish at Culpeper, Virginia.

Western Theater Morgan takes Lebanon. Two of the Federal defenders are killed and 65 are captured.

The Seven Days' Battle was part of the continuing Federal effort to besiege Richmond during June and early July 1862.

Federal commander McClellan moves the bulk of his force south of the Chickahominy River, leaving a small force behind. This is promptly attacked by the Confederates under Lee, who had planned a three-pronged assault, but because the forces needed did not arrive on time, the Federals were able to beat off all attacks. McClellan, after a series of indecisive actions, decided to withdraw to Harrison's Landing, and eventually the Federal Army was recalled to Washington.

Illustration shows Battle of Malvern Hill, with the Confederates trying to wrest control of the high ground.

QUAKER ROAD

BERDEN'S GREEN

WEST HOUSE

UNION DEFENDING FORCE

EXTREME EDGE OF UNION ARTILLERY

July 1862

Sunday, July 13, 1862

Eastern Theater President Lincoln still requires an attack on Richmond at the soonest possible moment, but General McClellan, with whom the president is rapidly losing faith, urges a more cautious approach. This does not stop him from making his usual requests for more troops.

Western Theater Another Confederate raider stings the Union by taking Murfreesboro, Tennessee. Nathan Bedford Forrest is a self-taught cavalry commander, possibly the most able of the war. Although famed for saying that generalship boiled down to "git thar fust with the most men," he is just as effective when fighting against the odds. Even though his thousand-strong force is outnumbered by the defenders, his opening cavalry charge settles the fate of the town. Confederate losses are 50 killed and 100 wounded, while the Union loses 33 killed, 62 wounded, and over 800 taken prisoner (including an entire Michigan regiment).

At the same time as Forrest's action, Morgan's raiders in Kentucky are moving on towards the small Federal garrison of Cynthiania, Kentucky.

Monday, July 14

The North Congress approves the establishment of the state of West Virginia, made up from the part of the pre-war state of Virginia that remained loyal to the Union. It does not approve of the president's proposed bill to compensate any state abolishing slavery.

Eastern Theater General Pope advances the Union Army of Virginia toward Gordonsville.

Trans-Mississippi A small cavalry skirmish is reported at Batesville, Arkansas.

Tuesday, July 15

Western Theater The Confederate ironclad *Arkansas* engages the Federal gunboats *Carondelet*, *Queen of the West*, and *Tyler* as they probe the Yazoo River near Vicksburg. Driving the Federal vessels aside, the Confederate armored ram breaks out into the Mississippi, and sails downriver to shelter under the guns of Vicksburg. In the process, the *Arkansas* steams right through Farragut's Federal fleet, which is lying at anchor and unable to get up steam fast enough to chase the rebel ironclad.

Trans-Mississippi A cavalry detachment under the command of Major W.H. Miller captures 150 Confederates near Fayetteville, Arkansas.

Far West There is a skirmish at Apache Pass, Arizona.

Confederates captured in the valley campaigns in 1862 are accommodated in a prison camp. Neither side in this war could be proud of their treatment of prisoners, although as much suffering was caused by shortages or ignorance as by brutality or deliberate policy.

Wednesday, July 16

The North Although the president's bill to provide financial assistance to states willing to abolish slavery has foundered, due to opposition from the border states, it is clear that slavery is becoming the major factor in a war which ostensibly broke out over states' rights. The next week will see a number of new bills and proposals on the subject.

Thursday, July 17

The North The president signs the Second Confiscation Act, which amongst other things grants freedom to slaves entering Federal jurisdiction.

Western Theater Morgan's Confederate raiders surround and capture Cynthiania. Seventeen Federal troops are killed and 34 wounded in the action, in exchange for eight dead and 29 wounded in the Southern force.

Friday, July 18

Trans-Mississippi There is a skirmish at Memphis, Missouri.

Saturday, July 19

Trans-Mississippi The guerrilla war in Missouri continues to give concern, even though a number of the more draconian examples of military law have been relaxed following the expulsion of the last major Confederate force from the state.

Sunday, July 20

Trans-Mississippi Currently, the Department of Missouri is commanded by General John M. Schofield. The Federal forces in the state now embark on an anti-guerrilla campaign that over the next two months will cost the Union 77 dead, 156 wounded and 347 missing and captured. Confederate and guerrilla losses will be much higher: 506 killed, 1800 wounded and 560 missing.

Abraham Lincoln had only one aim at the start of the war, and that was the preservation of the Union. However, the slavery question grew and grew, until his emancipation declaration of 1863 turned him into one of the great liberators of history.

Monday, July 21

Eastern Theater Pope's campaign in Virginia now begins to take shape. His army comprises Sigel's and Banks's corps from the Shenandoah, together with McDowell's corps. The Union line stretches 40 miles from Sperryville, east of the Blue Mountains, down to Fredericksburg. On July 14, Pope orders Banks's cavalry under John P. Hatch to seize Gordonsville, an important junction on the railroad uniting Richmond with the south. They fail to do so, and after a second attempt Banks's cavalry commander is relieved and replaced by John Buford.

Meanwhile Lee is taking steps to protect the capital of the Confederacy from the threat posed by Pope. With the immediate threat from McClellan eased, he has detached Stonewall Jackson with orders to take possession of Gordonsville. Once in position, Jackson considers the threat from Pope to be too great to consider offensive action, and he is content to hold his position until it is clear that McClellan has no immediate plans to move on Richmond. When that occurs, Lee will be free to reinforce the army facing Pope.

Tuesday, July 22

The North President Lincoln presents his Cabinet with the draft of an emancipation proclamation, calling for the freeing of slaves in states in rebellion against the Union.
The North/The Confederacy A cartel, or agreement to the exchange of prisoners, is signed by both North and South.

General Joseph E. Johnston was a master of defensive tactics. West Point trained, he was involved in the first battle at Manassas, and later in his career would conduct a masterly retreat to Atlanta in the face of Sherman's powerful armies. Although he was seriously wounded at Fair Oaks, it was not a tragedy because he was eventually replaced by General Robert E. Lee.

Wednesday, July 23

Western Theater Confederate General Braxton Bragg advances on Chattanooga from his base at Tupelo, Mississippi.
Trans-Mississippi There are skirmishes in the Missouri guerrilla war, with action at Florida and Columbus in that state.

Thursday, July 24

Western Theater Action is reported at Trinity, Alabama when a company of the 31st Ohio Regiment kills 12 rebels and wounds 30 for the loss of two dead and 11 wounded.
Trans-Mississippi Skirmishing at Santa Fe, Missouri will last through the night.

Friday, July 25

Western Theater Confederates take 100 Union soldiers prisoner at Courtland Bridge, Alabama.

Saturday, July 26

Trans-Mississippi There are skirmishes at Mountain Store, Missouri, and at Big Piney, Missouri.

Right: *Although McClellan's deliberate approach was not popular with the powers that be, he was liked by private soldiers such as this one because the general's administrative gifts meant that there was food to eat, clothes to wear, and powder and shot to fire.*

Above: *Many of McClellan's problems in the peninsula and afterward were caused by faulty intelligence, and the blame could be laid at the feet of his chief of intelligence. Allan Pinkerton (in the background with a pipe) went on to found the famous detective agency which bears his name, but as a purveyor of military intelligence he was a disaster.*

July–August 1862

Fierce fighting at Baton Rouge, which forced Butler to withdraw mainly through lack of troops. Later the Confederate forces would be driven out of town as the tide of war changed against them.

Sunday, July 27, 1862

Trans-Mississippi Skirmishes are reported at a number of locations in Missouri, including Brown's Spring, Carroll County, Ray County, and Livingstone County. Further west, there is a small action near Fort Gibson in the Indian Territory.

Monday, July 28

Trans-Mississippi In a sharp fight at Moore's Mills, Missouri, Confederate guerrillas are routed by a Union force including troops from Missouri, Iowa and Indiana. Confederate losses are variously reported at between 36 and 60 killed, with 100 wounded. Losses to the Union force total 19 killed and 21 wounded. In the Indian Territory there is a brief exchange of fire at Bayou Bernard, but no casualties are recorded.

Tuesday, July 29

Western Theater Brief skirmishes occur at Russelville, Kentucky and at Brownsville, Tennessee.

Trans-Mississippi Two companies of the 13th Missouri Regiment assault and capture a Confederate camp at Bollinger's Mills, Missouri, killing 10 rebels in the process.

Overseas/Naval Operations In spite of representations by the United States Minister to London, the steamer *290* sets sail from the Port of Liverpool. She has been built for the Confederates as a commerce raider, but Federal pressure on the British Government means that if she remains in port any longer she will be arrested. Under a British commander and crew, *290* is heading for the Portuguese island of Terceira, where she will be equipped and armed. Also heading for the island is Raphael Semmes, formerly commander of the CSS *Sumter* and now to convert the *290* into the most famous raider of the war, under the new name of the CSS *Alabama*.

Wednesday, July 30

Western Theater The 9th Pennsylvania Cavalry roughly handle a Confederate force at Paris, Kentucky, killing 27 rebels and wounding 39.

Thursday, July 31

Eastern Theater Four weeks of quiet on the peninsula, after the battle of Malvern Hill, are rudely interrupted in the night. The Federal fleet of gunboats is spread a mile up and down the James River by Harrison's Landing. Daniel Harvey Hill, in command of the Confederate forces south of the river, moves some 43 guns to be placed in a battery on Coggin's Point, which juts out into the James and narrows the river to 1000 yards at that point. Opening fire in the night, the Confederate guns lob 1000 shells into the Union positions on the other side of the river. In spite of the lights of the Federal camp and aboard the vessels in the river, the Confederate fire does little damage. Total Union casualties are 10 killed and 15 wounded.

Friday, August 1, 1862

The Confederacy Following General Pope's anti-rebel proclamations which promise harsh treatment to anybody helping the Southern cause in the Department of Virginia, the Confederate Government issues General Order Number 54. This states that General Pope, and the commissioned officers serving under him, would not be entitled to treatment as prisoners of war, and if captured would be held in close confinement; and if any persons were executed in pursuance of Pope's general orders, then a similar number of these prisoners, selected by lot, should be hanged.

Trans-Mississippi In an action lasting several hours, 73 men of the Missouri State Militia are defeated by the Confederates. Union losses are four killed, four wounded, and some 60 men taken prisoner. Confederate casualties are reported to be between 70 and 100 killed and wounded.

Saturday, August 2

The North Secretary of State Seward instructs Charles F. Adams, the Minister in London, to decline any British offer of mediation in what is, after all, a civil war which should be of no concern to outsiders.

Another view of the Battle of Malvern Hill, this time from the Confederate viewpoint as they skirmish in the wheatfield on July 1, 1862.

Eastern Theater Federal raiders from General Pope's Army of Virginia cross the Rapidan to seize Orange Court House, Virginia. In the process they beat off the Confederate Cavalry regiment which had been in occupation, killing 11 and capturing 52 for the loss of four troopers.

Western Theater A minor skirmish is reported in Coahomo County, Mississippi.

Trans-Mississippi The guerrilla war in Missouri continues unabated, with clashes occurring at Ozark and at Clear Creek.

Sunday, August 3

Eastern Theater General Halleck, the general-in-chief of the Union Army, orders General McClellan to move the Army of the Potomac back to Alexandria, Virginia. This is much closer to Washington and more suitable for the defence of the capital. McClellan, for all his faults, feels that sitting back defensively is wrong and that his army will be of more use threatening the Confederate capital. Of course, he cannot do anything until he gets more troops.

On the peninsula itself there is an exchange of shots when the Federal Cavalry probe toward Petersburg.

Trans-Mississippi Today's action in Missouri is at Chariton Bridge. Further south in Arkansas, the 1st Wisconsin Cavalry are roughly handled by the Confederates, losing 21 killed, 40 wounded and 21 missing in two actions at Jonesboro and at Lauguelle Ferry.

Monday, August 4

The North Because of the failure of the call for three-year volunteers in July, the president issues a new call for 300,000 nine-month volunteers. However, even though manpower is a problem he refuses to accept two black regiments raised in Indiana.

Eastern Theater There is a skirmish at White Oak Swamp Bridge, when 28 rebels are captured by troopers from the 3rd Pennsylvania Cavalry.

Western Theater A minor action is reported at Sparta, Tennessee.

Tuesday, August 5

Western Theater A Confederate division under General John C. Breckenridge attacks Baton Rouge, Louisiana, from its base at Tangipahoa some 50 miles away, after a two-day march through the southern summer heat. Just before the attack, which is supposed to be made in conjunction with the armored ram *Arkansas*, there is an exchange of fire with Confederate partisans who think the column is of Union troops. Among those killed is Captain Alexander A. Todd, who, although fighting for the South, is a brother-in-law to President Lincoln. After driving in the Federal pickets, and capturing some outlying encampments, the Confederate commander realizes that in the face of Northern artillery supported by fire from Federal gunboats, he cannot hold the position, especially as the *Arkansas* fails to arrive. The Confederates withdraw leaving Baton Rouge to the Union. Casualties are high, with rebel losses tallied at 84 killed, 316 wounded and 78 missing, while the Federal casualty bill includes 82 killed, 255 wounded and 35 missing. Among the dead is the Federal commander, Brigadier General Thomas Williams.

Wednesday, August 6

Eastern Theater Skirmishes are reported at Beech Creek, West Virginia and at Thornburg, Virginia.

Western Theater There is a skirmish at Tazewell, Tennessee, with Federal forces reporting three killed, 23 wounded and 50 missing. Confederate losses are nine killed and 40 wounded.

Trans-Mississippi In fierce action in Missouri, the Missouri State Militia inflict over 325 casualties on a rebel guerrilla force while losing 28 dead and some 60 wounded.

Thursday, August 7

Western Theater Thirty Confederates are killed by Union cavalry at Trenton, Tennessee,

Far West Confederates are forced out of the area around Fort Fillmore, New Mexico.

Friday, August 8

The North Steps are taken to ensure that anybody seeking to evade conscription shall be breaking the law and so subject to arrest.

Western Theater Skirmishing begins in the Cumberland Gap of Tennessee.

Saturday, August 9

Eastern Theater Stonewall Jackson's seeming period of inactivity facing Pope comes to an end when his intended strike on Pope's army is forestalled by General Nathaniel Banks striking at the Confederate force first. At Cedar Mountain, Banks throws two divisions at what he believes to be a small Confederate force. At first, the powerful Union attack almost turns the flank of the Confederates, but the fortuitous arrival of A.P. Hill's division, detached from Lee's army at Richmond some days before, turns the battle. This accidental encounter could almost be called a skirmish were it not for the size of the forces involved and the scale of the losses. Banks's casualties are reported at 450 killed, 660 wounded and 290 missing, most of whom have been captured. Confederate losses total 229 killed, with over 1000 wounded and 31 missing.

Union attack upon Cedar Mountain; troops prepare to attack the position on the right. The artillery duel is now getting under way as the columns of troops mass.

August 1862

Sunday, August 10, 1862

Trans-Mississippi Four days of running fights commence in Missouri, with skirmishes taking place at Grand River, Lee's Ford, Chariton River, Walnut Creek, Compton Ferry, Switzler's Mills, and Yellow Creek.

Far West In an action on the Neuces River, Texas loyalists are defeated by Confederate troops. Forty Union sympathizers are killed while eight Southern troops are killed and 14 wounded.

Monday, August 11

Eastern Theater A brief exchange of fire occurs at Wyoming Court House, West Virginia.

Western Theater General Ulysses S. Grant makes it clear that fugitive slaves will be employed by the military under his jurisdiction.

Trans-Mississippi The 7th Missouri Volunteers are badly beaten by Confederates in an action at Independence, Missouri. Further to the south, there is a skirmish at Helena, in Arkansas.

Tuesday, August 12

Western Theater Morgan's Confederate raiders are still raising havoc behind the Union lines. They take the town of Gallatin, Tennessee, capturing over 200 prisoners in the process.

Wednesday, August 13

Eastern Theater Robert E. Lee's Army of Northern Virginia begins to advance on Gordonsville, even though McClellan's Army of the Potomac is still within 25 miles of Richmond. It is clear, however, that the Union Army is preparing to withdraw from the peninsula, and the threat from Pope's army is much greater.

Eastern Theater/Naval Operations Eighty-three die in a collision between the Federal steamers *George Peabody* and *West Point* on the Potomac River.

Western Theater A large Union force drives Morgan's raiders out of Gallatin, Tennessee.

Trans-Mississippi Four days of skirmishing that started at Grand River, Missouri come to an end. The 9th Missouri Militia have suffered 100 casualties, but Confederate losses are not recorded. Further south, Union General Alvin P. Hovey's division captures 700 rebels at Clarendon, Arkansas.

Thursday, August 14

Western Theater Confederate troops under Major General Edmund Kirby Smith move out from Knoxville, Tennessee. His aim is the fertile valley of the Kentucky River, and his march will cause considerable excitement in Kentucky and Ohio.

Friday, August 15

Western Theater There is a skirmish at Merriweather's Ferry, Tennessee.

Saturday, August 16

Eastern Theater McClellan begins to embark the Army of the Potomac out of Harrison's Landing on the James River. He is under orders to join with General Pope's army in northeastern Virginia, from where the Union will again attempt to drive toward Richmond.

Trans-Mississippi The fighting in Missouri continues. At Lone Jack, a fierce engagement sees Union Cavalry take 160 casualties including 60 dead. Confederate losses are 110 dead and wounded.

Sunday, August 17

Trans-Mississippi In Minnesota, there is a violent Indian uprising. The Santee Sioux, numbering about 1200 warriors, leave their reservations and begin killing white settlers. Rumours that the uprising is Confederate inspired are widely believed, though it is more probable that the Indians are taking advantage of the distraction of the Federal Government by the war. The total loss of life in the next month will approach 800, most killed in the first days. Colonel H.H. Sibley is sent with some companies of Federal troops to quell the rising, which he will do highly efficiently.

The beau sabreur *of the Confederate Army, Jeb Stuart was everything a cavalryman should be. But he was more than a dashing raider. Under proper control, he led the best cavalry units of the war. But if given his head he could go too far, as at Gettysburg, when his absence may have contributed to the Confederate defeat. But at this time he was still the man who could ride right around an enemy army without losing a man.*

Wednesday, August 20

Eastern Theater A cavalry clash at Brandy Station presages the advance of Lee's Army of Northern Virginia. It is now in the field on the west bank of the Rappahannock, at least 80,000 strong. Lee brushes aside Pope's pickets at Rappahannock Station, until his whole force opposes Pope across the river. Lee's march north has the purpose of turning the Federal troops right, and for the next two days Lee will try to force a way across the river. Pope is in a difficult position, while waiting for McClellan, but he is assured that he will have reinforcements by the 23rd.

Trans-Mississippi There is a skirmish at Union Mills, Missouri. Far to the north in Minnesota, Fort Ridgely is attacked by the Santee Sioux, but manages to hold off the Indian warriors.

Left: *Photographers rest just before the second battle at Bull Run. This time the Union Army does not consist of amateurs as in the year before, but they are run ragged by Lee and by Stonewall Jackson.*

the flank on the morrow. At the same time, Lee plans to cross the river in the opposite direction.

During the night, the 6th Virginia Cavalry, under Jeb Stuart, crosses the river further north and gets behind Union lines. In a daring move, Stuart penetrates Pope's headquarters at Catlett's Station, and seizes some Union staff officers. More importantly, he also finds Pope's dispatch book, which reveals the exact situation of the Federal Army, its need of reinforcements and the time they are expected to arrive.

Saturday, August 23

Eastern Theater Heavy rain during the night raises the level of the Rappahannock by 6 to 8 feet, sweeping away bridges and making fords unusable. This stops Pope from making his ill-advised attack and Lee from carrying out his own crossing of the river. Lee, with the aid of Stuart's prize discovery, evolves a plan to occupy Pope's attention with a holding force, while marching the rest of his army rapidly beyond the Federal right and into the Federal rear. This will cut Pope's line of communication with Washington and enable the Confederate general to use his superior number to destroy the smaller Union Army.

Monday, August 18

The Confederacy The second session of the Confederate Congress meets at Richmond, where President Jefferson Davis gives a "State of the Nation" address.

Eastern Theater Pope, currently on the Rappahannock and facing Lee's Confederate Army of Northern Virginia, retires northward while awaiting the arrival of McClellan's army from the peninsula.

Western Theater Union troops capture the Confederate steamer *Fairplay* near Milliken's Bend, Louisiana and seize 40 rebels.

Tuesday, August 19

Western Theater Two hundred soldiers of the 71st Ohio Regiment are captured by the Confederates at Clarksville, Tennessee. There is also a skirmish at White Oak Ridge, near Hickman in Kentucky.

Thursday, August 21

Eastern Theater There is a continuous exchange of artillery fire on the Rappahannock as Lee seeks to find a way across to get to grips with Pope.

Western Theater Confederate General Braxton Bragg moves on Chattanooga.

Friday, August 22

The North President Lincoln replies to a criticism of his policy by Horace Greeley, the highly influential editor of the *New York Tribune*. In answer to the assertion that he is doing too little to free the slaves, Lincoln makes it plain that his sole aim is to save the Union. "If I could save the Union without freeing any slave I would to it, and if I could do so by freeing all the slaves I would do it."

Eastern Theater Pope, possibly unaware of the true Confederate strength, resolves to cross the Rappahannock and attack Lee's column in

Above left: *Quaker guns are dummies, placed in positions so that from a distance they will look stronger than they in fact are. These Quakers are at Centreville, a few miles east of Manassas and the Bull Run battlefield.*

Above: *A pontoon bridge across the Bull Run. Pope, the Union commander, is no match for the wily Confederates, and he loses the battle. Although he blames everybody but himself, the president recalls General McClellan to the center of things, once again to create an army out of a beaten rabble.*

August–September 1862

Sunday, August 24, 1862

Trans-Mississippi While the war in the Eastern Theater is moving towards a major battle, the guerrilla war in Missouri continues, with skirmishes reported at Dalls, and at Coon Creek in that state.

Monday, August 25

Eastern Theater Stonewall Jackson sets the first part of Lee's plan in motion when he moves off from the Rappahannock up the valley between the Blue Ridge Mountains and the Bull Run Mountains. He reaches Salem by midnight, and prepares to cut through the Thorofare Gap and fall on Pope's rear the next day.

Pope knows about the move, however, since Jackson has been shadowed by Federal Cavalry under Colonel J.S. Clark. Clark reports that Jackson has some 30 regiments of infantry and a large cavalry force. Pope has been instructed to maintain communication with Fredericksburg to the south, and cannot stretch his force any thinner. He is assured that he will receive reinforcements directly, so he feels he will be able to contain Jackson. The only problem is the fact that Jackson's command is twice as large as reported, consisting of 66 regiments of infantry and all of Lee's cavalry.

Western Theater A Confederate force attacks Fort Donelson and the Cumberland Iron Works in Tennessee.

Tuesday, August 26

Eastern Theater Jackson moves through Thorofare Gap and seizes Manassas Junction, which holds the only sizeable Northern stores depot between Pope and Washington. Meanwhile, Longstreet moves off from his positions on the Rappahannock where he had been making demonstrations against Pope. His aim is to unite with Jackson at Manassas. Pope pulls back from the Rappahannock and moves his army rapidly north toward Manassas.

Trans-Mississippi The Confederate steamer *Fairplay* is taken on the Yazoo River by a combined Union expedition, with General Samuel Curtis moving down the river at the same time as Commodore Charles Davis moves up from the Mississippi.

Wednesday, August 27

Eastern Theater The situation in Virginia has Jackson in possession of Manassas Junction, the rest of Lee's army moving up the other side of Bull Run Mountains to cross through Thorofare Gap, and Pope concentrating his forces in the direction of Manassas. Hooker's division marches on Bristoe, but meets Ewell's division which Jackson has left there. In the fight at Kettle Run both sides lose some 300 killed and wounded. Another Federal force moves down the railroad to Manassas, and meets the Confederates at Bull Run Bridge. The Union force is unable to drive the Confederates from their position, and in the battle Union General G.W. Taylor is mortally wounded.

Thursday, August 28

Eastern Theater Jackson is in danger of being cut off by Pope before Longstreet arrives through Thorofare Gap. Jackson feigns a retreat to his old stamping ground in the Shenandoah Valley. Pope is not sure of Jackson's exact whereabouts until Jackson reveals it himself by mounting an evening attack at Groveton, by the old Bull Run battlefield. Pope's line of march has exposed his flank, and Jackson's artillery fire initiates the action. A sharp fight is brought to an end by nightfall.

Western Theater General Braxton Bragg leaves Chattanooga to join with General Kirby Smith's command advancing into Kentucky.

Friday, August 29

Eastern Theater Pope throws his army on Jackson's position. He orders each of his commanders to attack as they arrive on the battlefield, as he is under the impression that Jackson is fighting a rear guard action and will break off and run before long. Pope sends Fitz John Porter's corps to attack Jackson's right flank, but even as the assault begins Longstreet's divisions arrive on the field at that point. Porter breaks off the attack and digs in to stave off the Confederate counter offensive he believes will come. Night falls upon a stalemate.

Western Theater In an action at Manchester, Tennessee, three companies of Federal infantry inflict over 100 casualties on a Confederate force.

GROVERTON

Battle of Second Bull Run as it appeared on a hot summer's day at the end of August 1862, viewed from the embankment that protected the Confederate troops under Jackson from repeated attacks by Federal troops which had arrived from Groverton.

Meanwhile, Longstreet arrived upon the scene (extreme right) with 25,000 Confederate troops and saved the day. By bringing up his guns he changed the course of the battle within 15 minutes, as Jackson could not have held out much longer. This defeat halted any reinforcements reaching McClellan and put the Federals on the defensive.

JACKSON'S CORPS

UNFINISHED RAILROAD EMBANKMENT

Saturday, August 30

Eastern Theater Pope orders repeated assaults on the Confederate line, and Jackson's troops are hard pressed. Indeed some companies, running out of ammunition, resort to throwing stones and using their muskets as clubs. Even as Jackson's troops begin to yield, Longstreet's corps are thrown in to turn the left of the Union line. Jackson launches a counterattack after Union troops are withdrawn from that sector of the field to bolster the left flank. The day is lost to the Union cause, and Pope orders a retreat toward Washington. Unlike the battle at the same spot the previous year, there is no panic. The three days of the second battle of Manassas costs Lee's forces some 1400 dead and 7000 wounded. Federal losses are more difficult to assess, but are probably of the order of 2000 dead, and some 10,000 wounded or taken prisoner.

Western Theater General Don Carlos Buell orders the pursuit of the Confederate forces, led by Braxton Bragg and by Kirby Smith, that are pushing into Kentucky. At Richmond, Smith defeats a Federal force, capturing General Manson and wounding General Nelson. The Union forces flee the field, leaving dead and wounded and most of their artillery. Federal losses are 200 killed, 700 wounded, and as many as 4000 men missing or taken prisoner. Confederate losses are 250 killed and 500 wounded.

Sunday, August 31

Eastern Theater A heavy rainstorm at Manassas hampers Confederate pursuit of the defeated Federal Army, but Stonewall Jackson pushes on toward Fairfax. Pope is not entirely beaten: he has sent McDowell's, Heintzelman's and Reno's corps in the same direction with orders to attack on September 2nd.

Monday, September 1, 1862

Eastern Theater The Second Bull Run campaign closes with a clash at Ox Hill, near Chantilly. The heads of the two forces sent toward Fairfax come into contact in a torrential thunderstorm just before dark. In a confused battle, Union Generals Isaac Stevens and Philip Kearney are both killed. Total casualty tolls are 1400 killed, wounded and missing on the Federal side and 800 on the Confederate side.

Tuesday, September 2

Eastern Theater The president, in the face of Cabinet opposition, recalls McClellan to take command of the defense of Washington. Whatever his faults as a field commander, and they are many, "The little Napoleon" is a superb organizer. "If he can't fight himself" the president comments, "he excels in making others ready to fight."

Western Theater Kirby Smith occupies Lexington, Kentucky, from where the state legislature has fled to Louisville.

Wednesday, September 3

Eastern Theater Even while McClellan is riding out to see the wreckage of the army he has to work with, General Halleck is receiving a report from Pope blaming everybody but himself for the defeat at Manassas.

Thursday, September 4

Naval Operations The Confederate blockade runner *Oreto* evades the Federal gunboat *Oneida* and reaches Mobile, Alabama.

Friday, September 5

Eastern Theater Lee strikes into Maryland while the Union high command argue over who is to lead the army in the field. This first invasion of the North will threaten Washington, boost Southern morale, and hit at Northern spirits and, at the same time, allow the farmers of war-ravaged northern Virginia to gather what is left of their harvest while the army reaps a similar harvest of supplies in the fat fields and overflowing larders of Maryland.

Saturday, September 6

Eastern Theater In just four days, McClellan has an army of 90,000 men, mostly veterans, in seven corps. However, this incredible organizational feat will be wasted if the army is not used correctly. McClellan's indecision in the field is well known to Lee, and indeed the Southern commander will base much of the coming campaign around his reading of an administratively able but tactically very slow opponent.

WARRENTON TURNPIKE

CONFEDERATE INFANTRY UNDER LONGSTREET

CONFEDERATE ARTILLERY

September 1862

SHARPSBURG

TO HARPER'S FERRY

CONFEDERATES DRIVE OFF UNION FORCE AT END OF DAY

ANTIETAM CREEK

Sunday, September 7, 1862
Eastern Theater After crossing the Potomac near Leesburg, Virginia, Lee leads the Army of Northern Virginia into Maryland. Lee knows his army is not strong enough to storm Washington but is determined to retain the initiative after his victory at the second battle of Bull Run. By taking the war to the North, he plans to keep the Federals off balance and prevent another invasion of Virginia in the fall.

The Army of the Potomac recoiled on Washington. Assembled at Rockville, Maryland, now once again under the command of General McClellan, it remains a larger and better-equipped formation than the ragged rebel army marching north. But Lee's confident advance leads to panic in Washington, with ships standing by to evacuate the Cabinet, and another crisis of confidence in the army's senior offices.

Monday, September 8
Eastern Theater The Commission of Inquiry, investigating General Pope's claims against Franklin, Porter and Griffin and their behavior at Bull Run, meet and adjourn. As the recriminations continue, General Nathanial Banks takes charge of the defense of Washington. McClellan's 90,000 strong army prepares to march against Lee who issues a proclamation to the people of Maryland, urging them to rally to his standard and restore Maryland to her rightful place in the Confederacy. But although he outnumbers the Confederates by nearly two to one, McClellan is acutely conscious of his army's demoralization.

Tuesday, September 9
Eastern Theater Lee's proclamation promises Marylanders a free choice: the Confederate Army would not compel them to join the cause. They take him at his word. Hardly a man joins and there is no rush to help provision the hungry rebel troops. The long summer's campaigning has reduced Lee's soldiers to rags: to a wavering Marylander they looked more like a beaten rabble than victorious veterans. Lee resolves to press north into Pennsylvania, issuing Special Order 191 ordering his forces to march by divergent routes to concentrate again at Hagerstown, Maryland, where he will draw on his supply base at Winchester in the Shenandoah Valley.

Wednesday, September 10
Eastern Theater McClellan warily leads the Army of the Potomac towards Lee's encampments at Frederick. Lee's army depart the same day. Longstreet and D.H. Hill cross South Mountain and march on Hagerstown. Jackson attacks Harper's Ferry while McLaws occupies the Maryland Heights which overlook the town from the north side of the Potomac. Walker approaches from the east and seizes the Loudon Heights across the Shenandoah from Harper's Ferry. True to form, Jackson ensures he is overheard asking about the best roads leading to Pennsylvania and few on his staff know of his real objective.

Thursday, September 11
Eastern Theater Having halted overnight near Boonsboro and narrowly avoided capture by Federal Cavalry in the town the previous evening, Jackson leads his troops to Williamsport, ford the Potomac and then head for Martinsburg to drive the Federal garrison there into the trap at Harper's Ferry.
Western Theater Without consulting General Bragg, President Davis appoints Van Dorn to command the Confederate Armies fighting in Mississippi. Van Dorn receives his orders by telegraph, but Price, ignorant of the change of command, is already marching on Iuka, Missouri, intent on striking into Tennessee.

Friday, September 12
Eastern Theater McClellan's vanguard enters Frederick. Stuart's cavalry rear guard manages to capture a Federal brigade commander in a surprise counter-attack before withdrawing down the Hagerstown road. Frederick then loudly demonstrates its loyalty to the Union.

Saturday, September 13
Eastern Theater Fortune smiles on George McClellan: two soldiers from Indiana find some cigars wrapped in paper on the site of Lee's encampment. The paper is a missing copy of Special Order 191. On a fair and sunny morning McClellan receives a hero's welcome in Frederick before closeting with Burnside and his staff to join their attack.

Sunday, September 14
Eastern Theater The Confederates have withdrawn west over three narrow roads leading over the timber-clad slopes of South Mountain. Their rear guards are attacked early in the afternoon. By evening, Crampton's Gap, the southernmost position, is in Union hands while Burnside's corps batter through the others. Discouraged at the speed of the Union pursuit, Lee writes orders cancelling the offensive that evening. But then a messenger gallops in with news from Jackson: Harper's Ferry is as good as taken.
Western Theater Price's army enters Iuka, Missouri.

Monday, September 15
Eastern Theater By establishing cannon on the heights overlooking Harper's Ferry, McLaws and Walker render the town untenable. A brief bombardment shatters the Union able. Miles hoists the white flag. Ironically he is killed by one of the rebel batteries unaware a surrender is about to take place. Some 12,000 troops pass into captivity, leaving A.P. Hill's division to take charge of the prisoners. Jackson leads his men on a forced march to join Lee before McClellan can close on the divided Confederates. In fact McClellan's army is already assembling before Sharpsburg where Lee has just 18,000 troops with him.

Tuesday, September 16
Eastern Theater Although the rolling countryside around Sharpsburg offers great possibilities for a strong defense, Lee has his back to the Potomac and is hopelessly outnumbered. But McClellan proves true to form. As the morning fog lifts, his cannon open a desultory bombardment while 75,000 Federal troops deploy at a torpid pace. Jackson arrives with 9000 footsore troops and joins the Confederate line which is stretched thinly over a four-mile front. During the afternoon McClellan despatches the fire-eating Joe Hooker to turn Lee's left with I Corps but the movement is detected at 6 p.m. and leads to a short exchange of fire as Hooker crosses Antietam Creek to the north of Sharpsburg.

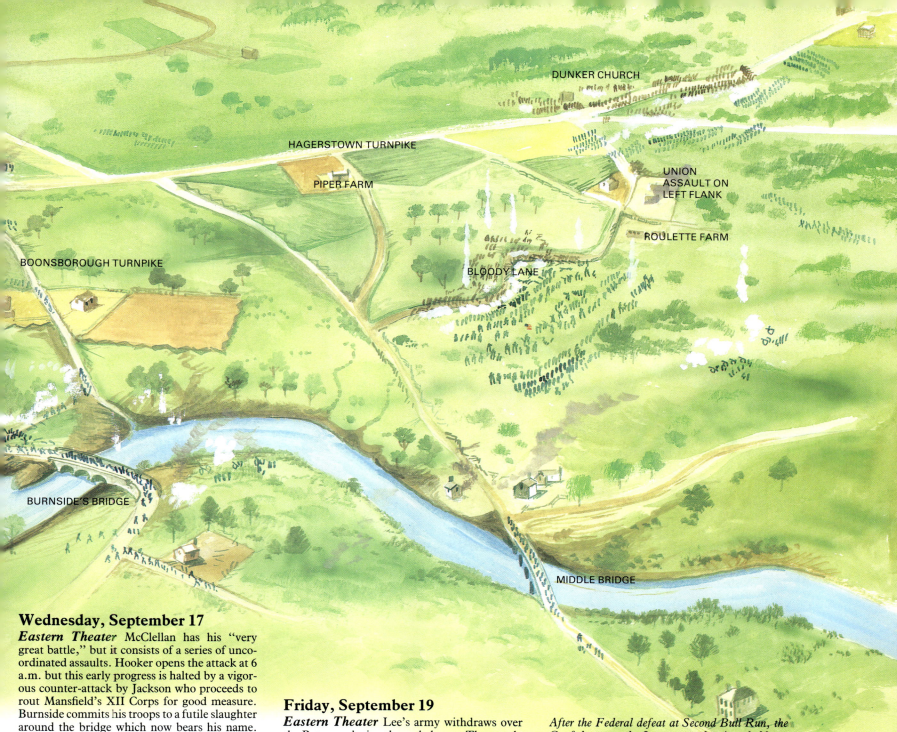

DUNKER CHURCH

HAGERSTOWN TURNPIKE

PIPER FARM

UNION
ASSAULT ON
LEFT FLANK

ROULETTE FARM

BOONSBOROUGH TURNPIKE

BLOODY LANE

BURNSIDE'S BRIDGE

MIDDLE BRIDGE

Wednesday, September 17

Eastern Theater McClellan has his "very great battle," but it consists of a series of uncoordinated assaults. Hooker opens the attack at 6 a.m. but this early progress is halted by a vigorous counter-attack by Jackson who proceeds to rout Mansfield's XII Corps for good measure. Burnside commits his troops to a futile slaughter around the bridge which now bears his name. A.P. Hill's division marches the 17 miles from Harper's Ferry to deliver a surprise attack at 4 p.m. and save Lee's right flank. All day, thousands of Federal troops remain unengaged as the commanders wait for orders which McClellan fails to issue. By nightfall the Confederate line is still held, but Lee's invasion of the North is over.

Western Theater General Bragg accepts the surrender of Mumfordsville, Kentucky.

Thursday, September 18

Eastern Theater The armies at Antietam remain in position. Two fresh Union divisions under Generals Couch and Humphreys arrive, but McClellan will not employ them until they have received "rest and refreshment." The contrast with A.P. Hill's devoted troops needs no comment. That afternoon, Lee orders the Army of Northern Virginia to withdraw. Longstreet leads the way over Blackford's Ford at midnight.

Friday, September 19

Eastern Theater Lee's army withdraws over the Potomac during the early hours. The supply trains and wounded are all evacuated without any interference from the Union Army.

Western Theater Price has command of 14,000 Confederate troops strung out around Iuka, a small village on the Memphis and Charleston railway, 30 miles east of Corinth where General Grant has his headquarters. Rosecrans' Army of the Mississippi advances to recapture Iuka but an encircling maneuver fails to trap the rebel army. Rosecrans advances 18 miles today and is assaulted straight off the line of march.

At 4.30 p.m. the leading Union division attacks Little's division at Iuka. Federal troops continue to arrive until 9000 men are in action with General Ord's 8000 men now just five miles away. Little's 3000 troops are driven back towards dusk and Price retreats during the night. Losses are light: 790 Union casualties and 535 Confederate although the latter are concentrated in Little's division.

After the Federal defeat at Second Bull Run, the Confederates under Lee turn north to invade Maryland, but this plan was foiled at Antietam Creek on September 17, 1862.

Action commenced at dawn with a Union attack on the Confederate left flank. After many actions the battle moves south where fierce fighting at Bloody Lane causes huge losses to the Confederates but the Union Army does not follow up this success.

Meanwhile, more Confederate forces under Hill arrive from Harper's Ferry and drive back the Federals, thus saving the day.

Saturday, September 20

Eastern Theater McClellan is still at Sharpsburg and has no thought of aggressive pursuit.

Western Theater Price organizes a successful withdrawal from Iuka, getting his cannon and trains away in the early hours. His infantry rear guards slowly fall back along the narrow roads and the thick forest prevents a flanking attack on his columns.

September – October 1862

Sunday, September 21, 1862

Eastern Theater Skirmishing occurs at Blackford's Ford, near Sheperdstown, Virginia as Federal troops from Fitz John Porter's V Corps cross the Potomac. The strong reconnaissance force is turned on by A.P. Hill's division, bringing up the Confederate rear. The Union troops are forced back, losing 92 killed, 131 wounded and 103 missing. Confederate casualties are estimated at 33 killed and 231 wounded.

Western Theater Braxton Bragg pushes on from Mumfordville, Kentucky towards Bardstown, with the intention of uniting with Kirby Smith. However, in so doing he allows Union General Don Carlos Buell to push through to Kentucky, a move he had previously been unable to accomplish because Bragg was sitting astride his route.

Monday, September 22

The North President Lincoln regards the battle of Antietam as being of advantage to the Union. While neither side could claim victory, at least the Federal Armies have stopped Lee's invasion of the North. The president takes this opportunity to present the draft of his emancipation declaration to the Cabinet. This firmly makes the total abolition of slavery a major aim of the Union war effort.

Western Theater Braxton Bragg reaches Bardstown, Kentucky in his attempt to merge his forces with those of Kirby Smith, leaving Louisville to Buell's Union Army.

Tuesday, September 23

Eastern Theater The beautiful fall weather looks down on almost total inactivity in Virginia and Maryland.

McClellan, believing his army to be in no fit state to fight, posts it along the banks of the Potomac, at Harper's Ferry and at the fords above and below that point. With his usual misreading of the situation he believes that Lee will still try to force a crossing, when in fact the Confederate general is pulling back with the remnants of his army, gathering stragglers on the way. His first destination is Martinsburg, but he has instructed the Confederate troops to reassemble at Winchester in the Shenandoah Valley.

Wednesday, September 24

The North President Lincoln suspends the writ of habeus corpus in certain instances, most particularly for those who interfere with volunteer enlistment or evade the militia draft.

Thursday, September 25

Eastern Theater The old bickering between McClellan and the authorities in Washington resumes. The general demands supplies, clothing, horses, and above all reinforcement. The first three are not forwarded in anything like the numbers McClellan wants, and Washington will not give up a single man from the 73,000 manning its defenses.

A blacksmith and his traveling forge at Antietam at about the time of the savage battle. Lee had invaded Maryland, and in an extremely costly action McClellan had stopped him on the Antietam Creek. Tactically it was a drawn battle, but Lee had to retire back into Virginia afterward, so it removed the threat to Northern territory.

Friday, September 26

The Confederacy The Foreign Policy Committee lays a report before the Confederate Congress recommending that the Mississippi and its tributaries should be declared free for navigation after the war, and that the northwestern states should be free to trade with the Confederacy on most favored terms.

Western Theater General Braxton Bragg issues a proclamation from his position at Bardstown making much the same offer. He also makes an appeal to the desire for peace on the part of the citizens of the northwest. "So far, it is only *our* fields that have been wasted, our people killed, our homes made desolate, our frontiers ravaged by rapine and murder." He goes on to ask the citizens of the northwest to prevail upon the general government to desist from war.

Saturday, September 27

Western Theater Alarm at the Confederate advance into Kentucky rises to panic in Louisville. General Nelson is within a day of abandoning the city, and non-combatants are being sent out of the city. Many lack confidence in the ability of General Buell to reach the city before Bragg. Buell suffers under the handicap that, like McClellan, he is not wholly trusted, having been politically affiliated with some of the leaders of the rebellion before the war.

Antietam Bridge, where Burnside threw his division across in the teeth of withering Confederate fire. Unfortunately, the enormous casualty bill was unnecessary: the river under the bridge is so shallow that the Northerners could have waded across at most points.

Sunday, September 28

Eastern Theater Lee's command is concentrating at Winchester. He has 53,000 men. McClellan at the same time is still demanding reinforcements to deal with Lee. He has 100,000 effective men in the field, not counting the 73,000 defending Washington.

Monday, September 29

Western Theater General Don Carlos Buell wins the race for Louisville, Kentucky after the way has been opened by Confederate General Bragg's move towards Bardstown a week before.

Tuesday, September 30

Trans-Mississippi In a battle at Newtonia, Missouri, a brigade of the Army of Kansas reinforced by Missouri Volunteer Cavalry lose 50 killed, 80 wounded, and 115 missing. Confederate losses are 220 killed and 280 wounded.

Wednesday, October 1, 1862

The Confederacy Lincoln's emancipation declaration is regarded by the press in Richmond as an invitation to the horrors of a slave insurrection.

Eastern Theater President Lincoln goes to Harper's Ferry to discuss the situation of the Army of the Potomac following the battle at Antietam, and to formulate future strategy with General McClellan. Meanwhile, in further skirmishing at Shepardstown, Union troops kill 60 Confederates losing only 12 wounded in the clash.

Western Theater There is a bloodless exchange of fire at Floyd's Ford, Kentucky.

Thursday, October 2

Western Theater Bragg's advance into Kentucky had left a considerable Confederate force in northern Mississippi. Split into two parts under Van Dorn and Price, they confronted Grant at Corinth. Now their strategy becomes plain: Price is to push into Tennessee to take Buell in the rear. Grant will then leave Corinth to deal with Price, and Van Dorn can move in and take the town. However, Grant's maneuvers have made it impossible for Price to co-operate with Bragg as planned, and Van Dorn does not move fast enough to take Corinth. The Confederates concentrate at Ripley and prepare to attack Corinth.

Grant has moved to Jackson to protect the railroad, and the defense of Corinth is in the hands of Major-General William S. Rosecrans.

Friday, October 3

Western Theater The Confederate attack on Corinth, under the overall command of Van Dorn, forces back the Federal troops on the Chewalla road with severe loss. Van Dorn's plan is to come upon Corinth from the northwest, where he believes the Federal defenses are weak. But for 10 days Rosecrans has been strengthening this sector, and the Union line is a tough proposition.

Saturday, October 4

Western Theater At 9.30 in the morning, Price's column makes an all-out assault on the defenses of Corinth. In a sharp but notably bitter battle, during which strongpoints are taken and retaken, the Confederates are pushed back and routed by an advance along the whole Union line. Van Dorn, whose attack was supposed to go in at the same time as Price's, is delayed. In spite of Price's repulse, the Texas and Mississippi regiments push forward into a maze of entanglements and pointblank fire from batteries of 30-pounder Parrott guns. The Confederates push on, overcoming all obstacles, until Colonel Roger's Ohio brigade rises from its place of concealment behind a ridge and pours six volleys into the Texans. Even then it takes bitter hand-to-hand fighting before Van Dorn's men are repulsed. The battle of Corinth costs the Confederates 1423 killed, 5692 wounded, and 2248 missing or captured. Federal losses are 315 dead, 1812 wounded and 232 missing.

October 3, and the president visits with General McClellan. Once again, McClellan resisted President Lincoln's urge to speedy action, but this time the president had had enough, and decided to replace him with someone who would act.

October 1862

Sunday, October 5, 1862

Eastern Theater President Lincoln orders McClellan to "cross the Potomac and give battle to the enemy, and drive him south." As usual. McClellan pays no attention to the order, instead requesting more supplies and reinforcements. He will move when he is ready, and not before.

Western Theater The rebels retreating from Corinth are pursued by Rosecrans's army. General Hurlbut, who during the previous day's fighting had been sent on a circle to take the Confederate rear, intercepts the beaten force at Metamora, on the Big Hatchie River. In a brief but fierce fight, 500 Union troops are killed and wounded, while Confederate casualties number 400, plus several hundred prisoners. The remnants of the Confederate force break off the battle and head for Holly Springs. The result of the fighting around Corinth means that Bragg's column in Kentucky, currently under pressure from General Buell, is in danger of being cut off.

Monday, October 6

Western Theater Buell's troops occupy Bardstown, Kentucky as Bragg pulls his force back towards Harrodsburg.

Tuesday, October 7

Western Theater Nashville, the Union's military center in Tennessee is cut off by Confederates a number of times in 1862. It is currently under threat from a force at La Vergne, Tennessee, which is commanded by Generals J.R. Anderson and Nathan B. Forrest, the noted cavalry leader. However, their combined column is brought to action and driven off by a Federal brigade under General John M. Palmer. For the loss of five killed, Palmer inflicts 80 casualties on the Confederates. After the battle, 175 rebels are reported missing.

Wednesday, October 8

Eastern Theater There is a minor skirmish at Fairfax, Virginia.

Western Theater General Buell catches up with General Bragg at Perryville. Gilbert's corps has been harassing the Confederate rear since the previous day. Bragg decides to give battle.

McCook's corps has been on the march since 2 a.m. and make contact with Gilbert at Perryville at about 11 a.m. Bragg mounts his attack just after noon, and the Federal left flank, manned largely by raw recruits, is quickly driven back. However, some of Rousseau's division are also on this flank and they stand fast in the face of strong Confederate pressure. The rest of the divison are on McCook's right flank, and are also pushed back. In spite of the pressure, the corps hold on to the field, and at nightfall the Confederates fall back. Although Gilbert's corps of some 20,000 men lie to the right of McCook, they play virtually no part in a desperate fight.

Perryville is a particularly bloody battle for the troops involved: Union losses are 916 killed, 2943 wounded, and 489 missing. Most of these losses are in McCook's I Corps, which had started the day some 15,000 strong. Confederate losses are estimated at over 500 killed, 2635 wounded and 251 missing out of a total strength of some 16,000.

Thursday, October 9

Eastern Theater J.E.B. Stuart takes a force of 1800 Confederate cavalrymen on a raid deep into Federal territory which will last for several days.

Western Theater General Braxton Bragg withdraws from Perryville towards Harrodsburg, where he unites with Kirby Smith. From there the Confederates move south towards Camp Dick Robinson and out of the state of Kentucky.

Friday, October 10

The Confederacy President Jefferson Davis requests that 4500 blacks be drafted to assist with the fortification of Richmond.

Eastern Theater Stuart crosses the Potomac, above the positions held by the Army of the Potomac. The Confederate raiders destroy property at Chambersburg, Pennsylvania.

Western Theater Union Cavalry commanded by Lieutenant-Colonel Boyle capture over 1000 Confederates left behind at Harrodsburg.

Saturday, October 11

The Confederacy The Confederate Congress excludes those owning 20 or more slaves from the draft. Many feel this inequitable measure makes the struggle a "rich man's war and a poor man's fight."

Eastern Theater Stuart's cavalrymen begin to circle right around the unmoving Army of the Potomac.

Trans-Mississippi A skirmish is reported at La Grange, Arkansas.

Sunday, October 12

Eastern Theater Stuart re-crosses the Potomac below the Union Army, having completed his second ride around McClellan, without losing a man.

Trans-Mississippi A Federal expedition sets off from Ozark, Missouri, in the direction of Yellville, Arkansas.

Monday, October 13

Eastern Theater The president again writes to McClellan, urging him on. ". . . You remember my speaking to you of what I called your over-cautiousness. Are you not over-cautious when you assume that you cannot do what the enemy is constantly doing? Should you not claim to be at least his equal in prowess, and act upon that claim?"

Tuesday, October 14

Western Theater Although the Confederate drive into Kentucky has been a military failure, the booty acquired in four weeks has been considerable. According to the *Richmond Examiner*, "the wagon train of supplies brought out of Kentucky by Kirby Smith is 40 miles long, containing a million yards of jeans, a large amount of clothing and boots, together with two hundred wagon loads of bacon, six thousand barrels of pork, fifteen hundred horses and mules, eight thousand cattle, and a large lot of swine."

Wednesday, October 15

Eastern Theater Troops from the Army of the Potomac mount a reconnaissance along the Potomac from Harper's Ferry towards West Virginia.

Left: *The former revenue cutter* Harriet Lane *led an eventful career. She was captured by Confederate forces at Galveston in January 1863 after a fierce fight. She then served the Confederate Army marine, and later became a blockade runner. She had been named after President Buchanan's niece, his official hostess.*

Thursday, October 16

The North Lincoln continues to press McClellan to action. As he has earlier written, "In coming to us, [the enemy] tenders to us an advantage we must not waive. We should not so operate so as merely to drive him away. As we must beat him somewhere, or fail finally, we can do it easier near to us than far away. If we do not beat the enemy where he now is, we never can, he again being within the entrenchments of Richmond."

Friday, October 17

Western Theater Confederate John Hunt Morgan with 1500 men attempts to interfere with Federal lines of communication to Nashville. He defeats detachments of Federal Cavalry defending Lexington, Kentucky. Union losses are four killed, 24 wounded, and 350 missing including 125 taken prisoner.

Saturday, October 18

Eastern Theater There is a small skirmish at Haymarket, Virginia.

A cross section of the vessels pressed into service to act as warships by both sides.

Almost anything that could float was eagerly seized and armed, especially on the Confederate side, where the shortage of newly built craft, coupled with the lack of building capacity, was a constant headache to those with responsibility for defending the South.

Manning this motley fleet also presented problems, as desertion was rife. At one time, Selma *(above), had only 15 men available to crew her. The situation was made worse as she was one of only three vessels available to defend Mobile Bay.*

US Rattler *(top), was typical of the vessels pressed into Union service. She served before Vicksburg and more than paid for her original purchase price of $24,000.*

October–November 1862

Sunday, October 19, 1862
Western Theater Confederate General Earl Van Dorn is collecting the remnants of his army, scattered after the battle of Corinth, and has taken up a position at Holly Springs, on the Cairo to New Orleans railroad. General Grant now contemplates moving on him.

Further south, General Butler continues with his controversial administration of New Orleans. He is responsible for two important acts. Raising three regiments of "free colored men," necessary because Washington cannot send him reinforcements due to the battles of Virginia and Maryland, he shows for the first time that blacks are perfectly capable of becoming soldiers, and consequently of becoming free men. More importantly, his administration establishes a legal precedent, that blacks are equal with whites in the eye of the Law.

Monday, October 20
Western Theater Skirmishes are reported at a number of places. Forrest's raiders are pushed away from Nashville, while at Bardstown, Kentucky, Southern troops seize or destroy two complete trains of Federal supply wagons.

Tuesday, October 21
The North Tennessee is currently under military government, but the president announces his support for state elections.

Wednesday, October 22
Eastern Theater Union positions on Port Royal and Hilton Head dominate the South Carolina coast, threatening the rail communications between Charlestown and Savannah. Although the siege of Charleston is on hold, there is skirmishing in the region, and this occasionally grows to serious proportions. A large Union force suffers 43 killed and 258 wounded in an action at Yenassee which costs the Confederates 116 casualties, 14 of which are fatalities.
Western Theater A Union force leaves Fort Donelson in a reconnaissance towards Waverly, Tennessee. In Kentucky, Confederate cavalry seizes Loudon.
Trans-Mississippi Confederate troops are forced out of the area around Maysville, Arkansas.

Thursday, October 23
Western Theater The reconnaissance of Waverly by the 83rd Illinois Regiment encounters rebels, and in the action which follows the Northern soldiers sustain only three casualties while inflicting 40.

Friday, October 24
Western Theater The military authorities in Washington relieve General Buell of command in Kentucky and Tennessee. He is to be replaced by General Rosecrans, whose success at Corinth is fresh in the mind. Meanwhile, skirmishes are reported at Brownsville, Tennessee, and at Morgantown, Kentucky.
Trans-Mississippi Two battalions of Missouri Militia cavalry set out from Independence, Missouri, on a three-day expedition. There is a skirmish at Grand Prairie.

Saturday, October 25
Eastern Theater President Lincoln is still eager to get the Army of the Potomac moving, and he is increasingly annoyed with General McClellan. McClellan does not appear to have told the president that in one day's time he will be moving the army back into Virginia.

Sunday, October 26
Eastern Theater After several weeks of inactivity following Antietam, the Army of the Potomac is on the move once again. McClellan begins pushing Federal troops across the Potomac.

Monday, October 27
Western Theater General Butler has undertaken few military operations around New Orleans, having barely enough men to garrison what he holds. However, a four-day expedition to occupy Bayou Lafourche, west of the Mississippi, is punctuated by one short action at Labadieville. The Federals under Godfrey Weitzel rout Confederate opposition, taking over 200 prisoners.

Tuesday, October 28
Eastern Theater Robert E. Lee edges his army southward up the valley of the Shenandoah to avoid being encircled by McClellan's Army of the Potomac, which is moving on Warrenton, Virginia.
Trans-Mississippi Some 6000 men of Schofield's "Army of the Frontier," organized to fight guerrillas in Missouri, are operating in Arkansas. One cavalry column of 1000 men under General Herron encounters a rebel encampment at Fayetteville Hollows. In spite of being outnumbered three to one the federal troops drive the Confederates before them for four miles.

Wednesday, October 29
Eastern Theater The Army of the Potomac continues to cross the Potomac. McClellan has more than 130,000 men at his disposal, compared with the Confederate Army of 70,000 in the Shenandoah Valley. Lee orders Jackson's corps and Stuart's cavalry to remain in place to observe the Federal movement, and to take any chances of making spoiling attacks. For two days the armies march parallel with each other only a few miles apart, but with the Blue Ridge Mountains in between.

Thursday, October 30
Western Theater General Rosecrans replaces General Buell as commander of the Federal Department of the Cumberland, with responsibility for Tennessee east of the Tennessee River and those parts of Alabama and northern Georgia under Federal control. In a further reorganization of the western armies, Grant's troops now constitute the XIII Army Corps while those under Rosecrans become the XIVth.

Friday, October 31
Western Theater General Grant gathers troops at Grand Junction, Tennessee, preparatory to a move against Vicksburg, the last major Confederate stronghold on the Mississippi

Saturday, November 1, 1862
Eastern Theater Pleasanton's Union Cavalry begin several days of skirmishing in Virginia with an action at Philomont.

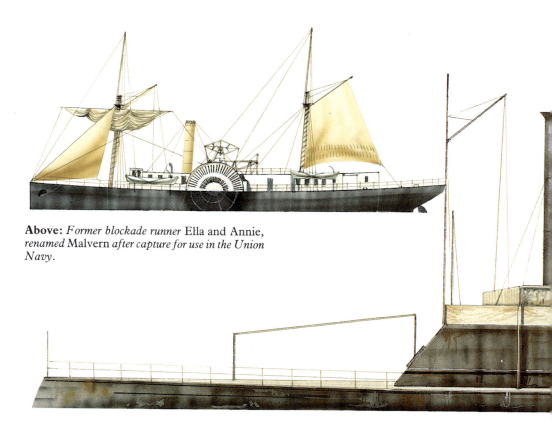

Above: *Former blockade runner* Ella and Annie, *renamed* Malvern *after capture for use in the Union Navy.*

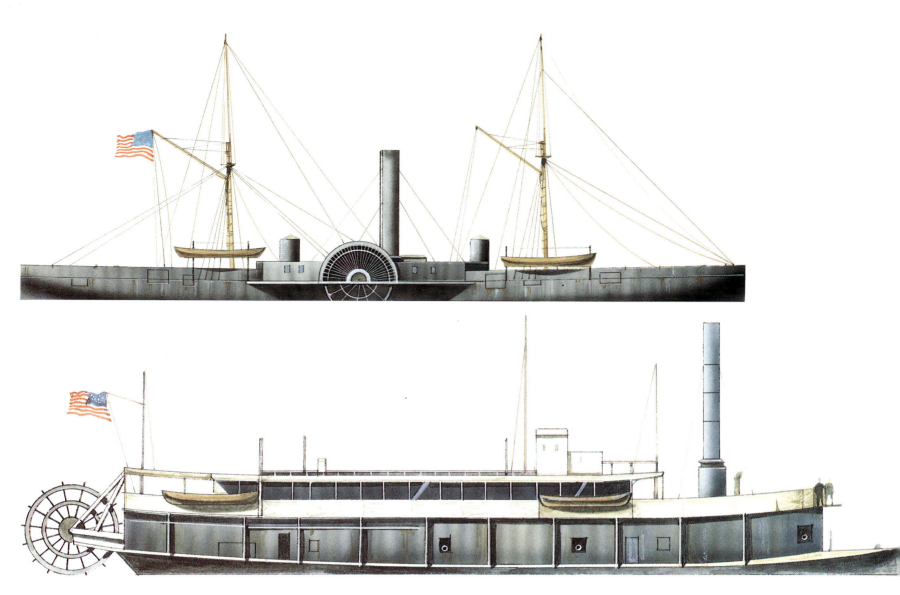

An assortment of Union vessels.
Top: *The purpose-built, double-ended gunboat US* Iosco, *was one of many highly maneuverable gunboats that could easily turn round in the narrow rivers of the Confederacy.*

Above: *Typical sternwheel steamer, this time US* Mamora, *demonstrates the lengths the Union went to in order to build up its navy.*

Below: *Ugly yet impressive profile of the armed ram USS* Vindicator. *Like so many Union vessels hastily purchased at the start of the war, she was eventually sold in 1865 for a mere fraction of her original cost.*

November 1862

Sunday, November 2, 1862

Eastern Theater The series of actions fought by Pleasanton's Union Cavalry continues at Bloomfield, in Loudon County, Virginia.

Western Theater General Grant sets his campaign against Vicksburg in motion. Advancing from Bolivar and Jackson, he follows the line of the Cairo and New Orleans railroad, toward Van Dorn and the remnants of his Confederate Army at Holly Springs. In spite of being considerably reinforced by new levies, Grant is hampered by his long lines of communication. In order to protect it, he must detach a significant number of troops to garrison Columbus, Humboldt, Trenton, Jackson, Bolivar, Corinth and Grand Junction. He is also short of cavalry.

Monday, November 3

Eastern Theater Pleasanton's cavalry continues to skirmish in Loudon County, Virginia. In the last two days he has lost two troopers, with 10 wounded. Confederate losses are three dead and 15 wounded.

Tuesday, November 4

The North The lack of decisive Federal victories in the war is reflected in the results of the Congressional and state elections. The opposition receives a majority in the popular vote, while the Republican majority of 41 seats in the election of 1860 is turned into an opposition majority of 10.

Wednesday, November 5

The North Washington has finally grown tired of McClellan's slow, cautious approach to fighting, and the decision is made to replace him as commander of the Army of the Potomac.

Eastern Theater Pleasanton's cavalry is now skirmishing at Barbee's Cross Roads and in Chester's Gap, Virginia. In today's fighting the Union loses five troopers killed and 10 wounded. Confederate casualties include over 30 dead.

Western Theater Union troops defending Nashville take 23 Confederate prisoners in a skirmish which costs the North a similar number of wounded.

Thursday, November 6

Western Theater In a skirmish at Gerrettsburg, Kentucky, the 8th Kentucky Cavalry inflict over 100 casualties on the Confederates, including 17 dead.

Ambrose Powell Hill was a Confederate commander who fought with distinction in many of the battles of the Eastern Theater. At Fredericksburg he commanded a division of Stonewall Jackson's corps, which had been operating in the Shenandoah Valley but was reunited with the rest of Lee's army in time to defend against Burnside's attack.

Friday, November 7

Eastern Theater McClellan has concentrated the Army of the Potomac at Warrenton, Virginia, barely 10 miles from Lee who is at Culpeper. The Union general has been seeking a way to split the Confederate force, and now he discovered that Lee, by detaching Jackson's corps and Stuart's cavalry, has done it for him. For once, he seems sure that he has the advantage, and he prepares orders for his army to move vigorously on Lee. If his plan is carried out, then the chances are the Confederacy can be dealt a crippling blow in the field. However, even as he is finalizing his plans, a messenger arrives with two brief messages. The first states:

"By direction of the President of the United States, it is ordered that Major General McClellan be relieved from the command of the Army of the Potomac, and that Major General Burnside take command of the army. By order of the Secretary of War."

The second is from General Halleck, who dislikes McClellan intensely:

"General; on the receipt of the order of the President, sent herewith, you will immediately turn over your command to Major General Burnside, and repair to Trenton, New Jersey, reporting on your arrival in that place, by telegraph, for further orders."

Trans-Mississippi In an action at Big Beaver Creek, Missouri, no less than 300 Union soldiers are captured. Further south, there is a skirmish at Marianna, Arkansas.

Saturday, November 8

The North Further changes in the high command of the Union include the recall of General Butler from New Orleans, where he is replaced by General Nathaniel Banks. The reasons for this action are not clear: Butler is received with all due ceremony, but rumours persist that the general has been recalled because he has used his position in Louisiana for personal gain.

Western Theater There is a skirmish at Hudsonville, Mississippi, during which Union cavalry men capture nearly 200 Confederates.

Sunday, November 9

Eastern Theater General Ambrose E. Burnside officially takes command of the Army of the Potomac at Warrenton. A Union reconnaissance patrol, consisting of 54 cavalrymen, enter Fredericksburg and take 34 Confederate prisoners.

Monday, November 10

Eastern Theater McClellan takes leave of the army which he has in large part created. He is well-liked by the troops and many are saddened by his departure.

Tuesday, November 11

Eastern Theater McClellan's plans to bring Lee to decisive battle within days are changed by the new commander. Burnside, who is not convinced that he is competent to do the job, is certain that the way to proceed is to take Richmond. Plans to bring Lee to battle are changed, as Burnside intends to move on Richmond by land via Fredericksburg. Thus Burnside, with a two-to-one superiority in men, throws away the best chance of a decisive victory for the Union.

Wednesday, November 12

Western Theater Although Braxton Bragg's invasion of Kentucky has been a failure, Rosecrans, the new commander of the Department of the Cumberland faces a number of problems. Provisions are short, for two armies have campaigned over the region for most of the summer. He must therefore establish long lines of com-

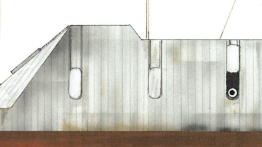

munication, and as he cannot use the Cumberland River because it is too low, he must use the railroad. Railroads use bridges, and bridges are vulnerable to lightning raids by gifted Confederate cavalry commanders such as Forrest and Morgan. The Confederates could use Rosecrans' difficulties to their advantage, but fortunately for the Union they lack the commander to carry out operations. Bragg is superb at planning a campaign but lacks executive ability.

Thursday, November 13

Western Theater Skirmishing occurs at Nashville. Bragg, looking to join with another Confederate force under Breckenridge, pushes his command towards Murfreesboro. In Mississippi, Grant's force takes Holly Springs after Van Dorn evacuates.

Friday, November 14

Eastern Theater Burnside reorganizes the Army of the Potomac before setting off for Fredericksburg. He divides the army into three Grand Divisions. Sumner's Grand Division, the "Right," comprises Couch's II Corps and Wilcox's IX Corps, formerly Burnside's command. Hooker's Grand Division, the "Center," has Stoneman's III Corps and Butterfield's V Corps. This had been Fitz John Porter's command until he was removed. Franklin's Grand Division, the "Left," takes in Reynold's I Corps (Hooker's old corps) and W F. Smith's VI Corps, which had previously been commanded by Franklin. Burnside also has XI Corps near Manassas Junction and XII Corps guarding Harper's Ferry.

Saturday, November 15

Eastern Theater Burnside begins moving the Army of the Potomac from Warrenton, directly away from Lee's positions, on the start of his drive toward Fredericksburg.

Right: When the war started, it was considered unsoldierly to dig in and fight a defensive battle, but bitter experience taught the lesson that field fortifications were essential. Artillery redoubts like this could be put together in days, the Confederates being particularly adept at such activity.

McClellan's plan to engage the main Confederate Army as it retired from Antietam did not get under way until six weeks after the battle, when the Army of the Potomac crossed the river after which it had been named. Concentrating at Warrenton, Virginia (the main street of which is seen here), McClellan was about to go in pursuit of Lee when he was replaced by General Burnside.

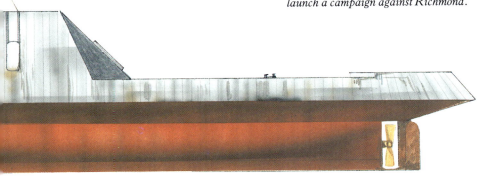

Confederate ironclad Atlanta *was converted from the blockade runner* Fingal. *She fell victim to two Union monitors at dawn on June 17, 1863, after a short fight.*

Scouts like these from the Army of the Potomac had located Lee's army when Burnside took command, but he decided instead to change the direction of the attack and take Fredericksburg to the south. He planned to use the town as a base from which to launch a campaign against Richmond.

November 1862

Sunday, November 16, 1862

Eastern Theater Burnside's strategy for the Army of the Potomac has a number of objectives. By making his advance upon Richmond from Fredericksburg, he can cover Washington from Confederate attack. At the same time, Fredericksburg is near the Potomac, and supplies can be brought in via Acquia Creek. There is then a 75-mile overland approach to the Confederate capital, rather than the 150 miles from Warrenton through Culpeper and Gordonsville.

Monday, November 17

Eastern Theater The advance units of the Federal Army, part of Sumner's Grand Division, reach Falmouth, on the north bank of the Rappahannock River opposite Fredericksburg. The plan is that they should cross at once and seize the heights above Fredericksburg. But the river is not suitable for crossing large numbers of men, and the pontoon bridges necessary have not yet arrived. Sumner comes under fire from a Confederate battery, but this is silenced with ease, indicating that the town is till only lightly held. The general considers sending a detachment across one of the few usable fords, but Burnside's orders are explicit that he should do nothing until the army's communications are established. The defenses will not remain weak for long, however, since Lee is sending two divisions with artillery and cavalry to bolster the defenses of Fredericksburg.

The view across the Rappahannock toward Fredericksburg. Burnside's attack on the town was delayed, mainly because the river was not passable by large formations, and the bridging units which should have been there took a long time to arrive. The delay was enough to allow the Confederates to get back from the Shenandoah Valley and to take up extremely strong defensive positions on the heights around the town.

Naval Operations The Confederate steamer *Alabama*, now fully equipped for action, sails into Martinique after crossing the Atlantic. It is closely followed by the USS *San Jacinto*, which stands off outside the harbor waiting for the Southern vessel to leave.

Tuesday, November 18

Eastern Theater A reconnaissance by Jeb Stuart's Confederate Cavalry confirms that the Federal Army has left Warrenton, and Lee immediately sends Longstreet's command toward Fredericksburg.

Western Theater Sixteen Confederate soldiers are killed by Kentucky cavalry at Rural Hills, Tennessee.

Naval Operations *Alabama* leaves Martinique, giving the *San Jacinto* the slip.

Wednesday, November 19

Eastern Theater Lee orders Jackson to leave the Shenandoah Valley and bring his command to rejoin the main army. Lee has a number of options: he can move back down the valley, re-invade Maryland, and threaten Pennsylvania; he can make a demonstration against Washington, and so force Burnside to pull back from Fredericksburg; he can fall back at once toward Richmond; he can throw his army across Burnside's route and force an engagement; or he can do nothing and await events. The last is by far the least likely, but it is what Burnside seems to suppose that Lee will do.

Thursday, November 20

Eastern Theater Lee arrives at Fredericksburg.

Friday, November 21

Eastern Theater Burnside requests that the mayor of Fredericksburg surrender the town. Instead, he sends non-combatants to safety while Lee's army entrenches.

Saturday, November 22

Eastern Theater Sumner sends a message to the mayor of Fredericksburg that he will not fire on the town if there is a promise of "no hostile demonstrations" on the part of the townspeople.

Sunday, November 23

Eastern Theater Although the Federal Army has been on the banks of the Rappahannock for a week, only now does any means of bridging the river begin to arrive—too late to allow an easy occupation of the city.

Monday, November 24

Trans-Mississippi There is a skirmish at Beaver Creek, Missouri.

Tuesday, November 25

Western Theater General Grant, having secured his long lines of communications, is almost ready to restart his operations against Vicksburg.

Wednesday, November 26

Western Theater In a skirmish at Summerville, Mississippi, 28 Confederate soldiers are captured by Union cavalrymen.

Thursday, November 27

Eastern Theater President Lincoln visits the Army of the Potomac, where he confers with General Burnside. The president is unable to persuade his commander to change the plan of attack, which will commit the Union Army to an assault across a river against a fully prepared enemy.

Friday, November 28

Western Theater General Ulysses S. Grant moves out from his position at Lagrange. General Earl Van Dorn withdraws his Confederate force from Holly Springs in the face of Hamilton's advancing division. At the same time as Grant's advance, a column from Arkansas is crossing the Tallahatchie River. Under the com-

mand of General Hovey, it is intended to work in conjunction with Grant by striking at Van Dorn's flank.

Saturday, November 29

Eastern Theater The Confederate Army of Northern Virginia is at this time adopting a formal corps structure. Longstreet commands I Corps, with the divisions of Anderson, Pickett, Ransom, Wood, and M'Laws, totalling 21 brigades. Jackson's II Corps includes the divisions of A.P. Hill, Ewell, and Taliaferro, to which will be added D.H. Hill's division when the rest of the force arrives from the valley. Stuart's cavalry is largely independent, but will operate with Jackson's corps for much of the Fredericksburg campaign. Both Jackson and Longstreet are promoted to lieutenant-general. While this is occurring, the Federal Army of the Potomac waits on the north bank of the Rappahannock for means to cross the stream, and for a supply base to be built up at the mouth of Acquia Creek.

Western Theater The advance guard of Hamilton's division enters Holly Springs to find it deserted of Confederate troops. Van Dorn has retreated to a position on the Tallahatchie River. However, Hovey's column of 7000 men is on his flank, and aggressive Union Cavalry patrols and the destruction of the railroad forces the Confederate commander to retreat toward Oxford.

Trans-Mississippi There is a battle at Cane Hill, Arkansas, between three Federal brigades under General James G. Blunt and a larger force of Confederate soldiers commanded by General James Marmaduke. The outnumbered Union force drives the rebels back and pursues them into the Boston Mountains. Federal losses in killed, wounded, and missing total less than 40 men, while Confederate losses are more than ten times higher.

Ambrose E. Burnside was a commander of the Rhode Island Militia. When President Lincoln appointed him commander of the army, he accepted reluctantly, knowing he was not really up to the job. When he took command, he dropped McClellan's plan of finding and beating Lee's army and instead evolved a plan to advance on Richmond.

Union Cavalry troopers ride along the banks of the Rappahannock River during the advance on Fredericksburg. The plan was to take the town quickly, then use it as a base from which to supply the advance over 70 or so miles to Richmond.

November–December 1862

Sunday, November 30, 1862

Eastern Theater Stonewall Jackson arrives at Fredericksburg with his corps, bringing Confederate strength in the town up to approximately 80,000 men.

Naval Operations USS *Vanderbilt* attempts to bring the Confederate raider *Alabama* to action, but is unsuccessful. Currently cruising the Atlantic coast, the Southern steamer poses a considerable threat to Northern shipping.

Monday, December 1, 1862

The North The third session of the 37th Congress of the United States gets under way in Washington. The president's State of the Union message covers a number of topics, including the state of the war and economic conditions. President Lincoln also repeats many of the points made in the Emancipation Declaration, announcing the abolition of slavery in all the insurrectionary states, and pledging that all the military power of the United States shall be used in the attainment of that goal.

Eastern Theater There is a skirmish at Charleston and Berryville, Virginia. It involves Federal troops from Slocum's XII Corps, left behind to cover Harper's Ferry when the rest of the Army of the Potomac was moved south to Fredericksburg.

Tuesday, December 2

Eastern Theater Burnside's plan, proposed to the president the week before, depends for its success on assaulting Fredericksburg quickly without giving Lee the chance to dig in. However, the Northern Army makes no move, and Burnside's hesitation will prove costly.

Wednesday, December 3

Western Theater Hovey's column from Arkansas continues its operations on the flanks of Van Dorn's retreating Confederate force. Federal troops seize Grenada, Mississippi, but not before the Southern garrison destroys a number of locomotives and wagons to prevent their being used by the North. Elsewhere, there is action along the Hardin Pike near Nashville, where Federal soldiers are attacked.

Thursday, December 4

Eastern Theater Winchester, all but deserted by the Confederates, is taken by Union troops operating in the Shenandoah Valley. At Fredericksburg there is small-scale skirmishing between patrols from the armies facing each other on either side of the Rappahannock.

Friday, December 5

Eastern Theater Union and Confederate cavalrymen fight a minor action at Coffeeville, Mississippi. Union casualties total 64, including 10 dead. Confederate losses are slightly less.

Trans-Mississippi In Arkansas Confederate units scattered through the state are being concentrated into a single force under General T.C. Hindman. Following Union General James G. Blunt's defeat of Marmaduke's Confederates at Cane Hill a week before, Hindman is advancing north with some 15,000 men in an attempt to cut the Union column's lines of communication. However, Blunt has sent for General Francis J. Herron's column, the two divisions of which are 100 miles away at Wilson's Creek. Herron is now on the march, covering 30 miles per day.

Saturday, December 6

The North President Lincoln orders that the ringleaders of the Santee Sioux uprising in Minnesota be hanged.

Trans-Mississippi Hindman's Confederates have slipped past Blunt at Cane Hill and now lie between him and Herron's approaching column. Hindman is stronger than each of the Federal columns and plans to engage them separately before they can combine.

Sunday, December 7

Western Theater While Confederate fortunes in the rest of the theater remain at a low ebb, Confederate Cavalry raiders are still harassing Union lines of communication. At Hartville, Tennessee, John Hunt Morgan takes 1800 Federal prisoners in a battle which costs him 21 killed and 114 wounded.

Trans-Mississippi Herron's column has reached Fayetteville by dawn and, marching on toward Blunt at Cane Hill, collides head-on with Hindman's Confederate Army at a village called Prairie Grove. He has only 4000 men, having previously detached his 3000 cavalrymen to join Blunt. The Confederates are positioned on a ridge by a creek, and at 10 o'clock Herron attacks, trusting that Blunt is within sound of the gunfire and will come to join the battle. Although outnumbered, the Federal assault is assisted by highly effective artillery. Blunt is, in fact, five miles away, and sets out immediately on hearing the cannon. He reaches the battlefield by 2 o'clock in the afternoon, and immediately falls on the Confederate left. The battle lasts until nightfall, when Blunt's and Herron's commands bivouac on the battlefield, ready to resume the next day.

Monday, December 8

Trans-Mississippi During the night the Confederates have slipped away from Prairie Grove and retreated toward the Boston Mountains. Union losses in the previous day's battle are 167 killed, 798 wounded, and 183 missing. Confederate losses are estimated at 300 killed, over 800 wounded, and 250 missing.

Tuesday, December 9

Western Theater There is a skirmish at Dobbin's Ferry, Tennessee.

Wednesday, December 10

The North The House of Representatives passes the bill to create the state of West Virginia five months after its passage through the Senate.

Thursday, December 11

Eastern Theater The Army of the Potomac moves across the Rappahannock River and begins to occupy Fredericksburg. Lee maintains his army in its strongly fortified positions on the wooded heights around the town, where he resolves to await the Federal attack.

Western Theater Brigadier-General Nathan Bedford Forrest, with 2500 Confederate cavalrymen, moves out from Columbia, Tennessee, at the start of an operation against General Grant's long lines of communication.

Friday, December 12

Eastern Theater A Federal expedition to Goldsboro, North Carolina, commanded by John G. Foster, gets under way.

Trans-Mississippi A skirmish is reported at Little Bear Creek, Alabama.

Saturday, December 13

Eastern Theater Burnside launches the attack against the Confederate positions around Fredericksburg. Franklin's Grand Division attacks Jackson's corps to the south of the city, while Sumner attacks to the north against Longstreet's corps. Franklin, by a misunderstanding of Burnside's orders, does not make an all-out assault but mounts what might be called a reconnaissance in force. Meade's division makes the first assault, outpacing Gibbon's division, which is supposed to be in support. Federal troops manage to penetrate a gap in Jackson's line, but Early's division is thrown in to fill the gap and the Federal troops are repulsed. By the time Burnside orders Franklin to launch a full-scale assault, the Grand Division commander considers it too late to make any change in his dispositions.

The battle of the north is very different. In repeated assaults, brigade after brigade from French's division and Hancock's division charge the guns and massed musketry of Longstreet's corps dug in on the wooded slopes of Marye's Heights. The slaughter is terrible. The final assault of the short December day is made by troops from Hooker's Grand Division, but they are no more successful in the face of the terrible Confederate small-arms fire. By the end of the day, the Army of the Potomac has lost 1200 killed, over 9000 wounded, and 2145 missing. Confederate losses are 570 killed, 3870 wounded, and 127 missing. Many of the Federal casualties have occurred at the sunken road and stone wall at the base of Marye's Heights, upon which so many brave assaults had been smashed. Lee, looking at so many Federal bodies on the small area of open ground before the heights, remarks, "It is well that war is so terrible; we should grow too fond of it."

After the battle of Antietam Creek, McClellan remained north of the Potomac until late October, when he began a move south.

Lincoln then replaced McClellan with Burnside, who planned to threaten Richmond by moving via Fredericksburg on the Rappahannock River where he arrived in mid-November.

Lee had now established himself around Fredericksburg and awaited the Federal assault. This came in the cold, gray morning of December 13, 1862, when heavy fighting broke out on the Confederate right, but the Federals were unable to break the Confederate hold.

Later the Federals launched an attack upon the Confederate center at Marye's Heights, where the Southern troops occupied a formidable defensive position. The Federals launched continuous attacks, which caused heavy losses among the Northern troops as they met an almost unceasing rain of small-arms fire, backed up by carefully placed artillery.

Burnside ordered the attacks to continue in spite of heavy losses. At dusk the final assault got under way, but the open ground between them and the Confederate position gave no protection and they fell in their hundreds. The losses eventually reached 12,500 killed and wounded.

As the battle raged on, reports came in to the Confederate H.Q. of a shortage of ammunition for the Confederate artillery, but the action ended before this became an embarrassment to the Confederates.

The night after the action brought terrible suffering to the wounded left upon the field of battle, and many died as a result of the cold. Their frozen bodies were used as shelters by the living. The scene below depicts the closing stages of the battle.

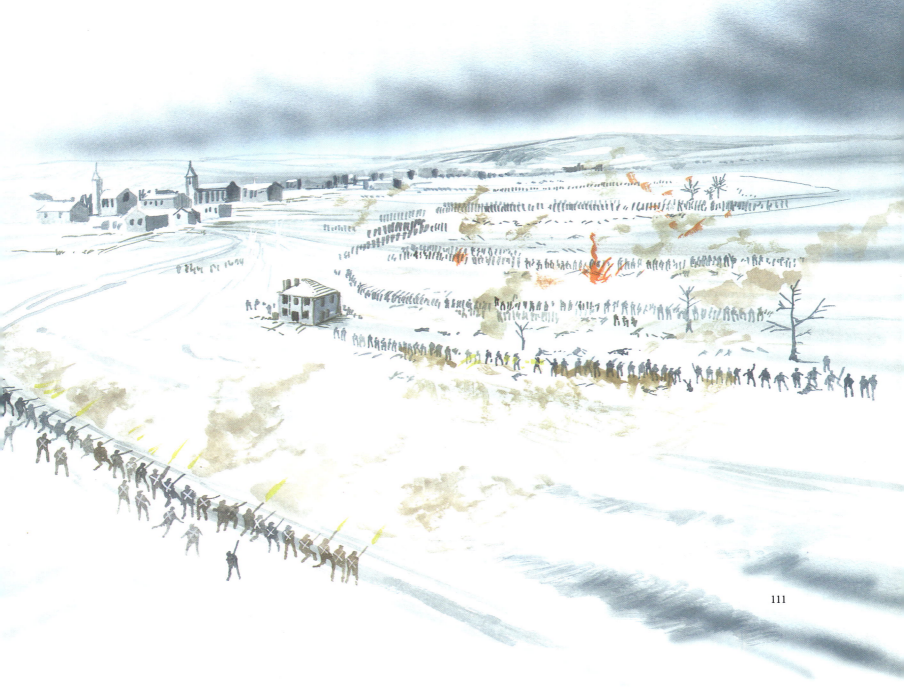

December 1862

Sunday, December 14, 1862

Eastern Theater The Confederates at Fredericksburg stand ready to receive another assault, but to their surprise it does not come. Burnside indeed wishes his army to attack again, and he is willing to lead it in person, but Sumner, Hooker, and Franklin persuade him to retire beyond the Rappahannock. There the Union Army will sit, facing a numerically inferior opponent but with the morale of the troops sinking like a stone.

In North Carolina Foster's expedition of some 10,000 men encounters a Confederate force at Kingston. In a sharp action the Southerners are forced back, leaving 50 killed, 75 wounded, and over 400 missing. Union casualties total 40 dead and 120 wounded. Foster then presses on toward his ultimate goal, the important rail junction at Goldsboro.

Monday, December 15

Eastern Theater Burnside's Army of the Potomac continues to retire north across the Rappahannock.

Western Theater Forrest's Confederate raiders strike at Grant's lines of communication as the Federal Army advances toward Vicksburg.

General Nathaniel Banks arrives in New Orleans to take command of the Department of the Gulf.

Tuesday, December 16

Eastern Theater Foster's North Carolina expedition reaches Whitehall, where in another brisk skirmish a Confederate force is pushed back, and two gunboats under construction are destroyed.

Western Theater General Banks officially takes command of the Department of the Gulf, relieving General Butler. After his controversial administration, few of the inhabitants will miss Butler.

Wednesday, December 17

Eastern Theater In North Carolina the Union expedition engages a third Confederate force near Goldsboro. Foster is aware that the Confederates are concentrating a superior force nearby and decides it would be unwise to proceed any further. He begins a rapid retreat back to New Berne.

Western Theater General Grant's reputation is sullied by his General Order Number 11, which expels Jews from his department because they are "a class violating every regulation of trade established by the Treasury Department."

Thursday, December 18

Western Theater Forrest's raiders skirmish with Federal Cavalry at Lexington, Tennessee. Confederate losses total seven killed and 28 wounded. Northern losses are seven killed, 10 wounded, and over 100 missing.

Friday, December 19

The North A row at the highest levels in the administration has caused problems, with disagreements between Treasury Secretary Chase and Secretary of State Seward leading to the latter tendering his resignation two days previously. The president refuses to accept the resignation and calls a meeting of the Cabinet to discuss and, if possible, defuse the situation.

Western Theater Skirmishes are reported at Spring Creek and at Jackson, in Tennessee.

Saturday, December 20

The North The Cabinet crisis worsens, with Secretary of the Treasury Salmon P. Chase also tendering his resignation, which is again refused by the president.

Western Theater Van Dorn takes advantage of Grant's extended lines by launching an attack on his supply base at Holly Springs, Mississippi. Some 22 Confederate Cavalry regiments sweep into the town, seizing over $1 million worth of supplies and burning several thousand bales of cotton. Six companies of the 2nd Illinois Cavalry manage to cut their way out of the trap, but the rest of the Federal troops in the town are overwhelmed. The Confederates take over 1000 prisoners. With other stations along the railroad line being attacked, Grant has to postpone his part in the attack on Vicksburg to secure his rear. However, General Sherman has been ordered to move on Vicksburg from Memphis,

and this part of the operation goes ahead.

At the same time as Holly Springs is falling, a Confederate attack on Trenton, Tennessee, nets a further 250 prisoners.

Sunday, December 21

Western Theater To add to the confusion in the Western Theater, Confederate Brigadier-General John Hunt Morgan launches yet another cavalry raid on the Union supply lines in central Tennessee.

In an action at Davis Mills, Mississippi, Federal Cavalry kill 22 Confederates and wound or capture a further 70 of the enemy.

Monday, December 22

Western Theater Rosecrans, in command of the Department of the Cumberland, has moved his army to Nashville where to all intents and purposes he is settling down to winter quarters. In fact, he is clothing and equipping his army for a strike on General Braxton Bragg at Murfreesboro. Bragg has 60,000 men under his command, compared to Rosecrans' 40,000. Fortunately, while Bragg has a preponderance of cavalry, he has sent Forrest and Morgan, his ablest commanders, on independent operations. Bragg is also of the opinion that Rosecrans will not attack, so makes few preparations to meet him.

Tuesday, December 23

The Confederacy The bitterness caused by General Benjamin Butler's period in New Orleans causes President Jefferson Davis to declare him an outlaw and enemy of mankind, who will be hanged if captured.

Wednesday, December 24

Eastern Theater Foster's expedition arrives back at New Berne. In 10 days it has marched over 200 miles and lost 90 men dead and 478 wounded. Confederate losses are 71 killed, 268 wounded, and 476 captured. Most of these last were taken at Kingston, and almost immediately paroled. The expedition has accomplished very little.

Western Theater Skirmishes are reported at Middleberg, Mississippi, and at Glasgow, Tennessee.

Thursday, December 25

Western Theater Christmas Day is celebrated with gunfire and bloodshed at a number of locations. Glasgow, Tennessee, is captured by Confederates, and there are skirmishes at Green's Chapel, Kentucky, and at Brentwood and along the Edmondson Pike in Tennessee.

Friday, December 26

Western Theater In Tennessee Rosecrans sets out from Nashville to attack Bragg at Murfreesboro.

General William T. Sherman, advancing on Vicksburg, reaches the Yazoo River.

Trans-Mississippi The ringleaders of the Santee Sioux uprising in Minnesota are hanged at Mankato in that state.

Saturday, December 27

Eastern Theater There is a skirmish at Dumfries, Virginia, in which three Union soldiers are killed. Confederate losses are 26 killed and some 40 wounded.

Western Theater The Vicksburg and Shreveport railroad is destroyed in an attempt to cut Confederate supply lines into Vicksburg. Federal gunboats shell Confederate batteries at Haine's Bluff.

Morgan's raiders capture Elizabethtown, Kentucky, taking more than 500 Federal prisoners.

An action at Elk Fork, Tennessee, sees Federal Cavalry from Kentucky roughly handle a Confederate force, killing 30 and wounding 176 rebels.

Sunday, December 28

Western Theater Sherman continues his march on Vicksburg. He has crossed the Yazoo, having driven the Confederate pickets back, but is confronted by a force fully the size of his own, fighting from well-nigh impregnable defenses at the base of a high bluff. Sherman resolves to attack, but unfortunately the approach is blocked by the Chickasaw Bayou, which has only two favorable crossing places, both of which are covered by Confederate fire.

Trans-Mississippi General James Blunt commands the Union force involved in a skirmish at Van Buren, Arkansas, where 100 Confederate prisoners and a considerable amount of supplies are captured.

Monday, December 29

Western Theater Sherman makes repeated attacks on the Confederate positions at Chickasaw Bayou, but without success. Sherman accepts the blame for the repulse. It is interesting to note that Grant, after the eventual capture of Vicksburg, will look over the ground and comment that "General Sherman's arrangement . . . in the attack on Chickasaw Bluffs was admirable. Seeing the ground from the opposite side afterwards, I saw the impossibility of making it successful." Federal losses in the battle are 191 killed, 982 wounded, and 756 missing. Southern losses total 63 killed, 134 injured, and 10 missing.

Tuesday, December 30

Western Theater Sherman resolves to make one more attempt on Chickasaw Bayou and the bluffs, this time working in cooperation with the mortar boats of Rear Admiral Porter.

Raids and skirmishes continue in the region, with Morgan's raiders pulling out of New Haven, Kentucky, and Union raiders under General Samuel Carter attacking Union, Tennessee. Also in Tennessee, Rosecrans is approaching Murfreesboro.

Wednesday, December 31

The North President Lincoln meets General Burnside to discuss the defeat at Fredericksburg.

Western Theater Bragg's and Rosecrans' armies meet at Stone's River, Murfreesboro. Both generals plan on attacking the other on the left, but Bragg gets his troops in first, just after dawn. McCook's corps, on the right of the Union line, is heavily pressed and soon being driven backward. On the defensive, the Federal forces regroup in a strong position to the rear, on to which a number of Confederate assaults are dashed. As the night draws in, the armies pause to wait for the New Year and the battles which will surely follow the next day.

Naval Operations The revolutionary ironclad *Monitor* sinks in a storm off Cape Hatteras.

During the Yazoo River Expedition in December 1862, which came about in an attempt to approach Vicksburg from the rear, Benton comes under heavy fire in the narrow river as she leads the Union warships. Her commanding officer, Lieutenant Commander Gwin, is mortally wounded but refuses to enter the pilot house and continues to direct the ship in the open.

There were numerous Union expeditions up the Yazoo in an attempt to isolate Vicksburg, but all were very costly and not entirely successful.

113

January 1863

Thursday, January 1, 1863

The North In a move which changes the whole character of the war, and which puts the North firmly in possession of the moral "high ground," President Lincoln signs the emancipation declaration. Included in the declaration are the statements, ". . . . I do order and declare that all persons held as slaves in the said and designated states and parts of states are and henceforward shall be free; and that the executive government of the United States, including the military and naval authorities thereof, will recognize and maintain the freedom of said persons. And I hereby enjoin upon the people so declared to be free to abstain from all violence, unless in necessary self defense; and I recommend to them that, in all cases when allowed, they labor faithfully for reasonable wages. And I further declare and make known that such persons, of suitable condition, will be received into the armed services of the United States to garrison forts, positions, stations and other places, and to man vessels of all sorts in said service."

Eastern Theater Although General Burnside feels that he did not receive adequate support from his subordinates, he accepts responsibility for the Federal reverse at Fredericksburg, and offers to resign. The president persuades him to reconsider.

Western Theater The battle near Murfreesboro, Tennessee, continues. Bragg and Rosecrans spend the day repositioning troops, attempting to gain advantage for the resumption of fighting expected on the morrow. Elsewhere in the theater, General William T. Sherman starts to pull his troops back after the fruitless assault on Vicksburg, Mississippi.

Trans-Mississippi Galveston, taken by Union gunboats in October, is attacked by a Confederate force under "Prince John" Magruder. An attack by land and sea sees four Federal gunboats taken or destroyed, while the three companies of Union infantry in the town are taken. Total Federal losses are 600 wounded and captured.

Friday, January 2

Western Theater Bragg renews the battle at Stone's River, near Murfreesboro. Confederate artillery directs a heavy cannonade on the Federal center, but in return a crossing of the river by Van Cleve's division threatens one flank of the Confederate line. Van Cleve is pushed back by a Confederate assault, but at the same time an attack on the other flank of the Union line is pushed back, forcing a general Confederate retreat. Losses in the battles of the last few days are reported as 1533 killed, 7245 wounded and 2800 missing on the Union side, and a total Confederate casualty bill of 14,560 killed, wounded and missing.

Saturday, January 3

Western Theater In spite of having a slight tactical advantage at Murfreesboro, General Braxton Bragg decides to break off the action and retreats to very strong positions on the Duck River. Even if Rosecrans wishes to follow, however, heavy rain makes the going virtually impossible. In any case, he has no cavalry, troops on both sides are exhausted, and the Federal artillery horses are completely unable to move the vital cannon in the mud.

Sunday, January 4

Trans-Mississippi An expedition is launched up the Mississippi against Fort Hindman, Arkansas (also known as Arkansas Post). It is commanded by General McClernand, who has been using his political connections in Washington to divert troops gathered for Grant's attack on Vicksburg to his own ends.

Naval Operations USS *Quaker City*, patrolling off the South Carolina coast, captures a Confederate vessel attempting to run the Federal blockade into Charleston.

Monday, January 5

Western Theater With the retreat of Bragg's army from Murfreesboro, the whole of the west and center of Tennessee are virtually under Federal control. Although a provisional state government has been set up, it is in no way a permanent fixture while the Confederate raiders Forrest and Morgan are active in the state. It will be a year at least before the military governor can call for state elections.

In spite of being a pre-war critic of Abraham Lincoln, Edwin Stanton was an honest and capable man who, although a Democrat, served for most of Lincoln's presidency as secretary of war. He did much to remove fraud and patronage from military contracting, and even though personally friendly with McClellan, he supported the general's dismissal when it became necessary.

Horace Greeley, editor of the New York Tribune, *was an extraordinary man who espoused the abolitionist cause with all his considerable energy. He thought President Lincoln was too soft on the South, even after the Emancipation Proclamation of January 1.*

General William S. Rosecrans commanded the Army of the Cumberland and over the New Year period forced the Confederate Army of Braxton Bragg into a series of battles at Stone River near Murfreesboro. An able strategist, he was slow and methodical but lacked dash, and he was to come badly unstuck at Chickamauga later in the year.

Tuesday, January 6

Trans-Mississippi McClernand's expedition up the Arkansas River is made up from two corps, McClernand's own and that of Sherman (now withdrawn from the futile assault on Vicksburg).

Wednesday, January 7

The Confederacy Confederate secretary of the navy Stephen Mallory writes to Commander James Bullock, now established at Liverpool UK as the main warship purchasing agent in Europe, to urge him to speedily push forward with plans to build much needed warships for the South. Mallory suggests ironclads of about 2000 tons and drawing only 14 feet of water to enable them to operate in the shallow inshore coastal areas of the Confederacy as well as up the rivers where the Union would be hard pushed to match such powerful vessels. Bullock is able to contract for such vessels in the UK and France, but out of the four ordered only one will see service in the Confederate Navy and that will not be until near the war's end. Bullock would suffer at the hands of the ever-diligent Union spies, who seem to know his every move, making it difficult to get things done without fear of the host government putting a stop to his activities. Money is a serious problem as funds are now exhausted and Mallory tells his subordinate that he with be receiving cotton certificates sooner or later.

Lack of funds would dog the Confederate cause in its dealings with European supplies.

Trans-Mississippi A large Confederate force commanded by General Marmaduke moves on Springfield, Missouri, but the defenses of the town have been thoroughly prepared by Brigadier General Browne. A scratch force of defenders, made up from Missouri Militia, convalescent soldiers and citizens of the town man the lines, but the Southern attack makes no headway.

Thursday, January 8

The North Caleb B. Smith is replaced as US secretary of the interior by John P. Usher.

Trans-Mississippi The Confederate attack on Springfield is finally beaten off. Union losses are 14 killed and 144 wounded (including General Browne) while Confederate casualties total 40 dead and over 200 wounded and missing. The Confederates move on looking for an easier target, and capture Ozark, Missouri.

Friday, January 9

Western Theater There is a skirmish at Ripley, Tennessee in which 46 Confederates are captured. Elsewhere, Confederate General Joseph Wheeler leads a six-day raid into Federal-controlled territory, attacking Mill Creek, Harpeth Shoals, and Ashland.

Saturday, January 10

Overseas While the British government has postponed any thoughts about offering to mediate between North and South following the battle of Antietam, the French Foreign Minister is today discussing with the French Ambassador to Washington the possibility of French involvement in such a move.

Eastern Theater There are skirmishes at Suffolk, Virginia and at Fairfax Court House. In the former, General Pryor's Confederates are defeated by a Federal force under General Corcoran.

The unknown soldier was typical of many thousands of young men called to the colors of both sides. They would be faced with hardship, and much worse, as the long, bitter war dragged on. Eventually over 620,000 would die before it ended, bleeding both sides of valuable manpower and leaving families grieving for those who would not return.

The Charleston Light Artillery, seen early in 1863, was typical of the Confederate artillery of the period. Although starting the war with many of the professionals of the pre-war army, Southern gunners were never as plentifully supplied with weapons as those of the industrial North, and by the middle of the war the artillery advantage was beginning to swing toward the Union.

January 1863

Sunday, January 11, 1863

Western Theater A Federal riverboat is sunk near Memphis.

Trans-Mississippi McClernand's expedition attacks Fort Hindman on the Arkansas River. The fort, also known as Arkansas Post, is on the north bank of the river on the first high ground overlooking the river, moving up from the Mississippi. Well fortified, it is defended by 5000 men under General T.J. Churchill, who has been instructed to "hold on till help arrived, or until all are dead." The night before, Federal gunboats had landed troops three miles downstream, and then moved on to bombard the fort. At midday the expedition is ready to attack and the gunboats again commence their bombardment. By mid-afternoon the Confederate guns have been silenced and several Federal brigades are pressing the enemy lines. When the last enemy gun falls silent, McClernand orders a general assault and the fort quickly surrenders. Union losses in the battle are 129 killed and 831 wounded, while Confederate casualties total 100 killed, 400 wounded, and the remainder of the 5000 strong garrison taken captive.

Naval Operations The Confederate raider *Alabama* approaches Galveston, Texas at night with a view to attack the large Union transport fleet assembled there. Instead the Confederates discover a strong blockading force who send out one of their number, ex-ferry boat *Hatteras*, to examine the suspicious vessel. Semmes turns and lures the unsuspecting Union gunboat away from support before turning on the vessel. In a brief 17-minute action fought at point blank range the *Hatteras* sinks.

Alabama pauses long enough to rescue the crew before speeding off into the night. As Semmes can not cater for the 114 prisoners from the crew of the *Hatteras* he makes for Jamaica to set them ashore on neutral land.

Monday, January 12

The Confederacy The Third Session of the First Congress of the Confederate States meets in Richmond, where they hear an opening address by President Jefferson Davis.

Tuesday, January 13

Trans-Mississippi Fort Hindman, the object of General McClernand's expedition, is of little use to the Union, so General Burbridge, who has been assigned to command the Federal force occupying the position is ordered to dismantle and blow up the defenses.

A joint army–navy expedition from Memphis destroys buildings at Mound City, Arkansas as a reprisal for the numerous Confederate attacks on Union river steamers. Anyone caught harboring Confederate guerrillas is immediately made prisoner.

Wednesday, January 14

Western Theater Union troops from New Orleans and under the command of General Godfrey Weitzel attempt to advance up the Bayou Teche into Louisiana. They are supported by the gunboats *Calhoun*, *Diana*, *Estrella*, and *Kinsman*, but are unable to make much progress in the face of determined Confederate opposition, aided by the gunboat *Cotton*. However, in the action the Confederate vessel is burned. Union losses are reported at 10 killed (including Flag Officer Buchanan, in command of the gunboats) and 27 wounded. Confederate losses are estimated at 15 dead.

Thursday, January 15

Western Theater Jefferson Davis writes to close personal friend General Braxton Bragg suggesting that the Confederates in Tennessee should go on the defensive, by developing a strong fortified position and awaiting, if not inviting, a Federal attack.

The North Lincoln makes another trip to Washington Navy Yard to confer with Captain John A. Dahlgren. They observe various tests on new weapons being developed. Lincoln is greatly impressed by the inventive Captain Dahlgren and will later in the year promote him to command the powerful Union fleet assembled before Charleston.

Friday, January 16

Naval Operations The Confederate commerce raider *Florida* eludes the Federal blockade and slips out of Mobile Bay. Over the next year and a half the raider will take some 15 Northern vessels as prizes, mostly in the waters of the West Indies.

Saturday, January 17

Eastern Theater The Army of the Potomac is in a low state of readiness, with numbers and efficiency considerably reduced in only three months. General McClellan had handed to General Burnside command of an army strong in numbers, discipline and spirit. It is not all Burnside's fault however. The emancipation declaration is not popular in the army; many regular officers being far from hostile to slavery and large numbers of recruits from the northern industrial cities "looking with bitter aversion upon the Negro."

Sunday, January 18

Western Theater Grant's Army of Tennessee has been organized into four corps, the XIIIth, XVth, XVIth, and XVIIth under the commands of McClernand, Sherman, Hurlbut, and McPherson respectively.

Grant meets with McClernand and Sherman, along with Commodore Porter near the mouth of the White River, as the Arkansas expedition returns to the Mississippi. Traveling onward with them to Helena, he consults them with regard to further operations against Vicksburg.

Porter points out that the next stage in the siege will be of a more tedious nature although he expresses satisfaction at the way the earlier attacks had been carried out. The clearing of eight miles of Yazoo River of torpedoes has not been easy especially as the crews of the Union vessels had been continuously fired upon from the river banks by unseen riflemen.

Monday, January 19

Eastern Theater General Burnside continues in his belief that the way to defeat the Confederacy is to attack Richmond using Fredericksburg as a base. He makes preparations to move the Army of the Potomac back across the Rappahannock in another attempt to take control of the area.

Tuesday, January 20

Eastern Theater Burnside's plans depend upon being able to move the Army of the Potomac in a wide-sweeping movement, but the snow which had kept the ground hard underfoot has been replaced by heavy rain which will turn every road to a mud track.

A constant source of anxiety to the Army Command is the possibility of disease breaking out among the troops who are often forced to exist in dreadful conditions. The daily exposure combined with crowded and badly ventilated barracks, cause much sickness, with the easy spread of epidemics. Most camps have hospitals but these frequently prove inadequate and the medical service is likely to be poor. Local doctors are often called in to help back up the military staff. Even in the New York camps an eastern army surgeon discovers a great deal of sickness is caused by bad food and poor whiskey, to which the men resort.

The United States Sanitary Commission, organised by civilians, does much to correct the insanitary conditions of the camps but the government fails to cooperate and even hinders those who struggle with this immense problem of health care. Of the 359,528 deaths in the Union Army, nearly a quarter million of them are from other reasons than enemy action. Five men die of disease for every two that die on the battlefield.

One army officer later wrote "I have ridden through a regimental camp whose utterly filthy condition seemed enough to send malaria through a whole military department, and have been asked by a colonel, with tears in his eyes, to explain to him why his men are dying at the rate of one a day."

Many men on the march resort to foraging to obtain food but often a frightful revenge is metered out to offenders. One was found hanged with a placard around his neck, which warned others against foraging. On another occasion 21 soldiers were reported found in a ravine with their throats cut in punishment for foraging.

Fresh water is essential for health, and several wells are required to supply the needs of an army of 100,000 men and their horses. Water pollution is common place. Around Vicksburg the Confederates pollute the local streams with dead horses. Whilst serving along the muddy banks of the Mississippi a choice has to be made between thirst and risking sickness from drinking contaminated water. The soldiers who know nothing of the causes of disease soon suffer fever, become unable to walk and die. Those that are transferred to healthier surroundings do not always fully recover.

Wednesday, January 21

The North General Fitz John Porter is dismissed from military service, having been blamed by Pope for the Union failure at Second Bull Run. Believing with some justification that he has been made a scapegoat, Porter will spend the next 23 years in an ultimately successful attempt to clear his name.

Eastern Theater Thirty hours of continuous rain make any Federal crossing of the Rappahannock a risky affair and even if the army can get across, the mud will make any meaningful operations almost impossible.

Naval Operations The ceaseless, but not always dramatic, operations of the various blockading squadrons maintain a constant pressure on the South to be on the defensive. Even the rivers are closely watched as the Confederates attempt to smuggle goods from shore to shore.

Thursday, January 22

Eastern Theater Burnside gives up the struggle to get his army across the Rappahannock, and after three days of the "Mud campaign," pulls his troops back to the camps they have held since the battle of Fredericksburg.

Western Theater General Grant has the Federal forces in Arkansas added to his command.

Friday, January 23

Eastern Theater General Burnside, frustrated in a job for which he is not suited and feeling that his subordinates have not been giving him the support he needs, decides to purge the Army of the Potomac. He prepares orders relieving a number of generals, some of whom he intends to dismiss entirely from the United States Army. Among those named are Grand Division commanders Joseph E. Hooker and William B. Franklin, corps commander William F. Smith, and divisional commanders Brooks, Newton, Cochrane, Sturgis and Ferrero.

Saturday, January 24

Eastern Theater Burnside goes to Washington to confront the President with his list of dismissals. He claims that ". . . This is the only way in which I can retain the command of the Army of the Potomac; otherwise here is my resignation; accept it, and here is the end of the matter as far as I am concerned."

Western Theater In action at Woodbury, Tennessee soldiers from the Second Division of Crittenden's corps lose two men killed and one wounded in a skirmish in which they inflict 135 casualties on the Confederates, including 35 killed.

Trans-Mississippi A Union Army starts to land on the neck of the land opposite Vicksburg. Porter, with his large fleet of gunboats, protects the fleet and sends patrols up the Yazoo River. He is rightly convinced that only the army laying siege from the landside could force Vicksburg to surrender.

One successful outcome of the Union activity up the Yazoo is the isolation of 11 Confederate transports loading up supplies for Port Hudson.

Union forces under McClernand arrive at Milliken's Bend in early January 1863, and within a few days the 32,000-strong army launches a fierce attack against the 5000 garrison of Fort Hindman. The action lasts for two days before the Confederates surrender, having caused just over 1000 casualties to the Union side.

This setback, yet another in the continuing train of disasters to the Confederate cause, does little to boost their morale. The serious weakening of the Southern forces enables the Union to redeploy their forces where additional strength would be needed.

January–February 1863

Sunday, January 25, 1863

Eastern Theater President Lincoln removes General Burnside from command of the Army of the Potomac, replacing him with General Hooker. No one is more relieved than Burnside himself, who announces to the president, "If Hooker can gain a victory, neither you nor he will be a happier man than I shall be." Burnside still wishes to resign from the army, but the president refuses to accept the resignation, giving him instead leave of absence. This is probably because Burnside had not wanted the command in the first place, so any failings could not be said to lie with him, and in any case he remained a capable commander who could profitably be employed elsewhere in a less onerous position.

Monday, January 26

Eastern Theater General Joseph E. Hooker officially takes command of the Army of the Potomac. An assertive, self-confident man, Hooker is in marked contrast to the self-doubting Burnside. Known as "Fighting Joe," although he himself dislikes the name, the general takes over a dispirited army of reduced fighting power.

Tuesday, January 27

The North The editor of the Philadelphia *Journal* is arrested on a charge of publishing anti-Union material.

The Confederacy President Jefferson Davis urges increased production of basic foodstuffs and of cash crops like cotton, recognizing that shortages will add to the South's difficulties in fighting the war.

Wednesday, January 28

Eastern Theater Desertions in the Army of the Potomac are running at over 200 per day, and it is estimated that as many as 85,000 Union soldiers are absent from their posts. General Hooker has a number of additional problems, foremost of which is the distrust of much of the army. Many of the senior officers are McClellan partisans, and do not forget that Hooker accused their favorite commander of incompetence during the Peninsular campaign.

Thursday, January 29

Eastern Theater Skirmishes are reported in Virginia at Suffolk, and at Turner's Mills, although no casualties are recorded. There is an exchange of fire on the Stono River of South Carolina between Confederate batteries and the Federal gunboat *Isaac Smith*, which is run aground and captured.

Western Theater The Confederates, knowing that Vicksburg will soon be the subject of an all-out assault by General Grant's army, look for ways of interfering with the Union advance. President Davis asks in a letter to General Pemberton whether it is possible to do something to obstruct the Yazoo River.

Friday, January 30

Eastern Theater In Virginia there is a skirmish at Deserted House, also known as Kelly's Store, near Suffolk. Troops from General Peck's command suffer 24 killed and 80 wounded while Southern casualties are tallied at 50 wounded.

Trans-Mississippi Meantime Grant informs Porter of his plans to cut a canal through Lake Providence, Louisiana, so that troops can be easily moved to the rear of Vicksburg. The Union command had been informed that the lake connects with the Black and Red rivers and these waters were wide and navigable. Porter immediately orders the gunboat US *Linden* to escort the troop-carrying transport. The expedition along this twisting route comes upon endless difficulties in trying to force its way through the winding rivers. Porter is not aware that there would be miles of forests jutting up out of the water to work through. Troops are frequently landed to cut down the obstructions but the swift current running down the shallow waters forces the vessels against the trees causing damage that can not be readily repaired. One by one the transports withdraw and the expedition is abandoned.

Saturday, January 31

Western Theater In an action at Dover, Tennessee, the 4th Ohio Cavalry defeats a Confederate force, taking some 300 prisoners while suffering only five casualties, none of which are fatal.

Naval Operations In a fight off Charleston, two iron-clad Confederate gunboats get the better of two Union blockading vessels. The Confederates claim Charleston harbor is open, but it will take a very powerful or lucky ship to get through the Northern blockade.

"Fighting Joe" Hooker was another in the series of President Lincoln's attempts to find a winning commander. He succeeded Burnside after Fredericksburg, and although partially successful in the task, personal animosity between himself and General Halleck led to Hooker's resignation just before Gettysburg.

Fighting is never easy, but adding the vagaries of climate to the exhausting work of building defenses makes it even harder: in summer the heat and humidity; in winter the rain and mud. Fighting in close woodland like this made it even more difficult, even though a battle would tear away the foliage leaving nothing but stumps of trees to scar the landscape.

Eastern Theater Correspondence between the army and naval commanders stress the need to keep open the Cumberland River between its mouth and Nashville so that the army supply vessels can still get through. The huge amount of supplies these shallow draft vessels could shift is vast and there is no way such amounts could be moved by road, especially in the impossible winter conditions.

Sunday, February 1, 1863

The Confederacy Inflation has reduced the value of the Southern dollar to one fifth its pre-war value.

Eastern Theater The Federal forces continue to use their foothold on the coast of the Carolinas for mounting raids inland. An expedition sets off from New Berne in the direction of Plymouth.

Western Theater Union forces take Franklin, Tennessee.

Trans-Mississippi Confederate agents start to remove large amounts of cotton away from plantations along the river to safer places inland. Cotton that can not be moved is simply burnt to avoid it falling into Union hands. Porter quickly organizes a force to seize as much cotton as possible as it is a major source of income to the Confederate Government. Porter reckons that if he can seize even eight thousand bales it will finance his large squadron for one year.

Monday, February 2

Eastern Theater Skirmishes occur at Rappahannock Station as Hooker sends reconnaissance patrols out to update the information he has on opposing strengths.

Western Theater General Ulysses S. Grant continues to bend all his efforts to the taking of Vicksburg. The Federal ram *Queen of the West* runs past the city, suffering some damage from Confederate batteries. Meanwhile Grant cuts the levee, or embankment, of the Yazoo River as a start in opening a passage via the Yazoo around the back of Vicksburg, avoiding Confederate guns.

Tuesday, February 3

The North Secretary of State Seward confers with the French Minister to Washington regarding French proposals for mediation in the war, but is unlikely to agree to anything the French may say.

Western Theater Fort Donelson is attacked by Confederates under the command of Generals Wheeler and Forest. Unlike the battle of the previous year, the attacking force has no gunboat support, so the Union garrison is able to hold out. Colonel Harding reports the garrison's losses at 16 killed, 60 wounded and 50 missing. Confederate losses in the unsuccessful attack are 140 killed, 400 wounded and 130 captured or missing.

At Vicksburg, the *Queen of the West* seizes three Confederate vessels.

Trans-Mississippi Skirmishes are reported at Mingo Swamp, Missouri.

Wednesday, February 4

Western Theater Louisiana Confederates sustain 30 casualties while routing a Federal force at Lake Providence, Louisiana.

Thursday, February 5

Eastern Theater General Hooker's reorganization of the Army of the Potomac gets under way. Skirmishes are reported at Rappahannock Bridge and at Grove Church.

A Federal expedition to Wyoming County gets under way in West Virginia.

Overseas The British policy on mediation is in marked contrast to the French, with the government stating any such action will have little probability of success.

Friday, February 6

The North Secretary of State Seward officially announces the Federal Government's rejection of French offers of mediation in the war.

Eastern Theater General Samuel P. Heintzelman is given command of the newly organized Department of Washington, charged with defending the national capital.

Saturday, February 7

Eastern Theater Confederates successfully ambush a Union Cavalry force at Williamsburg, Virginia.

Naval Operations Just over a month after retaking the city, and in spite of Union bombardment, the Confederates announce that the Texas port of Galveston is open. On the Atlantic coast, three blockade runners slip through the patrolling US Navy vessels into Charleston, South Carolina.

Charleston, like other major seaports in the South, is vital as a place from which blockade runners can operate, but even their activity can not cope with the needs of the Confederacy; the general tightening of the blockade forces the Southern economy into decline. As the blockade runners insist on payment in gold for the goods brought in, the Confederacy's slim gold reserve is quickly drained, so cotton has to be taken in exchange for goods.

Although over one million bales of cotton are run out through the blockade to Europe between 1862 and 1864, it is a mere one-tenth of pre-war exports. The situation is made worse when cotton production is reduced in favor of food, thus decreasing the South's main income even further. Ordinary necessities of life become scarce and prices rise to horrendous levels, with tea fetching $500 per pound.

When the Civil War was in its early stages and the blockade at its weakest, no effort was made to bring in railroad equipment and other materials from Europe as no one thought the war would last long. Consequently, the Southern railroad system fell into rapid disrepair once the crippling demands of the war effort were made on it. By the end of the war, when General Lee's army was starving in Virginia, food intended for that force was rotting in Carolina and Georgia depots for want of an effective railroad system.

General Henry W. Halleck became general-in-chief of the Union armies on the strength of his performance in the Western Theater, although most of the work had been done by able subordinates like Grant. An intelligent, even intellectual soldier, he offended everybody with his bluntness, yet seemed unable to come up with any coherent, overall strategy.

James Longstreet was known as Lee's "Old War Horse." His corps inflicted the major part of the Union casualties at Fredericksburg, and he fought solidly from Bull Run to Appomattox. His cautious nature was a failing, as he often obeyed orders in his own time, rather than at once. Indeed, some authorities claim that it was his slowness which lost the battle of Gettysburg.

February 1863

Sunday, February 8, 1863

Eastern Theater General Hooker's reorganization of the Army of the Potomac begins to take effect. He breaks up Burnside's Grand Divisions, re-establishing the former corps structure. Each corps is placed under the command of an officer in whom the General has confidence.

Monday, February 9

Eastern Theater General Hooker takes steps to improve the intelligence position of the Army of the Potomac. Outpost duty had been neglected, and it was said that the Confederates knew what was happening within the Union lines as well as the Union commanders did. On taking command, Hooker had found not one record or document at his headquarters that gave any information with regard to the enemy. General Butterfield, one of his corps commanders, will write "There was no means, no organization, and no apparent effort to obtain such information. We were almost as ignorant of the enemy in our immediate front as if they had been in China. An efficient organization for that purpose was instituted, by which we were soon enabled to get correct and proper information of the enemy, their strength and movements."

Naval Operations Du Pont experiences delays in obtaining supplies for his fleet. This also applies to the other Union commands who likewise run short of machine oil, clothes, and dried fruit. Coal is not always such a serious problem since it could often be obtained locally. Freshwater supplies for the smaller vessels, on station for weeks at a time, are always a source of concern as they lack facilities for producing their own water.

Tuesday, February 10

Eastern Theater Hooker continues to reconnoiter the Rappahannock line in his attempt to gain more accurate information regarding Confederate dispositions. There is a skirmish at Chantilly, Virginia.

Western Theater There are minor actions at Camp Sheldon, Mississippi, and at Old River, Louisiana.

Trans-Mississippi The *Queen of the West* sets off on another expedition up the tributaries of the Mississippi. Heading down the river, she makes for the mouth of the Red River.

Wednesday, February 11

Eastern Theater The reorganization of the Army of the Potomac continues. The problem of desertion is taken into hand, with disloyal officers being weeded from command, and furloughs being much more tightly controlled. The living conditions of the army itself also receive attention. Comfortable winter huts are built, and the regular issue of fresh bread and fresh vegetables is instituted. Results are rapid; desertions almost cease, absentees return to their regiments, and the proportion of the army unfit through illness drops from 10 percent to under 5 percent.

Naval Operations Porter is the next major commander to voice his opinions on the supply situation. His large fleet needs a constant supply of coal, so he asks for 160,000 bushels to be sent to the Yazoo River, plus a monthly supply of 70,000 bushels. Some 40,000 are needed at White River plus 20,000 at Memphis. Keeping up with these demands is a nightmare as never before have such large forces existed and been concentrated in one area.

Thursday, February 12

Western Theater A skirmish at Bolivar, Tennessee sees a small Federal force beaten by the Confederates.

Trans-Mississippi The *Queen of the West* accompanied by the *De Soto* passes up the Red River, after looking into the mouth of the Atchafalaya River and destroying several Confederate ammunition-loaded wagon trains on the river bank. In an unconnected action on the White River of Arkansas, the USS *Conestoga* captures two Southern vessels.

Naval Operations In the West Indies, the Confederate raider *Florida* captures and destroys the tea clipper *Jacob Bell*, with its cargo valued at more than $2 million.

Friday, February 13

Eastern Theater General Hooker makes a change to the Army of the Potomac which will be of supreme importance later in the war. Union Cavalry had been scattered amongst the Grand Divisions, but in the reorganization of the army it is collected into a separate cavalry corps. This will eventually grow into a powerful arm which will at last be able to take on the swashbuckling Confederate cavalrymen like Jeb Stuart. However, the one thing lacking is a commander fit to wield the weapon, and it will be some time before the new Northern Cavalry organization begins to match its potential.

Western Theater As night falls, the new Federal ironclad *Indianola* sets off from the mouth of the Yazoo down the Mississippi. She drifts past the Confederate batteries of Vicksburg without detection, although close enough to hear the voices of Southern sentries.

Saturday, February 14

Eastern Theater A Federal Cavalry force is defeated in a skirmish at Brentsville, Virginia.

Trans-Mississippi The *Queen of the West* captures the Confederate vessel *New Era Number 5*, together with 14 Texan soldiers, $28,000 Confederate dollars, and 4500 bushels of corn. Twenty miles further up the river, the *Queen* runs aground directly under the Confederate guns at Fort Taylor, and is abandoned by its crew. Many drift downstream to the steamer *De Soto*, which itself is almost unmanageable. The crews transfer to the captured *New Era* and retire back to the Mississippi, chased by the Confederate ram *Webb*.

Naval Operations Efforts steadily increase to maintain the tight blockade of the Confederacy but still blockade runners manage to slip in and out of numerous harbors and inlets. The seamanship and nerve of some of the blockade-running captains is of a high order. Off Fort Fisher, Wilmington it is common practice to track along the beach well within the inner line of Union blockaders and so slip in unseen as the outline of the runner is lost in the night against the darkness of the coastline.

Sunday, February 15

Western Theater Minor actions with Federal troops successfully holding off Confederate raiders are reported at Nolansville and at Cainsville, Tennessee. In the latter action the unsuccessful Confederates are commanded by General John

Hunt Morgan. On the Mississippi, the captured steamer *New Era Number 5* moves up a foggy river chased by the rebel ram *Webb*. When they meet the powerful Federal ironclad *Indianola* coming downriver, the Confederate vessel immediately turns about and runs.

Monday, February 16

The North The Senate approves the Conscription Act, which is designed to fill out the Union armies since voluntary enlistment is not providing adequate manpower for the armies of the Union.

Eastern Theater A force made up from detachments of the 116th and 122nd Ohio regiments is involved in a skirmish near Romney, West Virginia. Some 72 Northern soldiers are wounded or captured.

Western Theater Yazoo Pass, where the meandering of the Yazoo River and the Mississippi bring the rivers close together, is the scene of skirmishing. A canal joining the Mississippi with a tributary of the Yazoo would allow Grant to move Federal forces down the Yazoo to positions on Haine's Bluff, overlooking Vicksburg. The Confederate attacks aim to interfere with this plan.

US ironclad Winnebago *was one of a group of shallow-draft, screw-driven warships of the monitor type. They were ordered for use in shallow rivers to work alongside the more conventional paddle-driven type. In service they proved successful.*

Tuesday, February 17

Western Theater Federal troops leave Lexington, Tennessee on an expedition to take them towards Clifton. The Federal ironclad *Indianola* takes station on the Mississippi downriver from Vicksburg, with the aim of interdicting Southern vessels moving upstream to supply the town.

Wednesday, February 18

Eastern Theater The Confederate Army of Northern Virginia moves several divisions from the positions overlooking Fredericksburg which they have held since November. The divisions are positioned closer to Richmond, the Confederate capital.

Thursday, February 19

The North Federal soldiers convalescing in Keokuk, Iowa, ransack a local newspaper office for publishing anti-Union articles.

The Confederacy Jefferson Davis writes to General Joseph E. Johnston regarding the Confederate armies of the west. Although Braxton Bragg's generalship is causing unrest amongst his officers, the Confederate President is reluctant to relieve his close friend of command.

Friday, February 20

Western Theater Yazoo Pass, Mississippi is the target for another Confederate attack, but it is repelled by the Federal troops in that location.

Saturday, February 21

Western Theater There is a skirmish at Prairie Station, Mississippi.

As the war progresses and in spite of strenuous efforts on the part of the appropriate departments, the supply of suitable equipment to the South presents a serious problem. The Confederacy, with its almost non-existent manufacturing base, relies for its armies' material needs on the success of the blockade runners bringing their precious cargoes of uniforms, shoes, medicine and artillery. Not so with the North. Here the industrial might of the Union continues to provide every conceivable item to sustain a modern war.

However, the desire for profit soon prevails and many purchasing agents fall victim to the temptation to line their own pockets, as well as those of the suppliers. Prices are boosted out of proportion as the Federal Government proves a ready customer with a seemingly endless supply of money.

By the end of 1861 the Federal Government has spent nearly $50 million on subsistence, with a similar amount being spent on supplies by quartermasters' departments. The subsistence cost for the entire war amounts to nearly $370 million with $678 million being spent by quartermasters' departments. All in all, nearly three-quarters of a billion dollars are spent by departments. Add to this the cost of transportation and $163 million spent by the Ordnance Bureau, means that army contractors handled more than a billion dollars of government money. It will be estimated that profiteers secured half of that total.

Profiteering on a vast scale exists, and when compared to the total population and overall wealth of the Union, it represents a huge proportion of the wealth available to the North. Even worse, this graft robs the soldiers, who suffer deprivation and unnecessary casualties caused by contractors supplying poor food, clothing and general supplies. Often, because the food is inedible, the hungry soldiers spend their limited pay with the sutler. Soldiers' clothing does not stand up to the hard wear and needs frequent replacing at their own expense. Uniforms and army blankets of inferior quality are claimed to be made from horsehair and broom corn. Harper's Weekly points out that during the Crimean War the English Army hanged a few contractors who supplied the troops with poor meat. The paper hints that McClellan should copy the English!

The opportunities for swindling are plentiful. Colt revolvers normally selling at $15, are purchased by the army for $25 and Colt record in one year excess profits of £325,000. Remington offer a similar weapon for $15, but they would receive a contract for only 5000 guns. Numerous corrupt politicians make it clear which way they want many contracts to go.

February–March 1863

Sunday, February 22, 1863
Eastern Theater After nearly a month as commander of the Army of the Potomac, General Hooker sees his reforms take effect. Better food and efficient sanitation sharply reduces the level of scurvy and diarrhea in the army's winter quarters.
Western Theater There are minor actions at Tuscumbia, Alabama, and on the Manchester Pike, Tennessee.

Monday, February 23
The North Former secretary of war Simon Cameron resigns as minister to Russia.
Eastern Theater Confederate Cavalry raids continue to penetrate the 100-mile outpost line now policed by the reorganized Union Cavalry. Under General Stoneman's command, the Federal Cavalry regiments have an impossible task as their enemies know every track through the dense, second-growth timber. Local women and children contribute to the Confederate intelligence operation, providing details of Union patrols, and guiding small parties of rebel horsemen over the Rappahannock. Lying up in isolated farms deep in the woods, the Confederate Cavalry pounce on Union vedettes and escape back to their own lines with prisoners and booty.

Tuesday, February 24
Western Theater The Confederate ram *Webb*, with two cotton-clad steamers and the recently captured *Queen of the West*, intercept the Union ironclad *Indianola* near Warrenton. *Indianola* had passed the Confederate batteries at Vicksburg and Warrenton at night, steaming south to assist the crew of *Queen of the West* who were manning prizes taken before their vessel grounded. *Webb* overhauls the *Indianola* at night and the Union vessel is disabled by seven ramming attacks. Her crew run her ashore and abandon her.

Union troops on the Yazoo River expedition continue their advance, planning to get to the rear of Vicksburg via the Yazoo, Coldwater, and Tallahatchie rivers.

Wednesday, February 25
The North Congress authorizes a national system of banking as planned by Secretary of the Treasury Salmon P. Chase.
Eastern Theater Jeb Stuart's raiders continue to harass the Union outposts. Several Federal officers suggest a large counter-raid to attack the rebel cavalry on its home ground.
Naval Operations USS *Vanderbilt* seizes a British merchantman, the *Peterhoff*, as a blockade runner. But the vessel is bound for Matamoros, Mexico, and Great Britain protests strongly. The courts will eventually rule that the USA has no right to stop neutral shipping entering neutral ports, despite the fact that shipments made to Mexico are finding their way into Texas.

Thursday, February 26
The North The Cherokee Indian National Council overturns its ordinance of secession and declares its support for the Union.
Eastern Theater Major General Longstreet is appointed to command Confederate troops in the Department of Virginia and North Carolina. In a skirmish near Woodstock, Virginia, Confederate troops are defeated, with 200 casualties.

Western Theater Porter sets adrift a dummy monitor: a coal barge with a turret made of barrels. It drifts past Vicksburg under heavy fire from the Confederate batteries and approaches the grounded *Indianola*. The rebel picket, *Queen of the West*, flees downstream and the Confederates aboard *Indianola* set fire to their prize.

Friday, February 27
Eastern Theater The headquarters of the Army of the Potomac warns its cavalry patrols to take more care in their assessments of enemy strength. The aggressive raids of the Southern horsemen have made the Union patrols so nervous that minor parties of Confederate troops are being reported as whole regiments on the loose.

Saturday, February 28
Western Theater The USS *Montauk*, flying the pennant of Commodore J.L. Worden, former commander of the *Monitor* in the battle with CSS *Merrimac*, attacks and destroys Confederate steamer *Nashville* on the Ogeechee River.

Sunday, March 1, 1863
The North President Lincoln confers with Secretary of War Edwin Stanton over future military appointments.
Western Theater At Bradyville, Tennessee, the 1st Tennessee and the 3rd and 4th Ohio Cavalry overwhelm a Confederate Cavalry force, killing five, wounding 27, and capturing 100 rebel horsemen at a cost of one killed and six wounded.

Monday, March 2
The North Congress approves a long list of military appointments and promotions submitted by the president. Some 33 officers are dismissed from the service for a variety of offences. Meanwhile, the army sings a ditty ending with "Joe Hooker is our leader, he takes his whiskey strong." Hooker takes a lot else besides—his voracious appetite for women leads to his name becoming a synonym for "prostitute." But his leadership and thorough organization fill the army with confidence.

Tuesday, March 3
The North The Enrollment Act passes both houses of Congress. It calls for the conscription of all able-bodied men between 20 and 45 years old for a period of three years. These men can be called up by Federal decree, to the delight of the military command. Wild estimates of the numbers of recruits now available go to over 3,000,000, but the political and economic consequences rule out any such decision. In fact, only 21,000 men are drafted during the rest of the year, and by the end of the war, only 6 percent of the Union forces will have been raised by the draft—and most of these are substitutes provided by the men whose names were called. Congress also approves the suspension of habeas corpus in the face of bitter opposition from some Democrats.

Wednesday, March 4
Western Theater General Van Dorn takes the offensive, attacking Rosecrans' forces near Spring Hill, Tennessee. A small Union force of

five infantry and three cavalry regiments, supported by a single battery, have advanced from Franklin when they are attacked by Confederate infantry and ringed by Southern cavalry under Nathan Bedford Forrest. The Federal brigade is shattered. The cavalry break out but the rest of the force is compelled to surrender on Thursday. Total Union losses are 400 killed and wounded and 1300 prisoners. Confederate losses are 150 dead and 450 wounded.

Thursday, March 5
Western Theater Union engineers organize the construction of a canal across from Vicksburg under sporadic fire from the Confederate batteries. The idea is to create a short cut at Young's Bend, avoiding the hairpin at Vicksburg. A vital Southern position on the Mississippi, Vicksburg is now protected by extensive fortifications.

Friday, March 6
Eastern Theater The Army of the Potomac's cavalry continues to re-equip with Sharps breech-loading carbines, which gives the 12,000 troopers unrivalled close-range firepower.

Saturday, March 7
The North The military authorities in Baltimore forbid the sale of "secession music" and confiscate pro-Confederate music sheets.
Western Theater General Banks advances on Baton Rouge, Louisiana, while General Grant's campaign against Vicksburg begins to develop. He still hopes to ship his troops against the city by water, although as the Mississippi begins to fall, a land advance down the Louisiana bank will become feasible.
Trans-Mississippi Lieutenant-General E. Kirby Smith assumes command of all Confederate forces west of the Mississippi River.

The sinking of the Nashville
Lying behind a protective line of torpedoes (mines) on the Ogeechee River, the CSS Nashville *was believed to be safe. Any Union vessel approaching to within gun range would have had to brave the fire of heavy guns mounted in Fort McAllister. But the US Navy now had the first of its new monitors, the USS* Montauk, *available.*

Ordered to prevent the Nashville *from departing on a commerce-raiding voyage, Commodore Worden steamed up the Ogeechee on February 28. Trusting to the strength of construction of the* Montauk, *he approached to within 1200 yards of* Nashville *and opened fire with his 15-inch Dahlgren. Fort McAllister opened a heavy fire on the monitor, pounding the vessel from the flank. But the* Montauk's *fire soon told on* Nashville; *after five rounds, a thick column of black smoke rose into the sky. Several more 15-inch shells were fired into the stricken vessel and the* Nashville *burned fiercely for a short time. Then the flames reached her magazine and she exploded.*

Montauk *withdrew, still under fire from the shore batteries, but she suffered no significant damage from them. She struck a torpedo on the way out and had to effect temporary repairs while grounded on a bank, and she put in to Port Royal to make good the damage.*

March 1863

Sunday, March 8, 1863

Eastern Theater Lieutenant John S. Mosby, already nicknamed the "Gray Ghost" for his raids into Union lines this year, leads 29 men to Fairfax, Virginia. Passing through six Federal regiments, as well as the 2nd Vermont Brigade, their target is a Union colonel who has called Mosby a horse thief. But Fairfax Court House has become the temporary HQ of General Edwin H. Stoughton. Mosby captures the general and over 90 Union troops without firing a shot. Taking his prisoners with him, he slips back to the Confederate lines without mishap. Mosby is promoted to major for what Lee calls "a feat unparalleled in the war."

Monday, March 9

Western Theater General Banks concentrates 17,000 men at Baton Rouge. Supposed to advance up the Mississippi while Grant comes south from Vicksburg, communications between the two Federal armies are very poor. Washington intended Banks to join Grant in the assault on Vicksburg but the Confederates had fortified Port Hudson, 135 miles above New Orleans. Some 12,000 rebel troops and 21 heavy guns blocked Banks' advance. Meanwhile, at Vicksburg, a second "Quaker ironclad" made from logs with pork barrels piled up as a fake funnel, is set adrift to run past the batteries during the night. Confederate gunners treat it to a warm reception, wasting much precious ammunition.

Tuesday, March 10

The North President Lincoln is reduced to proclaiming an amnesty for Union deserters to stem the steady tide of men going absent without leave. Men who return to active duty by April 1 will not be punished.
Western Theater Federal troops re-occupy Jacksonville, Florida.

Wednesday, March 11

The North Federal authorities in Baltimore continue their campaign against rebel propaganda, banning the sale of pictures of Confederate leaders.
Western Theater Grant's latest attempt to approach Vicksburg is foiled. Gunboats advancing down the Yalobusha River find their way blocked by a new Confederate position christened Fort Pemberton in honor of the commander of the Vicksburg defenses. The hastily constructed earthwork is reinforced with cotton bales—a simple solution to the problem of digging trenches in such flooded ground.

Thursday, March 12

Western Theater Learning of the capture of *Queen of the West* and *Indianola*, Admiral Farragut plans to run his river flotilla past the guns of Port Hudson. His aim is to establish his warships on the long reach above Port Hudson and cut off Confederate supplies from the Red River country. Meanwhile, a Union force under Colonel Granger returns from a raid along the Duck River, Tennessee.

Union prisoners of war at Salisbury, North Carolina, play a game of baseball. In early 1863 conditions were still fairly reasonable in most prisoner of war camps. The most famous figure in the game's development, Abner Doubleday, was promoted major-general in November 1862 and served at Chancellorsville. At Gettysburg he took over I Corps on the death of Reynolds.

Friday, March 13

The Confederacy An explosion at the Confederate Ordnance Laboratory at Brown's Island near Richmond kills 69 workers, 62 of them women. The haphazard Confederate efforts to mobilize their economy involve a sharp increase in the use of female labor.

Saturday, March 14

Western Theater Admiral Farragut attempts to run the Confederate batteries at Port Hudson during the night. His advance betrayed by a small steamer, the squadron comes under a ferocious barrage. The Confederates fire piles of pine-knots on the right bank of the river, silhouetting the Federal warships for the rebel gunners. Farragut's flagship *Hartford* and *Albatross* succeed in making the passage, but *Richmond*, *Monongahela*, *Genesee*, and *Kineo* are compelled to withdraw. The *Mississippi* passes the lower batteries, running at high speed despite the four-knot current. Unfortunately, she strikes the spit opposite Port Hudson and goes hard aground.

Sunday, March 15

Western Theater Under fire from three Confederate batteries, Captain Smith evacuates the sick and wounded from the *Mississippi*. Unable to refloat her, he orders off the crew and sets his command on fire. At 3 a.m. the blazing vessel floats off and drifts downstream through the Federal fleet before blowing up.

California In San Francisco the authorities seize the schooner *J.M. Chapman*, about to depart with 20 alleged seccessionists and six cannon.

Monday, March 16

Eastern Theater General William W. Averell plans a retaliatory raid against Confederate cavalry outposts commanded by Fitzhugh Lee. The two officers had been classmates at West

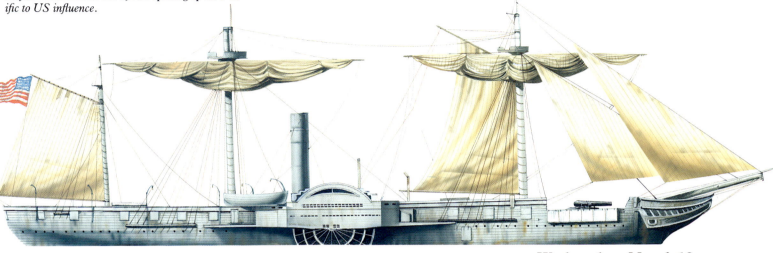

The wooden 3220-ton sidewheel steamer Mississippi was already 20 years old at the war's start. She went on to take part in numerous actions, until set on fire at Port Hudson in 1863. Her executive officer, Commander George Dewey, was later to become the famous admiral who defeated the Spanish fleet at Manila in 1898, thus opening up the Pacific to US influence.

The US Military Railroads' engine "General Haupt" was built in 1863. On the outbreak of war, the South had some 8500 miles of railroad compared to 22,000 in the North. The Federal railroads also included many more connecting lines, so long-distance transportation was far easier. Northern factories expanded the engines and rolling stock during the war, but the Confederate network suffered as worn-out machinery could not be replaced.

Point and Fitzhugh Lee had taken to sending taunting messages to annoy Averell as rebel horsemen continued to beat up the Union picket lines. The most recent asked Averell to bring some coffee with him if the Yankee cavalry could summon the nerve to cross the river. Hooker warmly approves the plan, observing sarcastically that he had not seen many dead cavalrymen lately.

Western Theater Grant and Porter make another attempt to maneuver past Vicksburg, this time via Steele's Bayou. Some 200 miles of narrow, twisting waterways connect the Yazoo with Steele's Bayou, and small parties of Confederates have already begun to fell trees into the bayous to obstruct the advance.

Tuesday, March 17

Eastern Theater Averell avenges himself on Fitzhugh Lee by taking 2000 cavalry and six cannon to attack his classmate's 800-strong command. Crossing the Rappahannock at Kelly's Ford, Averell barrels into Fitzhugh Lee's men and a furious succession of saber charges begin. The Confederates fight gamely but numbers begin to tell. Just then, Averell is told Jeb Stuart has arrived, and instead of over-running Fitzhugh Lee, he sounds the recall and his men trot back to their side of the river. Stuart had arrived, but on his own. Hooker is furious at this lost opportunity but the Union troopers are delighted at winning for a change. They lose 78 men, while inflicting 133 casualties on the Confederates, including the gallant 25-year-old commander of Stuart's horse artillery, John Pelham. He died at Culpeper, still carrying the Bible given him by the Confederate spy Belle Boyd, bearing inscription: "I know thou art loved by another now, I know thou wilt never be mine . . ."

Wednesday, March 18

Eastern Theater Hooker fulminates against "imaginary apprehensions" which tempered Averell's attack at Kelly's Ford. In "Fighting Joe's" army, there would be none of this sort of behavior.

France The Erlanger Bank agrees to lend the Confederacy £3 million at 7 percent interest for 20 years.

Thursday, March 19

The North Two divisions of the IX Corps embark at Newport News, bound for the Department of the Ohio. The superior communications in the North allow the numerically superior Federal forces to concentrate faster than the Confederates and rapidly shift troops from one theater to another.

Western Theater Admiral Farragut passes Natchez, Mississippi, and the batteries at Grand Gulf with *Hartford* and *Albatross*. He is now in position below Vicksburg.

Friday, March 20

Western Theater Another attempt on Vicksburg comes unstuck in Steele's Bayou. Eleven Union vessels try to break through but are beaten back by Confederate fire at Rolling Fork. Sherman lands troops to help Porter's ships, which are imperilled by rebels cutting trees to block the waterway and constant sniping at the crews.

Saturday, March 21

The North Major-General Edwin Vose Sumner dies at Syracuse, New York. Despite his advanced years, he had performed creditably in the peninsula operations and at Antietam.

Western Theater A series of skirmishes occur in Tennessee. Confederate troops attack a Federal railroad train between Grand Junction and Bolivar while Union forces head for Saulsbury, and there is fighting at Salem.

March–April 1863

Sunday, March 22, 1863

Western Theater Commanded by Basil Duke, John Morgan's raiders capture a Federal garrison at Mount Sterling, Kentucky. Other raiders under John Pegram raid into Kentucky throughout this week.

Monday, March 23

Western Theater *Hartford* and the gunboat *Albatross* bombard the Confederate shore batteries at Warrenton on the Mississippi, below Vicksburg.

Tuesday, March 24

Western Theater The last Federal attempt to advance on Vicksburg by water fails. The objective this time was to use the Black Bayou but an active Confederate defense frustrates all efforts to break through. The Mississippi continues to run very high for this time of year and the damage to the levees, both by neglect and sabotage, makes navigation especially difficult. Sherman's infantry wade through swamps and tangled brushwood.

Above: *Many foreign nations attached military observers to both Union and Confederate armies to study the Civil War. This group are with Major-General Stoneman, commander of the Army of the Potomac's cavalry. His slowness moved Lincoln to write Hooker on April 15, expressing concern over the lack of action along the Rappahannock.*

Above: *Battery "A" 1st US Artillery during the siege of Port Hudson, Louisiana. General Banks opened the siege on May 21 and the position surrendered six weeks later. Over 7000 Confederates were taken prisoner by Bank's 33,000-strong army.*

Blakely 7.5-inch rifled gun
Overlooking the river, this 3½-ton gun was one of the most powerful cannon in the Vicksburg defenses. The barrel was originally 8 feet 4 inches long, but lost 2 feet at the muzzle when a shell exploded prematurely in May 1863.

Below: *Soldiers recuperate in Carver General Hospital, Washington, D.C. War Department figures state that 110,100 men were killed in action or mortally injured, while 275,175 were wounded. The large numbers of wounded, particularly after major actions like Gettysburg, swamped the medical services and men frequently lay where they fell for many hours before rescue.*

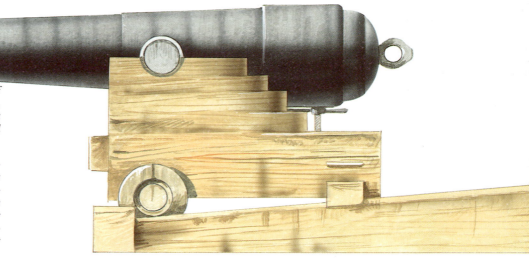

Wednesday, March 25

The North General Burnside, unemployed since the fiasco of his command of the Army of the Potomac, is appointed to command the Department of the Ohio.

Western Theater Two Union rams, *Lancaster* and *Switzerland*, are attacked by Confederate field batteries while withdrawing from the Black Bayou. *Lancaster* is destroyed and *Switzerland* damaged. A Union detachment at Brentwood, Tennessee, is surprised by a Confederate attack. Some 300 Federals are captured, while Southern losses are one killed and five wounded.

Thursday, March 26

The North West Virginia votes to emancipate its slaves. President Lincoln writes Governor Andrew Johnson of Tennessee, saying, "The sight of 50,000 armed and drilled black soldiers on the banks of the Mississippi would end the rebellion at once." The employment of black troops will increase steadily, despite opposition in the North and threats of reprisals from the South.

Friday, March 27

The North President Lincoln meets with a delegation of Indians and advises them to turn to agriculture.

Western Theater Union naval forces withdraw from Steele's Bayou just in time, as Confederate obstructions and a sudden fall in the waters threaten to strand them. The attempt to reach the Sunflower and Yazoo rivers above Haynes' Bluff is defeated.

Saturday, March 28

Western Theater Anticipating further Union naval attacks, S.H. Lockett, chief engineer of the Vicksburg defenses, supervises the expansion of the batteries at Grand Gulf. The Federal gunboat *Diana* is captured at Pattersonville, Louisiana.

Left: *Federal soldiers pose for the camera at Fairfax Court House. On March 8, Confederate raider John S. Mosby led his men into this small Virginia town and captured Union General Stoughton in his bed.*

Mexico Two battalions of the French Foreign Legion land at Vera Cruz to join French forces besieging Juarez at Puebla.

Sunday, March 29

Eastern Theater Skirmishing continues between the cavalry outposts along the Rappahannock. There is another action at Kelly's Ford.

Western Theater General Grant directs General McClernland to establish a route to Vicksburg from Milliken's Bend to New Carthage. Admiral Porter plans the naval support which will provide transport and supplies.

Monday, March 30

The North President Lincoln announces that April 30 will be a day of fasting and prayer throughout the Union.

Western Theater At Dutton's Hill, Kentucky, four Union Cavalry regiments defeat a Confederate force, inflicting 290 casualties for the loss of 35 of their own men.

Tuesday, March 31

Eastern Theater Mosby's raiders are in action again, defeating Union cavalry at Drainesville, Virginia.

Western Theater Union troops evacuate Jacksonville, Florida. Admiral Farragut takes *Hartford*, *Albatross*, and *Switzerland* past the Confederate batteries at Grand Gulf, Mississippi.

Wednesday, April 1, 1863

Eastern Theater Hooker warns the War Department that he will need siege equipment to the tune of 10,000 shovels and 5000 picks for his forthcoming assault on Richmond.

Western Theater Grant's plan to attack Vicksburg from the left and rear will require Porter's fleet to fight its way past the formidable shore batteries to break into the southern stretch of the Mississippi. The rebels continue to strengthen their defenses.

Thursday, April 2

The North Major-General Howard succeeds Major-General Carl Schurz as commander of the largely German XI Corps.

The South A riot in Richmond is quelled by the personal intervention of Jefferson Davis. The disturbances are symptomatic of the collapsing Southern economy: internal trade is breaking down, leading to food shortages in

Farragut's famous flagship Hartford. *She was almost constantly in action up the Mississippi many miles from her natural element.* Hartford *had a long and distinguished career but unfortunately she sank at her berth at the Norfolk Navy Yard on November 20, 1956, nearly 100 years after launching.*

some cities. But although the Richmond "bread riot" begins with a mob plundering a bread wagon, it soon turns into general looting. President Davis addresses the crowd from the wagon and throws them the money he has in his pocket. Judicious action by the militia and the president's personal example quell the mob without bloodshed.

Western Theater More cavalry patrol actions occur in Tennessee as the 3rd and 4th Ohio Cavalry defeat a small Confederate force at Snow Hill.

Friday, April 3

The North President Lincoln decides to visit Hooker's reformed Army of the Potomac and press the general for an early action against Lee. Hooker issues orders for the commissary department to have 1.5 million rations on boats, ready to be floated up the Pamunkey River.

Saturday, April 4

Eastern Theater Hooker readies the Army of the Potomac for action. All surplus baggage equipment begins to move to the rear. The Army Secret Service Department is ordered to update its maps of Richmond's defenses.

April 1863

Sunday, April 5, 1863
Great Britain Several Confederate vessels are detained at Liverpool, where the *Alexandria* is being prepared as a blockade runner. The war has already lasted far longer than British opinion had predicted, and there is little prospect of active help for the South from any quarter.

Monday, April 6
Eastern Theater Lincoln is not impressed with Hooker. The general talks with swaggering self-confidence, arousing the president's suspicions by beginning sentences, "After we have taken Richmond . . ." Lincoln takes a correct, Clausewitzian view: the real objective is Lee's Army of Northern Virginia. It might be outnumbered 2:1, but its veteran soldiers remain the sweeping sword of the Confederacy. Until that weapon is broken, the war will continue.

Tuesday, April 7
Naval Operations The South Atlantic squadron of the US Navy attacks Fort Sumter. Flying his flag in the *New Ironsides*, Admiral Samuel Du Pont leads eight other ironclads—*Keokuk, Weehawken, Passaic, Montauk, Patapsco, Catskill, Nantucket,* and *Nahant*—against the Confederate batteries. What follows is a classic ships *versus* fort encounter, ending as usual in defeat for the warships. The Union flagship suffers frequent hits, and only the *Catskill* and *Nahant* escape without significant damage. Although Union casualties are light (two killed, 20 wounded), the battered fleet has to withdraw.

Wednesday, April 8
Naval Operations The ironclad *Keokuk* founders owing to the damage inflicted by the Confederate batteries in Forts Sumter and Moultrie.
Western Theater Still smarting from being placed under Grant's command, McClernand's XIII Corps presses forward through the tangled Louisiana waterways. Several vicious skirmish actions occur near New Carthage, as the Confederates contest the slow Federal advance.

Thursday, April 9
Western Theater McClernand's troops continue to clear a route for Grant's forthcoming assault on Vicksburg. Plantation houses are ripped down to provide planking for the innumerable bridges required.

Friday, April 10
Eastern Theater President Lincoln reviews the Army of the Potomac at its winter quarters in Falmouth, Virginia. The troops make a fine sight and display every confidence in Hooker's leadership.
Western Theater Van Dorn's Confederates are driven off in a minor engagement with General Granger's Union forces near Franklin, Tennessee.

Saturday, April 11
The North Lincoln confers with the Cabinet. Hooker, mindful of security, has briefed the president only on his future plans, and even the formidable secretary of war does not know exactly what the general intends.
Eastern Theater Longstreet begins a month-long siege of Suffolk, Virginia. Hooker is aware of this further reduction in Lee's strength and gleefully anticipates a major victory.

Sunday, April 12
Western Theater With Union warships controlling the mouth of the Red River, General Banks resumes his plan to take Port Hudson with a turning movement by the Atchafalaya. To affect this, he must first deal with 4–5000 Confederate troops under Taylor, entrenched on the Teche River below Franklin. Banks begins to land troops behind Taylor's force while keeping them busy in front. His objective is to surround and annihilate the Confederates.

Monday, April 13
The North General Burnside publishes his infamous General Order 38, threatening the death penalty to anyone found guilty of treasonable behavior.
Western Theater Banks' troops debark behind Taylor's positions. The troops are ashore by 4.00 p.m. but the 2nd Louisiana and 4th Texas Cavalry take advantage of the thick woods and undergrowth to obstruct the Union advance. Meanwhile, Taylor retreats, fighting a brief engagement at Fort Bisland. During the night he falls back on Franklin.

Tuesday, April 14
Western Theater With his plan for a dawn assault frustrated by the Confederate withdrawal, Banks orders his troops in pursuit. Grover's division threatened Taylor's retreat along Irish Bend, the great bow in the Teche River. Although both sides had about 5000 troops, the rebels successfully batter their way through with the assistance of the captured Union gunboat *Diana*. The gunboat was subsequently burned by the retreating Confederates when their small naval squadron was assailed by a Union gunboat force under Lieutenant Commander A.P. Cooke, CSS *Queen of the West* is destroyed during the naval fight.

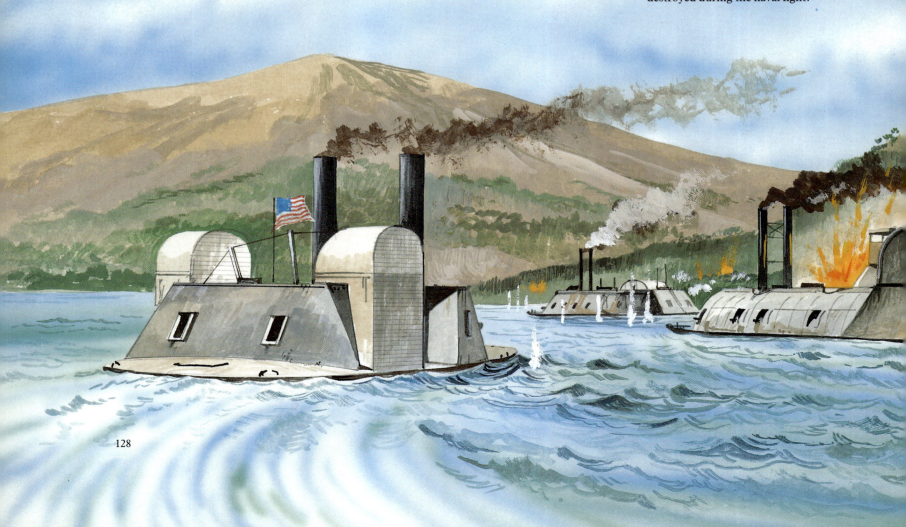

The battle of Grand Gulf, April 29

Twenty miles southwest of Vicksburg, the Mississippi is overlooked by steep bluffs rising over 100 feet above the water. At this bend in the river, known as Grand Gulf, the Confederates had established several batteries, including two 8-inch Columbiads and two 100-pounder rifles.

The Union river squadron, which ran the Vicksburg batteries on April 16, attacked Grand Gulf at the end of the month. Seven ironclads—Trenton, Tuscumbia, Louisville, Carondelet, Pittsburgh, Mound City, and Lafayette—opened fire at 7.55 a.m. In a four-hour bombard-

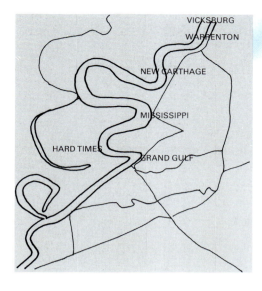

ment they gradually gained the upper hand, even shooting down the Confederate flagstaff at 9.05.

The 5-knot current made maneuvering difficult enough without heavy artillery fire. Benton was hit 47 times, most Confederate rounds penetrating her armor. Tuscumbia received 81 hits and was forced to withdraw. But one by one the Confederate guns ceased fire and the fleet eventually withdrew. The Confederates fired a defiant, parting shot, but their position at Grand Gulf was doomed. Union troops were later landed downstream and the position was evacuated on May 3.

Wednesday, April 15

Naval Operations Two Union whaling ships are seized by the Confederate raider *Alabama* off the Brazilian island of Fernando de Noronha.

Thursday, April 16

Western Theater During the night, Admiral Porter leads six warships and several transports in a bold attempt to run past the guns of Vicksburg as part of Grant's plan to take the city from the south. The river steamboats are protected by cotton bales and by coal barges lashed alongside. Confederate pickets land on the Union-held bank at De Soto and fire several houses to illuminate the Federal vessels for the gunners in Vicksburg. Eight ships succeed in breaking through, one transport is sunk, and several barges disabled.

Friday, April 17

Western Theater Thanks to Porter's gamble, the Union now has a formidable gunboat squadron below Vicksburg at New Carthage, and enough transport to make a major troop movement across the river. Colonel Benjamin H. Grierson leaves La Grange, Tennessee, with 1700 cavalrymen on what will become one of the most famous raids of the war: a 16-day, 600-mile sortie deep into the heart of the Confederacy.

Saturday, April 18

Western Theater Grierson's cavalry brush aside Confederate patrols near New Albany, Mississippi.
Trans-Mississippi There is a minor action at Fayetteville, Arkansas.

April–May 1863

Sunday, April 19, 1863

Western Theater Grierson's raiding column continues its progress through Mississippi. There is a brief skirmish at Pontotoc.

Monday, April 20

The North President Lincoln declares that the bill allowing West Virginia to enter the Union will take effect on June 20, 1863.

Western Theater General Banks' forces enter Opelousas, Louisiana, as Taylor's Confederates continue their retreat. Butte-à-la-Rose, a fortified position containing two heavy cannon and 60 crew, surrenders to Commander Cooke's Union naval squadron.

Trans-Mississippi A Federal detachment is defeated in a minor action at Paterson, Missouri.

Tuesday, April 21

Eastern Theater The Army of the Potomac's secret preparations continue. Hooker plans to keep Confederate attention directed at Fredericksburg, while several Union corps cross the Rappahannock upstream and move against Lee's left flank. To improve the torpid pace of wagon transport, 2000 mules are assembled to carry supplies during the advance.

Wednesday, April 22

The South President Davis resumes his attempt to run the Vicksburg campaign from Richmond. Today he orders Pemberton to attack the Union warships with fire rafts floated downstream.

Western Theater Eighteen Union supply ships run the Vicksburg batteries. One transport and six barges are destroyed but Grant's troops receive adequate supplies from the 11 vessels which make it.

Thursday, April 23

Western Theater General Banks receives his first communication from Grant. Dated March 23, Grant's letter arrives via Admiral Farragut's fleet. This begins a correspondence coordinating the two Union armies' efforts to control the Mississippi. Banks is told he can expect a corps of troops from Grant to assist in the assault on Port Hudson.

Friday, April 24

The South The Confederate Congress approves an 8 percent tax on all agricultural products grown last year, and a 10 percent tax on profits made from the sale of food, clothing, and iron. There is considerable opposition to a 10 percent tax-in-kind levied on this year's crops, but many Confederate leaders recognize that unless they deal with the food problem, the Southern economy will collapse. Unfortunately, too much land remains devoted to producing cotton instead of food.

Saturday, April 25

Western Theater Grant's forces skirmish with elements of the Vicksburg garrison at Hard Times Landing.

WILDERNESS CHURCH

DOWDALL'S TAVERN

ORANGE PLANK ROAD

SCOTT'S RUN

Sunday, April 26

Eastern Theater Hooker's long awaited offensive begins. Leading elements of the Army of the Potomac's XI Corps (Howard), XII Corps (Slocum), and V Corps (Meade) march on Kelly's Ford. Torrential rain has reduced many roads to mud troughs.

Trans-Mississippi General John Marmaduke leads a Confederate attack on the Federal garrison of Cape Girardeau, Missouri. The rebels are repulsed, with 40 dead and 200 wounded; Union losses are just six dead and nine wounded.

Monday, April 27

Eastern Theater The main bodies of XI, XII, and V Corps advance along the north bank of the Rappahannock. Each man carries eight days' rations instead of the usual four. Rations for one day weigh three pounds and consist of hardtack, salt pork, coffee, sugar, and salt.

Tuesday, April 28

Eastern Theater Hancock's and French's divisions of II Corps (Couch) demonstrate at Banks Ford while engineers repair the road leading to United States Ford. The heavy rains finally subside, but many tracks need to be corduroyed with logs to bear the weight of army wagons. Sedgwick's VI Corps crosses the Rapidan below Fredericksburg and digs in.

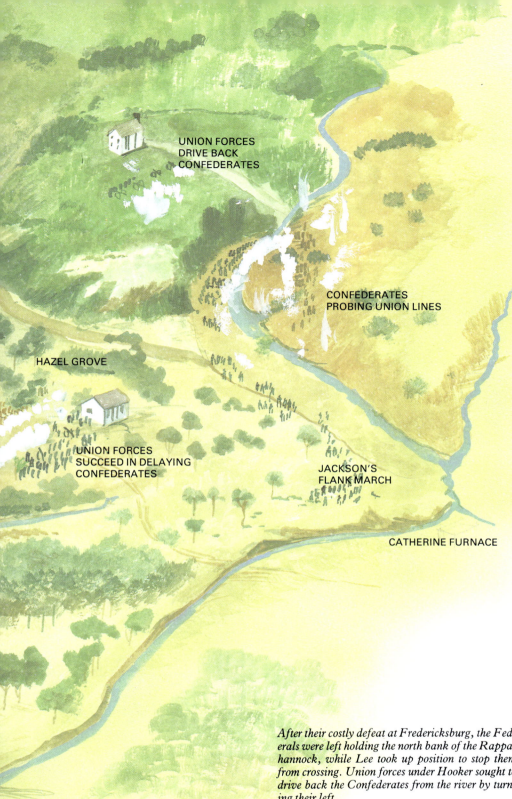

UNION FORCES
DRIVE BACK
CONFEDERATES

CONFEDERATES
PROBING UNION LINES

HAZEL GROVE

UNION FORCES
SUCCEED IN DELAYING
CONFEDERATES

JACKSON'S
FLANK MARCH

CATHERINE FURNACE

Wednesday, April 29

Eastern Theater Stonewall Jackson presses Lee to be allowed to launch an attack on Sedgwick's bridgehead. But Lee has numerous reports from Stuart's cavalry that major Union forces have crossed the Rappahannock and are advancing on his left flank. The Federals are now deep in The Wilderness, a dense forest of second-growth timber, with heavy underbrush clogging its innumerable creeks and gullies. Lee concludes that the maneuvering around Fredericksburg is a feint.

Western Theater Admiral Porter's squadron attacks the Confederate batteries at Grand Gulf but the forts remain operational.

After their costly defeat at Fredericksburg, the Federals were left holding the north bank of the Rappahannock, while Lee took up position to stop them from crossing. Union forces under Hooker sought to drive back the Confederates from the river by turning their left.

The Confederates are now caught between two Federal armies: Lee turns to face Hooker, while Jubal Early's force holds off Sedgwick in the east.

On the second day, May 2, 1863, Confederate Jackson begins a flank march across the Union front. This force is successfully attacked and gives the impression that the Confederates are in retreat.

Jackson takes up a fresh position and sweeps up the turnpike until the Union forces make a determined stand at Dowdall's Tavern. Massed Union artillery at Fairview Cemetery finally halts the Southern advance.

As Jackson returns from a reconnoiter, he is fatally wounded by nervous Confederates thinking they are under attack from Union forces.

Thursday, April 30

Eastern Theater Hooker launches General Stoneman and 10,000 cavalry to raid Lee's communications and do to the Army of Northern Virginia what Stuart's horsemen have been doing to the Federals. But although Hooker has succeeded in training the Union cavalry into an effective force, the grand raid achieves little. Half the force, under Averell, contents itself with occupying Rapidan Station. Stoneman splits his men into small raiding parties which fail to attack Lee's transport massed at Guiney's Station with the lightest of escorts. Stoneman has concealed from Hooker the embarrassing problem that he is suffering badly from piles. No medication can ease the agony of staying in the saddle. He is simply incapable of the hard riding an aggressive cavalry raid demands.

Mexico At the abandoned hamlet of Camerone 62 officers and men of the French Foreign Legion make one of the most famous last stands in military history. Attacked by 2000 Mexicans, they fight until just five men are left standing—and *they* make a last counter-attack with fixed bayonets. Meanwhile, the main French Army continues the siege of the Juarista fortress of Puebla.

Friday, May 1, 1863

Eastern Theater III, XI, and XII Corps are now concentrated at Chancellorsville, a farmhouse on a strategically important crossroads some two miles from the edge of The Wilderness. But Hooker delays the advance and does not move until 11.00 a.m. He never makes it into open country. Confederate troops under Jackson halt the Union advance, the tanglefoot underbrush preventing the Federals from knowing the strength of the opposition and making coordinated attacks impossible. Hooker astounds his corps commanders in the evening by announcing his intention to remain on the defensive. He has some 90,000 men in the front line, facing half that number of Confederates.

Saturday, May 2

Eastern Theater Jackson leads 25,000 Confederates on a flank march around the Union army, while Lee faces the Army of the Potomac with just 15,000 men. It is one of the greatest gambles in military history, but the supine Hooker allows it to work. Jackson's corps takes all day to outflank the six-mile front of the Union Army. Lee shuttles empty trains along the Richmond-Fredericksburg railroad, which helps convince Hooker that the Confederates are retreating. By early evening Jackson is in the rear of the Union Army and launches a surprise attack, routing XI Corps and driving the Federals back in confusion. Fighting continues into the night and parts of the dry undergrowth catch fire, burning alive some of the wounded. Planning to continue the attack through the night, Stonewall is accidentally shot by his own men while scouting ahead with members of his staff.

May 1863

Right: *Wounded are tended in the open after the battle of Chancellorsville. Both armies had over 9000 of their men wounded; but since there were 133,000 Federals to about 60,000 Confederates, Lee's men suffered a much greater percentage loss. It remains one of the most remarkable victories in military history.*

Pontoon bridges
No army could afford to have its movement channeled by the location of existing bridges, so both sides used pontoon trains. They were hinged skeleton frames which traveled as a wagon body. Inside were the canvas covers, lashings, anchor, and chains. Armies of all sizes used pontoon bridges: Sheridan's 10,000-strong cavalry force brought eight pontoon boats with them and used them to cross the swollen Shenandoah in March 1865. During the March to the Sea, Sherman arranged for each of his four corps to have enough pontoons to bridge 300 yards of river.

Sunday, May 3, 1863

Eastern Theater "Fighting Joe" Hooker loses all control at the battle of Chancellorsville. The outnumbered Confederate Army rolls up the Union position early in the morning and Hooker orders his engineers to prepare for a retreat over the River Rappahannock. Meanwhile, the 23,000 men of Sedgwick's VI Corps attack Early's 10,000 troops at Fredericksburg. Just before 6 a.m. on a beautiful spring morning, the Union troops rush the heights south of the town and drive the rebels from the field. Capturing 15 cannon and 1000 prisoners, Sedgwick presses forward but by the evening Lee has reacted. Leaving Stuart to mask Hooker with just 25,000 men, he prepares to annihilate the isolated corps.

Western Theater Grierson reaches Union lines at Baton Rouge, having devastated the Mississippi and Louisiana countryside in a raid covering 600 miles.

Monday, May 4

Eastern Theater Sedgwick's corps receives the Confederate attack but, although soon cut off from Fredericksburg, he holds his ground while Howe's division protects pontoon bridges built below Bank's Ford the previous evening. By nightfall the approaches to the bridges are shrouded in thick fog forming over the river, and VI Corps is able to retreat to safety during the night. A gloomy council of war summoned by Hooker agrees to begin a general retreat back to the winter quarters at Falmouth.

Western Theater General Grant's forces penetrate south of Vicksburg. Federal gunboats bombard Fort De Russy on the Red River in Louisiana but are repelled, with damage to the gunboat *Albatross*.

Tuesday, May 5

The North Former congressman Clement Vallandigham is arrested for treason by General Burnside, now commander of the Department of the Ohio. Vallandigham is a leading "copperhead", or anti-war Democrat (the name comes from their emblem: copper heads from pennies, mounted on pins and worn as a badge). On May 1 he made a fire-eating speech denouncing the war, "King Lincoln," and Burnside's General Order 38, which threatened arrest for "declaring sympathy for the enemy."

Eastern Theater Lee leaves Early to remain in observation at Bank's Ford and Fredericksburg, and marches the remainder of his army back to Chancellorsville, intending to assault the much larger Union Army the next day. Torrential rain swells the Rappahannock, wrecking some of the Federal pontoons but masking Hooker's withdrawal.

Wednesday, May 6

Eastern Theater By dawn the last Federal rear guard is away, leaving Lee in possession of five miles of empty trenches. The victory at Chancellorsville is a magnificent feat of arms: outnumbered 2:1, Lee attacked and defeated the Army of the Potomac. But although he inflicted 17,000 casualties, 13,000 Confederates fell too. The South cannot afford victories at this rate of exchange.

Europe Commander James D. Bullock, CSN, is appointed to superintend Confederate naval construction in Europe. £2 million is allotted under the South's European Act for the Confederate naval program. The vessels are required to be able to withstand 15-in gunfire, seaworthy enough to operate in the Atlantic, but also capable of navigating the Mississippi. The hope of a European-built ironclad squadron shattering the Union blockade will endure until the end of the war.

Thursday, May 7

Eastern Theater Although back at Falmouth, the Army of the Potomac is by no means despondent. With the exception of the humiliated XI Corps, many formations were not engaged and do not consider themselves beaten. It is a far cry from the demoralization which followed Burnside's bloody repulse at Fredericksburg.

Western Theater Still outnumbered by Pemberton's Confederates, Grant takes advantage of the rebels' failure to concentrate their troops. McClernland's corps advances on Raymond, Mississippi, while Sherman's corps pushes through Cayuga to Dillon's Plantation.

Friday, May 8

Eastern Theater Stonewall Jackson's condition worsens. His arm was amputated on May 2 after he was wounded in error by troops from North Carolina during the battle of Chancellorsville. With his iron constitution, Jackson was expected to make a full recovery, but infection sets in. Attended by his wife and devoted friends, the general drifts in and out of consciousness.

Right: *A copyist in a Washington patent office at the beginning of the war, Clara Barton became a legendary figure among the Army of the Potomac. She traveled with the troops, dispensing supplies and medication. Never part of an official aid group, she spent the war helping wounded soldiers. In 1881 she founded the American Red Cross.*

Below: *Marye's Heights, Fredericksburg, after Sedgwick's corps drove off Jubal Early's outnumbered Confederates on their third assault.*

Saturday, May 9
Eastern Theater Lee reorganizes the Army of Northern Virginia into three corps instead of two.
Western Theater Grant continues to threaten Vicksburg, the key to the Mississippi. An anguished President Davis promises Pemberton every support.

Sunday, May 10
Eastern Theater At 3.15 p.m. Stonewall Jackson raises his head and says, "No, no, let us pass over the river and rest under the shade of the trees." Then he closes his eyes for ever. The Confederacy has lost a soldier whose brief military career established him as one of the greatest commanders in history. He is irreplaceable and his death casts a deep shadow over the victory of Chancellorsville.

Monday, May 11
The North Clement Vallandigham applies for a writ of habeas corpus while languishing in a military prison at Cincinnati, Ohio. Mobs supporting him burn the premises of a Republican paper in Dayton.

Tuesday, May 12
Western Theater Having dispersed much of his infantry and all his cavalry to hunt for Grierson's raiders, Pemberton has no accurate intelligence on Grant's movements. As a result, Gregg's Confederate brigade is surprised by a whole Union corps at Raymond. But Gregg holds his ground, counter-attacking vigorously. McClernand assumes he is facing major opposition. Some 5000 rebels and two batteries hold off an army corps all afternoon.

Wednesday, May 13
Western Theater Pemberton deploys troops at Edward's Station, Mississippi, as Grant's Federal Army advances on this position and Jackson, near Vicksburg.

Thursday, May 14
Eastern Theater Hooker, who had won command of the Army of the Potomac by assiduously criticizing his fellow officers, now receives the same treatment. The army's senior commanders jostle to unseat him.
Western Theater McPherson and Sherman's corps take Jackson. Johnston has just 6000 men to oppose two army corps and he evacuates the town without delay. Grant sleeps the night in the house occupied by Johnston earlier in the day.
Europe Commander Sinclair informs Lieutenant North that Bullock's ships will be sent to France for completion. Federal pressure on Great Britain to halt the construction of warships for the Confederacy is succeeding.

Friday, May 15
Western Theater Outmaneuvered by Grant, Pemberton spends the day in a futile attempt to cut the Federal's supply lines. Sherman stays in Jackson, destroying manufacturing centers and railroads in a grim foretaste of his future campaigns of devastation.

Saturday, May 16
The North Vallandigham is found guilty of treason and sentenced to be confined for the duration of the war.
Western Theater McPherson's and McClernand's corps attack Pemberton at Champion's Hill, a small knoll between Vicksburg and Jackson. The 29,000 Federal troops attack in succession, allowing Pemberton to shift his 22,000 men in response. After six hours of indecisive combat in which both sides suffer over 2000 casualties, the rebels retreat to the Big Black River. Instead of marching north to link up with Johnston's command, Pemberton makes a fatal error. Leaving a rear guard, he falls back toward the already doomed defenses of Vicksburg.

May 1863

Sunday, May 17, 1863

Western Theater With the excellent staffwork which characterized Grant's command, Sherman's and McClernand's corps are on the road by 3.00 a.m., pursuing Pemberton's beaten army. At dawn the leading troops run into a new Confederate defensive position on the Big Black River. A charge led by Lawler's brigade overruns the trenches before the Confederates can get off a second volley. Some 1700 Confederates and 18 guns are captured. Union losses are 39 dead and 237 wounded. Just as the attack is launched, Grant receives a letter from General Halleck ordering him back to Grand Gulf. He is to assist Banks in the attack on Port Hudson, then make a joint attack on Vicksburg. Grant ignores Halleck's orders and cuts short an argument with the messenger by riding into the battle.

Monday, May 18

Western Theater Grant's engineers have worked through the night to prepare four bridges over the Big Black River. Three corps begin to cross early in the morning, and by the evening Sherman's leading troops reach the defenses of Vicksburg. Pemberton withdraws his troops to defend the city.

Tuesday, May 19

The North Secretary of War Edwin Stanton directs that Clement Vallandigham be handed over to the Confederates.

Western Theater Grant launches a hasty assault on the Vicksburg defenses, hoping to capitalize on the rebels' demoralization after Champion's Hill. But the Confederates repulse the assault, inflicting over 900 casualties.

Wednesday, May 20

Western Theater Grant's army entrenches itself around Vicksburg. Pemberton has missed his last opportunity to save his command from destruction. Union engineers make roads between Grant's lines and the Yazoo River and Chickasaw Bayou. Grant's troops have had only five days' rations of hardtack to sustain them for the last three weeks. Porter detaches *Choctaw*, *De Kalb*, and four light-draft gunboats to attack the Confederate base at Yazoo City. The Confederates fire their navy yard to deny its facilities to the Union. The Federals complete the destruction, burning three warships under construction.

Thursday, May 21

Western Theater Banks' advance on Port Hudson continues, two brigades skirmishing at Plains Store. Grant's troops receive bread and coffee in the evening as the Union supply line is re-established.

Friday, May 22

Western Theater Grant launches an assault on Vicksburg, but although McClernand's corps breaks into the Confederate trenches, Sherman and McPherson are repulsed. A second attack in the afternoon to support McClernand's success fails. Union losses are 500 killed and 2500 wounded. This evening, Grant determines on a regular siege—to "out-camp the enemy," as he later describes it.

Saturday, May 23

Western Theater Banks' army crosses the Mississippi during the night and advances to the rear of Port Hudson. Grant's troops dig in around Vicksburg as his army settles down to siege operations. The Federal lines stretch for 15 miles between Haynes's Bluff to Vicksburg, and south to Warrenton.

Sunday, May 24

Eastern Theater Hooker readies the Army of the Potomac at Fredericksburg, anticipating another Confederate attack. However, Lee is busy planning another invasion of the North.

Western Theater Grant writes a report of Friday's unsuccessful attack in which he unfairly criticizes McClernand (who broke into the enemy trenches), and overlooks the failure of Sherman and McPherson. Grant is not the only professional soldier angered by McClernand's carping criticism of West Pointers, and it is no secret that he would dearly love to be rid of this political general.

Monday, May 25

The North Spirited to Tennessee, Clement Vallandigham is handed over to his erstwhile friends in the Confederacy. It is a compromise which pleases neither the ardent loyalists, who want him hanged, nor the "copperheads" and their allies, who wish him released.

Tuesday, May 26

Western Theater Banks' investment of Port Hudson is now completed. Some 14,000 Union troops surround 7000 entrenched Confederates under Major-General Frank Gardner. Eager for victory, Banks orders an assault for tomorrow.

Wednesday, May 27

Western Theater Banks attacks Port Hudson with similar results to Grant's assault on the 22nd. The Confederate positions are well sited in dense magnolia forest. The Union troops have to maneuver through broken ground within it. The Confederates have felled trees in front of their redoubts, giving them a clear shot at the advancing Union troops and hampering the attackers' movement. The Union troops are repulsed with 293 killed and 1545 wounded. Banks, too, begins regular siege operations. At Vicksburg Porter's fleet attacks the Confederate shore batteries. The *Cincinnati* is sunk by the guns of Fort Hill, the principal redoubt above Vicksburg.

Naval Operations CSS *Chattahoochie* is destroyed on the Chattahoochie River, Georgia, by an accidental explosion.

Thursday, May 28

Western Theater Grant has no proper siege artillery, just six 32-pounders. Admiral Porter supplies a battery of large-caliber naval guns instead, and they are installed ashore to reduce the Confederate redoubts.

Friday, May 29

The North The Vallandigham affair continues to have repercussions. General Burnside tenders his resignation as commander of the Department of the Ohio in protest at Vallandigham's release. President Lincoln refuses to accept it.

Saturday, May 30

Western Theater Grant's army continues to fortify its positions. Johnston's Confederate Army is known to be concentrating somewhere to the east, preparing to march to the relief of Vicksburg.

The defenses of Vicksburg
The Confederates began to fortify Vicksburg immediately after the fall of New Orleans on April 25, 1862. Unless the Confederacy could maintain a powerful fortress, dominating the Mississippi with cannon, Union warships would be free to pass up and down the river, cutting off the whole Trans-Mississippi theater. Confederate engineers supervised hired Negro labor in constructing extensive earthworks along the hills and ridges which towered 200 feet above the water. By Farragut's first naval attack on June 26, the Confederates had two 10-inch Columbiad guns and 27 old-model 32- and 42-pounders. For the rest of 1862 the lines were regularly bombarded by the heavy mortars of the Union river fleet.

In early fall, as a land attack became more likely, slaves from nearby plantations were hired from their owners to expand the defenses facing inland. Hayne's Bluff on the Yazoo River and Warrenton, some six miles below Vicksburg, were fortified as flanking positions. These defenses were not seriously tested in 1862 and were not maintained during the winter. But after the defeat at the Big Black River, the Confederates withdrew into Vicksburg and regular siege operations commenced.

The extensive defensive works were manned by 30,000 troops under General John Pemberton, who faced 41,000 Union troops. Later this figure rose to over 70,000 when Vicksburg was eventually sealed off in the summer of 1863. When the city finally surrendered, the Union acquired 172 cannon and about 60,000 rifles, many of superior quality to the Union weapons.

Life for the citizens of Vicksburg during the long siege was extremely hard, many seeking shelter from the Union bombardments in caves cut into the cliffs and in sheltered areas.

ORD'S XIII CORPS

LAUMAN'S DIVISION

FEDERAL WORKS

CONFEDERATE WORKS

HERRON'S DIVISION

CONFEDERATE WORKS

MARINE HOSPITAL

MISSISSIPPI RIVER

May–June 1863

Sunday, May 31, 1863
Western Theater As the brooks and creeks dry up in the early summer heat, life in the trenches surrounding Port Hudson becomes increasingly unpleasant. The river falls, exposing a wide expanse of stinking mud. The situation is particularly grim for the Confederates as the Union artillery already dominates their trenches. Supplies of both food and ammunition are only good for a few weeks.

Monday, June 1, 1863
Naval Operations This was the original completion date for the Confederate ironclads building at the Laird's yard in England. Still several months from launching, the desperate Southern naval officers plan to spirit their ships away to France for completion. The British government seems increasingly hostile to the Confederates, and there is now a strong possibility that the British may seize the vessels before she can be moved.

Tuesday, June 2
Eastern Theater The Army of Northern Virginia receives its marching orders. Lee plans to strike north again, intending to draw Hooker after him and save Virginia from another Union onslaught. Although launching a strategic offensive, Lee plans to fight a defensive battle, confident after Chancellorsville that he can outmaneuver Hooker's larger army and inflict heavy losses on the enemy. Another Union defeat would, with luck, shatter confidence in the leadership of the Army of the Potomac and buy the Confederacy another year.

Wednesday, June 3
The North General Burnside incenses local opinion by sending cavalrymen to stop publication of the *Chicago Times*. Burnside suppresses the paper because of its staunchly Democrat stance. The general's decision places the president in a difficult position: Burnside had already suppressed freedom of speech by his arrest of Vallandigham; muzzling the press as well would inevitably outrage a wide spectrum of opinion. Lincoln revokes the order and warns Burnside not to shut down any papers without authorization from Washington.
Eastern Theater The vanguard of Lee's army leaves its quarters at Fredericksburg, 70,000 strong with 300 guns. Hooker now commands 120,000 troops but he is unsure if Lee really intends another invasion, and if so, by what route. Union officers monitor Confederate troop movements from observation balloons on the Stafford Heights. Two Confederate deserters enter Falmouth during the night, saying their division had received the order to march.

Thursday, June 4
Eastern Theater Lee advances with Longstreet's I Corps and Ewell's II Corps. A.P. Hill's III Corps remains in the trenches at Fredericksburg to block any Federal attempt on Richmond. Stuart concentrates his cavalry at Brandy Station, 25 miles upstream from Fredericksburg.

Western Theater Food is running out in Vicksburg. Pemberton orders the seizure of all private stocks of provisions, and organizes rationing for the garrison and civilian population alike. The ration for each soldier is 5 oz of peas, 10 oz of meal, 8 oz of beef (including bones), plus small quantities of lard, sugar, soap, and salt.

Friday, June 5
Eastern Theater Stuart puts on a great cavalry review, culminating in a mock battle calculated to impress the local ladies. Delighted with the show, Stuart decides to keep his 10,000 horsemen together and repeat the performance when Lee arrives on Monday. At Fredericksburg three Union regiments probe the Confederate lines. The ensuing skirmish, christened the battle of Franklin's crossing, proves that Lee's trenches are still strongly held. The Confederate commander delayed his departure from Fredericksburg until he was sure the Union attack was merely a demonstration to test his strength.

Saturday, June 6
Eastern Theater Lincoln is at odds with General Hooker over Union strategy. The president wants Hooker to go after Lee if the Confederates invade the North, but "Fighting Joe" argues for a counter-invasion of Virginia. Had they but known, Lee has already told his corps commanders that a Union advance on Richmond would force him back to the defense of the Confederate capital. However, Hooker's credibility has still not recovered from the Chancellorsville fiasco. The Army of the Potomac will dance to Lee's tune.

Sunday, June 7
Western Theater A small Union force at Milliken's Bend, 20 miles upstream from Vicksburg, is attacked by Taylor's Confederates from Arkansas. The garrison consists of the 23rd Iowa Regiment and three regiments of black troops, only recruited in the last few weeks. The

BALTIMORE PIKE

CEMETARY HILL

CODORI HOUSE

TROSTLE FARM

EMMITSBURG ROAD

CONFEDERATES SEIZE WHEATFIELD

PEACH ORCHARD

ROSE HOUSE

Federals are driven from their defenses down to the levee, but the Union ironclad *Choctaw* saves the day by firing over 100 rounds of heavy shell into the Confederates. Although the ironclad cannot see its target due to the intervening bank, Union troops on the shore direct the fire with surprising accuracy. The Confederates retreat with 125 killed and 400 wounded. Union losses are proportionately heavy: 154 killed and 223 wounded in a savage battle in which no quarter was given.

Monday, June 8

Eastern Theater Jeb Stuart's cavalry are reviewed by General Lee, but they are soon to have a rather different audience. The Army of the Potomac's cavalry, now under the command of General Alfred Pleasanton, plan a large-scale raid for tomorrow.

Tuesday, June 9

Eastern Theater On a fine misty morning, the Union cavalry crosses the Rappahannock and drives in Stuart's picket line. Some 11,000 Federal troopers surge from the riverbank toward Brandy Station, and Stuart counter-attacks with a similar number of horsemen. It is the greatest cavalry fight of the war and the Union cavalry come within an ace of overrunning Stuart's headquarters. But the Confederates hold their ground and reports of Confederate infantry arriving lead Pleasanton to withdraw. However, the Union troopers know they have held their own against Stuart's cavalry on their home ground, and their confidence soars.

Wednesday, June 10

Eastern Theater Ewell's II Corps departs Culpeper and heads along the Rappahannock, intending to advance north up the Shenandoah Valley.
Naval Operations The Union vessel *Maple Leaf*, shipping Confederate prisoners from Fort Monroe to Fort Delaware, is forced ashore by its unwilling passengers at Cape Henry, Virginia. The prisoners then make good their escape.

Thursday, June 11

The North Ohio Democrats nominate Clement Vallandigham for governor. Their candidate, already weary of life with his Confederate allies, has now gone into exile in Canada.

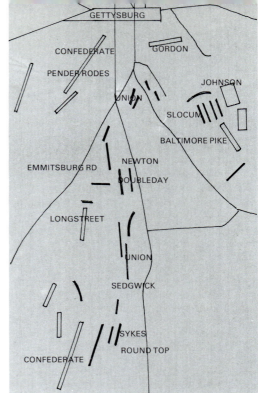

The three-day Battle of Gettysburg, fought from July 1 to July 3, 1863, between the Confederates under Lee and the Union forces under Meade, was a crucial turning point in the war, yet both sides stumbled across each other almost by chance.

It was Lee's second and final invasion of the North, and with the defeat of the Confederate forces, the South was forced over to the defensive.

The inset map shows the Confederate forces in their last-ditch throw at the Union lines on the afternoon of July 3.

Western Theater A cool and pleasant break in the weather at Vicksburg is spoiled for the Confederates by the arrival of two 10-inch Columbiads within 100 yards of the rebel trenches. Union guns now bombard the city daily, and many citizens live an underground existence in caves where they are safe from the shelling.

Friday, June 12

The North Rumors of another Southern invasion fly around communities north of the Potomac. Governor Curtin of Pennsylvania calls out the State Militia and requests assistance from New York State. Response to the creation of a militia corps is dismal, and refugees trickle northward to escape the fighting. Pennsylvania is denied Federal aid but New York supplies 26 regiments of State Guard from June 15 to July 3.
Eastern Theater Ewell's 23,000 men and 20 artillery batteries take 18 hours to pass through the defile of Chester Gap, but the move remains undetected by the Union cavalry. A reinforced Federal division sits unperturbed at Winchester. Its commander, Major General Robert H. Milroy, refuses to withdraw to Harper's Ferry, believing he is opposed by only a couple of cavalry brigades.

Saturday, June 13

Eastern Theater Milroy is staggered when leading elements of Ewell's corps attack the positions in what becomes known as the second battle of Winchester. The Federal lines are driven in but Milroy makes no attempt to withdraw.

CONFEDERATES UNDER EARLY DRIVEN BACK

CEMETARY RIDGE

CONFEDERATES ATTACK CENTER OF UNION LINE

TANEYTOWN ROAD

CONFEDERATES PROBE GAP IN UNION LINE

LITTLE ROUND TOP

DEVIL'S DEN

PLUM RUN

ROUND TOP

June 1863

Sunday, June 14, 1863

Eastern Theater Lee and Longstreet cross the Potomac near Sharpsburg. In the Shenandoah Valley, meanwhile, Ewell surrounds Winchester during the night.

Western Theater General Banks makes a second assault on the defenses of Port Hudson. His besieging army is suffering steady attrition, from sickness rather than enemy action, and Taylor's Confederate forces now threaten his communications on the west bank of the Mississippi. The Federals attack at dawn, preceded by an hour-long intensive cannonade. Brigadier-General Thomas Sherman's division is led by his second-in-command, Brigadier-General William Dwight, as Sherman is still incapacitated by his wound received during the assault on May 27. Dwight's men are misdirected by their guides and fail to make any progress. Brigadier-General Paine's division breaks into the rebel trenches, but Paine falls at the head of his troops, severely wounded. Intense Confederate musketry repels the attack. Banks' XIX Corps has now suffered 4000 casualties in its two assaults. The siege must continue.

Monday, June 15

Eastern Theater Ewell attacks Winchester just before dawn and overruns Milroy's 9000 troops, capturing half of them, and considerable quantities of booty. This includes 300 wagons, 300 horses, and 200,000 rounds of rifle ammunition. Rodes' division chases away Federal detachments at Berryville and Bunker Hill. Ewell's cavalry crosses the Potomac at Williamsport and penetrates Pennsylvania as far as Chambersburg. General Hooker marches the Army of the Potomac to Fairfax Court House, Virginia, abandoning the line of the Rappahannock. In blistering weather the army tramps along dusty roads in what will be remembered by many veterans as the worst march of the war.

Occupying a line from Leesburg to Thoroughfare Gap, Hooker sits and waits for Lee to attack him.

Western Theater Soldiers of the 27th Louisiana Regiment are enduring another sultry day in the Vicksburg trenches when a Union regiment launches a raid. The attackers are met with a hot fire, enfiladed by a rifled cannon, and driven back to their own lines.

Tuesday, June 16

Eastern Theater Hill and Longstreet's corps head northwest along the Shenandoah. Longstreet advances through the foothills east of Blue Ridge, while Hill follows Ewell's route through Chester Gap and on to Front Royal and Berryville.

Western Theater A continued flow of reinforcements brings Grant's strength to 77,000. Fewer than 30,000 Confederates are holding Vicksburg.

Wednesday, June 17

Naval Operations The latest Confederate ironclad, the CSS *Atlanta*, heads down the Savannah River into Wassaw Sound. She was originally an English blockade runner, the *Fingal*, which had landed 10,000 Enfield rifles and a million rounds of ammunition back in November 1861. Bottled up by Union warships, she was converted into an ironclad along the lines of the *Merrimac* in order to protect the city against a Union amphibious assault. Money was raised from many quarters and the ladies of Savannah sold their jewelry to finance her construction.

Atlanta's main deck was cut down and she was fitted with a central casemate holding two 7-inch and two 6·4-inch Brooke rifles: one at the bow and stern, and one on each broadside. The casemate was protected by 4 inches of iron over 18 inches of teak, angled at 30 degrees. Dark and poorly ventilated, she was a far cry from the armored leviathan depicted in Northern newspapers, but the addition of a spar torpedo to her deadly ram gave her a fighting chance in a close action.

Accompanied by the wooden gunboat *Isondiga*, the *Atlanta* steams to attack the Union blockaders, but a navigational error grounds her on a sandbar. Two monitors then engage her: USS *Weehawken* and the *Nahant*. *Atlanta* heels over, so her guns cannot depress far enough to fire back. *Weehawken*'s 11-inch Dahlgren fires two rounds, one missing and one scoring a non-penetrative hit from 300 yards. But her 15-inch gun hits three times, even penetrating the armor from an acute angle rather than straight on. One round alone injures 40 crewmen by the blast and splinters. *Atlanta* strikes her colors.

Although not widely reported in the USA, this battle causes enormous concern in the British and French navies: their great ironclad battleships *Warrior* and *Gloire* have little more side armor than *Atlanta* and are clearly vulnerable to the giant 15-inch guns of the Federal monitors.

Thursday, June 18

Western Theater Major-General John A. McClernland is relieved of his command for leaking an order of congratulations to his XIII Corps. This awards all the credit for the Vicksburg operations to his own men and, as Sherman observes, is intended for the Illinois voters. One of the archetypal political generals, his poor performance at Shiloh helped persuade Lincoln to allow him to stay in the North to recruit troops. McClernland believed he would lead them against Vicksburg and never forgave Lincoln for subordinating him to Grant. A standing War Department regulation stipulates that any papers released to the press must go through army headquarters. Grant has his excuse and replaces McClernland with E.O.C. Ord.

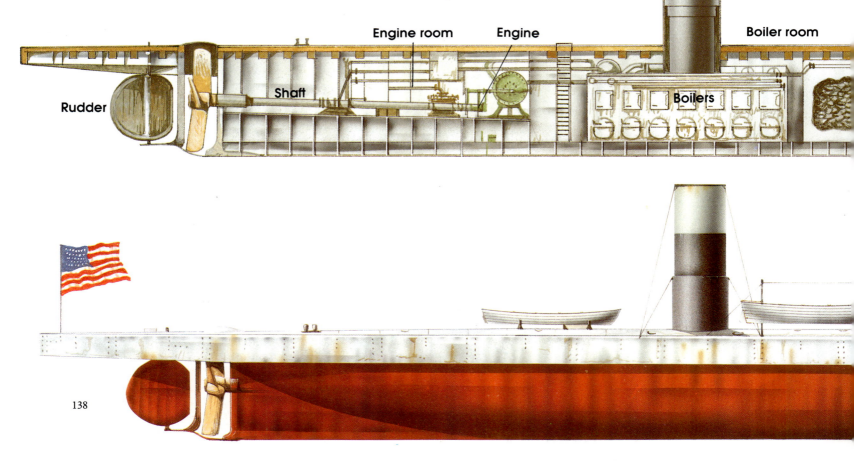

Friday, June 19

Eastern Theater Lee's three army corps continue to advance northward, while the Army of the Potomac waits to see which way the Confederates will turn. The rival cavalry formations are now clashing regularly, probing for the information their commanders need. At Middlesburg there is a fierce cavalry action.

Saturday, June 20

The North Concerned citizens in Baltimore begin to construct field works around the city to defend it against Confederate raiders.

Western Theater Grant's artillery continues to pound the defenses of Vicksburg. At La Forche crossing, Louisiana, elements of Taylor's 4000-strong Confederate force is driven off by a Federal detachment under the command of Lieutenant-Colonel Albert Stickney. Taylor's troops suffer 53 killed and 150 wounded, Union losses are eight dead and 40 injured.

Trans-Mississippi Union troops skirmish with Indians at Government Springs, Utah Territory.

Sunday, June 21

Eastern Theater Further cavalry skirmishes occur as both sides attempt to penetrate the other's outposts. There is a fierce fight at Upperville, before Stuart withdraws through Ashby's Gap. Lee orders Ewell to take Harrisburg, state capital of Pennsylvania.

Monday, June 22

Eastern Theater Stuart's cavalry blocks Ashby's and Snicker's Gaps to prevent the Federals discovering the location and activity of the main Confederate forces. Lee's main body rests today on the Shenandoah at Berryville.

Tuesday, June 23

Eastern Theater Seated under a tree in a driving rainstorm at midnight, Jeb Stuart receives an order directing him to take three brigades of cavalry, and harry the Union lines of communication. Whether he cuts in front of the Federals when they move north, or sweeps right around behind them, is left to his discretion. Lee simply stipulates that he must rejoin the main army at York in four days' time.

Western Theater Since the battle of Stones River in January, Rosecrans' Union Army has remained at Murfreesboro, Tennessee. Now fielding 40,000 infantry and 7000 cavalry, Rosecrans is faced by Bragg's 30,000 infantry and 13,000 horsemen. The Confederates have half their force in extensive field works south of Murfreesboro on the Duck River at Shelbyville. The rest occupy equally formidable defenses at Tullahoma, 18 miles to the southeast on the Nashville–Chattanooga railroad. Rosecrans orders his three army corps to march, preceded by his cavalry, which swings southwest.

Wednesday, June 24

Eastern Theater Stuart assembles his three brigades at Salem. Lee retains two cavalry brigades to cover the gaps and shield the army as it crosses the Potomac.

Western Theater Rosecrans' cavalry advances boldly on Shelbyville, as if screening the main force. That night it halts within view of the Confederates and lights masses of camp fires behind it to simulate the arrival of Rosecrans' infantry. Meanwhile, two of Rosecrans' army corps march directly on Tullahoma and one heads into the uplands to the east.

Thursday, June 25

Eastern Theater Stuart unexpectedly runs into Hancock's II Corps which is on the march toward Frederick. The Army of the Potomac has started to move! Stuart dispatches a messenger but he never arrives, and Lee remains ignorant of Hooker's actions. Hooker is actually locked into a bitter fight with Halleck and Stanton, who are refusing him reinforcements to replace the men prostrated by marching in the heat, and the loss of 20,000 short-term troops who had left the army since Chancellorsville.

Western Theater Drenching rains transform the roads into rivers of mud in Tennessee. Rosecrans' ruse has worked and Bragg's troops at Shelbyville remain in place.

Friday, June 26

Eastern Theater Jubal Early's division of Ewell's II Corps enters Gettysburg on its way to York and Wrightsville where Lee wanted Early to take the bridge over the Susquehanna. Early demands that the town officials supply him with several tons of provisions, plus 1000 pairs of shoes and 500 hats, or pay him $10,000 cash. The officials plead poverty and simply open the stores, but Early does not insist on the requisition and his troops pass through.

Saturday, June 27

Eastern Theater Hooker resigns in protest at Halleck and Stanton's refusal to let him withdraw the garrison at Harper's Ferry. The dispute is merely a symptom of the deep antipathy between the general and Washington. Only Secretary Chase seems prepared to allow Hooker to command in another major battle—others cannot forget Hooker's loss of nerve at Chancellorsville. The resignation, made in a fiery rage, is accepted with bland courtesy. During the night, General George Meade is woken by a War Department messenger and told that he now commands the Army of the Potomac.

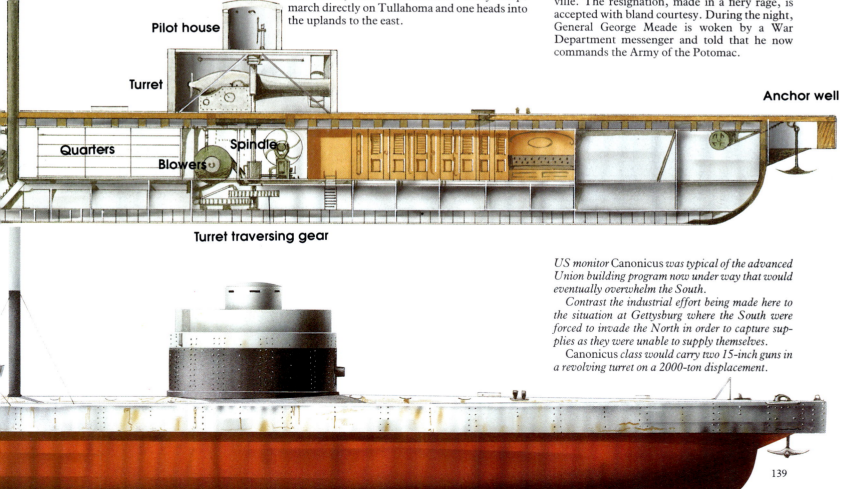

Pilot house

Turret

Anchor well

Quarters

Spindle

Blowers

Turret traversing gear

US monitor Canonicus *was typical of the advanced Union building program now under way that would eventually overwhelm the South.*

Contrast the industrial effort being made here to the situation at Gettysburg where the South were forced to invade the North in order to capture supplies as they were unable to supply themselves.

Canonicus *class would carry two 15-inch guns in a revolving turret on a 2000-ton displacement.*

139

June–July 1863

Sunday, June 28, 1863

Eastern Theater A Confederate scout reaches Longstreet's headquarters during the evening with detailed news of Union troop movements. He had been drinking with Federal officers in Washington, then followed the Army of the Potomac on its march to Frederick, Maryland. Lee learns of Hooker's resignation.

Western Theater 1500 Texans from Taylor's Confederate force attack Donaldsonville, Mississippi, but are repulsed by the 200-strong garrison under Major J.D. Bulle, 28th Maine. The citizens of New Orleans rejoice loudly to hear that rebel forces are within a few miles of the city, but firm leadership by General Emory prevents any serious threat to Union control.

Monday, June 29

Eastern Theater Meade sets the Army of the Potomac back on the road. He heads for Harrisburg, intending to fight Lee before the Confederates can cross the Susquehanna. Stuart's cavalry passes through Westminster, having paroled their prisoners but retained the captured wagons. After a sharp skirmish against a squadron of Delaware horse he reaches Union Mills. Now he knows the Union Army is on the move, Lee sends messengers ordering his army corps to concentrate at Cashtown, Pennsylvania.

Western Theater Rosecrans' advance continues with a series of minor actions as his army nears Bragg's entrenched positions.

Tuesday, June 30

The North President Lincoln comes under intense pressure to place General McClellan back in command of the Army of the Potomac; but he refuses to change his mind.

Eastern Theater Lee's reaction to the Federal advance is unknown to Stuart, whose exhausted troopers cover another 70 miles today and fight Kilpatrick's Union cavalry division at Hannover, Pennsylvania. As Lee's army advances on Cashtown, Heth's division of A.P. Hill's III Corps sends a brigade down the road to Gettysburg where a cache of shoes has been reported. The Confederates encounter Brigadier-General John Buford's Union cavalry division and withdraw.

Western Theater His entrenchments at Tullahoma now turned by the advance of Rosecrans' army, Braxton Bragg retreats his troops across the Tennessee River to defend Chattanooga. General Rosecrans has achieved a bloodless strategic victory.

Wednesday, July 1, 1863

Eastern Theater Assuming the Gettysburg garrison must be militia, not regulars as his brigade commander reports, Heth's division advances on the town to secure the much-needed shoes, and runs into the Union picket line at 7.00 a.m. Promised infantry support from Reynold's I Corps, Buford's 2500 cavalry, fight a dismounted action to hold their ground. Just as their line begins to give way, Union infantry arrive, delivering a surprise attack which overruns Archer's Confederate brigade, capturing Brigadier-General Archer and 1000 rebel troops. But as Reynolds supervises the deployment of

the Iron Brigade, he is shot in the head by a Confederate sniper. His death, at 43, deprives the Union of one of its most promising officers. His second-in-command, Major-General Doubleday, conducts a brilliant defensive action against increasing numbers of Confederates.

The ill-fated XI Corps, still under a cloud after its collapse at Chancellorsville, arrives to support I Corps but is ignominiously defeated once again. Ultimately, 22,000 Confederate troops are engaged against 16,500 Union soldiers, of which 4000 become casualties and 5000 are captured. By nightfall both sides have concentrated the greater part of their strength around Gettysburg, and it seems that the superiority of Lee's soldiers remains as great as ever.

After dark, eight selected Confederate horsemen fan out along different roads to locate Stuart.

Thursday, July 2

Eastern Theater Confident in the individual superiority of his troops, Lee abandons his plan to fight a defensive action and attacks the Union line. By noon the full strength of the Army of Northern Virginia is engaged—against the fully concentrated Army of the Potomac, of which some units, like Sedgwick's VI Corps, have marched 30 miles through the night to get there. Longstreet is unhappy with the change of plan, yet leads 15,000 men to attack Meade's left flank. Faced by 30,000 Federals, his assault comes within an ace of taking Little Round Top from where Confederate cannon could have enfiladed the Union position. Ewell attacks the Federal right late in the afternoon, and also comes very near to breaking through. By nightfall the Union defense is confused and disorganized, with units muddled up and the chain of command unclear. Major-General Sickles' III Corps is badly mauled in its forward position and the "Dutchmen" of XI Corps take to their heels again.

Stuart is found at Carlisle by one of Lee's messengers and races his tired troopers to the battlefield, arriving at 11.00 p.m. Lee's chief of staff argues that Stuart has flagrantly disobeyed orders and should be shot.

Friday, July 3

Eastern Theater Distracted by dysentery, Lee makes the greatest error of his career. Believing Meade will have weakened his center to defeat the heavy attacks on his flanks, Lee plans to assault the heart of the Federal position. But contrary to the Confederate commander's expectations, the Union troops are not demoralized. Although the Federals have so far suffered heavier losses, the 25,000 men of Slocum's XII

and Sedgwick's VI Corps have not been engaged, and Meade now outnumbers Lee by 85,000 to 75,000.

At 1.00 p.m. 150 Confederate guns open fire on the Union center. After two hours, their ammunition runs low and the infantry assault begins. Major-General Pickett's division of Longstreet's corps leads what becomes the most famous charge in American history. The division meets a storm of fire. Although the heroic assault is pressed home to bayonet point, Pickett's men are outnumbered and outgunned: of the 13,000 men engaged, some 7000 are killed or wounded, and the division is driven back in disorder.

With typical greatness of spirit, Lee takes his hat off and rides among the beaten soldiers as they stream back from Seminary Ridge. "This was all my fault," he says. "It is I that have lost this fight, and you must help me out of it the best you can."

Western Theater At 10.30 a.m. two horsemen approach Vicksburg into the Union lines. Pemberton offers to capitulate. Grant demands unconditional surrender but the Confederate commander holds out for his men to be paroled rather than become prisoners of war. He knows from intercepted messages that to transport 30,000 prisoners up the Mississippi would place an impossible burden on Porter's river fleet. Grant accepts, and agrees to a formal surrender on Independence Day tomorrow.

Saturday, July 4

Eastern Theater The armies face each other at Gettysburg but neither side attempts any action. That night Lee accepts the inevitable and orders a withdrawal. Over the last three days the Army of the Potomac has sustained 23,000 casualties,

The bizarre rock formations at Devil's Den were a strange feature of Gettysburg: a tangled mass of giant boulders jutting out of the Pennsylvania farmland. Devil's Den was captured after bitter fighting, then sharpshooters from Arkansas and Texas regiments sniped at the Union positions on Little Round Top throughout the second day. This dead Confederate lies behind an improvised stone breastwork, but the careful placing of his rifle suggests the photographer rearranged the subject and his equipment.

and the Army of Northern Virginia 22,000. Of the men who marched into battle around this small Pennsylvania town, one in four lie dead or wounded.

Western Theater Vicksburg surrenders. Grant's campaign has been a dazzling success. Surprising Pemberton by his ability to break loose from his supply lines, Grant concentrated his army to outnumber the Confederates at each decisive encounter, even when the Southern forces had overall superiority. Coming hard on the heels of the disaster at Gettysburg, Pemberton's surrender is a bitter blow for the South.

Sunday, July 5

Eastern Theater Lee's troops retreat, untroubled by any serious attempt at pursuit by the Army of the Potomac.

Western Theater The defenders of Vicksburg are paroled, agreeing not to bear arms against the Union again until exchanged for a Federal prisoner. A Union detachment at Lebanon, Kentucky, is overrun by 2500 mounted infantry under Brigadier-General John H. Morgan. Detached by Braxton Bragg to cover his retreat by threatening Louisville, Morgan has more ambitious plans for his brigade.

Monday, July 6

Eastern Theater Buford's cavalry skirmishes with Lee's advance guard at Williamsport, Maryland. The main body of Meade's army begins to leave Gettysburg and follow the retreating Confederates.

Tuesday, July 7

Eastern Theater The Army of Northern Virginia digs in at Hagerstown. The Potomac, swollen by heavy rain, is too high to cross.

Western Theater Braxton Bragg concentrates his army at Chattanooga after his withdrawal from Tennessee. Meanwhile, at Port Hudson, the Union forces have driven a saphead to within 16 feet of the Confederate trenches, and a 1000-man storming party is ready to assault. Then the news of Vicksburg arrives and the attack is called off. There is no need for it now.

Wednesday, July 8

Eastern Theater The first train-loads of wounded are shipped out of Gettysburg. Local farmers charge exhorbitant rates to carry wounded men to the station, and the railroad company dumps the injured in filthy cattle cars. Army medical officers protest vehemently and this appalling behavior is soon checked.

Western Theater Port Hudson surrenders. By order of General Banks, General Gardner's sword is returned to him in recognition of his brave defense. Of the 6000 defenders, only half were still fit to be in the line, and supplies of food and ammunition were all but exhausted. They also surrender 20 cannon and 7500 rifles.

Thursday, July 9

Western Theater Eluding Union troops now in pursuit, Morgan's raiders reach Brandenburg on the Ohio and cross over in two captured steamboats. By midnight his men are in Indiana.

Confederate prisoners taken at Gettysburg. Both sides lost about 5000 men missing and taken prisoner, and it is often forgotten that Lee's army marched back to Virginia with a long column of Union prisoners. Yet the simultaneous defeats at Gettysburg and Vicksburg did not augur well for the future of the Confederacy.

Friday, July 10

Eastern Theater There are several minor actions as the Army of the Potomac regains contact with Lee's Confederates, now concentrated around Williamsport, Maryland. Confederate wounded are shipped over the river, along with some 4000 Union prisoners taken at Gettysburg.

Saturday, July 11

Eastern Theater Meade begins to organize the Army of the Potomac to attack Lee's positions before the Confederates can withdrawn across the Potomac.

July 1863

Sunday, July 12, 1863

Eastern Theater Advancing on a six-mile front, the Army of the Potomac finally runs into Lee's outpost line. The Confederates are dug in with their backs to the Potomac. The situation is similar to that before Antietam—indeed, they are only a few miles from the battlefield. Meade baulks at ordering an assault, despite his superior numbers.

Monday, July 13

The North The first names drawn in the draft in New York include O'Reilly, McGuire, O'Shaugnessy, and McManus. Irishmen are incensed at what they see as blatant discrimination. Feelings are already running high as some political leaders, including the newly elected Democratic governor, Horatio Seymour, have linked opposition to the draft with fears over emancipation. By playing on worries that Irishmen would go to war only to return and find their jobs taken by blacks, Seymour and his associates help create a climate of race hatred. Long standing racial tension has also been exacerbated by some major employers using blacks as strike-breakers earlier in the year. What begins as a mob protesting the Federal Enrollment Act turns into the ugliest race riot in American history. The draft office is burned down, followed by several public buildings and the houses of prominent Republicans. Then the rioters turn on local blacks, lynching any they can find.

Eastern Theater During the night the main body of the Army of Northern Virginia crosses the subsiding Potomac, leaving its campfires burning to deceive the Union forces.

Tuesday, July 14

The North The rioting continues in New York, with several hundred already reported dead. Blacks are hanged from lampposts or burned in their houses. Widespread looting cannot be stopped, and troops are summoned from the Army of the Potomac.

Eastern Theater Meade finally orders his men forward, only to find that the Confederate positions around Williamsport are held by a small rear guard. The Federals overrun it and capture some wounded and a few stragglers. Brigadier-General James Pettigrew, whose brigade had opened the battle of Gettysburg, is killed in this last skirmish of the campaign. Lincoln is furious at Meade for allowing the beaten Confederates to escape so easily. "We had them within our grasp," he rails. "We had only to stretch forth our hands and they were ours."

Wednesday, July 15

The North The New York riots are finally quelled by armed troops. The majority of the 1000 slain die at the hands of the army, who fire rifles into the mob. The Irish community never forgives the government for this outrage and opposition to the draft will continue. Relations between the blacks and the Irish could not be worse.

Eastern Theater The Army of Northern Virginia withdraws along the Shenandoah Valley.

Thursday, July 16

The North Morgan's brigade raids through southern Indiana, robbing a bank with a loaded 12-pounder Napoleon, and pillaging freely. His men burn bridges and steal horses as they press on into Ohio. Union forces are now scouring the area for him.

Western Theater General Johnston withdraws his Confederate forces from Jackson, Mississippi, after Sherman advances on the town with elements of the victorious Union Army from Vicksburg.

Friday, July 17

The North Feinting toward Hamilton, Morgan's raiders ride through the suburbs of Cincinnati, heading east for the Ohio River.

Eastern Theater Major-General Quincy Gillmore's X Corps, deployed on Morris Island outside Charleston, bombard Battery Wagner, a Confederate redoubt on the north end, 2600 yards from Fort Sumter. If they can take the position, siege guns can begin the reduction of Fort Sumter.

Saturday, July 18

Eastern Theater In the early evening 5000 Union troops assault Battery Wagner, which is held by 1000 of the 8500 Confederate soldiers deployed under Beauregard for the defense of Charleston. The bombardment ceases when further fire would endanger the advancing troops, but Confederate riflemen issue forth from underground bunkers and shoot down the attackers at pointblank range. The assault is led by Brigadier-General George C. Strong, who is mortally wounded at the head of his brigade. After two hours of desperate fighting, the Union troops capture the southeast corner of the redoubt, but they are ejected at nightfall. The 1515 Union casualties include the divisional commander, Brigadier-General Truman Seymour, who is wounded, and six out of ten regimental commanders. Colonel Robert Shaw dies leading the 54th Massachusetts, one of two colored regiments present. Confederate losses are 174.

Western Theater Morgan reaches the bank of the Ohio near Buffington Bar during the evening. Federal troops are closing in on his tiring troops.

Below: *At the start of the war the South had no regular warships it could let loose on Northern merchant vessels, so a thriving trade in privateering, carried out by privately owned vessels operating with a letter of marque given by the Confederate Government, was started up by Southern businessmen. One such early example was the former tug Calhoun, which netted $27,000 for her owners during her first cruise.*

The South was the only nation still to operate privateers, as it has been abolished by European powers in 1856.

Sunday, July 19

Eastern Theater The Army of the Potomac finally crosses over at Harper's Ferry in pursuit of Lee.

Western Theater Morgan's brigade is cut to pieces by superior Union forces. Some 120 of the raiders are killed and 700 captured. Morgan himself escapes with 300 riders. Reaching the West Virginia shore, he then heads north for Pennsylvania.

Monday, July 20

The North New York is quiet after the suppression of the riots. Merchants meet to organize compensation for the black victims.

Eastern Theatre Meade's advance guard occupies the passes through the Blue Ridge Mountains.

Tuesday, July 21

Eastern Theater Meade deploys the army to assault Manassas Gap and batter his way into the Shenandoah to intercept Lee's retreating columns.

Wednesday, July 22

Eastern Theater Elements of the Union III Corps attack at Manassas but fail to make rapid progress against a Confederate rear guard. Meanwhile, Lee's rear guard, Longstreet and Hill, slip away along the Shenandoah Valley. Once again, the tardy Federal pursuit has failed to achieve anything.

Thursday, July 23

Western Theater Morgan's surviving raiders spend over 20 hours in the saddle in a frantic attempt to shake off Union pursuit.

Friday, July 24

Far West Since the defeat of the Sioux Indians in Minnesota during the fall of 1862, the most implacable Indian bands have retreated to the Dakota Territory. Today part of the forces pursuing them intercept a large group of Sioux near what will later become Bismarck, North Dakota. The 1st Minnesota Mounted Rangers, three volunteer infantry regiments, and an artillery battery are engaged all day, the Indians breaking off the fight at nightfall.

Saturday, July 25

Eastern Theater Union siege artillery continues the reduction of Battery Wagner, supported by ironclad warships. As usual, the ability of earthworks to withstand shellfire proves much greater than pre-war artillerists had predicted. The Confederates have several hundred cannon deployed around Charleston, and the Union trenches receive their share of fire too.

Far West The Minnesota Mounted Rangers pursue the beaten Indians.

Below: *Confederate raider* Georgia *was a fast, screw, iron merchant ship typical of the newer types entering service during the 1860s. Although not a success as a raider, her exploits occupied the attention of numerous Union warships. Off the coast of Morocco she was in action against a group of hostile Arabs, the only time the Confederacy became involved in combat with a foreign power.*

Bottom: *The unique, privately funded submarine* Pioneer *was intended for use as a privateer, the only time a submarine was ever put to such use. Her owners were to be paid 20 percent of the value of any warship sunk.*

Her hull survived the war, and in 1952 was set up in the Presbytere Arcade, Louisiana State Musuem.

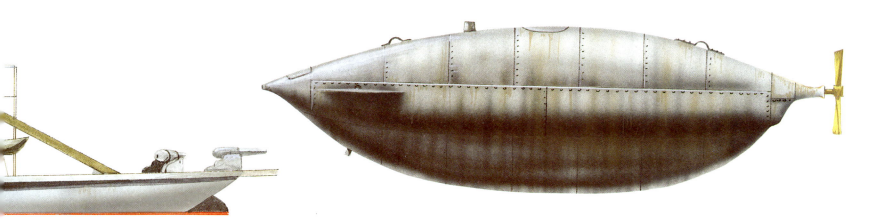

July–August 1863

Sunday, July 26, 1863

Western Theater John Morgan and his surviving raiders are cornered at New Lisbon, Ohio. As nothing came of the hopes of a copperhead rising in support of the Confederates, Morgan's men were left to face overwhelmingly superior Union forces. Morgan and his officers are sent to Ohio State Penitentiary.

The South Elder statesman Sam Houston dies in retirement at Huntsville, Texas. He had opposed secession. John J. Crittenden dies in Kentucky; he had fought hard to keep the state in the Union, but opposed many government policies, including emancipation. At his death he has one son in the Union Army and one in the Confederate.

Far West The 1st Minnesota Mounted Rangers overrun a Sioux village at Dead Buffalo Lake. The warriors fall back in front of them, observing but not attacking.

Monday, July 27

Western Theater Minor actions occur at Rogersville, Kentucky, Cassville, Missouri, and Bridgeport, Alabama.

Far West Reunited and marching toward Stony Lake, the brigade is attacked by a large force of Sioux. Mounted warriors rush the head of the column but are driven back by volley fire, and withdraw. They do not renew their attack, but turn away and travel toward Missouri. The Union troops reach Stony Lake, then return to Minnesota.

Tuesday, July 28

Eastern Theater Confederate partisan leader John S. Mosby commences a series of guerrilla-style tip and run raids in the rear of the Army of the Potomac. His elusive cavalry plague Union outposts around Fairfax Court House and Aldie, Virginia.

Wednesday, July 29

Eastern Theater Colonel Edward W. Serrell, Volunteer Engineers, finalizes his plans to build a battery in the marshes of Morris Island to bombard the city of Charleston. Union troops now occupy all of the four-mile long island, except the northern tip, which is defended by the Confederate Battery Wagner.

Great Britain Addressing the British Parliament, Her Majesty Queen Victoria restates the British Government's policy of strict neutrality. Fear in some quarters that the Federal Government regards Britain as pro-Confederate has led

to pressure for intervention, but few major political leaders oppose the neutrality policy. The continuing French involvement in Mexico is widely welcomed by the British who regard it as a useful counterweight to American power.

Thursday, July 30

The North President Lincoln retaliates to Confederate threats against black troops and their white officers in Union service. President Davis has announced that captured black troops will be handed over to State authorities. Since it is a capital offense for a black man to bear arms, their fate is fairly obvious. Davis had also threatened legal action against the white officers. Lincoln's statement today promises to shoot one Confederate prisoner for every Union soldier executed as a result of Davis's policy, and one rebel prisoner will be put to hard labor for every Federal black prisoner of war sold back into slavery.

Western Theater Minor skirmishes continue, with actions at Lexington and Marshall, Missouri, Grand Junction, Tennessee, and Barnwell's Island, South Carolina.

Friday, July 31

Eastern Theater With the main armies returned to their traditional lines, cavalry outposts once again face each other along the Rappahannock.

Western Theater Skirmishes occur at Paint Lick Bridge, Kentucky, and St Catherine's Creek near Natchez, Mississippi.

Saturday, August 1, 1863

The North The Federal IV and VII Army Corps are disbanded. The Confederate spy Belle Boyd is imprisoned in Washington after her arrest at Martinsburg, West Virginia.

The South President Davis offers an amnesty to Confederate soldiers absent without leave. The chronic desertion rate in the Southern armies has to be arrested soon or the already large Union forces will be unbeatable. In fact, the Union armies have similar problems.

Eastern Theater Buford's cavalry engages Confederate pickets along the Rappahannock, with actions again at Brandy Station and Kelly's Ford. Union losses are 16 dead and 134 wounded. Meanwhile, Federal troops begin a week-long penetration of the country between the Blue Ridge Mountains and Bull Run.

Western Theater A small Federal column advances from Columbus to Hickman, Kentucky, and there is a skirmish at Smith's Shoals on the Cumberland River.

Sunday, August 2

Eastern Theater Colonel Serell submits his technical plans for the construction of a battery to fire on Charleston. His experiments on the swampy ground have established that there is a suitable area which can bear up to 600 pounds per square foot. By building foundations of sandbags at the end of a two and a half mile trestle-work roadway, Serrell calculates he can raise a firing platform for one heavy cannon. Charleston is 7900 yards away—long-range, even for a large-caliber rifle. Skirmishing continues between the rival outpost lines along the Rappahannock River.

Monday, August 3

Eastern Theater Union troops begin construction of the road across the marsh of Morris Island, near Charleston.

Western Theater The Union IX Corps leaves Vicksburg for Kentucky.

Tuesday, August 4

Eastern Theater The Union engineers come under long-range fire from Confederate batteries of James Island. They plan to build a dummy battery alongside the real one to distract the attention of the Confederate gunners. Outpost battles continue along the Rappahannock, with skirmishes at Brandy Station and Fairfax Court House. Meanwhile, a small Federal amphibious force probes up the James River.

The large-caliber bullets fired by Civil War rifles inflicted wounds to which contemporary medicine had only one answer. This is an amputation tent at Gettysburg. The field hospitals established there were busy until August and the last patients were not discharged until November.

Union and Confederate dead lie in the baking July heat at Gettysburg. Governor Curtin of Pennsylvania visited the battlefield a week after the fighting and immediately ordered the purchase of land for a national cemetery. But by President Lincoln's visit in November, the cemetery was still only a quarter completed. The local contractor charged $1.59 per body but could move only 100 per day.

Wednesday, August 5

Eastern Theater The foundation of Serrell's battery is sunk into the marsh. The engineers need to drive piles 20 feet down through the mud to reach the sand substratum. It takes 30 men to sink each pole. The Confederates continue to strengthen their works at Charleston, concentrating on Fort Sumter and Battery Wagner.

Federal cavalry under William W. Averell raid Confederate territory in West Virginia, skirmishing today at Cold Spring Gap. More minor actions take place at Little Washington and Muddy Run, Virginia. The sidewheel ferry USS *Commodore Barney* is damaged by an electric torpedo near Dutch Gap, Virginia.

Thursday, August 6

The North Following President Lincoln's proclamation, today is a day of thanksgiving for the succession of Union victories. Business is suspended in favor of church services in many cities.

Eastern Theater Mosby's guerrilla raid continues; his men seize a Union wagon-train near Fairfax Court House.

Naval Operations CSS *Alabama* captures the Federal bark *Sea Bride* off the Cape of Good Hope. Semmes now plans to sail into the Indian Ocean.

Friday, August 7

The North President Lincoln refuses Governor Seymour of New York's request to suspend the draft in the city.

Western Theater There is a small skirmish at New Madrid, Missouri.

Saturday, August 8

Eastern Theater Still in poor health, Robert E. Lee offers his resignation as commander of the Army of Northern Virginia. He takes full responsibility for the defeat at Gettysburg and makes not the slightest attempt to blame any of his subordinates. President Davis refuses Lee's request, recognizing that the Confederacy's only hope of survival now lies with Lee's generalship.

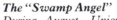

The "Swamp Angel"
During August, Union engineers built a gun emplacement on the low-lying swamp known as Morris Island, some four miles outside Charleston. Logs were driven vertically downward by 30-man teams. The logs were slowly forced 20 feet through the soft mud to the sand substratum below. Pine logs were then laid on top, followed by 800 tons of earth in 13,000 sandbags. The 8-inch 200-pounder Parrott rifle was eventually installed on August 17.

145

August 1863

Sunday, August 9, 1863
Eastern Theater Siege operations continue against Battery Wagner, the Confederate redoubt on Morris Island. Union troops have dug two parallel lines of trenches already. During the night they dig another sap—a trench running toward the Confederates—then branch out either side to start a third parallel. From here they can bring the rebel position under close-range fire.

Monday, August 10
Trans-Mississippi A Federal force commanded by General Frederick Steel departs Helena, Arkansas, to march on Little Rock.

Tuesday, August 11
Eastern Theater The defenders of Battery Wagner bombard the Union lines, supported by the remaining guns of Fort Sumter.

Wednesday, August 12
Eastern Theater Union boats armed with naval howitzers picket the streams and inlets surrounding Morris Island to prevent Confederate interference with the construction of the battery aimed at Charleston.

Thursday, August 13
Eastern Theater Battery Wagner's guns continue to duel with the Union heavy cannon dug in on Morris Island. The Confederate position began as a simple field battery covering the south of the island. It now holds 11 guns, of which only two, a pair of 10-inch Columbiads, are capable of effective counter-battery fire. The battery's single 32-pounder rifle burst and cannot be repaired. The rest of the guns are 32-pounder carronades (short cannon designed to repel infantry assaults or sweep a ship's deck at close range), and 12-pounder mortars. Ceaseless labor by the defenders improves the defenses to incorporate a bomb-proof shelter to hold 750 of the 1000-strong garrison.

Friday, August 14
Eastern Theater Serrell's battery is nearing completion. According to his original calculations, 2300 troops would be able to dump enough sandbags onto the sunken foundations to provide a firm firing position.

Saturday, August 15
Eastern Theater Around 13,000 sandbags, weighing 800 tons, are now piled on the foundations of the Union battery on Morris Island. Following Bonaparte's artillery transportation system used in the crossing of the Alps, Serrell prepared to transport the gun across the marsh road on skids.

Sunday, August 16
Western Theater Rosecrans orders the Army of the Cumberland toward the Tennessee River. His delay after the spectacular bloodless victory of the Tullahoma campaign has already led to much official prodding from Washington. But Rosecrans has never yet moved before he is ready, and the results he has achieved once on the march have protected his position from too much interference. Meanwhile, General Burnside marches from Lexington, Kentucky, as part of a combined move on Chattanooga.

BATTERY GLOVER

ASHLEY RIVER

CHARLESTON

BATTERY RAMSAY

WAPPOO CREEK

LIGHTHOUSE CREEK

FORT JOHNSON

BATTERY SIMKINS

FORT SUMTER

VINCENT'S CREEK

SOUTH CHANNEL

MORRIS ISLAND

BATTERY GREGG

BATTERY WAGNER

MARSH BATTERY

CUMMING'S POINT

MAIN SHIP CHANNEL

Monday, August 17

Eastern Theater Some 450 soldiers drag an 8-inch, 200-pounder Parrott rifle into the battery on Morris Island. It is christened the "Swamp Angel." All day soldiers ferry up the huge quantities of powder and shot required for long-range fire on Charleston. Meanwhile, the Union cannon emplaced in the north of the island begin a week-long bombardment of Fort Sumter. By concentrating their fire over such a period, the Union artillery officers hope to prevent any Confederate attempt at repairing the fort. Many of Sumter's cannon have already been removed to safer, sand and log batteries ashore, but the garrison returns fire with the remaining armament. Private John Drury, 1st South Carolina Artillery, replaces the Confederate flag several times until the 80-foot flagstaff is brought down by the bombardment.

Tuesday, August 18

The North President Lincoln tries a few rounds with the new Spencer Repeating Carbine—a weapon which will further increase the technological superiority of the Union forces. Eventually, Spencer will supply over 60,000 of these .52 caliber rifles and carbines.

Wednesday, August 19

Eastern Theater All the Union batteries opposite Battery Wagner are now in action, pounding the sand and log parapet to pieces while mortars drop their bombs into the rear of the Confederate position. The bombardment of Fort Sumter continues, with some 540 rounds striking the old brickwork walls every day.

Thursday, August 20

Trans-Mississippi Colonel "Kit" Carson leads a column against the Navaho Indians in New Mexico territory.

Friday, August 21

Western Theater Rosecrans' forces reach the Tennessee River near Chattanooga. General Gillmore demands Beauregard evacuate Battery Wagner and Fort Sumter or he will fire on Charleston. Beauregard claims this is contrary to the laws of war as he needs several days to evacuate women and children. But by the time the message reaches the Confederate commander, the Union deadline has already expired. During the afternoon, the Union officers hammer in range stakes for the Swamp Angel's gunners to aim by since they cannot see Charleston from the battery itself.

Trans-Mississippi William C. Quantrill leads a gang of 450 raiders against Lawrence, Kansas, a town which has incurred his particular hatred for its strong Union and abolitionist sentiment. Quantrill's band is regarded by many Confederate officers as nothing but a haven for deserters and, although he calls himself a Confederate officer, Quantrill himself has already been outlawed by the Federal authorities. His men burn the town to the ground, killing 150 people and wounding 30 in the process.

Saturday, August 22

Eastern Theater The Swamp Angel opens fire at 1.30 a.m. Emergency bells and whistles from Charleston reveal the shell has struck home. Sixteen rounds are then fired in rapid succession: 12 incendiary rounds filled with combustible fluid of William Parrott's own design, and four packed with "Short's Solidified Greek Fire."

MAGNOLIA   BELVIDERE   DANIEL'S ISLAND   COOPER RIVER

WANDO RIVER

CASTLE PINCKNEY

HADRELL'S POINT

BATTERY BEE

HOG ISLAND CHANNEL

MOUNT PLEASANT

The defenses of Charleston

Clearly shown here is the outer ring of defenses that resisted every effort made by the Union Navy to gain access to the city of Charleston, looked upon by many Northerners as the seat of the rebellion.

As soon as hostilities broke out in 1861, every effort was made to strengthen the defenses, which in many ways had been allowed to run down, but by summer of 1862 any defects had been mostly remedied.

On August 18, 1863 the Union batteries on the north of Morris Island began a seven-day bombardment of Fort Sumter, which reduced the brickwork to rubble. Four days later the 8-inch Parrott rifle, nicknamed the "Swamp Angel," opened fire on the city itself. In addition to Fort Sumter, Charleston's defenses consisted of a number of pre-war batteries in the bay and on shore, supplemented by earthworks built as the threat of a Union assault increased.

Fort Sumter

In the fall of 1862 Sumter's armament included 79 guns, from 8-inch Columbiads in the lower casemates to 32-pounders mounted above the second tier of heavy guns. The fort's armament was sharply reduced after the August bombardment, but during the naval attack on April 7, Sumter engaged the Union warships with the following guns: 2 × 7-inch Brooke rifles; 2 × 9-inch Dahlgrens; 4 × 10-inch and 4 × 8-inch Columbiads; 4 × 8-inch navy guns; 6 banded and rifled 42-pounders; 8 × 32-pounder smoothbores, and 3 of her 7 10-inch sea coast mortars.

Fort Moultrie

A pre-war brick work on Sullivan's Island, this mounted 38 guns en barbette, i.e. the cannon fired over the parapet without overhead protection. During the US Navy's attack, Fort Moultrie engaged the ironclads with: 9 × 8-inch Columbiads; 5 × banded and rifled 32-pounders; 5 × 32-pounder smoothbores; and two 10-inch mortars.

Battery Beauregard

Planned by P.G.T. Beauregard in 1861, this five-gun battery protected Fort Moultrie from the east. It included an 8-inch Columbiad and several 32-pounders.

Battery Wagner

Originally called the "Neck" battery, this open position covered the approach to Fort Sumter. It fell to Union ground assault after a protracted struggle.

Sand Battery

Four sand batteries protected the floating boom across the Sumter channel.

Battery Bee

On the tip of Sullivan's Island, this earthwork included 5 × 10-inch and 1 × 8-inch Columbiads.

Castle Pinckney

An old brick fort designed to beat off wooden warships of the early nineteenth century, this was of little value and its armament of 10 24-pounders could not stop an ironclad.

Fort Johnson

Another old battery, this had just one 32-pounder at the beginning of the siege of Charleston.

SULLIVAN'S ISLAND

FORT MOULTRIE

BATTERY BEAUREGARD

147

August–September 1863

Sunday, August 23, 1863

Eastern Theater Beauregard wrote Gillmore yesterday saying: "Your firing a number of the most destructive missiles ever used in war into the midst of a city taken unawares and filled with sleeping women and children will give you a bad eminence in history." Gillmore replies that the city has been under siege for seven weeks and nothing blocks the retreat of non-combatants. Gunboats are under construction in Charleston and the waterfront is defended by batteries.

The dispute over the ethics of bombarding Charleston is resolved by the Swamp Angel herself when her breech explodes just behind the vent, throwing the barrel forward onto the parapet. They had fired 20 more incendiary rounds but six had exploded in the breech, no doubt contributing to the accident. After the war, the gun is rediscovered among scrap metal at Trenton, New Jersey, and set up on a granite plinth as a monument on the corner of Perry and Cinto streets.

Monday, August 24

Eastern Theater The seven days' shelling of Fort Sumter is over. The commander, Colonel Alfred Rhett, reports he has just one 11-inch Dahlgren left operational. Of the 5009 rounds fired at the fort, roughly half hit home. The brickwork is smashed to powder and the crumbled mass of masonry looks finished as a defensible position.

John Singleton Mosby continues his epic raid in northern Virginia. Large numbers of Union troops search for his men along the Rappahannock. Minor actions with Lee's outposts lead to fights at Barbee's Cross Roads and Coyle's Tavern near Fairfax Court House.

Tuesday, August 25

Eastern Theater A Federal attempt on the rifle pits in front of Battery Wagner is repulsed. Skirmishes take place along the Rappahannock and Chickahominy rivers. In West Virginia Averell's cavalry destroy the Confederate saltpeter works on Jackson's River.

Trans-Mississippi Brigadier-General Thomas Ewing issues General Order 11 at Kansas City. It is a brutal reaction to Quantrill's raid, expelling 20,000 people from their homes in Bates, Cass, and Jackson counties. Federal troops seize and destroy property and crops. This retaliation is extremely counter-productive, creating a legacy of hatred and fertile grounds for anti-Union guerrilla warfare.

Wednesday, August 26

Eastern Theater The 24th Massachusetts Infantry storm the Confederate rifle pits in front of Battery Wagner. Now just 240 yards from the rebel defenses, the Union troops dig in to create another parallel line of trenches. Averell's raid in West Virginia continues, with a sharp fight at Rock Gap near White Sulphur Springs. In Virginia a small Federal expedition sets out from Williamsburg to Bottom's Bridge.

The South Former US secretary of war and lately Confederate general, John B. Floyd, dies at Abington, Virginia.

Thursday, August 27

Eastern Theater The Federals in front of Battery Wagner encounter large numbers of "subsurface torpedo mines"—black powder charges

buried in the mud and detonated by foot pressure. The approaches to the Confederate position are littered with them.

Western Theater A series of minor actions occur near Vicksburg.

Friday, August 28

Eastern Theater Beauregard recognizes that Battery Wagner cannot be expected to resist for very much longer. The Confederates begin to plan their evacuation.

Saturday, August 29

Eastern Theater Charleston's newest defensive weapon, the submarine *H.L. Hunley*, sinks in the harbor, drowning several of its crew. Constructed at Mobile by its inventor, the submarine is financed entirely by private capital after the Confederate government showed no interest. Hunley shipped his creation to Charleston by rail and plans to use it to attack the blockading Union fleet with a spar torpedo—a bomb mounted on a pole attached to the bow of the submarine.

Western Theater McCook's corps of Rosecrans' Army of the Cumberland crosses the Tennessee River at Caperton's Ferry, 35 miles below Chattanooga. Once again, Rosecrans is attempting to maneuver Bragg out of his positions by a series of turning movements.

Far West Federal troops are deployed against the Navaho Indians in New Mexico Territory.

Sunday, August 30

Eastern Theater Union batteries resume their firing on Fort Sumter while the Confederates withdraw workable cannon, redeploying them in batteries around the harbor. Confederate batteries fire on one of their own steamers by mistake and sink her.

Monday, August 31

Eastern Theater The siege guns fire another 627 rounds at Fort Sumter. The fort is now reduced to rubble and cannot fire back. The garrison looks anxiously toward the magazine which is in danger of penetration by heavy shell.

Tuesday, September 1, 1863

Eastern Theater *New Ironsides* and six monitors steam into Charleston harbor to bombard Fort Sumter. The shattered fort cannot reply but other Confederate batteries do so with vigor. In Virginia minor actions occur near Leesburg and at Barbee's Cross Roads.

Western Theater Rosecrans' main body begins to cross the Tennessee River, beginning operations against Bragg's Confederates.

Trans-Mississippi Skirmishes take place at Devil's Backbone and Jenny Lind, Arkansas.

Wednesday, September 2

Eastern Theater Union cavalry wreck two steamers captured by the Confederates at Port Conway on the Rappahannock.

Western Theater Burnside occupies Knoxville, Tennessee, cutting the railroad link from Chattanooga to Virginia. Confederates will now have to travel via Atlanta and Tennessee.

Mexico The French troops in Mexico hold part of the coast and Mexico City but the rest of the country is in the hands of rival bandit gangs. One group under Zapata is routed today by Confederate troops at Mier. This band had been raiding across the border into Texas.

Thursday, September 3

Western Theater Bragg recognizes he is being outmaneuvered again. He remarks to Daniel H. Hills, "It is said to be easy to defend a mountainous country, but mountains hide your foe from you, while they are full of gaps through which he can pounce upon you at any time. A mountain is like the wall of a house full of ratholes. The rat lies hidden at his hole to pop out when no one is watching."

Far West The Sioux Indians suffer their worst defeat in all their wars. Brigadier-General Sully with the 4th Iowa and 6th Nebraska cavalry is attacked at Whitestone Hill, near present-day Ellendale, North Dakota. His initially divided forces manage to concentrate and fight the most bitterly contested battle of the Indian wars. Sully drives the Sioux into a ravine and by nightfall, 300 warriors are dead, wounded, or captured. The cavalry suffer 22 dead and 50 wounded.

Friday, September 4

Western Theater Rosecrans completes his crossing of the Tennessee downriver from Chattanooga. Bragg, who has been expecting an attack from upstream, has been outmaneuvered.

The South Shortages of food and clothing result in rioting in Mobile, Alabama. Federal gunboats set out from New Orleans as part of an operation against the Texas/Louisiana coastline. Meanwhile, in the city, General Grant is injured falling from his horse. His enemies say, with some evidence in their favor, that he was drunk. The allegations of drunkenness will continue for years to come.

Saturday, September 5

Western Theater The confident Rosecrans splits his army into three columns to pass rapidly through the gaps in the mountains and attack Chattanooga. Meanwhile, at Charleston, Union batteries open their final bombardment on Battery Wagner as troops dig a sap close enough to make an infantry assault.

Great Britain Under constant pressure from the Federal Government, the British seize the two ironclad rams building in Liverpool for the Confederacy. Twin-turreted, 1800-ton warships, their high speed and four 9-inch guns would have made them a serious menace to the US Navy. They had already been sold to a sympathetic British company, ostensibly for transfer to Egypt, but Washington and London knew of the deception. Confederate endeavors to build powerful warships in Europe will continue but their greatest effort has now been frustrated.

Top left: *Diplomatic representatives in New York state, August 1863. Not until the 1890s did the European powers upgrade their diplomatic representation to ambassadorial level.*

Left: *The Slave Pen of Price Birch & Co, Alexandria, Virginia.*

Above: *Early in the morning of June 17 the CSS* Atlanta *was engaged by USS* Weehawken *and* Nahant *at the mouth of the Wilmington River in Wassaw Sound, Georgia. The monitor* Weehawken *fired five rounds, hitting with four and convincing the Confederates to surrender. The damaged ironclad was towed to Port Royal, repaired, and taken into US service.*

Below left: *Confederate submarine* Hunley *was built in 1863 as a private venture for use against Union warships blockading Charleston. Propulsion was by hand power geared to a single screw at the stern.* Hunley *was lost in the attack upon USS* Housatonic, *the first successful attack carried out by a submarine.*

149

September 1863

Sunday, September 6, 1863

Western Theater Braxton Bragg orders the evacuation of Chattanooga—a strategic disaster for the Confederacy. At Charleston Battery Wagner is still under fire, the Union engineers illuminating the defenses with calcium lights to prevent the Confederates repairing their position under cover of darkness. During the 42-hour bombardment, 1663 artillery rounds and 1553 mortar bombs are fired at the beleaguered position.

Monday, September 7

Eastern Theater The Union assault on Battery Wagner is scheduled for 9.00 a.m. but they find that the Confederate garrison has withdrawn. After 58 days of resistance, they have bowed to the inevitable and evacuated their defenses, taking their operative cannon and their wounded with them. Luckily for the Union occupiers, powder trains lit to fire the magazines fail to burn properly and they do not explode. The monitor USS *Weehawken* maneuvers to block any Confederate attempt to re-establish forces on Morris Island, but she grounds within easy range of rebel batteries on Sullivan's Island. USS *Patapsco* runs a gauntlet of Confederate fire to test the channels either side of Fort Sumter and to make a close inspection of the defenses.

Tuesday, September 8

Eastern Theater The Union ironclads steam to Sullivan's Island and shell the batteries there all day, while *Weehawken* struggles to refloat herself. She finally escapes at 4.00 p.m. During the night, the US fleet lands 400 sailors and marines by boat to storm Fort Sumter but the Confederates are alert and ready. The landing party suffers a bloody repulse with 124 casualties out of the 400 men engaged.

Wednesday, September 9

Eastern Theater Recognizing the importance of Chattanooga, President Davis authorizes James Longstreet to take 12,000 troops from the Army of Northern Virginia and travel by train to join Bragg's forces.

Western Theater Believing he is again pursuing a beaten enemy, Rosecrans advances on a 40-mile front. Crittenden's XXI Corps advances through Chattanooga while XIV Corps (Thomas) and XX Corps (McCook) move through separate gaps through Lookout Mountain well to the south. The three Union corps are now separated by several days' marching. But Bragg is not fleeing; he is concentrating his forces to attack and defeat Rosecrans in detail.

Thursday, September 10

Western Theater Bragg springs his trap but it fails to achieve any significant successes. He remains ignorant of the Federal deployment, Rosecrans' exact strength, and the lie of the land. The scattered Union divisions straggle through the densely forested terrain in happy ignorance of the huge concentration of Confederate troops close by.

Friday, September 11

Western Theater Bragg learns he is to be reinforced by Longstreet's men who are changing trains and rail lines every few hours as they are shuttled over the chaotic Southern rail network. With no trusted force of scouts such as Lee used in the east, Bragg relies solely on his cavalry for reconnaissance. But although his horsemen are superb, the Federal cavalry screen has infantry support which cannot be brushed aside. Bragg orders the fiery General Leonidas Polk to attack, but nothing happens.

Saturday, September 12

Western Theater Crittenden's XXI Corps is exposed and isolated but Polk refuses to attack as he has no way of telling what he is facing. Previous experience of Bragg's poor intelligence information does not encourage him. Bragg himself cannot make up his mind where to mount his main attack. Hill believes his commander is indeed bewildered by "the popping out of the rats from so many holes."

Sunday, September 13

Eastern Theater Weakened by the loss of Longstreet's troops, Lee withdraws across the Rapidan. Meade advances from the Rappahannock to the Rapidan, occupying Culpeper Court House.

Western Theater Rosecrans realizes that Bragg is not retiring and rushes to concentrate his forces. McCook's XX Corps, his southernmost wing, is ordered to hasten north. So begins a 57-mile epic march that will save the Union Army.

Monday, September 14

Western Theater Bragg rails at his subordinates, refuses to believe how scattered the Federals are, and continues to issue orders bearing no relation to what his corps commanders encounter on the ground. His habit of demanding a scapegoat for every failure has stifled initiative in his army and the antipathy between him and his subordinates severely hampers coordinated action.

Tuesday, September 15

Western Theater Bragg plans to maneuver between Rosecrans and Chattanooga to bring the Union forces to battle on Friday. Once again, poor staffwork delays the dissemination of the Confederate orders.

Wednesday, September 16

Western Theater Rosecrans now has his forces well in hand. The Army of the Cumberland occupies an 11-mile front from Lee and don's Mills to Steven's Gap in a line running from east to southwest. Bragg's headquarters is at Lafayette and his troops hold the gaps in Pigeon Mountain plus the fords to Lee and Gordon's Mills.

Thursday, September 17

Western Theater Rosecrans correctly divines Bragg's operational plan 12 hours before the Confederate commander issues his orders. During the afternoon, Rosecrans orders McCook to take the place of Thomas at Pond Spring, while Thomas occupies Crawfish Springs, and Crittenden extends to the left to cover the road to Chattanooga. The Union corps begin to march into position during the night.

Friday, September 18

Western Theater Bragg issues his orders just one day too late to catch Rosecrans' forces dispersed. It is a fateful day for the Confederacy since Bragg, unusually for a Confederate commander, has a substantial numerical advantage. Boosted by the arrival of Longstreet, he now has 75,000 troops against Rosecrans' 57,000.

Saturday, September 19

Western Theater Now he has redeployed, the Confederate attack hits Rosecrans' Federals head-on rather than on their left flank. The battlefield is a vast natural amphitheater bounded by Missionary Ridge and Pigeon Mountain. The area is densely forested, making command and control a nightmare for both sides. Thomas's corps bears the brunt of the Confederate attack but he fights a brilliant defensive action and is still in good order when the fighting dies down late in the evening. The rival commanders both convene councils of war at 11 p.m.

Fort Hindman was an example of the many lightly protected river steamers taken over by both sides in large numbers in the continuing struggle for control of the rivers.

In 1862 about 20 such vessels were pressed into Union service alone. They were given a light protection of thin iron plates and carried a few guns. With a draft of only 3 feet, sometimes only 18 inches, they were able to operate up shallow tributaries, fighting Confederates forces who constantly harassed Union supply lines. Without their help the Union Army would have been sorely pressed.

September–October 1863

Sunday, September 20, 1863

Western Theater Bragg's Army of the Tennessee resumes its attack on Rosecrans, but the assault is delayed until 9.00 a.m. due to typically poor staffwork. Lieutenant-General Leonidas Polk displays no sense of urgency and, when finally prodded into action by the apoplectic Bragg, commits his troops in piecemeal attacks. The Confederates concentrate on attacking the Union left, ably commanded by Major-General Thomas. Two hours of fighting fail to break through. One notable Southern casualty is Ben Hardin Helm, brother-in-law to President Lincoln's wife, mortally wounded in one of the attempts to flank Thomas's line.

Rosecrans feeds more and more troops to support Thomas but a disastrous misinterpretation of orders leads Brigadier-General Wood to withdraw his troops from the center right at 11.00 a.m. Ordered to close up on Reynolds' division, Wood pulls out of the line and circles around, rather than shifting directly to his left. This mistake leaves a gap in the Union front in the exact spot selected by Longstreet for the major thurst. At 11.15 Longstreet launches three divisions, stacked one behind the other, into the vacuum and shatters the Federal Army. It is perhaps the most decisive battlefield stroke of the war. Their center and right penetrated by the dashing Southern attack, XX and XXI Corps rout, leaving Thomas unsupported. He rescues the day for Rosecrans by an epic rear guard action which wins him the sobriquet "The Rock of Chickamauga."

By nightfall Thomas is withdrawing his battered corps in good order toward Chattanooga. Of the 57,000 Union soldiers, 1656 are killed, 9749 wounded, and 4774 captured for a total of 16,179. Confederate casualties are 2389 slain, 13,412 wounded, and 2003 missing; severe losses, but a vigorous pursuit will destroy the Union Army completely.

Monday, September 21

Western Theater The beaten Union Army straggles into Chattanooga. Officers work desperately to re-establish order but the troops are scattered. Brigadier-General Nathan Bedford Forrest soon detects the vulnerability of the Federal Army, reporting artillery batteries jumbled up with trains of wagons as disorganized bands of troops hastened away from the battlefield. The retreat is a rout. But Bragg's army spends the day burying the dead and looting captured stores. Forrest sends back word that "every hour is worth a thousand men," but Bragg was slow to comprehend the magnitude of his victory. Not until late afternoon did some elements of the Confederate Army begin to follow up. Rosecrans spends all night hurrying his trains out of Chattanooga and reorganizing his command.

Tuesday, September 22

The North A series of telegraphs from Rosecrans admit the scale of the Union defeat. The news is a bitter blow to President Lincoln, who had regarded the capture of Chattanooga as the first step toward an advance into the heart of the Confederacy. Receiving a message from Rosecrans that "our fate is in the hands of God" is anything but reassuring.

Western Theater The belated Confederate advance runs into entrenched Union positions. Bragg has fumbled his second opportunity to destroy the Army of the Cumberland. Fortune will never offer such chances again.

Wednesday, September 23

The North President Lincoln receives a wire from Rosecrans announcing that he is secure in Chattanooga and can hold it unless menaced by superior Confederate forces. Lincoln rides to the Soldiers' Home to sleep but is woken by John Hay with the news that Stanton has convened a special war council. This is distressing, indeed: Stanton had never previously summoned the president from his sleep—not even during the desperate days of 1862.

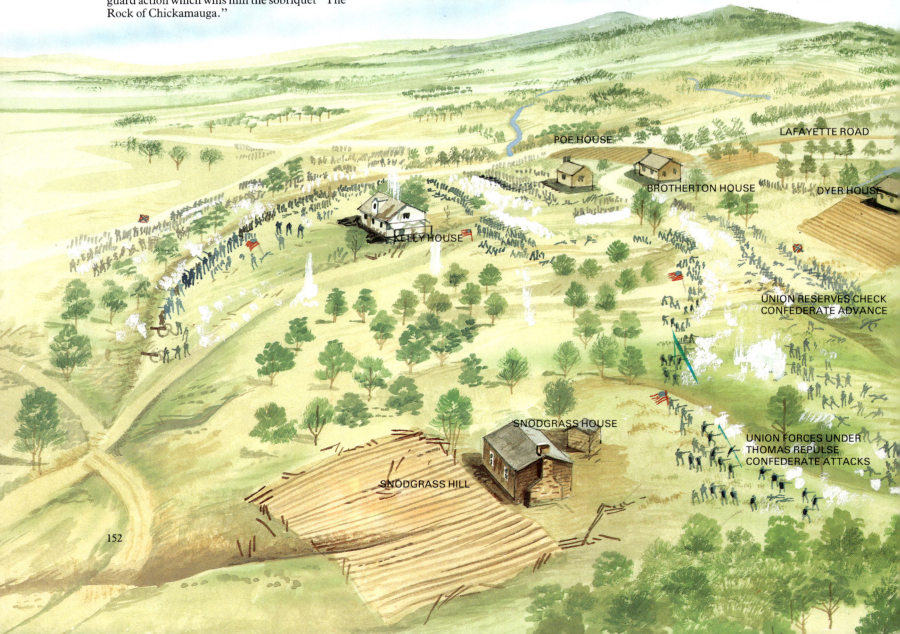

POE HOUSE

LAFAYETTE ROAD

BROTHERTON HOUSE

DYER HOUSE

KELLY HOUSE

UNION RESERVES CHECK CONFEDERATE ADVANCE

SNODGRASS HOUSE

UNION FORCES UNDER THOMAS REPULSE CONFEDERATE ATTACKS

SNODGRASS HILL

Thursday, September 24

The North Lincoln rides back to Washington by moonlight. He meets with Stanton, Halleck, Seward, and Chase at the War Office, and they discuss the news from Chattanooga until dawn. They recognize that Chattanooga is the key to middle Tennessee and an essential base for any future offensive into the Deep South. Grant and Burnside are ordered to dispatch reinforcements to Rosecrans and the meeting decides to send 20,000 men from the Army of the Potomac. After the conference, Hay shows Lincoln a Confederate dispatch: Mary Lincoln's brother-in-law, the Confederate Brigadier-General Ben Hardin Helm, was killed in action at Chickamauga. Helm was not the only member of Mrs Lincoln's family to die for the South: three of her half-brothers had already given their lives.

Western Theater Bragg's army occupies Missionary Ridge and Lookout Mountain, connecting the two by entrenchments across Chattanooga Valley. By deploying troops in Lookout Valley, Bragg commands the Union's 26-mile wagon route to Bridgeport, cutting Rosecrans' supply line.

Friday, September 25

The North Lincoln is let down yet again by General Burnside, who fails to support Rosecrans and marches instead on Jonesboro. He is equally annoyed with Rosecrans, describing him as "confused and stunned like a duck hit on the head."

Eastern Theater Hooker takes charge of XI Corps (Howard) and XII Corps (Slocum), ready to move to reinforce Rosecrans. The 20,000 troops leave the Army of the Potomac's lines along the Rappahannock and head north to join the rail system.

Saturday, September 26

Eastern Theater Hooker's command reaches Alexandria, Virginia, where it begins to entrain for the west.

Sunday, September 27

Eastern Theater The combined artillery of XI and XII Corps, plus the officers' horses, are loaded onto trains and begin their journey to Chattanooga.

Monday, September 28

Western Theater Recriminations begin in the Army of the Cumberland. Rosecrans brings charges against his corps commanders McCook and Crittenden and they are ordered to Indianapolis for a court of inquiry. This does not inspire the Union soldiers with great confidence in their leaders. Rations are already short as the Confederates continue to block the Federal supply line.

Tuesday, September 29

Western Theater Halleck telegraphs Ulysses S. Grant, informing him of Rosecrans' disaster at Chickamauga and directing him to dispatch as many troops as he can spare to march on Chattanooga. Grant has already sent Sherman off, and McPherson is leading the bulk of the Vicksburg garrison east.

Wednesday, September 30

Western Theater Recognizing that Rosecrans shows no signs of retreating, Bragg orders Wheeler's cavalry to raid the rear of the Union Army.

Thursday, October 1, 1863

Western Theater The Union supply line between Bridgeport and Chattanooga is cut by Confederate Cavalry. Rosecrans' only supply route is a tortuous 28-mile mountain road along the north side of the Tennessee River. To supply 50,000 men along this single route during the coming winter is clearly impossible. Rosecrans orders the construction of flat-bottomed steamers able to navigate the river from Bridgeport.

Friday, October 2

Western Theater The leading elements of Hooker's troops begin to arrive in Bridgeport, Alabama. Some 20,000 men, with 3000 horses and mules, are traveling 1159 miles by railroad. It takes just over a week for this transfer to take place—another example of the strategic flexibility conferred by the railroad.

Saturday, October 3

Western Theater As Wheeler's Confederate cavalry continue to raid into the surrounding area, Hooker establishes his headquarters at Stevenson, and Howard occupies Bridgeport. Grant is ordered to transfer his headquarters to Cairo.

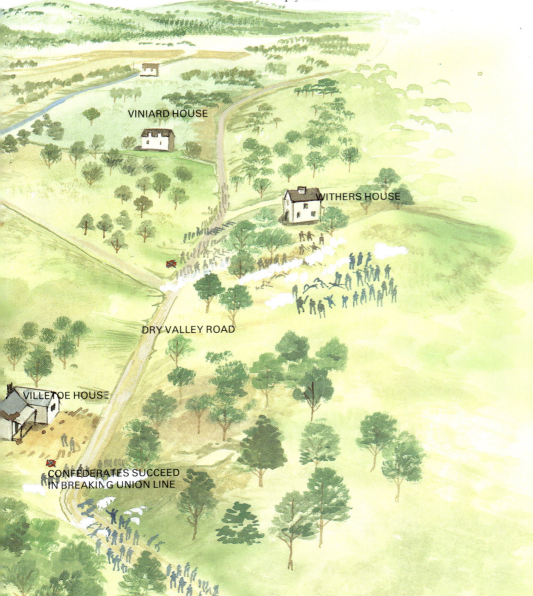

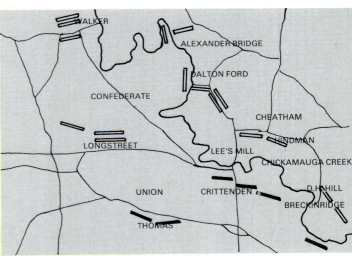

After a long period of inactivity following the Battle of Murfreesboro at the end of 1862, Confederate forces started to concentrate near Chickamauga Creek. Initial actions on September 1, 1863 left a Union salient at Kelly's House. A hole had been left in the Union center on the second day at Brotherton House and this was pierced by the Confederates, with disastrous results for the Federals. However, they recovered and retired to safety at sundown.

Small map shows the opening phase of battle.

153

October 1863

MEN WANTED FOR THE NAVY

All able-bodied men not in the employment of the Army, will be enlisted into the Navy upon application at the Naval Rendezvous, on Craven Street next door to the Printing Office.

H. K. DAVENPORT,
Com'r. & Senior Naval Officer.

New Berne, N. C.,
Nov. 2d, 1863.

Sunday, October 4, 1863

Western Theater Major-General Hooker examines a boat under construction by Federal engineers at Bridgeport. By mounting an engine, boiler, and sternwheel on a flat-bottomed scow, the Union engineers plan to fashion a supply vessel to revictual the Army of the Cumberland by steaming directly down the Tennessee River. Hooker is impressed and orders Brigadier-General William E. Le Duc to send a report to Rosecrans, and press on with the work in the meantime.

Monday, October 5

Western Theater Wheeler's cavalry destroys the bridge at Stone's River near Murfreesboro, cutting another important link in the Union supply line.
Naval Operations The semi-submersible CSS *David* attacks the Union ironclad *New Ironsides* at Charleston. The detonation of a spar torpedo causes extensive damage, although two of the four crew members are captured and the *David* ships a great deal of water. The others take the *David* back to Charleston where she runs aground.

Tuesday, October 6

Western Theater The heat of late September fades rapidly this week as the heavy rain lashes the Chattanooga area. The situation is unpleasant for both sides, but the Confederates find it easier to drain their trenches and rifle pits along the slopes of Missionary Ridge and Lookout Mountain. Down by the Tennessee River, the hungry Union soldiers have to bail out their positions.

Wednesday, October 7

Eastern Theater Alerted by a flurry of Confederate signals from their flag stations, the Army of the Potomac responds to Lee's attempt to march around its flank. Meade withdraws the Union forces to the Rappahannock. The army which had followed Lee all the way from Gettysburg withdraws the moment Lee turns to fight. In fact, Lee is merely making a demonstration to attract Union attention and prevent further troops being dispatched to the Western Theater.
Western Theater There is little shelter available in Chattanooga now since all the wooden houses have been pulled down to shore up the trenches and redoubts, and provide firewood. Most of the town's 2500 citizens have lost their homes and huddle together in the few stone buildings available for their use.

Thursday, October 8

Western Theater Food is running out in Chattanooga. Poor diet and the cold, wet weather causes a steep increase in sickness among the Union troops. Most of the army's draft animals have been eaten and the daily 4-inch square piece of hardtack is christened "Lincoln's Platform."

Friday, October 9

Western Theater Wheeler's cavalry return from their raid, having narrowly escaped defeat by the large concentration of Union cavalry ranged against them. Although some of their booty is lost, the Confederates have burned hundreds of Union wagons—a crippling blow to Rosecrans' supply system.

Saturday, October 10

Eastern Theater A series of minor skirmishes take place along the Rapidan as the Army of Northern Virginia maneuvers around Meade's right flank and the Union forces continue to fall back.
Western Theater President Davis meets with Braxton Bragg and his senior officers who are seething with discontent. Davis asks them to speak frankly and is disagreeably surprised when Longstreet does just that. Buckner, Cheatham, Cleburne, and D.H. Hill all agree that Bragg's talents would be "better employed elsewhere." Davis is furious; what he wants is another ringing declaration of support for his friend Bragg, such as the one wrung out of Joe Johnston after Stone's River.

Sunday, October 11

Western Theater Davis takes Longstreet for a walk. The veteran general offers to resign, which the president refuses; he then asks Davis to replace Bragg with Johnston, which meets with the same stony response. The Confederacy is paying dearly for the friendship forged at the battle of Buena Vista. On February 23, 1847 Bragg commanded an artillery battery and

Left: *Lord Richard Lyons was the British minister in Washington from December 1858 until February 1865. Anglo-American relations were soured early in the war by the* Trent *affair but there was never any serious prospect of British intervention on the Confederate side.*

Below: *Lee and Gordon's Mill on Chickamauga Creek. The Union right flank to the north of here collapsed in the face of Longstreet's brilliantly orchestrated attack which sent Rosecrans, McCook, and Crittenden fleeing.*

achieved instant fame when, at the height of the battle, Zachery Taylor ordered, "A little more grape, Captain Bragg." The then Colonel Davis had commanded the Mississippi Rifles who had supported Bragg's battery, and the two became firm friends. It was to have fatal consequences for the Confederacy.

Sherman departs Memphis for Corinth, ordered to repair the roads behind him so the army can be supplied. He has 330 miles of hostile country to contend with; the bridges are all down and Confederate guerrilla bands lurk around his line of march.

Monday, October 12

Eastern Theater The Army of the Potomac continues to retreat as Lee once again advances on Manassas.

Tuesday, October 13

The North Republican Union candidates win a series of state elections. Clement Vallandigham, who has run his campaign from exile in Canada, is defeated in Ohio.

Wednesday, October 14

Eastern Theater Lee endeavors to cut off Meade's withdrawal. A.P. Hill attacks Warren's V Corps at Bristoe Station, but a day of maneuver in close country fails to produce any decisive result. Union losses are 51 dead and 329 wounded; the Confederates sustain 750 killed and wounded, plus 450 missing.

Thursday, October 15

Naval Operations H.L. Hunley takes personal command of his privately financed submarine, the *Hunley* or *Fish* as she is also called. His plan is for the submarine to tow an explosive charge and, by diving beneath an enemy warship and surfacing the other side, to drag the "torpedo" against the target's hull. But although the boat has had several successful trial runs in Mobile, this second attempt in Charleston also ends in disaster. The ballast tanks fail and the *Hunley* sinks, suffocating its inventor and the crew. The boat is soon raised and its ill-fated crew are later interred in Charleston with full military honors.

Friday, October 16

The North In a major reorganization, the Departments of the Ohio, Cumberland, and Tennessee are combined into the Military Division of the Mississippi under the command of General Grant.

Western Theater Brigadier-General Le Duc saves the Union supply ship at Bridgeport. The rapidly rising waters of the Tennessee River threaten to overwhelm the vessel before she can be caulked and pitched. Le Duc has engineers run partially submerged pontoons under her and keeps her unprotected timbers dry.

Saturday, October 17

Eastern Theater With no wish to actually bring on another major engagement, Lee withdraws his troops from the Bull Run area and heads back to the Rappahannock.

Major-General George H. Thomas was a loyal Virginian aged 47 when he won the sobriquet the "Rock of Chickamauga" by his dogged defense on September 20, 1863. A solid 200 pounds, his imposing figure saved the Union Army that day and he would go on to win one of the few decisive victories of the war at Nashville. Wounded only once—by an Indian arrow in 1860—he was one of the most capable Federal commanders. He died in 1870.

October 1863

Sunday, October 18, 1863

Western Theater William S. Rosecrans is relieved of his command and replaced by Major-General George H. Thomas. Standing 6 feet 4 inches and weighing 200 pounds, Thomas is a confident leader whose enthusiasm proves infectious. He declares, "We will hold this town till we starve." Rosecrans leaves Chattanooga and journeys north, a beaten man. Although he remains in the army until 1867, he will never receive another important command.

Monday, October 19

Western Theater Hooker's engineers plan to complete the unfinished railroad grade to Jasper, first for wagons, and then for trains, if they can find the iron. They are exasperated by the local citizens employed as extra labor, Le Duc describing them as "dull to comprehend, slow to execute and needing constant direction."

Tuesday, October 20

Eastern Theater The Army of Northern Virginia returns to its old line across the Rappahannock. The last two weeks' maneuvers have cost the Army of the Potomac 2292 killed and wounded, and Lee, 1381.

Wednesday, October 21

Western Theater Grant leaves Nashville and reaches Stevenson, Alabama, before dark. He encounters Rosecrans travelling in the opposite direction and the former commander at Chattanooga briefs him on the situation there. Grant describes being impressed by Rosecrans' ideas for action, but puzzled as to why he had not pursued them himself.

Thursday, October 22

Western Theater Grant travels on to Bridgeport. Burnside, who has yet to contribute anything positive to the Union campaign, has his outposts at Sweetwater and Philadelphia overrun.

Friday, October 23

Western Theater Grant, still suffering from a fall from his horse, finally arrives in Chattanooga. He has experienced for himself the problems of the Union supply line. The bitter personal battles continue in the Confederate camp as the incompetent Leonidas Polk is at last removed—posted to Mississippi. Bragg has never forgiven him for his failure to attack on September 20.

Saturday, October 24

The North Lincoln presses Meade for an offensive against Lee. Once again he despairs at the Army of the Potomac, which still seems incapable of attacking Virginia.

Sunday, October 25

Western Theater Grant's arrival in Chattanooga coincides with the launching of the river boat—a coincidence which will later lead to arguments over whose idea it was to supply the town by river.

Monday, October 26

Western Theater Hooker's troops, under orders from Thomas, cross the Tennessee to take part in a joint operation with the defenders of Chattanooga. The objective is to seize Brown's Ferry, the old high-water route across the neck of Mocassin Point below Raccoon Mountain. If Union forces could capture the crossing before Longstreet's men on Lookout Mountain could intervene, the supply line to Chattanooga will be open.

Tuesday, October 27

Western Theater At 5 a.m. the Confederate picket guard at Brown's Ferry is surprised by 1800 troops on pontoons, floated down from Chattanooga right past the Confederate positions on Lookout Mountain. Commanded by General Hazen, the assault force captures many of the Confederates and controls both banks. A separate detachment from Chattanooga marches across the rear of Mocassin Point, links up with Hazen, and is ferried over to the west bank. The crossing is now in the hands of some 4000 Union troops who speedily entrench themselves. Engineers have a pontoon bridge in position by 10 a.m., so the defenses of Chattanooga now extend into Lookout Valley.

Wednesday, October 28

Western Theater Advancing into Lookout Valley, Hooker reaches Brown's Ferry. The siege of Chattanooga is over. Hooker's frontline strength is about 12,000, as Slocum had refused to serve under "Fighting Joe" after the Chancellorsville debacle. Lincoln allowed him to work independently, protecting Hooker's supply line with one division. The Confederates on Lookout Mountain are not strong enough to attack immediately, so a night assault is organized instead. Longstreet plans to attack the weaker end of Hooker's line around the railroad depot at Wauhatchie, three miles from the river. Bragg cancels the participation of McClaw's division without informing Longstreet. As a result, Jenkins' division attacks alone.

Thursday, October 29

Western Theater One of the most confused fights of the war is already underway at midnight and it lasts until the early hours of the morning. Jenkins' 4000 men run into about 5000 troops of John W. Geary's 2nd division of the Union XII Corps. There was a full moon on Monday night and the sky is clear, so Longstreet is able to direct the fight from a promontory subsequently christened "Signal Rock," but his flare signals are read by Union observers who have cracked the Confederate code. However, no one can actually control the fighting, which results in Union losses of 77 killed and 339 wounded. Jenkins is beaten off, with some 300 dead and wounded, plus 100 captured. Geary can take little pleasure in his successful defense; his son is shot dead commanding an artillery battery during the action.

LOOKOUT MOUNTAIN

MOCASSIN POINT

FORT NEGLEY

CHATTANOOGA CREEK

ROSSVILLE ROAD

Friday, October 30

Western Theater The scratch-built steamship, now named the *Chattanooga*, travels up the Tennessee and arrives in Chattanooga after dark, towing several barges. She delivers 40,000 rations, plus 39,000 pounds of forage. Hooker's men have just half a breakfast ration left in their haversacks, while in the town itself, just four boxes of hard bread remain in the commissary warehouse.

Saturday, October 31

Western Theater The news flies through the town. The cry goes up: "The Cracker Line is open. Full rations boys!" The prospect of regular supply transforms the spirit of the Federals in Chattanooga.

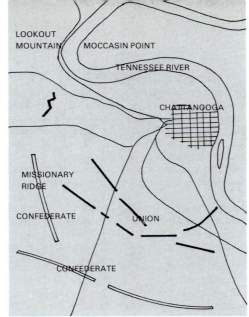

In November 1863 the Union Army was besieged within the defenses of Chattanooga and dominated by the Confederates who occupied Missionary Ridge and Lookout Mountain. The Federals seized the initiative and captured Orchard Knob on the high ground in the plain before Missionary Ridge.

Next day, November 24, Lookout Mountain was attacked, while to the north Sherman crossed the Tennessee River to attack the Confederate right.

After a slight pause, the center section of the Union Army succeeded in overrunning the Confederate position on Missionary Ridge and stormed on over the crest, forcing the Confederates to flee the field.

157

November 1863

Sunday, November 1, 1863

Eastern Theater The Federal siege batteries treat Fort Sumter to another 786 rounds. In West Virginia Averell leads Union cavalry on another raid into Confederate lines.

Western Theater Sherman reaches Eastport where his troops cross the Tennessee River. Supplies have arrived from St Louis and are stockpiled, awaiting his arrival. In Louisiana Federal troops under General Franklin move to New Iberia, completing their operation in the Bayou Teche area.

Monday, November 2

The North President Lincoln is invited to say a few words at the dedication of a new cemetery at Gettysburg.

Eastern Theater President Davis arrives in Charleston as the Union guns subject Fort Sumter to another heavy barrage. In a speech to the embattled troops and citizens, Davis states his confidence that the city will never be taken.

Western Theater General Banks' Union expedition takes Brazos Island on the Rio Grande, establishing a foothold on the Texas coastline. There is a series of skirmishes throughout the west—at Bayou Bourbeau in Louisiana. Bates Township, Arkansas, and Corinth, Mississippi.

Tuesday, November 3

Western Theater Sherman marches toward Chattanooga, dropping off G.M. Dodge's division to rebuild the railroad from Decatur to Nashville. Grant is anxious about relying solely on the single track line from Nashville to Stevenson. Dodge, an experienced railroad builder, has no proper tools for the job and must contend with constant raiding by small parties of Confederate guerrillas.

The destruction of Fort Sumter

Charleston harbor was dominated by the imposing five-sided fort in the center. Fort Sumter was built of gray bricks laid with mortar, and concrete made from cement and pounded oyster shells. The walls rose 40 feet above the water and were between 5 and 10 feet thick.

The Union naval attack in September 1863 inflicted enormous damage, exposing the upper casemates. After the Union attack in small boats, the Confederates added wire entanglements and sharpened stakes to the sloping piles of rubble which had once been their walls. Maintaining these defenses

Wednesday, November 4

Western Theater Partly at President Davis's instigation, Bragg rids himself of Longstreet, his main opponent. Longstreet is dispatched with his corps and Wheeler's cavalry to reinforce Confederate troops around Knoxville where Burnside's small Union Army remains halted. By detaching 20,000 of his best troops at the moment the Union Army receives substantial reinforcements, Bragg makes it obvious that his decisions are now governed mainly by personal animosity rather than military strategy. Over the next two weeks, he will act to rid himself of all the officers who opposed his continued leadership of the Army of the Tennessee.

Thursday, November 5

Eastern Theater John S. Mosby leads his elusive band behind the Union lines in northern Virginia for most of the month. Again, their effect is out of all proportion to their numbers.

Western Theater Grant ignores the Confederate threat to Knoxville, biding his time until Sherman's arrival will give him enough men to attack the Confederate lines around Chattanooga. Burnside is confident he can hold Knoxville, providing his ammunition supply does not fail.

Friday, November 6

Eastern Theater A mixed brigade of Union troops—two regiments of infantry and two of cavalry, plus one battery—under Brigadier-General Averell runs into a smaller Confederate detachment at Droop Mountain, West Virginia. Averell divides his command and attacks the Southern force from two directions at once. The Confederates are dispersed with the loss of 50 men dead, 250 wounded, and 100 prisoners. Federal losses are 31 killed and 94 injured. Averell continues his raid against Confederate rail links in West Virginia.

Western Theater Banks' expedition moves deeper into Texas along the Mexican border, occupying Point Isabel and Brownsville.

Saturday, November 7

Eastern Theater Meade attacks Lee's positions along the Rappahannock. The V and VI Corps under Sedgwick attack the Confederate redoubts near the site of the old railroad bridge. The rest of the army, under General French, forces the passage at Kelly's Ford. Held by two brigades of Early's Corps, the rebel positions on the Rappahannock are well constructed and a bombardment by Federal cannon produces little effect. Sedgwick asks his divisional commanders

cost the life of Captain Frank H. Harleston, 1st North Carolina Artillery on November 24, 1863.

The Confederates eventually fortified a citadel from which they could fight on, even if Union troops seized the outer part of the fort. They planned to use the guns in Charleston to sweep the attackers off.

The blue outline depicts the former height of the once proud fort.

The United States Christian Commission field headquarters photographed near Germantown, Maryland, in September 1863. The overhead cover helps keep the fierce, late summer heat off the tents.

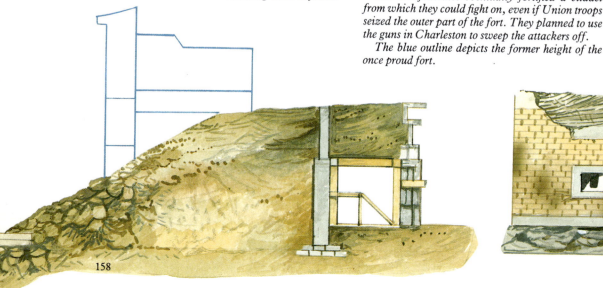

whether an infantry assault might work. Wright is noncommittal, but General David A. Russell, says, "I think I can." His men rush the Confederate works near dusk and, to the astonishment of the Confederates, they overrun the whole position. Upton's brigade gets behind the defenders to complete an amazing minor victory. Union losses are 83 dead, 330 wounded, and six missing. Confederate losses are six killed, 39 wounded, and 1629 captured.

Western Theater A Federal column departs Fayettville, Arkansas, on a week-long expedition to Frog Bayou, which generates several sharp skirmishes.

Sunday, November 8

Eastern Theater Colonels Penn and Godwin, commanding the two brigades of Hay's Confederate division, have breakfast with their captors. They are complimentary to the Union officers, saying ruefully that they had only just reported to Lee that they could hold their positions against anything the Yankees could throw at them. The Army of the Potomac continues its probe over the Rappahannock, with skirmishes at Warrenton and around Culpeper Court House. The Federal raid into West Virginia continues, with a minor action at Second Creek.

Western Theater At Vermillionville and Bayou Junica in Louisiana's Teche country there are brisk skirmishes. Bragg's purge of the Army of the Tennessee continues with Major-General John C. Breckinridge replacing the outspoken Lieutenant-General Daniel H. Hill in command of the II Corps.

Monday, November 9

The North President Lincoln goes to the theater to see a play called *The Marble Heart*. It stars the actor John Wilkes Booth.

Eastern Theater Federal troops from Williamsburg probe toward New Kent Court House, east of Richmond. Heavy snow falls early in Virginia as President Davis returns to the Confederate capital.

Far West There is a skirmish between Union troops and Indians in the Choctaw Nation, Indian Territory.

Tuesday, November 10

Eastern Theater Fort Sumter withstands its third consecutive day of bombardment from the Union batteries outside Charleston. The federal cannon fire nearly 600 rounds a day at the shattered fort.

Wednesday, November 11

Western Theater Longstreet's 20,000 men have reached no further than Loudon, the end of the Confederate railroad. He halts here to organize wagons to shuttle his supplies forward as he advances on Knoxville. Skirmishes take place at Greenleaf Prairie, Indian Territory, Natchez, Mississippi, and at Vermillion Bayou, Louisiana.

Thursday, November 12

Western Theater Longstreet completes his preparations and departs Loudon. Burnside learns that the Confederates have bridged the river at Huff's Ferry near Loudon.

Friday, November 13

Western Theater Longstreet advances on Knoxville where Burnside's men are well entrenched, expecting the Confederate assault. Minor actions occur at Palmyra and Blythe's Ferry, Tennessee.

California Union troops skirmish with hostile Indians near the Big Bar on the Trinity River.

Saturday, November 14

Western Theater Sherman arrives in Bridgeport at the head of 17,000 men. His troops have covered 675 miles by boat, rail, and foot in the last two weeks. Grant briefs him on the situation at Chattanooga, explaining that nothing much can be expected from the Army of the Cumberland. In Grant's opinion, they will be reluctant to leave their trenches, so the men from Vicksburg will have to lead the way.

The South The Confederate Government threatens to use force and confiscate property to collect taxes from the farmers of North Carolina. The whole episode illustrates the central weakness of the Confederacy: the self-sufficient agrarian economy can only sustain a limited burden of taxation. With few banks and little capital to work with, the government's resources are quite inadequate for this prolonged struggle.

Part of the headquarters of the Army of the Potomac, Fall 1863.

Below: The railroad station at Hanover Junction, Pennsylvania. Lincoln passed through here on his way to the ceremony at Gettysburg. His five-minute speech followed a two-hour address by Edward Everett and it attracted little attention at the time. But when it was printed in the newspapers it caught the imagination of a nation and is remembered as one of the greatest speeches of Lincoln's career.

November 1863

Sunday, November 15, 1863

Western Theater Wheeler's cavalry cross the Tennessee to accompany Longstreet on his advance to Knoxville. Meanwhile, Grant begins to issue orders for the breakout from Chattanooga. In accordance with his remarks to Sherman, Grant plans a largely static role for the Army of the Cumberland. Hooker's men from the Army of the Potomac and Sherman's veterans will launch the main effort.

Monday, November 16

Western Theater Longstreet tries but fails to cut off Burnside's rear guard as the Federals withdraw into their defenses at Knoxville. Confronted now by regular field works, Longstreet lacks the heavy guns and numbers of troops demanded for a siege.

Tuesday, November 17

The North President Lincoln writes the address he will deliver at Gettysburg. Contrary to later legend, it is a carefully prepared speech, not something hastily thought out on the train. Like that later great orator, Winston Churchill, Lincoln knows that even a ten-minute talk takes many hours of careful planning if it is to be effective.

Wednesday, November 18

The North President Lincoln leaves Washington by special train, heading for Gettysburg. Secretary of State Seward and the French ambassador accompany him.

Thursday, November 19

The North Edward Everett delivers a brilliant two-hour lecture to 15,000 people assembled at Gettysburg. Using detailed information provided by several officers of the Army of the Potomac, including Meade, Everett explains the course of the campaign and the epic events of the three-day battle. After he finishes, Lincoln rises to give his short speech. It receives only polite applause and Lincoln considers it a failure, an opinion shared by the London *Times*. In fact, few people even hear the speech and the president is gone before some realize he has spoken. His observation that "the world will little note, nor long remember what we say here" is only proved wrong due to extensive press coverage.

Friday, November 20

Western Theater Heavy rain delays Sherman's move into Chattanooga. His men continue to cross over at Brown's Ferry, passing through the remains of the town to a start line opposite the Confederate right.

Saturday, November 21

The North President Lincoln is taken ill with a mild form of smallpox. Forced to stay in bed, he has a consoling thought: "At last I have something I can give everybody."

Western Theater Sherman's men assemble for the attack. Grant plans a preliminary operation by the Army of the Cumberland to clear Orchard Knob, a foothill between Chattanooga and Missionary Ridge.

Sunday, November 22

Western Theater The Army of the Cumberland has now been reorganized and reduced. Brigadier-General Jefferson C. Davis's 1st division of XX Corps is deployed to support Sherman, and most of XIV Corps—Thomas's old command—is detached to Hooker. XX and XXI Corps, both driven from the field at Chickamauga, have been combined and renumbered IV Corps, under the command of Major-General Gordon Granger. Two divisions of the new corps, Wood's and Sheridan's, are chosen for the attack on Orchard Knob.

Monday, November 23

Western Theater Wood and Sheridan parade their troops, accompanied by bands, while Union batteries exchange shots with their Confederate opposite numbers atop Missionary Ridge. Under the eyes of both armies, the two Federal formations abruptly end their parade and charge Orchard Knob *en masse*. The surprised defenders are overrun and retreat up the slopes to join the main Confederate position. The Knob is swiftly entrenched and will be Grant's headquarters tomorrow. Bragg continues to allow personal feeling to dictate his plans; in response to a request for reinforcements from Longstreet, he orders Cleburne's division away to Knoxville. Longstreet, Polk, Buckner—and now Cleburne: Bragg has removed all the senior officers who asked Davis to dismiss him.

Tuesday, November 24

Western Theater Continual drizzle, punctuated by bursts of heavy rain, soak both armies at Chattanooga. Lookout Mountain and Missionary Ridge are lost to view, shrouded in thick fog. Hooker mounts a diversionary attack on Lookout Mountain, designed to pave the way for Sherman's main effort on the right against Missionary Ridge. Hooker's assault becomes known as "The Battle Above the Clouds"—a romantic name for a fog-bound action in which the Confederate defenses are overcome with surprising ease. Sherman advances during the afternoon, capturing what his map shows as the end of Missionary Ridge, but it is really only an outlying hill.

Wednesday, November 25

Western Theater At dawn the Union troops in the valley see the Stars and Stripes flying above the Confederate positions on Lookout Mountain. Cleburne's division is hurriedly ordered back and races over to the Confederate right to defend Missionary Ridge. Joined in the early hours of the morning by Hardee, the Confederates have little time to organize their dispositions. Sherman's powerful force of three corps, plus Baird's and Davis's divisions of the Army of the Cumberland, assault at 11.00 a.m. But the ruthless Sherman once again proves a lackluster tactician, and a series of frontal assaults fail to dislodge Cleburne's tough Confederates.

Hooker's advance stalls. Moving down from Lookout Mountain, he is confronted by Chattanooga Creek where the Confederates have destroyed the bridge. He orders up pontoons and halts.

At 3.00 p.m. Wood's and Sheridan's divisions begin a demonstration in force to tempt Bragg into reinforcing his center. Thomas orders them to seize the Confederate rifle pits at the base of Missionary Ridge and halt there. Both with two brigades up and one back, the divisions advance, preceded by a swarm of skirmishers. The brigades are deployed on a frontage of two regiments—the same formation used by Pickett at Gettysburg.

They overrun the Confederate forward position, but do not stop. In defiance of their orders, the troops surge up the ridge, driving the defenders of the Confederate first line before them. A confused mass of blue and gray scrambles up the steep ridge under fire from Confederate guns along the crest. Grant countermands this unplanned advance, but the officers bearing his orders fail to reach the leading troops, who storm the Confederate center. Thomas orders his whole line forward as soon as the extent of the advance becomes obvious.

Its center penetrated, the Army of the Tennessee collapses. Only opposite Sherman does the line still hold. Cleburne and Hardee cover the withdrawal of their comrades. Seven Congressional Medals of Honor are granted to the troops involved in storming Missionary Ridge. One first lieutenant so honored, Arthur MacArthur, will become a lieutenant-colonel at 19 and eventually commander of the Philippines. His son will be Douglas MacArthur.

Thursday, November 26

Eastern Theater Meade maneuvers against Lee along the Rapidan. This time the greatly superior Army of the Potomac tries to turn Lee's right and threaten Richmond.

Western Theater Bragg retreats on Ringgold, Georgia. Casualties at Chattanooga amount to about 10 percent for either side. The Confederates suffer 6667 out of 64,000 men; the Federal forces lose 5824 from their 56,000-strong army. By abandoning their defenses immediately Missionary Ridge fell, the Confederates avoided heavy losses and their army is still an effective force.

Friday, November 27

The North After 26 days of labor, digging through a 6-foot wall, the Confederate raider John Morgan tunnels out of the Ohio State Penitentiary at Columbus. With six of his officers, Morgan breaks out of the cells and climbs over the wall. Having bribed a guard with $15 to get him a paper, Morgan times his escape so he can board the train to Cincinnati. Jumping from the train outside Xenia, Morgan slips away into Kentucky. Reaching Confederate lines, he is given command of the Department of Southwest Virginia.

Eastern Theater Meade runs into the Army of Northern Virginia well entrenched at Mine Run, a minor stream which runs north into the Rapidan.

Saturday, November 28

Eastern Theater Meade convenes a council of war, which decides to dispatch General Warren's corps around Lee's southern flank near Antioch church, 10 miles south of the Rapidan. Warren moves off on a bitterly cold night, passing through wooded country dotted with the occasional farm.

Union forces storm Confederate defenses on Lookout Mountain on November 24, 1863. This was the midway period in raising the siege of Chattanooga.

On the following day the Confederates were driven from the field at the critical fighting along Missionary Ridge which ran off to the left of Lookout Mountain.

The Federal force had withdrawn into Chattanooga after its defeat at Chickamauga and faced starvation because of its tenuous supply line. Lincoln made Grant overall commander in order to retrieve the situation and fortunately for the Union, he was successful.

Both sides fielded large armies; the Federals had 56,000, while the Confederates, under Bragg, had 64,000.

After the action the Confederates withdrew to Dalton, Georgia, having had their lateral line of communication in the South cut. The Federals were now free to advance upon Atlanta.

November–December 1863

Sunday, November 29, 1863

Eastern Theater While Warren's corps, reinforced by A.H. Terry's division of VI Corps and 300 cavalry, marches around Lee's right flank, Sedgwick discovers that the northern end of the Confederate position is unprotected by earthworks. He urges Meade to allow another flanking movement. If successful, the Confederates will find themselves practically surrounded.

Western Theater Longstreet assaults Burnside's lines at Knoxville. The attack centers on a redoubt called Fort Saunders by the Union, and Fort Loudon by the Confederates. McClaw's division charges in several columns. The men have fixed bayonets and do not stop to fire. The garrison consists of nearly 400 infantry plus four 20-pounder Parrotts, six 12-pounder Napoleons, and two 3-inch rifles. Checked by abatis and wire entanglements, the Confederates become pinned down in the ditch. A gallant few plant the flags of the 13th and 17th Mississippi and the 16th Georgia on the Union parapet, but every man rallying to them is killed. The attack is repulsed, with 129 Confederate dead, 458 wounded, and 226 captured. Twenty men in the fort are injured.

Monday, November 30

Eastern Theater Sedgwick maneuvers V and VI Corps around the Confederate left during the night. The plan calls for a bombardment all along the line at 7.00 a.m., followed by simultaneous attacks on Lee's flanks. But Sedgwick's assault is called off, even as his guns open fire. Warren's advance has brought him up against well-entrenched Confederate troops, and he reports that an attack on them would be futile. Both Union flanking operations are cancelled and the troops return to the original lines. Throughout this abortive march, the troops suffer terribly from rain, which freezes as it falls.

Tuesday, December 1, 1863

Eastern Theater Meade abandons his maneuvering against Lee and withdraws the Army of the Potomac back across the Rapidan.

Western Theater Writing from the headquarters of the Army of the Tennessee at Dalton, Georgia, Braxton Bragg tenders his resignation to President Davis. Of the defeat at Chattanooga, he writes, "The disaster admits of no palliation, and is justly disparaging to me as a commander." But he goes on to describe Breckinridge as a drunk and Cheatham as equally unfit.

Wednesday, December 2

Western Theater Lieutenant-General W.H. Hardee assumes temporary command of the Army of the Tennessee. Bragg appeals to the army to support him and urges President Davis to consider a new Confederate offensive in the west. Longstreet is now threatened by a Federal column marching to the relief of Knoxville.

Thursday, December 3

Western Theater Longstreet concludes that there is nothing to be gained at Knoxville. Contrary to earlier expectations, he does not significantly outnumber Burnside and lacks the large-caliber guns and the ammunition for a successful attempt on the Federal lines. His forces begin to withdraw toward Greeneville to go into winter quarters. Skirmishes take place at Log Mountain and Wolf River Bridge near Moscow, Tennessee.

Friday, December 4

Eastern Theater Fort Sumter has survived another seven consecutive days' shelling, with 1307 rounds directed at the pulverized rubble.

Western Theater Just after last light, Longstreet's rear guard pulls out of the Confederate lines before Knoxville. Marching through the night, the Confederates are drenched by heavy rain, which churns the roads into a fearful state.

Saturday, December 5

Western Theater Longstreet's men finish their march 18 miles away at Blain's Cross Roads. The columns of troops are frequently delayed as wagons sink up to their axles and require double teams to haul them out of the mire. Despite orders to the contrary, the troops fire many miles of fences to light up the road. The rear guard brushes off Federal pursuit.

Trans-Mississippi Federal troops from Little Rock move out on an eight-day probe toward Princeton.

Sunday, December 6

Western Theater William T. Sherman leads his troops into Knoxville, while Longstreet continues to head for Greeneville. There are skirmishes at Clinch Mountain and near Fayetteville, Tennessee.

Naval Operations The ironclad USS *Weehawken* founders in an accident when a powerful tide washes over her and floods through an open hatch. She was loading ammunition and too much had been stored forward, upsetting her trim. The ingress of water is not noticed until it is too late, and she sinks in Charleston harbor with the loss of 24 men.

Two views from Sumter looking at the shores around Charleston, which were well defended and did not fall until near the war's end.

FORT MOULTRIE

MORTAR BATTERY

Monday, December 7

The South The fourth session of the first Confederate Congress meets in Richmond. The mood is as bleak as the weather, although President Davis attempts to put a brave face on this disastrous year for the Confederacy.

Tuesday, December 8

The North President Lincoln announces a Proclamation of Amnesty and Reconstruction at the end of his annual message to Congress. He offers a full pardon to all Confederates, except former officers in the US forces who resigned their commissions to fight for the South, senior government or military officials, and anyone who has mistreated Union prisoners of war. All property, except slaves, will be restored. He also offers Federal statehood to any Southern state in which 10 percent of the citizens swear allegiance to the Union and abandon slavery.

Wednesday, December 9

Western Theater General Burnside is once again relieved of his command, this time at his own request. He is replaced by Major-General J.G. Foster. His failure to assist Rosecrans at

Left: Retained by Grant in 1864, Major-General George G. Meade became the Army of the Potomac's longest serving (and only successful) commander. Badly wounded in the Seven Days' Campaign, he had distinguished himself at Fredericksburg by breaking into Jackson's lines—the only bright spot in an otherwise bleak day for the Union. He had not sought the command and was surprised to be given it at all, let alone on the eve of Gettysburg.

Chattanooga and reluctance to pursue Longstreet have aroused much criticism. Meanwhile, Longstreet continues the political battles which dominate Confederate operations in the west; he fires several members of his staff for alleged incompetence during the Knoxville campaign. The charges are later withdrawn.

Black troops mutiny at Fort Jackson near New Orleans. The revolt is quelled by white officers.

Thursday, December 10

Eastern Theater The soldiers of the Army of the Potomac finish their earth and log shelters ready for the Christmas season's inactivity. Horse races, cockfights, and greased pigs and poles are arranged to break the monotony. The officers organize a series of balls, and a large wooden dancehall is soon under construction.

Western Theater Federal troops destroy the Confederate salt works in Choctawatchie Bay, Florida.

Friday, December 11

Eastern Theater Union siege guns outside Charleston continue their bombardment of Fort Sumter's tortured rubble. Today a shell finally penetrates one of the powder magazines, touching off an explosion which kills 11 and wounds 41 of the garrison. Union cavalry raiding Confederate railroads in West Virginia are in action at Big Sewell and Meadow Bluff.

Saturday, December 12

Eastern Theater Anticipating another Union attempt to capture Fort Sumter now most of its guns are silent, the Confederates fortify the interior with sandbags, loopholed for rifles and howitzers. Should the Federal fleet effect a landing, the attackers can be raked from neighboring Confederate batteries and the garrison can fight on from within its casemates. Any troops breaking into the interior of the fort would be shot down from the barricades.

SOUTH CHANNEL BEACON

MOULTRIE HOUSE

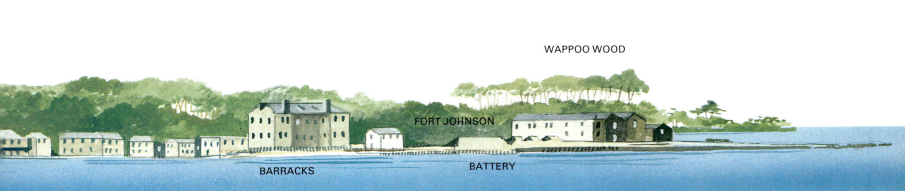

WAPPOO WOOD

FORT JOHNSON

BARRACKS

BATTERY

December 1863

Sunday, December 13, 1863

Western Theater At Knoxville it becomes apparent that Major-General Foster is incapable of exercising command owing to disability. Authority devolves on Parke, but he passes responsibility to Granger, who in turn unloads it on the prickly Major-General Sheridan.

Monday, December 14

The North President Lincoln gives his wife's half-sister amnesty after she swears allegiance to the Union. Her husband, Brigadier-General Helm, died for the Confederacy at Chickamauga, and his distraught widow comes to live with the Lincolns. Dark murmurings about Southern influence in the Lincoln household will continue.

Western Theater Having rested at Rogersville since Thursday, Longstreet suddenly doubles back toward Bean's Station where 4000 Federal cavalry under Shackleford had advanced unsupported. Gracie's brigade leads the attack but the early winter darkness brings the fighting to a close before enough Confederates can be concentrated. A column of troops under Parke block Longstreet's outflanking maneuver, and the Union forces retreat after dusk.

Tuesday, December 15

Western Theater Longstreet's troops march back to Rogersville. The collapse of the Confederate economy is so complete that many of the man are without proper footwear. Brigadier-General E.P. Alexander records seeing the bloodstains on the frozen ground where barefooted Southern soldiers had marched. The soldiers rely on raw beef-hide mocassins, but they are no protection against the winter weather. The only way to obtain reasonable footwear is to capture a Union soldier. Longstreet authorizes his men to "swap" shoes with prisoners.

Wednesday, December 16

The South Despite the deep personal differences which arose in the past, President Davis appoints General J.E. Johnston to succeed Braxton Bragg as commander of the Department of the Tennessee. General Leonidas Polk succeeds Johnston in the Mississippi. Bragg joins his friend the president in Richmond, appointed to act as a military adviser.

Trans-Mississippi A strong detachment from General Banks' XIII Corps lands at Corpus Christi, Texas. Banks landed on the Texas coast 10 days ago, capturing Brownsville as part of

Halleck's orders to raise the Union flag in the state and deny anchorages to Confederate shipping.

Thursday, December 17

Naval Operations The Union merchant ship *Chesapeake*, seized by a copperhead gang off Cape Cod, is retaken near Nova Scotia.

Friday, December 18

Western Theater In the mountains of East Tennessee the snow falls to a depth of several inches. Longstreet's men are not the only ones suffering. Sheridan observes that the Union troops at Knoxville are still without winter clothing; nor do they have proper accommodation. In bivouac their sole protection against the elements is the army poncho, rigged to make rudimentary shelters. There is not a tent in the command. Small wonder that the armies continue to suffer far more casualties through disease and ill-health than in combat.

Saturday, December 19

Western Theater Sherman files his official report, praising Burnside's fortifications at Knoxville for their excellence of siting and construction, especially given the haste with which they were thrown up.

Sunday, December 20

Naval Operations The Confederate commerce raider *Alabama* reaches Singapore. Having crossed the Indian Ocean, her presence in Far Eastern waters paralyzes US shipping, which dare not venture to sea. Neutral merchant ships soon take over all the carrying trade. Captain Semmes now plans to double back across the Indian Ocean, round the Cape of Good Hope, and head for South American waters.

Above Right: *Part of the commissary, Army of the Potomac, February 1864. By this time the Federal forces enjoyed substantial material superiority—better rifles, cannon, and equipment—as well as their traditional advantage in numbers. Yet the margin was not great enough to overwhelm the veteran Army of Northern Virginia.*

Right: *Ambulance drill for the 57th New York. The armies carried out surprisingly little military training in the modern sense during their annual withdrawal into winter quarters. Even weapons drill was unusual, and practice firing rare enough to attract comment if someone organized it.*

Monday, December 21

Eastern Theater Averell's cavalry return from a two-week foray behind Confederate lines in southern West Virginia. Elsewhere in the theater, military operations are effectively suspended by the weather.

Tuesday, December 22

Western Theater Longstreet's Confederates at Rogersville lose some of their foraging wagons to guerrilla bands. Recruited from the local area, these irregular groups in Federal service cut off small detachments and do not take prisoners. In turn, the "bushwackers" receive little quarter from Confederate soldiers.

Wednesday, December 23

Eastern Theater The Federal cannon on Morris Island continue to batter Fort Sumter.

Thursday, December 24

Western Theater The 7th Illinois Cavalry engage Confederate cavalry pickets at Bolivar, Tennessee.

Friday, December 25

Naval Operations Federal warships engage Confederate shore batteries at John's Island and Stone River, South Carolina. USS *Marblehead* is damaged.

Saturday, December 26

The South The muster rolls record Confederate strength at 465,000 men, but only 278,000 troops are actually present with the colors. Some are temporarily absent, many are sick, and thousands have deserted. But although few Southerners can look forward with any optimism, at least the troops who remain in the Confederate armies are battle-hardened veterans, whereas the North continues to have severe trouble enforcing conscription. One of Lee's troops had shouted to him at the very moment of defeat at Gettysburg: "We'll fight them till hell freezes over—and then we'll fight them on the ice!"

Sunday, December 27

Western Theater Grant visits Knoxville and arranges to run the railroad direct from Chattanooga so the troops in East Tennessee can be supplied by rail instead of through Cumberland Gap by slow convoys of wagons.

Monday, December 28

Western Theater Elements of the 2nd Missouri and 4th Ohio cavalry defeat a Confederate raid on a Union supply column. Their defense of the wagons is so successful that they take 121 prisoners, as well as killing eight and wounding 39 of the attackers. Federal losses are two dead and 15 wounded.

Tuesday, December 29

Western Theater Elements of the 2nd division of the Union XXIII Corps stand to against a Confederate raid on Talbot's Station, Tennessee. In the camps of all armies, but particularly the Confederates, the shortage of fresh fruit and vegetables produces the first signs of scurvy. Until a proper diet can be reinstituted in the spring, the health of the soldiers will continue to suffer. Poor sanitation does not help; dysentery and other disorders, known in the west as "The Mississippi Two-Step," will be rife all winter.

Wednesday, December 30

Trans-Mississippi Banks' operations continue on the Texas littoral. Leaving one force on the Rio Grande, his detachment landed at Corpus Christi assaults a Confederate position at Pass Cavallo. The earthwork, Fort Esperanza, commands the entrance to Matagorda Bay. The garrison is driven out and retires to the mainland. Banks intends to occupy all inlets and passes connecting the Gulf of Mexico to the lagoons and sounds of the Texas coast from the Sabine River to the Rio Grande.

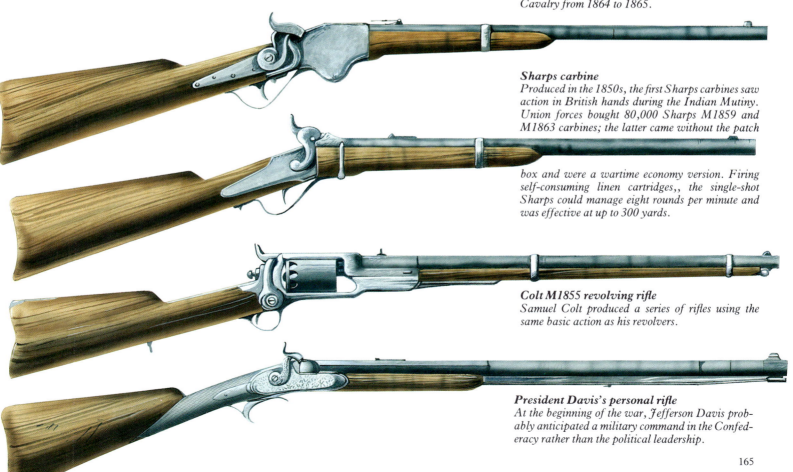

Spencer carbine
This was produced in 1860 by a 27-year-old inventor, Christopher Spencer, who designed all manner of industrial machinery. It was ignored by General Ripley, head of the Ordnance Department, so Spencer offered the president a personal test in August. With a seven-shot tubular magazine housed in the butt, the Spencer had a realistic rate of fire of 10 rounds a minute and produced 6-inch groups at 100 yards. It became highly popular with Union Cavalry from 1864 to 1865.

Sharps carbine
Produced in the 1850s, the first Sharps carbines saw action in British hands during the Indian Mutiny. Union forces bought 80,000 Sharps M1859 and M1863 carbines; the latter came without the patch box and were a wartime economy version. Firing self-consuming linen cartridges,, the single-shot Sharps could manage eight rounds per minute and was effective at up to 300 yards.

Colt M1855 revolving rifle
Samuel Colt produced a series of rifles using the same basic action as his revolvers.

President Davis's personal rifle
At the beginning of the war, Jefferson Davis probably anticipated a military command in the Confederacy rather than the political leadership.

January 1864

The famous raider CSS Alabama *had crossed the Indian Ocean during the fall of 1863. By late December she was passing through the Straits of Malacca and headed back across the Bay of Bengal during early January 1864. She took two more prizes off India in the middle of the month.*

A Union station on the James River where powder was extracted from salvaged Confederate mines. Called torpedoes during the Civil War, they were detonated either by a variety of percussion fuzes or by electric command wire.

Friday, January 1, 1864

Eastern Theater The armies' winter quarters are blanketed with snow, and military operations are effectively suspended. Temperatures fall below zero as far south as Memphis, Tennessee. The Union siege guns at Charleston fire a few rounds at Fort Sumter, but the bombardment will not continue with the same vigor this month.

Saturday, January 2

The South The Confederate Senate confirms Senator George Davis of North Carolina as attorney-general, replacing Wade Keyes who had held the post temporarily since September.
Trans-Mississippi General Banks leads his men against Galveston, continuing his winter campaign along the coast of Texas.

Sunday, January 3

The South After two and a half years of conflict, the Confederate economy continues to collapse. Inflation is out of control; prices this winter are now, on average, 28 times their 1861 levels. Wages have risen by a factor of three or four.
Eastern Theater Union cavalry occupy Jonesville, Virginia. Other Federal cavalry patrol between Charles Town and Winchester, West Virginia.

Monday, January 4

The South President Davis authorizes General Lee to commandeer food supplies in Virginia.

This harsh measure may be needed to feed Lee's hungry troops and starving animals, but the state's capacity to feed itself is already doubtful.
Trans-Mississippi General Halleck renews his instructions to Banks for an offensive along the Red River during the spring. He is to cooperate with Steele's Union forces in Arkansas in a pincer movement against Kirby Smith's Confederates. The plan makes the ambitious assumption that two Union armies, separated by 500 miles of hostile territory and unable to communicate properly, can somehow coordinate themselves against an aggressive and resourceful enemy.

Tuesday, January 5

The North President Lincoln urges Congress to continue paying bounties to volunteers.
Eastern Theater Confederate cavalry recapture Jonesville, taking 200 prisoners.
The South Food shortages are not restricted to Virginia. The loss of the pork-producing states of Tennessee and Kentucky severely weakens the Confederacy's ability to feed its people.

Wednesday, January 6

Western Theater The Union steamer *Delta* is attacked by Confederate guerrillas on the Mississippi.
Trans-Mississippi Colonel "Kit" Carson traps a large number of Navaho Indians in the Canyon de Chelly area in New Mexico Territory.

Thursday, January 7

The North President Lincoln commutes the death sentence of an army deserter, unable to add to "the butchering business." The desertion rate in the Federal armies, particularly the Army of the Potomac, is now a severe problem. Field punishments are more common and more brutal than in the far-off "volunteer days" of 1861–2.

Friday, January 8

The South John H. Morgan returns in triumph to Richmond after his spectacular escape from Ohio State Penitentiary. In New Orleans pro-Union activists meet to consider reconstruction in the state of Louisiana. David O. Dodd, convicted as a Confederate spy, is hanged at Little Rock, Arkansas.
Trans-Mississippi Federal artillery bombards Confederate defenses at the mouth of Caney Bayou, Texas.

Saturday, January 9

Trans-Mississippi Arkansas is in the iron grip of winter. All operations give way to the daily struggle to stay warm and find something to eat. The hostile armies are ranged along the line of the Arkansas River. Confederate general Kirby Smith now has one of the most independent commands of the war; with the Mississippi controlled by the Union, southern Arkansas is isolated from the rest of the Confederacy.

Left: *A Dahlgren gun aboard USS* Mendota *during 1864. These large-caliber cannon saw widespread service on both the river fleets and ocean-going warships. The design was perfected by Rear Admiral John A. Dahlgren during his time with the Ordnance Bureau before the war. He left in 1861 to take command of the South Atlantic blockading squadron.*

Below left: *Many blacks served in the US Navy; some vessels of the river fleet were crewed almost entirely by Negroes. This is the crew of the gunboat* Mendota. *Note the sailor with a banjo, center left; the Civil War left an enduring musical legacy.*

Below: *"The value of the magnetic telegraph in war cannot be exaggerated."—General William T. Sherman. Federal engineers added over 15,000 miles of line during the war, enabling commanders to confer as never before. However, it could provide a mixed blessing: both presidents indulged in some "back-seat driving" from their capitals, although Lincoln's judgements were generally more sound than Davis's.*

Sunday, January 10

The South Although inflation is eating away at the Confederate economy, the government continues to print more paper money. Taxing land and slaves is failing to generate significant income. With few banks in the South, there is no liquid capital; borrowing from abroad is becoming impossible, and supplies of foreign weapons demand foreign currency or gold. The flood of paper money is deliberately increased by the Federals who are now faking Confederate money as a tool of economic warfare. But the remorseless blockade claims its price today; the blockader USS *Iron Age* runs aground at Folly Inlet, South Carolina, and is lost after Confederate batteries bombard her.

Monday, January 11

The North Senator John B. Henderson of Missouri proposes a joint resolution in the Senate abolishing slavery throughout the United States.

One reason for the appalling desertion rate in the Union armies is the bounty system. Since the number of men to be drafted in any state, city or county is inversely proportional to the number of men who volunteer, larger and larger cash bounties have been offered to attract volunteers. Towns and cities have escalated the bounties throughout the fall. This has succeeded in keeping down the number of men to be conscripted, but has filled the army with the worst sort of recruit. Men join up to get the bounty, then desert at the earliest opportunity, only to re-enlist in another town and repeat the process. Despite opposition in Congress, the system continues to thrive.

Tuesday, January 12

The North Anyone whose name comes up in the draft is allowed to avoid military service if he can pay a $300 fee. This gives exemption until his name is called again. However, if a drafted man can hire a substitute, his liability is at an end and he is permanently exempt. To service the increasing demand for substitutes, a class of "substitute brokers" is doing a roaring business this winter, charging a fee to find potential soldiers and inducing them to enlist. A lot of men make fast money providing the army with the sick, the useless, and the retarded. The 57 men recruited by the 6th New York Heavy Artillery this winter include 17 physically disabled and several congenital idiots.

Mexico Federal troops intervene in Matamoros, Mexico, to rescue the US consul. French efforts to subdue the guerrilla armies continue.

Wednesday, January 13

The North President Lincoln presses Federal officials in Louisiana and Florida to form Union governments.

Thursday, January 14

The South President Davis writes General Johnston, now commanding the Department of the Tennessee, warning that he may have to provide troops for the defense of Alabama or Mississippi during the spring. But, he continues, Johnston's army must not retreat if pressed by Union forces from Tennessee.

Friday, January 15

The North At the roll call of one regiment in the Army of the Potomac, many of the new recruits forget which name they enlisted under. The combination of bounty jumpers and new immigrants is the despair of veteran soldiers. The despair of President Lincoln is that many of these veterans will finish their term of enlistment during the spring. They cannot be compelled to stay with the colors, but if they leave, the Federal Army will be in no condition to take the field.

Saturday, January 16

Europe Prussia and Austria present their ultimatum to King Christian IX of Denmark, bringing Europe to the brink of war. Bismarck orchestrates the Prussian demand for Denmark to abandon its new constitution and Schleswig-Holstein. Prussian troops occupied the Duchy of Holstein during December. In Britain Palmerston thunders against the Prussian aggression but is privately aware that intervention is militarily and politically impossible. In France Napoleon III is equally horrified but powerless. The smallest, lingering hope that Britain or France might recognize the Confederacy is snuffed out by the European crisis.

January 1864

Sunday, January 17, 1864

Eastern Theater Commander James Wallace Cooke journeys to Edward's Ferry on the Roanoke River, North Carolina, to take command of an ironclad under construction there. Cooke, who commanded the *Ellis* during the battle for Hatteras inlet, has several wounds and a spell in Federal prison behind him, but he is enthusiastic about his new command. The vessel is the *Albemarle*, brainchild of another Confederate captured at Hatteras Island, Gilbert Elliot.

Monday, January 18

Eastern Theater Protest meetings in North Carolina voice the widespread opposition to the Confederacy's conscription law, which renders all white males between 18 and 45 liable for service. They will achieve nothing; the law will soon extend conscription to 17-year-olds and men up to 60.

Tuesday, January 19

Eastern Theater In a cornfield belonging to William Ruffin Smith, the ironclad *Albemarle* begins to take shape. Yellow pine planking for the ship comes from the farm of Smith's son, and his grandson works as a courier for the builders.
Trans-Mississippi In Arkansas the pro-Union Constitutional Convention meeting at Little Rock adopts an anti-slavery measure.

Wednesday, January 20

The North President Lincoln responds to the news from Arkansas, telling General Frederick Steele, commanding Federal forces there, that an election should be held at once.
Western Theater There is a minor skirmish at Tracy City, Tennessee. The Union forces deployed around Knoxville continue to suffer from supply shortages, particularly animal fodder.

Thursday, January 21

The North Due to a shortage of grain, the authorities in Ohio ban the distillation of whiskey.
Western Theater Pro-Union leaders in Tennessee meet at Nashville to plan a constitutional convention which will create a new government and abolish slavery in the state.

Friday, January 22

Western Theater With animals dying of starvation and the men on short rations, some of the Union troops near Knoxville are directed to march closer to their depots. Sheridan's division is ordered to march on Loudon, Tennessee. Major-General Rosecrans is appointed commander of the Department of the Missouri, succeeding General J.M. Schofield.
Trans-Mississippi Isaac Murphy is inaugurated provisional governor of Arkansas in the restored pro-Union administration, pending the elections which will be held in March.

Saturday, January 23

The North President Lincoln approves a policy by which slaves would be freed by plantation owners who would then hire them to continue working the land. The Treasury Department cancels most of the restrictions on trade in Kentucky and Missouri.
Trans-Mississippi In a minor action at Rolling Prairie, Arkansas, 11 soldiers from the 11th Missouri Cavalry are killed.

Sunday, January 24

Trans-Mississippi Cavalry actions continue in Arkansas, with another skirmish at Baker Springs.

Monday, January 25

Eastern Theater Fort Sumter suffers another day's shelling. The bombardment has continued with hardly a pause since August, but the tortured rubble still flies the Confederate Flag, and the Union fleet does not contemplate another amphibious assault.
Western Theater Union troops evacuate Corinth, Mississippi.

Tuesday, January 26

The North President Lincoln suspends another nine executions. He approves new trade regulation for dealing with former Confederate territory now under Union control again.
Western Theater Sheridan's men march along frozen roads, glad of the activity. They have still been sleeping under ponchos as their promised tents have failed to materialize.

Wednesday, January 27

The South President Davis invites his old friend Braxton Bragg over to Richmond where he will become the president's military adviser.

Western Theater Sturgis's cavalry fight Confederate horsemen at Kelly's Ford, Tennessee, suffering 100 casualties. They kill 65 rebel troops and capture 100. Meanwhile, Sheridan's division reaches Loudon.

Thursday, January 28

Western Theater Elements of the Union XIV Corps are engaged in a minor action at Tunnel Hill, Georgia.

Friday, January 29

Eastern Theater A small Union infantry brigade and two regiments of cavalry are engaged at Medley, West Virginia. Around 100 Confederate casualties are reported in an action that leaves 10 Federal troops dead and 70 wounded. At Charleston the Confederates finish fitting out another ironclad, the CSS *Charleston*. She is known unofficially as "The Ladies' Ironclad Gunboat," as much of the money for her has been raised by bazaars and fund-raising fairs organized by the ladies of the city.
Western Theater Sheridan's division receives its long overdue tents and winter clothing. The Union steamer *Sir William Wallace* is attacked by Confederates on the Mississippi River.

Saturday, January 30

Eastern Theater General George E. Pickett marches from Kinston, North Carolina, to attack New Berne, held by 3000 Federals under General I.N. Palmer. Pickett's force consists of three infantry brigades, 14 guns, and 600 cavalry—about 4500 men. He is supported by 10 rowboats, manned by 300 men armed with muskets and cutlasses, under the command of Colonel John Taylor Wood. The Union garrison is supported by the steamers *Lockwood*, *Commodore Hull*, and *Underwriter* stationed on the Neuse and Trent rivers.

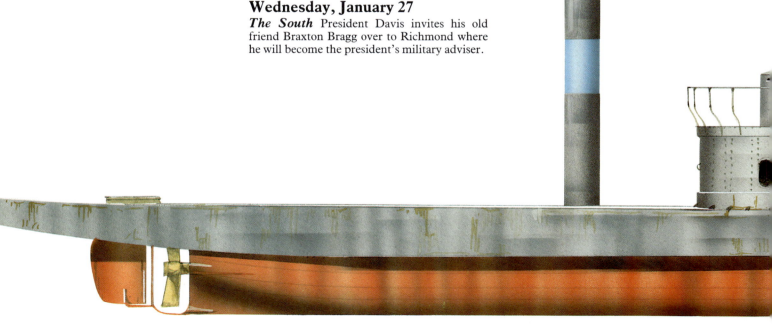

Right: *One of the most obvious advantages enjoyed by the Union soldiers was their food; this is a company kitchen preparing dinner. The starved condition of Confederate dead left on the field of battle had been observed during 1863. In the spring battles of 1864 it would be noticed that Yankee dead bloated and festered much faster than the empty-bellied rebels.*

Below right: *Religious service aboard the monitor USS* Passaic *while she was serving with the block-ading squadron off Charleston in 1864. The* Passaic *was involved in the epic duel with the Confederate batteries in April 1863. She suffered 35 hits in the futile 40-minute engagement.*

Below: Passaic *class monitors of the US Navy were the backbone of the naval forces and proved invaluable in all the actions they took part in.*

These 1875-ton vessels armed with two guns in a single, revolving turret were an improvement over the original Monitor *upon which Ericsson based the design. Delays were experienced in their construction because armor manufacturers were already busy working on existing orders. The same applied to the construction of the machinery as all well established companies were swamped with work. Even companies of doubtful financial stability were considered in order to overcome the problem.*

The first completed batch of Passaic *monitors took part in the abortive attack upon Charleston in April 1863 and sustained heavy damage in the day-long action. The Navy Department had had high hopes of these vessels, expecting them to take Charleston without the support of the army.*

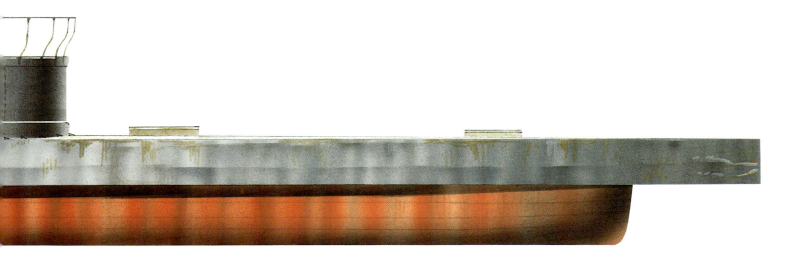

January–February 1864

Matthew Brady (1823–96) spent his entire fortune of over $100,000 to take more than 3500 photographs during the war. He trained a team of photographers in the wet plate process he pioneered. This enabled him to take large numbers of pictures, but they still required long exposure times. The stilted poses of his subjects are mostly due to this problem.

Sunday, January 31, 1864
The North President Lincoln writes General Banks, now returned to New Orleans to plan his campaign up the Red River. Lincoln hints that he will accept "unquestionably loyal free state men" being given the vote without them fulfilling all requirements demanded by the Proclamation of Amnesty and Reconstruction. All the same, he continues, "I do wish they should all take the oath."

Monday, February 1, 1864
The North President Lincoln orders another 500,000 men drafted on March 10. They will serve for three years, or the duration of the war. Grant's patron, Elihu Washburne, succeeds in persuading Congress to revive the rank of lieutenant-general for Grant's benefit.
Europe Prussian troops invade the Duchy of Schleswig, beginning the Danish war.

Tuesday, February 2
Eastern Theater During the early hours of the morning, Wood's Confederates seize the Union steamer *Underwriter* as she lies at anchor under the guns of Fort Stevenson. They kill her commander, acting master Jacob Westervelt and, three crew before the others surrender. But the ship's boilers are cold so the Confederates cannot make away with their prize. Instead, they set fire to her and escape.

Wednesday, February 3
The South Increasingly harsh government from Richmond has fanned opposition to President Davis, but today he suspends habeas corpus for those accused of spying, desertion, or association with the enemy.
Eastern Theater Pickett abandons his plans for an assault on New Berne after a study of the defenses.
Western Theater General Sherman leaves Vicksburg with 20,000 troops. His objective is to destroy the Mobile and Ohio railroad from Okolona southward, and to capture or burn as much Confederate property and supplies as possible. His infantry will march on Meridian, where they plan to link up with a cavalry force under General W. Sooy Smith, Grant's chief-of-cavalry.

Thursday, February 4
Western Theater The Confederate troops opposing Sherman's winter offensive are commanded by the irascible Leonidas Polk. He has some 20,000 men available but they are widely dispersed. Sherman's men advance over the old battlefields of 1863.

Friday, February 5
The South General Gillmore orders General Truman Seymour to land a division at Jacksonville, Florida. The objective is to press westward to block the movement of supplies from southern Florida and, more importantly, to form a rallying point for pro-Federal citizens who might wish to form a quasi state government and rally to the Union.
Western Theater Advancing in two columns of infantry under McPherson and Hurlbut, Sherman's troops reach Jackson, Mississippi.

Saturday, February 6
The South The fourth session of the Confederate Congress bans the import of luxury goods and the circulation of US paper currency. Neither measure will be fully obeyed.
Eastern Theater A Federal sortie over the Rapidan meets tough resistance from the Confederates and has to withdraw during the night.

Sunday, February 7
The South Seymour lands with 7000 troops at Jacksonville, Florida, assisted by Admiral Dahlgren and five gunboats. As well as engineering Forida's return to the Union, he hopes to recruit local blacks into the Federal Army.
Western Theater Sherman continues his advance on Meridian. Unknown to him, the cavalry raid has not started yet as Sooy Smith's forces have failed to concentrate in time.

Monday, February 8
Western Theater General Sooy Smith's command consists of three cavalry brigades and 20 guns. The first brigade left Union City, Tennessee, on January 22 but does not arrive until today, delayed by flooding as the swamps and rivers burst their banks.

Tuesday, February 9
Eastern Theater 109 Union officers dig their way out of Libby Prison, Richmond. It is the largest escape of the war; 59 men reach Union lines, 48 are recaptured, and two drown. The leader of this audacious escape, Colonel Thomas E. Rose, is unfortunately among those returned to the prison.

Wednesday, February 10
Western Theater Sooy Smith's cavalry complete their preparations for the raid which should have begun over a week ago. Today the pack train, which could have been prepared earlier, is finally organized.
France The Confederate raider *Florida* slips out of Brest, where she has been laid up since August, and evades the watching USS *Kearsage*.

Thursday, February 11
Eastern Theater Confederate guerrillas under Major H.W. Gillmore derail a train in West Virginia, then rob the passengers.
Western Theater General Sooy Smith finally begins his long awaited cavalry raid, one day after he was supposed to link up with Sherman's infantry. Heavy rains continue to hamper movement.

Friday, February 12
Western Theater There are skirmishes at Chunky Station and Decatur as Sherman's columns head for Meridian. Other minor actions occur at Macon and California House, Missouri.

Saturday, February 13
The South Confederate forces assemble in Florida in response to the Union invasion. At Lake City 4600 infantry, 600 cavalry, and 12 guns are now ready under the command of Brigadier-General Joseph Finegan. At Hilton Head General Gillmore issues a proclamation announcing the occupation of Florida, calling on the people to take the oath of allegiance to the Union. But Seymour remains unconvinced that there is much pro-Union sympathy in Florida and marches his troops toward the Suwanee River to break down the bridges.

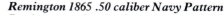

Remington 1865 .50 caliber Navy Pattern
Remington produced a large number of different handguns during the war. This Navy Pattern, built on the success of the Army .44 New Model and M1861 .36 caliber revolvers which were widely used by Federal forces. Pistols were especially popular with naval boarding parties. The 1600 US Navy sailors attacking Fort Fisher in January 1865 were solely armed with cutlasses and revolvers, ready for a hand-to-hand fight. Their repulse clearly demonstrated the pistol's limitations as a military weapon.

A four-tier railroad trestle bridge 780 feet long stretches over a gully at Whiteside, Tennessee. Advancing the railroad was crucial to the forward movement of troops. Sherman estimated that the furthest an army could operate from a railhead was about 100 miles—the furthest distance a wagon could cover before the teams consumed all its contents en route.

The imposing signal tower which stood on Cobb's Hill, New Market, Virginia, during 1864. "Wig-Wag" signal flags were used extensively by both sides. Posted on such vantage points, the semaphore operators could also observe troop movements themselves. A Confederate "Wig-Wag" station spotted and betrayed the Union flanking maneuver at First Manassas. Both sides struggled to develop codes unintelligible to enemy observers. The Union adoption of the Myer cypher disc was a major breakthrough in this respect but it was not as widely used as it could have been.

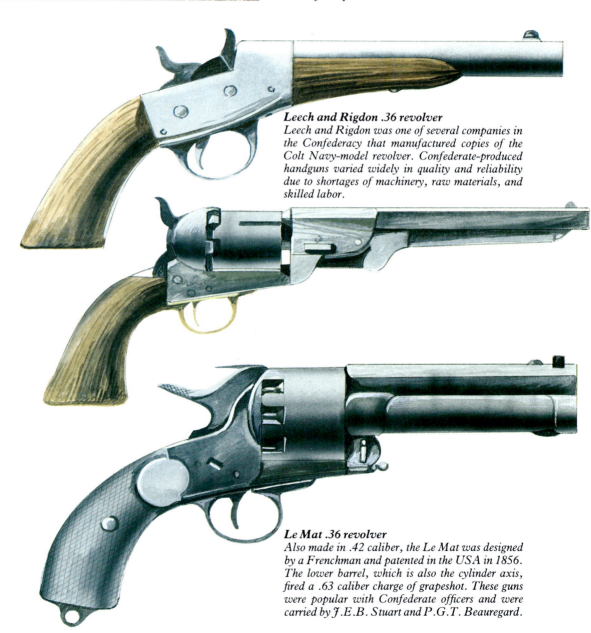

Leech and Rigdon .36 revolver
Leech and Rigdon was one of several companies in the Confederacy that manufactured copies of the Colt Navy-model revolver. Confederate-produced handguns varied widely in quality and reliability due to shortages of machinery, raw materials, and skilled labor.

Le Mat .36 revolver
Also made in .42 caliber, the Le Mat was designed by a Frenchman and patented in the USA in 1856. The lower barrel, which is also the cylinder axis, fired a .63 caliber charge of grapeshot. These guns were popular with Confederate officers and were carried by J.E.B. Stuart and P.G.T. Beauregard.

171

February 1864

Sunday, February 14, 1864

Western Theater Sherman's men enter Meridian and commence the systematic destruction of the town. In addition to the strategically important railroad, Sherman destroys the hotels, offices, hospitals, and storehouses. There is still no sign of Sooy Smith's cavalry.

One of the methods used by the Confederacy in their struggle with the Union was that of letting raiders loose upon the merchant marine of the North. Although only a few vessels ranged across the oceans of the world, they were able to drive the US merchant marine from the sea, and it was not until the turn of the century that the US merchant marine got back to its former position of 1860.

A typical raider was the former blockade runner Edith, *now renamed* Chickamauga. *Placed under the command of the South's leading blockade runner John Wilkinson, she enjoyed a brief but successful cruise as a raider before reverting to her former trade.*

Monday, February 15

Eastern Theater The Confederate forces, assembled at Ocean Pond on the Olustree River, Florida, work to improve their defenses. The low-lying country is flat and covered with open pine forest unobstructed by undergrowth.

Tuesday, February 16

Western Theater There is a minor action at Lauderdale Springs near Meridian. Sherman has about half his command engaged in destroying Meridian, while the other 10,000 are deployed against Polk.

Naval Operations Two blockade runners are intercepted off Wilmington, North Carolina. Wilmington remains the ideal haven for the blockade runners because the Federal fleet cannot effectively blockade the mouth of the Cape Fear River. This is divided by an island and blocked by a shallow bar. Just at the entrance, dominating the approaches to Wilmington, is Fort Fisher. Two-thirds of the runs from Wilmington will be successful in early 1864.

Wednesday, February 17

The South Conscription is extended to all white men aged between 17 and 50. The chorus of opposition to the measure is led by the vice-president himself.

Naval Operations The Confederate submarine *Hunley* makes its first and last attack, sinking the Union sloop *Housatonic* off Charleston. The Federal sailors spot a dark shape in the water, 100 yards from their vessel. Beating to quarters, they find they cannot depress their cannon to fire on the mysterious object. The *Hunley* continues its painfully slow, hand-cranked progress toward the target, which ups anchor and begins to drift away. *Hunley* eventually strikes home with a spar torpedo which explodes to devastating effect. *Housatonic* settles in 28 feet of water, all but five crew making it to the nearby USS *Canadaigua*. The gallant Confederate submariners are all killed as *Hunley* is dragged to the bottom along with its victim.

Thursday, February 18

Europe Bullock notifies Mallory that the two ironclads building in France will not be allowed to sail. With the Danish crisis commanding his attention, Napoleon III is in no mood to further antagonize the United States.

Western Theater Sooy Smith's cavalry reaches the prairie country to eastern Mississippi around Okolona. A few skirmishes take place, but the Union troops do not meet with serious resistance.

Friday, February 19

Western Theater Sooy Smith continues his advance, pressing on toward West Point, 30 miles south of Okolona.

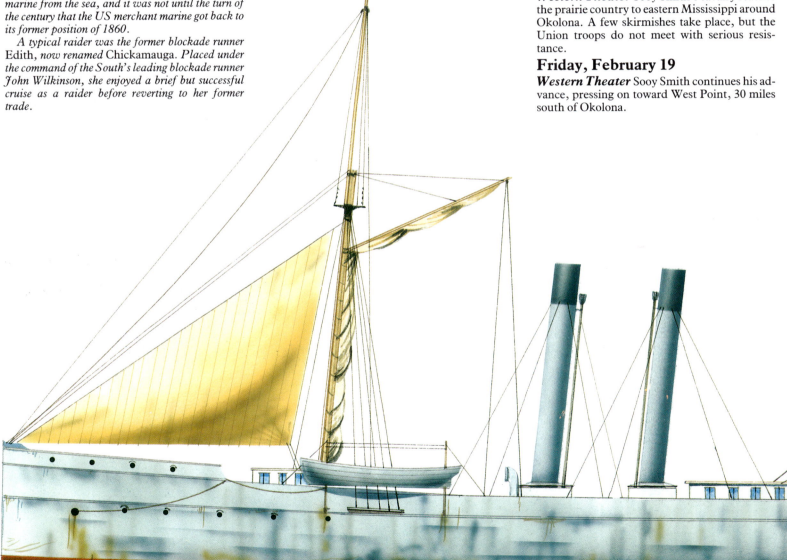

Saturday, February 20

Western Theater Sherman begins to withdraw back to Vicksburg, despairing of ever linking up with Sooy Smith's elusive cavalry division.

The South Seymour's Union troops march 18 miles from the south fork of the St Mary's River to Olustree, Florida. Some 5500 Federal troops and 16 guns are soon engaged against a similar number of Confederates, who advance out of their defenses believing that the Union forces would be unlikely to attack them. At the start of the battle the 64th Georgia, a new regiment, forms square, believing it is to face a cavalry attack, but Brigadier-General Colquitt shakes them into line before the Union guns can concentrate on this dense target.

A bitter musketry duel begins at a range of 250 yards in the open pine forest. The 7th New Hampshire, a veteran regiment whose ranks have been diluted with substitutes and inferior conscripts, breaks and flees. The 8th US Colored Regiment fights on, suffering 300 casualties out of 500. Despite several of their regiments being armed with Spencer carbines, the Union forces are driven back and defeated. Federal casualties are 1861; Confederate losses, 940. The Union forces leave 1600 rifles and five field guns behind.

Sunday, February 21

Western Theater Sooy Smith's cavalry runs into Nathan Bedford Forrest's troops, entrenched at West Point. Sooy Smith orders an immediate retreat, urging his men on to out-distance the Confederates, who actually consist of Forrest's personal escort and part of Faulkner's regiment.

Monday, February 22

Western Theater Forrest concentrates his cavalry and pursues Sooy Smith, overhauling the Union troops by dawn. Sooy Smith begins a rear guard action at 5.00 a.m. but the 7th Indiana flee after the first shots, abandoning five guns to the enemy. During the day the Union cavalry retreat nine miles. A charge by the 4th Missouri Cavalry temporarily checks the Confederate pursuit but does not make up for the scale of this humiliating defeat. Around 7000 Union cavalry have been herded back toward their own lines by 2500 Confederates.

Tuesday, February 23

The North President Lincoln's Cabinet meets without Secretary of the Treasury Chase. He is compromised by the "Pomeroy Circular"—a paper produced by Senator Pomeroy calling for Chase to run for the presidency.

Wednesday, February 24

Europe Since the British government will never countenance its sailing, North's ironclad is sold to Denmark. Of the rams building in France, one is also sold to the Danes and the other to Prussia. It seems that the Confederate naval programme in Europe is finished.

The North Congress approves the revival of the rank of lieutenant-general, enabling Grant to become the supreme commander of the Union Army. President Lincoln approves a plan to free slaves who enlist, paying their former masters $300 compensation.

The South President Davis appoints General Bragg to control the conduct of military operations. The outspoken Longstreet bitterly denounces this blatant favoring of an incompetent officer purely on the basis of personal friendship.

Western Theater General Thomas decides to break from his winter quarters on a reconnaissance against Johnston's Army of the Tennessee. Federal troops drive in Confederate outposts at Tunnel Hill, Georgia.

Thursday, February 25

Western Theater Thomas's troops attempt to break through at Buzzard Roost Gap. By placing this pressure on Johnston, Thomas is trying to see whether the Army of the Tennessee has been weakened to provide reinforcements for Polk's command in Mississippi.

Friday, February 26

Western Theater Sooy Smith's defeated cavalry arrive back in Memphis. Sherman's troops withdraw to Canton. Confederate engineers begin to assess the damage caused by Sherman.

Saturday, February 27

The South At Andersonville, Georgia, Union prisoners of war begin to arrive at a log stockade. Built because Richmond can no longer accommodate the numbers of Federal prisoners, this crudely built prison will become the most notorious prison camp of the war.

February–March 1864

Sunday, February 28, 1864

Eastern Theater Brigadier-General Judson Kilpatrick leads 3500 Union cavalry on an ambitious raid against Richmond itself. To the anger of his commander, Pleasonton, Kilpatrick had submitted his plan to President Lincoln and Secretary of War Stanton. Recognizing that the Confederate capital's defenses are lightly manned, Kilpatrick's plan is to break into Richmond by surprise, free the 15,000 Federal prisoners held at Belle Isle, and race back to Union lines before Lee's army can react. He is joined on the raid by Ulric Dahlgren, son of the famous Federal admiral.

Monday, February 29

Eastern Theater Kilpatrick leads the main body of the Federal raiders straight toward Richmond. The one-legged Dahlgren (he lost it in a cavalry action after Gettysburg) takes 500 men and rides toward Goochland. The Confederates in Richmond learn of the operation and begin to concentrate forces against it.

Tuesday, March 1, 1864

The North President Lincoln nominates Ulysses Grant for lieutenant-general.

Eastern Theater Kilpatrick's raid begins to go badly wrong. His command has hardly stopped moving for 36 hours, a pace which exhausts men and horses alike. At dawn he demonstrates in front of Richmond; according to the plan, Dahlgren was to have infiltrated the city by now, but the defenses reply with a steady stream of cannon shot. Kilpatrick withdraws. He makes another attempt near evening, only to run into Wade Hampton's cavalry drawn down from Lee's army. The Federal brigade is chased through the darkness.

Meanwhile, Dahlgren reaches the James River and dallies at the house of Confederate Secretary of War Seddon, drinking blackberry wine with Mrs Seddon before rejoining his men. Guided to a ford by a colored guide named Martin, Dahlgren is furious to find the river in full spate. Crying treachery, he has the guide hanged and heads toward Richmond on the north bank. By the time he reaches Richmond, Kilpatrick has already retreated.

Wednesday, March 2

The North Grant is confirmed as lieutenant-general by the Senate. As the highest ranking officer, he assumes the title general-in-chief of the Army of the United States.

Eastern Theater Dahlgren is ambushed during the night and shot dead at the head of his troops. His artificial leg is stolen and documents found on his body state that his objective was to fire Richmond and kill the Confederate Cabinet. There is understandable doubt about the authenticity of these notes but General Lee sends photographic plates of them to General Meade, along with a vigorous protest.

174

Thursday, March 3

Eastern Theater Kilpatrick's cavalry continue their retreat, riding hard to evade the Confederate pursuit. Dahlgren's body is stripped and carted into Richmond in an open pine box.

Friday, March 4

The North Andrew Johnson is confirmed by the Senate as Federal military governor of Tennessee.

Eastern Theater Kilpatrick, dubbed by his men "Kill Cavalry," raids the area where Dahlgren met his death before retreating back to the Union lines. The raid has cost the Federals 340 men, over 500 horses, and many Spencer carbines.

Western Theater Sherman's infantry returns to Vicksburg.

Saturday, March 5

The South The Confederate Government demands half the cargo space on all blockade runners. The fabulous profits realized by the blockaders are not entirely related to war material; handsome sums are being made bringing in luxury goods. Not willing to rely on private enterprise, the resourceful Confederate Ordnance Bureau and the state of North Carolina commissioned their own vessels.

Sunday, March 6

The North Northern newspapers celebrate Kilpatrick's raid as a great success and take delight in describing the dilapidated state of northern Virginia. Southern papers make the most of Dahlgren's incriminating papers and denounce the whole affair as Northern barbarity.

Monday, March 7

Eastern Theater The first load of armor for the *Albemarle* arrives at Halifax, North Carolina.

Tuesday, March 8

The North President Lincoln meets Grant for the first time. At a White House reception, the embarrassed general has to stand on a sofa to shake hands with a cheering crowd.

Wednesday, March 9

The North Grant receives his command in a ceremony attended by the Cabinet. Afterward he has a long talk with Lincoln, quickly winning the president's confidence. Following his interview, Grant leaves Washington, announcing to some people's surprise that his headquarters would not be in the capital, but in the field, next to that of the Army of the Potomac.

Thursday, March 10

Eastern Theater Grant meets Meade at Brandy Station. The smartly turned out Zouave regiment, the 114th Pennsylvania, parade in his honor and the band plays on, oblivious to the fact that the new commander is tone deaf and cannot tell one tune from another.

Friday, March 11

Western Theater The expected spring rise in the Red River has not yet begun. Halleck's plan for a major offensive along this waterway will go into action tomorrow, but if the waters do not rise soon, the powerful Union river fleet will be helpless.

Saturday, March 12

Western Theater Admiral Porter leads a fleet of 13 ironclads and seven light-draft gunboats into the mouth of the Red River. With the fleet are 10,000 of Sherman's troops and 17,000 from Banks' command. In theory they are to cooperate with Steele's 15,000 men in northern Arkansas, but this proves to be impossible. Halleck's plan still makes no allowance for any defensive action by Kirby Smith's 30,000 Confederates.

Left: *Major-General Meade, embattled commander of the Army of the Potomac, 1864. Radical members of Congress were pressing for his removal and his caution during the fall of 1863 had led to widespread criticism. But when Grant set up his headquarters in the field with the army, he expressed full confidence in Meade's leadership.*

Below: *Federal engineers bridge the Tennessee River at Chattanooga in March 1864. Sherman's advance on Atlanta greatly extended his supply line and large numbers of troops had to be left behind to protect such valuable assets from Confederate raiders like Bedford Forrest.*

Bottom: *Awnings rigged against the baking summer heat, the monitor USS* Onondaga *lies in the James River during 1864. The four gunboats with her departed at the end of the year to take part in the attack on Fort Fisher. This prompted the Confederate James River squadron to attack the isolated monitor; but their raid, in January 1865, was frustrated by obstructions in the river.* Onondaga *inflicted serious damage on the CSS* Virginia II *before she was floated off and escaped.*

March 1864

Sunday, March 13, 1864

The North President Lincoln hints to the recently elected free-state governor of Louisiana, Michael Hahn, that some of the "very intelligent" blacks be seated in a convention which would define the elective franchise.

Trans-Mississippi Two divisions of the Union XVI Corps plus Kilby Smith's division of the XVII land from Porter's fleet at Simsport, near the head of the Atchafalaya River.

Monday, March 14

Trans-Mississippi Commanded by Brigadier-General A.J. Smith, the three Federal divisions overrun Fort De Russy near Simsport. The Confederate defenders, Walker's division commanded by General Richard Taylor, fall back on Bayou Boeuf, covering Alexandria, Louisiana. The assault on Fort De Russy costs 34 Union casualties but results in the capture of eight heavy guns, two field pieces, and 260 prisoners. Meanwhile, Porter's fleet breaks through the dam nine miles downstream and steams toward Alexandria.

Tuesday, March 15

The South Federal governor Michael Hahn of Louisiana is invested with powers formerly held by the military governor.

Trans-Mississippi Porter's fleet steams up the Red River and arrives at Alexandria.

Wednesday, March 16

Western Theater Bedford Forrest's cavalry begins a raid into Tennessee and Kentucky.

Trans-Mississippi Kilby Smith's division is shipped up the Red River and lands at Alexandria. Taylor's Confederates retreat on Natchitoches, summoning Mouton's division from the country north of the river.

Thursday, March 17

The North President Lincoln writes Representative John A.J. Creswell pushing for emancipation in the state of Maryland.

Western Theater At Nashville, Tennessee, Grant, conferring with Sherman, formally assumes command of the armies of the United States. Halleck, relieved at his own request, will be chief-of-staff. Grant announces: "Headquarters will be in the field, and until further notice, will be with the Army of the Potomac." He recognizes that the key to victory is the destruction of the Army of Northern Virginia.

Friday, March 18

Western Theater Major-General William T. Sherman officially assumes command of the Military Division of the Mississippi.

Trans-Mississippi Arkansas voters ratify the new pro-Union constitution which ends slavery in the state. Taylor's Confederates concentrate at Carroll Jones' Plantation, in the pine forest, covering the roads to Sabine and Shreveport, 36 miles above Alexandria.

Saturday, March 19

The South The Georgia legislature, knowing an invasion from Tennessee is imminent, resolves that the Confederacy should offer peace after each victory. This would be based on independence for the South and self-determination for the border states.

Trans-Mississippi Banks' advance guard enters Alexandria. Delayed in New Orleans, Banks sends forward 15,000 infantry and 4600 cavalry under the command of General Franklin, Departing from the Teche River, 175 miles away on March 13, their journey was hampered by bad weather ruining the roads.

Sunday, March 20

Naval Operations The CSS *Alabama* arrives off Cape Town, South Africa.

Monday, March 21

The North President Lincoln approves an act of Congress enabling the territories of Colorado and Nevada to become states in spite of their small populations.

Trans-Mississippi Taylor's Confederates suffer a major disaster at Bayou Rapides. At night, in a heavy rainstorm, their sole cavalry unit, the 2nd Louisiana, is captured by the enterprising Union general A.J. Mower. Crossing the Bayou 23 miles above Alexandria. Mower's men capture 250 troops, 200 horses, and four guns of Edgar's battery before returning to Alexandria.

Tuesday, March 22

The North Major-General Lewis Wallace supersedes Brigadier-General Henry H. Lockwood in command of the Middle Department, with headquarters in Baltimore.

The South Heavy snow falls in Richmond.

Wednesday, March 23

The North General Grant returns to Washington. Major-General G.K. Warren replaces Major-General George Sykes in command of the Army of the Potomac's V Corps. Some members of congress press for the removal of General Meade.

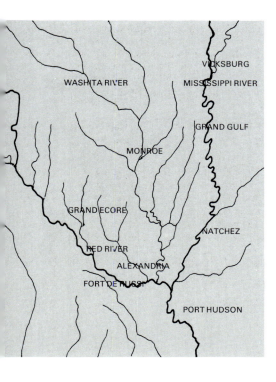

The Red River campaign

In the fall of 1863 Union forces seized several key points along the Texas coastline. General Halleck was particularly concerned to establish a large Union presence in Texas and he ordered Major-General Nathaniel Banks to organize a major offensive up the Red River during the spring. The river was only navigable for a few weeks of the year, and the operation hinged on the water level rising on time. But in 1864 the river did not rise to its usual level, limiting the advance of the large Union river fleet. After Banks's defeat at Sabine Cross Roads on April 8, there was a serious danger that the US warships would be cut off as the Red River began to fall. Only timely and ingenious damming of the river saved the ships.

Trans-Mississippi General Frederick Steele's Union Army advances south from Little Rock, Arkansas. The Confederates now face a two-pronged assault: Steele in the north, and the large concentration assembling at Alexandria.

Thursday, March 24

Western Theater Confederate cavalry under Bedford Forrest capture Union City, Tennessee.

Trans-Mississippi There is a skirmish at Oil Trough Bottom, Arkansas. Federal troops operate from Batesville to Coon Creek and Devil's Fork at the mouth of the Red River.

Far West A Federal expedition against the Indians leaves Camp Lincoln near Canyon City, Oregon.

Friday, March 25

Western Theater Bedford Forrest's cavalry attack Paducah, Kentucky, on the Ohio River. They make two assaults but are unable to subdue the Union garrison. News of their arrival causes panic along the valley of the Ohio.

Trans-Mississippi Banks' main column begins to arrive in Alexandria. The waters of the Red River are rising, but not fast enough for the Federal fleet which needs to pass the rapids near the city in order to continue upstream in support of the army operations.

Saturday, March 26

Western Theater Bedford Forrest retreats towards Fort Pillow on the Mississippi as Union cavalry respond to his raid. Major-General James B. McPherson assumes command of the Army of the Tennessee under Sherman.

March–April 1864

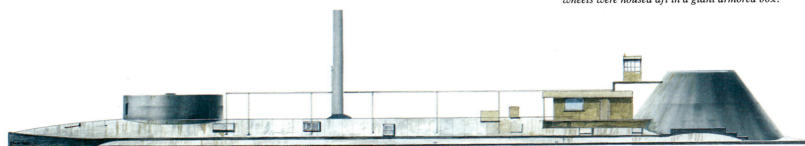

USS Osage *was one of the shallow-draft warships built to back up the earlier gunboats. The paddle-wheels were housed aft in a giant armored box.*

Sunday March 27, 1864

Trans-Mississippi At his headquuarters in Alexandria, Louisiana, General Banks receives orders from Lieutenant-General Grant, dated March 15. A.J. Smith's corps is ordered to join Sherman's army at Vicksburg for the coming Atlanta campaign, and Banks is to attack Mobile. Yet Halleck's original orders are not cancelled. Banks confers with his staff and decides to rush ahead with the Red River campaign, aiming to conclude operations quickly before he has to lose Smith's troops.

Monday, March 28

The North A mob of about 100 copperheads vent their hatred on Federal soldiers on furlough at Charleston, Illinois. Five men are killed and 20 wounded in a savage anti-war riot.

Trans-Mississippi Banks' troops advance from Alexandria. The Confederate Army of General Richard Taylor concentrates in readiness for battle.

Tuesday, March 29

The North Stung by newspaper criticism of his handling of the Gettysburg battle—probably fed to the press by hostile officers of his own army—General Meade is on the verge of demanding a public inquiry. Knowing that this would serve no useful purpose, President Lincoln dissuades Meade from making such a request.

Trans-Mississippi The Union river fleet assembled at Alexandria heads up the Red River. Thirteen ironclads are led by *Osage* and *Eastport*. As they advance upstream, the Confederates burn vast stockpiles of cotton along the riverbank to prevent it falling into Union hands.

Wednesday, March 30

Western Theater As the spring weather arrives, more skirmishes take place between Union and Confederate outposts. Bedford Forrest raids Bolivar, Tennessee, while minor actions take place at Caperton's Ferry, Alabama, Monett's Ferry and Cloutierville, Louisiana, and Arkadelphia, Arkansas.

Thursday, March 31

Western Theater There are skirmishes at Arkadelphia, Arkansas, at Patlatka, Florida, and Forks of Beaver in east Kentucky.

Trans-Mississippi Banks' troops clash with Taylor's outposts at Natchitoches, Louisiana.

Friday, April 1, 1864

Trans-Mississippi Frederick Steele's Union troops advance south to join Banks on the Red River.

Naval Operations CSS *Albermarle* is towed to Hamilton, North Carolina. The US transport *Maple Leaf* sinks after striking a torpedo in the St John's River, Florida.

Sasturday, April 2

Eastern Theater The Confederates destroy Cape Lookout Light, North Carolina.

Western Theater Minor actions occur all over the theater of war, with fights at Cleveland, Tennessee, and Grossetete Bayou and Crump's Hill, Louisiana.

Sunday, April 3

Eastern Theater Union siege mortars open fire on Fort Sumter once again. Their heavy bombs are clearly visible in the night sky, arcing slowly across the bay to smash into the rubble.

Trans-Mississippi The last of the Union gunboats and transports pass the rapids at Alexandria, still gravely hampered by the unusually low water level. Acting Volunteer Lieutenant J.P. Couthouy, commanding the ironclad *Chillichothe*, is shot dead by a Confederate sniper on the bank near Grand Ecore.

Monday, April 4

The North Concerned over the continued French involvement in Mexico, the House of Representatives passes a joint resolution saying the USA will not tolerate a monarchy in Mexico. There is growing evidence that the French plan to instal Ferdinand Maximilian of Austria, the brother of the Hapsburg emperor, as ruler of Mexico. The guerrilla war in Mexico is costing France dear, and Napoleon III is anxious to create a Mexican government that can shoulder the border of the war so that he can bring French troops home. Maximilian, who knows nothing of the country, is fooled by conservative Mexican exiles in Europe, who convince him that their nation is crying out for a European sovereign. A former London *Times* correspondent warns the young Austrian that there is not a Mexican alive who would not forego his dearest principles for $500.

The photographer Matthew Brady in one of the Union redoubts opposite Petersburg, June 21, 1864. Grant's spring campaign inexorably forced the Confederates back toward Richmond. But the shovel had become as important a tool as the rifle by this period: ten months of trench warfare began, anticipating the conditions at Plevna in 1877, and on the western front 1914 to 1918.

The Confederate ironclad Arkansas was eventually completed under difficult circumstances owing to the rapidly advancing Union forces. In spite of her great weight, she was quite fast thanks to the tapered stern and hull form improved over those of some of the earlier Southern ironclads.

Tuesday, April 5

Trans-Mississippi Taylor concentrates 16,000 Confederates at Mansfield, covering the roads to Marshall, Texas, and Banks' current objective, Shreveport. Banks has 26,000 men but they are strung out along a single narrow road through the pine forest, encumbered by a 12-mile column of wagons bearing his ammunition and provisions through the barren country.

Wednesday, April 6

The South The Constitutional Convention of Louisiana, meeting at New Orleans, adopts a new state constitution, abolishing slavery.

Thursday, April 7

Western Theater Longstreet's corps, which has wintered in east Tennessee, is ordered to return to Virginia to rejoin Lee.
Trans-Mississippi Banks' advance guard skirmishes with Confederates near Mansfield at Wilson's Plantation.

Friday, April 8

The North The US Senate passes a joint resolution, voting 38 to 6 to abolish slavery and approving the thirteenth amendment to the constitution. Unthinkable before the war, the lack of opposition reflects the change of attitude resulting from three years of conflict.
Trans-Mississippi Without waiting for General E. Kirby Smith to arrive General Richard Taylor advances with 9000 Confederates and

Above left: *As of April 4, 1864, the Army of the Potomac had yet another cavalry commander: Major-General Philip H. Sheridan. This cold and ruthless officer continued to improve the Union mounted arm, ready for the coming campaign. Sheridan was not one of the most charismatic soldiers of the Civil War, but his reputation for energy and efficiency was thoroughly deserved.*

Left: *Burying the dead at Fredericksburg after The Wilderness campaign, May 1864. Not long after the war veterans began to visit the battlefields, but whereas Gettysburg drew crowds, few men ever returned to The Wilderness or Cold Harbor. These chilling battles of attrition had only bitter memories for the poor bloody infantry.* .

occupies a defensive position at the edge of one of the few clearings in the forest at Sabine Cross Roads. Banks' column arrives and the leading brigades, some 4500 men, deploy for action. After two hours' indecisive skirmishing, Taylor launches his men forward and crushes the head of Banks' army. The superior Union artillery is helpless in the forest and several batteries are overrun immediately. The defeated Union troops recoil onto the front of the wagon train, panicking the drivers and those troops hurrying forward to join the battle. In scenes of great confusion, Banks' men are routed for over three miles. The retreat is checked by Emory's division, which stands firm. Union losses are 113 dead, 581 wounded, and 1541 missing or captured, for a total of 2235. Taylor's troops suffer about 1000 killed and wounded.

Saturday, April 9

Eastern Theater General Grant issues his campaign orders. The Eastern Theater has been quiet since the early fall, but Grant intends to win the war here now. Making Lee's army his objective, he says to Meade's Army of the Potomac, "Wherever Lee goes, there you will head also."
Western Theater Bedford Forrest continues to raid Federal communications in western Tennessee.
Trans-Mississippi With all hope gone of taking Shreveport before he has to relinquish A.J. Smith's corps to Sherman, Banks orders his army to retreat. At Pleasant Hill the Union troops form a line of battle to deal with Taylor's Confederates, who pursue impetuously through the woods. A Confederate assault breaks into the Federal position but they are dislodged by a counter-attack and ultimately driven from the field. Both sides subsequently claimed to have fought a superior enemy force, but the numbers engaged were actually about 12,000 on either side. Confederate losses are 1200 killed and wounded, plus 426 missing. Union casualties are 150 dead, 844 wounded, and 375 missing for a total of 1369.
Naval Operations USS frigate *Minnesota* is damaged by a torpedo from the Confederate torpedo boat *Squib* off Newport News, Virginia.

April 1864

Sunday, April 10, 1864

Trans-Mississippi Banks withdraws toward Alexandria, while Steele's Union Army in Arkansas retires on Little Rock. The projected Union pincer movement is over and there will be no further Federal invasions of the Red River country.

Europe An assembly of Mexican émigrés, led by Gutierrez and Hidalgo, journey to the castle

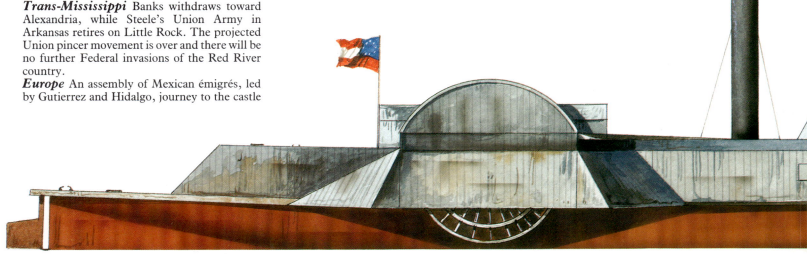

of Miramar, Austria, to offer Ferdinand Maximilian the crown of Mexico. Dressed in the uniform of an Austrian vice-admiral, the 31-year-old archduke and his 23-year-old archduchess sit beneath a canopy of rose silk embroidered with gold. Speaking in Spanish, Ferdinand accepts the crown, taking the name Maximilian I rather than Ferdinand—Hernando in Spanish—which would remind everyone of Cortés.

Monday, April 11

Trans-Mississippi Banks reaches Grand Ecore and entrenches, throwing a pontoon bridge over the river and asking for reinforcements from New Orleans. Porter's fleet is now in dire peril as the waters of the Red River are falling, threatening to maroon his warships in Confederate territory.

A pro-Union state government is inaugurated at Little Rock, Arkansas, with Dr Isaac Murphy as governor.

Tuesday, April 12

Western Theater In one of the most notorious minor actions of the war, Bedford Forrest's Confederate cavalry storm Fort Pillow, Tennessee. Held by 557 Federal soldiers, including 262 black troops, the position is rapidly overwhelmed by Forrest's veteran cavalry. The Confederates suffer 14 dead and 86 wounded. Federal losses are 231 dead, 100 wounded, and 226 captured—an exceptionally high ratio of dead to wounded, which Union soldiers subsequently claim was the result of a cold-blooded massacre after the surrender. Later, the Joint Committee on the Conduct of the War will hear bitter accusations from Union soldiers that the rebels had committed numerous atrocities after the fighting was over, concentrating with particular viciousness on the black soldiers. This is hotly denied by the Confederates, Forrest stating that the Union commander had continued the action long after his defeat was inevitable. On the other hand, the Confederate commander and subsequent KKK founder, writes a letter describing the scene and saying: "It is hoped that these facts will demonstrate to the Northern people that Negro soldiers cannot cope with Southerners."

Trans-Mississippi A Confederate cavalry brigade led by General Thomas Green, the former guerrilla commander, ambushes Porter's fleet from the bluff near Blair's Landing. The water is so low that vessels of the *Osage* type are almost unmanageable. *Osage* herself is only steerable with the transport *Black Hawk* lashed to her, but she goes aground at 2 p.m. For an hour and a half, Confederate troops engage the ships with rifles at less than 100 yards. The ships return fire with grape and cannister, and when this runs out, they use shell with the fuze cut to one second. The Southern forces eventually retreat, their commander being among the killed.

Wednesday, April 13

Western Theater Forrest's cavalry are again in action, this time at Columbus, Kentucky.

Trans-Mississippi Admiral Porter reaches Grand Ecore with most of his river fleet.

Thursday, April 14

Eastern Theater Charleston's Fort Moultrie fires on the US tug *Geranium*.

Western Theater Forrest's cavalry raids toward the Ohio River, skirmishing at Paducah, Kentucky.

Trans-Mississippi There are minor actions at Bayou Saline, Dutch Mills, and White Oak Creek in Arkansas.

Friday, April 15

Trans-Mississippi The river fleet is finally assembled at Grand Ecore, the larger ironclads having great difficulty getting over the bar below the town. The large ironclad *Eastport*, joining the squadron for the first time, strikes a Confederate torpedo eight miles below Grand Ecore. Her bottom is ripped open, but Lieutenant-Commander Phelps rallies the crew and bulkheads the leak. *Eastport* makes it 40 miles downstream before grounding.

Saturday, April 16

The North A report on prisoners shows the Federal authorities have captured 146,634 Confederates since the beginning of the war between the states.

Western Theater The Union transport *General Hunter* is destroyed when she strikes a Confederate torpedo on the St John's River, Florida.

Sunday, April 17

The North General Grant orders that there will be no further exchanges of prisoners until the Confederates balance Union releases. As his forthcoming military campaign will show, Grant knows that he can win the war by exhausting the limited Confederate manpower reserves. This measure further damages the Confederacy but condemns prisoners in Southern hands to severe hardship since the Confederacy can barely feed itself, let alone its prisoners.

Eastern Theater Confederate forces, soon to be aided by the new ironclad ram *Albemarle* attack Plymouth, North Carolina. The ram departs Hamilton, headed for Plymouth. Drifting backward downstream, she has chains and anchors fixed to her bows to control her in the fast-flowing current.

Monday, April 18

The South General P.G.T. Beauregard leaves Charleston to command the Department of North Carolina and Southern Virginia.

Eastern Theater *Albemarle* is delayed after the main coupling bolts of one of her propeller shafts come loose. Repairs take six hours before she continues her journey. By evening, she is tied up three miles from Plymouth.

Trans-Mississippi At Poison Springs, Arkansas, Sterling Price's Confederates attack a Federal supply column, capturng 198 wagons.

Tuesday, April 19

Eastern Theater The *Albemarle* passes Union obstructions placed in the Roanoke and attacks the Federal squadron at Plymouth. Challenged by the fast sidewheeler *Miami* and the armed ferry boat *Southfield*, the *Albemarle* sinks the latter by ramming. Nearly pulled down with her victim, the Confederate ram then engages in a pointblank range action with the *Miami*. The Union captain, Commander Flusser personally fires his 100-pounder Parrott rifle with a 10-second fuzed shell, but it bounces off *Albemarle's* armor and explodes in his face, killing him instantly. After a failed attempt to board, *Miami* retires past Plymouth into Albemarle Sound. *Albemarle* now commences a leisurely bombardment of the Federal earthwork called Fort Williams, the key Federal position in the Plymouth defenses.

Eastport *started life under the Confederate flag, but before completion she was seized by a force of raiding Union gunboats. She grounded while taking part in the Red River Expedition during 1864, and was destroyed to prevent the ironclad from falling into enemy hands.*

Wednesday, April 20

Eastern Theater Fort Williams was not built to withstand fire from the river, which had always been dominated by Union warships. *Albemarle's* two English Armstrong 100-pounders make short work of the position, and the Federal garrison at Plymouth surrenders at noon. The Confederates capture 2800 men and a large quantity of supplies, including 200 tons of fine anthracite coal for the ironclad. It is the first Southern victory in this area for a long time and, if the port itself is not of great strategic importance, the moral value of a victory is cheering news for the embattled Confederacy.

Thursday, April 21

Trans-Mississippi Banks withdraws from Grand Ecore, heading for Alexandria as his Red River campaign fizzles out. The crew of the *Eastport* work desperately to save their ship before the surrounding country is abandoned to the Confederates.

Friday, April 22

The South President Davis writes Lieutenant-General Polk in Alabama, saying that if captured black soldiers turn out to be escaped slaves, they should be held for recovery by their owners.
Trans-Mississippi There are skirmishes at Cotton Plant and Jacksonport, Arkansas.

Saturday, April 23

Trans-Mississippi Federal troops are attacked at Camden, Arkansas, and Swan Lake. Banks' rear guard is attacked at Monett's Ferry.

Above left: *Union soldiers pose in front of Robert E. Lee's home, Arlington Mansion, June 28, 1864. The Confederacy's renowned commander was painfully aware that only the continued resistance of his army was staving off total defeat.*

Left: *Seated on pews "borrowed" from the nearby church, Grant's staff confer at Massaponax, Virginia, May 21, 1864. Grant is looking over General Meade's shoulder at the map. The Army of the Potomac was advancing past Guiney's Station while Lee's battered forces withdrew to the North Anna River.*

April–May 1864

Sunday, April 24, 1864
Western Theater Skirmishes occur at Decatur, Alabama, and at Pineville and Ringgold in Georgia.
Trans-Mississippi There are minor actions near Camden, Arkansas.

Monday, April 25
Europe A temporary armistice is agreed between Denmark and her enemies, Prussia and Austria.
Trans-Mississippi The minor actions continue in Arkansas, with fights at Mark's Mills and Moro Bottom.

Tuesday, April 26
Eastern Theater Following the loss of Plymouth, Federal troops evacuate Washington, North Carolina, which Grant does not consider worth defending.
Trans-Mississippi Steele's Union force at Camden, Arkansas, retreats north, completing the Confederate victory in the Red River campaign. At Alexandria Banks receives new orders from General Grant, firmly instructing him to bring the Red River operations to a close. Attempts to save the *Eastport* have to be abandoned now the army has retreated, and Commander Phelps reluctantly blows up his vessel. The three Union light-draft gunboats remaining up the Red River are attacked as they withdraw, running a gauntlet of field guns and musket fire. The *Cricket* (flagship) suffers 38 hits in five minutes, losing 12 dead and 19 wounded out of a crew of 50, which included many Negroes. Admiral Porter pilots the vessel himself after the pilot is wounded. The unarmed pump boat *Champion No. 3* is destroyed when a shell explodes her boiler, scalding to death her captain, three engineers, and all but 15 of her 200 Negro crew.

Wednesday, April 27
The North Grant issues his orders for the Union spring offensive. Recognizing that previous Union offensives had been characterized by poor coordination and lack of determination, he plans to strike a death blow to the Confederacy. The Army of the Potomac will attack Lee head on. Grant cannot rid the Union Army of three of its worst political generals—Banks, Sigel, and Butler—but the first is harmless after the Red River fiasco. Sigel's independent command is to press down the Shenandoah, and Butler's Army of the James is to attack the Southern capital from the rear, while the Army of the Potomac assaults from the north.
The South President Davis dispatches Jacob Thompson as a special commissioner to Canada. He is instructed unofficially to put out peace feelers via sympathetic elements in the North.

Thursday, April 28
Eastern Theater The Federal siege guns at Fort Sumter embark on another seven-day shoot against this embattled symbol of the Confederacy.

Friday, April 29
Trans-Mississippi Another skirmish takes place at Grand Ecore. In Arkansas the Union withdrawal from Camden is marked by minor battles on the Quachita River and at Saline Bottom.

Saturday, April 30
The South President Davis writes General Polk that captured slaves should be returned to their masters. Then the Davis household is struck by personal tragedy: his five-year-old son Joe falls to his death from the Confederate White House veranda.
Trans-Mississippi The Union fleet at Alexandria, Louisiana, is trapped by the unusually low waters of the Red River. The chief engineer of the army's XIX Corps, Lieutenant-Colonel Joseph Bailey of the 4th Wisconsin, begins the construction of a dam across the rapids. While the larger ironclads discard whole sections of their armor and ship some of their 32-pounder guns ashore, army soldiers work up to their waist in water, blocking the river to raise the water level in the rapids.

Sunday, May 1, 1864
Western Theater At Stone Church, Georgia, a cavalry skirmish opens the battle of outposts, which precedes Sherman's advance against General Johnston's Army of the Tennessee.
Trans-Mississippi Confederate troops capture the Union transport *Emma* at David's Ferry.
Far West Union troops in California skirmish with Indians at Booth's Run.

Monday, May 2
The South President Davis addresses the first session of the Second Confederate Congress. Admitting there is no current hope of foreign recognition, he tries to sound optimistic about the immediate military future. Condemning Northern "barbarism," he rails against the deliberate destruction of private property and war against civilians, which now characterize Federal operations.
Western Theater Sherman's outposts clash with Johnston's near Tunnel Hill and Ringgold Gap.
Far West After more skirmishing, the uprising in northern California is extinguished. Two of the three remaining bands agree to surrender. The third—whittled down to 15 braves—will surrender in June. The war leaders will find themselves working on the San Francisco harbor defenses.

Tuesday, May 3
The North President Lincoln and the Cabinet discuss the alleged Confederate atrocities during the fall of Fort Pillow in Tennessee. Orders go out to the Army of the Potomac for the crossing of the Rapidan tomorrow. Practically dormant since Gettysburg, the Army of the Potomac is at last in business again. Grant says it is in splendid condition "and evidently feels like whipping somebody."
Trans-Mississippi Steele's defeated Union force arrives back in Little Rock.
Far West Federal troops are in action against Indians at Cedar Bluffs, Colorado Territory.

Wednesday, May 4
Eastern Theater The 122,000 strong Army of the Potomac crosses the Rapidan once again.

APPROACHING UNION SUPPORT

UNION LOG BREASTWORK

Old hands warn this winter's recruits not to tear down their winter quarters huts. From previous experience, the veterans expect to be back. In fact, this is the last time the army will cross this familiar waterway; under Grant's new management, they will not return until the war is won.

The Army of Northern Virginia, 66,000 strong, reacts with customary vigor. Grant's choice of route allowed Lee to accept battle in the tangled undergrowth of The Wilderness where he and Jackson had humiliated Hooker a year ago. In the thick brush, the Federal advantage in artillery will be nullified.

Butler's Army of the James assembles in transports in Hampton Roads. Intending to move up the James and operate against Richmond from the south side, Butler faces empty defenses as Confederate troops are concentrated against Grant.

Western Theater Sherman's 98,000 strong army prepares for its advance from Chattanooga to Atlanta.

Thursday, May 5

Eastern Theater Battle begins among the tangled thickets of stunted pine, scrub oak and sweet-gum that is The Wilderness. Warren's V Corps of the Army of the Potomac engages Richard Ewell's Confederate II Corps on the Orange Turnpike during the morning. In a separate action later, Hancock's II Corps fights A. P. Hill but neither battle is decisive. The close country helps to disguise the Confederates' numerical inferiority.

General Butler meanwhile lands 30,000 Federal troops at City Point and the Bermuda Hun-

Battle of The Wilderness, May 5 and 6, 1864, fought between Grant with 119,000 troops and 316 guns, and Lee with 64,000 men and 274 guns.

Grant took overall command of the Union forces after he dispatched Sherman against Atlanta. Grant planned to go around the Confederate right front and advance upon Richmond. He knew Lee would have to protect the Southern capital and he therefore planned to start a campaign of attrition that would bleed the South dry as they were now less able to replace lost troops.

Main picture shows the height of battle where Confederates captured the Union earthworks only soon to be driven off as they lacked adequate back-up.

Small map shows overall battlefield.

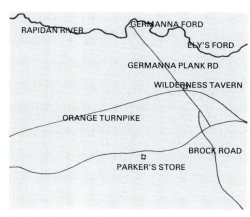

dred on the south side of the James River. Butler proposes a night assault on Fort Darling but allows his officers to talk him out of it.

Naval Operations The ironclad ram CSS *Albemarle* escorts two steamers, *Cotton Planter* and the ex-Federal *Bombshell*, down the Roanoke. The steamers carry troops which are to be

shipped up the Alligator River. The Federal flotilla intercepts them, chasing off the *Cotton Planter*, which retires into Plymouth, and battering the *Bombshell* into submission. But *Albemarle* fights on, scoring repeated hits on her opponents, the double-enders *Mattabesett*, *Sassacus*, *Wyalusing*, and *Miami*, supported by three smaller warships. Even 100-pound solid shot bounces off the iron hull of the Confederate like giant marbles, the captain of the *Sassacus* remarking that they may as well have been firing blanks. He rams the *Albemarle* square on after a 400-yard "run up," by which time the *Sassacus* is traveling at 11 knots. The ram is tilted over and takes on water, but rights herself and fires back. The crippled *Sassacus* limps away with her bows stoved in. The Confederate withdraws to Plymouth, fighting off the *Miami*, which attacks with a spar torpedo.

Friday, May 6

Eastern Theater Once again it seems as if Lee's ragged veterans are going to triumph over the odds. As A.P. Hill is driven back by the Union forces, Longstreet's corps arrives in the nick of time and overruns part of the Federal left. Hancock's corps is severely mauled, and Longstreet is beginning to roll up the Union line when he is shot in error by his own men, only five miles away from where Stonewall Jackson met the same fate. He is badly wounded, General Jenkins is killed outright, and the Confederate attack stalls for want of leadership. Lee takes personal charge of the battle late in the afternoon, but is pulled away from the frontline by his men. A day of close-range fighting in the twilight world of The Wilderness leaves both armies exhausted. Of the 100,000 Federals engaged, 2236 are killed, 12,037 wounded, and 3383 missing for a total of 17,666. The 60,000 Confederates lose about 7500 killed, wounded, and missing. Many of the wounded are burned to death in brush fires started by the musketry.

Butler's Army of the James can see the steeples of Petersburg seven miles away. Now fielding nearly 39,000 men against the fewer than 10,000 Confederates available in Richmond and Petersburg, Butler makes an inept attempt to break the Richmond–Petersburg railroad but his corps commanders, W.F. Smith and Quincy A. Gillmore, fail to act.

Saturday, May 7

Eastern Theater Instead of withdrawing as usual, the Army of the Potomac begins to advance again. Shifting toward Spotsylvania Court House, Grant is heading toward Richmond, forcing Lee to conform to his movements. The rival armies advance at best speed along tiny country roads to their next battle.

The fumbling, incompetent Butler continues to do nothing. Some 8000 Federals briefly occupy the railroad, then withdraw, menaced by less than 3000 Southerners.

The Confederate ironclad ram *Raleigh* steams out of Wilmington to attack the blockaders, chases them off, but grounds when re-entering harbor, destroying herself.

Western Theater Sherman's forces probe Johnston's defenses at Dalton, Georgia, before beginning a turning movement around the Confederate left flank.

CONFEDERATES STORMING UNION LINE

FEDERAL ABATIS

May 1864

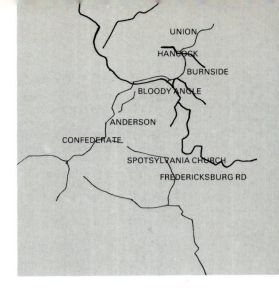

Sunday, May 8, 1864

Eastern Theater General Richard H. Anderson, commanding Longstreet's corps in his absence, gets his men on the road four hours earlier than Lee ordered. His enterprise enables the Confederates to beat Warren's Union V Corps in a race for the Spotsylvania Cross Roads. Marching through the night, Anderson's corps is soon in action, rescuing Fitzhugh Lee's cavalry from an unequal contest against Warren's infantry. Heavy fighting continues until after dark, but Grant's attempt to get between Lee and Richmond has failed. The Confederates entrench themselves with customary skill and repel a series of Federal attacks.
Western Theater Sherman continues his efforts to bypass Johnston's defenses. McPherson's corps enters Snake Creek Gap to turn the Confederate left.

Monday, May 9

Eastern Theater The Army of the Potomac concentrates against Lee's defenses between the Ny and Po rivers. There are no major assaults today but sporadic firing continues along the line of Confederate entrenchments. The Union suffers a serious loss when the popular Major-General John Sedgwick, the Commander of VI Corps, goes forward to supervise the deployment of his infantry. Chiding his troops for going to ground under sniper fire, he says, "I'm ashamed of you dodging that way. They couldn't hit an elephant at this distance." Seconds later he is shot in the face and killed instantly.
Western Theater Sherman's troops probe Johnston's defenses at Buzzard Roost near Dalton, McPherson moves through Snake Creek Gap but does not attack the strong Confederate position he finds at Resaca. In fact, the Confederate defenses here are held by only a single 4000-strong brigade, but they make a bold front.
Trans-Mississippi The dam across the Alexandria rapids is finished. *Lexington* leads the way through and the Federal warships are saved.

Tuesday, May 10

Eastern Theater Sheridan's Union cavalry ride along the North Anna, drawing Stuart's Confederate horsemen after them and fighting a brisk skirmish at Beaver Dam Station. Lee's entrenchments at Spotsylvania are in the shape of an inverted "V," the apex covering important high ground. Union probes continue all day but a sharp attack at 6 p.m. breaks into this central salient, christened "The Mule Shoe."
Western Theater Johnston learns of McPherson's attempt to turn the Confederate left through Snake Creek Gap. Polk's Confederates are hurrying to join Johnston's badly outnumbered army. Sherman issues orders for his whole force to swing past Johnston's left.

Wednesday, May 11

Eastern Theater There is little action at Spotsylvania as Grant maneuvers 60,000 men from four army corps into position for a concerted attack tomorrow. Unfortunately, Lee withdraws the 30 cannon which dominate the Mule Shoe, planning to withdraw from the Spotsylvania lines soon. Six miles north of Richmond at Yellow Tavern, J.E.B. Stuart's cavalry hold off superior numbers of Union cavalry. Sitting on his horse behind a line of dismounted troopers, Stuart fires his pistol at the advancing Federals, crying, "Steady, men, steady. Give it to them!" Then he reels in the saddle, mortally wounded. Handing command to Fitzhugh Lee, the "Cavalier of Dixie" is taken to the rear to die. The Confederacy has lost one of its most skilful and courageous officers.

Thursday, May 12

Eastern Theater At 4.30 a.m. the 20,000 men of Hancock's II Corps attack and overrun the Mule Shoe, capturing General Johnston and almost the entire "Stonewall" brigade. In pouring rain, the Confederates counter-attack and block further Union progress. Further assaults by Burnside's IX Corps and Wright's VI Corps get nowhere but in some of the bitterest fighting of the war, waves of troops battle for the northwest face of the Confederate position. Known as "Bloody Angle," the battered entrenchments are fought over from 10.00 a.m. without a break.

General Franz Sigel had been an albatross around the neck of the Union Army for several years. His habit of communicating with the War Department via influential politicians had earned him a just rebuke from Grant, and his semi-independent command was stirred into action at the head of the Shenandoah Valley. To prevent the traditional Confederate assault up the valley, which tended to occur whenever the situation in Virginia became unfavorable, Sigel was ordered to march down the valley. At the head of 6500 troops, the German-born Sigel cautiously advances south. Brigadier-General John D. Imboden's 2000 Confederates fall back on the village of New Market where they await reinforcements. Hurrying up from southwest Virginia, John C. Breckinridge brings 2500 veteran infantry to oppose the Union offensive.
Western Theater General Johnston evacuates Dalton, withdrawing to a new defensive line at Resaca.

Friday, May 13

Eastern Theater The savage battle for Bloody Angle finally dies away at about 4 a.m. Federal losses in the battle for Spotsylvania are 6800; Confederate casualties are estimated at 5000. But the Army of the Potomac still does not retreat. Instead, Grant sends Warren to extend the Union lines to the south and east. This aggressive leadership maintains confidence, despite the lengthening butcher's bill.

Butler continues to fumble the Army of the James' attack. While he does nothing, General Beauregard hastily improves the fortifications at Drewry's Bluff.
Western Theater Johnston's Confederates are joined by reinforcements under Polk in their new positions at Resaca. Sherman begins a series of probing attacks, searching for a weakness in the extensive Confederate entrenchments.
Trans-Mississippi Banks continues his retreat on the Red River, while Steele's Union forces complete their withdrawal to Little Rock. The Federal offensive across the Mississippi has been a complete failure.

Saturday, May 14

Eastern Theater The heavy rain continues, flooding the armies' trenches. A planned Union assault is cancelled as the state of the ground slows all preparatory movement. Grant sends Wright's VI Corps after Warren, continuing to shift his weight to the south.

Sigel's advance continues, his little army brushing into the Confederate forces at New Market. Breckinridge's Confederate reinforcements reach Lacy Springs, 10 miles away, and hear the sound of cannon as Sigel's men drive back Imboden's small command. Breckinridge marches his men on through the night to arrive behind the Confederate positions west of the village by dawn.

After the Battle of The Wilderness, which ended in deadlock, Grant moved his force to seize New Spotsylvania Court House, a vital junction on the road to Richmond. However, a fast march by part of Lee's force blocked the move.

The main action was fought on May 10 to 12, 1864, with various Federal frontal assaults on the strong Confederate defenses being beaten off.

On the 11th a massed attack was launched against Lee's center at the Bloody Angle, causing a great setback to the Confederates as they lost some ground. Elsewhere they stood firm, as Grant, during the next six days, probed the Confederate flanks looking for a way to Richmond but without success.

Sunday, May 15

Eastern Theater Once the youngest vice-president in American history, Major-General John C. Breckinridge attacks and defeats Sigel's Union force at New Market. Although the two small armies are of similar size—5500 Federals versus 5000 Confederates—Breckinridge deceives Sigel into believing he is attacked by superior numbers. At the height of the battle, Breckinridge unwillingly commits his last reserve—the 247 cadets from the Virginia Military Institute. In a charge which passes into legend, they take part in a Confederate counter-attack which defeats the Union force. The Union loses 831 men, the Confederates 577, including 10 dead and 47 wounded cadets. Losses are concentrated among several Virginia regiments, especially the 62nd, which suffers 50 percent casualties attacking a Federal battery. The 22nd Virginia is commanded by Colonel George S. Patton. His grandson and namesake will be one of America's greatest commanders in World War II.

Western Theater Sent west to redeem his reputation, former commander of the Army of the Potomac, "Fighting Joe" Hooker leads a corps in Sherman's army. Hooker batters away at Hood's Confederate corps before Resaca but there is no breakthrough.

Monday May 16

Eastern Theater Having prevaricated for weeks while the Confederates had almost nothing in front of him, Butler is now attacked by P.T. Beauregard at Drewry's Bluff. Coming on in dense morning fog, 18,000 Confederates break into the Union lines, but Butler's 16,000-strong army clings to its lines despite heavy and accurate rebel fire. Butler withdraws toward Bermuda Hundred, having lost over one-fourth of his men: 390 dead, 2380 wounded, and 1390 missing—a total of 4160. Southern losses are 355 dead, 1941 wounded, and 210 missing—2506 altogether.

Tuesday, May 17

Eastern Theater At Spotsylvania the torrential rain finally stops. The narrow country roads are washed away and the troops are still bailing out their trenches, but everyone knows that the fine sunshine is the cue for another assault. Meanwhile, Butler's retreat leaves him bottled up between the Appomattox and James rivers with a Confederate Army blocking the way to Richmond. Sigel's retreat up the Shenandoah is actually well conducted, but Halleck wires a vitriolic message to Grant: "He will do nothing but run. He never did anything else." The German-born general is relieved of his command on Thursday.

Western Theater Sherman maneuvers Johnston's Confederates out of another position at Adairsville, Georgia, sending troops around both flanks while Thomas's corps menaces the Confederate front.

Wednesday, May 18

Eastern Theater Grant hurls Hancock's depleted corps at Lee's entrenchments, but the assault withers away in the face of a ferocious fire from the Confederate lines. Meade calls it "knocking our heads against a brick wall," and even Grant recognizes the futility of further attacks. Once again, he maneuvers southward.

Thursday, May 19

Eastern Theater Lee orders Ewell's II Corps, now reduced to about 6000 men, to probe the Union lines and determine if Grant is shifting past the Confederate right. This demonstration leads to more savage fighting, mainly against the former heavy artillerists from Washington, dragged by Grant from their comfortable billets to the delight of the Army of the Potomac's veterans. The gunners fight well and Ewell withdraws, ending the fighting at Spotsylvania. Of the 110,000 Federals engaged in this series of battles, 17,500 become casualties. Added to the losses in The Wilderness battles, Union casualties exceed 33,000. Lee's 50,000-strong army suffers badly too (exact figures have never been recorded). The South cannot afford this continual attrition.

Friday, May 20

Western Theater Johnston's Confederates withdraw again, slipping away through Cartersville, across the Etowash River. Sherman's advance continues, with Schofield's troops entering Cartersville after a skirmish.

Saturday, May 21

Eastern Theater Grant shifts the Army of the Potomac to the south and east around Guiney's Station. Lee orders his men to fall back to the North Anna. Major-General David Hunter replaces Franz Sigel in the Department of West Virginia.

Western Theater Johnston entrenches his army around Allatoona Pass.

CONFEDERATE ADVANCE LINE

UNION FORCE PENETRATING CONFEDERATE SALIENT

McCOULL HOUSE

DRIVING BACK UNION FORCE

185

May–June 1864

Part of the vicious fighting around Atlanta when Union and Confederate forces engage around the unfinished Troup Hurt House.

In the distance Union forces bear down upon the Confederate line, while more Union troops advance from the extreme right.

Sunday, May 22, 1864

Eastern Theater The rival armies race each other south. Only a few miles apart, the Army of the Potomac marches from Guiney's Station toward the North Anna River, while Lee's Confederates fall back on a parallel route. Ewell's corps wins, and digs in at Hanover Junction before the Federals arrive.

Western Theater Sherman issues orders to march on Dallas, Georgia, bypassing Johnston's left flank.

Monday, May 23

Eastern Theater Warren's V Corps crosses the North Anna but is counter-attacked by A.P. Hill in the evening near Jericho Mills. During the night, Wright's VI Corps crosses to support Warren. Hancock's II Corps is in action to the east against the remaining Confederate positions on the north bank. Thus Lee has a fleeting opportunity to attack Grant's army while it is divided. The odds are 2:1 in the Union favor, but they were as bad as that at Chancellorsville. However, Lee succumbs to a serious fever and is confined to his tent.

Western Theater Sherman's army marches on Dallas, Georgia, crossing the Etowah River.

Tuesday, May 24

Eastern Theater The Union VI Corps joins V Corps south of the North Anna River, while II Corps crosses separately at the Chesterfield Bridge, and Burnside's IX Corps begins to cross over at Ox Ford. Sheridan's cavalry returns from its raid along the James. Lee is still sick. At Charleston, the *Albemarle* is out again, dragging for torpedoes in the Roanoke River.

Western Theater Wheeler's Confederate cavalry raid Sherman's lines of communication, destroying large quantities of supplies. This hampers the Federal advance, but the absence of his cavalry reduces Johnston's ability to discern Sherman's movements in front of him. Johnston retreats from the Allatoona Pass, heading for Dallas via New Hope Church.

Trans-Mississippi Colonel Colton Greene's Confederates begin a two-week campaign against Union shipping from the west bank of the Mississippi.

Wednesday, May 25

Eastern Theater Once again, Grant's advance is blocked by a formidable line of entrenchments, and he begins to plan another outflanking maneuver.

Western Theater Running into Johnston's hastily-constructed defenses at New Hope Church, Sherman deploys for an assault. At 6 p.m. Hooker's corps begins a series of desperate assaults over a rain-filled ditch and muddy field. Sixteen cannon pour caseshot into the Union ranks, and some 5000 Confederate rifles dominate the ground. The Federal soldiers christen the area the "Hell Hole."

Trans-Mississippi Greene's Confederates fire on the USS *Curlew* and capture the *Lebanon*.

Far West Federal troops depart Fort Wingate, New Mexico Territory, on an expedition which lasts until 12 July, heading to the Gila and San Carlos rivers in Arizona Territory.

Thursday, May 26

Eastern Theater Grant withdraws from the Confederate lines and re-crosses the North Anna, planning to head around Lee's right flank. The new Union commander in the Shenandoah, David Hunter, leads 16,000 troops from Strasburg and Cedar Creek. Breckinridge too has been replaced, and the 8500 Confederates in the valley are now commanded by W.E. "Grumble" Jones.

Western Theater Sherman's right wing under McPherson enters Dallas, Georgia, while the main body digs in opposite Johnston's entrenchments. There is heavy firing all along the line at various times during the day.

Far West Montana Territory is formally established.

Friday, May 27

Eastern Theater Leading Grant's advance, the cavalry under Sheridan occupy Hanovertown, Virginia, while the long columns of infantry march from the North Anna to the Pamunkey River. The rival cavalry outposts clash all along the line as Confederate cavalry seek to determine Grant's line of march. The Army of Northern Virginia begins to move too, heading south and east once more.

Western Theater Heavy firing continues along the rival lines between New Hope Church and Dallas. Howard's corps assaults Pickett's Mills but is repulsed. Movement in this largely uninhabited country is difficult; few roads pass through the dense forests, and a large coordinated attack is difficult.

Saturday, May 28

Eastern Theater The Army of Northern Virginia hurries past Mechanicsville, swings south toward Cold Habor, and gets between Grant and Richmond. Cavalry actions take place at Crump's Creek, Haw's Shop, and along the Totopotomoy River.

Western Theater Johnston's counter-attack on Sherman is frustrated by John B. Hood, whose night approach march leaves him further from the Union lines than when he started. Realizing he has lost the advantage of surprise, Johnston cancels the attack.

Mexico Maximilian arrives in fever-stricken Vera Cruz. There is no welcome; the French troops required to escort them to Mexico City are delayed, so the royal party remains on board ship until tomorrow.

Sunday, May 29

Eastern Theater Lee entrenches his new line. The Army of the Potomac continues its advance on Richmond.

Western Theater Firing continues in the forests near Dallas. Having repulsed several Union assaults with little loss, the Confederates now find their own casualties mounting as this daily attrition takes its toll.

Monday, May 30

Eastern Theater The Army of the Potomac arrives in front of Lee's new line, as close to Richmond as McClellan was two years ago. Grant begins a series of probes, searching for any weak points in the Confederate entrenchments.

Western Theater John H. Morgan sets off on another raid, heading into Kentucky to attack Sherman's lines of communication.

Tuesday, May 31

The North Radical Republicans meet at Cleveland. Furious over Lincoln's policy of emancipation, they nominate General John C. Frémont—arguably the most incompetent officer on either side during the war—for president. Although this group has little immediate support, Lincoln is painfully aware that he needs a military victory before the election in November.

Eastern Theater Grant shifts the Army of the Potomac east toward Cold Harbor. Lee follows suit, barring the way again.

Western Theater Sherman too is stalled in front of a resourceful commander. Outnumbered over 2:1, Johnston has slowed the Federal advance to an average of about a mile a day, protecting the strategically vital city of Atlanta.

Wednesday, June 1, 1864

Eastern Theater Grant begins to batter at Lee's positions around Cold Harbor, near the Seven Days' battlefields of 1862. The Union troops make a few limited gains and immediately entrench themselves.

Western Theater Stoneman's Union cavalry seize the Allatoona Pass through which the vital railroad to Chattanooga runs. This will allow Sherman to advance his railhead closer to his army. Meanwhile, General S.D. Sturgis leads a force of 3000 cavalry, 3800 infantry, and 18 guns from Memphis to chase Bedford Forrest's cavalry, which continues to harry Sherman's supply line.

Thursday, June 2

Eastern Theater Grant's planned morning assault is delayed, and finally postponed until tomorrow. Lee sends Early to probe the Union left but to little effect. In blisteringly hot and humid weather, the rival armies improve their positions.

Western Theater Sherman takes advantage of his improved railroad communications and begins to shift northeast toward the Atlanta–Chattanooga railroad. Skirmishes follow at Acworth and Raccoon Bottom.

Friday, June 3

Eastern Theater Grant hurls three corps against Lee's defenses at 4.30 a.m. If he breaks through, Richmond will fall—but the massed charges are received by a storm of fire. Well-sited Confederate guns sweep every angle of approach, and the Army of the Potomac sustains 7000 casualties in just one hour. Grant calls off the attack at noon. Confederate losses are under 1500. Once again, Lee's outnumbered veterans have stopped the Federals dead in their tracks. But the cannon can clearly be heard in Richmond, just eight miles away.

Saturday, June 4

Eastern Theater At Cold Harbor the armies bury their dead and snipe at the enemy lines, often just a few yards apart. The humidity is almost unbearable and the stink of decaying bodies is everywhere.

Western Theater Marching through a stormy night, Johnston withdraws to defensive positions he had already created on Lost, Pine, and Brush mountains. Federal forces continue to scour Tennessee and Kentucky for Forrest and Morgan.

Cold Harbor Battle was fought between June 3 and 12, 1864. Grant moved his force toward the road junction of Cold Harbor only 10 miles from Richmond. Lee moved his army to cover Richmond once again and established a seven-mile front, beating off determined Federal attacks.

Grant now took advantage of his greater numbers, but Lee received reinforcements from the Shenandoah and James valleys and was able to withstand further Union attacks which caused heavy losses to the Federal Army. Grant retired South across the James River to threaten Richmond via Petersburg.

187

June 1864

Sunday, June 5, 1864

Eastern Theater The battle of New Market is avenged. Breckinridge was ordered back to rejoin the Army of Northern Virginia, leaving John Imboden with a handful of men to hold the Shenandoah Valley. By calling out veterans, reserves and militia, the Confederates scrape together about 5000 men and 12 guns. General William E. Jones leads the little force to Piedmont, where it is attacked and destroyed by 8500 Federals under Hunter. Jones is killed and the Confederates suffer some 1500 casualties, including 1000 captured. Union losses are 780 killed, wounded, and missing.

Monday, June 6

Eastern Theater Hunter's Union troops enter Staunton in the Shenandoah Valley where they burn much private property. The lines are quiet at Cold Harbor, apart from a tentative move by Early against the Federal right flank.

Western Theater Sherman continues to shift positions. There are skirmishes at Raccoon Creek and Big Shanty.

Tuesday, June 7

The North The National Union Convention, representing most Republicans and those Democrats who support the war, meets in Baltimore to nominate a candidate for president.

Eastern Theater Grant dispatches Sheridan with two divisions of cavalry to join Hunter in the Shenandoah and attack Confederate railroads.

Western Theater S.D. Sturgis's column skirmishes with Confederates at Ripley, Mississippi, as his attempt to run down Bedford Forrest continues.

Wednesday, June 8

The North Lincoln is nominated for president, with Andrew Johnson, military governor of Tennessee, as the vice-presidential candidate. The party platform calls for no compromise with the South and a constitutional amendment to end slavery.

Eastern Theater In the Shenandoah Valley, Hunter's Federals are joined by columns under Crook and Averell, bringing their combined strength to 18,000 men. John Imboden's Confederates fall back to Waynesboro, 11 miles east, occupying the Rockfish Gap where the Chesapeake and Ohio railroad passes through the Blue Ridge Mountains.

Western Theater John Morgan's raiders capture Mount Sterling and its Federal garrison. Some of the Confederates also rob the local bank of $18,000. The complicity of their leader has never been established. Sherman's army marches on Marietta to face Johnston's latest line of defenses.

Mexico Emperor Maximilian enters Mexico City. Benito Juarez refuses an invitation to peace talks, vowing to fight on against the French and their imperial regime.

Thursday, June 9

Eastern Theater General Butler attacks Petersburg, Virginia, with 4500 men, but is driven off by P.T. Beauregard with 2500 troops. At Cold Harbor the Army of the Potomac begins to extend its lines. Grant is planning to shift his operations to the James River.

Friday, June 10

The South The Confederate Congress authorizes military service for men between 17 and 50 years of age.

Western Theater Morgan's raiders attack Lexington, Kentucky, and burn the depot and stables. At Brice's Cross Roads in Mississippi General Samuel D. Sturgis finally catches up with Bedford Forrest. The Union cavalry —3000 men in two brigades under B.H. Grierson—is attacked by Forrest with 3500 men. The first Southern advance is driven back, the leading Union troopers firing rapidly with revolving rifles. But when the Confederates advance again and get to within 50 yards, the Union cavalry gives way. Sturgis's three infantry brigades are five miles away when the fighting begins but they hurry forward through waterlogged roads under a burning sun. They form a new line to face Forrest's attack but the cavalry retires again, exposing its flanks. After three hours fighting, the Union Army disintegrates. Of the 8000 Union troops engaged, 223 are killed, 394 wounded, and 1623 missing or captured for a total of 2240. Forrest loses 96 dead and 396 wounded for a total of 492. It is Forrest's most brilliant tactical performance.

Saturday, June 11

Eastern Theater Sheridan's cavalry, on its way to join Hunter's forces in the Shenandoah, finds the way blocked by Fitzhugh Lee and Wade Hampton's Confederate cavalry. The battle which follows at Trevilian Station is indecisive. George A. Custer has a narrow escape when he unknowingly drives his brigade between the two Confederate forces. His wagons and colored cook Eliza are captured, but the girl, called the "Queen of Sheba" by his soldiers, escapes, bringing Custer's valise with her. Sheridan learns that Hunter is not at Charlottesville where he was expected, but at Lexington where he burns down the Virginia Military Institute.

Sunday, June 12

Eastern Theater Sheridan attacks Hampton's cavalry again at Trevilian Station. The Confederates are now well entrenched and the assault is driven off. Learning also that Jubal Early's corps had been detached from the Army of Northern Virginia and is now marching on Lynchburg, Sheridan abandons his attempt to join Hunter. He has lost 1007 of his 8000 men but Confederate losses are similar.

The Army of the Potomac pulls out of the lines of Cold Harbor. Several days of painstaking preparation pay off. Using newly constructed roads and a 700-yard pontoon bridge over the James River, Grant's men file over to the south bank. One corps travels down the Pamunkey and York rivers to be shipped back up the James. Warren's corps remains at Cold Harbor to keep the Confederates busy.

Western Theater Still leading 300 prisoners taken yesterday at Cynthiana, Morgan's raiders are attacked and defeated by 1500 Federals under General Burbridge. Morgan flees towards Abingdon, Virginia.

Monday, June 13

Eastern Theater Robert E. Lee withdraws toward Richmond in the belief that Grant is trying to assault the Confederate capital via Malvern Hill and White Oak Swamp. But he is wrong. By late afternoon Hancock's II Corps reaches the James at Wilcox Landing.

Tuesday, June 14

Eastern Theater The Union II Corps crosses the James River in boats. Smith's XVIII Corps reaches the Bermuda Hundred by water. Union and Confederate cavalry clash at Harrison's Landing. Lee still believes that Grant's next attack will be north of the James.

Western Theater Skirmishing and desultory firing continues along the Confederate entrenchments in the mountains near Marietta, Georgia. General Johnston confers with Hardee and Polk on Pine Mountain, concluding that the position should be abandoned during the night. But they are observed by a Union Parrott battery which opens fire at about 4000 yards. The third round passes straight through General Polk's chest, killing him instantly. No great commander, the bishop of the Episcopal Church nevertheless exerted a great influence on his men and his loss is a bitter blow to the Army of the Tennessee.

Naval Operations USS *Kearsage* arrives off Cherbourg, France, where the notorious Confederate raider *Alabama* has been reported.

Wednesday, June 15

The North The House votes 95 for to 66 against a joint resolution abolishing slavery. But the measure fails as a two-thirds majority is required.

Eastern Theater Generals Smith and Hancock fumble the chance to end the war at a stroke. Poised before Petersburg, the back door to the Confederate capital, their combined forces of 16,000 men are opposed by about 5000 men under Beauregard, but the morning attack is postponed until evening. Appalling staffwork leads to muddled orders, incorrect maps, and unnecessary stops for rations. When finally launched, the attack makes good progress and

Hancock argues they should continue into the night since the moon is illuminating the battlefield well. Smith disagrees and the Federals stop and entrench.

Thursday, June 16

Eastern Theater Beauregard strips the Bermuda Hundred defenses and manages to muster nearly 14,000 men to defend Petersburg. But he now faces all the Army of the Potomac, except Wright's VI Corps, and a series of assaults overrun several Confederate earthworks. Union troops overrun the Bermuda Hundred front but Lee, still believing the main Federal effort would be north of the James, sends Pickett with two divisions to counter-attack and he regains the Bermuda Hundred by early evening.

Friday, June 17

Eastern Theater Against all the odds, Beauregard manages a limited counter-attack in the battle outside Petersburg. Finally convincing Lee that he faces Grant's main body, he is reinforced by A.P. Hill and R.H. Anderson's corps.

Saturday, June 18

Eastern Theater Lee's main army arrives at Petersburg as Meade supervises the last attempts to carry the defenses by direct assault. The four days' fighting have cost the Army of the Potomac 8000 casualties. Confederate losses are unknown. In the Shenandoah Valley, Hunter begins to withdraw as he is threatened by Jubal Early's advance from Lynchburg.

Western Theater Johnston withdraws again, this time to the Big and Little Kennesaw mountains.

Confederate lines at Grace's Salient, Petersburg, the scene of severe fighting. Life in these trenches was bleak, with little chance of leave.

June–July 1864

Sunday, June 19, 1864

Naval Operations Having waited since June 11 to refit his vessel, Captain Raphael Semmes takes the Confederate raider *Alabama* out of Cherbourg. Stationed just outside the three-mile territorial limit, the USS *Kearsage* engages her on a bright, sunny morning. The battle attracts huge crowds along the cliffs, and an English yacht, *Deerhound*. The two cruisers circle each other at about 500 yards, but although the Union warship has only a marginally superior broadside to her opponent on paper, the *Alabama's* powder is defective. *Kearsage's* guns report with a sharp crack, giving off a thin vapor, but the *Alabama's* guns produce thick clouds of dirty smoke. Neither is the Confederate ammunition any better. Although many defective rounds had been removed after a practice shoot off Brazil, her best shot of the battle—a 100-pound shell which lodges in *Kearsage's* stern post—fails to explode. After less than an hour's fighting, the *Alabama* is sinking. An attempt to nurse the crippled vessel back into neutral waters fails and the Confederacy's proud raider slips below the waves. Her captain and 40 of the crew are rescued by the *Deerhound* and escape to Southampton.

Monday, June 20

Eastern Theater The rival armies continue to entrench at Petersburg. Grant is settled on a siege as attempts to break through have merely led to heavy losses. Meanwhile, in South Carolina, the bombardment of Fort Sumter continues once more.

Western Theater Sherman advances against Johnston's new positions. Confederate sorties disrupt the Union deployment, leading to a series of skirmishes.

Tuesday, June 21

Eastern Theater President Lincoln visits the army before Petersburg, touring the lines on horseback with General Grant. General David B. Birney replaces Hancock in charge of II Corps and leads his new command to extend the Union lines. Wright's VI Corps does likewise as Grant attempts to occupy a semi-circular line around Petersburg. The Confederate squadron on the James River engages in a long-range gun duel with Union warships.

Wednesday, June 22

Eastern Theater Birney's new command does not start well. As II and VI Corps march out to extend the Union line to the south and west, they run into A.P. Hill on the Jerusalem Plank Road. The Confederates launch a vigorous attack and drive back the Federals, killing 604, wounding 2494, and capturing 1600. Hill's men lose just 500 killed, wounded, and missing. Meanwhile, James H. Wilson leads two divisions of Union cavalry against the Confederate railroad at Burkeville. Pursued by W.H.F. Lee's cavalry, they fight a series of skirmishes for the rest of the week. Another Union cavalryman on the run is Phil Sheridan, who breaks up his supply depot and heads for the James with 900 wagons. Wade Hampton follows closely.

Thursday, June 23

Eastern Theater Sheridan's column is attacked as it crosses the Chickahominy by Jones' Bridge. In a brisk skirmish, the Confederates are driven off. In the Shenandoah, Hunter continues his retreat before Early, withdrawing up the Kanawha Valley into West Virginia.

Friday, June 24

The North The constitutional convention of Maryland votes to abolish slavery.

Eastern Theater Sheridan is attacked again, this time at St Mary's Church. The Federal cavalry is driven back in disorder.

Trans-Mississippi Three US steamers on the White River are attacked by Shelby's Confederates, USS *Queen City* is captured and burned.

Saturday, June 25

Eastern Theater At Petersburg engineers begin to dig a tunnel underneath one of the main Confederate redoubts. The mine is the brainchild of former mining engineer Lieutenant-Colonel Henry Pleasants, 48th Pennsylvania Volunteers. His men are mostly miners from the upper Schuylkill coal region. From an advanced section of the Union lines, 130 yards from an earthwork called Elliott's (or sometimes

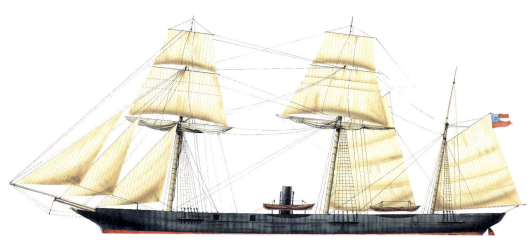

The famous Confederate raider Alabama. *Under the command of Captain Semmes, she destroyed or* captured 64 *vessels worth over $6 million in a 22-month cruise.*

Above: *Union sloop* Kearsage, *which eventually caught up with and sank the* Alabama *off the coast of France after a hotly contested action. Semmes was able to escape and made his way to the South where he commanded the fleet at Richmond, Virginia.*

Above: *Never the most elegant of generals, Grant patiently waits for the photographer to finish at Cold Harbor, June 1864. His steady battering against the Army of Northern Virginia was deliberately calculated to bleed the Confederate Army white. It did the same to the Army of the Potomac, but the Union had the deeper purse.*

Pegram's) Salient, the miners tunnel away, taking pains to conceal their labor from the Confederates.

Europe Prussia and Austria resume hostilities against Denmark after the expiry of the armistice.

Sunday, June 26

Eastern Theater Sheridan reaches the main army, crossing the James at Couthard's Landing. In the Shenandoah Early's 14,000 men reach Staunton. Their rapid marching over bad roads has been accomplished despite the fact that nearly half the infantry have no shoes. Early pauses, ordering shoes and other supplies—his men have not eaten since Friday—but is determined to press on. His object is to threaten Washington and take the pressure off the Confederates at Petersburg.

Western Theater There is a minor action at Olley's Creek, Georgia.

Monday, June 27

Western Theater Perhaps hoping for another Missionary Ridge, Sherman hurls his men at Johnston's formidable entrenchments on Kennesaw Mountain. The Armies of the Cumberland and Tennessee make the assault, while the Army of the Ohio menaces Johnston's left. But

after nearly three hours, the assault is driven back. Coming on in seven waves, the Federals are stopped just short of the Confederate parapet and the following troops pile up until a dense mass of soldiers in pinned down under heavy fire. Of the 16,000 attackers, 1999 are killed or wounded, and 52 missing. Confederate losses are fewer than 500.

Tuesday, June 28

Eastern Theater Early leaves Staunton before his supplies arrive and strikes north, planning to attack Harper's Ferry.

Western Theater Although his line at Kennesaw Mountain holds, Johnston is under no illusions that his outnumbered army can block Sherman indefinitely. He begins to construct another line of defense along the Chattahoochee River.

Wednesday, June 29

Eastern Theater Early's advance continues. He has five days' rations in the wagons and two days' in the men's haversacks. Imboden leads a small brigade of cavalry through Brock's Gap to the south branch of the Potomac to destroy the railroad bridge there, and all bridges on the Baltimore and Ohio railroad from there to Martinsburg.

Thursday, June 30

The North Secretary of the Treasury Salmon P. Chase resigns once too often. This time, to his surprise, Lincoln accepts.

Eastern Theater Early's Confederates reach New Market.

Friday, July 1, 1864

The North President Lincoln appoints Senator William Pitt Fessenden of Maine as secretary of the treasury. Fessenden has served on the finance committee for some time and, although taking the office with some reluctance, he soon proves a great success.

Far West Federal troops skirmish with Indians in Minnesota. Major-General Irwin McDowell, who presided over the shambles at Bull Run, is appointed to command the Department of the Pacific.

Saturday, July 2

Eastern Theater Early reaches Winchester where he receives fresh orders from Lee. He is directed to remain in the lower valley until he has sufficient supplies to cross the Potomac, and to destroy the Baltimore and Ohio railroad to prevent the Union moving troops from the west over to Washington.

Western Theater Before Sherman can begin an outflanking maneuver, Johnston evacuates the Kennesaw Mountain position during the night, withdrawing to his new entrenchments below Marietta.

July 1864

Sunday, July 3, 1864

The North Secretary of the Treasury Fessenden tries to decline the post but Lincoln talks him round. One of Chase's closest allies, Fessenden was an unexpected choice. But left in the finance committee he would have given the president serious trouble. Another liberal Republican, his inclusion in the Cabinet stops a major threat of defections to Frémont's leadership challenge.

Eastern Theater Franz Sigel, still commanding troops in the Shenandoah despite his demotion, evacuates Martinsburg in the face of Early's advance. During the night he falls back over the Potomac to Maryland Heights. Apprehension grows in Washington amid inflated reports of Early's strength.

After six months of sporadic bombardment of Fort Sumter, the Federal forces before Charleston launch another offensive. Troops are landed from barges in a dawn attack on Fort Johnson, Morris Island, but they are repulsed. A second attack on James Island also meets with failure.

Western Theater Sherman advances through Marietta toward the new Confederate defenses at Nickajack Creek. Confederate cavalry continue to menace Sherman's rear.

Monday, July 4

The North President Lincoln pocket-vetoes the Wade-Davis reconstruction bill which calls for harsh settlement with rebel states. Lincoln refuses to abandon his policy of lenient reconstruction, already in operation in Louisiana and Arkansas.

Eastern Theater During the night Federal forces evacuate Harper's Ferry once again, burning the railroad bridge over the Potomac. Heavy guns on the Maryland Heights dominate the town, so the Confederates occupy it only with skirmishers.

Western Theater Sherman's forces lap around Johnston's defenses until McPherson on the right flank is actually nearer to Atlanta than the Confederates. Johnston withdraws to new positions along the Chattahoochee.

Tuesday, July 5

Eastern Theater Early leaves Ramseur's and Rodes' divisions to demonstrate at Harper's Ferry. During the afternoon Breckinridge's division marches on Shepherdstown and crosses the Potomac. Panic reigns in the North, with the call going out for 24,000 militia from New York and Pennsylvania to defend Washington.

Western Theater Sherman probes Johnston's defenses on the Chattahoochee. A Union cavalry column under A.J. Smith leaves La Grange, Tennessee, bound for northern Mississippi as part of the hunt for Bedford Forrest's raiders. President Lincoln proclaims martial law in Kentucky and suspends the writ of habeas corpus on the grounds that many citizens are aiding "the insurgents."

Wednesday, July 6

Eastern Theater Early's Confederates levy $20,000 from Hagerstown in retribution for Hunter's destruction in the Shenandoah, while working parties destroy the aqueduct of the canal over the Antietam. The 3rd (Rickett's) division of Wright's VI Corps is withdrawn from the Petersburg lines to defend Washington; Early's invasion is at last drawing off troops from Lee.

Thursday, July 7

Eastern Theater Rickett's division of VI Corps arrives in Baltimore. Early demonstrates against the strong positions on the Maryland Heights, but plans to move through the gaps of South Mountain rather than assault the position. During the night the desperately needed supplies of shoes arrive for his footsore infantry. At Petersburg the rival armies improve their trenches but neither plans an immediate offensive. The Confederates at Charleston counter-attack on James Island, storming the newly won Federal entrenchments. Union siege guns continue to batter Fort Sumter, firing 784 rounds at the rubble.

Western Theater Smith's Union cavalry force skirmishes with Forrest's men near Ripley, Mississippi. President Davis writes General Johnston saying he can offer no reinforcements, but criticizing him for withdrawing.

Friday, July 8

Eastern Theater Early's men pass through the gaps in South Mountain in three columns. General Lew Wallace gathers a scratch force of troops at Frederick, Maryland.

Western Theater Sherman's left wing under Schofield crosses the Chattahoochee near Soap Creek, while McPherson on the right makes a demonstration at Turner's Ferry. Johnston plans to withdraw across the river himself and fall back on Atlanta.

Saturday, July 9

Eastern Theater Early finds his path blocked by Lew Wallace's hastily assembled force of raw recruits and Rickett's division, hurried forward on the railroad. The Federal force of 6000 occupies a strong position on the east bank of the Monocacy near Frederick, Maryland. Having already marched 14 miles today, the Confederates attack immediately. Early's 10,000 veterans batter their way through by sunset, Wallace's green troops disintegrating. Union losses are 90 dead, 579 wounded, and over 1200 missing—mostly "helping the wounded to the rear." The battle delays Early's advance on Washington by a day, gaining vital time for the capital's defenses to be organized. Early levies $200,000 from Frederick.

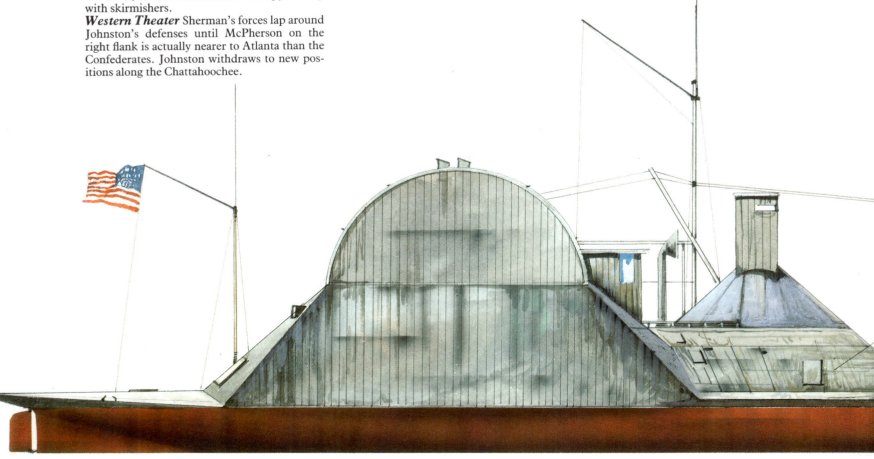

Western Theater Johnston withdraws across the Chattahoochee, destroying all the bridges as he goes and occupying new entrenchments around Atlanta itself. President Davis dispatches Braxton Bragg to meet Johnston and ask what he is planning to do next.

Sunday, July 10

Eastern Theater Early's Confederates march another 20 miles in blistering summer heat. There has been no rain for several weeks and the troops are enveloped in clouds of dust, but at least they all have shoes now. They camp at Rockville on the Georgetown Pike.
Western Theater Sherman plans to invest Atlanta rather than attempt an assault. He sends Lovell Harrison Rousseau with 2500 cavalry from Decatur, Alabama, to raid the railroad between Columbus, Georgia, and Montgomery, Alabama.

Monday, July 11

Eastern Theater The fast marching in the oppressive heat reduces Early's strength to some 8000 men. They arrive in front of the Federal fortifications in the early afternoon. Early has 40 cannon with him but nothing heavier than a 12-pounder Napoleon. The Washington defenses are now reinforced by two regular divisions; with invalids, short-term men, and raw recruits, the number of men defending the capital reaches 20,000. That night Early plans an assault, but then learns of the reinforcements and orders a retreat.

Tuesday, July 12

Eastern Theater Early turns his men around, his rear guard sniping at Fort Stevens where President Lincoln is standing on the parapet. "Get down you damned fool or you'll be killed," shouts a young officer as a man near Lincoln is hit. Ducking down, Lincoln observes, "Well, Captain, I see you have already learned how to address a civilian." The officer is Oliver Wendell Holmes, Jr.

Wednesday, July 13

Eastern Theater Early's footsore veterans march away from Washington pursued by the Union VI and XIX Corps.
Western Theater A.J. Smith leads 14,000 Federal troops to Tupelo, Mississippi. Bedford Forrest launches two attacks but they are driven off.

Thursday, July 14

Western Theater Bedford Forrest launches a succession of attacks against A.J. Smith at Tupelo. But the Union line does not give way and the Confederates are driven back. Union losses are 77 dead, 559 wounded, and 38 missing—a total of 674. Confederate casualties are 153 killed, 794 wounded, and 49 missing for a total of 996. Although repulsed, Forrest's men still have enough fight in them to shell the Federal camp that night.

Friday, July 15

Western Theater Low on ammunition and supplies, A.J. Smith's command begins a slow retreat to Memphis. Although he has defeated Forrest, the Confederate raiders are still active and the action at Tupelo has not changed anything.

Saturday, July 16

Eastern Theater Jubal Early's Confederates outpace the pursuing Federals and head back into the Shenandoah Valley, much to Lincoln's irritation.
Western Theater Sherman begins to advance across the Chattahoochee, around the north side of Atlanta. President Davis wires General Johnston, demanding to know what action is planned. Johnston is noncommittal, pointing out that the Union Army outnumbers him 2:1, but saying that he hopes to hold Atlanta with the Georgia militia for a day or so to allow him to maneuver his field army against Sherman.

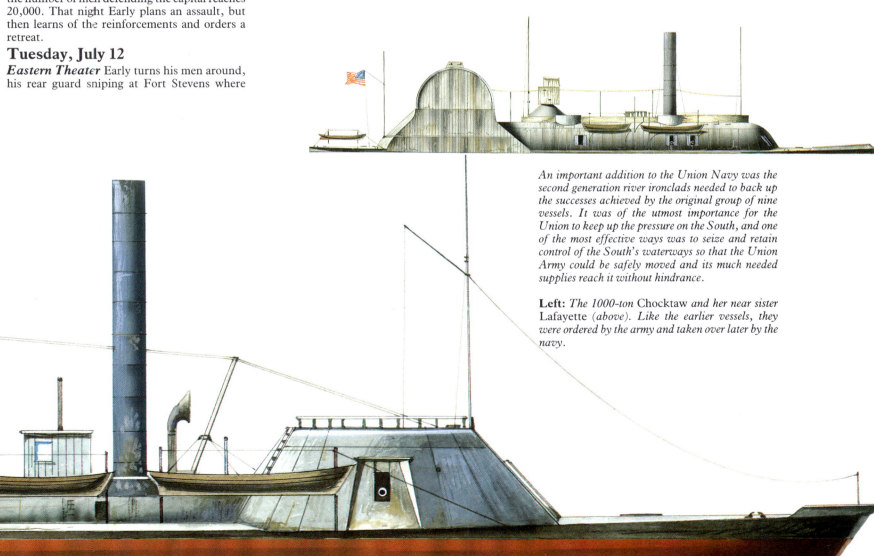

An important addition to the Union Navy was the second generation river ironclads needed to back up the successes achieved by the original group of nine vessels. It was of the utmost importance for the Union to keep up the pressure on the South, and one of the most effective ways was to seize and retain control of the South's waterways so that the Union Army could be safely moved and its much needed supplies reach it without hindrance.

Left: *The 1000-ton* Chocktaw *and her near sister* Lafayette *(above). Like the earlier vessels, they were ordered by the army and taken over later by the navy.*

193

July 1864

Sunday, July 17, 1864

Western Theater President Davis, relying on Braxton Bragg's judgment, relieves Johnston of his command and appoints 33-year-old John B. Hood in his place. Once again, Bragg's judgment is highly questionable. Hood is the youngest man to command a full army during the war; having lost his left arm at Gettysburg and his right leg at Chickamauga, no one could doubt his courage. But as a Kentuckian reported to Sherman, he had been known to bet $2500 with only a pair in his hand. President Davis hoped Hood's aggressive leadership would lead to a change in fortune for the Army of the Tennessee. It would indeed.

Monday, July 18

The North President Lincoln rejects tentative peace overtures conducted via Horace Greeley, editor of the *New York Tribune*. The Confederate proposals still insist on recognition of an independent South.

Tuesday, July 19

Eastern Theater Early's Confederates are closely followed up now, leading to a brisk skirmish at Berry's Ford. During the night Early retires toward Winchester.

Western Theater Sherman's command is divided as he spreads his force around Atlanta. Thomas leads the Army of the Cumberland around the north; Schofield's Army of the Ohio moves to the east, and McPherson's Army of the Tennessee is at Decatur. Hood lays his plans to attack Thomas without delay.

Wednesday, July 20

Eastern Theater The bombardment of Fort Sumter continues, fatally wounding the commandant, J.C. Mitchell. Over the last two weeks the battered fort has taken another 4890 rounds. Some 2000 Union troops under Averell attack Ramseur's division of Early's command at Winchester and defeat him, inflicting 400 casualties for the loss of 214.

Western Theater At Peachtree Creek Hood sends 20,000 Confederates against Thomas, who has a similar number of troops engaged, the brunt of the attack falling on Hooker's XX Corps, which had crossed the creek on improvised bridges. Hood is too ill to command personally and blames the failure of the assault on General Hardee, author of the infantry tactical manual used by both sides during the war. Hardee's attack does go in three hours late, but in the fighting which follows the Confederates lose four brigadier-generals: Featherstone, Long, Pettis, and Stevens. The total Southern loss is over 4000, while Thomas loses 300 dead and 1300 wounded.

Thursday, July 21

Western Theater Hood sends Hardee on a wide outflanking maneuver to attack McPherson between Atlanta and Decatur. But there are further delays in getting the troops organized and the columns are still in Atlanta at midnight. McPherson moves west toward the city, and his XVII Corps storms a Confederate redoubt on Bald Hill.

Friday, July 22

Eastern Theater Wright's VI Corps returns to Washington, leaving Hunter to look after the Shenandoah.

Western Theater Hardee's men finally leave the city at 3 a.m. Marching 15 miles on a humid summer night, the columns become confused. Major-General W.H.T. Walker takes the wrong road, and, riding ahead to check the route, is shot dead by a Union rifleman. Finally clearing the ponds and dense brush thickets which obstructed their night march, Hardee's men attack the Union XVI Corps at noon. McPherson gallops to the front to see what is happening and rides into Cheatham's Confederates who shoot him dead. But the Federals hold off the attack at a cost of 3772 casualties, including 1733 missing. Confederate losses are never properly assessed; best estimates are 6500 killed and wounded, and 2000 missing. Hood claims the action as a success, citing the 13 guns captured by his men, and claiming that his offensive policy improved morale, stemming the desertions that weakened the army during Johnston's long rear guard action.

Saturday, July 23

Eastern Theater Jubal Early turns on his pursuers, marching north on the Valley Turnpike toward Stonewall Jackson's old battlefield at Kernstown.

Western Theater General A.J. Smith's command returns to Memphis, while Bedford Forrest continues his raiding.

Sunday, July 24

Eastern Theater Early attacks Union troops under General George Crook near Kernstown and inflicts a sharp reverse on the Federals. Crook's line breaks and his men suffer 1200 casualties, inflicting 600 killed and wounded in return. Crook's men flee in disorder, reaching Bunker Hill, West Virginia, by nightfall.

Monday, July 25

Eastern Theater Early follows up his victory at Kernstown, pursuing Crook's men through a torrential rainstorm. At Petersburg Grant determines to send troops north of the James River against the Confederate rail network. The tunneling operation continues as suspicious Confederates begin to countermine, digging several listening galleries underground to try to locate the Union tunnel.

Tuesday, July 26

Eastern Theater Crook retreats into Maryland. Early's men break up the Baltimore and Ohio Railroad near Martinsburg. At Petersburg the tunnel is ready and Brigadier-General Edward Ferrero's colored division is completing its rehearsals for the attack. After the detonation, Ferrero's men will enter the hole in the Confederate line and fan out right and left to widen the breach and allow a follow-on attack against Cemetery Hill.

Wednesday, July 27

Eastern Theater Hancock's II Corps and two cavalry divisions cross to the north bank of the James ready to launch a diversionary raid toward Richmond.

Western Theater Sherman detaches large formations of cavalry to cut the railroads south of Atlanta. Major-General Oliver O. Howard is appointed to command the Army of the Tennessee in place of the gallant McPherson. This is the last straw for Joe Hooker, commanding XX Corps, who holds Howard responsible for his defeat at Chancellorsville and subsequent demotion. Hooker resigns.

Thursday, July 28

Eastern Theater Hancock's II Corps and Sheridan's cavalry discover new Confederate defenses north of the James and abandon their expedition after a skirmish at Four-Mile Creek.

Western Theater Hood launches another attack on the Union Army of the Tennessee, which is now threatening Atlanta from the southwest. Generals S.D. Lee and A.P. Stewart attack Howard's men during the afternoon at Ezra Church, where the Federals had hastily dug in that morning. The Confederates are repelled, with 4600 casualties, inflicting a loss of only 700 on the Union Army.

Far West At Tahkahokuty Mountain in Dakota Territory, Brigadier-General Sully's small brigade forms rallying squares to beat off an attack by Sioux Indians, covering the retreat of their village. Brackett's Minnesota Cavalry Battalion charges near the end of the day and disperses the Indians. The column will now head into Yellowstone country, driving the Sioux further westward.

Friday, July 29

Eastern Theater Early sends his cavalry under John McCausland over the Potomac to raid Maryland and Pennsylvania. During the evening the Union commanders at Petersburg make a series of decisions which will bear bitter fruit tomorrow. General Meade refuses to allow Ferrero's colored division to lead the assault after the explosion of the mine. He is afraid that if the attack miscarries and the black soldiers suffer heavy losses, it will seem as if the Federal Army is employing its Negro regiments as mere cannon fodder. Grant agrees and compels Burnside to change his plans. He meets his four divisional commanders that night and they draw straws. Ledlie's men get the short straw—they have under 12 hours to prepare for an assault Ferrero's men have been training for days to undertake.

Saturday, 30 July

Eastern Theater The Union soldiers gather in their trenches before dawn. A stomach-churning hour's delay occurs because the mine does not go off. Sergeant Harry Reese goes back along the tunnel to find the fuze has gone out. Finally, the 900 pounds of powder detonate, creating a smoking crater 170 feet long, 30 feet deep, and between 60 and 80 feet wide. Some 278 Confederates die in the explosion, which showers the surrounding area with cannon barrels, caissons, and shattered bodies.

The assault goes disastrously wrong from the beginning. Ledlie remains in his shelter as his division pours into the crater, promptly followed by the second wave. Instead of fanning out either side, the first two waves of Union soldiers crowd into the crater and the Confederates recover fast. Guns are soon in place, sweeping the crater with cannister from either side, while infantry assemble in the dead ground behind the crater. With his three white divisions crammed helplessly in the crater, Burnside commits the black division which attacks in splendid style and manages to gain a little ground. But they take heavy losses from the Confederate cannon and are driven back by a counter-attack; the whole Union force then retreats over ground swept by Confederate guns. In three hours' fighting over 4000 Federal troops are killed or wounded out of the 20,000 engaged. Confederate losses are about 1500 out of 11,000.

The Confederate raid into Pennsylvania continues. McCausland's cavalry enter Chambersburg and demand $500,000 cash or $100,000 in gold in exchange for not burning down the town. The money is not forthcoming so Chambersburg is put to the torch.

The defenses of Atlanta

Built at the crossroads of Georgia's four main railroads, Atlanta was one of the Confederacy's most important industrial centers. Its factories produced iron for the Confederate gunboats and railroads; its warehouses supplied food to Southern armies in Tennessee and Virginia.

As the Union forces continued to make progress in the Western Theater during 1863, Colonel L.P. Grant, chief engineer of the Department of Georgia, planned Atlanta's defense. By the summer of 1864 a 12-mile line of earthworks surrounded the city. Rifle pits supported a total of 20 major redoubts studded with cannon. The approaches were cleared of cover and the immediate front of the lines choked with abattis and other obstacles. After early reconnaissance, Sherman's chief engineer, Captain Poe, described Atlanta's defenses as "too strong to assault and too extensive to invest." He was certainly correct, but Sherman did not need to invest the city completely—merely to cut it off from the rest of the Confederacy and starve it out.

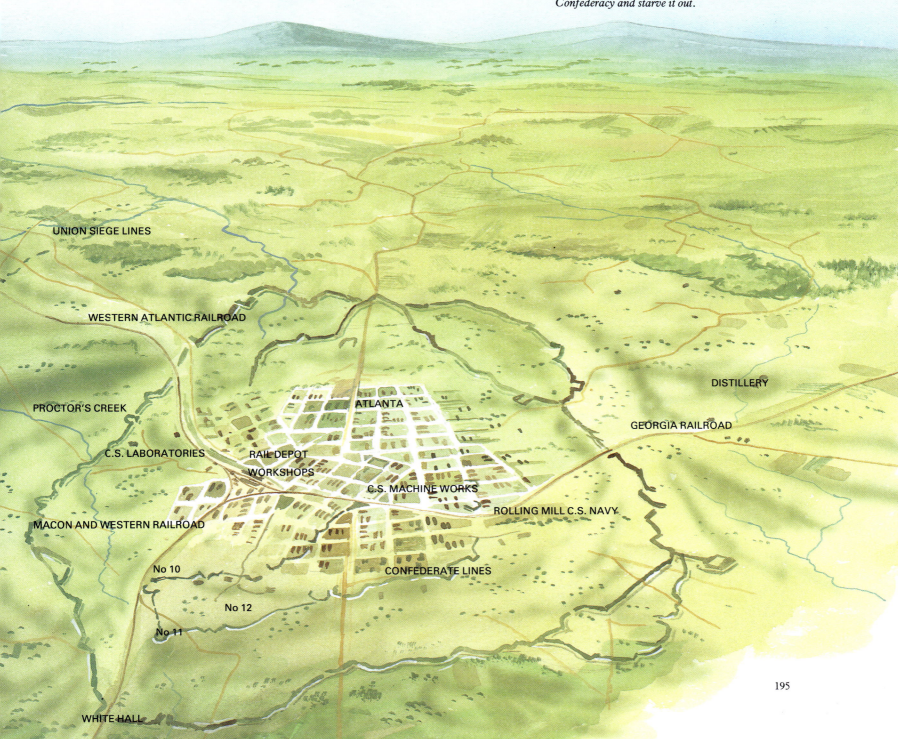

UNION SIEGE LINES

WESTERN ATLANTIC RAILROAD

PROCTOR'S CREEK

DISTILLERY

ATLANTA

GEORGIA RAILROAD

C.S. LABORATORIES

RAIL DEPOT

WORKSHOPS

C.S. MACHINE WORKS

ROLLING MILL C.S. NAVY

MACON AND WESTERN RAILROAD

No 10

No 12

No 11

CONFEDERATE LINES

WHITE HALL

July–August 1864

The crater at Petersburg

Well before dawn, Union soldiers had assembled in their trenches ready to storm the Confederate positions after the mine was fired. They ate their usual breakfast, as it was believed that a hearty meal helped a man survive much loss of blood. No fires could be lit, so they fed on raw, fat salt pork sandwiched between two pieces of hard tack.

At about 4 a.m. the Confederate redoubt vanished in a thunderous explosion and Ledlie's division charged into the smoking wreckage. But the last-minute decision to use his men rather than Ferrero's colored troops spelt disaster. Unprepared for the operation, the Union troops failed to exploit the impact of the explosion and the Confederates soon rallied.

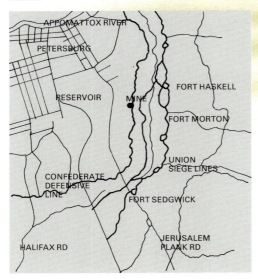

Sunday, July 31, 1864

The North President Lincoln confers with General Grant at Fort Monroe. Grant knows that the army's fortunes are closely allied to Lincoln's, and promises to send Sheridan after Jubal Early to prevent any more politically embarrassing raids over the Potomac.
Eastern Theater McCausland's cavalry retire from the flaming ruin of Chambersburg but are intercepted at Hancock, Maryland, by Averell's Federal cavalry.

Monday, August 1, 1864

Eastern Theater McCausland's cavalry slip through the Union net to raid Cumberland, Maryland. Major-General Philip H. Sheridan is named as the commander of the Army of the Shenandoah.

Tuesday, August 2

Eastern Theater McCausland's cavalry are in action again at Hancock, Maryland.
Europe Denmark makes peace with Prussia and Austria, ceding Schleswig-Holstein. Confederate naval officers abandon their attempts to fit out the CSS *Rappahannock* as a raider. Having slipped from Sheerness, England, over the Channel to Calais, hours ahead of a British order to seize her, the *Rappahannock* was repaired, but the French authorities will only allow her a 35-man crew, not enough to work her at sea. She remains in port as a depot ship and will be sold off at the end of the war.

Wednesday, August 3

Eastern Theater McCausland's men slip back into West Virginia.
Western Theater Federal troops under General Granger land on Dauphin Island at the entrance to Mobile Bay, Alabama. Admiral Farragut completes his plans to mount a naval attack on this strategically important Confederate port. Using wooden blocks as model ships, he "wargames" an attack on the powerful forts guarding the three-mile channel into the bay. By maneuvering the models, he calculates the best courses and bearings for his vessels to concentrate their fire on the Confederate defenses.

Thursday, August 4

Western Theater A detachment of US Army signal officers join Farragut's fleet before Mobile. Posted on several of the Union warships, they will communicate with Granger's troops ashore during tomorrow's naval attack. During the afternoon Admiral Farragut conducts a last personal reconnaissance of the Confederate defenses in the steam-tender *Cowslip*. The channel is defended by Fort Gaines on the west—a small brick and earth battery over a mile from the route the warships have to take, and not a significant threat. But on the eastern side of the channel the defenses are right at the water's edge, with a powerful battery on the beach and the mighty Fort Morgan commanding the channel with three tiers of heavy guns. Built of old brick, Fort Morgan has been substantially strengthened with sandbags. Behind the land defenses wait the powerful ironclad ram CSS *Tennessee* and three small gunboats. Under water lurk numerous torpedoes, many of them beer kegs filled with powder, with fulminate primers projecting from their sides.

Friday, August 5

The North Radical Republicans issue the Wade–Davis Manifesto, accusing Lincoln of overweening ambition and encroaching on the authority of Congress by his pocket-veto of their reconstruction bill.

Western Theater Admiral Farragut leads his warships past Fort Morgan into Mobile Bay. His ships take a pounding from the fort but subject the Confederate gunners to a formidable weight of fire in return. Their vitals protected by chain armor, none of Farragut's ships suffer serious damage from the fort, although men on the exposed decks receive hideous injuries. The leading monitor *Tecumseh* heads directly for the CSS *Tennessee*, but strikes a torpedo and sinks like a stone, drowning all but four of her 98 crew. Confusion in the Union fleet is overcome by Farragut, who takes the lead in *Hartford* and steers over the Confederate minefield. His reported cry of "Damn the torpedoes, full speed ahead," goes into legend. Admiral Franklin Buchanan aboard the *Tennessee* then takes on the whole Union fleet and, after a gallant action, is forced to strike his colors.

Saturday, August 6

Western Theater At Mobile Bay the Confederates evacuate the small battery called Fort Powell, untenable now the Union warships are in the bay. The sole major Confederate port is now Wilmington, North Carolina, from where the former blockade runner *Atlanta*, now named CSS *Tallahassee*, sets off on a commerce raiding mission up the Atlantic coast.

Sunday, August 7

Eastern Theater Major-General Sheridan assumes command of the new Middle Military Division and the Army of the Shenandoah.
Western Theater Fort Gaines surrenders, but the officer who gave the order, Colonel Anderson, is overruled by his superiors and hostilities are resumed.

Monday, August 8

Western Theater Fort Gaines finally surrenders to the Federal troops under General Granger.

Far West Federal columns range across Kansas and Dakota Territory on operations against hostile Indians.

Tuesday, August 9

Western Theater Sherman's artillery, reinforced by two 32-pounder Parrott guns, bombard Atlanta, inflicting civilian casualties. The first victims of the shelling are a little girl and her dog, blown to pieces on East Ellis and Ivy Streets. Sherman has no intention of assaulting the formidable defenses; his plan is to maneuver south to cut Hood's supply line and starve out the defenders.

At Mobile, Union troops go ashore at Navy Cove under protection of the monitors. They invest Fort Morgan and its 400-strong garrison.

Wednesday, August 10

Eastern Theater Sheridan marches his new command south from Harper's Ferry, while Early's Confederates move from Bunker Hill, West Virginia, to Winchester. The outnumbered Early plans to follow Stonewall Jackson's example and maneuver rapidly to confuse the Federal commanders as to his real strength and intentions.

Western Theater Joe Wheeler leads the Army of the Tennessee's cavalry in a raid on Sherman's lines of communication, heading into northern Georgia. But Sherman has stockpiled supplies with his troops and Hood has left himself with few horsemen to reconnoiter around Atlanta itself.

Naval Operations CSS *Tallahassee*'s cruise begins well. The fast 500-ton raider takes seven prizes off Sandy Hook, New Jersey.

Thursday, August 11

Eastern Theater Early withdraws from Winchester and heads south toward Cedar Creek as Sheridan's troops advance.

Friday, August 12

Eastern Theater Sheridan's leading cavalry catch up with Early's rear guard, leading to a skirmish at Cedar Creek.

Naval CSS *Tallahassee* captures six Union vessels off New York.

Saturday, August 13

Eastern Theater Sheridan's cavalry discover Early's men strongly posted around Fisher's Hill, with an unknown number of reinforcements joining him. On the James River, the Confederate ironclads *Richmond*, *Fredericksburg*, and *Virginia* engage in a long-range duel with Union monitors.

August 1864

Sunday, August 14, 1864
Eastern Theater Sheridan withdraws from Early's Confederate Army in the Shenandoah, planning to go on the defensive until he receives reinforcements.
Western Theater Sherman's bombardment of Atlanta continues, while his troops extend their trenches toward the Southern lines.

Monday, August 15
Eastern Theater Minor actions take place at Cedar Creek and Strasburg as Sheridan retreats from Cedar Creek to Winchester. Elements of the Union Army before Petersburg again operate north of the James River at Chaffin's Bluff.
Western Theater Confederate cavalry raid the Nashville and Northwestern Railroad in Tennessee. Lieutenant-General Richard Taylor is appointed to command the Confederate Department of Alabama, Mississippi, and East Louisiana.
Naval Operations CSS *Tallahassee* continues to wreak havoc, taking another six schooners off New England.

Tuesday, August 16
Eastern Theater Sheridan reaches Winchester, the rapidity of his withdrawal not yet apparent to Early who has occupied Cedar Creek. North of the James River, Hancock's II Corps attacks Confederate entrenchments near Fussell's Mill, but is repulsed. Hancock withdraws toward the Union lines at Petersburg.
Naval CSS *Tallahassee* captures five more Union vessels.

Wednesday, August 17
Eastern Theater Jubal Early's Confederates advance north from Cedar Creek, his leading troops running into Sheridan's rear guard at Winchester. But the Federal main body has already fallen back on Berryville.

Thursday, August 18
Eastern Theater Warren's V Corps advances westward from the siege lines at Petersburg, seizing over a mile of the strategically important Weldon Railroad, which runs south from Petersburg. Warren then swings north toward the stricken town and runs into Heth's Confederates, who block further progress. For the second time, Grant refuses to exchange any more prisoners; this exacerbates the Confederate's crippling manpower shortage but condemns many Federal prisoners to chronic malnutrition in Southern camps. The Confederacy can barely feed and clothe its own armies, and can spare little for its prisoners of war.

In the Shenandoah Valley Sheridan marches toward Charles Town, West Virginia, while Early heads for Bunker Hill north of Winchester.
Western Theater Sherman sends two cavalry brigades under Judson Kilpatrick to raid Hood's lines of communication. Their primary target is the Macon and Western railroad.

Friday, August 19
Eastern Theater Warren's V Corps, reinforced by elements of II and IX Corps, are attacked by a Confederate force under A.P. Hill. The Confederates come on the old style, supported by 30 guns. Charging through the forest, they overrun S.W. Crawford's division, capturing 2000 prisoners and 3000 rifles. But by nightfall, Warren still holds Globe Tavern, a station on the Weldon Railroad four miles south of Petersburg.
Western Theater Cavalry actions take place around Atlanta as both sides raid the enemy supply lines.

Saturday, August 20
Eastern Theater Skirmishing continues around Globe Tavern but the railroad remains cut. Minor actions also take place in the Shenandoah as Early's Confederates press Sheridan's troops at Berryville.
Western Theater Kilpatrick's cavalry continue their raid against Confederate supply lines.

Sunday, August 21
Eastern Theater A.P. Hill makes another attempt to drive the Federals away from the Weldon Railroad, but the Union troops are now solidly entrenched and the assault fails. This series of actions since Thursday has cost the Confederates about 1600 casualties from the approximately 14,000 troops engaged. Total Union losses are 198 dead, 1105 wounded, and an incredible 3152 missing—over 2000 of them captured. Their numbers made up with green troops, some Union formations seem to be of

The south side of Fort Morgan after its fall on August 23. Union infantry had cut the fort off from Mobile on August 17 and sapped toward the walls, making surrender inevitable. Although the Confederates still held the town of Mobile, it was finished as a port. The Confederacy had one remaining outlet to the world: Wilmington, North Carolina.

Below: *Confederate raider* Tallahassee *was a fast, cross-Channel steamer before being taken into Southern service in 1864. Unlike others raiders who cruised worldwide looking for prey,* Tallahassee *spent her time hunting along the US coast, capturing 39 vessels.*

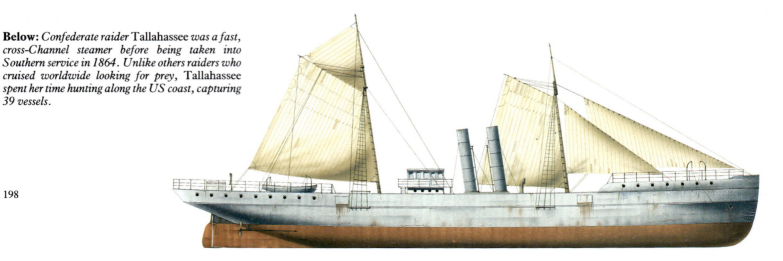

very low fighting quality, to the distress of their commanders.

In the Shenandoah Sheridan withdraws to near Harper's Ferry after a series of actions around Charles Town. Early and R.H. Anderson fail to coordinate a combined attack on the Federal Army, which escapes to a strong defensive position.

Western Theater Bedford Forrest mounts a daring dawn raid on Memphis, Tennessee, coming within an ace of capturing Union Major-Generals Hurlbut and Washburn. After all the effort expended to track down and vanquish the elusive Confederate leader, this audacious assault is a humiliating defeat for the Union.

Monday, August 22

Western Theater The Union forces ashore near Fort Morgan outside Mobile, Alabama, have been sapping steadily forward. Covered by the guns of the fleet, they opened their first line of approach on August 10 and by yesterday they had sapped to within 200 yards of the fort. Today the fleet closes in for a concentrated bombardment. The Confederate gunners are unable to fire back as they are picked off by riflemen in the Union trenches. Eventually, all the fort's cannon are knocked out and several breaches made in the walls. Accurate mortar fire during the night threatens to penetrate the magazine,

which contains 80,000 pounds of powder. The commander reluctantly floods the magazine, although not before a serious fire threatens to blow up the whole position.

Tuesday, August 23

The North President Lincoln seems resigned to defeat in the forthcoming election. He asks the Cabinet to sign a memo affirming the administration's commitment to cooperating with "the new president" in the vulnerable time between the election and inauguration.

Western Theater Brigadier-General R.L. Page, commanding Fort Morgan, surrenders his command to the Union forces under General Granger. Although the port of Mobile remains in Confederate hands, Union troops now control the entrance to the bay. Wilmington, North Carolina, is the South's only remaining port.

Wednesday, August 24

Eastern Theater Early's forces demonstrate against Sheridan's defensive line near the Potomac. Small parties of Confederates continue to attack the Union troops along the Weldon Railroad.

Thursday, August 25

Eastern Theater A.P. Hill leads nine Confederate brigades against the Union troops engaged in breaking up the Weldon Railroad. Entrenched in the woods, Hancock's II Corps receives the brunt of the attack. When the Confederates surge across their cleared fields of fire, Hancock's infantry begin to abandon their trenches and flee to the rear. The line holds briefly as gunners from Battery B, 1st Rhode Island Artillery, and the 10th Massachusetts Battery fight on, but they are overrun and the guns captured. Gibbon's division, ordered to counter-attack the disorganized Confederates, refuses to fight, and falls back. Hancock's line is driven back and the casualty figures again reveal the demoralization of the Union troops: 140 dead, 529 wounded, and an astonishing 2073 missing and captured. Confederate losses are 720.

Western Theater Sherman begins to march again, sending troops toward Jonesboro on the south side of the city.

Naval Operations CSS *Tallahassee* breaks through the blockading squadron and returns to Wilmington with her coal supply running low. Her three-week cruise has netted 31 Union ships.

Friday, August 26

Western Theater Sherman's new advance threatens Hood's last exit from the city of Atlanta. Skirmishes take place along the Chattahoochee River.

Saturday, August 27

Eastern Theater Early retires to Bunker Hill, West Virginia, abandoning any pretense of assaulting Sheridan's defenses at Harper's Ferry.

Western Theater Sherman deploys his army southwest of Atlanta, poised to cut the only remaining railroads into the city.

Left: Lines of chevaux-de-frise *at Atlanta. These barriers of sharpened stakes were mentioned in Caesar's account of the Gallic War. Classic siege defenses, they were making their last appearance during the Civil War; the development of barbed wire rendered them obsolete.*

Left: Contrary to some accounts of the war, the notorious Confederate prisoner of war camp at Andersonville, Georgia, was not established until February 1864. Conditions were appalling, but the Union record in this respect was not much better. It has been calculated that almost one Union prisoner in six died in captivity. One in eight Confederates perished in Northern camps.

August–September 1864

Sunday, August 28, 1864

Western Theater Sherman continues his efforts to isolate Atlanta and with it Hood's Confederate Army. Federal forces destroy 10 miles of the West Point road, leading from Atlanta to the Alabama state line.

Farther west, Union Cavalry skirmish with Confederate raiders south of the large Federal supply base of Holly Springs, Mississippi.

Monday, August 29

In Chicago, the Democrats convene to select a presidential and vice-presidential candidate. One faction of the party seeks to end the war immediately, whatever the military situation.

Eastern Theater Shenandoah Valley. In the continual skirmishing between Jubal Early's Confederates and Union troops under Sheridan the 3rd Division of the Union's VI Corps get the better of a Confederate force at Smithfield, Virginia.

Tuesday, August 30

Western Theater Generals Thomas and Howard cut the rail line from Atlanta to Montgomery, leaving the line to Macon as Atlanta's only lifeline. Hood has still not fathomed Sherman's entire plan, but can recognize his own vulnerability. He sends two corps under Hardee and Lee to take up positions at Jonesboro, on the Macon line. He does not realize that the Federal armies of Thomas, Howard, and Schofield are already within striking distance, and are concentrating to finally isolate Atlanta.

Battle of Fisher's Hill, September 22, 1864, when the Confederates were forced to abandon this strong position. Under Early they had stopped at Fisher's Hill to resist any enemy moving South.

Here the valley narrowed down to four or five miles. Early's right was protected by impassable mountains and by the north fork of the Shenandoah River as it sweeps around. However, his left flank was rushed and his army scattered by troops concealed in the timber north of Cedar Creek.

Wednesday, August 31

General George B. McClellan is nominated as the Democratic presidential candidate in the forthcoming election.

Western Theater Lee's and Hardee's corps reach Jonesboro at about 3 p.m. Hardly have they left their trains when scouts report that Howard's Army of Tennessee is close by, dug into defensive positions. Hardee immediately launches a fierce attack, "but neither in weight nor persistence was it equal to former Confederate efforts," reports Union Brigadier General Cox. Hardee is well aware that the loss of the last rail link will be the end of Atlanta, but after two hours of battle has to withdraw. Confederate losses amount to almost 2000 killed and wounded, against less than a tenth of that figure for the Federal Army. Even as the battle is fought, Schofield's army lunges to capture the station at Rough and Ready, isolating Atlanta. Hood's last telegraph message to Jonesboro before the wires are cut recalls Lee's corps to Atlanta.

Thursday, September 1, 1864

Eastern Theater The stalemate before Petersburg continues.

Western Theater Wheeler, who had been sent by Hood to harass Sherman's supply lines to Tennessee, is himself being pursued by a powerful Union Cavalry force under Rousseau.

At Atlanta, Sherman throws his entire force against the remains of Hardee's command at Jonesboro. The Confederates hold out until the end of the day, pulling out as night falls, but leaving 3000 prisoners in Union hands. Hood, bowing to the inevitable, begins to evacuate Atlanta. The last to leave are the cavalry, who destroy stockpiles of much-needed supplies and ammunition before departing. As the tattered Confederate columns move down the McDonough Road, they are joined by what is left of Hardee's corps.

Friday, September 2

Eastern Theater Lee proposes to draft slaves for laboring tasks in the Army of Virginia, freeing white laborers for military service. Other measures suggested to ease the South's crippling manpower shortage include tightening up the system of exemptions from military service.

Western Theater The 2nd Massachusetts Infantry, part of Slocum's XX Corps, are the first Union troops into Atlanta. Sherman's telegraph message to Lincoln states that "Atlanta is ours, and fairly won."

Saturday, September 3

President Lincoln declares 5 September to be a day of national celebration, following the occupation of Atlanta and Farragut's victory at Mobile Bay in August.

Eastern Theater Lee requests the return of Anderson's corps which had been lent to Early in the valley. On the way to Richmond, however, they encounter part of Sheridan's command at Berryville, and after a sharp fight they withdraw to the main Confederate force at Winchester, Virginia.

Western Theater Sterling Price prepares a large Confederate raid into Missouri, which will be launched two weeks later.

Sunday, September 4

Eastern Theater In front of Petersburg, Grant orders a salute to Sherman's victorious armies, "with shotted guns, from every battery bearing on the enemy."

Western Theater The noted Confederate raider John H. Morgan is surprised by Federal Cavalry while in bivouac at Greenville, Tennessee. In the battle, Morgan is killed.

At his new headquarters, Sherman determines to make Atlanta an exclusively military post. He orders all citizens to leave, and prepares to destroy all structures other than private residences and churches.

Monday, September 5

National day of celebration. Citizens in Federal-occupied Louisiana who have taken the loyalty oath vote to abolish slavery in the state.

Eastern Theater Early moves his command south along the valley. Clashes with Sheridan's troops continue along the Opequon creek.

Tuesday, September 6

After a two-day pause, Federal Naval forces resume the bombardment of Fort Sumter. They will continue until September 14.

Wednesday, September 7

Eastern Theater Sheridan and Early continue to skirmish near Winchester in the Shenandoah Valley.

Western Theater Minor actions are reported at Searcy, Arkansas, and Centralia, Missouri.

Thursday, September 8

George B. McClellan formally accepts the Democratic presidential nomination in Chicago, although he distances himself from the copperhead, or anti-war section of the party. Nevertheless, Atlanta has given the Republicans a significant boost, and McClellan's own cause is not helped by questions as to the propriety of a major general in the United States Army standing against his own commander-in-chief.

Friday, September 9

Western Theater Action is reported at Warrensburg, Missouri, and the Federal steamer *J.D. Perry* is attacked at Clarendon, Arkansas.

Saturday, September 10

Eastern Theater Federals take Fort Hell, Virginia, capturing 90 rebels in the process. Grant telegraphs Sherman, urging him to continue his offensive. Both generals consider Hood's army to be the primary target.

Confederate flanking column surprises at night a Federal force at Cedar Creek as it attacks from the rear. The Union troops were able to reform on the reverse side of the rifle pits and beat off the attack.

The battle of Allatoona on October 5, 1864, where a Federal force successfully held off the Confederates who were trying to disrupt Sherman's tenuous supply line by seizing the rail depot there.

September 1864

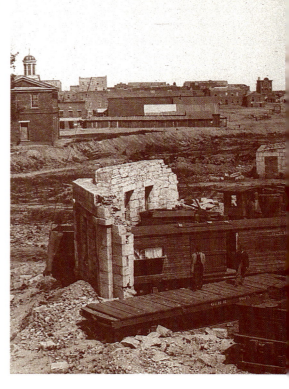

Sunday, September 11, 1864

Western Theater A 10-day truce begins at Atlanta to allow the citizens to depart in obedience to Sherman's ruthless order.

Far West Groups of Indians fighting for the Union, the Confederacy, and each other are engaged in a series of minor actions in the Cherokee Nation, Indian Territory. Federal troops depart Fort Rice, Dakota Territory, to relieve an emigrant train.

Monday, September 12

Eastern Theater President Lincoln, irritated by the apparent lack of action in the Shenandoah, presses Grant to reinforce Sheridan rapidly to knock out Early's force in a lightning blow. Remaining in the lower Shenandoah, Early continues to threaten Maryland and Pennsylvania. His main object is to prevent movement along the Baltimore and Ohio railroad and the Chesapeake and Ohio canal, and to draw as many of Grant's troops as possible away from Lee's embattled army at Petersburg. But staying in the north of the Shenandoah exposes his army to a Union attack on his lines of communication—a danger he has to live with as there is no forage in the upper Shenandoah for his horses.

Tuesday, September 13

Eastern Theater Skirmishing continues in the Shenandoah, with actions at Bunker Hill at the two fords over Opequon Creek.

Wednesday, September 14

Eastern Theater R.H. Anderson's Confederate Corps leaves the Shenandoah to join Lee's army at Petersburg. The continual attrition of the siege is bleeding the Army of Northern Virginia to death. But this withdrawal leaves Early badly outnumbered in the valley. He now has about 20,000 men of all arms facing 43,000 Union troops, plus 7000 in garrison at Harper's Ferry.

Thursday, September 15

Eastern Theater Grant leaves the siege lines of Petersburg to confer with Sheridan.

Western Theater There is a minor action at Snake Creek Gap, Georgia, on Sherman's supply line.

Friday, September 16

Eastern Theater The Army of Northern Virginia ran out of corn by the beginning of the month and Lee's food supply is practically exhausted. Wade Hampton brings temporary relief by a daring raid behind the Union lines with 4000 cavalry. Departing last Sunday, his men have now captured 2400 head of cattle and 300 prisoners for the loss of only 61 troopers.

Saturday, September 17

The North John C. Frémont, nominated as a presidential candidate by radical Republicans, withdraws from the race. Although still no friend of Lincoln, he fears a Democratic victory might to lead to peace based on recognition of the Confederacy and the survival of slavery.

Eastern Theater Wade Hampton's column returns in triumph to Petersburg. In the Shenandoah Valley, Early receives reports of Union troops working on the railroad at Martinsburg, and sets off during the afternoon, reaching Bunker Hill by evening.

Sunday, September 18

Eastern Theater Early advances to Martinsburg and learns from the Federal telegraph office there that Grant is visiting Sheridan. Pulling back toward Bunker Hill, his four small divisions are too spread out for safety; unknown to the Confederates, Sheridan is already on the march, hoping to catch his outnumbered opponent by surprise and defeat him in detail.

Bottom: *Atlanta was a powerhouse of Confederate industry, which was why the South fought so hard to defend it. Here, precious railroad engines lie in the ruins of the engine house. The systematic destruction of the city by Sherman's army signalled that a new and even uglier phase of the war had begun.*

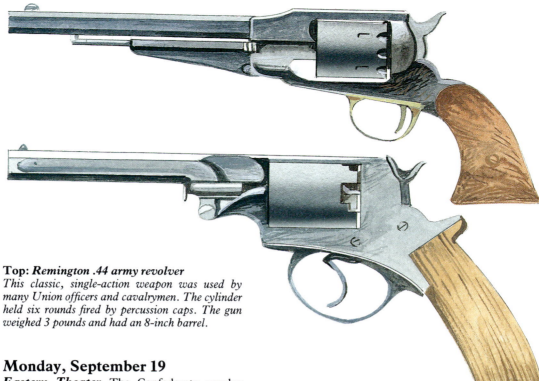

Top: *Remington .44 army revolver*
This classic, single-action weapon was used by many Union officers and cavalrymen. The cylinder held six rounds fired by percussion caps. The gun weighed 3 pounds and had an 8-inch barrel.

Above: *Adams dragoon revolver*
American handguns like the Colts or Remingtons were mass-produced. This made them cheap, and Colt made sure that plenty of spares were available. British manufacturers concentrated on quality. Adams revolvers were forged from a single piece of high-grade iron, making them very tough indeed. Their superb double-action offered the shooter rapid fire without loss of accuracy. The Adams was one of the Confederacy's most popular British imports.

Monday, September 19

Eastern Theater The Confederate cavalry pickets on the crossing of the Opequon Creek on the Berryville Road are driven in at first light. Ramseur's division bears the brunt of the Federal attack, and his men are driven back before Early counter-attacks with his other three divisions. By mid-afternoon the hopelessly outnumbered Confederates are driven back, Early ordering a retreat from their position near Winchester. Extracting his army in the face of a greatly superior cavalry force, Early retreats to Newtown. His 12,000-strong army suffers 3921 casualties, including 1818 missing. Sheridan's 40,000 men lose 697 killed, 2983 wounded, and 338 missing for a total of 4018. Sheridan has fumbled the chance to annihilate Early's army.
Trans-Mississippi General Sterling Price leads a last Confederate offensive in this theater. He enters Missouri with some 12,000 troops, although only two-thirds of his men are equipped with firearms.

Tuesday, September 20

Eastern Theater Sheridan's men pursue Early's defeated Confederates with rear guard actions taking place at Middletown and Strasburg.
Western Theater Bedford Forrest is on the move in northern Alabama, heading for Tennessee.
Trans-Mississippi Keytesville, Missouri, surrenders to Sterling Price's rag-tag Confederate Army.

Wednesday, September 21

Eastern Theater Sheridan's army catches up with Early on the banks of Cedar Creek, four miles from Fisher's Hill. The Union troops immediately entrench themselves, while the cavalry reconnoiter the Confederate position. Sheridan dispatches most of his cavalry into the Luray Valley, which leads to a skirmish at Front Royal. During the night, Brigadier-General George Crook's Army of West Virginia lies concealed near the Confederate left, hidden in the woods near Cedar Creek.

Thursday, September 22

Eastern Theater Crook's men advance around Early's left flank. The Confederate commander, suspecting an attack tomorrow issues orders for a retreat during the night; but shortly before dusk, Crook attacks the Confederate lines from the left and rear. Then Sheridan's whole line advances. Ramseur's division, attacked from two sides at once, collapses, and the Confederates are routed. Like the Union gunners in the recent action before Petersburg, the Confederate gunners stand by their pieces while the infantry break. Twelve of Early's guns are captured and his army sustains another 1200 casualties, of which only 30 are dead and 210 wounded. Union losses are 528.

Friday, September 23

Eastern Theater Early's shattered army withdraws toward New Market. Sheridan does not pursue with vigor; most of his cavalry are absent and his infantry cannot outmarch the rapidly retreating Confederates.

Saturday, September 24

Eastern Theater Sheridan's army begins to burn the crops in the Shenandoah, following Grant's orders to destroy this Confederate granary.
Western Theater Bedford Forrest captures Athens, Alabama.
Trans-Mississippi Price's Confederates attack Fayette, Missouri.

September–October 1864

Sunday, September 25, 1864

Eastern Theater Early's demoralized army falls back to Brown's Pass in the Blue Ridge, while Sheridan's men continue to lay waste the Shenandoah.

Western Theater Bedford Forrest continues his assault on the Federal rail network, capturing Sulphur Branch Trestle in northern Alabama. President Davis visits General Hood's headquarters at Palmetto, Georgia, to discuss the ominous military situation in the west.

Monday, September 26

Eastern Theater Skirmishes occur in the Shenandoah at Port Republic and Brown's Gap as Sheridan harries Early's army.

Western Theater Bedford Forrest attacks a Federal garrison at Richland Creek, near Pulaski, Tennessee.

Trans-Mississippi Price's Confederates are in action at Arcadia Valley, Shut-in-Gap, and Ironton, Missouri.

Tuesday, September 27

Trans-Mississippi Sterling Price's invasion of Missouri leads to bloody fighting at Pilot Knob, near Iron Mountain, 86 miles from St Louis. The Union defense centers on a position known as Fort Davidson, and General Thomas Ewing, Jr. holds off Price's attack with 1051 men and 11 guns. Recognizing that he cannot hold on for ever, Ewing breaks out at midnight, blowing up the fort's magazine and retreating toward St Louis.

At Centralia, Missouri, Bloody Bill Anderson and 30 Confederate guerrillas, including the James boys, loot the town. They ambush a train arriving in the station, slaying 24 unarmed Union soldiers on board. Leaving the town, they are pursued by three companies of the 39th Missouri. Anderson's men ambush them, killing 116.

Wednesday, September 28

Western Theater President Davis wires General Hood, relieving Lieutenant-General Hardee of his command and appointing him instead to the Department of South Carolina. Hood had not gotten along with Hardee and the new posting is designed to restore harmony in the Army of the Tennessee.

Trans-Mississippi Price continues his advance into Missouri, setting out in pursuit of Ewing's men after the spectacular explosion of Fort Davidson's magazine told him the Union forces were retreating.

Thursday, September 29

Eastern Theater After several weeks of static siege operations, Grant launches two major assaults on the Confederate lines before Richmond and Petersburg. Birney's X Corps and Ord's XVIII Corps attack north of the James against the defenses of the Confederate capital. One important Southern bastion, Fort Harrison, is taken, but X Corps' assault on Fort Gilmer is repulsed. Meanwhile, General Meade presses further west of the Weldon Railroad with some 16,000 men, threatening the important South Side Railroad.

Western Theater Forrest's raiders are in action near Lynchburg, Tennessee. A Federal column departs Vicksburg heading for Port Gibson, Mississippi.

Trans-Mississippi Sterling Price's invasion continues, with minor actions at Leesburg and Cuba, Missouri.

Friday, September 30

Eastern Theater Meade's new advance had extended the siege lines another three miles. As the front lengthened, so Lee's much smaller army was being stretched dangerously thin. He now has fewer than 50,000 men to hold 35 miles of trenches and his dispatches to Richmond are becoming pessimistic. There is no relief in prospect and the position of the armies allows the Union to concentrate men for a breakthrough without the Confederates knowing about it. Lee has so far managed to rush reserves to a threatened point just in the nick of time, but he is aware that one day they may lose the race and the defenses will be broken.

Lee personally directs a series of counterattacks on Fort Harrison, but the Union troops have entrenched rapidly and many are armed with repeating rifles. The attacks are defeated, forcing the Confederates to construct new defenses facing their former strongpoint. At Peeble's Farm, southwest of Petersburg, Warren's V Corps and Parke's IX Corps are driven back by a counter-attack led by A.P. Hill. The Union troops fall back to Squirrel Level Road and entrench.

Saturday, October 1, 1864

Eastern Theater A Confederate soldier finds the body of a woman on the beach near Wilmington, North Carolina. She is attached to a bag containing $2000 in gold coin, which he relieves her of—only to return the money when he learns that the body is that of Mrs Rose O'Neal Greenhow, one of the Confederacy's most famous spies. This former queen of Washington society, rumored mistress of President Buchanan, had passed details of McDowell's plans for the Army of the Potomac to General Beauregard on the eve of Bull Run. She was returning from Europe aboard the English blockade runner *Condor* when the vessel went aground. Fearing the ship would be boarded by one of the blockading vessels, she made for the shore in a boat which overturned in the surf, drowning her.

Western Theater While Bedford Forrest's cavalry skirmish with Union garrison posts at Athens and Huntsville, Alabama, Hood prepares to mount a major Confederate counter-offensive in the west. Having conferred with President Davis, Hood marches around Atlanta, aiming to strike Sherman's supply line which runs all the way from Chattanooga.

Sunday, October 2

Western Theater Hood's advancing army skirmishes with Sherman's troops at Big Shanty and Kenesaw Water Tank, Georgia, where the Confederates cut the Western and Atlantic Railroad, breaking Sherman's line of communications. In Augusta, Georgia, President Davis instructs General Beauregard to assume command of the two western departments currently under Hood and Taylor.

Trans-Mississippi Price's Confederates occupy Washington, Missouri, 50 miles from St Louis.

Monday, October 3

The South President Davis stops at Columbia, South Carolina, on his way back to Richmond. He makes an optimistic speech, anticipating the defeat of Sherman if enough Southerners shoulder their responsibilities and soldier with Hood.

Western Theater Hood's men break up the track of the Chattanooga–Atlanta railroad. Sherman responds by sending troops north to deal with what is obviously more than another cavalry raid. George H. Thomas is sent back to the headquarters of his department at Nashville; Schofield to his at Knoxville, while Sherman remains at Atlanta.

Trans-Mississippi Price's Confederates continue their advance along the Missouri River at Hermann and Miller's Station.

Tuesday, October 4

Western Theater Hood's army marches toward Dallas, Georgia, detaching a strong force of cavalry which tears up 15 miles of railroad above Marietta.

Trans-Mississippi With his small army and only 14 guns, Price has no realistic prospect of assaulting St Louis. His men are involved in a minor action near Richwoods.

Wednesday, October 5

Western Theater From his new headquarters on Kenesaw Mountain, Sherman watches the smoke rise from the railroad pass at Allatoona, where Major-General S.G. French's Confederate division attacks a Union division under Major-General J.M. Corse. In a savage battle, Corse beats off the assault, winning handsome praise from Sherman. Casualties are proportionally heavy: Union losses are 142 killed, 352 wounded, and 212 missing, a total of 706 out of the 2000 men engaged. The similar sized Confederate force loses 122 dead, 443 wounded, and 234 missing for a total of 799.

Thursday, October 6

The South The *Richmond Enquirer* prints an article favoring the employment of blacks in the Confederate Army. With the writing on the wall for the Confederacy, there is increasing support for such a measure of desperation.

Eastern Theater Jubal Early's Confederates are recovering from their recent defeats. General Thomas L. Rosser leads a cavalry raid down the Shenandoah and attacks two regiments of General George A. Custer's cavalry at Brock's Gap, but the Confederates are driven off.

Friday, October 7

Naval Operations Commander Napoleon Collins of the cruiser USS *Wachusett* attacks the Confederate commerce raider CSS *Florida* in the Brazilian port of Bahia. In defiance of international law, Collins rams the *Florida* and fires on her. With her commander and most of her crew ashore, *Florida* surrenders and both vessels put out to sea under fire from the Brazilians. Collins wins public acclaim in the US, but is criticized by Secretary of State Seward.

Saturday, October 8

Naval Operations The last great Confederate commerce raider, the *Shenandoah* leaves London, England, to rendezvous with her supply ship off Madeira, where she will be commissioned into the Confederate Navy on October 19.

The Dutch Gap Canal

The Union Army of the James fell back into a defensive line at Bermuda Hundred after its repulse on May 16, 1864. But its positions were matched by equally strongly posted earthworks soon thrown up by the Confederates. Further Union progress along this axis was hampered by a strong artillery battery dominating the James River. This prevented Federal warships pressing any closer to Richmond. General Butler's solution was to dig a canal, cutting off a five-mile stretch of the river which rounded a neck of land called Dutch Gap, but the area was within easy range of Confederate gunners.

Excavation began on August 10 and Confederate artillery immediately began to shell the area. The black soldiers tasked with the digging frequently had to take cover, and bombproof shelters had to be constructed. The work was advancing well when Butler's troops overran the outer defenses on September 29. The canal lost its importance and was not completed until December 30. The final bulkhead, consisting of some 6000 cubic yards of earth, was blown up by 12,000 pounds of powder on January 1, 1865. When most of the earth fell straight back into the ditch, filling it in again. The project was abandoned until after the war, when it was enlarged and finally became the main channel.

October 1864

Sunday, October 9, 1864
Eastern Theater Sheridan counter-attacks in the Shenandoah, sending his cavalry under Meritt and Custer to respond in force to the Confederate cavalry raids of the last week. The Union cavalry defeat Early's horsemen under Rosser and Lomax, taking 300 prisoners for the loss of nine dead and 48 wounded.

Monday, October 10
Eastern Theater Sheridan withdraws north over Cedar Creek, while VI Corps moves toward Washington via Front Royal.

Western Theater An amphibious assault against Bedford Forrest's men on the Tennessee River at Eastport fails disastrously. Confederate fire from the bank damages the gunboat *Undine* and disables some of the transports. Fortunately, the troops who are landed manage to escape.

Tuesday, October 11
The North Lincoln's supporters win in elections in Pennsylvania, Ohio, and Indiana, showing the president's pessimistic view of his political fortunes is not at all accurate. Lincoln stays up past midnight at the War Department telegraph office to discover the election results.

Wednesday, October 12
Naval Operations Rear Admiral David D. Porter assumes command of the North Atlantic Blockading Squadron, relieving Acting Rear Admiral Lee.

Thursday, October 13
The North Maryland votes to adopt a new constitution which includes the abolition of slavery, but only by a hair's breadth: the vote is 30,174 in favor and 29,799 against—a majority of just 375.

Eastern Theater Early's Confederates are at their old position on Fisher's Hill while Sheridan advances to Cedar Creek. Mosby's raiders are active behind him, taking up the Baltimore and Ohio Railroad west of Harper's Ferry and wrecking a train. They also take $173,000 from two US Army paymasters.

Western Theater Hood threatens Resaca, Georgia, but declines to attack, preferring to destroy the railroad for 20 miles and capture the Federal garrison at Dalton.

Friday, October 14
Trans-Mississippi Sterling Price issues a public call for recruits in Missouri. He subsequently claims that in his 1434-mile march his ill-equipped army was joined by 5000 men, but it took a dedicated Southerner to join the Confederate armies in the fall of 1864.

Center right: *The Army of the Potomac's voracious appetite for supplies was fed from City Point, Virginia. Light railroads supplemented horse- and mule-drawn transport in carrying food, ammunition, and other equipment to the troops entrenched opposite Lee's lines at Petersburg.*

Right: *Building transport steamers at Chattanooga during 1864. Both sides built ships where they needed them, but the Confederates achieved some incredible successes, even assembling ironclad warships in cornfields.*

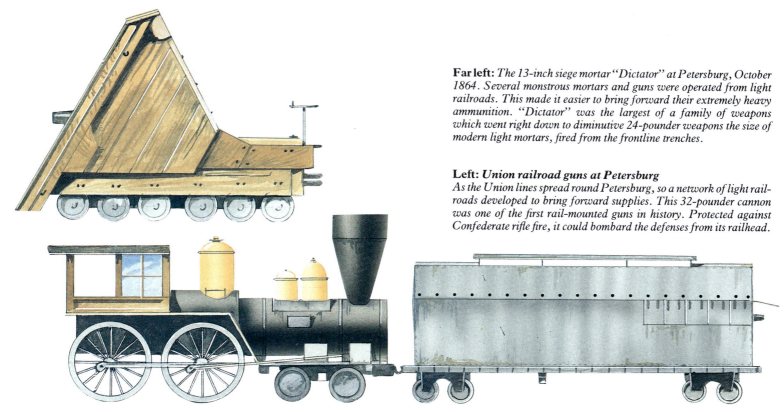

Far left: *The 13-inch siege mortar "Dictator" at Petersburg, October 1864. Several monstrous mortars and guns were operated from light railroads. This made it easier to bring forward their extremely heavy ammunition. "Dictator" was the largest of a family of weapons which went right down to diminutive 24-pounder weapons the size of modern light mortars, fired from the frontline trenches.*

Left: *Union railroad guns at Petersburg*
As the Union lines spread round Petersburg, so a network of light rail-roads developed to bring forward supplies. This 32-pounder cannon was one of the first rail-mounted guns in history. Protected against Confederate rifle fire, it could bombard the defenses from its railhead.

Armored train
This armored train was used by Union troops detached to repair bridges burned by Confederate raiders. Protected against rifle fire, it offered a reasonable defense against a small party of hostile cavalry. The Civil War was the first conflict in history in which the railroad played an important strategic role.

Saturday, October 15

Trans-Mississippi Jo Shelby of Price's command attacks Sedalia, Missouri. Local citizens aid the Federal garrison before they are defeated and surrender. Shelby's "Iron Brigade" of cavalry also storm Glasgow, Missouri, capturing 400 Union troops.

Sunday, October 16

Western Theater Skirmishing continues between elements of Hood's Army of the Tennessee and Sherman's troops hurrying north to defend their supply lines. There is a minor action at Ship's Gap, Georgia.
Trans-Mississippi Price's Confederates occupy Ridgely, Missouri, as they continue their advance northwestward along the Missouri River.

Monday, October 17

Western Theater Hood marches away from Sherman's Chattanooga–Atlanta railroad line and heads for Gadsen, planning to invade Tennessee.
Trans-Mississippi Price's Confederates are near Lexington, Missouri, and he is now aware that Union forces are gathering around him. From the west he is threatened by General S.R. Curtiss, commander of the Department of Kansas; behind him is a Federal cavalry force under Alfred Pleasonton; and to the south is General A.J. Smith. Price's cavalry burn Smithville and occupy Carrolton.

Tuesday, October 18

Eastern Theater Hopelessly outnumbered, Jubal Early plans to attack. He and his staff scout Sheridan's positions at Cedar Creek, knowing they had fought great odds throughout the war and that those odds were tipping further in favor of the Union.

Wednesday, October 19

The North About 25 Confederates under Lieutenant Bennett H. Young attack St Albans, Vermont, from across the Canadian border. They rob three banks of over $200,000 and shoot to death one of the citizens who resists. Fleeing back to Canada, Young and half his men are arrested, but only $75,000 is recovered.
Eastern Theater With just 8800 infantry and 1200 cavalry, Lieutenant-General Jubal A. Early attacks Sheridan's 30,000 troops at Cedar Creek. Marching during the night and concealed by an early morning fog, the Confederates achieve complete surprise. Both Kershaw and Gordon's divisions were supposed to attack before dawn, but Gordon's assault is delayed until after sunrise. However, the attack overruns Crook's corps and Emory's XIX Corps, capturing many prisoners, guns, and supplies. Sheridan is absent, on his way back to the army from a conference in Washington. Horatio Wright's VI Corps falls back, maintaining a steady line while many Confederates fall out to loot the captured encampment.

After the night march and the inevitable disorder following a successful attack, Early's men are too weak to mount another major effort against VI Corps. Sheridan arrives on the field by 10.30 a.m. and the Union Army counterattacks late in the afternoon. After an hour and a half of heavy fighting, the exhausted Confederates finally break, despite last ditch resistance by a few groups led by Major-General Stephen D. Ramseur who is captured mortally wounded, "fighting like a lion at bay," as Early describes him. The collapse of a bridge between Strasburg and Fisher's Hill dooms Early's artillery and train to capture by Sheridan's cavalry as no formed bodies of troops remain to defend them. The defeat costs the Confederates about 3000 casualties, and the Union sustains 644 killed, 3490 wounded, and 1591 missing for a total of 5665.

Thursday, October 20

Eastern Theater Early's broken Confederates rally at Fisher's Hill, the infantry retreating toward New Market covered by Rosser's cavalry. There is no serious pursuit by Sheridan's victorious army and Early's men still have 1500 Union prisoners of war in their hands.
Trans-Mississippi Sharp fighting occurs near Lexington, Missouri, as a Federal force composed largely of volunteers engages Price's army before falling back to the Little Blue River.

Friday, October 21

Western Theater Sherman halts at Gaylesville, Alabama. He plans to detach part of his army to deal with Hood while concentrating the bulk of his forces to continue the invasion of the South.
Trans-Mississippi Jo Shelby, commanding Price's advance guard, defeats the Union forces of Major-General James G. Blunt on the Little Blue River. Blunt withdraws, joining the assembled Kansas State Militia who had consented to cross the state line into Missouri at the request of their commanders.

Saturday, October 22

Western Theater Hood marches from Gadsen to Guntersville, Alabama, planning to invade Tennessee. But the Tennessee River is running high and his lack of supplies is already giving cause for concern. Hood continues to believe that a steady advance will improve his army's morale sufficiently for him to engage Sherman.
Trans-Mississippi Price drives back the Union forces from Lexington to the Big Blue River. Threatened from the rear by Pleasonton, the Confederate commander plans to assault Blunt's troops tomorrow, while a rear guard under John S. Marmaduke holds off Pleasonton.

October–November 1864

Sunday, October 23, 1864

Trans-Mississippi While the major battles in the Eastern and Western Theaters grab the headlines, this has tended to obscure the fact that more fighting takes place in Missouri than any other states except Virginia and Tennessee. Today, about 8000 of Price's Confederates attack Major-General S.R. Curtis's troops under Major-General Blunt. The Federals are posted along Brush Creek two and half miles south of Westport, Missouri, with a second force under Pleasanton approaching Price's rear. The leading Confederates under Jo Shelby batter their way over the Creek, but the Union soldiers counter-attack and a ferocious close-quarter battle continues for several hours. Meanwhile, Pleasanton crosses the Big Blue River and defeats the Confederate rear guard, capturing Marmaduke. The victorious Union force attacks Price's main force in the rear and the Confederates are routed. Exact casualties are unclear but the 20,000 Federal troops are estimated to have lost about 1500 killed and wounded, the Confederates at least as many.

Monday, October 24

Trans-Mississippi Sterling Price retreats south along the Kansas state line, trying to escape with his wagon train. Pleasanton's and Curtis's cavalries are launched in pursuit.

Tuesday, October 25

Western Theater Elements of Hood's army attack Federal forces at Round Mountain, near Turkeytown, Alabama.

Trans-Mississippi Price's Confederates are forced to make a stand against the pursuing Federals to allow their artillery and wagon train to cross the Marais des Cygnes River. Driven back from there, they form a line of battle at Marais des Cygnes, near Mine Creek, Kansas. Federal cavalry charge his position and overrun most of his artillery. Two of Price's divisions break and he is compelled to burn many of his wagons and flee south.

Wednesday, October 26

Western Theater Sherman said of Hood, "He can turn and twist like a fox and wear out my army in pursuit." The young Confederate general does just that, surprising the Union command by a rapid march on Decatur. The 12,000-strong Union IV Corps is immediately ordered up from Gaynesville.

Trans-Mississippi Bloody Bill Anderson dies in an ambush at Richmond, Missouri. The Federal pursuit of Price's beaten Confederates begins to slacken as the commanders wrangle over whether to follow up their victory or not. This inter-departmental dispute gives Price the delay he needs to make good his escape. His withdrawal ends the last Confederate offensive in this theater. Price summarizes his achievements as having fought 43 battles and skirmishes, captured and paroled 3000 Federals, captured large quantities of stores, and destroyed $10 million worth of property. On the other hand, most of the booty is recaptured, and most of the 5000 recruits he claimed to have picked up during the campaign promptly desert during his retreat.

Thursday, October 27

Eastern Theater Grant launches another offensive against Petersburg's railroad lifeline, this time sending 20,000 men under Hancock and Warren against the South Side Railroad. A spirited defense by Heth and Mahone's divisions, supported by Wade Hampton's cavalry, beat back the assault and the Confederates remain in control of the vital railroad. Union losses are 166 dead, 1028 wounded, and 564 missing for a total of 1758. Confederate casualties are not recorded.

The formidable Confederate ironclad CSS *Albemarle* is sunk at her moorings in the Roanoke River by Lieutenant William B. Cushing, USN. The US Navy had no ironclad available with a light enough draft to cross the Hatteras bar and enter the sounds of North Carolina, and it was impossible for warships to force the defenses of Plymouth, recaptured by the Confederates with the aid of the *Albemarle*. Cushing attacks the ram at 3 a.m. in a 15-man steam launch armed with a torpedo projecting on a long spar. The warship is surrounded by a log boom, but Cushing bumps over at full steam, the logs having become slimy from long immersion. Under heavy fire from the *Albemarle*, the launch places the charge squarely against the ironclad's hull and Cushing detonates it. All the crew but one are picked up by the Confederates. Cushing swims ashore and hides.

Friday, October 28

Eastern Theater Lieutenant Cushing steals a skiff from a party of Confederate soldiers and rows out to the US warships. He is rescued by the picket boat *Valley City* at midnight.

Western Theater Hood demonstrates against the Union garrison in Decatur but has no intention of assaulting their defenses. Sherman decides to rejoin his main force at Atlanta and continue with his invasion of the South, leaving Thomas at Nashville to deal with Hood.

Saturday, October 29

Eastern Theater US gunboats probe the defenses of Plymouth, North Carolina, now unprotected by the *Albemarle*, which has settled on to the bottom of the Roanoke, water washing through the gunports. The Confederates have sunk schooners around the wreck of the *Southfield* and the Federals cannot pass up the channel.

Western Theater Bedford Forrest, lying in wait on the Tennessee River near Fort Henry, captures the Union transport *Mazeppa*, which is carrying 9000 pairs of shoes—desperately needed by the Confederate armies.

Sunday, October 30

Western Theater The Union IV Corps marches from Chattanooga toward Pulaski, Tennessee, while Hood's vanguard reaches Tuscumbia, Alabama. Bedford Forrest's artillery badly damages the gunboat *Undine*, which his men capture along with two more transports, soon christened "Forrest's Navy."

Monday, October 31

Western Theater Hood arrives at Tuscumbia. One month after his departure from Palmetto, the Confederate Army is once again on the banks of the Tennessee. But Hood has failed to draw Sherman north; the two great armies are heading in opposite directions, while Thomas masses sufficient men to block Hood's progress.

Tuesday, November 1, 1864

Western Theater Hood is frustrated to discover that the railroad to Decatur has not been repaired, despite his orders issued on October 9. Neither has the promised stockpile of supplies been assembled.

Trans-Mississippi While columns of Federal troops operate in central Arkansas against Confederate guerrillas, the two divisions of XVI Corps detached to fight Price now head back to join Thomas at Nashville.

Wednesday, November 2

Western Theater Forrest's navy receives a setback when the *Venus* is driven ashore by Federal gunboats six miles below Johnsonville, Tennessee. The *Undine* escapes.

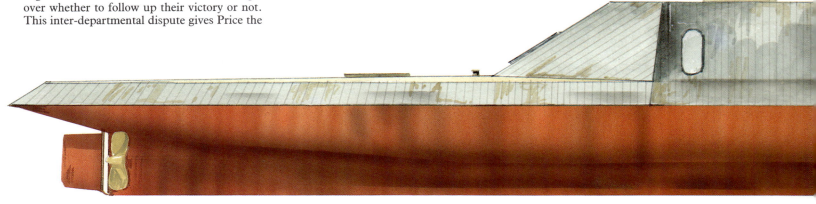

Thursday, November 3

Western Theater The Union IV Corps reaches Pulaski, Tennessee, while Forrest's gunboat *Undine* drives back three Federal gunboats on the Tennessee River.

Friday, November 4

Western Theater Bedford Forrest's river ambush site at Reynoldsburg Island is attacked by Federal gunboats and the Confederates are forced to abandon and burn the *Undine*. But Forrest then deploys his artillery on the west bank of the river and shells the important US supply base at Johnsonville. Warehouses and supply ships are badly damaged. Meanwhile, Major-General John C. Breckinridge leads a small raiding force from southwest Virginia into east Tennessee.

Saturday, November 5

Western Theater Hood remains at Tuscumbia, in conference with General Beauregard. Hood favors a continued offensive north, while most of his officers are alarmed at Sherman's apparent intention to plunge into the heart of the Confederacy.

Above right: *Sutler's Row at Chattanooga: troop concentrations were a source of big business throughout the war. Both sides exploited this reliance on civilian suppliers for intelligence gathering.*

Right: *US Military Railroads engine number 137 was constructed in the Chattanooga yards in 1864. While the Union steadily increased its rolling stock, the Confederates could barely maintain their existing railroad.*

Confederate ironclad Albemarle *was originally built in a cornfield where few construction facilities were available. This highlights the permanent problems which faced the South as they tried to assemble warships.*

Albemarle *controlled the waters around Plymouth until sunk by Lieutenant Cushing in a daring attack using a launch in October 1864.*

209

November 1864

Sunday, November 6, 1864

The North The ringleaders of a Confederate plot to free the prisoners of war held at Camp Douglas and burn down Chicago are arrested by Colonel Benjamin Sweet. Exactly how serious a threat this really was will never be established, but the houses of some of the plotters contain large arms caches.

Monday, November 7

The South The Congress of the Confederate States of America meets in Richmond for the second session of the Second Congress. President Davis sends an optimistic message, minimizing the loss of Atlanta. But he recommends the army buys slaves for laboring tasks, freeing them on discharge. Davis also wires General Hood, urging him to defeat Sherman's divided forces in detail, then advance to the Ohio River! But Hood remains doubtful of his army's fighting spirit and plans to attack Tennessee and Kentucky prior to rescuing Lee by an offensive into the Eastern Theater. Neither strategy seems based on the true military situation.

Tuesday, November 8

The North President Lincoln defeats George B. McClellan in the presidential election. Winning 55 percent of the popular vote, the Republicans carry every state except Delaware, Kentucky, and New Jersey. For all Lincoln's worries, popular discontent with the war is not sufficient to produce a Democratic victory and possible peace talks with the Confederacy. Republicans and Unionists increase their majority in the House and the Senate. There will be no negotiations with the South, and the second session of the Confederate Congress will be its last.

Wednesday, November 9

Western Theater Major-General J.M. Schofield's 10,000-strong XXIII Corps passes through Nashville *en route* for Pulaski to join Thomas. At Kingston, Georgia, Sherman issues the orders for a resumption of the advance into Georgia. He has collected substantial quantities of supplies in Atlanta, where four corps and one cavalry division—a total of 60,000 men—are poised to strike with 65 guns. Sherman recognizes that once the armies of Lee and Hood have been destroyed, the Confederacy is at an end. Leaving Thomas to tackle Hood, Sherman plans to march to the Eastern Theater of operations to join Grant against Lee. The siege of Petersburg is 1000 miles away, too far for a single march, so Sherman elects to head for the Atlantic coast to establish a new base at Savannah, 300 miles distant.

Thursday, November 10

Eastern Theater Jubal Early leads the remnant of his command from New Market toward Sheridan's forces in the Shenandoah, but he lacks the strength to offer effective opposition.
Western Theater Bedford Forrest is back at Corinth, Mississippi, heading over to join Hood for the invasion of Tennessee.

Friday, November 11

Western Theater Union troops at Rome and Atlanta, Georgia, begin the systematic destruction of everything that could conceivably be used by the Confederates after Sherman departs. No army dependent on wagons can move more than 100 miles from its base—the wagons will consume their loads just coming and going—so Sherman will have no base. He plans to live off the country, seizing Confederate supply depots, fodder, and livestock until he can re-establish communications from a new base on the coast, supplied by sea.

Saturday, November 12

Western Theater Sherman's men tear down every building in Atlanta, except the churches and some houses.
Eastern Theater Early's men skirmish at Middletown and Cedar Creek.

Sunday, November 13

Eastern Theater Early detaches most of his men to join Lee at Richmond and Petersburg. This marks the end of his valley campaign, which, since June, has occupied greatly superior Union forces. If he failed to achieve the incredible success of Stonewall Jackson in 1862, it was nevertheless an outstanding effort considering the odds against his little army.
Western Theater Hood establishes his headquarters at Florence.
Far West Federal troops are in action against Indians near Fort Larned, Kansas.

Above left: *Major-General George H. Thomas, seen here with his staff, refused to be hurried into attacking Hood's Confederates at Nashville. His apparent caution angered Washington, but no one could complain after his methodical demolition of the Army of the Tennessee in December.*

Left: *John B. Hood was one of the most controversial Confederate generals. His indisputable courage cost him two limbs and he had to be strapped to his horse to ride. His winter offensive ultimately destroyed the Army of the Tennessee and it failed to arrest Sherman's march into the heart of the Confederacy.*

Monday, November 14

The North President Lincoln accepts the resignation of Major-General George B. McClellan and appoints Sheridan to the rank of major-general.
Western Theater Major-General Schofield reaches Pulaski, Tennessee, with his leading division. There are now 18,000 Union troops concentrated there, with another 5000 men nearby. Bedford Forrest joins Hood at Florence. Judson Kilpatrick leaves Atlanta at the head of Sherman's cavalry vanguard. Slocum leads XX Corps to Decatur, tearing up the railroad.

Tuesday, November 15

Western Theater Sherman's forces complete their work of destruction in and around Atlanta. The former economic center is totally destroyed, ruining thousands of people and creating a legacy of bitterness in Georgia.

Wednesday, November 16

Western Theater Carrying 20 days' rations, Sherman's 60,000 men leave the ruins of Atlanta and march into the heart of Georgia. Opposing them are just 10,000 infantry and 300 state militia, plus 10,000 cavalry under Wheeler. Sherman advances in two main columns, one down the Macon railroad toward Lovejoy Station where the Confederates are driven off, and the other along the Georgia railroad toward Augusta. Meanwhile, in eastern Tennessee, John C. Breckinridge's force skirmishes with Union troops at Strawberry Plains.

Thursday, November 17

The South President Davis writes a group of Georgia senators denouncing any plans by individual states to negotiate their own peace with the Union.
Western Theater Sherman's mighty columns march eastward into Georgia with nothing to impede their progress. Breckinridge's men skirmish at Flat Creek in eastern Tennessee.

Friday, November 18

Western Theater Sherman rides with the left wing of his army as it passes between the Ocmulgee and Oconee rivers. President Davis orders General Howell Cobb, commander of the Georgia reserves, to muster every man he can to resist Sherman, and to employ blacks building obstructions on the roads.

Saturday, November 19

Western Theater Governor Brown of Georgia calls to arms all men between the ages of 16 and 55, but there is no rush to join the colors. Hood's Army of the Tennessee finally begins the Confederate offensive, and his cavalry vanguard departs Florence. Hood believes he can get between Thomas's forces and Nashville to score a desperately needed Southern victory.
Far West Federal troops engage Indians near Plum Creek Station, Nebraska Territory.

The bizarre wreckage of Hood's 28-car ammunition train destroyed at Scholfield Rolling Mill near Atlanta in September. The vulnerable rail lines were the target of cavalry raids by both sides during the fall campaign in Tennessee and Georgia.

Above: *Butler's Folly: digging the canal at Dutch Gap, Virginia. This was to have been a short cut to bypass a bend in the James River. The excavation culminated in a giant powder blast on New Year's Day 1865. Intended to complete the job, it went disastrously wrong, and the huge volume of earth displaced promptly filled in the trench already dug. It proved to be the last failure Butler presided over.*

November–December 1864

Sunday, November 20, 1864

Western Theater Sherman's progress through Georgia continues with skirmishes at Clinton, Walnut Creek, East Macon, and Griswoldsville. But Wheeler's cavalry and the local militia cannot seriously obstruct the Union advance. Sherman's men do more than live off the land: they destroy a great deal of property besides. Hood's army completes its preliminary moves as A.P. Stewart's corps crosses the Tennessee River.

Monday, November 21

Western Theater Hood's main body begins to move; 30,000 infantry and 8000 cavalry are now racing Schofield's smaller Union force to the crossings over the Duck River. If Hood wins, he will be able to attack the Union forces while they are still divided.

Tuesday, November 22

Western Theater Sherman's left wing under Slocum enters the Georgia state capital at Midgeville. The Georgia legislature has just enough time to issue a *levy en masse* before fleeing. Hood's vanguard—6000 cavalry under Bedford Forrest—reaches Lawrenceburg, 16 miles west of Pulaski, but his advance is hampered by rain and snow. The condition of the roads is appalling, bogging down his wagons. The first two divisions of Schofield's force at Pulaski pull out and head for Columbia.

Wednesday, November 23

Western Theater Schofield's other two divisions, plus artillery and train, leave Pulaski, Tennessee. In Georgia the burning and looting continues around Midgeville. General William J. Hardee assumes command of the handful of troops available to oppose Sherman's march.

Thursday, November 24

Western Theater Bedford Forrest narrowly fails to storm the crossings of the Duck River before Schofield's main body reaches the bridges. Brigadier-General Jacob D. Cox's division reaches the Mount Pleasant Pike just in time to save the small detachment by the crossings from being overwhelmed by Forrest's men.

Nashville seen from the Capitol, December 1864. Many of the city's citizens watched in despair as Thomas's Union Army smashed Hood's tattered forces. The retreat of the ragged Confederates was marked by bloody footprints in the snow left by barefooted infantrymen. Although Nashville is often regarded as one of the few truly decisive battles of the war, Hood's army was only really destroyed by its withdrawal over a desolated countryside in the dead of winter.

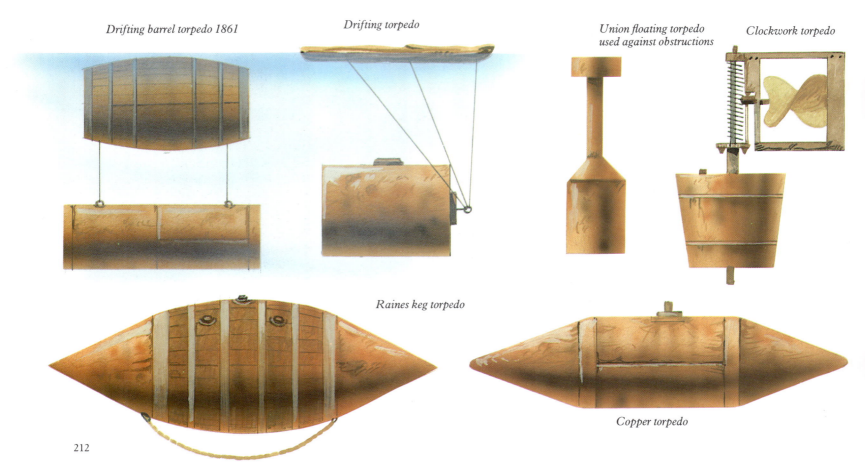

Drifting barrel torpedo 1861

Drifting torpedo

Union floating torpedo used against obstructions

Clockwork torpedo

Raines keg torpedo

Copper torpedo

Friday, November 25

The North Confederate agents start fires in 10 New York hotels and Barnum's Museum, but they are all extinguished without serious problems.

Western Theater Slocum's wing of Sherman's army skirmishes with Wheeler's Confederate cavalry as they approach Sandersville, Georgia. Sherman is no longer in communication with Washington and no one in the North knows the details of his progress. Schofield's army digs in at Columbia on the Duck River, hoping to get across before Hood's superior forces can attack.

Far West Federal troops are in action against Indians in Nebraska Territory and New Mexico Territory.

Saturday, November 26

Western Theater Schofield's army is ordered to cross the Duck River but a heavy storm makes this impossible. Hood's main body now arrives opposite the Federals' hastily dug entrenchments.

Far West Fighting continues in Nebraska Territory at Plum Creek Station and Spring Creek between Indians and Federal troops.

Sunday, November 27

Eastern Theater On the James River, Virginia, General Butler's headquarters, the steamer *Greyhound*, explodes and sinks. Confederate sabotage is suspected.

Western Theater Schofield's army waits until darkness before beginning to cross the Duck River. In Georgia Wheeler's Confederate cavalry fight Kilpatrick's cavalry at Waynesborough.

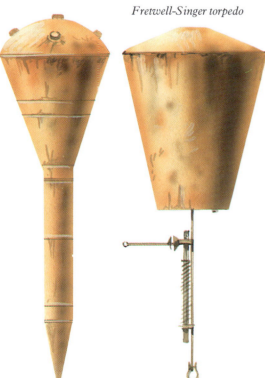

Copper torpedo

Fretwell-Singer torpedo

Because of their weakness in warships, other methods had to be devised by the Confederates to slow up Union progress along southern rivers. A vast number of mines, known in the 1860s as torpedoes, were used, many of an ingenious nature. Over 20 Union vessels were lost by these devices and they were greatly feared.

Monday, November 28

Eastern Theater Thomas L. Rosser leads a Confederate cavalry raid down the Shenandoah Valley to New Creek, attacking the Baltimore and Ohio Railroad.

Western Theater Schofield's army completes its crossing of the Duck River at 5.00 a.m., burning the railroad bridge and sinking its pontoons behind it. Confederate deserters paint an exaggerated picture of Hood's strength as the Union troops hurry away toward Franklin on a bright fall day. Bedford Forrest crosses the river later in the morning, and during the night Confederate engineers under Colonel Presstman lay their own pontoons three miles above Columbia.

Tuesday, November 29

Western Theater Hood's Army of the Tennessee crosses the Duck River, hoping to cut Schofield off at the road junction at Spring Hill before he can reach Franklin. Forrest's cavalry arrive at noon and skirmish with the Union division of Brigadier-General Wagner. Cleburne's Confederate division arrives in the afternoon but delivers only a half-hearted attack. Wagner's 4000 men cling to the junction, and by nightfall Schofield's army is retreating along the sole metalled road to Franklin. Hood's army is in many cases within a few hundred yards of the road, and why they do not attack and destroy Schofield's inferior force as it runs for safety will remain the subject of bitter controversy. Appalling staffwork certainly plays its part, with wrong orders delivered to several formations, and Stewart's whole corps taking the wrong road. But only the odd group of Confederates leave their campfires to snipe at the retreating Federals, who even manage to get their wagon train away.

Far West The central plains had been quiet from 1862 to 1863, defended by volunteer cavalry from California, Kansas, and Ohio. But this summer parties of Indians had conducted a series of raids, stinging the citizens of Denver into recruiting more troops. The Hundred-day Volunteers of the 3rd Colorado Cavalry join the 1st Colorado led by Colonel John M. Chivington on campaign. Other US forces scouring the territory include the 11th Ohio, 7th Iowa, 7th Nebraska, and 16th Kansas cavalry. The Indians soon give up, but Chivington and his

men want blood, not peace. At Sand Creek Chivington finds a peaceful village flying the US flag and orders his men to attack. The 1st Colorado refuse, but the 3rd charge into the village of Arapahoe and Cheyenne, killing, raping, and mutilating the dead. He claims several hundred victims, but only 30 are males of warrior age. This appalling massacre scandalizes the east but attracts general support locally. The incensed Indians promptly rise: Brulé Sioux, Northern Arapaho, and Cheyenne war parties all setting out to avenge the atrocity.

Wednesday, November 30

Western Theater Schofield's army is attacked at Franklin, Tennessee, where his army hastily dug in while the wagon trains waited to cross the damaged bridges over the Harpeth River. In bright sunshine Hood hurls his troops at the Union defenses, Cleburne's men overrunning two Union brigades who, lacking any tools, had not entrenched. The defeated Federals are chased back into the main defenses, Union guns unable to fire for fear of hitting their own men. But a vigorous counter-attack by Brigadier-General Emory Opdycke's brigade catches the Confederates in disorder as they swarm over the parapet. Without a breath of wind, the cannon smoke shrouds the battlefield, as wave after wave of Confederate infantry assault the Union entrenchments. The ground is devoid of cover but Hood's infantry slog it out in an unequal exchange of fire until well after dark. Then Schofield's men slip away in the night, crossing the Harpeth and retreating on Nashville. Both sides had approximately 23,000 men engaged. The Federals lost 189 killed, 1033 wounded, and 1104 missing—a total of 2326. But the attack cost Hood's army dear: six general officers died, including the gallant Pat Cleburne, 1750 troops were killed, 3800 wounded, and 702 are posted missing. The loss of 6252 men makes this one of the most disastrous attacks of the war.

Thursday, December 1, 1864

Western Theater Schofield's army reaches Nashville, joining with Thomas's command to form a numerically superior force to Hood's badly shaken army. Hood's troops arrive shortly afterward, but their hard marching avails them nothing. The Union position is strongly entrenched, with both flanks rested on the Cumberland River.

Friday, December 2

Western Theater Sherman's army reach Millen, Georgia, halfway to the sea. Hood probes the Union defenses at Nashville, while Thomas receives orders from Washington demanding immediate action against Hood.

Saturday, December 3

Western Theater Sherman's remorseless advance continues, his columns now converging on Savannah with no significant opposition to their progress.

December 1864

Sunday, December 4, 1864

Western Theater At Waynesborough, Georgia, Kilpatrick's cavalry, guarding infantry detachments tearing up the railroad, are attacked by Confederate cavalry under Wheeler. At Nashville Thomas prepares to obey the flood of telegrams from Washington demanding he attack Hood, but the weather has deteriorated, and freezing rain makes life miserable for both armies in their entrenchments.

Monday, December 5

Western Theater Hood detaches Bedford Forrest toward Murfreesboro, supported by a division of infantry. General Grant joins the War Department in urging Thomas to attack. Both fear that Hood will bypass Nashville and march to the Ohio River.

Tuesday, December 6

The North President Lincoln appoints former Secretary of the Treasury Salmon P. Chase as chief justice, thus removing a potential presidential rival.

Eastern Theater Federal forces on the Atlantic coast demonstrate against the Confederate defenses of Charleston and Savannah. But Sherman will receive no great assistance from the small Federal enclaves on the coast of the Confederacy.

Wednesday, December 7

Eastern Theater Federal warships, transports, and troops assemble at Fort Monroe, Virginia, for an attack on Fort Fisher, North Carolina, the guardian of the Confederacy's only major port.

Western Theater Sherman's army is nearing the coast; his troops skirmish today at Jenk's Bridge on the Ogeechee River, and near Sister's Ferry, Georgia.

Thursday, December 8

The North Grant tells Halleck that Thomas mut be replaced by Schofield if he does not attack Hood without delay. Grant and Thomas exchange telegrams, Thomas pointing out that many of his cavalry are still waiting for their horses and that without a powerful mounted force an attack is pointless.

Friday, December 9

Western Theater Sherman's leading troops are just south of Savannah. Skirmishing takes place along the Ogeechee Canal. The Confederates have flooded the rice fields, hampering the Union approach to the city. At Nashville the freezing rain continues; the roads are quagmires by day and frozen solid by night.

Saturday, December 10

Western Theater Sherman's army arrives before Savannah where Hardee commands a garrison of some 18,000 troops strongly entrenched around the city. Although Sherman's men still have enough to eat, the same cannot be said of his horses, which require immense quantities of fodder. A large army can only live off the land if it keeps moving; if it stops in the same place, it soon eats up all available supplies. Knowing he must break through to contact the Union fleet, Sherman orders a reconnaissance of Fort McAllister on the Ogeechee River.

Sunday, December 11

Western Theater Sherman's troops rebuild the King's Bridge over the Ogeechee, destroyed by the retreating Confederates. The Union Army deploys before Savannah but fails to cut the road north to Charleston. Grant continues to badger Thomas.

Monday, December 12

Western Theater General Stoneman leads 4000 Federal cavalry from east Tennessee, heading toward southwest Virginia. The Confederates under Breckinridge have fewer than 1500 troops available as the area has been stripped of men to reinforce Lee's embattled army at Petersburg. Thomas wires Halleck, promising to attack the Confederates before Nashville the moment there is a break in the weather.

Tuesday, December 13

Western Theater Elements of the US XV Corps assault Fort McAllister below Savannah. Attacking late in the afternoon, they capture the position for the loss of 24 killed and 110 wounded. Contact is now established with the fleet, and Sherman's army can be supplied by sea. Stoneman's cavalry defeat the remnants of Morgan's cavalry at Kingsport, east Tennessee. The sleet and snow continue at Nashville. Grant travels to Washington, intending to journey to Nashville himself. Meanwhile, he appoints Major-General John A. Logan to succeed Thomas.

Wednesday, December 14

Western Theater The weather improves at Nashville and Thomas wastes no time ordering his men to attack. With the briefings completed and his officers dispersing to issue their orders, Thomas wires Halleck, saying he will attack tomorrow. In east Tennessee Stoneman's cavalry raid continues; his men capture 300 prisoners at Bristol.

FERRY

HYDE'S FERRY

LINE MANNED BY QUARTER MASTERS' FORCES

FORT GILLEM

BOSLEY

SUGAR TREE CREEK

GRANNY WHITE PIKE

HILLSBORO PIKE

Thursday, December 15

Western Theater Thomas attacks Hood's lines around Nashville with some 35,000 troops. A feint against the Confederate right flank is followed by a major effort against the left. Outnumbered nearly 2:1, the Confederate line is rolled up and several formations crack, including Johnson's division, which retreats the moment it is pressed. Fortunately for the Confederates, the short winter's day gives way to darkness before they can be completely destroyed. The Union Army camps in the cold, wet fields around Nashville, confident that Hood will retreat. Sixteen guns and 1000 prisoners are taken back into Nashville.

Friday, December 16

Western Theater Thomas wires the news of his attack and Grant cancels his plan to travel to Nashville. Thomas has saved his command by a day. Logan has not yet arrived, but Hood has not yet left. He defiantly deploys his army for battle along a contracted line dug in during the night. At dawn Thomas renews the battle as rain alternates with snow. Thomas deploys his full strength: over 50,000 troops against Hood's force of fewer than 30,000. During the morning and early afternoon, Federal forces probe Hood's flanks, while the Union artillery assembles, forming a gunline on three sides of Hood's position. Thomas's cavalry passes along Granny White Pike, turning Hood's left before the main assault is delivered at 3 p.m. Hood's right holds, repelling an attack led by Major-General Steedman's black troops and Post's brigade from XXIII Corps. Post is killed by grapeshot at the head of his command. But the Confederate center gives way and the vital position of Shy's Hill on Hood's right is stormed under cover of a ferocious artillery barrage. The Army of Tennessee disintegrates, fleeing in confusion. Over 4500 dejected Confederates surrender; Hood's losses in killed and wounded are estimated at 1500. Fifty-nine of Hood's 156 cannon are taken. Federal casualties are 387 killed, 2562 wounded, and 112 missing for a total of 3061. The last major Confederate Army in the west has been eliminated. Although Hood will rally the survivors, they must now retreat over a barren land in the dead of winter and will cease to be an effective military force.

Saturday, December 17

Eastern Theater Stoneman's cavalry destroy the railroad in southwestern Virginia, while Breckinridge guards the Salt Mines with his small force of troops.

Western Theater Hood's surviving troops tramp over rain-lashed roads toward Columbia. His rear guard fights off Federal pursuit at Hollow Tree Gap and along the West Harpeth River.

Defensive lines of Nashville in December 1864 showing the situation on December 15. Confederates had retreated into Nashville with a force of 31,000 men and awaited the attack. After several classic assaults, a major Federal attack drove in part of the defensive line, which was only saved at nightfall by the timely arrival of help from one of the unengaged wings.

On the 15th the attack was renewed with determination, and again the Confederate line caved in. Only darkness and heavy rain enabled the Confederate Army to escape.

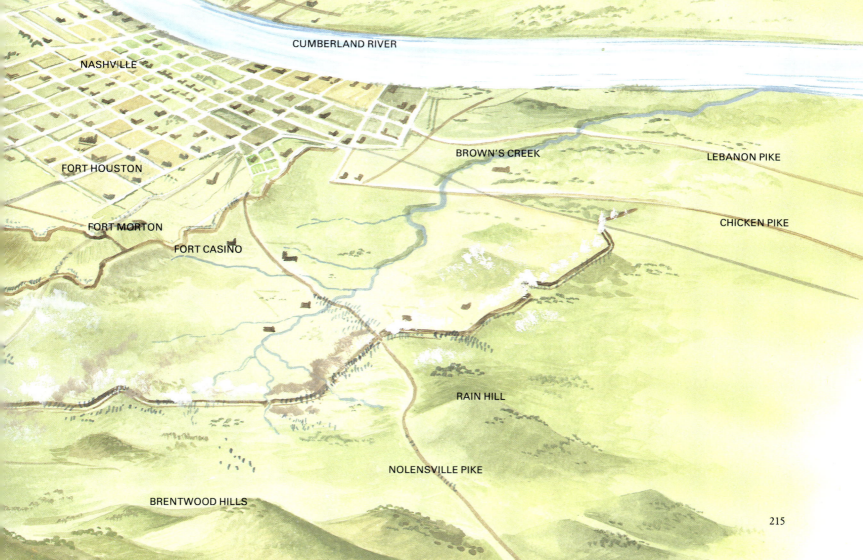

CUMBERLAND RIVER

NASHVILLE

FORT HOUSTON

FORT MORTON

FORT CASINO

BROWN'S CREEK

LEBANON PIKE

CHICKEN PIKE

RAIN HILL

NOLENSVILLE PIKE

BRENTWOOD HILLS

December 1864

Sunday, December 18, 1864

Eastern Theater John C. Breckinridge's scratch force of about 1000 men fight off part of Stoneman's Federal cavalry at Marion, south-west Virginia. Bitter winter weather soaks both sides in freezing rain, and tactical movement is hampered by the mud. But Stoneman is able to detach part of his force to destroy one of the nearby saltworks.

Western Theater General Hardee rejects Sherman's demand to surrender Savannah. But his engineers are working on an escape route: by passing along a two-mile causeway and over an improvised pontoon bridge, his men may be able to escape into South Carolina if Sherman's troops fail to block it.

Monday, December 19

Eastern Theater The Union and Confederate forces in the Shenandoah both detach more men to join the siege lines before Richmond and Petersburg. Sheridan also detaches 8000 cavalry under A.T.A. Tolbert to attack the Confederate railroads. Colonel John G. Clarke, chief engineer at Savannah, supervises the completion of a pontoon bridge made of rice flats anchored with wagon wheels. His efforts were slightly delayed when a party of Confederate cavalry burned some of his boats, believing them to belong to Union forces.

Western Theater Skirmishing continues at Rutherford Creek north of Columbia, where the Federal pursuit of Hood is frustrated by the Confederate rear guard and the much-swollen river.

Tuesday, December 20

Eastern Theater Hardee's 10,000 troops escape from Savannah during the night, taking their field artillery, baggage, and stores with them. It is a brilliant achievement, saving the last Confederate field force from capitulation. However, his little army is still outnumbered 6:1 by Sherman, and the loss of Savannah is another blow to Southern morale. Hardee leaves behind 250 heavy guns and 25,000 bales of cotton. The ironclad CSS *Savannah* is brought under fire by field guns at her anchorage.

Wednesday, December 21

Eastern Theater CSS *Savannah* is blown up by her crew to avoid capture. Sherman occupies Savannah.

Western Theater Hood's army retreats from Columbia toward Pulaski. Heavy rain swells the rivers and streams, hampering the weary Confederates and the Union pursuit. A Federal column leaves Memphis to raid the Mobile and Ohio railroad.

Thursday, December 22

Eastern Theater Sherman sends President Lincoln the famous message, "I beg to present you, as a Christmas gift, the city of Savannah." Hardee's men make good their escape into South Carolina.

Western Theater Hood's men are back at the Duck River where their rear guard skirmishes with Thomas's pursuing columns.

Friday, December 23

Eastern Theater Buffeted by heavy seas off Cape Hatteras, a massive Federal fleet assembles off Beaufort for a combined assault against Fort Fisher, North Carolina. It is the largest concentration of US naval strength ever seen: 60 warships, including five ironclads. The only hope for the Confederates is that the US Army element is commanded by that notorious political general, Ben Butler, the "Beast" of New Orleans. During the night the Federals explode an old gunboat, *Louisiana*, near the fort but, as many naval officers had predicted, it fails to damage the defenses.

Saturday, December 24

Eastern Theater Fort Fisher, guarding the entrance to the Confederacy's last port at Wilmington, is bombarded by the US Navy. *New Ironsides* leads the monitor force against the northeast face, while the powerful steam frigates *Wabash*, *Minnesota*, and *Colorado* batter the earth and sand emplacements with their powerful broadsides of 8- and 9-inch smoothbores. With broadsides of over 20 heavy guns, these warships dominate the bombardment; the Confederate batteries consist of 44 guns and three mortars. For their best gun, a 150-pounder Armstrong, they only have 13 rounds. The mile-long line of emplacements is deluged with shell, but at least a third of the Union rounds sail over the low fort and plunge into the Cape Fear River. The fleet mistakes the slow return fire of the Confederates as marking the defeat of the fort, but in fact the gunners are ordered to fire no more than one round every 30 minutes to conserve ammunition. The fleet sustains a few casualties when some ships' 100-pounder Parrott rifles burst.

Sunday, December 25

Eastern Theater Butler's 6000 troops are landed two miles north of Fort Fisher, but when they arrive before the fort they find it largely intact. In fact, only three guns were disabled yesterday, and another eight today by the continuing naval bombardment. A few rounds of canister from the batteries, and news that Confederate reinforcements are on their way, convince Butler that an assault cannot succeed, and he re-embarks most of his men. Some 700 are abandoned on shore as the weather worsens.

Western Theater Hood's army reaches the Tennessee River at Bainbridge.

Monday, December 26

Eastern Theater The US Navy manages to evacuate the remaining troops ashore near Fort Fisher. The transports return to Hampton Roads, while the fleet returns to Beaufort. Recriminations begin immediately.

Tuesday, December 27

Western Theater Hood's army crosses the Tennessee River and marches toward Tupelo, Mississippi.

Wednesday, December 28

The North President Lincoln speaks to Grant about the Wilmington operation. The general, already incensed by Butler's incompetence on the James River during the summer, is in no doubt where responsibility lies for this humiliating defeat.

Thursday, December 29

The North The debate over Butler's future continues. His political influence has won him a series of commands, but from New Orleans to the recent James campaign, his military incompetence has become too conspicuous to ignore. President Lincoln, fresh from his election victory, is now in a strong position to deal with such officers.

Friday, December 30

The North The Cabinet meets to discuss Benjamin Butler. Lincoln says he will remove him from command of the Army of the James.

The South Francis P. Blair, an elder statesman from Maryland, writes President Davis, requesting an unofficial visit to explore peace terms.

Saturday, December 31

Eastern Theater The siege lines at Richmond and Petersburg have turned the whole area into a desolate wasteland. The once extensive woods have been chopped down to make supports for the trenches, walls for huts, and as fuel. Soldiers and civilians alike wonder how much longer this dismal business must continue. The South is clearly defeated militarily and thoughts turn to the future. Will the Southern states be treated as a defeated enemy—as radical Republicans are demanding—or will they be welcomed back into the Union on Lincoln's generous terms?

Western Theater Sherman continues to rest and refit his army at Savannah.

The fall of Fort McAllister.
Situated on the Ogeechee River below Savannah, Fort McAllister was garrisoned by 230 men commanded by Major G.W. Anderson. At 5 p.m. on December 13, Hazen's division of the Union XV Corps launched an attack watched by Sherman from a nearby rice mill. The fort had been attacked by the US Navy once in 1862 and three times in early 1863, but even the heavy guns of the USS Montauk had failed to inflict much damage. The main strength of the fort lay in its heavy guns, which scored repeated hits on attacking ironclads and were moved under cover when bombardments became too fierce. The landward side was defended by obstructions and mines, but the garrison lacked the manpower to beat off a major ground assault.

Hazen's troops stormed the fort, inflicting 35 casualties on the garrison, while suffering 24 dead and 110 wounded themselves. With the capture of Fort McAllister, Sherman's army had finally reached the sea and regained contact with the North.

January 1865

Sunday, January 1, 1865
Eastern Theater General Butler's men on the James explode a large charge of gunpowder to complete the excavation of a canal, bypassing a large bend in the river. But the explosion fills in the ditch instead and the project is abandoned.

Monday, January 2
Western Theater The Federal raiding column attacking the Mobile and Ohio railroad in Mississippi skirmishes with Confederate forces at Franklin and Lexington.

Tuesday, January 3
Western Theater Sherman begins to ready his army for a renewed advance, shifting some troops to Beaufort, South Carolina.

Wednesday, January 4
Eastern Theater Federal troops embark on transports at Bermuda Hundred for a second attempt on Fort Fisher. Once again, the second division of XXIV Corps will provide most of the infantry but they are reinforced by the third division, XV Corps—two brigades of colored troops under Brigadier-General Charles J. Paine. The force of nearly 8000 men is commanded by a capable officer, Major-General Alfred H. Terry.

Thursday, January 5
The North President Lincoln issues a pass to James W. Singleton, one of several self-appointed go-betweens, allowing him to cross through Union lines. Military defeat is staring the South in the face, although leaders as different as President Davis and General Robert E. Lee continue to make optimistic statements.

Friday, January 6
The North Although passed by the Senate, the Thirteenth Amendment failed to achieve a two-thirds majority in the House of Representatives. The Republicans know that they will be able to pass it in the Thirty-ninth Congress, but that will not meet until December 1865, and they are anxious to pass this measure as soon as possible. The Administration works hard to persuade enough Democrats to change their votes.
Eastern Theater General Grant wires Lincoln asking for Butler to be removed. Such is the politician's seniority that he would command the Army of the Potomac in Grant's absence.
The South There is an angry exchange of letters between President Davis and his vice-president, Alexander H. Stephens, who has criticized Davis repeatedly and is rumored to be active in the Georgia peace movement.

Saturday, January 7
The North Major-General Benjamin Butler is removed from his command of the Army of the James and the Department of Virginia and North Carolina, and replaced by Major-General E.O.C. Ord.
Europe One of the two powerful Confederate ironclad cruisers built at Bordeaux and seized by the French Government last summer was sold to Denmark, the other to Prussia. After her defeat, Denmark could not afford to maintain her naval strength, so the French builder buys back the warship and secretly sells her to the Confederacy. The 1560-ton ironclad leaves Copenhagen, bound for Quiberon, France.

UNION TRANSPORTS

UNION ATTACKING FORCE

LAND TORPEDOES

PALISADES

FORT FISHER

TELEGRAPH STATION

RIFLE PITS

CAPE FEAR RIVER

Sunday, January 8

Eastern Theater Porter's fleet meets Terry's transports off Beaufort, North Carolina. He meets with the naval officers to plan the assault on Fort Fisher. Lying at the end of a long, narrow peninsula, the fort is supported by about 6000 Confederate troops in Wilmington itself. The assault force is liable to be attacked in the rear as it tackles the defenses.

Monday, January 9

The North The influential Democrat Moses Odell of New York changes his mind and supports the Thirteenth Amendment as the debate continues.

The South The Constitutional Convention of Tennessee adopts an amendment abolishing slavery.

Tuesday, January 10

Western Theater Cheatham's corps, bringing up the rear of the Army of Tennessee, reach Tupelo, Mississippi, and go into camp. The exhausted Confederate troops have suffered badly on their bleak winter retreat but they are desperately needed to defend the Carolinas from Sherman.

Wednesday, January 11

The South The Constitutional Convention of Missouri adopts an ordinance abolishing slavery.

Eastern Theater Some 300 Confederate cavalry under Thomas L. Rosser brave heavy snowfalls to attack Federal forces in West Virginia. Achieving complete surprise, they capture twice their strength in prisoners at Beverly.

Europe A party of Confederate officers and sailors arrives at Gravesend, England, ready to man the ex-Danish ironclad, soon to be named the CSS *Stonewall*.

Thursday, January 12

The South Francis P. Blair meets with President Davis, who hands him a letter to pass on to President Lincoln. Davis is willing to enter into negotiations, but still insists on independence for the South.

Friday, January 13

Eastern Theater The US fleet covers the landing of Terry's troops two miles above Fort Fisher. During the morning the monitors exploit their shallow draft to approach within 1200 yards and trade shots with the Confederate batteries. In the early afternoon, with all the troops and their stores safely landed, the fleet assembles before Fort Fisher and begins a concentrated bombardment. The 800 defenders are reinforced by 700 men, including 50 sailors and marines of the Confederate Navy. The Confederate department commander at Wilmington is none other than Braxton Bragg. His troops in the city do not respond to Fort Fisher's telegraph for help, and Terry's landing is unopposed.

Western Theater Having gotten his surviving troops into winter quarters, John Bell Hood telegraphs Richmond asking to be relieved of his command.

Saturday, January 14

Eastern Theater The bombardment of Fort Fisher continues during the night and all through today. Many guns are dismounted and the Confederate gunners suffer heavy losses when they try to fire on the approaching Union infantry. Inside the fort, the commander, Colonel William Lamb, and the district commander, Major-General W.H.C. Whiting, telegraph Bragg to attack at night when the fleet cannot support Terry's troops. They receive no reply. Bragg does not stir and a Confederate transport sails into the arms of the Union forces and is captured. She is later fired on and sunk by the CSS *Chickamauga*, which is lurking in the Cape Fear River.

Western Theater General Beauregard takes temporary command of the Army of Tennessee. Lieutenant-General Richard Taylor is named as Hood's successor.

UNION FLEET

MOUND BATTERY

FORT BUCHANAN

The capture of Fort Fisher

The Confederacy's last point of contact with the outside world, the port of Wilmington, North Carolina, was cut off on January 15. The mouth of the Cape Fear River was controlled by a mile-long line of earthworks known as Fort Fisher. Bombarded by the US Navy, it resisted the attack over Christmas 1864, but the reinforced Union assault in January was another matter. Entrenching themselves midway between Wilmington and the fort, the Union troops isolated Fort Fisher from Bragg's 6000 troops in the city itself. The officers of the fort were critical of Bragg for his failure to intervene during the assault. Some 3000 Federal troops broke into the defenses on the Cape Fear side of the peninsula, although a US Marine and Navy attack on the Atlantic side was defeated with heavy losses. The Confederate gunners fought for every battery and the garrison launched several spirited counter-attacks. But after six hours of fighting, the defenses were overrun, and those Confederates still fighting had been driven back to the Battery Buchanan which surrendered well after dark at about 10 p.m.

219

January 1865

Sunday, January 15, 1865

Eastern Theater At 3 p.m. the Federals mount a combined attack on Fort Fisher. Leaving nearly 5000 men dug in across the neck of the peninsula facing Wilmington, Terry sends 3000 troops against the western end of Fort Fisher's landward defenses. At the same time a force of 1200 sailors armed with cutlasses and pistols land from the fleet. Covered by 400 US marines, they rush the eastern side, but the Confederates pour a heavy fire into the naval column. Drawn from 35 different ships, in many cases unfamiliar with each other and not having rehearsed the operation, the sailors' assault fails. Pinned down by the Confederate fire, they suffer 300 killed and wounded before they break.

Terry's infantry are engaged in bitter, hand-to-hand fighting as they break into the western end of Fort Fisher. They are fortunate that the naval gunfire has cut the wires to an electrically detonated minefield in front of the Confederate defenses. Maneuvering out three 12-pounder Napoleons, the Confederates sweep the first wave of troops off their parapet, but with the sailors out of the way, the Union gunboats close in to rake the eastern part of the defenses, while Terry's infantry batter their way in. After six hours of close-quarter fighting, the fort is finally overrun. Combined US Army and Navy casualties are 226 dead, 1018 wounded, and 57 missing—a total of 1341. Confederate losses are reported by General Bragg as 500 killed and wounded. Over 2000 officers and men are captured, although some were taken in outlying batteries rendered untenable by the fall of Fort Fisher. Both senior Confederate officers were wounded; Whiting was captured and died in New York on March 10. Both heavily criticized Bragg for his inaction. He retorted that the Federals were too well entrenched across the peninsula for his 6000 men to have broken through.

Top right: *A 200-pounder Parrott rifled cannon at Fort Gregg, Morris Island, Charleston, South Carolina. The heavy shells fired by such guns wrought havoc on Fort Sumter but they had an unenviable reputation for bursting.*

Monday, January 16

The North Francis P. Blair meets with Lincoln, revealing the details of his discussions with Jefferson Davis. He outlines the Confederate peace plan, based on recognition of the Confederacy, followed by joint action against Maximilian's Imperial government in Mexico.

Eastern Theater Two drunken sailors wander into the magazine of Fort Fisher with lanterns. Moments later the 13,000 pounds of powder detonate, killing 25, injuring 66, and leaving 13 men unaccounted for. Many of the casualties are from the 169th New York who were sleeping on the grassy mound above the magazine. President Davis wires Braxton Bragg urging him to counter-attack and retake the fort. With Fort Fisher in Union hands, Wilmington is now shut off and the Confederacy is completely isolated.

The South By 14 votes to two, the Confederate Senate passes a resolution that Robert E. Lee should be appointed commander-in-chief of the armies of the Confederacy. Beauregard is appointed to command in South Carolina, Georgia, and Florida. while Joe Johnston regains command of the Army of Tennessee.

Tuesday, January 17

Western Theater As the Confederate authorities desperately try to raise fresh troops in the Carolinas, Sherman stands ready to march once more. His army was followed into Savannah by over 10,000 black refugees, and to accommodate them he issued special Field Order Number 15 yesterday. This hands the refugees much of the confiscated or abandoned land along the Georgia coast, 40 acres per man. Although a temporary war measure, this creates great hope among Southern blacks that freed men will receive land of their own.

Wednesday, January 18

The South The Senate urges Lee to accept the post of general-in-chief, in addition to commanding the Army of Northern Virginia.

Left: *The mile-long line of earthworks known as Fort Fisher guarded the Confederacy's last port, Wilmington, North Carolina. After an abortive attack in December, the Union forces stormed the fort in one of the most successful amphibious operations of the war.*

Thursday, January 19

The South General Lee reluctantly becomes general-in-chief. Opposition to President Davis's handling of Confederate Grand Strategy had grown throughout the war. But it is now far too late for even a soldier of Lee's caliber to mastermind a military recovery for the doomed Confederacy.

Western Theater Sherman starts to march again, heading north into South Carolina, the cradle of the rebellion. Many soldiers of his army keenly anticipate the opportunity to avenge the years of fighting and hardship on the citizens of the first rebel state.

Friday, January 20

Western Theater Heavy rains hamper Sherman's advance. Slocum's corps is unable to leave Savannah as the roads are in a terrible condition.

Far West Federal troops skirmish with Indians near Fort Larned, Kansas.

Saturday, January 21

Eastern Theater Sherman moves his headquarters to Beaufort, South Carolina. No significant Confederate force can oppose his advance.

Sunday, January 22

Trans-Mississippi A skirmish takes place near Little Rock, Arkansas. Federal action continues against bands of Confederate guerrillas.

Monday, January 23

Eastern Theater The Confederate ironclads *Virginia*, *Richmond*, and *Fredericksburg* leading the gunboat *Drewry*, Davidson's torpedo boat, and three torpedo launches, attempt to pass the obstructions placed by Union engineers at Trent's Reach on the James River. With most of the Union fleet concentrated at Fort Fisher, only the monitor *Onondaga* remains to resist the attack. But the obstructions, laid on Grant's orders six months earlier to prevent just such a sortie, cause *Virginia*, *Richmond*, and *Drewry* to go aground. At daybreak they come under fire from the Union guns in Fort Parsons. *Onondaga* steams to within 900 yards and shells *Virginia*. The Confederate flagship is struck about 150 times by the 100- and 200-pounder Parrotts of the fort, and the monitor's 150-pounders and two 15-inch smoothbores. Penetrated twice, she is badly battered before escaping on the flood-tide. *Drewry* is destroyed.

Western Theater Richard Taylor assumes command of the Army of Tennessee, now reduced to fewer than 18,000 men. He is ordered to dispatch a large proportion of his forces to defend the Carolinas, but most of them will desert along the way.

Tuesday, January 24

The South The Confederate Congress offers Grant an exchange of prisoners. This time he accepts—no amount of returned Southern prisoners can affect the outcome of the spring campaign.

Europe The powerful Confederate ironclad CSS *Stonewall* meets her tender off Belle Isle, France, and prepares to cross the Atlantic.

Wednesday, January 25

Eastern Theater The siege lines of Petersburg remain frozen, but in South Carolina Sherman's advance guard skirmishes along the Salkehatchie River.

Western Theater A Union column journeys from Irish Bottom to Evan's Island, Tennessee.

Thursday, January 26

Eastern Theater Sherman's chosen objective is Goldsborough, North Carolina, but he dispatches troops toward Charleston to confuse the Confederates as to his real line of march.

Friday, January 27

Eastern Theater General Lee writes the governor of South Carolina, who has been pleading for troops to stop Sherman taking Charleston: "Should our whole coast fall in the possession of our enemies, with our people true, firm, and united, the war could be continued and our purpose accomplished. As long as our armies are unsubdued and sustained, the Confederacy is safe." But the Southern armies are neither. Today Lee again complains to Richmond that the pitiful rations provided for his men are a major cause of his serious desertion problem.

Saturday, January 28

The South President Davis appoints Vice-President Stephens; R.M.T. Turner, president of the Senate; and former US Supreme Court Justice John A. Campbell to hold informal talks with the Union.

Large Union monitor Miantonomoh *was a successful type that entered service toward the end of the war. Armed with 15-inch guns, she needed a crew of only 150.*

January–February 1865

Sunday, January 29, 1865

Eastern Theater Southern efforts to concentrate forces against Sherman continue. The only sizable force is the garrison of Charleston plus Hardee's troops from Savannah, but on its own this is no match for Sherman's four corps.

Monday, January 30

Western Theater Major-General John Pope is assigned the command of the new Military Division of the Missouri. There is a skirmish at Chaplintown, Kentucky.

Tuesday, January 31

The North The US House of Representatives passes the Thirteenth Amendment by a two-thirds majority. It will only become part of the Constitution after two-thirds of the states have given approval; radical Republicans naturally press for the Confederate states to be excluded from the calculation. Although the news of this decision will stiffen the resolve of some Southerners to fight to the last, the futility of continued resistance is becoming obvious to many more.

The South President Davis recommends Lee's appointment as general-in-chief to the Confederate Senate, so the commander of the Army of Northern Virginia receives this empty title officially.

Wednesday, February 1, 1865

The North Illinois becomes the first state to ratify the Thirteenth Amendment.

Eastern Theater Sherman's advance begins in earnest. His right wing continues to feint toward Charleston, while his left threatens Augusta, Georgia. Confederate cavalry skirts around the edge of his columns but can do no more than delay their progress and cut off small detachments.

Thursday, February 2

Eastern Theater Skirmishes occur along the Salkehatchie River, and among the swamps and waterways of South Carolina.

Far West Federal troops fight Indians along the North Platte River in Colorado, as war parties begin to exact revenge for the Sand Creek massacre.

Europe The CSS *Stonewall* arrives at Ferrol, Spain.

Friday, February 3

The North President Lincoln and Secretary of State Seward meet the three Confederate representatives aboard the *River Queen* in Hampton Roads. Lincoln scotches the Confederate plan for peace and an alliance against Mexico; he maintains that they are one country. There can be no independent nation of Confederate States. Lincoln also rejects an armistice until the Union is restored.

Eastern Theater Sherman's troops wade through the swamps along the Salkehatchie and head north toward Columbia, South Carolina.

Saturday, February 4

Western Theater Slocum's corps struggles across the swollen Savannah River. Skirmishes take place at Angley's Post Office and Buford's Bridge, South Carolina.

Sunday, February 5

Eastern Theater The year's first major action on the Petersburg siege lines takes place as the Union II and V Corps march out and occupy the Boydton Plank Road, further extending the Federal lines south and west of the town. Confederate opposition is light. The long winter in the trenches has eaten away at the once proud Army of Northern Virginia. Living on little more than a pint of oatmeal a day, disease and hunger tempt many men to desert the colors. Nearly 3000 Confederate troops have deserted in one five-week period. Lee's attempts to secure more rations for his men met with failure in Richmond, Lee complaining to his son Custis

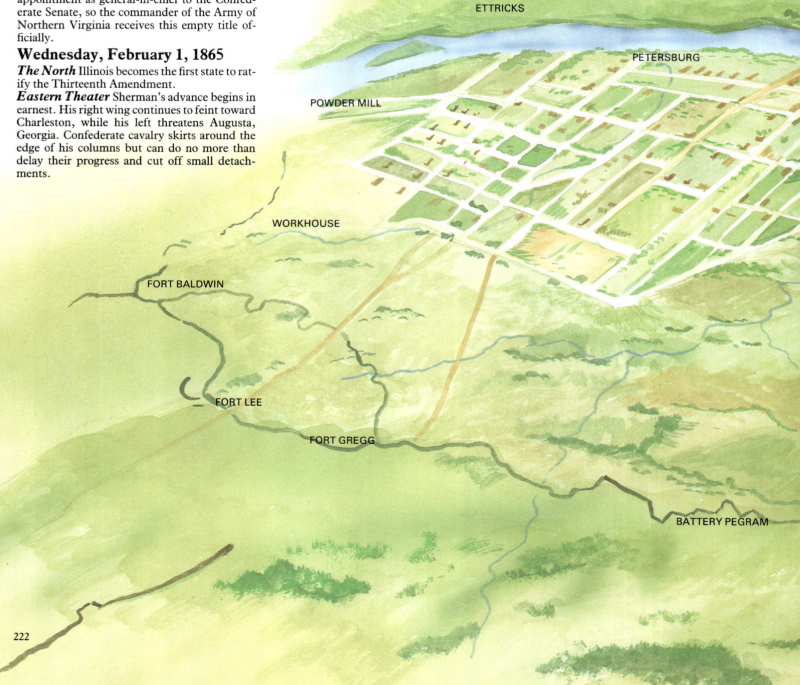

that the Confederate Congress seemed happy to eat peanuts and chew tobacco while his army starves.

Monday, February 6

The South In another belated change of command, John C. Breckinridge is appointed Confederate secretary of war in place of James A. Seddon.

Eastern Theater Brigadier-General Pegram is killed as his division counter-attacks the Union forces on the Boydton Plank Road.

Tuesday, February 7

Eastern Theater Further fighting at Petersburg forces the Federals back from the Boydton Plank Road, but their new line at Hatcher's Run holds. Lee's 46,000 troops now have to defend 37 miles of trenches and many of his men are ill.

Wednesday, February 8

Eastern Theater General Wheeler, commanding the Confederate cavalry skirmishing around Sherman's army, complains to the Union commander that Federal troops are wantonly destroying private property. Sherman has issued orders to respect occupied dwellings but empty buildings are fair game for the looters.

Far West Fighting continues along the North Platte in Colorado and near Rush Creek, Nebraska Territory.

Thursday, February 9

Eastern Theater General John M. Schofield assumes command of the Department of North Carolina, joining his XXIII Corps at Fort Fisher, ready for an assault on Wilmington. Robert E. Lee persuades President Davis to offer amnesty to deserters who return to their regiments within 30 days.

Friday, February 10

Eastern Theater Skirmishing takes place on James Island and at Johnson's Station, South Carolina, as the defenders of Charleston fight Union troops from the sea and inland. Return-

ing from England, Captain Semmes of the *Alabama* is promoted rear admiral and given command of the James River squadron.

Saturday, February 11

Eastern Theater Sherman's army cuts the Augusta–Georgia railroad, dividing the Confederates assembling at Augusta, Georgia, and the forces at Charleston, South Carolina. Beauregard urges the evacuation of Charleston to avoid one of the South's few remaining armies being besieged.

Siege lines before Petersburg during the mild and wet winter of 1864/65.

Grant had moved on Petersburg in order to threaten Richmond. His army now mustered 125,000 men against the Confederate 57,000. He constantly probed around the defenses but they held. Later Lee launched his last offensive but this in turn failed.

Grant now extended the siege lines to such an extent that the Confederates could not adequately man them. The Confederate defeat at Five Forks, only 11 miles away, convinced Lee that both Petersburg and Richmond would have to be evacuated.

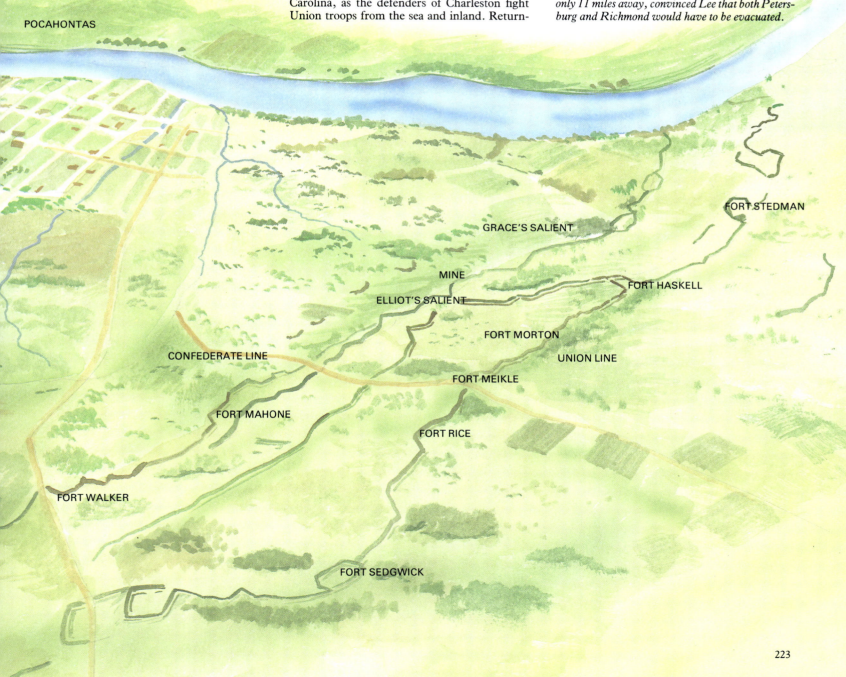

February 1865

Sunday, February 12, 1865
The North The electoral college meets and officially elects Lincoln, 212 to 21.
Eastern Theater Sherman's march continues, still hampered by the rain, which forces his engineers to corduroy many of the roads with logs so the wagons can pass.

Monday, February 13
England Lord John Russell complains to Federal commissioners about the increased US military presence on the Great Lakes. The US action is in response to the St Albans raid of October 1864, the perpetrators of which have been released for lack of evidence. Canadian authorities are very anxious about this display of American strength, and demand extra British troops and improvements to Canadian defenses along the St Lawrence.

Tuesday, February 14
Eastern Theater Sherman's army heads for Columbia, crossing the Congaree River. Skirmishes take place on the North Edisto. President Davis urges Hardee to hold Charleston until the last possible moment.

Wednesday, February 15
Eastern Theater Sherman's approach to Columbia is marked by skirmishes at Bates' Ferry on the Congaree and at Red Bank Creek and Two League Cross Roads near Lexington, South Carolina. Confederate cavalry patrols surround the advancing Union columns, picking off stragglers and, especially, anyone caught burning houses.

Thursday, February 16
Eastern Theater Sherman's troops arrive on the south bank of the Congaree opposite Columbia. Beauregard evacuates the city during the afternoon, and a series of skirmishes take place as Union troops practically surround the city. A few field guns are fired into the houses. Meanwhile, at Charleston Hardee prepares to evacuate; with Sherman's army between him and his only possible reinforcements at Augusta, Georgia, he has little choice.

Friday, February 17
Eastern Theater A black day indeed for the Confederacy: Sherman's men occupy Columbia, and much of the city is burned to the ground during the night. Charleston, birthplace of secession, is also evacuated. Sherman's army has cut a swathe of destruction through South Carolina, and the burning of Columbia is laid at his door by most Southerners. Among the houses destroyed is Wade Hampton's magnificent residence with its fine library. Ironically, some Union officers claim the fires were started by Hampton's cavalry rear guard igniting cotton bales. But the real culprits are drunken soldiers looting the city, pursued by Sherman's provost guard. Like the burning of Moscow in 1812, exact responsibility will never be determined.

As Hardee's troops withdraw from Charleston, Captain Thomas A. Huguenin evacuates Fort Sumter. Last to depart, he goes the rounds of the deserted casemates for one final time during the night, then boards a little boat waiting at the wharf. Four years of defiant resistance are over.

Top right: *One of the many black families which flocked to follow Sherman's army on its march into the heart of the Confederacy.*

Right: *Former vice-president John C. Breckinridge was the Southern Democrats' choice for president in 1860. Opposed to war, he resigned from the Senate with deep reluctance before joining the Confederate Army and rising to the rank of major-general. He was appointed minister of war on February 4, 1865.*

Below: *The blackened ruins of the once-proud city of Columbia. It is unlikely Sherman actually ordered it to be put to the torch, but his subsequent refusal to express any sorrow damned him in Southern eyes.*

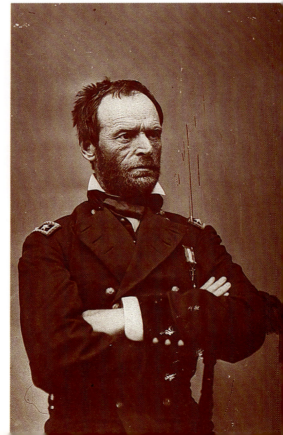

Saturday, February 18

The South Replying to Mississippi Congressman Ethelbert Barksdale, Robert E. Lee endorses the idea of arming blacks to bolster the Confederacy's exhausted reserves of manpower.
Eastern Theater Sherman may not have given orders to burn the whole city of Columbia, but today he instructs his men to pull down the railway depots, warehouses, and all military installations. The people of Columbia pick through the blackened ruins of their homes. Federal troops under General Alexander Schimmelfennig receive the surrender of Charleston.
Naval Operations The Confederate commerce raider *Shenandoah* completes her refit at Melbourne, Australia, and sails for the North Pacific.

Sunday, February 19

Eastern Theater Federal troops commanded by Jacob D. Cox, architect of the Union victory at Franklin, march 15 miles around the Confederate lines at Wilmington. The defenders block this outflanking maneuver, leading to fighting at Town Creek. During the night the Confederates withdraw on the east side of the Cape Fear River. At Columbia Sherman's troops wreck the railroad installations and the factories which supplied the Confederate armies for so long.

Monday, February 20

The South The Confederate House of Representatives passes a bill authorizing the use of slaves as soldiers.
Eastern Theater Cox's Union troops have outflanked the Confederates on the west bank of the Cape Fear River and press toward Wilmington, North Carolina. Federal warships bombard the defenses.

Tuesday, February 21

The South The Confederate Senate, unable to grasp the nettle, postpones debate on the vexed question of employing blacks as soldiers.
Eastern Theater The defenders of Wilmington bow to the inevitable and begin to destroy those military stores they cannot take with them. Evacuation is unavoidable as Cox's troops close in.

Left: *The classic portrait photograph of Sherman—an old man at 44 years of age. His record as a battlefield commander was by no means outstanding but his ability to manage and maneuver large bodies of troops was undoubted. A ruthless man, he proved the truth of his own maxim that "war is hell."*

Wednesday, February 22

Eastern Theater Union troops enter Wilmington unopposed. General Lee assigns Joseph E. Johnston to the Department of South Carolina, Georgia, and Florida. Beauregard, although ill and unhappy about being replaced, cooperates with Johnston. Lee begins to plan his last campaign, as it is obvious that the Army of Northern Virginia must act soon, or be crushed between Grant and Sherman.

Thursday, February 23

Eastern Theater Sherman's troops resume their advance, the XX Corps crossing the Catawba River as it nears the border with North Carolina. Torrential rain begins to fall.

Friday, February 24

Eastern Theater Sherman complains to Wade Hampton that some Union foragers, or "bummers" as they have become known, have been shot out of hand by Confederate cavalry. Wade Hampton denies knowledge of the incident mentioned but affirms his order to shoot on sight all Union troops engaged in burning private homes.

Saturday, February 25

Eastern Theater General Joe Johnston assumes command of the Army of Tennessee, now reduced to about 25,000 men, including state militia mustering in the Carolinas. Federal forces occupy Camden on the Wateree River, South Carolina.

A group of typical Confederate blockade runners: the standard merchant steamer Peterhoff *(top); the highly successful* Lizzie *(center); and the steel-hulled* Hope *(bottom) that was only eventually captured after a 65-mile chase. The last two were especially built as blockade runners able to steam swiftly in and out of Southern ports, bringing in much needed supplies and leaving with cotton.*

Blockade runners were an essential part of the Confederate war effort. At first, anyone could purchase or charter suitable craft, but as the war progressed and the Union blockade of the 3000-mile Southern coastline became more effective, so purpose-built vessels were obained. These were low, sleek vessels, lightly built to achieve maximum speed at the critical moment of entering or leaving the blockaded ports. They could carry only about 850 bales of cotton, but even so vast profits were made, especially on the luxury items being carried into the South. Captains of these unique craft could earn massive fees—$5000 per round trip—and each vessel could pay for its own cost in two or three trips.

The Confederate Government eventually stepped in to ensure that blockade runners carried only essential supplies, such as medicine and military equipment. They even organized their own fleet headed by John Wilkinson, who managed to make 20 successful trips.

Union troops in the trenches before Petersburg. Grant was going to win the war by the steady attrition of siege warfare. But this was cold comfort to the troops fed into this mincing machine.

Some of Sherman's veterans—men of the 21st Michigan Infantry. The contrast between the spic and span Army of the Potomac and the informality of the western armies was clearly demonstrated when they paraded through Washington, D.C. after the end of hostilities.

Sunday, February 26, 1865

Eastern Theater The US XX Corps reaches Hanging Rock, South Carolina, as Sherman's advance continues to be slowed by the torrential rain. There is a skirmish at Lynch's Creek.

Monday, February 27

Eastern Theater General Wesley Merritt leads 10,000 of Sheridan's cavalry up to the Shenandoah Valley with orders from Grant to destroy the Virginia Central Railroad and the James River Canal. Sheridan no longer trusts his cavalry to Torbert who, he feels, lacks the initiative for independent command. To oppose them, Jubal Early has two weak brigades at Staunton. All the rest of his infantry, except Echol's brigade, which is in southwest Virginia, has been withdrawn to bolster Lee's depleted ranks at Petersburg. Fitz Lee's two brigades of cavalry have also been sent east, leaving Early with the small mounted forces under Rosser and Lomax. Rosser's men have been allowed to disperse to their farms as the army has no fodder for their horses or food for the men.

Tuesday, February 28

Eastern Theater The surrounding mountains still capped with snow, Merritt's column crosses the north fork of the Shenandoah River during a heavy rainstorm. The two cavalry divisions under Custer and Devin carry 15 days' rations with them as there is nothing left to requisition in the exhausted land.

Wednesday, March 1, 1865

Eastern Theater Sheridan had attempted to disguise his new offensive by announcing yet another fox hunt, but the news of the Federal advance has travelled fast. Rosser musters about 600 cavalry and burns the bridges over the middle Shenandoah. Early summons Echol's brigade and concentrates his small army at Waynesborough.

Thursday, March 2

Eastern Theater Covered in mud from head to toe, Custer's 5000-strong cavalry division hurries along the miry roads to Waynesborough where Jubal Early has entrenched himself with 2000 troops and 11 guns. Custer dismounts one brigade to flank the Confederate position, while leading two brigades against the entrenchments. The turning movement succeeds and a mounted charge through the broken Confederate center led by the 8th New York and 1st Connecticut completes the rout. Most of the Confederates are taken prisoner; Early and a handful of his officers manage to escape but the Confederate presence in the valley is at an end. Meanwhile, at Petersburg, General Lee writes Grant, proposing a meeting.

Friday, March 3

The North The Thirty-eighth Congress of the United States holds its final session. It establishes a Bureau for the Relief of Freedmen and Refugees. This will supervise abandoned lands and will aid and provide work for the displaced black population.

Eastern Theater Union troops enter Cheraw, South Carolina, where men from Blair's XVII Corps discover a large cache of vintage wine,

Confederate ironclad Fredericksburg *was one of the last vessels completed for the Confederate Navy. She led the only fleet ever assembled by the South, and this operated around Richmond.*

As can be seen, the same basic design for Southern ironclads was followed throughout the war, with a few exceptions.

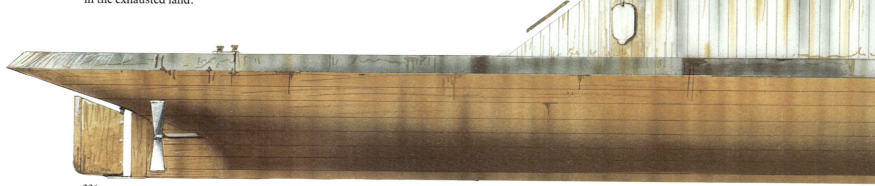

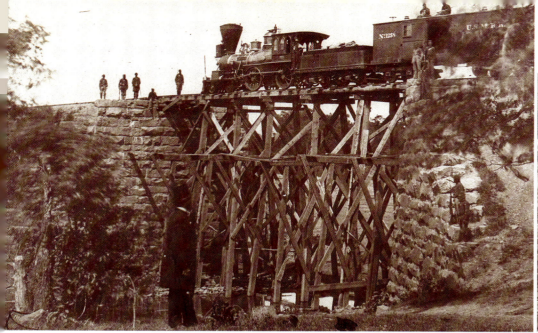

The engine "Firefly" of the US Military Railroad poses confidently on a trestle bridge on the Orange and Alexandria line.

Major-General Philip Sheridan and his staff. Critical of his superiors, Sheridan was correspondingly tough with his subordinates. Had Custer been the incompetent he is often shown as, he would never have commanded one of Sheridan's divisions.

brought from the cellars of Charleston for safe-keeping. Blair organizes a fair distribution. His soldiers drink the fine wines from their tin cups—the taste of victory. The Confederates retire across the Pee Dee River and burn the bridges. At Petersburg Grant receives a message from Lincoln forbidding any military convention. Political questions were not to be decided by the army.

Saturday, March 4

The North President Lincoln is inaugurated for his second term of office. His eloquent inaugural address is in sharp contrast to his vice-president's, which is rendered confused after a little too much medicinal whiskey.

The South Still fiddling while Rome burns, the Confederate Congress approves a new design for the Confederate national flag.

Sunday, March 5

The North President Lincoln asks Hugh McCulloch to become secretary of the treasury. William Fessenden has resigned after being re-elected to the Senate.

Monday, March 6

Eastern Theater Sherman's advance resumes as his men march on Fayetteville, North Carolina, crossing the Pee Dee River. General Joseph E. Johnston assumes command of all Confederate forces in the Department of North Carolina and south of the siege lines of Petersburg.

Tuesday, March 7

Eastern Theater Jacob Cox's Union troops at Wilmington, North Carolina, establish themselves at New Berne and repair the railroad to Goldsborough. This will provide a short supply line to Sherman's army from the North Carolina coast. Once again, the power of the US Navy allows Union forces to be supplied by sea, enabling them to march through the Confederate heartland.

Wednesday, March 8

The South Voting nine to eight, the Confederate Senate approves the use of black troops.

Eastern Theater Braxton Bragg makes the first significant Confederate counter-attack this spring by attacking Cox's troops at Kinston,

near New Berne. An inexperienced Union brigade breaks and runs but Bragg lacks the strength to inflict a major defeat.

Thursday, March 9

Eastern Theater Bragg's battle at Kinston continues with heavy skirmishing but no breakthrough. The veteran Confederate cavalry leaders Wade Hampton and Joe Wheeler surprise Judson Kilpatrick's Union troopers in their night camp at Monroe's Cross Roads, Virginia. The unpopular Union commander is nearly captured in bed, and the rumor that he fled without his trousers leads the battle to become known as the "Battle of Kilpatrick's Pants."

Friday, March 10

Eastern Theater Kilpatrick's cavalry rally and eventually beat off the Confederate raiders during the early hours of the morning. Bragg's men withdraw from Kinston after failing to defeat the Federal forces under Cox.

Saturday, March 11

Eastern Theater Sherman's troops enter Fayetteville, North Carolina. Their long train of black refugees follows the Union soldiers into the town. At times, the vast numbers of refugees crowding along the roads has seemed to exceed the number of soldiers. Thousands of families have fled the plantations and farms to follow the Federal Army.

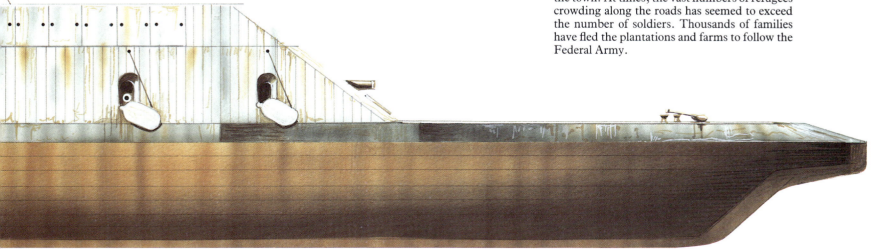

March 1865

Sunday, March 12, 1865

Eastern Theater Sherman's forces at Fayetteville, North Carolina, destroy the arsenal buildings, machine shops, and foundries, including the machinery brought over from the Harper's Ferry arsenal in 1861. A tug traveling up the Cape Fear River from Wilmington re-establishes communications between Sherman's army and the rest of the Union. The Federal soldiers receive their mail and much-needed new uniforms, and the thousands of refugees with the army are shipped to safety.

Monday, March 13

The South The Confederate Congress sends President Davis the bill putting Negroes in the army and he signs without delay. The unspoken assumption is that individual states will grant freedom to slaves who fight for the Confederacy. Recruiting begins immediately and within weeks there will be small numbers of blacks in Richmond wearing the gray uniform of the Confederacy.

Tuesday, March 14

Eastern Theater Cox's Federal Army occupies Kinston, North Carolina, while Sherman's advance guard skirmishes along the Black River. His troops at Fayetteville cross the Cape Fear River. Sheridan's cavalry have continued their advance and now skirmish at the South Anna Bridge as they move to join Grant's army.

Wednesday, March 15

Eastern Theater Sherman's army marches, ready to do battle with the Confederate forces known to be concentrating ahead. Colonel Rhett, former editor of the *Charleston Mercury*, one of the strongest secessionist newspapers, is captured by Union troops as Kilpatrick's cavalry overrun part of the rear guard which he is commanding.

Thursday, March 16

Eastern Theater Sherman's left wing under Slocum runs into a line of Confederate entrenchments four miles north of Averasborough, North Carolina. Sherman directs Slocum to outflank the defenses while deploying two divisions of XX Corps in front of them. The Confederates under Hardee retreat with the loss of over 800 men. Federal casualties are 95 killed, 533 wounded, and 54 missing. The Confederates fall back to another defensive line and the Union forces camp immediately in front of them.

Friday, March 17

Eastern Theater Hardee's men withdraw toward the little hamlet of Bentonville where Johnston is concentrating all available Confederate forces.

Western Theater Major-General E.R.S. Canby begins land operations against Mobile, Alabama. Commanding elements of XIII Corps and XVI Corps, plus a powerful siege train, Canby has 32,000 men. He is supported by 13,000 troops under Major-General Steele operating from Pensacola. Against them, General Maury can muster fewer than 10,000 troops.

RICHMOND

DRURY'S BLUFF

JAMES RIVER

CONFEDERATE IRONCLADS

FORT DARLING

Saturday, March 18

The South The Confederate Congress ends its session in bitter arguments with President Davis. It will not meet again.

Eastern Theater Wade Hampton skirmishes with Union troops near Bentonville as Joe Johnston marches his infantry forward to attack Sherman's left wing. Johnson has managed to assemble about 17,000 men. They are opposed by a similar number of Federals, although Sherman's total army is over 60,000 strong, and there are nearly 40,000 other Union troops now active in the Carolinas. Both sides entrench their positions during the night.

Western Theater Some 1700 Union troops demonstrate from Dauphin Island against the west side of Mobile Bay. The real assault is intended to come from the east.

Sunday, March 19

Eastern Theater Johnston's Confederates attack the Union forces at Bentonville, North Carolina. Elements of the US XIV Corps are defeated and driven back on XX Corps. The swamps and thickets impede both sides' movement, but this is a more serious problem for the Confederates who find several of their columns delayed. After heavy fighting, the Confederates withdraw to their original entrenchments. Sherman hurries the rest of his mighty host toward Bentonville. Meanwhile, Sheridan joins Grant's army at Petersburg after wrecking the Virginia Central Railroad and destroying the locks on the James River Canal. His column is followed by several thousand blacks who help move his wagons through the muddy roads.

Monday, March 20

Eastern Theater The Union troops at Bentonville are reinforced as Sherman's army concentrates against Johnston. Wheeler leads 3000 Confederate cavalry in skirmishes against the advancing columns. The Union line laps around that of the Confederates, who are compelled to extend their frontage to avoid being outflanked. A series of Federal attacks begin, mainly against Johnston's center.

Tuesday, March 21

Eastern Theater The US XX Corps under Major-General Mower attempts to turn Johnston's left, cutting his line of retreat. Hardee and Wade Hampton hastily gather a small force of troops and counter-attack, stopping the Federal advance. Hardee's only son, 16 years old, is

Scene at the closing stages of the war along the James River, as it twists its way from Richmond in the distance down to Fort Darling and Drury's Bluff already in action against Union forces. The small fleet of Confederate ironclads was frequently in action supporting troops along the riverbanks and was the largest concentration of armored vessels the Confederates were able to gather together at one time.

RIFLE PITS

killed charging with the 8th Texas Cavalry which he had joined a few hours earlier. During the night, Johnston withdraws across Mill Creek and camps two miles beyond the bridge. Union losses in the fighting at Bentonville are 1500 killed and wounded. The Confederates lose 2600, many of them prisoners.

Naval Operations The powerful Confederate ironclad *Stonewall* vainly tries to provoke a fight with US cruisers *Niagara* and *Sacramento* off Ferrol, Spain.

Wednesday, March 22

Western Theater Major-General James Wilson leads his 13,000-strong cavalry corps across the Tennessee River from Waterloo, Alabama, where they had been encamped on the north bank. In an offensive delayed three weeks by the torrential rain, they marched to threaten Tuscaloosa and the last Confederate manufacturing center at Selma. They find the valley of the Tennessee utterly devastated by the last two years' fighting, and the three divisions have to spread out widely to forage as the land is all but destitute of supplies.

Thursday, March 23

Eastern Theater Sherman joins Schofield's forces at Goldsborough, North Carolina, forming an irresistible concentration of over 90,000 troops. The 425-mile march from Savannah has taken the 50 days Sherman predicted. "Like the thrust of a sword through the heart of the human body," as Sherman describes it, his advance has crushed what pitiful opposition the Confederates could offer and consumed the supplies badly needed by Lee's beleaguered men at Petersburg.

Friday, March 24

Eastern Theater With fewer than 35,000 men left fit for duty, Lee knows that he must be defeated if he remains at Petersburg. He orders General John B. Gordon to select part of the Union line and attempt to break through. During the night, Gordon's three divisions assemble, bolstered by elements of Anderson's and Hill's corps.

Saturday, March 25

Eastern Theater In the early hours of the morning a handful of Confederate deserters cross the Union lines near Fort Stedman, a powerful redoubt near Grant's major supply line, the City Point Railroad. Grant had recently offered Confederate soldiers a bounty if they deserted with their weapons, but these men had not come to collect it. They silence the Federal pickets and remove some of the abatis and *chevaux-de-frise* in front of the position. Then Gordon's attack goes in; Confederate troops seize the battery at Fort Stedman and fan out to occupy over 1000 yards of the Union front. But time is wasted looking for other reported Federal earthworks behind the fort. As dawn breaks, the Confederates are counter-attacked and driven back to Fort Stedman. Gordon is forced to cancel the attack as Union forces regain the battery. Federal losses are 1500 but the Confederates lose 4000, many of them troops caught in the Union front line who elect to surrender rather than face the storm of shot and shell sweeping no man's land.

March–April 1865

Sunday, March 26, 1865

Eastern Theater Sheridan's cavalry crosses the James River. Grant is planning another extension of the Union siege lines at Petersburg, this time to cut off Lee's line of retreat and box in the Confederacy's last major army.

Monday, March 27

Eastern Theater President Lincoln meets Generals Grant and Sherman, plus Admiral Porter, aboard the *River Queen* at City Point, Virginia. Sherman will later say that the president was prepared to grant the rebels US citizenship directly they laid down their weapons—the basis for Sherman's future peace agreement with General Johnston.

Western Theater Canby's XIII and XVI Corps besiege Spanish Fort and the defenses of Mobile, Alabama. Steele's advance from Pensacola is badly delayed by the state of the roads.

Tuesday, March 28

Eastern Theater The Army of the Potomac prepares for its final offensive against the Army of Northern Virginia. Some 125,000 Union troops are massed against Lee's fewer than 50,000. Meanwhile, the Confederates continue their own preparations. Lee hopes to break out to join Johnston for a last stand in North Carolina; even if they combine, the two Confederate armies could not hope to defeat either Sherman or Grant, let alone both together.

Wednesday, March 29

Eastern Theater General Lee's nephew, Major-General Fitzhugh Lee, leads the Confederate Cavalry to Five Forks to support Pickett's division against the inevitable Union assault around the Confederate left flank. The Federal attack is made by Warren's V Corps, and II Corps under Humphreys, with Sheridan's cavalry sweeping westward.

Thursday, March 30

Eastern Theater The US II and V Corps press the Confederate left on the line of Hatcher's Run and Gravelly Run as torrential rain turns the already poor roads into deep mire. Part of Sheridan's cavalry under Merritt is repulsed at Five Forks, but by concentrating over 10,000 troops on his far left flank, Lee has fatally over-extended his dwindling army.

Naval Operations CSS *Stonewall* sails from Tenerife.

Friday, March 31

Eastern Theater Pickett's men drive back Sheridan's dismounted cavalry around Dinwiddie Court House. But the Confederates withdraw during the night as the heavy columns of Union infantry begin to arrive. His 10,000 troops are now facing nearly five times their number.

Western Theater As operations against Mobile continue, the besieging Union forces send commissary wagons to Steele's column advancing from Pensacola. The bad weather has so delayed his march that supplies are running desperately low. The Confederate ironclad *Nashville* supports the defenders of Mobile.

Saturday, April 1, 1865

Eastern Theater Attacked by Sheridan's cavalry in front and Warren's infantry corps in the flank, Pickett's men at Five Forks are crushed. Both Pickett and Fitzhugh Lee are absent at a fish-fry when the assault begins, Lee himself never forgiving Pickett for his crucial absence. Sheridan, having been given complete control over the Union assault at Five Forks, relieves Major-General Warren of his command for not moving fast enough. Sheridan leads a ferocious pursuit and nearly half the Confederate force is taken prisoner in the rout.

Western Theater Steele's 13,000 men arrive before Blakely, near Mobile, Alabama, to begin siege operations tomorrow. Union trenches snake ever closer to the city's defenses.

Sunday, April 2

Eastern Theater Before dawn, in a thick fog, the Army of the Potomac launches an assault all along the lines of Petersburg. The thinly stretched Confederate defense is broken everywhere, except at Forts Gregg and Baldwin, which hold out until midday preventing II, VI, and XXIV Corps from breaking into Petersburg itself. Lieutenant-General A.P. Hill is killed and the Army of Northern Virginia abandons the positions it has held for so long. The new concentration point is at Amelia Court House, 40 miles west of Richmond. Federal casualties are 625 killed, 3189 wounded, and 26 missing for a total of 4140 men. Confederate casualties

remain unknown. Richmond is abandoned amid scenes of wild grief, mad panic, and opportunist looting. The center of the city burns down and the James River squadron blows up its surviving ironclads before joining the retreat. Petersburg is occupied, Grant refusing to fire on the last columns of retreating Confederates, allowing them to depart in peace.

Western Theater Wilson's Federal Cavalry reach Selma, Alabama, and assault the defenses without delay. With one division detached, Wilson has about 9000 men against about 7000 Confederates. The Union Cavalry dismount and attack the enemy fieldworks, carrying them in a single charge. Nearly 3000 Confederates are taken prisoner as the surviving Confederates flee the city, pursued by the Federal Cavalry. Bedford Forrest and three other Confederate generals barely escape themselves.

Monday, April 3

Eastern Theater The US flag is unfurled over Richmond as Federal infantry march into the Confederate capital playing "The Girl I Left Behind Me." President Davis and most of the Confederate Cabinet are on board a special train taking them to Danville, Virginia. Lee's troops hurry westward, many formations in no proper order, a long line of men who knew in their hearts their cause was lost.

Tuesday, April 4

Eastern Theater To the cheers of thousands of Union troops and Richmond blacks, President Lincoln visits the fallen Confederate capital. Grant's army does not directly pursue Lee; instead, the Union forces march on a roughly parallel course, heading him off from Johnston's forces.

Wednesday, April 5

Eastern Theater Lee's army concentrates at Amelia Court House but the expected 350,000 rations ordered to be moved from Richmond on Sunday are not there. In fact, the War Department had queried his order but the message never reached Lee and the supplies were never dispatched.

Thursday, April 6

Eastern Theater Resuming the retreat, Lee's army becomes divided as Ewell halts his men to allow the wagon train to pass into the center of the Confederate columns, away from Federal raiders. Ewell is subsequently cut off at Sayler's Creek and compelled to surrender when his troops fail to respond to orders to fight their way through. Wise's brigade is the only Confederate formation to sustain a serious battle, and it breaks out to rejoin Lee. The Confederates lose nearly a third of their remaining strength.

Friday, April 7

Eastern Theater Grant calls upon Lee to surrender the Army of Northern Virginia as the Union forces have all but surrounded the Confederates. Lee's troops skirmish with Union troops before crossing the Appomattox River, but Sheridan's cavalry sweep around to block further retreat at Appomattox Court House.

Saturday, April 8

Eastern Theater Lee plans to break through Sheridan's cavalry to resume the retreat. But Lee and his officers agree that if the Federal horsemen are supported by infantry, they will have no choice but to surrender.

The battle of Bentonville
Union troops hurry forward to meet the Confederate attack. On March 19, 1865 20,000 Confederates under General Johnston counter-attacked the leading wing of Sherman's 100,000-strong army. Facing approximately 30,000 Union troops, the Confederates made some progress despite the Federal field defenses. But tough resistance from the troops of Jefferson C. Davis frustrated the

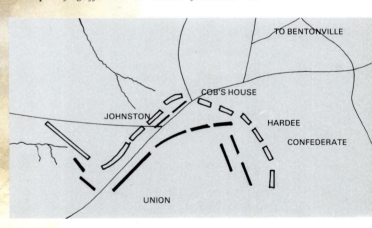

Confederate attack, and the Southern forces withdrew to their start line after dark. The third and final Confederate assault was delayed by poor staffwork and the difficulty of seeing what was happening in the dense undergrowth.

In the interval, the Union XX Corps hurried forward to reinforce XIV Corps and the Federal soldiers were able to improve their positions with hasty fieldworks. Union reinforcements continued to arrive during the night and the following day. By March 21, Johnston was facing an overwhelming force and had to order his men to retreat. With the fight for Richmond nearing its climax, Sherman's irresistible advance through North Carolina meant that the Confederacy was being crushed from two directions at once.

April 1865

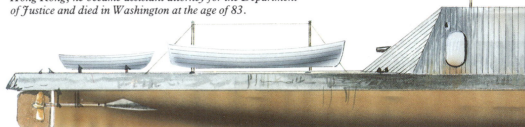

Sunday, April 9, 1865

Eastern Theater The Army of Northern Virginia fights its last battle. After making progress against the Union Cavalry screen, the Confederates encounter firm lines of Federal infantry. There is no escape. Lee bows to the inevitable and a white towel is borne aloft and carried through the Federal lines by an officer bearing Lee's request for an immediate truce. Lee and Grant meet in the house of Wilbur McLean at Appomattox Court House and the Union general scratches out the terms of surrender in pencil. Grant, observing the magnificent sword Lee is wearing, allows officers the right to retain their personal weapons. Lee reads the terms, mentioning that most of his cavalrymen and many of his artillerists own the horses they have been campaigning with. Grant immediately modifies the terms to allow all those who claim a horse to keep it.

Lee signs and rides back through the silent gray ranks. Looking neither right nor left, he tells them: "Go to your homes and resume your occupations. Obey the laws and become as good citizens as you were soldiers."

Western Theater In the early hours of the morning the Union forces at Mobile enter Spanish Fort, evacuated by the Confederate garrison after some 90 cannon were emplaced in the Federal siege lines during last week. A general assault in the afternoon by 16,000 Union troops overruns the Confederate defensive lines, capturing nearly 3500 men.

Monday, April 10

Eastern Theater Lee's surrendered men receive rations from the Union Army. News of the surrender reaches the fugitive Confederate Government at Danville and the leadership flees for Greensborough, North Carolina. Robert E. Lee issues his farewell address to his men. Written by Colonel Charles Marshall, the general order contained a paragraph of bitterness which Lee deleted before signing and issuing it. He concludes: "With an increasing admiration of your constancy and devotion to your country, and a grateful remembrance of your kind and generous consideration of myself, I bid you an affectionate farewell."

Tuesday, April 11

Eastern Theater Sherman's army is marching on Raleigh, planning to intercept Johnston's Confederates.

Western Theater The small defensive works, Forts Tracy and Huger, are blown up during the night at Mobile. General Maury prepares to evacuate the city.

Wednesday, April 12

Eastern Theater Sherman's army receives the news of Lee's surrender. In a deeply moving ceremony at Appomattox the Army of Northern Virginia formally surrenders its weapons and flags. General Gordon leads the Confederate column before the assembled ranks of Union troops under Major-General Joshua Chamberlain. Proud battle ensigns are laid down for the last time. One of the most famous military organizations of all time passes into history.

Western Theater Moving via the Blakely and Tensas, the Union fleet approaches the rear of Mobile, while Granger's troops are shipped across the bay to enter the Confederacy's last major city. The 4500 remaining troops of Maury's garrison slip away with 27 field guns and a wagon train, planning to join Johnston. Meanwhile, Wilson's 12,000 cavalrymen occupy Montgomery, Alabama, after some skirmishing.

Thursday, April 13

Eastern Theater Sherman's army enters Raleigh, North Carolina, while Kilpatrick's cavalry race ahead some 25 miles further on near Durham Station.

Friday, April 14

The North After meetings with the Cabinet and General Grant, President Lincoln visits Ford's Theater to see a comedy, *Our American Cousin*. He is acccompanied by his wife, Clara Harris, daughter of a senator, and her fiancé, Major Henry Rathbone. At 10 p.m. Lincoln is shot in the back of the head by John Wilkes Booth, who stabs the major too before leaping onto the stage to make his escape. The bullet passes through Lincoln's head to lodge by his right eye.

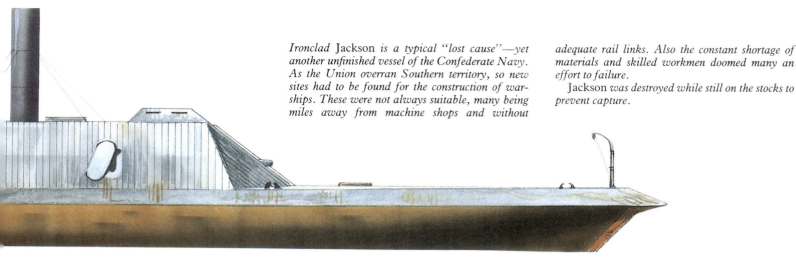

Ironclad Jackson *is a typical "lost cause"—yet another unfinished vessel of the Confederate Navy. As the Union overran Southern territory, so new sites had to be found for the construction of warships. These were not always suitable, many being miles away from machine shops and without* adequate rail links. Also the constant shortage of materials and skilled workmen doomed many an effort to failure.

Jackson *was destroyed while still on the stocks to prevent capture.*

Far Left: *On April 3, 1865 the Army of the Potomac finally entered Richmond. It had taken four years to advance the hundred miles between the U.S. and Confederate capitals. Here the Stars and Stripes flies over Libby Prison.*

Left: *There were refugees of all kinds on the roads in the spring of 1865. Slaves fleeing their masters traveled in one direction, while increasingly wild tales of Union atrocities had Southern civilians hurrying out of Sherman's path.*

The shooting is part of a conspiracy. Secretary of State Seward is attacked in bed where he is recovering from a carriage accident, but his attacker is driven off by his son and a male nurse.
Eastern Theater General Robert Anderson, who surrendered Fort Sumter to the Confederates four years before, raises the Union flag above the shattered rubble in Charleston harbor.

Saturday, April 15

The North President Lincoln lingered through the night before dying at 7.22 a.m. Andrew Johnson takes the oath at 11.00. Meanwhile, Booth is helped to the house of Doctor Samuel Mudd by an accomplice, David Herold. In his leap to the stage, Booth had broken his leg. Mudd treats the injury, a decision which will earn him a life sentence.

Sunday, April 16

Eastern Theater Troops scour Washington and the surrounding countryside, hunting for the conspirators. In North Carolina Sherman receives a request from General Johnston, asking for a cessation of hostilities with a view to negotiating a surrender.

Monday, April 17

Generals Sherman and Johnston meet near Durham Station and they discuss much more than the surrender of Johnston's Confederate Army. Johnston offers to surrender the armies of Kirby Smith across the Mississippi, and Richard Tay-lor's men down by the Gulf coast. The two commanders agree to meet again tomorrow.
Western Theater Wilson's cavalry raid continues; his men destroy 15 locomotives, and several bridges and factories at Columbus, Georgia. They also wreck the navy yard and destroy the ironclad ram CSS *Jackson*. Wilson captured over 1200 Confederates in the city, the surviving troops withdrawing downstream and burning the CSS *Chattahoochee*.

Tuesday, April 18

Eastern Theater Sherman and Jackson sign a conditional treaty which goes beyond immediate military matters and ventures into the political arena. The memorandum states that there will be an armistice and the Confederate armies will disband, handing their weapons to their state arsenals. Federal courts are to be re-established in the South, and Southerners' political rights guaranteed under the US Constitution. The US Government is not to "disturb any of the people by reason of the late war, so long as they . . . abstain from acts of hostility and obeys the law." Unprepared for the storm of criticism he will face, Sherman will later claim that he was following President Lincoln's wishes on reconstruction.

Wednesday, April 19

The North After a funeral service, President Lincoln's body is borne through Washington to the rotunda of the Capitol where it lies in state. Mournful lines of people file past and the bells of the city toll.
Eastern Theater President Davis is at Charlotte, North Carolina, where he learns of the death of Lincoln. Wade Hampton writes him, suggesting the Confederacy carries on the fight from across the Mississippi.

Thursday, April 20

Eastern Theater Still skirmishing with groups of Confederates, Wilson's cavalry reach Macon, Georgia. Wilson receives a letter from General Beauregard informing him of the armistice agreed between Sherman and Johnston. Robert E. Lee writes Jefferson Davis, arguing against the president's proposed guerrilla war.

Friday, April 21

The North President Lincoln's body leaves Washington bound for Springfield, Illinois.
Eastern Theater John S. Mosby disbands his famed Confederate partisans at Millwood, Virginia.

Saturday, April 22

The North Conspirators Booth and Herold escape across the Potomac River to Gumbo Creek, planning to flee south.
Eastern Theater Skirmish actions continue in Georgia between Wilson's Union cavalry and small parties of Confederates.

April–May 1865

Sunday, April 23, 1865

Eastern Theater Federal cavalry under Wilson and Stoneman continue to skirmish with the remnants of Confederate military strength. Wilson's forces divide with the intention of capturing President Davis.

Monday, April 24

The North The search for Lincoln's assassins continues but Booth and Herold manage to reach Port Conway, Virginia, and cross the Rappahannock. The president's body lies in state in New York City.

Eastern Theater General Grant arrives at Sherman's headquarters in Raleigh, North Carolina, bringing with him the letter he had received from Lincoln prohibiting him from entering into political negotiations. Sherman's treaty with Johnston's Confederates clearly exceeds a purely military surrender, but Sherman maintains he thought he was following Lincoln's intentions as he understood them from their last meeting. He certainly never received the sort of letter sent to Grant. Sherman is vilified in the New York newspapers, which are baying for blood in revenge for Lincoln's murder. His lenient settlement with the Confederates incenses radical Republican sentiment and Sherman is ordered to resume hostilities until a straight surrender has been achieved. Major-General Slocum discovers some of Sherman's soldiers burning a cartload of New York papers, furious at the treatment of their chief.

Tuesday, April 25

Eastern Theater Sherman and Johnston arrange to meet again after the Union commander notifies his opposite number that hostilities will have to resume within 48 hours. Johnston wires President Davis at Charlotte, North Carolina, informing him of the rejection of the peace terms but saying that he would have to surrender his command under whatever new terms Sherman would offer. Davis meets with his Cabinet and resolves to leave Charlotte and head for Alabama, where Richard Taylor's Confederate Army was still in the field. Federal cavalry pursuing Booth and his accomplice, Herold, trace the fugitives to the farm of Richard Garrett, south of the Rappahannock River.

Wednesday, April 26

Eastern Theater General Joseph E. Johnston surrenders 31,000 Confederates under the same terms as Lee's army. Once again, the Confederates can keep their horses and other private property. Sherman also provides for field transportation to be loaned to the troops for the journey home and for subsequent use.

A detachment from Company L, 16th New York Cavalry, surround Richard Garrett's barn and call upon Booth and Herold to surrender. Herold gives himself up but Booth shouts defiance and refuses to budge. The troopers fire the barn and rush it. In the confusion, Booth is shot dead, possibly by his own hand but more likely by one of the troopers. His body is taken to the Washington Navy Yard for the inquest. With Booth's death, all prospect of penetrating to the heart of the conspiracy vanishes. Although he and his gang were probably acting alone, many in the North believed that more senior figures were behind the assassination. Some pointed the finger at Jefferson Davis.

Thursday, April 27

Eastern Theater Jefferson Davis and the Confederate Cabinet head away from Charlotte. Their flight is not conducted at any great speed—no more than 12 to 15 miles a day. Five weak infantry brigades escort a lumbering wagon train, while Federal cavalry hover in the distance, observing the Confederates' progress.

Western Theater One of the riverboats carrying Union soldiers home from the Confederate prison camps suffers a catastrophic boiler explosion and sinks in the Mississippi River. Of the 2000-odd men aboard the *Sultana*, over 1200 are drowned.

Friday, April 28

The North Lincoln's funeral train reaches Cleveland, Ohio, where over 50,000 people pay him their last respects.

Eastern Theater Sherman's army marches toward Washington, intending to travel via Richmond.

Saturday, April 29

Far West Furious Indian reaction to Chivington's appalling massacre at Sand Creek was only blunted by the onset of the severe winter weather. As the prairie grass grows again in the spring, so the Indian ponies are once again ready for war. Large columns of Federal troops take the field in response. Today Brigadier-General James H. Ford leads 1200 cavalry against the tribes south of the Arkansas River, while a similar sized column passes north of the Black Hills in Dakota, bound for the Powder River. The Union commanders face a severe morale problem among many regiments; with the news of Lee's surrender, many volunteer soldiers demand demobilization.

Sunday, April 30

Western Theater Confederate commander Richard Taylor meets General Edward Canby near Mobile, Alabama, and agrees to a truce prior to the surrender of Confederate forces in Alabama and Mississippi.

Monday, May 1, 1865

The North President Johnson orders the appointment of nine army officers to form a military commission which will try the eight people accused of the Lincoln assassination conspiracy.

Tuesday, May 2

The North Falling prey to the hysteria sweeping the North in the wake of the assassination, President Johnson offers a reward of $100,000 for the capture of Jefferson Davis. He accuses the Confederate president of complicity in the plot.

Eastern Theater At Abbeville, South Carolina, Jefferson Davis calls a council of war with his five brigade commanders, plus Breckinridge and Bragg. He expresses his determination to continue the war, citing the way the American Revolution was saved by the steadfastness of a handful of patriots. He regards the few thousand troops remaining with him and the Cabinet as a nucleus around which the South will rally. But their commanders are under no such illusion. With deep reluctance, they tell Davis that their men are only soldiering on so their president can affect his escape. Neither Breckinridge nor Bragg intervene as they do not command the troops concerned, but afterward they express their support for the five officers. Further resistance is futile. The order to resume the retreat is issued during the evening. Brigadier-General Basil W. Duke supervises the transfer of the Confederate gold and silver reserve—half a million dollars in coin—from the railroad onto jealously guarded wagons.

Wednesday, May 3

The North President Lincoln's body arrives in Springfield, Illinois.

Eastern Theater Stephen Mallory resigns as secretary of the Confederate Navy. Judah Benjamin leaves Davis's party, escaping to Florida and thence to the Bahamas in an open boat. He will eventually reach Britain.

Thursday, May 4

The North President Lincoln is buried.

Western Theater At Citronelle, Alabama, General Richard Taylor surrenders 42,000 Confederates—the remaining forces in Alabama, Mississippi, and eastern Louisiana.

Trans-Mississippi Kirby Smith's Confederates are the last to remain in arms. There is a minor action near Lexington, Missouri.

Friday, May 5

Trans-Mississippi There is a skirmish in the Peche Hills, Missouri.

Saturday, May 6

Naval Operations The mighty ironclad ram CSS *Stonewall* arrives at Nassau *en route* for Havana after crossing the Atlantic.

Confederate Stonewall *was the only ironclad built in Europe to enter the Southern Navy. She briefly served the Confederacy before being laid up at Havana, Cuba. She went on to lead a varied career in the Japanese Navy until the 1880s.*

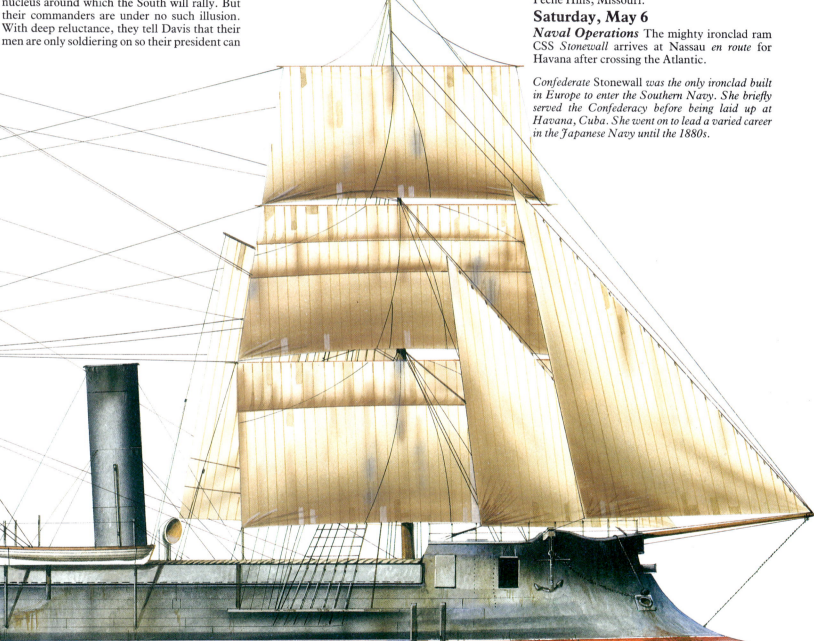

May 1865

Sunday, May 7, 1865

Western Theater Lieutenant-Colonel Benjamin Pritchard leads a detachment of his 4th Michigan Cavalry out from Macon, Georgia, as part of the continuing search for President Davis and the Confederate leadership. As the main Confederate armies surrender, so bands of troops all over the South quietly separate and go home.

Monday, May 8

Western Theater The Confederate soldiers under the command of General Richard Taylor come in to be paroled in Mississippi and Alabama. In the bitter fratricidal conflict in Missouri, there is another skirmish at Readsville.

Tuesday, May 9

Western Theater President Davis parts company from the five weak infantry brigades which have been accompanying him. The men are told they can go home but they initially separate in formed bodies, marching on divergent roads to confuse the Federal cavalry as to the whereabouts of the Confederate leaders. Davis now travels with a handful of picked cavalry with the declared intention of slipping across the south to the Trans-Mississippi theater. But he does not quicken his pace, resigned perhaps to capture now that the sands have run out for the Confederate States of America.

Wednesday, May 10

The North President Johnson proclaims that armed resistance "may be regarded as virtually at an end." He warns foreign powers against providing further assistance to those Confederate warships still on the open sea.

Western Theater Lieutenant-Colonel Pritchard's 4th Michigan Cavalry capture President Davis, his wife, and the few senior Confederate leaders remaining with him at Irwinsville, Georgia. General Breckinridge escapes with Colonel Wood, and they manage to reach Florida and sail to Cuba in an open boat. The fate of the Confederate president is open to much speculation, with many voices crying for a speedy trial and execution for treason.

After the fall of Mobile, CSS *Nashville, Morgan*, and some blockade runners retreated up the Tombighee River where they were soon sealed off by Federal warships. Union warships assembled for an attack by the Confederate flotilla commander, Captain Eben Farrand, who wrote Rear-Admiral Thater, USN, asking for terms. Today the surviving warships and their crews surrender at Nanna Hubba Bluff.

William C. Quantrill, one of the most notorious Confederate guerrilla leaders, is fatally wounded by Federal irregulars near Taylorsville, Kentucky. The 27-year-old ringleader will linger until June 6. His gang included Frank and Jesse James, plus Cole Younger.

Thursday, May 11

Trans-Mississippi General Jeff M. Thompson, renowned Confederate commander in Missouri and Arkansas, surrenders his brigade at Chalk Bluff, Arkansas.

Naval Operations The CSS *Stonewall* puts in at Havana, Cuba. The Confederates finally have a warship in American waters powerful enough to mount a serious attack on the US blockading squadrons. But she is too late.

Friday, May 12

The North The eight accused of the Lincoln assassination conspiracy all plead not guilty. This is probably a fair plea for Dr Mudd, who fixed Booth's leg, and Mrs Mary Surratt, who kept the boarding house where Booth stayed. But the others are whistling in the wind.

Far West A column of Union troops under Colonel Theodore H. Barrett captures a Confederate camp at Palmito Ranch on the bank of the Rio Grande. Confederate reinforcements arrive late in the afternoon, and the Federals withdraw during the evening.

The innovative Confederate semi-submersible torpedo boat David *lies forlornly aground at Charleston after the fall of the city to Union troops in February 1865.*

Imposing profile of the Confederate ironclad Nashville. *The massive paddle-boxes were 95 feet 6 inches across. Her construction was greatly delayed through lack of materials and part of her armor had to be taken from the worn-out* Baltic. *Even the engines were taken from abandoned steamers.* Nashville *was yet another example of what faced those trying to create a Southern Navy. Compare this with the building program of the North able to turn out many vessels of the same kind.*

Saturday, May 13

Trans-Mississippi Barrett's Federal force returns to the area of Palmito Ranch, Texas, where it is attacked by Confederates under Colonel John S. Ford. The Union troops are eventually compelled to withdraw, making the last significant land action a Confederate victory.

General Edmund Kirby Smith meets with the Confederate governors of Arkansas, Louisiana, and Mississippi at Marshall, Texas. They advise him to surrender under terms they have drawn up. Jo Shelby threatens to arrest his commander unless Kirby Smith agrees to continue the war.

Sunday, May 14

Western Theater Minor skirmishes continue to take place in Missouri. The irregular forces of either side have fought a bitter war; even where a Confederate band elected to give up the fight, there was deep reluctance to surrender to similar outfits loyal to the Union. This was not the relatively mannered, regular warfare of the main armies. The "rules of war" had seldom been observed in nearly five years of savage guerrilla warfare.

This famous view of Harper's Ferry was taken in July 1865 and the view has changed remarkably little since. Note how the bridges are dominated by the surrounding heights, the key to the series of actions which took place here.

Wednesday, May 17

The North Major-General Philip H. Sheridan is relieved of his command of the Middle Military Division and assigned command of US forces west of the Mississippi. Grant directs his ruthless subordinate to "restore Texas and that part of Louisiana, held by the enemy, to the Union in the shortest practical time." He will command some 25,000 troops: 12,000 men under Reynolds in Arkansas; IV Corps at Nashville; and XXV Corps currently at City Point, Virginia, ready to embark. Meeting with Grant, Sheridan is given additional verbal instructions. There is another objective in dispatching such an overwhelming force into Texas—to overawe the imperial regime in Mexico. Still locked in battle with Juarez's republicans and innumerable guerrilla bands, Maximilian's monarchy staggers on, propped up by French soldiers longing to escape this dreadful war. Grant tells Sheridan he wants to topple the imperial regime directly, but that he must act with caution since Secretary of State Seward is opposed to any action that could lead to conflict with France.

Naval Operations Also in Havana, Cuba, Captain C.S. Boggs of the USS *Connecticut* writes Captain Page of the *Stonewall*. He informs the Confederate captain that all states east of the Mississippi are now in Union hands and that President Davis is a fugitive. With hostilities all but over, further action against US forces by the *Stonewall* are not only futile but would probably leave Page and his crew open to the direst penalties when eventually cornered.

Friday, May 19

Naval Operations With the heartbreaking news of the fall of the Confederacy confirmed, Captain Page surrenders the ironclad *Stonewall Jackson* to the Spanish authorities in Havana. The Confederate account opened in Ferrol, Spain, had gone dry and Page arranges to sell the warship to the captain-general of Cuba in return for enough money to pay off his crew.

Saturday, May 20

Naval Operations Secretary Welles appoints a board headed by Vice-Admiral Farragut to produce a comprehensive review of the Naval Academy which had been badly disrupted by the war. The results were to produce some of the nation's greatest leaders.

Fort Sumter, pictured from a sandbar in Charleston Harbor after two years of Federal bombardment. The failure of their landing on the fort discouraged Union forces from further attempts at seizing the position, and they endeavored to subdue the fort by shelling alone.

May–June 1865

Sunday, May 21, 1865

Naval Operations Shenandoah enters the cold waters of the Sea of Okhotsk prior to running along the Kamchatka coast in search of Northern whalers.

Monday, May 22

The North President Johnson declares that from July 1 all trade restrictions with Southern ports will be lifted, except for four in Texas: Galveston, La Salle, Brazos Santiago, and Brownsville. President Davis is imprisoned at Fort Monroe, Virginia, and held in irons by order of General Nelson A. Miles after he had thrown his rations in the face of the corporal delivering them.

Tuesday, May 23

The North The Army of the Potomac marches through Washington in triumph. Cheering crowds line the streets and flags fly at full mast for the first time in four years. From its uncertain beginnings and the long years of depressing failure, the army of McClellan, Burnside, and Hooker was now the victorious army of George Meade and U.S. Grant. On this very day, the pro-Union government in Virginia is established in the former Confederate capital at Richmond.

Wednesday, May 24

The North Washington continues with the parade. Today is the turn of Sherman's army from the west, its slack drill and casual uniforms in vivid contrast to the smart precision of the Army of the Potomac. Sherman's men march with their pack mules and loot, and are even followed by some of the Negro refugees who had attached themselves to his army during its last campaign. At the reviewing stand Sherman shakes hands with President Johnson but cuts dead Secretary of War Stanton who had led the attack on the original peace terms offered to General Johnston.

Thursday, May 25

Western Theater A warehouse containing 20 tons of gunpowder captured from the Confederates explodes in Mobile, Alabama. Some 300 casualties are reported and extensive damage is caused to the dockyard area.

Friday, May 26

Trans-Mississippi General Simon B. Buckner, acting for General E. Kirby Smith, meets with Federal Major-General Peter J. Osterhaus in New Orleans to discuss surrender terms for the Confederate forces west of the Mississippi.

Saturday, May 27

The North President Johnson orders the release of most people held in prison by Federal military authorities.

Monday, May 29

The North President Johnson grants a general amnesty for all those who participated in the rebellion. All property rights are restored, except for slave ownership. There are a number of exceptions to the amnesty: senior political leaders and military officers, and people with over $20,000 of taxable income or who had left US military or judicial posts to join the Confederacy. All such persons must apply individually

to the president for a pardon, but Johnson will be very liberal in granting them; by the summer he will be issuing an average of 100 per day. Some 13,000 are granted by the end of the year.

Above: *Cannon barrels and ammunition lie abandoned before the ruins of Richmond around the Capitol. Confederates fired the supplies they could not evacuate, looters did some burning of their own, and the result was a good deal of damage of the former Confederate capital.*

Giant Union monitor Dictator *highlights the tremendous strides made by the North when this 4438-ton monster is compared to the Confederate vessel on the previous page. Dictator was a formidable ocean-going vessel considered able to match the warships of Europe.*

Left: *Spring leaves appear on the trees next to the US Sanitary Commission established in Richmond after the occupation. Soldiers would continue to die of disease, despite the guns falling silent.*

Friday, June 2, 1865

Trans-Mississippi General E. Kirby Smith surrenders the Confederate forces west of the Mississippi under terms similar to those offered to Lee at Appomattox. Eventually, some 17,600 of his men will be paroled, but others led by Jo Shelby refuse to surrender and head south toward Mexico. Others simply disperse to their homes.
Great Britain The British Government withdraws belligerent rights from the Confederacy.

Saturday, June 3

Trans-Mississippi Confederate forces on the Red River, including the ironclad *Missouri*, surrender.

Thursday, June 8

The North The Federal VI Corps, which had not been able to join the previous grand parades in Washington, has its own review in Washington.

Sunday, June 11

Far West The news of the Sand Creek massacre reached the Sioux and Cheyenne wintering around the headwaters of the Powder River in March. There was no doubt about their immediate hostility but the attitude of the 2000 or so "friendly" Indians near Fort Laramie remained unknown. By order of Secretary of War Stanton, they were regarded as prisoners and were being shepherded toward Fort Kearny when rival Indian factions came to blows. Captain William D. Fouts, commanding the 135-strong escort from the 7th Iowa, intervened and was shot dead. His men were then engaged in a running battle, as the Indian braves covered the retreat of their families and the whole mass of Indians fled for the Platte River.

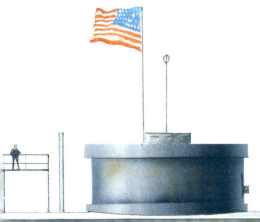

Saturday, June 17

Far West Colonel Thomas Moonlight led 234 California, Kansas, and Ohio cavalrymen from Fort Laramie to pursue the Indians on the very afternoon of the fight. During the week nearly half his command turned back with broken horses, but after 120 miles he found his foe—or rather, they found him. Some 200 Sioux warriors surprised the US camp at breakfast and ran off all the horses. The unfortunate soldiers were forced to burn their saddles and return on foot. Many of the Indians journeyed to the Powder River country, joining the hostile bands, but others eventually drifted back.

Thursday, June 22

Naval Operations The commerce raider CSS *Shenandoah*, unaware of the collapse of the Confederacy, attacks the Federal whaling fleet in the Bering Sea, capturing two whalers. A former British transport bought secretly in England, the *Shenandoah* had sailed on October 8, 1864, and reached Australia by January, capturing several US merchantmen *en route*. Captained by James I. Waddell of North Carolina—a tough officer who still limped from an old duelling wound—the *Shenandoah* was not designed for Arctic waters and it was a bold decision to brave the ice her hull could not withstand. Papers on one of his prizes tell of Lee's surrender at Appomattox, but mention President Davis's continued resistance. Waddell steers north through Arctic fog, seeking the bulk of the New England whaling fleet.

Friday, June 23

The North President Johnson declares the blockade of Southern ports lifted. The stranglehold established by the US Navy played a crucial role in the war. With its poor manufacturing base, the South urgently needed weapons from abroad at the beginning of the conflict. As the war dragged on, so the vastly superior industrial resources of the North made a Confederate military all but impossible. Union warships frustrated the export of cotton, blocking vital foreign earnings, and severely restricted the import of military supplies. The US Navy began the war with some 90 warships, only a third of which were modern vessels, and employed fewer than 8000 officers and men. By 1865, over 50,000 men were serving in a fleet of over 600 vessels. At the beginning of the year, before the blockading operations were scaled down, 471 warships were patrolling the Confederate coastline.

Top: *The McLean house at Appomattox was ransacked by relic-hunters after Grant and Lee signed the surrender terms. It was a cruel irony for Mr McLean whose last farm was ruined by the battle of Bull Run. He moved here to be away from the fighting!*

Above: *Robert E. Lee photographed by Matthew Brady in April 1865. One of the most charismatic generals in history, his achievement in defending Virginia against such odds for so long remains a remarkable triumph.*

July–December 1865

July 1865

The North On July 7 four of the Lincoln conspirators are hanged. Lewis Payne, George Atzerodt, David Herold, and Mary Surratt walk to the gallows in the Old Penitentiary, Washington, DC. There was considerable protest about the execution of Mrs Surratt, who merely kept the boarding house where Booth and his henchmen planned their attack. But President Johnson was not about to pardon anyone connected with Lincoln's murder. The other four conspirators are imprisoned at Fort Jefferson on Dry Tortugas off Key West, Florida. Michael O'Laughlin dies of yellow fever in 1867, Dr Mudd is pardoned a year later for his work during the epidemic, and Edward Spangler and Samuel Arnold are pardoned in 1869.

Far West Indian war parties had been cutting the telegraph to Fort Laramie and sniping at detachments throughout May and June. The botched attempt to herd the neutral Indians near Laramie away from trouble helped persuade the chiefs to agree on a major onslaught. In May and June a huge concentration of lodges spread along the Powder River and the sheer effort in killing enough buffalo to support this gathering had interrupted plans for a united attack.

The Indian assault took place on July 26 at Platte Bridge Station, a small post held by 96 officers and men under Major Martin Anderson. A train of five empty wagons was coming in and Anderson dispatched 20 men under Lieutenant Collins to support the 25-man escort. Half a mile from the stockade, the Indians spring their trap: up to 3000 Sioux, Cheyenne, and Arapaho warriors engulf them. Collins is shot through the head with an arrow, four of his men are killed, and the rest wounded as they shoot their way back to the fort. In the desperate melee the revolvers of the cavalrymen prove vastly more effective than a tomahawk. But the approaching wagon train, commanded by Sergeant Amos Custard, is surrounded by the warriors. Coralling the wagons, Custard and his men hold out for four hours before they are overwhelmed, killed, and mutilated. Satisfied that they had made their point, the great Indian gathering begins to disperse.

August 1865

Naval Operations On August 2 the CSS *Shenandoah* learns that the war is truly over when she hails a British ship two weeks out of San Francisco. Captain Waddell reluctantly ships his guns below, figuring it would be better to surrender a defenseless ship to the British courts, for he had no intention of handing himself or his crew over to Yankee justice. Keeping out of sight of land, the *Shenandoah* begins her 17,000-mile journey home to England.

Mexico Jo Shelby leads 1000 Confederate veterans into Mexico City to offer their services to Emperor Maximilian. The embattled Austrian ruler has enough trouble relying on French and other European troops to fight the Republicans and other guerrilla groups. To his dwindling number of Mexican supporters, reliance on Americans would be the last straw. But Maximilian and his wife are quite taken with the Confederates and provide land for them to settle.

Far West Brigadier-General Patrick E. Connor organizes three columns to sweep around the Black Hills where Sioux Indians, previously thought to be peaceful, were now assembling and donning war paint. The "right" column of 1400 men was to probe around the north of the Black Hills, while the "left," under Connor, marched up the Bozeman Trail from Laramie. The "center" column was to skirt the Black Hills from the west and link up with the others on Rosebud Creek, a tributary of the Yellowstone, on September 1.

September 1865

Trans-Mississippi The Cherokees, Creeks, Choctaws, Chickasaws, Osages, Seminoles, Senacas, Shawnees, and Quapaws sign a treaty of loyalty to the United States and renounce their previous commitment to the Confederacy.

Far West Not until September 11 did Brigadier-General Connor discover the fate of his other two columns. Beset by hit-and-run guerrilla attacks and weakened by scurvy which swept the ranks as rations ran low, their progress had been far slower than planned. The weather worsened, the first storms of the fall sweeping across the badlands and killing half their horses and mules in a single night. With the Indians still hovering around, they finally unite at Fort Connor on September 24.

By the end of the summer it was obvious that the army's operations on the frontier were an expensive failure. In addition to Connor's three columns, other forces had marched up the Missouri, along the Arkansas against the southern plains tribes, and a small force had scouted up the Republican River. Over 6000 troops had campaigned all summer at enormous cost, and they had killed fewer than 100 Indians. Morale among the soldiers was very low indeed; one of Connor's columns was only engaged on the march at gunpoint, while cavalry from Kansas were near the end of their enlistment and saw no reason to go fighting Indians now. Many of the volunteers were "Galvanized Yankees"—Confederate prisoners of war who had agreed to fight on the frontier rather than languish in jail. Planning for operations was frustrated as regiment after regiment came west, only to muster out within months or even weeks.

October 1865

The North On October 11 President Johnson paroles former Confederate vice-president Stephens and several members of Jefferson Davis's Cabinet.

Mexico On October 3 Maximilian announces the "Black Decree." Believing that Juarez had fled across the Rio Grande, he proclaims that the Republican forces have ceased to exist and any further action against his government will be regarded as criminal, punishable by death. In fact, Juarez never leaves the country, although his officers attend festivities organized by Sheridan's command.

Jamaica Free blacks riot on the British island of Jamaica, killing 21 people before British soldiers quell the disturbance. Southern fears about their own black population are increased when the news reaches America.

Far West Peace is established on the southern plains in treaties signed on the Little Arkansas on October 12 and 24. The Cheyenne, Arapaho, Kiowa, Kiowa-Apache, and Commanche tribes accept annual annuities in exchange for withdrawing to areas south of Kansas and east of New Mexico. The Cheyenne and Arapaho received extra payment—blood money for the "gross and wanton outrages" perpetrated by Chivington and his men.

November 1865

The North Only one man was branded a "war criminal" after the end of the Civil War—the Swiss-born Captain Henry Wirz, who had commanded the infamous prison camp at Andersonville, Georgia. Convicted of cruelty to prisoners of war by a military commission, he is hanged in the Old Capitol prison yard. The hangman had evidently not calculated the drop to kill him quickly; Wirz took over seven minutes to die.

Wirz's execution makes the name Andersonville synonymous with grim prisoner-of-war camps, but Andersonville was only in operation from February 1864, and the conditions at Union prisons like Camp Douglas, Chicago, or Johnson's Island on Lake Erie, were hardly pleasant. Federal records show that 211,000 US troops were captured, of whom 16,000 were paroled, and 30,000 died in captivity. Some 460,000 Confederates surrendered during the war; 247,000 were paroled and 26,000 died in prison. Thus the mortality rates were not vastly different—12 percent against 15 percent.

The South Mississippi adopts a series of laws regulating vagrancy and labor service. It is the first of a succession of Southern states to pass discriminatory laws intended to keep the freed black population firmly under white control. By continuing to oppose reform, these die-hard state adminstrations play into the hands of Northern radicals who are determined to see the Negro placed on an even legal footing.

December 1865

North Carolina, Georgia, and Oregon all approve the Thirteenth Amendment, although Mississippi rejects it. Oregon's decision on December 11 enables Secretary of State Seward to declare a week later that the Thirteenth Amendment is now in effect since it has been approved by 27 states.

Above right: *It fell to Major-General John B. Gordon to lead the last parade of the Army of Northern Virginia. On April 12 the colors of the Confederate regiments were laid to the ground before Union troops at Appomattox Court House. Gordon's gargantuan beard conceals a relatively young man: he was only 33 in 1865. He later became a champion of reconstruction, serving as Georgia's governor and three terms as a senator.*

Left: *The infamous box at Ford's Theater where John Wilkes Booth shot President Lincoln. The killing took place just five days after the surrender of Lee's army: a disaster not just for the Union, but for the Confederate States as well. Lincoln wanted a peace of reconciliation; his murder created a mood of vengeance instead.*

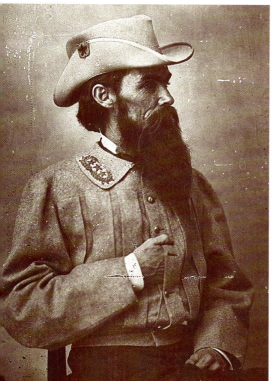

Above: *The execution of the Lincoln conspirators in the Old Penitentiary, Washington, D.C., July 7, 1865. President Johnson was in no mood to grant clemency and refused the many appeals against the hanging of Mrs. Surratt whose only crime was owning the lodging house where Wilkes had stayed.*

Left: *Major-General John Pope, relieved of his command in 1862 after Second Bull Run, was still in the field long after his former comrades had finished their war. Posted to the newly created Department of the Northwest, he oversaw the campaigns against the Sioux from 1862 to 1864. He clashed with the War Department in 1865, determined to impose tough treaties by force rather than relax military action as the volunteer regiments mustered out.*

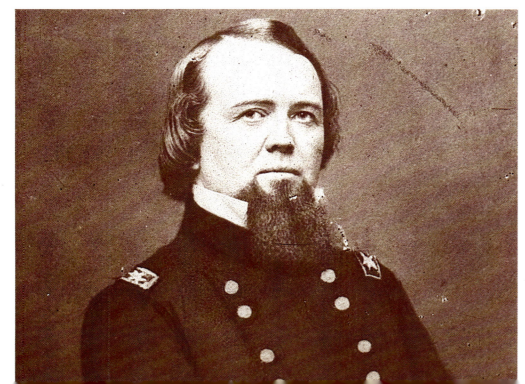

241

1866–1870 The South. Losing the Peace

With the exception of Texas, which had not been invaded until the end of the war, the Confederate States were in ruins. Where the armies of Sherman or Sheridan had passed, the destruction surpassed the damage that would be inflicted on Central Europe by 1945. Factories were burned-out shells, railroads pulled up, and bridges pulled down. South Carolina had been the third wealthiest state in the Union in 1860; ten years later she languished in fortieth place. From the total white population of the South—some 8 million people—nearly 750,000 had marched off to war. Over a third failed to return; the Confederates' battlefield losses are estimated at 94,000, while 164,000 died of disease.

The planter aristocracy lost control of the rural South. In fact, the "poor white trash" which seized and looted many estates probably did as much damage as the Union armies, before venting their spleen on the black population. No one had any money—least of all Southern banks. Many returning Confederate officers found nothing to come home to. A few went south to Mexico, others moved North. Baltimore became notorious for its concentration of ex-Confederate businessmen and professionals who had abandoned their ruined homeland.

Congress extended the powers of the Freedmens' Bureau in February 1866. Radical Republicans were determined that the civil liberties of the Negro would not be blocked by Southern obstruction. Yet that is exactly what proceeded to happen. Blacks were not yet entitled to vote; Southern state governments proceeded with the assumption that they never would be. Robert E. Lee, Wade Hampton, and former Confederate vice-president Stephens all spoke out against the prevailing climate of racial prejudice, urging that the vote be given to the property-owning blacks on the same basis as it was to whites. But their words fell on deaf ears. The middle- and lower-class whites were determined not to give an inch, and the new state governments responded with a series of discriminatory laws. The majority of the white population of the lower South was vehemently opposed to living on equal terms with a free black population. It would take over 100 years for this resistance to begin to weaken.

The evident defiance of the South played into the hands of the radical Republicans, who won sweeping victories in the elections of 1866. In March 1867 Congress imposed military rule. The South was divided into five military districts presided over by US generals Schofield, Thomas, Ord, Sickles, and Sheridan. Confederate veterans' organizations were banned, military tribunals replaced civil courts, and an army of occupation backed up the new regime with its bayonets.

The military governors began to register voters to elect conventions which would draft new constitutions. They excluded many former Confederate leaders and included blacks, which led to whites boycotting the subsequent elections. Anger mounted—against the Republicans and the blacks, and against two further groups. "Carpetbaggers" were Yankee adventurers, supposedly with their original possessions kept in a satchel made from two squares of carpet. According to Southern mythology they descended on the defeated land to loot, aided and abetted by "Scalawags"—Southerners who joined the Republicans, like former General Longstreet who worked to moderate the radicals' thirst for vengeance.

The new state conventions and legislatures included a black element. While some colored office-holders lived down to the worst expectations of the white opposition, and became tools in the hands of profiteers, they were a varied lot. In South Carolina, the only state ever to have a black majority in either house, their number included Robert B. Elliott, an old Etonian.

The radical Republican regimes imposed on the Southern states were a disaster. Although roads and bridges were repaired and free education provided for children of all races, corruption became endemic. Governor Warmouth's theft of $500,000 from state school funds in Louisiana set the pace. The poorer members of the white community directed their hate at the blacks and their newly imported teachers who found their schools burned down. The Ku Klux Klan was not the only paramilitary organization to materialize—but with Bedford Forrest as "Grand Wizard" and General Gordon as "Grand Dragon" in Georgia, it became the best-known force behind the "Invisible Empire of the South."

The landed gentry had its own ax to grind. The Carpetbagger regimes imposed high tariffs and tough taxation on real estate. Farms were first mortgaged, then sold to pay the taxes. Making common cause, the Southern leadership began to eject the new state governments, with the KKK orchestrating a campaign of violent intimidation against Republicans and blacks. Between 1869 and 1871, Tennessee, Virginia, North Carolina, and Georgia were all recaptured.

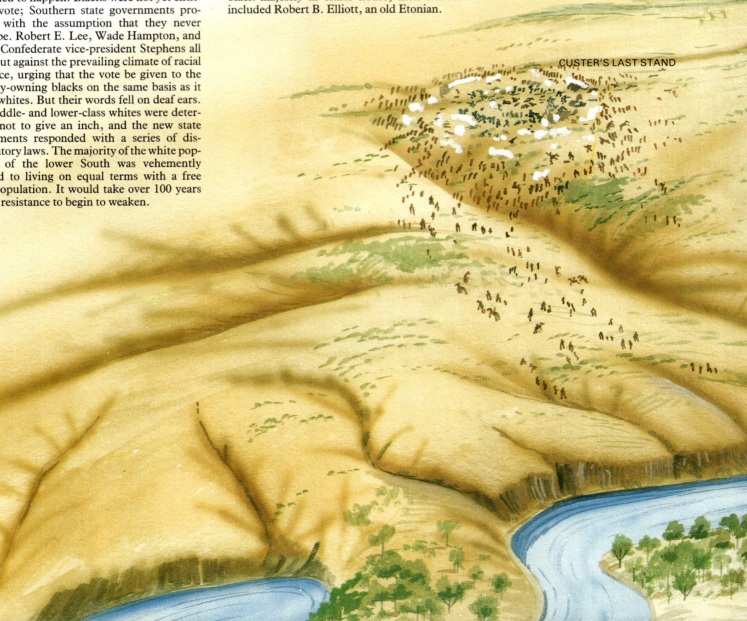

CUSTER'S LAST STAND

The Battle for the Presidency: Johnson and Grant, 1866–70

The congressional elections of 1866 pitted a Democratic president against the power of radical Republicanism. Johnson needed to fight an outstanding campaign to stave off defeat, but he failed miserably, and the Republicans swept back in triumph with a large enough majority to override the presidential veto.

The South must bear some of the responsibility for the vindictive mood of the congress in 1867. But in addition to imposing military rule on the former rebel states, the Republicans foisted on the president the Tenure of Office Act. This required Senatorial consent to removals as well as appointments. Johnson regarded this as unconstitutional and fired Secretary Stanton, who refused to leave the War Department. The Republicans countered by impeaching the president.

The impeachment was managed by a committee led by Benjamin Butler, and it resorted to every procedural device, bullying tactic, and cheap propaganda trick Butler's fulsome imagination could devise. Johnson escaped by a single vote.

Johnson was abandoned by the Democrats, who selected Horatio Seymour, wartime governor of New York, as their candidate, while the Republicans fielded none other than General U.S. Grant. Even with three Southern states not voting, Grant only won by a plurality of 300,000. His move to Washington would be, arguably, the worst of his career.

Death of an Emperor: Mexico, 1865–67

The French intervention in Mexico would never have been possible without the Civil War. Yet by the time the US Army was ready to oppose the French presence, Emperor Napoleon III had already abandoned his Mexican adventure. Four years of bitter guerrilla war had eaten into the French treasury and led to mounting political opposition in Paris. Emperor Maximilian wrote President Johnson soon after his inauguration, emphasizing that his regime has "not intended to be an empire on the European model, but a state of freedom and progress, and the home of most liberal institutions." But the president refused to accept the letter.

The US Army demonstrated American opposition to Maximilian before the administration. Major-General Sheridan missed the Army of the Potomac's victory parade to take over US forces in Texas. He concentrated large elements of his command along the Rio Grande and made no secret of the army's enthusiasm to cross the river in pursuit of some of their old enemies. A number of senior Confederate leaders—notably John Magruder, Jubal Early, Jo Shelby, Matthew Maury, and Edmund Kirby Smith—had sought refuge with the imperial regime. On half a million acres confiscated from the Church near Cordoba, a large number of Confederate exiles created the "Carlota Colony" named after Maximilian's empress.

Sheridan's demonstrations on the frontier gave heart to Juarez and his followers who had retreated to northern Mexico. He met the leader of the regime still recognized as the legitimate government by the USA, and openly supplied them with arms. During the winter of 1865–66, 30,000 muskets were supplied from the Baton Rouge arsenal alone. General Schofield, who coveted Sheridan's command and wished to lead an invasion, was sent instead to Paris. Secretary of State Seward told him to make US policy crystal clear: "Get your legs under Napoleon's mahogany and tell him to get out of Mexico." The Emperor of Austria was informed that a proposed shipment of 2000 troops to Mexico would mean war between the Hapsburg Empire and the United States. The troop ships stayed in port.

Marshal Bazaine, commander of the French troops in Mexico, was ordered to evacuate in early 1866. Remaining Belgian and Austrian contingents began to withdraw too, but Maximilian chose to battle on. Throughout 1866, the Republican forces closed on the center: Juarez's men from the north and Porfirio Diaz from the south. Much of Mexico remained in a state of savage anarchy.

In August Carlota fled to France, pleaded unsuccessfully with Napoleon, fell on her knees before the Pope, and had a nervous breakdown. She lived on until 1925 but never recovered her mental health. The French forces departed on February 5, 1867; Maximilian abandoned Mexico City a week later. His ragtag army marched to Queretaro, where it was besieged, and surprised most observers by holding out until May 15. Held to account for four years of bloody civil war, the unhappy emperor was executed by firing squad on June 19, 1867.

A Pact with the Devil: The US Army, 1865–70

To observers in Europe the immense strength of the Union Army at the end of the war was a source of considerable anxiety. The Federal forces had a million men in the field—more than enough to turn the French out of Mexico and the British out of North America. But despite the formidable military capability of the US armed forces, it was not to be the instrument of a new, aggressive foreign policy. Although Seward and Stanton both espoused Ben Franklin's view of the "unnatural division" of North America, there was little support for such intervention. The volunteer armies had done their job; now they were going home. By November 1865, army strength was already down to 183,000.

Rapid demobilization suited the volunteers, but career officers were soon engaged in heated debate over the ultimate size of the post-war army. They eventually made a pact with the Republicans: the army would not return to pre-war strength; instead of the 30 regiments of 1860, the new army of 1866 would field 60. In exchange, the army would provide about a third of its men to enforce Republican reconstruction policy in the South. This policing role practically became the army's primary task. Texas had one of the longest frontiers to be guarded, but between 1866 and 1870 there were always more troops deployed on internal policing than against the Indians or along the Mexican frontier.

Defeat at the Little Big Horn

The Army's campaigns against the Plains Indians were conducted on a shoestring budget after the Civil War. Only the icy shock of Custer's defeat temporarily loosened the pursestrings. Custer, the flamboyant "boy general" of 1864–65, had fought on the frontier with considerable success. Yet he became one of the most notorious American commanders of all time by his decision on June 25, 1876. After a long march, he attacked an Indian force of unknown size with exhausted men and horses. He split his command to attack from several directions at once, and paid the ultimate price. He, and every one of the 215 troopers with him, died in an hour of close-quarter fighting against up to 3000 Indians. The other half of his men were besieged on a hilltop for two days. In Custer's defense, experience had taught US commanders that only an immediate attack, preferably from several directions, could overrun an Indian camp before the ever-elusive enemy broke contact and vanished. American forces normally had great difficulty in bringing the Indians to battle; no one was prepared for the new-found resolution of Sitting Bull's tribal alliance that fateful summer.

1870–1880 Reconstruction Abandoned

President Grant's administration was soon marred by a series of financial scandals, and his choice of Cabinet appointments proved unfortunate. Grant rewarded his friends—hardly a unique feature of the presidency—but few of them proved fit for high public office. The close involvement of corrupt New York financiers became a running sore that the Democratic opposition worried at for four years. Failure to take action against the bloated Civil Service or reduce the wartime customs duties further demonstrated Grant's weakness as president.

The one success of his first presidency was the settlement of the *Alabama* claims. Semmes' famous cruiser, and those other British-built warships CSS *Florida* and *Shenandoah*, had inflicted colossal damage on the US merchant marine. The British government had only belatedly imposed restrictions on private companies building warships for the Confederacy, and to many American observers this looked suspiciously like collusion. But despite hotheads on either side, Sir John Rose, the Canadian finance minister, and Secretary Hamilton Fish agreed to submit the US compensation claims to an international tribunal. This opened at Geneva in December 1871 and eventually awarded $15.5 million to the US for the depredations of the Confederate cruisers. The British acceptance of the verdict smoothed Anglo–American relations, which had been rocky since the beginning of the war.

Opposition to Grant within the Republican Party led to a liberal Republican convention assembling in May 1872. Salmon P. Chase and Charles Francis Adams fought for the nomination on a platform which included Civil Service reform, withdrawal of the garrisons from the South, and a resumption of payments in coin. But the delegates eventually opted for Horace Greeley. As editor of the *New York Tribune* for 30 years, Greeley had clashed with Grant during and after the war. But the election pitted a controversial journalist against the nation's leading soldier: Grant won all but six states, winning the popular vote 3.6 million to 2.8 million.

Unfortunately, the president's re-election did not mean a change of direction for his administration. Corruption became endemic: the Union Pacific Railroad showered influential congressmen with stock; treasury officials were caught in a whiskey ring based in St Louis—an operation which had defrauded the treasury of millions of dollars' tax; and the navy yards became notoriously corrupt (the yacht *America* was refitted at taxpayer's expense for the personal use of Ben Butler).

Corruption in the administration reflected a general problem throughout the Northern states. The thriving business world expanded rapidly, but with a good deal of sharp practice along the way. "Boss" Tweed and his associates relieved New York City of an estimated $100 million; Jim Fisk and Jay Gould forced the treasury to release $4 million in gold to prevent them cornering the market. They were later involved in stockwatering on the Erie Railroad.

Cornelius Vanderbilt did the same for the New York Central. Collis P. Huntingdon effectively bought the entire California legislature for Transcontinental Railroad interests. John D. Rockefeller built Standard Oil by means which shocked even the most blasé observers.

Frenzied stock speculation and the overrapid expansion of the agricultural west coincided with a worldwide drop in demand to produce economic panic in 1873. It was the beginning of a three-year depression and marked the doom of the reconstruction program. In the elections of 1874 the Democrats captured the House of Representatives and they used their new-found strength to dig up scandal after scandal in Grant's administration.

The Stolen Election: 1876

The Republicans nominated Rutherford B. Hayes, an eminently respectable lawyer who had served three terms as governor of Ohio. But the odds against a Republican victory seemed long indeed. The Democrats chose Governor Samuel J. Tilden who had played a leading role in exposing Republican corruption. Fortunately for Hayes, Tilden was a rather reluctant candidate, and his lackluster campaign failed to capitalize on the Republicans' dismal record. Both sides charged and counter-charged in one of the dirtiest election campaigns in US history. The Republicans countered the corruption scandals with an orgy of flag-waving patriotism, reminding the electors that "every man that shot a Union soldier was a Democrat."

Tilden won the election, securing 184 electoral votes. But Oregon, South Carolina, Florida, and Louisiana returned two sets of votes. The Southern states, still under carpetbag rule, had thrown out thousands of Democratic votes on grounds of fraud or intimidation. An electoral commission was dispatched to investigate. Instead, the eight Republicans and five Democrats did a deal with Southern Democratic leaders: in return for letting Hayes win, the Republicans agreed to withdraw Federal troops and look the other way if the Fifteenth Amendment was not enforced. On March 2, 1877, the commission voted to disregard the Democratic returns from the disputed states, giving Rutherford Hayes 185 electoral votes.

Hayes did act against some of the worst of Johnson's and Grant's appointees, and his own choice of Cabinet proved highly successful. In accordance with the deal, Hayes removed Federal troops from Louisiana, paving the way for conservative victory over the Republican regime. Former Confederate General Wade Hampton had locked horns with General Daniel Chamberlain, US Army, in the South Carolina elections. Hayes resolved the impasse in Hampton's favor. With the exception of Texas, the former Confederate states were all back under the control of the old officer class.

The Battle for the Plains: The Army and the Indian, 1868–77

The US population doubled from 31 million in 1860 to 62 million by 1890. By 1910 it would reach 92 million. Although most of the new immigration and population growth was concentrated in the North, the consequences for the American frontier were equally dramatic. In the 50 years after the Civil War, the white population west of the Mississippi rose from 6 to 26 million. Expansion on the western frontier was rapid: the population increasing from 6 to 7 million between 1860 and 1870 and to 8½ million a decade later. Standing squarely in the way were the Indian tribes of the Great Plains.

In 1866 the US Government estimated the number of Indians in the American west at approximately 270,000. Some, like the Crows in Montana, had made their peace with the white man; others, like the Navaho in Arizona, had already fought and lost. Indian opposition to this tidal wave of white migration was probably limited to fewer than 100,000 individuals. On the Great Plains, the Sioux, Cheyenne, Arapaho, Commanche, and Kiowa were the most conspicuous opponents of white settlement. In the southwest the Apache tribes were not about to surrender lightly. Nez Percé, Bannock, and Ute Indians occupied the Rocky Mountains, while Modoc and Paiute still held the northwest.

The Indian tribes were as culturally diverse as the Russian, Irish, Greek, and Italian immigrants arriving at New York. Intertribal feuds continued to sap the Indians' military potential, which was fatally undermined by their ultrademocratic society. Often described as "the finest light cavalrymen in the world," their strength lay only in individual combat. Their warrior society, organized for war and exulting in martial prowess, was tailored only to semi-ritual tribal conflict.

As the expanding white population began to encroach on the Indian lands, there was no increase in US military strength to match. On the contrary, the strength of the army actually declined: from 54,000 officers and men in 1868, it fell to 37,000 by 1869. By 1874 it was down to 27,000. Between 1869 and 1872 the officer corps was slashed by one-third, and many of the newly appointed officers were civilians rather than West Pointers. Political patronage continued to dictate many military appointments. The army had gained its extra strength after the war by becoming the instrument of reconstruction. But with Grant in the White House and Republican domination in Congress, the politicians were now reluctant to fund a substantial military establishment.

Given its reduced size, the army was anything but the cutting edge of white expansion in the west. While it became the most conspicuous agent of destruction, fighting some 200 actions against the Indians between 1869 and 1876, it was not the only one. The great railroads spreading across the plains, the waves of miners and settlers, the incredibly rapid annihilation of the buffalo, and the debilitating effects of white man's diseases combined to doom the Indians to defeat.

War on the Plains

The post-war Indian wars began, ironically, with one of the few Indian victories of the nineteenth century. The Oglala Sioux chief, Red Cloud, successfully defeated the army's attempts to hold a line of forts along the Bozeman Trail—the route between the Oregon Trail and the newly discovered mines in Montana. On December 21, 1866, Captain William Fetterman, who once boasted he could destroy the Sioux nation with 80 men, was led into an ambush by a young chief called Crazy Horse. In less than an hour, Fetterman and 80 men lay mutilated in the snow outside Fort Phil Kearny in the Rockies. A series of fights in 1867 showed that while the army could control the trail by pouring troops into the field, the route remained closed to civilians. During the year Congress created the Indian Peace Commission to end the fighting, and do away with the frantic treaty-making which had already created 370 paper peace treaties. To the chagrin of the frontier officers, Congress conceded to Red Cloud's demands. Forts Kearny and Smith were abandoned and burned by celebrating Sioux warriors.

On the Southern plains, the Cheyenne were less disposed to make any sort of peace. In the fall in 1868 Sheridan oversaw the deployment of three columns to attack the Indians in revenge for a series of raids during the summer. Winter deprived the Indians of their mobility; their villages presented a static target and their horses were thin and weak. On November 27, Lieutenant-Colonel George A. Custer led his 7th Cavalry against the hapless chief Black Kettle, who had survived the Chivington massacre four years earlier. He had tried to negotiate a surrender at Fort Cobb only days before, but was killed in the attack. The village of some 50 Cheyenne lodges was overrun and their pony herd slaughtered by the cavalrymen.

The discovery of gold in the Black Hills of South Dakota doomed the Sioux to a last fight with the white man. They fought the prospectors during 1875 and inevitably faced the army the next year. In an action bearing certain similarities with his attack on the Washita, Custer once again force-marched deep into hostile territory and attacked the Indian village without delay—or reconnaissance. But this time he faced almost the entire Sioux nation: he and half the column under his command were killed in what became the most famous fight of the Indian wars. Subsequent US action forced many Sioux to accept peace, although Sitting Bull led a large number of his followers over the Canadian border in early 1877. By the summer, the last great concentration of Indian tribal strength had been dispersed.

US naval forces launch an attack upon Korean forts at the mouth of the river below Seoul in June 1871. This came about because of Koreans firing upon a party surveying the area. In spite of having only obsolete weapons, the Koreans remained at their posts in the forts and sustained many casualties.

PRIMANQUET BANKS

US ASIATIC FLEET

MARINE REDOUBT

MUD FLATS

US FORCE LANDING

245

1880s Awakening World Power

Death of a President: The Garfield–Arthur Administration

Rutherford Hayes refused to run for re-election in 1880, leaving the field open for a wide number of potential candidates. General Grant's supporters entered his name but he could never obtain a majority at the Republican convention. At last the delegates settled on General James A. Garfield. The Democrats picked one of Grant's better corps commanders, General Winfield Scott Hancock who, alone of the five military "satraps," had earned the confidence and respect of the South. But although Hancock carried the South, his campaign failed to make a wider impact, and Garfield won. The 1880 election was significant for the absence of one perennial issue: reconstruction. Radical Republicanism and the determination to enforce the rights of freedom had quietly subsided in the wake of the stolen election of 1876.

Four months after his inauguration, President Garfield was shot by a disappointed office-seeker and died in September 1881. He was succeeded by Chester A. Arthur, a gregarious, 51-year-old lawyer who surprised the party by championing Civil Service reform. The increasingly bloated bureaucracy had continued to expand, with offices regarded as rewards for services rendered, regardless of the applicant's ability. A Civil Service Commission was created in 1883, making a small proportion of offices dependent on competitive examination.

A Clean Sweep: Cleveland and Harrison

Arthur had little support within the Republican Party machine which nominated James G. Blaine for president. It was a controversial choice, even in an era of remarkably elastic moral attitudes. Blaine had a loyal cadre of supporters who would not believe the common accusations of corruption. But his nomination infuriated the more conscientious Republicans, who "bolted" and announced they would sup-

port any reasonable Democratic candidate. This turned out to be Grover Cleveland, whose election was notable for the reappearance of Ben Butler, nominated by two minor parties.

Deprived of office for a quarter of a century, the Democrats purged the Federal administration with vigor. The Tenure of Office Act had been repealed in 1886, enabling Cleveland to dispense with incumbents without reference to the Senate. Cleveland fought congressional attempts to provide pensions for their supporters, and he clashed with numerous interest groups—upsetting ranchers over the 1886 Dawes Act, and Texans over his refusal to offer Federal aid during the 1887 drought.

Cleveland was narrowly defeated by Benjamin Harrison of Indiana in the 1888 election. His Republican administration was noted only for the incredible penetration of Federal office by a clutch of politicians from the state of Maine. Congress continued to be dominated by men who sought merely to reward themselves and their backers from the public purse. The Republican grip on the Senate was increased in 1889 by the admission of the solidly Republican states of North Dakota, South Dakota, Montana, and Washington. Wyoming and Idaho were added in 1890, but sharply rising prices helped the Democrats sweep to power in the House of Representatives in the elections of that year. In 1892 Grover Cleveland returned to the White House in triumph.

The Railroad Revolution

The economic strength of the United States on the outbreak of the Civil War compared very favorably to the European powers. US manufacturing output exceeded that of Germany and Russia, and was similar to that of France. America boasted 30,000 miles of railroad: Russia had barely 1000 miles. The railroads were to be the arteries of American industry and their expansion paralleled the dramatic increase in US manufacturing power. By the end of the Civil War, the rail network had increased to 35,000 miles of track; by 1870 it passed 53,000, reached 93,000 in 1880, and 163,000 miles in 1890. The

invention of the refrigerated car allowed beef slaughtered in Chicago to reach the eastern cities in good condition, and eventually Californian fruit and vegetables undercut locally grown produce in New England.

The transcontinental railroads were a formidable source of political power and business muscle. The Union Pacific connected with the Central Pacific near Great Salt Lake in May 1869, the latter making enough profit effectively to buy the California legislature.

Three great lines were destined to change the American west with bewildering rapidity. The Northern Pacific ran from Lake Superior across Minnesota, through the Badlands of the Dakotas, up the Yellowstone River, and through the Rockies to Portland, Oregon. The Southern Pacific ran from New Orleans, across Texas, and on to El Paso and Los Angeles. The Santa Fé ran from Atchison, Kansas, along the Arkansas River to Trinidad, Colorado, and on to Sante Fé through Apache and Navaho country, before striking across the Mohave Desert to San Diego. Government land grants were offered to all three lines at 20 square miles per mile of track. Despite frequent upsets, bankruptcies, and other panics, all three reached the coast by 1884.

At the end of the war, huge tracts of the west were still the exclusive preserve of the Indians; the Great Plains west of Nebraska and eastern Kansas, and the High Plains and the Rockies were empty lands, supporting a proportionately tiny number of people. But the transcontinental railroads brought thousands of workers across the west. As the construction moved on, they bought land and settled down as farmers. Small settlements where the railroads joined became metropolitan cities within 30 years: Duluth, Kansas City, and Omaha sprang out of nowhere. The population of Kansas, Nebraska, and the Dakotas increased sixfold in the 20 years from 1870 to 1890. That of Utah and Colorado trebled in the same period.

American wheat production shifted westward as the railroads connected the northwest to the population centers of the east. Improved agricultural techniques and the newfound ability of the railroad and lake and river steamers to transport grain gave Minnesota and the Dakotas the distinct edge in low-cost grain. US production rose from 152 million bushels in 1866 to 612 million by 1891—and this despite the collapse of eastern wheat production after the crash of 1873.

Perhaps a strange by-product of the railroad bonanza was the collapse of America's merchant marine. Before the war, two-thirds of US imports and exports traveled in American hulls. In 1870 only a third did so, and by 1880 the proportion had sunk to one-sixth. A congressional investigation of 1882 reported that the railroads were widely regarded as the better investment—along with western land, manufacturing, and mining interests.

The Cowboy: A Legend Is Born: 1875–87

Perhaps the most enduring image of the American west, the cowboy driving cattle across the plains, was actually a short-lived phenomenon.

Mature cattle raised in southern Texas commanded up to $5 locally, but up to $100 in the east. By the mid-1870s, the great grasslands which ran from Texas, through Indian Territory, Kansas, and north to Wyoming were largely free of the millions of buffalo they had once supported. Exterminated with industrial zeal, the majestic herds which once supported the Indian were all but extinct by 1884. The cattlemen were presented with a belt of pasture running from Texas to Canada—and with the western termini of the great railroads just waiting to transport the beef to eastern cities.

The great drives involved groups of a dozen or more cowboys bringing a few thousand head of cattle on a journey of up to 1500 miles. Driven skilfully at no more than 20 miles per day, they could even fatten a little *en route* before being sold to Chicago or Kansas City dealers. The great cattle drives peaked in 1871 when 600,000 head made the journey north. But although Indian power on the plains had been effectively broken, the open range was soon menaced by the continuing development of the west. The dangers of Indian attack, stampede, rustlers, and prairie fires began to take second place to the steady encroachment of homesteaders. Barbed wire fences sprouted across the range, which was becoming too heavily pastured to sustain such long drives. The murderous winter of 1886–87 killed thousands of cattle caught in the open. Cattle owners stopped the drives and settled down, fencing off the land themselves. The free-ranging cowboy became the hired farm hand.

The End of the Frontier

As he retired in 1883, General Sherman wrote that "there may be spasmodic and temporary alarms but such Indian wars as have hitherto disturbed the public peace and tranquility are not probable." Three years later, with the surrender of Geronimo ending 20 years of guerrilla war in the southwest, the last major body of Indians in arms had passed into history. The tribes were all boxed into reservations. The Bighorn and Powder River country was occupied by stockmen. The mountains of the Chief Joseph's Nez Percé were dotted with mining communities, and the buffalo were a memory.

The last tragic confrontation between the Indian and the army stemmed from a religious leader who foretold of a new world, free from the white man. By praying and dancing the Ghost Dance, Indians could glimpse this paradise to come, and by strict moral behavior they would inherit the future. Wovoka, the Paiute shaman who preached the Ghost Dance, emphasized peace: the Ghost Dance was not a violent religious movement. But the militant Teton Sioux, recently tricked into signing away half the Great Sioux reservation, figured that the paradise free from white men could be hurried along.

The unrest among the Sioux soon led to a military response. But a bungled attempt by Indian police to arrest the veteran leader Sitting Bull resulted in a confused gunfight in which the great chief died. Several hundred Hunkpapa Sioux Ghost Dancers fled to join the Miniconjous led by Big Foot. The Indians eluded pursuit for two weeks before Colonel James Forsyth surrounded them with Custer's old regiment on December 29, 1890. An attempt to disarm the Indians peacefully went tragically wrong, leading to a chaotic gunfight in the middle of the Indian camp. Around 150 Indians died, including 62 women and children; 25 soldiers were killed and 39 wounded. General Nelson A. Miles relieved Forsyth of his command and convened a court of inquiry. This concluded that the fight was not a Chivington-style massacre, but a tragic accident.

In 1890 the statisticians of the Census Bureau found they could no longer identify an internal frontier to American settlement. The Indians had finally lost the 400-year struggle for North America.

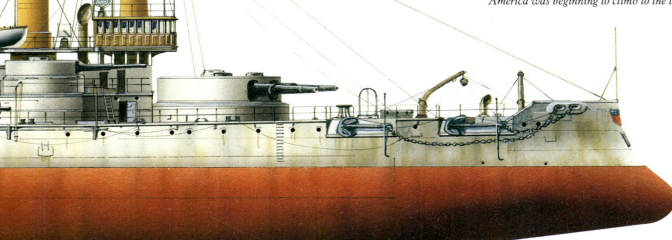

USS Oregon *launched in 1893 was the ultimate US achievement in warship construction as the century closed. Enormous strides had been made in US industry, even from the heady days of the Civil War. During the nineteenth century, countries were judged by the size of their navies, and by 1893 America was beginning to climb to the top.*

1890s Challenging World Power

Challenging the Old World: America in 1900

Forty years after the fateful fall of 1860, the United States of America was a world power. The incredible pace of American industrial growth catapulted the USA to great power status faster than many people realized at the time. The domestic concerns of most US politicians and the physical distance from Europe masked the extent to which America had advanced. During the 1870s, US industry was still primarily concerned with extracting mineral wealth, but by the turn of the century America was an industrial giant among manufacturing nations.

American business was able to exploit this rich land and its abundant raw materials with the latest technology, and untroubled by any outside threat. With no significant military power threatening the nation, less than 10 percent of the Gross National Product was consumed by defense expenditure. American economic progress is demonstrated by wheat and corn production, which quadrupled between 1865 and 1898. During the same period coal production jumped eightfold. At the end of the Civil War, America produced three million barrels of crude petroleum; by 1898 this had risen to 55 million barrels. Equally importantly, the developments in transportation enabled American goods to challenge for a place in the world market. In 1865 it cost some 40 cents to carry a bushel of wheat from Chicago to London; by the turn of the century, this had fallen to 10 cents. American wheat, pork, beef, and corn could arrive in Europe and undercut local produce.

The rise in US exports was accompanied by a continuing policy of high tariffs on foreign goods which kept imports from increasing at a similar rate. Despite the occasional panic induced by the frenzied economic cycle, there was nothing to check the onward march of American industry and commerce. Only a ruinous foreign war or conflict between the states could have arrested this expansion. The new importance of Washington, DC, in world affairs was recognized in 1892 when the great European powers upgraded their representation from ministerial to ambassadorial rank.

Battle of Manila Bay on May 1, 1898 between US forces under Dewey and the Spanish fleet. This action destroyed Spanish power in the Pacific and ensured that America would finally emerge as a world power.

Isolation and Segregation: The South in the 1890s

The exponential growth of US manufacturing was only matched by the agrarian sector in the mid- and northwest. Southern farms were not prospering and the small farmer identified four main enemies. First were the high tariff Republicans and mill-owners who paid low prices for cotton and minimal wages to mill hands recruited from the farming communities. The bankers and merchants loaned money at ruinous rates of interest, foreclosed, and took the land for themselves. The railroads had absolute control over access to markets and could dictate their price. Lastly, and by no means least, there was the Negro.

As poor whites felt themselves becoming poorer, their naked determination to keep down the Negro made itself felt. The Civil War leadership of Southern gentry lost its grip in the 1890s as a new generation succeeded to power in the state governments. Many new leaders eased themselves into office by pandering to the vociferous redneck vote, and new constitutions followed. Between 1890 and 1908 the South turned back the clock. The black franchise was steadily reduced—from 130,000 eligible voters in 1896, only 1342 were still entitled to vote by 1904. Equality of education had been theoretically imposed since the days of reconstruction, and in many areas theory and practice had matched up. But during the 1890s the schools were segregated. Passenger trains were divided, then the waiting-rooms, streetcars, theaters, factories, and public buildings. White nurses could no longer attend black patients and vice versa. The only colored man seen in a restaurant would be the waiter.

The majority of the racial laws stemmed from the Deep South, but some spread in the opposite direction. The legal zoning of cities began in Baltimore in 1910. By Wilson's administration, Washington government offices were segregated. There was some attempt to argue that segregation implied no difference in standards or opportunity—merely separation. But the most cursory examination of conditions in black schools, the colored sections of trains or streetcars gave the lie to it. The strong arm of the Invisible Empire continued to be active against any transgression, real or imaginary; at least 50 Negroes were lynched every year until 1918. This peaked in 1892 wih 226 mob killings, 156 of the victims being black. No one was punished for a lynching until 1918.

"A Splendid Little War"

Grover Cleveland's second administration witnessed the first rattling of an American saber against a foreign power since the expulsion of the French from Mexico. A border dispute between Venezuela and British Guiana looked like being resolved by British military intervention, Lord Salisbury refusing to accept arbitration. President Cleveland astonished the British—and many Americans—by a bellicose interpretation of the Monroe Doctrine. For all the consequent flag-waving, Wall Street panicked immediately. The fortunate intervention of the Kaiser, who publicly supported the Transvaal against a pro-

US ASIATIC FLEET

British coup attempt, concentrated British minds on real priorities. Salisbury agreed to arbitration; this went in favor of Britain and that was that.

The 1893 depression led to Republican victories in the 1894 elections and justified confidence of a presidential triumph in 1896. This election became a bitter fight between the new muscle of US industry and the old agrarian interest. A battle in which class struggle came to the forefront. "Pitchfork" Ben Tillman of South Carolina likened the power of big money to the tyranny of a slave owner, and the Democratic candidate, William Jennings Bryan, made an effective campaign; he carried the South and most of the far west. But Mark A. Hanna secured monstrous campaign contributions from industrial leaders, banks, and railroads; his presidential nominee, Congressman William McKinley, swept the north and Midwest.

McKinley's presidency began with the highest protective tariff yet seen—an appalling monument to monopoly-building. Fortunately for the Republicans, fortune offered a conspicuous diversion in the shape of Cuba. This major Spanish colony had been in a state of unrest for many years, but the endemic guerrilla war had become an issue thanks to the sensationalist coverage by the popular newspapers of William Randolph Hearst and Joseph Pulitzer. Spain was an isolated minor power in Europe and unable to sustain any prolonged campaign. In October 1897 military repression on Cuba was abandoned and limited home rule offered to the rebels.

The waning of popular interest in Cuba was arrested by the explosion of the battleship USS *Maine* in Havana on February 15, 1898. The American popular press blamed the Spaniards but a conspiracy theory also pointed the finger of suspicion at the rebels, anxious for American aid to achieve total victory. An inquiry, subsequently endorsed by examination of the wreck in 1911, concluded that the *Maine* was destroyed by a mine which detonated her forward magazine—but that it might have been an accident. Later studies have proved that the hapless vessel was actually destroyed by an internal explosion started by a spontaneous fire in her coal bunkers which were located next to the magazine. Some 260 men died as a result of the catastrophe.

Spanish prospects in Cuba sank as rapidly as the ill-fated battleship. President McKinley demanded an immediate armistice on the island prior to American arbitration. On April 9 the governor of Cuba offered an armistice and the American representatives in Madrid were soon cabling to say that Spain would abandon Cuba to independence or even US rule. A peaceful solution was not in doubt, but McKinley invited Congress to declare war instead.

The generation of Shiloh, Antietam, Gettysburg, and the Crater evidently failed to prevent a popular belief in successful war. A confidence in military glory which had already taken fatal root in Europe stampeded America into war with Spain. It was certainly an ideal choice of enemy: a small country with a weak European army, and a navy mostly made up of small cruisers only suitable for colonial work. Better still, she had no allies among the real powers, and although there was talk of a European peace initiative, Spanish colonies had been dropping off throughout the century and nobody was about to champion a once-great nation which was now a provincial backwater.

The war was extraordinarily popular throughout America. Democrats and Republicans at last had something they could agree on without reservation. North and South united against a common enemy. Young men flocked to the colors once again, and some old names reappeared: former Confederate commanders Joe Wheeler and Fitzhugh Lee were now generals in the US Army.

The US Navy had an overwhelming preponderance of powerful ships, crewed by professsional officers and men. The Great Pacific War of 1879–81 had made it plain to Congress that the great US Navy of the Civil War had never been updated, and that Chilean ironclads were now the ultimate arbiter of naval power in these waters. Since then, the US Navy had expanded to become the biggest fleet in the western hemisphere. Commodore Dewey set the precedent for the war by smashing the Spanish Philippines Squadron a week after the declaration of war. The Atlantic fleet rushed to seek out the Spanish warships approaching from Europe—exposing the US landings to attack and risking a humiliating defeat—but the morbidly gloomy Spanish Admiral Cevera led his doomed squadron meekly into Santiago. Emerging only after US ground forces menaced the anchorage, his ships were blown apart in a four-hour turkey shoot.

The Cuban campaign revealed gross deficiencies in an army which had been dispersed across the nation in penny packets and seldom used to managing even modest concentrations of soldiers. This was doubly humiliating since the US Army's textbooks had continued to instruct officers in conventional military tactics. Despite over two decades of Indian fighting, the manuals still dealt with infantry divisions facing similarly organized opponents. When the US Army finally met such an enemy, it won more by luck than judgment. The landings on June 20, 1898, were chaotic. The actions against the Spanish Army were a confused succession of frontal assaults which worked thanks to good junior leadership and the bravery of the troops, rather than any talent displayed at senior level. Medical facilities were dreadful and malaria inflicted many more casualties than Spanish rifles.

The Spanish–American War was the most spectacular manifestation of the arrival of the United States among the acknowledged great powers. Nothing could demonstrate more clearly America's recovery from the Civil War years than the sight of soldiers from North and South united against a common foe. Yet the war continued to exert a powerful influence. Between the death of President Lincoln and the end of McKinley's term in 1901, every president save Grover Cleveland had served in the US forces during the war. Few men gained political office unless they had fought in blue or gray. It would be many years before passions cooled, and there were men and women on both sides who could never bring themselves to bury the hachet.

If the thorny issue of states rights had been partially dealt with, the question of the status of the Negro had still to be resolved. While America achieved great power status at the turn of the century, the immediate future of the black population was bleak indeed. But nearly 100 years on from the beginning of segregation, a state now has a black leader; in 1989 Douglas Wilder became governor of Virginia.

ANCHORED SPANISH FLEET

CAVITE

Index

Page numbers in **bold** type indicate illustration.

Index

Index

Index